Walking in Australia

Andrew Bain
Lindsay Brown, Ian Connellan, John & Lyn Daly,
Grant Dixon, Glenn van der Knijff

Destination Australia

In Australia's most famous bush poem (and de facto national anthem), *Waltzing Matilda*, the tale begins with a swagman camped by a billabong. But for the subsequent sheep rustling, 'Banjo' Paterson had just created the prototype bushwalker, carrying his or her tent into the bush and settling each night by a welcome drink of water.

Australia's greatest feature is not its cities, or even its people – it has around 7000 beaches, 8000 islands, 60,000km of coast, more than 300 national parks and just five cities with populations above 500,000. It is clear that this enormous land is its own star feature. And while the celebrated outback might be among the harshest environments on earth, the country is gift-wrapped in flour-soft beaches and forests as cool as they are lush.

The most intimate way to experience great parts of Australia is on foot, and the options are as varied as the landscapes. You can haul food and water for weeks through the High Country of Victoria and New South Wales, or amble between restaurants and B&Bs beside the relentlessly scenic Great Ocean Road. You can discover Tasmanian mountains shaped as peculiarly as Australia's native wildlife, West Australian forests that scratch at the sky, or Queensland islands that will slow your step to an admiring, tropical stroll. Even the outback has its welcoming moments, with the Flinders and West MacDonnell Ranges among the country's unique natural treasures. Everywhere there are castaway beaches accessible only to those prepared to walk – often, you need barely leave the city to find them.

So take Banjo's lead and walk for a while, and discover the poetry of the Australian land.

ANDREW B

New South Wales

Taking a breather on the lower slopes of Mt Twynam (p92) in Kosciuszko National Park

Kangaroos browse among the distinctive blooms of Paterson's Curse in Warrumbungle National Park (p110)

Exposed granite tors of the Rams Head Range, seen on the Mt Kosciuszko & the Lakes Circuit (p88)

Victoria

Glorious vistas of the Victorian Alps from the top of the Crosscut Saw on the Mt Speculation & the Crosscut Saw walk (p168)

A chilly winter crossing of Thurra River, one of several fords to be negotiated along the Croajingolong Coast Walk (p182)

Gentle forest walking en route to Sealer's Cove on the Prom Southern Circuit walk (p176)

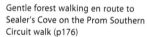

Tasmania

Deciduous beeches add stunning autumn colour to mountain slopes in Mt Field National Park (p206)

Overleaf:
Lush temperate rainforest in the Franklin-Gordon Wild Rivers National Park, encountered on sections of the Frenchmans Cap walk (p229)
RICHARD I'ANSON

Cliffs of Cape Pillar (p200), at 270m the highest vertical sea cliffs in Australia

The iconic profile of Cradle Mountain, seen from Cradle Plateau along the Overland Track (p214)

South Australia & Western Australia

Once the sandy floor of a warm shallow sea, 'The Terraces' at Alligator Gorge are a highlight of the Mt Remarkable Gorges walk (p263)

Walkers get a birds-eye view of the forest on the Tree Top walk, along the Bibbulmun Karri & Coast walk (p290)

The view from the top of Kangaroo Island's west coast cliffs on the Flinders Chase Coastal Trek (p258)

Northern Territory & Queensland

The extraordinary rock art at Nanguluwur Gallery is a major drawcard of the Barrk Sandstone Bushwalk (p312)

TOM BO

RICHARD I'ANSON

Upper Edith (Leilyn) Falls, the end-point of the four-day Jatbula Trail (p315) in Nitmiluk National Park

Little Ramsay Bay, an early taste of the spectacular coastal scenery along the Thorsborne Trail (p349)

WILL SA

Foreword Jon Muir

For many years my childhood dreams threw me into the high-altitude world of snow, rock and ice, but even from the earliest days I had an inkling that, in some shape or form, Australia held the potential for an extreme challenge. It wasn't until I stood alone on the summit of Everest and gazed out over the red and brown plains of the Tibetan Plateau that the desert came sharply to mind. Such similar landscapes, Tibet and Australia: both vast expanses of hauntingly isolated arid country.

In 2001 I walked across Australia, from the Spencer Gulf to the Gulf of Carpentaria, with my Jack Russell Seraphine – a journey that holds some of the richest memories of my life. The Australian desert has some of the most ephemeral and stunning landscapes that I've experienced anywhere. Mountains float like blue and purple hallucinations on the horizon, and the pure expanses of the salt lakes glow crystal-white like ice. It is an exquisite perfection of colours: the olive green of the desert oaks standing quietly in the deep-red sand; the twisted, stark, white ghost gums and orange rock against pulsing blue sky; and the soft contrast of the palest hues when the desert is sucked dry of both colour and moisture by the midday sun.

I've found through my prowls out and about into the Australian wilderness that it usually takes me a couple of weeks to experience that deep relaxation that comes as my mind drifts further away from the trappings of the modern world. Reducing my needs to the basics of water, food and shelter, I immerse myself in the incredible beauty of the isolated mountains, coastline or desert. What a privilege that is! To be able to allow myself the time to slow down. I see this 'time out', walking in our magnificent wilderness, as an essential balance to the paper-juggling mind strain that seems to be an inevitable consequence of our hectic world of 'progress' and consumerism. I wonder if anyone can truly escape this pressure without pulling on a pair of boots and taking themselves out for a walk amid the overwhelming magnificence of the land around us.

Walking gives me the opportunity to live totally in the moment, as my mind is absorbed in the sharp focus required to meet the challenges of survival in the wilderness – when I need to get my tarpaulin up quickly to avoid sudden rain or when I am intently studying the landscape for signs of water. At these times the rest of the world ceases to exist. Life becomes simple, uncluttered by the non-essential.

While on the march the steady rhythm of walking allows me the pleasure of letting my mind drift; to dream, plan, reminisce or simply to be. This freedom of mind, this unravelling from the snares and tangles associated with absorption in tasks, or relationships with other people, is deeply supported by walking at length through a natural landscape.

To experience the beating heart of Australia, forget about the Opera House, the Gold Coast or Lygon St, Melbourne – it's when you're out in the forest or the desert, or on an isolated stretch of coast, that the soul of the country becomes apparent. In the spirals on the bark of snow gums, or the meandering spine of mountain ridges, or the lonely cry of the dingo under a desert night sky, here is the essence of Australia.

Jon Muir has devoted his life to outdoor adventure, including five Mt Everest expeditions, a 52-day solo sea-kayaking journey and treks to both Poles, in addition to crossing Australia on foot in 2001. He was awarded the Order of Australia Medal in 1989 and named the Australian Geographic Society's Adventurer of the Year in 2001.

Contents

Regional Map Contents

NORTHERN TERRITORY
p306

QUEENSLAND
p329

WESTERN AUSTRALIA
p277

SOUTH AUSTRALIA
p250

NEW SOUTH WALES
pp50–1

VICTORIA
pp126–7

OVERLAND TRACK
p221 & p224

TASMANIA
p191

The Walks	Duration	Difficulty	Best Time
New South Wales			
Barrington Tops Plateau Explorer	3 days	easy-moderate	all year
Blue Gum Forest	2 days	moderate	Jun-Nov
Bouddi Coast	5 hours	easy-moderate	Aug-Nov
Bungonia Gorge	2 days	moderate-demanding	all year
The Chimneys	5-6 hours	easy-moderate	Nov-Apr
The Coast Track	2 days	moderate	Aug-Nov
Gorges, Caves & Plains	5-6 hours	easy	Nov-May
Heart of the Budawangs	4 days	moderate-demanding	Apr-Nov
Kanangra Walls to the Kowmung River	2 days	moderate-demanding	Jun-Nov
Mt Kosciuszko & the Lakes Circuit	3 days	easy-moderate	Dec-Apr
Mt Solitary	2 days	moderate	Jun-Nov
Pigeon House Mountain	3 hours	moderate	all year
Red Hands Cave	4-4½ hours	easy-moderate	Aug-Nov
Rosewood Creek Circuit	4 hours	moderate	all year
Six Foot Track	3 days	moderate-demanding	Apr-Oct
Warrumbungles Grand High Tops	3 days	moderate	all year
Wentworth Falls & the Valley of the Waters	5½-7 hours	easy-moderate	Jun-Nov
Victoria			
Bushrangers Bay	3½-4 hours	easy	year-round
Cathedral Range	2 days	demanding	Mar-Nov
Croajingolong Coast Walk	5 days	moderate	Sep-May
Great Ocean Walk Highlight	2 days	moderate	year-round
Mt Bogong	2 days	moderate-demanding	Dec-Apr
Mt Buffalo Plateau	5-6 hours	easy-moderate	Nov-Apr
Mt Difficult	2 days	moderate-demanding	Sep-Nov
Mt Feathertop & the Razorback	2 days	demanding	Dec-Apr
Mt Speculation & the Crosscut Saw	2 days	moderate-demanding	Nov-Apr
Mt Stapylton	4-4½ hours	moderate-demanding	Sep-Nov
Prom Southern Circuit	3 days	moderate	Nov-May
Surf Coast Walk	2 days	easy	year-round
Werribee Gorge	2½-3 hours	easy-moderate	Sep-Nov
Tasmania			
Cape Pillar	3 days	moderate	all year
Frenchmans Cap	4 days	moderate-demanding	Nov-Apr

The Walks	Duration	Difficulty	Best Time
Tasmania *continued*			
Freycinet Peninsula Circuit	2 days	easy-moderate	all year
Mt Anne & Eliza Plateau	7-8½ hours	moderate-demanding	Nov-Apr
Mt Field & Tarn Shelf Circuit	5-6 hours	moderate	Oct-Apr
Mt Rufus & Shadow Lake	6-8 hours	moderate	Nov-Apr
Mt Wellington & the Organ Pipes Circuit	5-7 hours	moderate	all year
Overland Track	6-7 days	moderate	Dec-Mar
South Coast Track	6-7 days	moderate-demanding	Dec-Mar
Walls of Jerusalem	3 days	easy-moderate	Nov-Apr
South Australia			
Flinders Chase Coastal Trek	2 days	moderate	Sep-Apr
Heysen Highlight	3 days	moderate	Aug-Oct
Mt Remarkable Gorges	2 days	moderate	Sep-Oct
Wilpena Pound	2 days	easy-moderate	May-Oct
Yurrebilla Trail	3 days	easy-moderate	all year
Western Australia			
Bibbulmun Karri & Coast	4 days	moderate	Sep-Nov
Bluff Knoll	2½-3 hours	moderate	Sep-Oct
Cape to Cape Track	7 days	moderate	Jun-Dec
Nancy Peak & Devil's Slide	2½-3 hours	easy-moderate	Sep-Nov
Toolbrunup Peak	2½-3 hours	moderate-demanding	Sep-Oct
Northern Territory			
Barrk Sandstone Bushwalk	5-7 hours	moderate-demanding	May-Sep
Jatbula Trail	4 days	moderate	May-Sep
Larapinta Trail Highlight	2 days	moderate	Apr-Sep
Ormiston Gorge & Pound	3½-4 hours	easy-moderate	Apr-Sep
Queensland			
Coomera Circuit	8 hours	moderate	May-Oct
Great Walk Fraser Island	5 days	moderate	Apr-Oct
Green Mountains	2 days	moderate	May-Oct
Mt Bartle Frere	2 days	demanding	May-Oct
Ships Stern Circuit	6 hours	moderate	May-Oct
Thorsborne Trail	4 days	moderate	Apr-Sep

The Authors

ANDREW BAIN

Growing up in Adelaide, Andrew once believed the great outdoors was a place far away, so it was with delight that he rediscovered his home state (among other places) for this book. A reformed sportswriter, he now writes about adventure and travel for publications around the world. He has trekked, cycled and paddled across parts of five continents and is the author of *Headwinds,* the story of a 20,000km bike ride around Australia, and Lonely Planet's *A Year of Adventures*.

Walk My Way

For me, Australian walking begins from the bottom up – in Tasmania, where nights on Wineglass Bay (p244) or days among the mountain assortments of Cradle Mountain–Lake St Clair National Park (p214) are unsurpassed. A couple of bushwalking's lesser lights, South Australia and Western Australia, deserve greater attention. The forests along the Bibbulmun Karri & Coast walk (p290) and the forest-less approach into Wilpena Pound along the Heysen Highlight (p268) are exceptional. The Victorian Alps are my mountain playground of choice – the Razorback (p164) and Crosscut Saw (p168) are as sharpening to the senses as their names might suggest. And all good things should end on Hinchinbrook Island (p349) – 32km, nine beaches, four days; leisure with your boots on.

LINDSAY BROWN

Having recently explored the Top End for Lonely Planet's *Northern Territory & Central Australia,* it was time to park the 4WD and hit the trails. As a Lonely Planet author Lindsay has contributed to several titles, including *Australia, Queensland & the Great Barrier Reef* and *East Coast Australia*. He has trekked in Pakistan, Nepal and India, and bushwalked in most states of Australia.

LONELY PLANET AUTHORS

Why is our travel information the best in the world? It's simple: our authors are independent, dedicated travellers. They don't research using just the Internet or phone, and they don't take freebies in exchange for positive coverage. They travel widely, to all the popular spots and off the beaten track. They personally visit thousands of hotels, restaurants, cafés, bars, galleries, palaces, museums and more – and they take pride in getting all the details right, and telling it how it is. For more, see the authors section on www.lonelyplanet.com.

IAN CONNELLAN

Ian's first bushland walking experiences were near his childhood Sydney home, and he'd graduated to multiday walks in the Blue Mountains and other national parks by his early years in high school. Alpine and cross-country skiing and bicycle touring were added to his outdoor-rec mix while he completed university studies in literature, history and professional writing. After this he somehow endured several years of ski-bumming before settling down as a journalist, editor and freelance travel writer/photographer. Widely published by anyone who'll put up with him, Ian is based near the coast in Sydney with his family (partner x 1, children x 2). This is his fourth Lonely Planet title.

JOHN & LYN DALY

Weekend forays into the bush after a torrid week in computers were the beginning. Outdoor escapes became addictive – no phones, no staff, no hassles! It was time for a career change. Wine tasters and restaurant critics were covered, so John and Lyn turned their long-time passion for bushwalking, travel and conservation into an occupation. They produced their first *Take A Walk* book and six others followed. Their 'job' allows them to pursue another passion: long-distance walking, highlighted by end-to-ending the Australian Alps Walking Track. They regularly write for outdoor and travel magazines and share experiences with conservation groups and bushwalking clubs. The pay might not be flash, but the memories and experiences are worth millions.

GRANT DIXON

Wandering in the wilderness of his native Tasmania provided inspiration for Grant's geological training, and subsequent work with nature conservation organisations and the Tasmanian Parks & Wildlife Service. Spending part of each year trekking, climbing and photographing wild and remote areas of the planet, Grant has explored parts of all seven continents and many different environments over the past 30 years, from the Antarctic to the Arctic and Himalayan summits to a South Pacific island. He is a co-author of Lonely Planet's *Trekking in the Central Andes* and *Walking in the Alps,* contributed to the previous edition of *Walking in Australia,* and is also a widely published photographer.

GLENN VAN DER KNIJFF

Glenn grew up in Bright, at the foot of the Victorian Alps, and completed his first walk at the tender age of 11. Living near the mountains ensured he acquired a passion for snow skiing as well as bushwalking. In the last 20 years Glenn has walked extensively in the High Country of Victoria and Kosciuszko National Park, and he's even written his own book, *Bushwalks in the Victorian Alps*. Though he's worked at Lonely Planet since 1997, his previous job for *Wild* (a magazine devoted to Australian rucksack sports) unwittingly gave him the impetus to travel overseas, and he's since visited Nepal, Canada, the USA and Europe to expand his walking and skiing experiences.

CONTRIBUTING AUTHORS

Jon Muir wrote the foreword (p9) and boxed text 'Bush Tucker' (p31) in the Environment chapter. Jon has devoted his life to outdoor adventure, including five Mt Everest expeditions, a 52-day solo sea-kayaking journey and treks to both Poles, in addition to crossing Australia on foot in 2001. He was named the Australian Geographic Society's Adventurer of the Year in 2001.

Tim Flannery wrote the boxed text 'Environmental Challenges' (p34) in the Environment chapter. Tim is a naturalist, explorer and and author of a number of award-winning books, including *Country* and *The Future Eaters*. Tim lives in Adelaide where he is director of the South Australian Museum and a professor at the University of Adelaide.

Walk Descriptions

This book contains 60 walk descriptions ranging from day trips to the multicountry megawalks, plus suggestions for other walks, side trips and alternative routes. Each walk description has a brief introduction outlining the natural and cultural features you may encounter, plus information to help you plan your walk – transport options, level of difficulty, time frame and any permits required.

Day walks are often circular and are located in areas of uncommon beauty. Multiday walks include information on camp sites, mountain huts, hostels or other accommodation, and places where you can obtain water and supplies.

Times & Distances

These are provided only as a guide. Times are based on actual walking time and do not include stops for snacks, taking photographs, rests or side trips. Be sure to factor these in when planning your walk. Distances are provided but should be read in conjunction with altitudes. Significant elevation changes can make a greater difference to your walking time than lateral distance.

In most cases, the daily stages are flexible and can be varied. It is important to recognise that short stages are sometimes recommended in order to acclimatise in mountain areas or because there are interesting features to explore en route.

Level of Difficulty

Grading systems are always arbitrary. However, having an indication of the grade may help you choose between walks. Our authors use the following grading guidelines:

Easy – a walk on flat terrain or with minor elevation changes usually over short distances on well-travelled routes with no navigational difficulties.

Moderate – a walk with challenging terrain, often involving longer distances and steep climbs.

Demanding – a walk with long daily distances and difficult terrain with significant elevation changes; may involve challenging route-finding and high-altitude or glacier travel.

True Left & True Right

The terms 'true left' and 'true right', used to describe the bank of a stream or river, sometimes throw readers. The 'true left bank' simply means the left bank as you look downstream.

Planning

Australian walking is an evolving creature. At its core it is about self-sufficiency; the simple act of dragging your food, water and bed with you through the bush, seeing only natural architecture along the way, and with wildlife as your major companion. This remains the essence of bushwalking, but it's no longer the only option. Paths such as the Bibbulmun Track (p290) and Larapinta Trail (p322) have redefined bushwalking infrastructure, alleviating some of the exhaustive forethought required to step out into the bush. Increasingly, there are also opportunities to make your planning as simple as calling ahead to book a bed at a B&B, or securing your place on a guided walk.

See Climate (p361) for more information.

Plan ahead according to your walk – a track in the Northern Territory or outback New South Wales might require copious preparation, while a stroll near the city might require no more than a packed lunch and a transport timetable. This book is designed to be one of your preparation tools as well as your track guide – it will be the first step of your walk.

WHEN TO WALK

Australia is a land for all seasons, balanced between north and south, tropical and temperate. Whenever you fancy a walk, somewhere in the country is in its prime. When the Northern Territory and Queensland are afloat in their wet season (October to March), southern regions such as Victoria, Tasmania and Kosciuszko National Park beckon. During winter (June to August), snow and severe weather can make walking hazardous, if not impossible, in much of Tasmania and the High Country of New South Wales (NSW) and Victoria, but it is gloriously warm across central Australia (if you can excuse the freezing nights); and Queensland and the Top End have wrung themselves dry of humidity.

Spring (September to November) and autumn (March to May) are anything but seasonal fillers, offering the finest walking conditions across much of the country. South Australia and Western Australia (WA) are at their best – spring means copious wildflowers in WA – while NSW and Victoria are also balanced between their summer heat and winter rains.

Australia's great holiday migration is primarily over the summer school holidays (late December through January), but it shouldn't mean any travel disruption – just a few more people to weave around if you are walking along the coast.

COSTS & MONEY

In recent years the Australian dollar has been holding its own against currencies such as the greenback and the euro, so it is a less economical destination than in the days when the Aussie dollar more resembled a peso. That said, daily living costs such as food and accommodation are

HOW MUCH?

Camping ground (tent & 2 people) $20-25

B&B (per person sharing) $60

Topographic map $10

Litre of Shellite $5

Post-walk pub meal $15-30

See also Lonely Planet Index, inside back cover.

DON'T HIT THE TRACK WITHOUT...

- getting over your fear of snakes (p384)
- checking for Total Fire Bans (p24)
- plenty of drinking water (p385)
- map and compass (p390)
- checking the permits and fees situation (p371)

still fairly inexpensive. The biggest cost in any trip to Australia will be transport, simply because it is such a large country.

As a walker you have an automatic financial advantage, since you will almost certainly be spending some nights sleeping in a tent, often free of charge. Off the trail, your budget will be determined by the kind of travel you are doing. If you are touring around between walks, doing some general sightseeing, prefer to stay in at least midrange accommodation and have a stomach that demands regular restaurant visits, then $90 to $110 per day (per person travelling as a couple) should do it.

If you are travelling more frugally, camping or staying in hostels, cooking your own meals, limiting your entertainment to the walking itself, and moving around by bus (or in your own vehicle), you could probably eke out an existence on $50 per day. For a budget that realistically enables you to have a good time, open your purse a little wider to allow $70 per day.

If you're not already geared up, a significant expense can be fitting yourself out with the appropriate clothing and equipment. See p389 for advice and options.

GUIDED & GROUP WALKS

Sometimes you just want somebody else to point the way or carry your stuff. Try the following walking organisations:

Australia

Auswalk (☎ 02-6457 2220; www.auswalk.com.au) Guided and self-guided walks along the east coast, Tasmania and central Australia.
Ecotrek (☎ 08-8346 4155; www.ecotrek.com.au) A large selection of South Australian walks, plus the High Country and Tasmania.
Nature Bound Australia (☎ 07-3254 1911; www.natureboundaustralia.com) Tours that include day walks along many of the trails in this book.
Parktrek (☎ 03-9486 7070; www.parktrek.com) Walks throughout Victoria, plus the Budawangs, Flinders Ranges, Kangaroo Island, central Australia, Snowy Mountains and Tasmania.
Willis' Walkabouts (☎ 08-8985 2134; www.bushwalkingholidays.com.au) Walks along the Larapinta Trail and through Kakadu.
World Expeditions (☎ 1300 720 000; www.worldexpeditions.com.au) Walks along the Overland Track, Freycinet Peninsula, South Coast Track, Walls of Jerusalem, Flinders Ranges, Larapinta Trail, Bibbulmun Track and Cape to Cape Track.

UK

HF Holidays (☎ 0208-905 9556; www.hfholidays.co.uk) A 16-day Tasmania tour focusing on the major walking areas.
KE Adventure Travel (☎ 0176-877 3966; www.keadventure.com) A 15-day trekking tour in the Blue Mountains and Snowy Mountains.
Walks Worldwide (☎ 0152-424 2000; www.walksworldwide.com) A broad range of walks in eastern Australia, including Lamington, the High Country, Overland Track, Blue Mountains, Croajingolong, Grampians and the Great Ocean Road.

USA

Wilderness Travel (☎ 1-800-368 2794; www.wildernesstravel.com) Offers a Wild Tasmania tour that includes walks at Cradle Mountain, Mt Field and Freycinet.

To find local operators on specific walks, see the relevant regional chapter. For information on walking clubs around the country, see p358.

BACKGROUND READING

The tradition of travel literature has barely touched the Australian walking scene. Not here do you find personal accounts of discovery through walking: Australia's *Snow Leopard* remains to be written. A recent exception was Jon Muir's diary-style *Alone Across Australia,* the story of his unassisted 128-day walk from Port Augusta to Burketown, one of the great contemporary Australian journeys.

Paddy Pallin's *Bushwalking and Camping,* first published in 1934 and now into its 14th edition, is something of a walkers' bible, covering everything from bushcraft and first-aid to tips on stuffing everything into your backpack. Paddy's autobiography *Never Truly Lost* is a fascinating account of bushwalking in a bygone era and of his personal philosophy (for more about Paddy Pallin, see the boxed text p389).

Being Outside by Everest summiteer Tim Macartney Snape is a comprehensive how-to guide to the outdoors – learn everything from types of sleeping bag to the pathology of hypothermia.

Classic Wild Walks of Australia by Robert Rankin takes a glance at walks in 25 regions of the country, complemented by a beautiful set of photos. *Classic Walks of Australia* by Sven Klinge features thumbnail descriptions of around 180 walks. Hardback and huge, both books are more for the coffee table than the backpack.

SEASONED WALKERS

Seasons, as much as scenery, can be a deciding factor in the tracks you choose to walk. If you want your visit to coincide with nature's moods, try one of the following.

Summer

Brutal heat across much of the country brings Tasmania and the High Country of NSW and Victoria into their own. Head out into Kosciuszko National Park (p82), the Victorian Alps (p155) or Tasmania's west (p204). If you are in northern Australia, you might join the summer exodus to Lamington National Park (p333) to beat the lowland heat.

Autumn

As a general rule, autumn provides the most stable weather conditions across much of the country, making it arguably the finest walking season of all. Australia's trees are not noted for the kind of deciduous colouring that so electrifies forests in many other parts of the world. One exception is the deciduous beech (or 'fagus') in Tasmania. This tree changes colour around late April, and is best sighted along the Overland Track (p214) or on Mt Field (p206).

Winter

Follow the migration north for the best of the walking conditions. Wander along the Jatbula Trail (p315) or sample the Larapinta Trail (p322). In northern Queensland, both the Thorsborne Trail (p349) and Mt Bartle Frere (p353) are exceptional in winter.

If you can brave the chill in the south, you will witness the ocean's full ferocity around Cape Pillar (p200) and the Great Ocean Walk Highlight (p143).

Spring

There is no better place to be during spring than in Western Australia, where the wildflowers turn the earth into a Monet canvas. All the walks in the WA chapter feature great spring floral displays. You need not venture far out of Sydney, however, to find a decent coating of wildflowers, with both the Bouddi Coast (p55) and Royal National Park Coast Track (p58) rich in flowering heath. This is also the most comfortable and beautiful season to walk in the Flinders Ranges (p261).

INTERNET RESOURCES

Australia Online (www.australiaonline.com.au) Includes an A-Z of all things ocker.

Australian Tourist Commission (www.australia.com) Official tourism site with nationwide info for visitors.

Bushwalking in Australia (www.bushwalking.org.au) NSW-centric – it is the website of the Confederation of Bushwalking Clubs NSW – but with links to walking clubs, and titbits on food and equipment.

Department of the Environment & Heritage (www.deh.gov.au/parks/links/index.html) Info on the handful of Commonwealth national parks and links to the state-run national park authorities.

Guide to Australia (www.csu.edu.au/australia) Links to sundry domestic sites focusing on attractions, culture, the environment, transport etc.

John Chapman – Bushwalking in Australia (www.john.chapman.name/bushwalk.html) Good overview of many of the country's major tracks.

LonelyPlanet.com (www.lonelyplanet.com) Talk the walk on the dedicated walking, trekking and mountaineering branch of the Thorn Tree forum.

Yahoo! Groups: bushwalking (http://groups.yahoo.com/group/bushwalking) Discussion group on all things bushwalking.

Environment

Separated from other lands for around 33 million years, Australia has been on a unique evolutionary journey, moulding wildlife as though it was an abstract art form – mammals with pouches, a pin-cushion that lays eggs, a monotreme with the bill of a duck – and grinding down its ancient mountains even as the rest of the world has been erecting theirs. Is it any wonder they call it the land down under?

THE LAND

Australia contains ancient rocks and evidence of the earliest life, but the landscape itself is very old in many areas. While northern hemisphere land masses were scraped clean by glaciers during recent ice ages, this was not so in much of Australia, which retains landscape and soil fea-

---

TREADING LIGHTLY

The Australian bush is more fragile than its sun-hardened image might appear, and hordes of bushwalkers can easily upset the ecological balance. To that end, national parks and bushwalking clubs have adopted Minimal Impact Bushwalking Codes – you will find an example at www.bush walking.org.au/code.html. You don't need to be able to recite them like a pledge of allegiance: everything in the codes is common bush sense. The following guidelines are based on these codes.

Rubbish

- Take plastic bags for your rubbish and if you have carried it in, carry it out. Carry out rubbish left by other people.
- Don't bury or burn rubbish. Burning creates pollution and buried rubbish might be dug up by animals and scattered.
- If walking in scrubby country, don't carry foam sleeping mats or items in plastic bags on the outside of your pack.

Human Waste

- It there is no toilet, bury your waste by digging a hole 15cm deep and at least 100m from any watercourse and camp site. Take a trowel or large tent peg for this purpose. Cover the waste and paper with soil.
- At many national park camp sites there are composting toilets. Do not place rubbish in these toilets as it can affect the composting process.

Feeding Animals

- Don't feed animals, no matter how cute they are, and secure rubbish and food away from prying paws. Feeding makes wild creatures dependent on humans for food and can cause diseases such as lumpy jaw – a fatal condition found in marsupials, causing them to starve to death.

Camping

- Use an existing camp site rather than creating a new one. Avoid grassed areas; choose sandy or hard surfaces.
- Don't dig trenches around your tent to divert rainwater; use a waterproof groundsheet.

tures caused by the cumulative effects of more than 100 million years of weathering.

In general, Australia has grown from west to east. Western Australia's Pilbara region contains both Australia's oldest rocks (3.3 billion years) and evidence of some of the oldest known organisms: stromatolites (more than 2.5 billion years ago). Younger (600 million years) rocks in the Flinders Ranges contain fossils of jellyfish-like organisms, the first evidence of multicelled life. Complex life burst forth worldwide soon after.

During the last billion years Australia has lain in the centre of two supercontinents, ancient Rodinia and more-recent Gondwana. The latter contained all the major southern landmasses and was assembled by 520 million years ago. During the subsequent 150 million years, warm and shallow seas covered parts of Australia, and volcanic arcs and deeper water lay to the east. Cycles of sedimentation and deformation built new crust, the present eastern Australia.

Global cooling about 330 million years ago, with Gondwana near the South Pole, plunged Australia into an extended glacial period. As the

Washing

- Don't use detergents or toothpaste in or near watercourses; try to use sand or a scourer (not detergent) to clean dishes.
- If washing with soap, use a water container at least 50m from any watercourse. Disperse the waste water widely so it filters through the soil before it returns to the creek.
- Strain food scraps from dishwashing water and carry them out in your rubbish.

Fires & Total Fire Bans

- Campfires are not allowed in fuel-stove-only areas.
- Carry a fuel stove to avoid campfires; fires inevitably result in some scarring of the land.
- Fires of any kind (including fuel stoves) are prohibited on days of Total Fire Ban. In remote areas, regard any hot, dry, windy day as a fire ban day.
- If having a campfire, use an existing fireplace rather than making a new one. If there are multiple fireplaces, use the major one – you might even consider dismantling the others.
- Don't surround fireplaces with rocks; instead, clear away all flammable material for at least 2m. Use the minimum of dead, fallen wood.
- Be absolutely certain the fire is extinguished. Drown the embers with water – sand and soil won't extinguish a fire. A fire is only safe to leave when you can comfortably put your hand on it.
- Place your stove on hard, nonliving surfaces, not vegetation. Cooking on vegetation can cause scorching from radiant heat – you may not see the effect but it can come through over subsequent days.

Low-Impact Walking

- Use existing tracks. Don't cut corners to bypass zigzags.
- Walk through muddy or waterlogged sections of track; walking around the edge only increases the size of the pool.
- Avoid walking on sensitive vegetation. Minimise walking on loose ground, scree, dunes and marshes.

climate thawed 40 million years later, sediments, then cold peat swamps, filled subsiding basins along the east coast: Australia's future black-coal deposits. Sands that would become the cliffs of the Blue Mountains and rocks of the Sydney region were deposited subsequently in deltas and floodplains. Despite Australia's polar location, the climate continued to warm, with the development of arid inland riverine plains. Lush vegetation developed in eastern Australia when warm and humid conditions developed, and dinosaurs and early mammals roamed the land.

Crustal extension within Gondwana began about 180 million years ago, heralded by the injection of molten rock into the crust – now Tasmania's dolerite. The separation of Australia and Antarctica and the opening of the Tasman Sea both began 100 million years ago, at about the same time the first platypus appears in the fossil record. The opening of the Tasman Sea ended after less than 20 million years, but the Australian Plate has continued to move northeast by 7cm per year since, with northern Australia reaching the tropics about 25 million years ago.

Read about the 400-million-year greening of Gondwana in Mary White's book of the same name.

The rise of Australia's Eastern Highlands, or Great Divide, and the formation of the Great Escarpment along its eastern margin, were associated with the opening of the Tasman Sea. But its subsequent erosion, in particular gorge incision and valley widening along the Great Escarpment, has been remarkably slow, a reflection of the tectonic stability of this part of Australia.

Australia and Antarctica had fully separated by 33 million years ago; Australia had finally become the island continent. The Antarctic Circumpolar Current then became established in the new Southern Ocean, triggering the refrigeration of Antarctica and increasing aridity in Australia about 15 million years ago, thus ending a 75-million-year period during which Australia and Antarctica were heavily forested and drained by abundant rivers and lakes.

Some uplift of the Central Australian mountain ranges occurred hundreds of millions of years ago. However, uplift of the Mt Lofty and Flinders Ranges has occurred over the last 50 million years, accelerating during the last 10 million, suggesting some of Australia's central mountains have formed from rejuvenated crustal activity and are not just worn down remnants of older, higher ranges. Further west, the Nullarbor Plain limestones were uplifted at the same time, facilitating the formation of one of the world's most extensive cave systems.

Australia is the only continent lacking active volcanoes, but this has not always been so and the most recent volcanic phase has barely ended. Basalt volcanoes and lava fields occurred all down the eastern margin from 70 million to just 4600 years ago, the latter eruption near Mt Gambier probably witnessed by the local Aboriginal people. Northern NSW's Border Ranges are the remnant of a 22-million-year-old basalt shield volcano, the eroded caldera being one of the largest in the world.

The Finke River, which runs through the West MacDonnell Ranges and floods out into the Simpson Desert, is claimed to be the world's oldest river, at around 350 million years.

The gross shape of the Australian coastline reflects the Gondwana break-up fracture pattern, but at a detailed level the coast has evolved from a combination of drowning and erosion of rocky coastal areas, and recent deposition in deltas and along sandy coastlines. Sea levels rose and fell by more than 100m over the last one to two million years, with shorelines migrating in response to the waxing and waning of several ice ages; the present level was attained only 6500 years ago.

Around 1300 sq km of Tasmania's highlands was glaciated during the last ice age, peaking 18,000 years ago, but on the mainland only a small area of ice formed near Mt Kosciuszko. However, the ice ages were periods of lowered precipitation as well as temperature, and did have a continent-wide effect with a dramatic influence on the character and distribution of vegetation. Many of Australia's desert dunes are probably relict features from the last ice age.

WILDLIFE

For all its visibility on postcard stands and road signs, Australia's wildlife can play pretty hard to get. In the main, the animals are more sensible than the walkers, avoiding the heat of day and stirring only for nocturnal activity. This means your days are unlikely to be spent among warm-blooded company, though wildlife parades past camp in the evenings and early mornings are common. If you are walking in Tasmania, where the animals think walkers are some form of butler service, you might even find yourself cursing the day possums were given dexterous, backpack-opening claws.

For a more complete look at Australian critters and their distribution, see Lonely Planet's *Watching Wildlife Australia*.

Animals
MAMMALS

The kangaroo is as symbolically Australian as Uluru, though it comes in about 39 flavours (counting wallabies). Fortunately, it seems to have so baffled the earliest settlers it finished up with a nomenclature that makes species simple to identify: if you see a kangaroo that is red in colour, it will be a red kangaroo; if you see a wallaby with yellowish feet in a rocky gorge, it will be a yellow-footed rock wallaby.

The most majestic roo is the **red kangaroo**, which can stand up to 1.8m tall. Restricted to the arid inland, only walkers in the Flinders Ranges (p261) are likely to see these bush giants. A more common sight is the **eastern grey kangaroo**, marginally smaller (and a lot greyer) than big red and found throughout eastern Australia. The **western grey kangaroo**, which looks very much like the eastern grey, isn't limited by its name, ranging across southern Australia.

Wallabies are classified as kangaroo species weighing less than 25kg, and there are several you might see on your wanders. The **red-necked wallaby**, with its characteristic reddish nape, is the most commonly seen along the east coast and Tasmania, while the dark **swamp wallaby** is also a frequent sight. Rock wallabies can be more reclusive than Ken Kesey, but early mornings and dusk in the gorges along the Larapinta Trail (p322) will reveal the endangered **black-footed rock wallaby**. On the Heysen Highlight (p269), watch for **yellow-footed rock wallabies**, the icon of the Flinders Ranges.

The **euro**, or common wallaroo, is found on rocky hillsides across the country. It is more solidly built and has a rougher, shaggier coat than red or grey kangaroos. The males' colouring varies from grey-black to reddish-brown to fawn, while the females are usually smaller and paler.

If you are going to reliably see any one mammal, it will be the **brushtail possum**, the largest and most boisterous of Australia's possums. Renowned for making a racket on suburban roofs, brushtails are no less bold in the bush, and on many walks, especially in Tasmania, you will need to guard your food against these bushy thieves. More reticent is the **ringtail possum**, with its white-ringed prehensile tail used for climbing.

The **koala** is atop everybody's list of wildlife darlings, at least until you have slept anywhere near a randy male koala grunting like a wild boar. With tufted ears and a hard black nose, it is among the easiest marsupials to spot during the day, often resting in a low fork of a eucalypt; manna gums are a favourite. You will find koalas along much of the east coast and also in South Australia, where they have been reintroduced after becoming extinct.

An apocryphal legend suggests that 'kangaroo' is an Aboriginal word for 'don't know'. When James Cook first saw this strange creature, he supposedly asked an Aboriginal man what it was. The man answered that he didn't know…'kangaroo'.

The **common wombat** is another bit of bush cuddliness that walkers in New South Wales, Victoria and Tassie might encounter. With its vaguely bear-like shape and amble, it looks cumbersome but can hit speeds of up to 40km/h. Those large burrows beside the track and the cube-shaped scat uncannily balanced atop rocks are the wombat's handiwork.

One creature you won't want to cuddle is the **short-beaked echidna**. It has a coat of long spines on its back and an elongated, beak-like snout perfect for catching ants and termites, its main food. It is often seen during the day in cooler climates, usually nosing about or ploughing open termite mounds and logs with its huge claws. If an echidna notices you, it will generally burrow frantically, leaving only its spines exposed. Echidnas are found throughout Australia.

Along with the echidna, the **platypus** is the world's last remaining monotreme, or egg-laying mammal. It is something of a jigsaw, with a softish, duck-like bill, short legs, webbed feet and a short, beaver-like tail. It is confined to the eastern mainland and Tasmania, and you are not going to see a platypus on many walks, though the two ends of the Overland Track (p214) – Lake St Clair and Dove Lake – offer hope.

As the name suggests, you will find the **Tasmanian devil** only in Tasmania. As stocky as a small pig, with white stripes across its black chest, its ferocious name gives it a largely undeserved notoriety, though watch a group of devils arguing over roadkill and you will wonder. It has solitary and nocturnal habits, either scavenging or hunting vertebrates. If you hear a banshee scream in the night, it is likely to be a Tassie devil but it is not about to come charging through your tent.

Perhaps the only mammal more notorious than the Tassie devil is the **dingo**, Australia's so-called native dog, which probably arrived about 4000 years ago with Asian sailors. Common in much of the outback (and prolific on Fraser Island, p346), it usually has a bronze tinge to its coat, and yips and howls rather than barks – if you hear barking, it is a wild dog not a dingo. The dingo is an efficient predator of rabbits but also attacks livestock.

BIRDS

Australia has around 800 recorded bird species and they're likely to be the most visible of the animals you'll see while walking. They are most

Discover the curious world of the wombat in James Woodford's *The Secret Life of Wombats*.

When the first platypus specimens were sent to England in the late 18th century, they were thought to be a hoax.

DEVIL OF A DISEASE

In the last decade, the Tasmanian devil population has been decimated by a fatal condition known as devil facial tumour disease (DFTD). Beginning as small lesions on the face and in the mouth, DFTD develops into large and hideous cancers around the face and neck. Affected animals usually die within six months of the appearance of lesions.

First found in Tasmania's northeast in 1996, DFTD has since become prevalent throughout eastern, central and northern parts of the island – currently the west coast remains free of the disease. There has been a dramatic population decline in some of these areas, with estimates that around 50,000 animals have died from DFTD. As a result, Tasmanian devils have been listed as a vulnerable species.

Researchers predict that DFTD isn't likely to result in the extinction of Tasmanian devils, but the decline in the population may result in increased cat numbers and could allow foxes to establish in Tasmania, making it difficult for the Tassie devil population to recover.

If you see a sick Tasmanian devil, leave it be but report it to the wildlife management branch of Tasmania's Department of Primary Industries, Water and Environment at http://wildlife .enquiries@dpiwe.tas.gov.au.

active in the early morning and you will have a better chance of seeing a good variety if you set off early each day.

Australia's most recognisable birds are the **emu** and the **laughing kookaburra**. The former looks like an ostrich baked dry by the sun and is found across most of the country. When startled, it can hit speeds of 50km/h. You will almost certainly hear the laughing kookaburra (the largest member of the kingfisher family) before you see it, with its loud, cackling laugh, though it is also easily spotted. Closely related is the **blue-winged kookaburra**, found in the tropics.

If you are walking in spring, the **Australian magpie** will probably find you before you find it. This large black-and-white bird has one of the bush's most melodious songs, but can be highly territorial when breeding, swooping anything that comes near, including humans. The good news for walkers is that swooping seems more prevalent in urban areas than on walking tracks.

Looking like a cross between a crow and a magpie, the **pied currawong** is one of the most regularly seen birds in the bush. This black bird has yellow eyes and a strip of white across its tail feathers. It is among the most gregarious of the birds you will encounter and has a piercing, almost parrot-like call.

The greatest sight you will see in the Australian skies is the freewheeling figure of a **wedge-tailed eagle**. The country's largest bird of prey has a wingspan of up to 2m and is named for the distinctive shape of its tail. Though 'wedgies' are found across Australia, they are most commonly seen in the interior.

Just as fascinating is the sight of a male bowerbird at work. This stocky, stout-billed bird builds a bower that he decorates with various coloured objects: the glossy-blue male **satin bowerbird** will use almost anything that's blue; the **golden bowerbird** uses pale-green moss, pale flowers and fruits; and the **great bowerbird** accumulates stones, shells, seeds and metallic objects.

Among the parrots and cockatoos you can expect to see, the **galah** and **sulphur-crested cockatoo** are prominent. The former is pink and grey in colour, while the latter is white and has a crest coloured like the rim of a volcano. It also has a shriek loud enough to wake the dead. The **black-cockatoo**, whether yellow-, red- or white-tailed, is another welcome sight. They can look like crows from a distance, but have a heavier, lazier wing motion and a call like a creaky door. The **crimson rosella** is a common sight – look for a flash of red through the trees – and the brilliantly coloured **rainbow lorikeet**, with its blue head, orange breast and green body, gathers in great numbers around flowering plants.

The **superb lyrebird**, which graces the Australian 10-cent coin, is a ground-dwelling bird. The male lyrebird has tail feathers that form a lyre shape when hoisted to attract a female. Its party trick is bush mimicry, copying almost any noise it has heard, from the calls of other birds to livestock and chainsaws. To hear a lyrebird running through its noises like a compilation CD is worth any amount of walking.

Walkers in Queensland will soon be aware of the **Australian brush-turkey**, with its bald red head and yellow wattles – it will be the bird trying to pilfer your food and rubbish bag. You might even start wishing Christmas dinner upon it.

REPTILES

It is true that Australia has a few reptiles, but work under the assumption that they are at least as frightened of you as you are of them. Make some noise as you walk and you will most likely go unbothered.

Learn to pick one poo and paw from another in *Tracks, Scats and Other Traces* by Barbara Triggs.

Magpies usually swoop from behind. Painting eyes on the back of your hat or wearing sunglasses backwards can dissuade them from attacking.

For a bird identification guide that won't break your back, carry the *Slater Field Guide to Australian Birds* by Peter, Pat & Raoul Slater.

Australia has 130 species of snake and, despite the negative press, the majority are harmless (though it is always wise to assume otherwise). Warm, sunny conditions, such as the start of spring, are best for seeing snakes. It is difficult at a glance to tell one snake from another – most come in fetching shades of brown or black – though walkers in Lamington National Park might be treated to an array of rainforest pythons and tree snakes.

One reptile you will want to see is the goanna, or monitor lizard, a primordial reptile with the swagger of a cowboy. Australia has around 25 species of goanna, which can stretch to 2.5m. **Gould's goanna**, with cream or yellow spots, and the **lace monitor**, with white, cream or yellow scales forming a lace-like pattern, are often seen ambling through camps.

Only walkers on Hinchinbrook Island (p347) need browse up on crocodiles. The **saltwater (or estuarine) crocodile** is the one that causes all the fuss. Growing to 7m, it will attack and kill humans. It lives in large numbers on mangrove-rimmed Hinchinbrook, though there have been no recorded attacks. The **freshwater crocodile** is smaller, not so interested in the taste of humans, and can be distinguished from 'salties' by its narrow snout (salties have wide, box-like snouts). Kakadu is flush with crocs, but not along the walking route described in this book.

> Bushfire-aware slogan in the Northern Territory: 'We Like Our Lizards Frilled Not Grilled'.

Plants

NATIVE GRASSES

Australia has more than 700 species of native grass, a couple of which will come to the particular notice of walkers.

Spinifex is the hardiest and most common desert plant, forming round clumps of needle-like leaves sprouting into softer, wheat-like seed stalks. The prickly dome is a haven for small desert mammals and reptiles, which shelter inside during the day.

WHERE THE WILD THINGS ROAM

Animals you might expect to see on walks in this book include the following:

Black-footed rock wallaby Larapinta Trail Highlight (p320)
Brushtail possum Warrumbungle National Park (p110), Croajingolong National Park (p180)
Common wombat Wilsons Promontory National Park (p175), Blue Mountains (p62)
Dingo Fraser Island (p341)
Eastern grey kangaroo Warrumbungle National Park (p110)
Eastern quoll Overland Track (p214)
Echidna Warrumbungle National Park (p110)
Emu Warrumbungle National Park (p110)
Frilled lizard Kakadu National Park (p311)
Great bowerbird Nitmiluk National Park (p315)
Koala Yurrebilla Trail (p253), Warrumbungle National Park (p110)
Lace Monitor Croajingolong National Park (p180)
Noisy pitta Lamington National Park (p333)
Platypus Overland Track (p214)
Red kangaroo Flinders Ranges (p261)
Ringtail possum Wilsons Promontory National Park (p175), Overland Track (p214)
Saltwater crocodile Hinchinbrook Island (p347)
Satin bowerbird Lamington National Park (p333)
Superb lyrebird Blue Mountains (p62), Cathedral Range (p135)
Tasmanian devil Overland Track (p214), Freycinet Peninsula (p242)
Western grey kangaroo Stirling Range (p298), Walpole-Nornalup National Park (p290)

Largely confined to poorly drained plains in southwest Tasmania, **buttongrass** grows in tall tussocks, separated by bare patches of bog, and is a dirty word among walkers who have ever wallowed through it. Its leaves are tough and the flower for which it is named is a small cluster of white spikelets.

SHRUBS & FLOWERS

The best known of the Australian shrubs (and among the easiest to identify) is the callistemon, or **bottlebrush**. Named for its brush-like flowers, it is found right across the country, and ranges in height from 1m to 10m. There are about 30 species with varying flower colours – red, white, pink and yellow among them – though species are difficult to distinguish. They are a favourite with some birds.

There are around 250 species of **grevillea**, of which 245 are endemic to Australia. They come in various sizes and flower colours and are found in the Australian Alps, forests, semi-arid country and near the coast. Most are small to medium in size, although the silky oak can grow to 25m and, covered with orange flowers, is one of Australia's most beautiful trees.

There are around 80 species of **tea-tree**, which are found in all states. Most species are large, dense bushes, not trees. Early settlers gave the tree its name after trying to brew tea from its leaves (what English settler

BUSH TUCKER *Jon Muir*

Australia supported a rich culture for thousands of years on food that was hunted and gathered. Most of these foods can still be found in wilderness areas, although few people today recognise them. To sample these wild foods you need to be able to positively identify what you are about to put in your mouth to avoid accidental poisoning. Many edible bush foods have closely related plants that look very similar but are poisonous. Fortunately, most plants that are toxic to humans make themselves known by an unpleasant taste or burning sensation to the mouth (however, there are a few poisonous plants that do taste OK!). Before sampling any bush food you should touch it to your lip to check for taste or burning.

It is also important to note that flora and fauna are protected in national parks. Nothing here can be sampled, be it water lily petals or red kangaroo. However, parks are a great place to learn about identification of food because there is such a diverse range of bush tucker found in these ecologically intact remnants of wilderness.

In dune fields you can find lizards, native pear (a green vegetable that grows on a low bush and needs baking), pigweed (which has sweet, fleshy red flower petals with a salty aftertaste) and bloodwood galls. These galls are often tennis-ball-sized knobbly growths on the western bloodwood. Both the gall itself and the grub found inside are edible.

Arid mountains are the home of the bush banana, which grows on spindly vines strung between trees and needs to be picked young and steamed or lightly roasted. In these rocky terrains, rock figs are often found above rock holes, with the fruit looking similar to (though smaller than) the common fig.

The Top End is probably the easiest place to find a diverse supply of bush foods, including burdekin plums, lilly pilly fruit, lady apples (crunchy and sweet) and the vicious green ant (if you are bold enough to disturb its nest!). Both the green ant larvae and the nests themselves are a source of food. The nest clump can be dropped into hot water to make a deliciously tangy lemon flavoured tea.

One of the best books on northern Australian bush food is *Bush Tucker Field Guide* by Les Hiddins, and for central Australia (and my all-time favourite), *Wild Food Plants of Australia* by Tim Low.

Australian adventurer Jon Muir completed an unassisted traverse across Australia, from the Spencer Gulf to the Gulf of Carpentaria, surviving largely on bush food.

could live without his tea, after all?). Flowers are mainly white and stalk-less, and leaves are small.

The **pandani** is the tallest heath plant in the world, and though it looks more like a tropical palm you will only find it in west and southwest Tasmania. It can reach a height of 12m, and has a crown of stiff leathery leaves 1.5m long, with old, dead leaves or fronds forming a huge skirt around the lower trunk.

CYCADS & FERNS

The **MacDonnell Ranges cycad** is one of about 25 Australian species of the ancient cycad family, and will become familiar to walkers on the Larap-inta Trail (p322). It is very slow-growing, and often found high on rocky hillsides and in gorges. It has palm-like fronds and seed cones grow at the tip of the short trunk on female plants; the male cones carry the pollen. The seeds are poisonous.

The **burrawang** grows along the NSW coast on sandy soils. The 2m-long palm-like fronds grow from ground level. Its red seeds are also poisonous.

The beautifully ornate **rough tree fern** and the **soft tree fern** are found in eastern Australia's temperate rainforests. Some reach a height of 20m and all are capped by a crown of green fronds.

TREES

First among equals for Australian trees is the ubiquitous **eucalyptus**, or gum tree. Of the 700 species, all but about eight are endemic to Aus-tralia. Eucalypts vary in form and height from the tall, ruler-straight karri (confined to WA) and the towering mountain ash to the twisted snow gum. River red gums typically line watercourses, permanent or ephemeral, where their deep roots tap underground water reserves. The most widespread eucalypt, these massive, spreading trees grow to 45m high and can live for hundreds of years. River red gums are notorious shedders of branches, so never camp under this tree; people have been killed by falling branches. The hardy, shrub-like mallee is widespread in the interior. There are over 100 species of this ground-branching tree, which grows from a massive underground root (lignotuber) that enables it to survive fire.

Two of Australia's most striking trees are eucalypts: the snow gum and the ghost gum. The snow gum flourishes at higher altitudes than any other eucalyptus – up to 1700m in the High Country and Tasmanian highlands. It ranges from 1m to 20m in height and has smooth, whitish bark, sometimes patterned in racing stripes of green, yellow and red. Walkers in the MacDonnell Ranges won't fail to notice the bone-white trunks of the ghost gum, immortalised in Albert Namatjira's distinctive paintings.

Australian acacias are commonly known as **wattles** and around 700 species have been recorded. They vary from small shrubs to the black-wood, which grows up to 30m in height. The flowers come in all shades of yellow; most species flower during late winter and spring, bring-ing brilliant splashes of colour to the bush. The golden wattle, with its masses of bright-yellow flowers, is Australia's floral emblem. A less-showy acacia is the mulga, found across the arid inland. Its wide, funnel-like shape acts as its own water catchment, channelling rain to its base.

Never again will you think of the humble gum tree as just a khaki-coloured bit of stick after reading Murray Bail's beautiful *Eucalyptus*.

(Continued on page 45)

BOOTS, BEACHES & BULLDUST

ISLANDS SHOULD FIGURE HEAVILY IN YOUR PLANNING IF YOU ARE HOPING TO SPOT WILDLIFE.

The wild beauty of the Gap, along the Bibbulmun Track (p290) on Western Australia's southern coast

They call it the wide brown land, but such a monochromatic description does Australia a disservice. It forgets the red rocks of the Centre, the dripping green forests of tropical Queensland, the buttery yellow of the outback spinifex at dusk, and the peacock-blue seas found almost anywhere around the country's massive coast. Australia is as varied as it is large, which means there is something for everyone – only if you have packed crampons and an ice-axe will the landscape disappoint.

Variety equals choice and choice can often equal confusion. Australia has thousands of kilometres of walking tracks, so how do you distinguish one from another? In order to help you choose the walks that will best suit your interests, we have herded the country's tracks into the following selection of themes, according to their natural or cultural features. And while we have highlighted the finest of Australia's walks throughout this book, you will also find a few suggestions for stepping out into less travelled places for new experiences.

WILDLIFE WATCHING

Like Africa and Antarctica, one of Australia's greatest attractions is the inimitability of its animals: who would believe the platypus if they hadn't seen it? Like wildlife the world over, the more quietly you move, the better your chance of seeing it. Which makes your feet the best vehicle for happening upon Australia's peculiar fauna.

Some of Australia's greatest animal concentrations are found within noted walking regions. Croajingolong (p180) and Kakadu (p311) National Parks each support around one-third of the country's recorded bird species, and at times in the former you will just about have to push aside the mammals and reptiles to see the birds.

ANDREW BAIN

Birds are also a feature on Tasmania's Bruny Island, home to all 12 of the island state's endemic birds. Here, you can walk a circuit around the Labillardiere Peninsula (p246), noted as a home for Tasmania's rarest bird: the forty-spotted pardalote (the peninsula is noted also for its snakes).

AUSTRALIA IS AS VARIED AS IT IS LARGE, WHICH MEANS THERE IS SOMETHING FOR EVERYONE.

Islands should figure heavily in your planning if you are hoping to spot wildlife. Fox-free Flinders Chase National Park (p258) is a preview of what Australia could look like without feral predators. The park's isolation also led to its selection last century as a place to rescue threatened species – koalas and platypuses, among others, were not native to the island but are now found here in great numbers.

Tasmania's Maria Island (p247) has a similar story. In the 1970s several mammals and birds were introduced to secure their survival. It worked beyond hope, and if you are walking through Darlington on your way up to Bishop and Clerk you will be all but stepping over forester kangaroos and Cape Barren geese.

Many of Australia's great walking areas are defined by a single creature: Fraser Island (p341) is renowned for its dingoes; Lamington National Park (p333) has beautiful regent bowerbirds; gorges along the Larapinta Trail (p322) share their fame with the resident black-footed rock wallabies; and on the newly created, 50km-long Mackay Highlands Great Walk (see www.epa.qld.gov.au/parks_and_forests/great_walks/mackay_highlands) you will

The common wombat (*Vombatus ursinus*) is easily spotted at Wilsons Promontory National Park (p175)   MITCH REARDON

wander along Broken River, noted as perhaps the country's best setting for spotting a platypus.

In sight of Adelaide, along the Yurrebilla Trail (p253), you will see more koalas and kangaroos than people, while almost as close to Melbourne, the three-day Burchell Walk through Brisbane Ranges National Park (p132) is also thick with koalas.

Not even marine life need be denied you if you are walking. Hit the track in the right season and you can witness whale migrations along the Cape to Cape Track (p279), Great Ocean Walk (p143) or Fraser Island Great Walk (p342).

For a fuller list of walks and parks most likely to reveal particular animals, see the boxed text on p30.

ABORIGINAL CULTURE

Kakadu National Park is one of only 24 places to be on Unesco's World Heritage list for both natural and cultural reasons,

an indication of the importance of its wetlands and the more than 5000 recorded Aboriginal rock art sites in the park. The Barrk Sandstone Bushwalk (p312) links two of the most important of these rock-art sites, and is a must for anybody with an interest in Aboriginal art. Trundle a short way down the Stuart Hwy to the Jatbula Trail (p315) and you will wander past the Amphitheatre, a curving rock-art site.

Nearer to home for most of the country, Red Hands Cave (p64) in the Blue Mountains is decorated with numerous stencils and solid images of hands, created with coloured clays.

Many other walking trails will bring you near to Aboriginal art sites. The trailhead for the Mt Stapylton walk (p151) is also near to Gulgurn Manja Shelter and Ngamadjidj Shelter, the only art site in Grampians National Park where white ochre was used. Walkers at Wilpena (p266) need only stray outside of the Pound to find

The cascades of Cave Creek, viewed on the Gorges, Caves & Plains walk (p94) in Kosciuszko National Park

ANDREW BAIN

Arkaroo Rock, its art telling the Dreaming story of the Pound's creation. Way out west, the remote trailhead for Mt Augustus (p302) also has engravings of animal tracks and hunters.

KAKADU NATIONAL PARK IS ONE OF ONLY 24 PLACES TO BE ON UNESCO'S WORLD HERITAGE LIST FOR BOTH NATURAL AND CULTURAL REASONS.

Queensland's Carnarvon Gorge (for more information see www.epa.qld.gov .au/projects/park/index.cgi?parkid=49) is home to three Aboriginal art sites. Walkers can follow the park's main trail through the gorge for 9km to the site at Cathedral Cave, passing the simply named Art Gallery along the way.

MOUNTAIN CHALLENGES

Less than 1% of Australia's land surface is higher than 1500m above sea level yet there is plenty here to keep walkers occupied – evidence of this is the Australian Alps Walking Track (p157), which could occupy you in the Great Dividing Range for up to two months.

Inevitably, it is the country's highest peak, Mt Kosciuszko (p88), that receives the most attention, though it is far from the most challenging outing in the country – until 1982 you could drive to its summit. Wander a short distance and you can sample summits such as North Rams Head and Mt Townsend that are arguably more interesting.

Victoria has some of the finest mountain walks (as well as the sharpest ridges)

Mt Hayward viewed at dawn on the Heysen Highlight walk (p269) in South Australia's Flinders Ranges ANDREW BAIN

in the country. Mt Feathertop (p164) has been called both 'Queen of the Victorian Alps' and Australia's most alpine mountain. Couple this with the Razorback Ridge, draping between Feathertop and Mt Hotham, and you have a mountain walk the equal of any in the country. If that inspires you, you can find other ridges atop the Crosscut Saw (p168) or in the Cathedral Range (p135).

If it is mountain shapes that inspire you, Tasmania will top your wish list. Wearing the scars of recent glaciation, peaks here range from the rounded Barn Bluff (p220), to the dolerite quills of Mt Wellington (p196), to the tall, sharp lines of Mt Geryon, best seen from atop the Acropolis (p228). One author was so inspired by this abstract Tasmanian landscape he fictionalised a theory that here was the location of the Garden of Eden.

Tasmania's west and World Heritage Area is arguably the finest mountain terrain in the country: along the Overland Track (p214) you can climb up to seven mountains, including Tasmania's highest; the Walls of Jerusalem (p232) is encased by peaks; the summit cliffs on Frenchmans Cap (p229) need to be seen to be believed;

TASMANIA'S WEST AND WORLD HERITAGE AREA IS ARGUABLY THE FINEST MOUNTAIN TERRAIN IN THE COUNTRY.

and there are difficult routes on Mt Anne (p209), Federation Peak (p247) and the ultimate walking commitment through the Western Arthurs (p247).

The only places on the mainland to match Tasmania's weird and wonderful

Belougery Spire, Warrumbungle National Park (p112)   RICHARD I'ANSON

Like the rest of the world, Australia's most fickle weather is to be found in its mountains. Snow is not unusual in Tasmania's west even in summer, while altitude and wind chill can transform a pleasantly cool day in a valley into a tussle with hypothermia on the mountain tops; as a vague rule, the temperature drops around 1°C for every 150m you climb.

The mountains are a place where half clothing measures may not be good enough. Certainly, you can wear your shorts and T-shirt, but always be prepared for the worst conditions a mountain might throw at you. Wear walking boots, as they offer better protection against the elements, and carry a spare pair of socks in case your walking socks get wet.

Swot up on the layering principle (p389) and be sure to pack the full measure of warm clothing – thermal underwear, a thick windproof fleece, and even a down jacket (although avoid getting the last item wet or it will lose its insulation). If you are going to spend big money on one item of clothing, make it your wet-weather gear – the last thing you want is to be cold *and* wet. Look for a Gore-Tex (or equivalent) rain jacket. Lightweight gloves come in handy in cool, damp conditions, and a warm hat is a must (up to half of your body heat can be lost through your head).

Nights in the mountains can be bitterly cold, so always carry a down sleeping bag (see p393 for info on sleeping bags) and a three- or four-season tent.

mountain shapes are the Warrumbungles (p110) and Glasshouse Mountains (p356).

For outback mountains there is nothing better than the Flinders and West Mac-Donnell Ranges. Most walks here thread below the peaks, not onto them, with a few wonderful exceptions. At Wilpena Pound (p266) you can scale Mt Ohlssen Bagge, or you can head further south to the Dutch-mans Stern (p273), Mt Brown (see www.flindersranges.com/attract/walkq.htm) or Mt Remarkable (p272). In the West Mac-Donnells you can walk west from Standley Chasm, along the Larapinta Trail (p323), for 10km to the summit of Brinkley Bluff, complete with camp sites and jaw-dropping sunset and sunrise views. At the trail's far western end you can scale shapely Mt Sonder (p326).

BEACHCOMBING

If the Australian landscape is famous for one thing it is beaches, and you don't need to be a beach bum to enjoy them. Throughout the country there are great coastal bushwalks, dipping in and out of gorgeous beaches. Many you will have to yourself; at others, such as Tasmania's Wineglass Bay (p246), you will be able to gain new perspective on well-known sights.

Most of the famous beaches are on Australia's east coast, though many of the best beaches are actually in the west. The Cape to Cape Track (p279) follows a chain of beaches, and you will be walking on

Guinness World Records once listed Hyams Beach, on NSW's Jervis Bay, as having the world's whitest sand; it's the end point of the bay's White Sands Walk.

Walkers take in the early morning sun on Jervis Bay's windswept Blenheim Beach ANDREW BAIN

them for up to 8km at a time. Around the coast, beyond Esperance, is Cape Le Grand National Park (p302) – see the beaches here and you will appreciate why Matthew Flinders called one of them Lucky Bay.

In the east there are good beach walks in every state. Sydney is renowned for its beaches so it is little wonder there are good walking beaches nearby on the Coast Track (p58) and on the Bouddi Coast (p55).

In Victoria, the Croajingolong Coast Walk (p182) is beach upon beach, while Refuge Cove (p177) on Wilsons Promontory is like a lovebite nibbled into the country. If you are imagining crowds on every beach along the Great Ocean Road, set out on foot for Milanesia Beach (p145) – if there is more than a handful of people here, register a complaint.

South Australia's best beach-walking destination is on Kangaroo Island – see West Bay (p260) at dusk and you will never want to leave. On Eyre Peninsula you can walk between beaches few people know exist on the Investigator Trail (p273) or on distant Boarding House Bay in Coffin Bay National Park (see www.tep.com.au /nationalparks/np_coffinbay.htm), which makes for a great, if long, day walk.

Then, of course, there is Queensland. If you believe the hype, this state is one giant tropical beach. There are few walking opportunities on mainland beaches – though a notable exception is Cape Hillsborough National Park (see www.epa.qld.gov.au/ projects/park/index.cgi?parkid=44) – but plenty among the 900-plus islands. The king of beach walks is the Thorsborne Trail (p349) on Hinchinbrook Island, Australia's largest island national park. In 32 idyllic kilometres you can stroll the sands of nine postcard-perfect beaches.

Fraser Island is the world's largest sand island, so it's unsurprising that it should have beaches. What is remarkable here is that the best beaches – and they are great

40

Adventure Bay on Tasmania's Bruny Island (p246)   ANDREW BAIN

TOP FIVES

Still can't decide which track to walk? Choosing five favourite mountains or beaches in Australia is fraught with dilemma (what about the other 6995 great beaches?) but in the interests of subjectivity (or just to spark a good tent debate at night) here are our best-of-the-best walking destinations.

MOUNTAINS

- Mt Feathertop (p164)
- Mt Townsend (p90)
- The Acropolis (p228)
- The Castle (p99)
- Frenchmans Cap (p229)

BEACHES

- Nina Bay (p350)
- Wineglass Bay (p242)
- Boranup Beach (p288)
- Refuge Cove (p177)
- Lucky Bay (p302)

CITY ESCAPES

- Mt Wellington & the Organ Pipes (p196)
- Yurrebilla Trail (p253)
- Cathedral Range (p135)
- Coast Track (p58)
- Lamington National Park (p333)

beaches – are inland, around the lakes pooled between the sand hills. Hit the trail on the Fraser Island Great Walk (p342) and you will visit most of them.

Tasmania has the kind of beaches that would bankrupt Queensland if only it had the weather to match. For walkers in the island state, this usually translates to a guided walk along the Bay of Fires (see www.bayof fires.com.au), a coast crowded with wildlife and basted in brilliant orange lichen.

CITY ESCAPES

Not everybody has the time to seek out walking nooks and crannies in the mountains or on distant beaches. If you are confined to walking near one of the capital cities, you need not limit yourself to footpaths; there are excellent trails within easy reach of every state capital.

Sydneysiders are invariably drawn to the Blue Mountains (p62) or Royal National Park (p58), though they also now have

the opportunity to amble along the Harbour Circle Walk (see www.planning.nsw .gov.au/harbour/walking.asp), a 26km trail that does exactly as it promises, circuiting Sydney Harbour. Sydney walkers are even able to set out on a long-distance trail – the Great North Walk (p55) – from the very heart of the city.

Melburnians don't have to give up mountains or beaches. In the Cathedral Range (p135) there is a ridge walk as sharp as any in the country, while Bushrangers Bay (p133) is a hideaway beach little more than an hour from the city, and accessible only to walkers.

Hobart doesn't simply have any mountain for a backyard – it has a great mountain. Mt Wellington (p196), wearing the dolerite Organ Pipes like a turtleneck

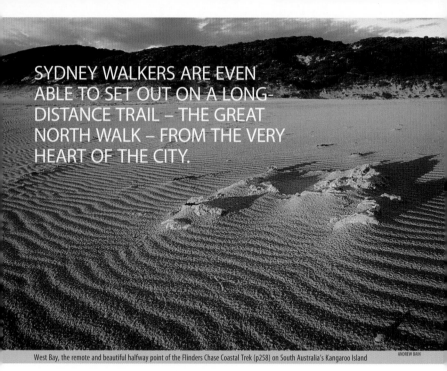

SYDNEY WALKERS ARE EVEN ABLE TO SET OUT ON A LONG-DISTANCE TRAIL – THE GREAT NORTH WALK – FROM THE VERY HEART OF THE CITY.

West Bay, the remote and beautiful halfway point of the Flinders Chase Coastal Trek (p258) on South Australia's Kangaroo Island   ANDREW BAIN

WALKING EPICS

Several walks in this book can keep you occupied on the track for up to a week, but you need not stop there. Fitting to its size, Australia has a number of long-distance trails, right up to the 5330km Bicentennial Trail between Healesville (Victoria) and Cooktown (Queensland).

In this book we have picked the eyes out of some of the country's major long-distance tracks – namely the Bibbulmun Track, Heysen Trail, Great Ocean Walk and Larapinta Trail – selecting what we consider to be their best sections. WA's Cape to Cape Track we have covered in its entirety.

Most of the long-distance tracks are covered in detail in dedicated guidebooks. At the time of writing no such books exist for the two newest walks, the Larapinta Trail and Great Ocean Walk, but by the time you read this they probably will.

The following is the pick of the long-distance walking tracks.

Walk	Distance	Duration	Page
Australian Alps Walking Track (Victoria, NSW & ACT)	680km	55-60 days	157
Bibbulmun Track (WA)	964km	55-60 days	293
Cape to Cape Track (NSW)	133.5km	7 days	279
Great North Walk (NSW)	250km	14 days	55
Great Ocean Walk (Victoria)	91km	5-8 days	148
Great South West Walk (Victoria)	250km	12-14 days	187
Heysen Trail (SA)	1200km	60 days	269
Hume & Hovell Walking Track (NSW)	450km	20-25 days	105
Larapinta Trail (NT)	223km	12-16 days	323

READING
& RAMBLING

Sometimes you don't have to leave the city to escape it. Within all of Australia's capital cities there are walking opportunities. To browse up on a few, consider picking up a copy of the following books:

- *50 Family Walks in & Around Hobart* by Jan Hardy
- *50 Real Bushwalks around Adelaide* by George Driscoll
- *Walking Brisbane* by Alison Cotes and Pamela Wilson
- *Walking Canberra's Hills & Rivers* by Graeme Barrow
- *Walking Melbourne* by Helen Duffy and Ingrid Ohlsson
- *Walking Perth* by Ron Crittall
- *Walking Sydney* by Jeff Toghill

Signature dolerite boulders of Mt Wellington (p196), overlooking the Tasman Sea high above Hobart

GARETH McCORMACK

sweater, is probably the ultimate city escape, offering solitude, great natural features and terrific views just 10km from the city centre.

Just as close to Adelaide are sections of the Yurrebilla Trail (p253), a three-day walk winding between national, state and conservation parks in the Mt Lofty Ranges. You will see Adelaide plenty of times but with a great sense of removal.

Brisbane's great walking pleasure is Lamington National Park (p333), a showcase of waterfalls and subtropical rainforest set in the hinterland of the Gold Coast.

Even Perth, so isolated from everything else, has a couple of walking options in near proximity. Head for the hills and the Eagle's View Walk Trail (p301) or stay on the plain for the Coastal Plain Walking Trail (p301).

Quininup Falls Cascades, an inviting rest stop on Day 2 of Western Australia's Cape to Cape Track (p279)

(Continued from page 32)

Banksias take their name from Sir Joseph Banks, the botanist who accompanied James Cook on his exploration of eastern Australia. Numbering about 70 species and confined to Australia, they are common on sandy soils. Most banksias sport upright cylindrical flower spikes up to 30cm long, covered with vibrant orange, red or yellow flowers. As the flowers die, the woody fruits appear. Aboriginal people dipped the banksia spikes in water to make a sweet drink.

Casuarinas, also known as she-oaks, are hardy trees characterised by wiry 'leaves' that are actually branchlets; the true leaves are small scales clustered in whorls along the branchlets. Casuarinas produce distinctive small knobbly cones, and are widely distributed from the desert to the coast.

The **melaleuca**, also called paperbark or honey-myrtle, is easily recognised by its pale papery bark, which peels from the trunk in thin sheets. It is widespread on rocky ground, from the coast to semiarid inland areas. The flower spikes consist of many tiny filaments and range from cream through crimson to purple.

Australia has several families of native **conifer**, but they rarely dominate the vegetation as pines and spruces can in the northern hemisphere. Endemic to Tasmania, the pencil pine is found in areas of high rainfall: the central plateau and the southwest. A graceful tree, it grows to a height of about 15m. In coastal areas and inland semi-arid country in all states except WA, the Oyster Bay pine has distinctive segmented cones and reaches 6m in height. Foliage is typical of the *Callitris* genus: tiny scaly leaves arranged along branchlets. The **cypress pine** has hard, furrowed bark and its resistance to termites has made it a favourite bush building material.

The unusual looking **grass tree** is widespread in southeastern and southwestern Australia, mainly on sandy soils. It has very thin long leaves, a short thick trunk and a distinctive flower spike up to 3m tall, with tiny flowers massed along the upper half of a long stem. Walkers on the Cape to Cape Track (p279) will see the biggest of them.

Australia has about 50 species of **mangrove** – trees and shrubs adapted to daily flooding by salt water. Along northern coasts and estuaries, various species grow to around 30m, while at the southern limit of their distribution, in Victoria, they rarely exceed 5m. Mangroves have various ways of coping with inundation, with some breathing through aerial roots that are exposed at low tide. Walkers on Hinchinbrook Island (p347) will get the best look at mangroves.

WORLD HERITAGE WANDERS

Australia has 16 sites inscribed on the Unesco World Heritage list, including six that feature walks in this book:

- Central Eastern Rainforest Reserves (p119)
- Fraser Island (p341)
- Greater Blue Mountains Area (p62)
- Kakadu National Park (p311)
- Tasmanian Wilderness (p204)
- Wet Tropics of Queensland (p352)

For a full list of World Heritage sites, log on to http://whc.unesco.org.

ENVIRONMENTAL CHALLENGES *Tim Flannery*

The European colonisation of Australia, commencing in 1788, heralded a period of catastrophic environmental upheaval, with the result that Australians today are struggling with some of the most severe environmental problems to be found anywhere. It may seem strange that a population of just 20 million, living in a country the size of continental USA, could inflict such damage on its environment, but Australia's long isolation, fragile soils and difficult climate have made it particularly vulnerable to human-induced change.

Damage to Australia's environment has been inflicted in several ways, the most important being the introduction of pest species, destruction of forests, overstocking of rangelands, inappropriate agriculture and interference with water flows. Beginning with the escape of domestic cats into the Australian bush shortly after 1788, a plethora of vermin (from foxes to wild camels and cane toads) has run wild in Australia, causing extinctions in the native fauna. One out of every 10 native mammals living in Australia prior to European colonisation is now extinct, and many more are highly endangered. Extinctions have also affected native plants, birds and amphibians.

The destruction of forests has also had a profound effect on the environment. Most of Australia's rainforests have suffered clearing, while conservationists continue to fight with loggers over the fate of the last unprotected stands of 'old growth'.

Many Australian rangelands have been chronically overstocked for more than a century, the result being the extreme vulnerability of both soils and rural economies to Australia's drought and flood cycle, as well as the extinction of many native species. The development of agriculture has involved land clearance and the provision of irrigation, and again the effect has been profound.

Clearing of the diverse and spectacular plant communities of the Western Australian wheat belt began just a century ago, yet today up to one-third of that country is degraded by salination of the soils. Between 70kg and 120kg of salt lies below every square metre of the region, and clearing of native vegetation has allowed water to penetrate deep into the soil, dissolving the salt crystals and carrying brine towards the surface.

In terms of financial value, just 1.5% of Australia's land surface provides over 95% of its agricultural yield, and much of this land lies in the irrigated regions of the Murray–Darling Basin. This is Australia's agricultural heartland, yet it is also under severe threat from salting of soils and rivers. Irrigation water penetrates into the sediments laid down in an ancient sea, carrying salt into the catchments and fields. If nothing is done, the lower Murray River will become too salty to drink in a decade or two, threatening the water supply of Adelaide, a city of over a million people.

Despite the scale of the biological crisis engulfing Australia, governments and the community have been slow to respond. In the 1980s coordinated action began to take place, but not until the '90s were major steps taken. The establishment of **Landcare Australia** (www.landcareaustralia .com.au), an organisation enabling people to effectively address local environmental issues, and the expenditure of $2.5 billion through the National Heritage Trust Fund have been important national initiatives. Yet so difficult are some of the issues the nation faces that, as yet, little has been achieved in terms of halting the destructive processes.

Individuals are also banding together to help. Groups such as the **Australian Bush Heritage Fund** (www.bushheritage.asn.au) and the **Australian Wildlife Conservancy** (AWC; www.australianwildlife .org) allow people to donate funds and time to the conservation of native species. Some such groups have been spectacularly successful; the AWC, for example, already manages many endangered species over its 5260-sq-km holdings.

So severe are Australia's problems that it will take a revolution before they can be overcome, for sustainable practices need to be implemented in every arena of life – from farms to suburbs and city centres. Renewable energy, sustainable agriculture and water use lie at the heart of these changes, and Australians are only now developing the road map to sustainability that they so desperately need if they are to have a long-term future on the continent.

Tim Flannery is a naturalist, explorer and writer. He lives in Adelaide where he is director of the South Australian Museum and a professor at the University of Adelaide.

NATIONAL PARKS & RESERVES

It is safe to suggest that Australia has more national parks than any other country on earth. While Britain has 15 national parks and the USA has around 60, Australia has about 330 national parks.

Around 7% of Australia's land is protected as either national park or as some other form of nature conservation reserve. It doesn't sound huge, but it represents an area about twice the size of New Zealand. South Australia has the greatest amount of protected land, both in area (203,700 sq km) and proportion (20.7% of the state). This is followed by Tasmania (20%), Victoria (13.4%), WA (6.1%), NSW (4.8%), Queensland (3.1%) and the NT (2.8%).

State governments have authority over their own national parks. Contact details for each national park authority are provided in the regional chapters.

Many national parks have entry fees; for an overview see p368.

ENVIRONMENTAL ISSUES

Romanticised around the world as an environmental exemplar, Australia has its share of ecological problems. It is also one of only four nations (with the USA, Monaco and Liechtenstein) yet to sign the Kyoto Protocol on the reduction of carbon dioxide emissions, so pack away any preconceptions that this green-and-gold nation is more interested in green than gold.

Wherever you wander, and as you drive to and from walks, you will encounter weeds, feral animals, deforestation, suburban sprawl and, most likely, salinity and water shortages. Even national parks are often located on previously logged or damaged lands.

Walking doesn't automatically remove you as part of the problem. The hardening of tracks and camp sites is evident throughout the country, while some responsibility for the spread or containment of *Phytophthora cinnamomi*, or dieback, rests with walkers. This destructive root rot affects a variety of woody species, and has killed great numbers of plants in many of the walking areas covered in this book. It is spread by the movement of dirt or plant material, so you should make certain that your gear is thoroughly washed after leaving an infected area. In many places, special cleaning stations are provided.

Conservation groups in Australia include the following:

Australian Conservation Foundation (ACF; ☎ 1800 332 510; www.acfonline.org.au)
Foundation for National Parks & Wildlife (☎ 02-9221 1949; www.fnpw.com.au)
Friends of the Earth Australia (☎ 03-9419 8700; www.foe.org.au)
Greenpeace Australia Pacific (☎ 02-9261 4666; www.greenpeace.org.au)
Landcare Australia (☎ 1800 151 105; www.landcareaustralia.org.au)
Wilderness Society (☎ 03-6270 1701; www.wilderness.org.au)

The first Green political party in the world was formed in Australia, arising from failed efforts to stop the flooding of Lake Pedder in Tasmania's southwest in the 1960s and early 1970s.

New South Wales

When it comes to bushwalking, New South Wales (NSW) can rightly claim to be Australia's state of variety. Dotted around the state's 800,000-or-so square kilometres are several of the country's highest peaks, lush pockets of temperate and subtropical rainforest, volcanic remains, desert ranges, isolated beaches and gorge-scarred tableland. There's empty space aplenty and it's possible to walk through almost all of it.

On a crowded walkers' highlights reel, the cool upper reaches of Kosciuszko National Park probably grab top billing. Here are relatively easy walks in a usually well-watered region, under wide skies and with stunning views. The dense eucalypt forests and shady, plunging canyons of Blue Mountains National Park would probably run a close second. Especially as the 'Blueys' are in an eponymously named World Heritage Area, and said area of world renown is right on the doorstep of Sydney, and Sydney is a jolly fine destination for walkers in its own right. North and south of the NSW capital are easy coastal walks through cliff top heathland of unrivalled beauty. From these ocean ramparts, you can gaze in silence at the tall towers of nearby Sydney with nothing but sea-eagles for company.

Of all the places to walk in NSW, the remarkable Warrumbungle Range might be the best in which to ponder NSW's diversity of terrain and experience. To the west of the 'Bungles stretch the tabletop plains of western NSW. East, a spur of the Liverpool Range bends back towards the Great Dividing Range, which includes the Blue Mountains, Kosciuszko Range and other distinctive walking destinations, such as the World Heritage-listed Barrington Tops and the rugged, hidden Budawangs. Big state. Big choice. Get started.

HIGHLIGHTS

- Wandering past sandy beaches, beautiful wind-fretted rock formations and soaring cliffs of the Royal National Park on the **Coast Track** (p58)
- Exploring the World Heritage–listed landscapes of the **Blue Mountains** (p62) and **Kanangra-Boyd National Parks** (p80)
- Climbing Australia's highest peaks in **Kosciuszko National Park** (p88)
- Savouring solitude and the extraordinary rock formations of **Monolith Valley** (p101)
- Scaling the ridges surrounding the volcanic spires of the **Warrumbungles** (p110)

■ TELEPHONE CODE: 03   ■ www.visitnsw.com.au   ■ www.nationalparks.nsw.gov.au

ENVIRONMENT

The Great Dividing Range dominates eastern NSW, running the length of the state and providing a key influence on climate, plant and animal distribution and human settlement. Most of the Great Dividing Range's ancient peaks have been worn down to a series of plateaus or tablelands, including the New England tableland, the Blue Mountains, the Southern Highlands and the Monaro Tablelands, most of which don't rise above 1200m to 1400m. By contrast, in the Snowy Mountains the high peaks top 2000m, culminating in Australia's highest point, Mt Kosciuszko (2228m). Here there's evidence of the last ice age in the moraines and lakes left by retreating glaciers.

East of the range, the coastal strip is (by Australian standards) heavily settled and much changed by human hand. To the west, the better watered and more productive agricultural lands on rolling land near the range give way to vast, empty, arid plains.

The walks in this chapter are concentrated in the ranges and coast, where there's generally a higher proportion of forested country and greater diversity of plant and animal life.

INFORMATION
When to Walk

For the most part NSW offers year-round walking conditions, with a few exceptions. Mid-winter snows generally prevent walking in Kosciuszko National Park, while high temperatures and lack of surface water can sometimes inhibit departures in certain parks (and even close some areas) in mid-summer. Generally, autumn and spring are the most popular seasons for walking.

Maps

If you're planning to do a lot of driving, take along the series of regional road maps by the National Roads & Motorist's Association (NRMA), which shows almost every road and track in the state, although not the topography. The descriptions of road conditions are accurate and up to date. You can order online (www.mynrma.com.au/maps_2.asp) or pick them up at NRMA offices – most will have the maps to their area and probably the whole set. They're free to members, and to the members of motoring organisations in other states.

The **NSW Department of Lands** (☎ 9228 6111; www.lands.nsw.gov.au), referred to as 'Lands', produces topographic maps at three scales – 1:25,000, which cover the coast and ranges; 1:50,000, for the western slopes and central region, and 1:100,000, for the far west. In the past, the state mapmaker has been known as Land & Property Information New South Wales (LPINSW) and Central Mapping Authority (CMA), and many Lands maps continue to be published under one of those imprints.

For maps covering individual walks, see Planning in the introduction to each walk.

BUYING MAPS

Sydney has the best range of maps (p52), available either in dedicated map shops or one of the many outdoor gear shops.

Books

For the most extensive coverage of the state's national parks, use the National Parks Association (NPA) guide in two volumes: *The NPA Guide to National Parks of Northern NSW* and *The NPA Guide to National Parks of Southern NSW*. Several walking books explore the state in fair depth. Tyrone Thomas's *120 Walks in New South Wales* and *70 Walks in Southern New South Wales and the ACT* are extremely useful. John and Lyn Daly's *Take a Walk in a National Park* series has four volumes covering NSW walks: *South-Eastern Zone, Blue Mountains, Sydney to Port Macquarie* and *Port Macquarie to Brisbane*.

Information Sources

Tourism NSW (☎ 13 20 77; www.tourism.nsw.gov.au) is the NSW government's peak tourism body. Almost every major town (and many minor ones) has a tourist office with local information that's not readily available from the larger state organisation; those relevant to individual walks are listed in this chapter.

For information on NSW national parks and bushwalking organisations (all based in Sydney), see Information (p51).

Park Fees & Regulations

National park fees and camping regulations vary across NSW. Just under 50 of the state's 100-plus parks charge vehicle-entry fees, which vary from $22 per day during the winter in Kosciuszko National

Park ($16 during the rest of the year) to $3 per day. If you're going to be a regular park visitor, a Country Park Pass ($45 for 12 months, allowing unlimited entry to all parks except metropolitan Sydney and Kos\ ciuszko), Multi-Park Pass ($65; entry to all parks except Kosciuszko) or All-Parks Pass ($145; all parks including Kosciuszko) is probably the best deal. The **National Parks Annual Pass Centre** (☎ 9585 6068, 1300 361 967; fax 9585 6831; www.nationalparks.nsw.gov.au) has all the details and you can purchase permits online.

Some parks have restrictions on camp sites and campfires, and some charge fees for camping, usually only at popular sites with vehicle access and facilities, but oc-casionally for the use of bush camp sites. Any relevant fees are listed in the Planning section for each park or area within this chapter.

Guided Walks

National Parks Association (NPA; ☎ 9299 0000; www.npansw.org.au) Conducts one or more overnight bushwalks per week, led by a member, on a bring-your-own gear and pay-your-own costs basis. The NPA's volunteer guides are often vastly experienced walkers with a detailed knowledge of the areas in which they lead walks.

Parktrek (☎ 03-9486 7070; www.parktrek.com) Has a program of all-inclusive walking tours from various bases in several states. Among its NSW offerings is a five-day Kosciuszko National Park trip, consisting of day walks

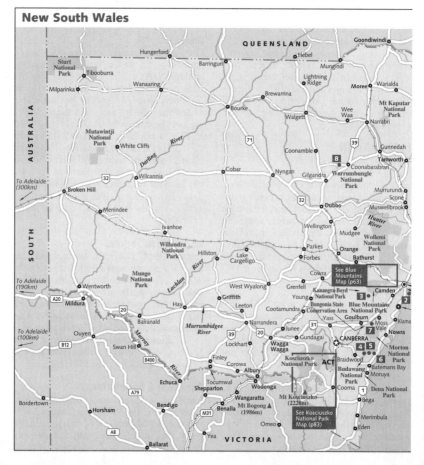

New South Wales

from a base, which usually runs late January. Pick-up is from Canberra, if required. Cost is from $132 to $165 per day.

River Deep Mountain High (☎ 4782 6109; www .bluemountainsguides.com.au; info@bluemountainsguides .com.au) Runs two- and three-day Blue Mountains overnight walks from Katoomba into the Blue Gum Forest and along routes such as the Six Foot Track. Costs range from $375 for a two-day carry-own-gear trek to $660 for a fully supported three-day walk.

Tread Lightly EcoTours (☎ 4788 1229, 0414 976 752; www.treadlightly.com.au) Does short, half- and full-day walks in the Blue Mountains.

Wildframe Ecotours (☎ 0500 505 056) Leads more tourist-oriented day walks in the mountains, picking up from city hotels. Cost is $82 per person and overnight walks can be arranged on application.

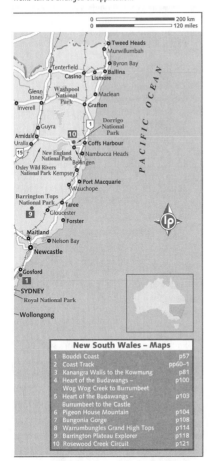

New South Wales – Maps	
1 Bouddi Coast	p57
2 Coast Track	pp60–1
3 Kanangra Walls to the Kowmung	p81
4 Heart of the Budawangs – Wog Wog Creek to Burrumbeet	p100
5 Heart of the Budawangs – Burrumbeet to the Castle	p103
6 Pigeon House Mountain	p104
7 Bungonia Gorge	p108
8 Warrumbungles Grand High Tops	p114
9 Barrington Plateau Explorer	p118
10 Rosewood Creek Circuit	p121

GATEWAY
Sydney
☎ 02 / pop 4 million

Conveniently, Australia's most populous city is the nearest centre to several of NSW's walking hot spots. There are excellent local, state, national and international transport connections and plenty of things to distract you during down time between walks.

INFORMATION

Information on Sydney and its vibrant suburbs is available at the **Sydney visitor information centre** (☎ 1800 067 676, 9240 8788; www.tourism.nsw .gov.au) The Rocks (cnr Argyle & Playfair Sts) Darling Harbour (33 Wheat Rd), open daily. The website includes a large database of hostels and hotels.

The NSW National Parks & Wildlife Service (NPWS) is the prime source of information about walking in the Sydney region and throughout NSW. Its **head office** (☎ 9585 6444; www.nationalparks.nsw.gov.au; 43 Bridge St, Hurstville) is rather inconveniently located, about 15 minutes' walk from Hurstville station. The information centre there is open weekdays and carries a comprehensive range of parks information and maps. Its website (www.npws.nsw.gov.au) is also a mine of information, with contact numbers for each park, details of activity programs and news of bushfires and park closures. For information on specific parks, it's usually better to call the ranger or district office (contact details are listed in the Information section for each park).

The **National Parks Association** (☎ 9299 0000; www.npansw.org.au; level 9, 91 York St) is one of the state's leading community conservation organisations, and has a very active walks program open to non-members.

The Confederation of Bushwalking Clubs NSW represents more than 60 clubs across the state and operates a volunteer wilderness search and rescue service. Although it cannot normally be contacted for inquiries (its office bearers are volunteers), it produces an informative magazine, *The Bushwalker,* and also maintains an excellent website (www .bushwalking.org.au), which includes a list of clubs, addresses of shops, information about current environmental issues and a list of national parks closed by bushfires.

The Sydney Morning Herald and *The Australian* daily newspapers carry detailed weather reports and forecasts.

Lonely Planet has two guides to Sydney: *Sydney* and *Best of Sydney*. The Lonely Planet *Sydney City Map* is a great help for getting around central Sydney and nearby suburbs.

SUPPLIES & EQUIPMENT

In the city, branches of the main outdoor gear shops cluster on Kent St, behind the Town Hall. The icon is **Paddy Pallin** (☎ 9264 2685; www.paddypallin.com.au) at No 507. Other worthwhile outdoor gear shops in Kent St are **Mountain Designs** (☎ 9267 3822; www.mountaindesigns.com) at No 499, and **Snowgum** (☎ 9261 0187; www.snowgum.com.au) at No 481. **Larry Adler Ski & Outdoor** (☎ 9264 2500; www.larryadler.com.au) at No 497, offers gear hire – a basic two-person tent rents for $30 and a sleeping bag $40 for one night (each $5 more per extra night). A credit-card imprint is required as security.

These shops also stock walking maps, but the best range can be found at **Map World** (☎ /fax 9261 3601; 371 Pitt St, Sydney) and **Sydney Map Shop** (☎ 9236 7720; Maps_Sydney@lands.nsw.gov.au; 1 Prince Albert Rd).

SLEEPING & EATING

The accommodation choice in Sydney is huge and prices competitive, with good options in every price range. Contact the **Sydney visitor information centre** (☎ 1800 067 676, 9240 8788; www.tourism.nsw.gov.au) for an extensive list of accommodation options.

It's a complex trek to the tent sites nearest to the city at **Lane Cove River Tourist Park** (☎ 9888 9133; www.lanecoverivertouristpark.com.au; Plassey Rd, North Ryde; unpowered/powered sites for 2 $30/$36, cabins from $121). To get there, take bus route 545 from Chatswood train station to Plassey Rd. The park is a few hundred metres north towards Lane Cove National Park. Access will improve from 2008 when Delhi Rd station opens on the new Epping–Chatswood train line.

Sydney Central YHA (☎ 9281 9111; www.yha.com.au/hostels; cnr Pitt St & Rawson Pl; dm members/nonmembers $35/39) is the nearest hostel to Central Station. Just to the southeast is **Railway Square YHA** (☎ 9281 9666; 8 Lee St; dm members/nonmembers $35/39).

Wake Up! Sydney Central (☎ 9288 7888; www.yha.com.au/hostels; 509 Pitt St; dm $24, d without/with ensuite $88/98) is central and has the Fed Up bistro in-house (mains $8 to $12).

Y On the Park Hotel (☎ 9264 2451; www.yhotel.com.au; 5 Wentworth Ave; dm/s/d $33/88/98, deluxe r with/without kitchenette $130/136) is close to the Oxford St buzz overlooking Hyde Park. Tariffs include breakfast.

Central Railway Motel (☎ 9319 7800; 240 Chalmers St; d $114), just south of Central station, has clean and neat rooms.

Medina Apartments (☎ 1300 633 462; www.medinaapartments.com.au; cnr Kent & Bathurst Sts; studio $180, 1-/2-bed r $240/316) are at the Medina Grand Sydney.

Star City Apartments (☎ 1800 700 700; www.starcity.com.au; 80 Pyrmont St; 1-/2-/3-bed apt $520/620/730) are right near the casino – get your yah yahs out after a lengthy stint in the bush.

Aarons Hotel (☎ 1800 101 100; www.aaronshotel.com.au 37 Ultimo Rd; s/d $110/$150) is a convenient 3½-star establishment central to theatres, entertainment venues, restaurants and markets.

Woolbrokers Hotel (☎ 9552 4773; http://members.ozemail.com.au/~woolbrokers; 22 Allen St Pyrmont; d $89) is on the corner of Pyrmont St near the Convention light rail stop and monorail station – slightly downmarket but close to Darling Harbour.

With great local produce, innovative chefs, inexpensive prices and BYO (Bring Your Own) alcohol licensing laws, Sydney is a fine place to eat out. Choices are nearly unlimited around Pitt and Goulburn Sts in Haymarket, and Chinatown's Dixon St.

Musashi (☎ 9280 0377; 447 Pitt St, cnr Campbell St; lunch $15-22, mains $19-25; ✆ lunch & dinner) has reliable Japanese cuisine including sushi and sashimi.

Encasa (☎ 9211 4257; 423 Pitt St; mains $19-$26; ✆ dinner Mon-Sat) offers a mix of international flavours, including tapas, pizza and pasta.

Diethnes (☎ 9267 8956; 336 Pitt St; mains $15-$26; ✆ lunch & dinner) is the place for traditional Greek food amid the skyscrapers. Sydney's biggest concentration of Greek restaurants is further out in the suburbs, so this is one to savour.

There's no shortage of Chinese food in this part of town, and **Seabay** (☎ 9267 4855; 372 Pitt St; mains $8-$12; ✆ lunch & dinner) is cheap and cheerful, with dumplings a speciality.

BBQ King (☎ 9267 2586; 18 Goulburn St; mains from $15; ✆ lunch & dinner) is a Sydney institution, stays open late (2am) and specialises in flamed flesh with a Chinese flavour.

Macchiato (☎ 9262 9525; 338 Pitt St; mains $16-23; ✆ lunch & dinner) offers mostly Italian cuisine as the name would suggest – filling pastas, lasagnes and wood-fired pizzas.

GETTING THERE & AWAY
Air
Sydney's **Kingsford Smith Airport** (☎ 9667 9111; www.sydneyairport.com.au) is 10km south of the city centre. Flights arrive from the usual international points and from all over Australia. **Qantas** (☎ 13 13 13; www.qantas.com.au), **Virgin Blue** (☎ 13 67 89; www.virginblue.com.au) and **Jetstar** (☎ 13 15 38; www.jetstar.com.au) all have frequent flights to other Australian capital cities and major airports. Regional carriers, such as **Qantaslink** (☎ 13 13 13) – comprising Airlink, Eastern Australia Airlines and Sunstate Airlines – and **Regional Express** (Rex; ☎ 13 17 13; www.regionalexpress.com.au) fly mainly within NSW.

The Sydney domestic and international terminals are 4km apart. A convenient free shuttle service operates between the terminals for transit ticket holders. **CityRail** (☎ 13 05 00; www.cityrail.info) run trains between the domestic and international terminals, connecting to the rest of the Sydney metropolitan network and to country services at Central Station. These are regular commuter services, so can get crowded and are not luggage-friendly.

Bus
Sydney Coach Terminal (☎ 9281 9366; Eddy Ave), outside Central Station, is a base for **Greyhound Australia** (☎ 13 14 99; www.greyhound.com.au). **Premier** (☎ 13 34 10; www.premierms.com.au) and **Firefly Express** (☎ 1300 730 740; www.firefly-express.com.au) have offices around the corner on Pitt St.

Car & Motorcycle
Major car-rental companies have offices at the airport and around the city: **Avis** (☎ 13 63 33; www.avis.com), **Budget** (☎ 1300 794 344; www.budget.com.au), **Europcar** (☎ 1300 131 390; www.deltaeuropcar.com.au), **Hertz** (☎ 13 30 39; www.hertz.com.au) and **Thrifty** (☎ 1300 367 227; www.thrifty.com.au).

The major roads leading out of Sydney are either motorways, on which a toll is charged, or freeways. Routes to know include the M4 from Strathfield to the Blue Mountains, the F3 to Newcastle (en route to Bouddi, Brisbane Water and Ku-ring-gai Chase National Parks), the F6 from Waterfall (Royal National Park) towards

TOLL CITY

Planning on using a rental car to get to various walks near Sydney? Consider this: a whopping share of recent Sydney transport infrastructure projects have been given to private enterprise, which has enterprisingly engineered deals that amount to the pro-verbial licence to print money. How bad can it be? Well, suppose you're a resident of Sydney's eastern suburbs faced with a busy day (Christmas?) visiting relatives. Leave the city via the Cross City Tunnel ($3.56) and pick up the M4 ($2.20) to get to Aunty Joan's at Penrith for lunch. Bail out midafternoon and pick up the Westlink M7 ($5.88) and M2 ($3.80) to get back to tea at Uncle Ted's place in Chatswood. Duck back home after dark through the Harbour Tunnel ($3). If you're driving an economical four-cylinder car, you've just spent more on tolls than you did on petrol.

Wollongong and the Budawangs, and the M5 towards Goulburn (Bungonia Gorge), Canberra and Kosciuszko National Park.

Train
All interstate and principal regional train services operate from Central Station, on Eddy Ave between George and Elizabeth Sts. For bookings and recorded information on arrival and departure times call **Countrylink** (☎ 13 22 32; www.countrylink.info) or try a **Countrylink Travel Centre** (☎ 13 28 29).

SYDNEY REGION

Amid the towering buildings of central Sydney it's difficult to believe that within 100km are several national parks and some of the state's largest wilderness areas. The parks protect a staggering variety of habitats – ranging from coastal heath to subalpine eucalypt woodland – and include unspoilt beaches, World Heritage–listed mountain vistas and rare plants and animals. It says much for the community's commitment to national parks that some of these have survived intact for as long as 120 years, in defiance of Sydney's relentless urban sprawl. Two outstanding and popular walks in parks flanking Sydney to the north and south are

---

WARNING

During summer, walkers must be alert to the ever-present threat of bushfires in Sydney's national parks. During the Bushfire Danger Period (usually 1 October to 31 March) it's always wise to contact the relevant park information centre to check on fire danger rating before setting out. If there isn't a park fire ban in place, you may be allowed to light a cooking or heating fire – although it's always advisable to use a fuel stove. Days of Total Fire Ban (p25) are widely publicised in the news media. Fire danger ratings are listed in the weather pages of the daily newspapers. You can also check the Total Fire Ban and Current Fire Danger map on the **NSW Rural Fire Service** (www .bushfire.nsw.gov.au) website, or contact the local park information centre.

Also ensure you're familiar with the advice on what to do if caught near a fire (p387).

---

described in this section – just a glimpse of the city's wealth of walking opportunities.

PLANNING
When to Walk
Sydney's climate is pleasant for walking during all but the hottest and most humid days of summer. Late winter through spring (wildflower season in the city's nearby national parks) is the most pleasant time to be out. September is the month with lowest average rainfall; blooming wildflowers and daily temperature averages of 10°C to 20°C add to September's charm for walkers. Flies are a distraction throughout summer; late summer is often uncomfortably humid and has the year's highest average rainfall. Check weather forecasts for thunderstorm activity from late spring through summer.

Maps
For general planning, there's not much difference between the many regional tourist maps on the market, although it's fair comment that the NSW government's Lands Department's tourist maps are probably less frequently revised than some of their commercial counterparts'. The LPINSW 1:25,000 series maps covering the region have mostly been recently updated.

For maps covering individual walks, see Planning in the introduction to each walk.

Books
The range of Sydney walking guides is undergoing a growth spurt. They now number in the dozens; some of the most recent are low-budget efforts that cover relatively small areas. The most comprehensive and detailed remains *Bushwalks in the Sydney*

HARBOUR WALKABOUT

More than anything, even real estate prices, Sydney Harbour defines the NSW capital and its inhabitants. It's the fluid space that makes the Opera House sails fly and reflects the famous Bridge's grandeur. Melbourne can keep its trams: Sydneysiders get to scoot home on ferries.

A new walk that loops around the western part of the harbour gives a fascinating perspective of this Sydney icon. The Harbour Circle Walk was mapped by volunteers who were determined to keep the harbour foreshores accessible for all to enjoy. Over a period of some years they explored the foreshore parks, long-forgotten rights-of-way and little-used footpaths that run within rock-skipping distance of the water. They dug into the history of various suburbs and colourful individuals, and finally they pulled all their knowledge together in a map and set of historical walking notes.

The walk has a main 'circle' of 26km and 13 scenic loops that add another 40km. It's possible to complete the main circle in one solid day but much more interesting to break it into sections and walk a bit at a time, travelling to harbourside starting points by (what else?) ferry. From the Harbour Bridge the main circle winds along the north shore of the harbour to Hunters Hill, then meanders south to Balmain and finally crosses the Anzac Bridge on the way back to Pyrmont, Darling Harbour and Observatory Hill. The more difficult north section is 12km and the south 14km; they each take about five hours to walk. You can download the walk map and the historical notes (one set for the main circle, another for the side-trip 'loops') from the **NSW Department of Planning** (www.planning.nsw.gov.au/harbour/walking.asp) website.

GREAT NORTH WALK

Opened in 1988 to celebrate the bicentenary of European settlement in Australia, the 250km Great North Walk (GNW) links the cities of Sydney and Newcastle via natural corridors – narrow strips of bushland and beaches in places – that extend virtually to the centre of both cities.

From Circular Quay, the route crosses Sydney Harbour by ferry to Valentia St wharf. It briefly parallels part of the new Harbour Circle and Loop walks (opposite) before going through Lane Cove National Park, along Berowra Creek and through Ku-ring-gai Chase National Park to Broken Bay. Walkers then take a ferry to Brisbane Water National Park. Beyond there, the GNW traverses state forest and private land northwards to Congewoi Valley, then heads east along the Myall Range, past Lake Macquarie and on to the coast and Newcastle. The route is a combination of fire trails, walking tracks and some specially built sections of walking track, and is well signposted and track marked. Simple camp sites have been provided at suitable intervals, and the GNW passes through some small towns with shops and accommodation. About 75km of linking tracks provide access to transport connections and, at the northern end, Hunter Valley wineries around Pokolbin.

The recommended time for the full distance is 14 days, although transport access means this can be split into shorter journeys, mainly in the south where the route regularly crosses the Sydney–Gosford railway line.

The walk is maintained by the **Department of Lands** (☎ 9228 6111, 9236 7720; www.lands.nsw .gov.au), which publishes a set of six colour brochures, each with a topographic map showing the route of the GNW and all the necessary practical information. It's available from the Department, local tourist offices, map shops and outdoor gear suppliers.

Region, Volumes 1 and 2, edited by S Lord and G Daniel and published by the National Parks Association of NSW. They describe 166 walks, all within about 120km of central Sydney. The contributors are all active bushwalkers; the maps are almost good enough to use on the walks. *Sydney and Blue Mountains Bushwalks* by Neil Paton describes 140 walks from two hours' to several days' duration, most in national parks.

BOUDDI COAST

Duration	5 hours
Distance	13.5km
Difficulty	easy–moderate
Start/Finish	Putty Beach
Nearest Town	Sydney (p51)
Transport	private

Summary A varied walk along Bouddi's unspoiled coast, featuring heath, woodland, beaches, cliffs and panoramic views across Broken Bay to Sydney's northern beaches and the city skyline.

The Bouddi Coast walk (one of the finest of its kind in NSW) links Putty Beach (towards the western end of the park) with Little Beach, on the northeast boundary. Boardwalks, walking tracks and fire trails generally keep close to the rugged cliff-lined coast, passing through most of the park's different vegetation types, from tall, cool forest in sheltered gullies to dense, low heath on exposed headlands.

It is described here as a return walk from Putty Beach, near Killcare, a small settlement on the shore of Brisbane Water. The moderate part of the grading is earned by the several steep ups and downs, and also by the occasional roughness of the track – although track work is improving several of the most eroded sections. You'll probably notice discrepancies in the distances given between places on signposts along the walk, although by no more than 1km; we've tried to reconcile these in this description.

A couple of worthwhile side trips to cliff-edge vantage points would add close to 2km and up to an hour.

ENVIRONMENT

Bouddi's distinctive suite of plants includes eucalypt-like angophoras, the intriguing scribbly gum and the burrawang, a type of cycad – an ancient group of palm-like plants that was once widespread but is now restricted to about 250 species, all in tropical and subtropical habitats. The burrawangs are especially noticeable from the track near Maitland Bay and Little Beach.

PLANNING
Maps & Books

The LPINSW 1:25,000 topographic map *Broken Bay* covers the walk described here. *Bushwalks in the Sydney Region* and *Take a Walk in a National Park Sydney to Port Macquarie* (p49) both include descriptions of six walks in Bouddi.

Information Sources

The park information centre beside the Maitland Bay car park, on the Scenic Rd about 2.5km east of the Putty Beach turn-off, is open only at weekends. A better alternative is **NPWS Central Coast** (☎ general inquiries 4320 4200, ☎ camping inquiries 4320 4203; central .coast@environment.nsw.gov.au; 207 Albany St North) in Gosford.

Permits & Regulations

Sites at bushland camping areas at either end of this walk – Putty and Little Beaches – require permits, which are available from the NPWS Central Coast Office (see Information Sources earlier). The fee per two people is $16; at Putty Beach there's an additional charge of $7 per day to park your car. Bring $1 and $2 coins for the ticket machines. No wood fires are allowed at these camps, but there are (free) gas barbecues; to be on the safe side you should bring a fuel or gas stove for cooking. Camping is not permitted elsewhere in the park. During times of extreme fire danger the park is closed to public access.

NEAREST TOWNS & FACILITIES

See Sydney (p51).

Putty Beach camping area & Killcare

For something a bit more natural before setting out, indulge in a spot of car camping at the national park site at Putty Beach (at the start of the walk); it's essential to obtain a permit first (see left).

The nearest food shops are on Araluen Dr in tiny Killcare – follow the Killcare road for 400m from the junction of Putty Beach Dr and the Scenic Rd. Killcare Cellars is a convenience store open daily with some supplies. The Old Killcare Store opposite has a small delicatessen and offers takeaway or eat-in sandwiches, burgers and quiches.

GETTING TO/FROM THE WALK

Drive north of Sydney on the Sydney–Newcastle Fwy. Leave the freeway at the Kariong and Woy Woy exit, then turn off the Pacific Hwy 1.5km southeast of the freeway along Woy Woy Rd. About 10.5km further south, at a right bend near the shore of Woy Woy Inlet, Woy Woy Rd becomes Rawson Rd, which in turn (at the intersection of Edward St) becomes Allfield Rd. Veer right off

---

MARIE BYLES & BOUDDI

The dense scrub and rugged terrain of the Bouddi area deterred European settlers and ensured that this coast remained more or less in its natural state well into the 20th century.

In 1922 a remarkable young woman, Marie Byles (1900–79), ventured onto Bouddi Peninsula and was captivated by its natural beauty. Soon after, she became the first female solicitor in NSW and began her lifelong campaign for equal rights for women. Mountaineering and bushwalking were enduring passions and she was naturally drawn to the concept of national parks to preserve natural areas.

In the early 1930s Byles and a group of fellow bushwalkers campaigned for the creation of a national park at Bouddi, and in 1935 the state government set aside 263 hectares for public recreation and named the area Bouddi National Park. Its administration was in the hands of trustees, one of whom was Byles; it's almost certain that she was responsible for having the trustees' meetings on a park beach.

As Bouddi State Park, the reserve was taken over by the NSW National Parks & Wildlife Service in 1967, and in 1975 it regained national park status; the area of the park is now 1189 hectares. The park's marine extension of 287 hectares, between Gerrin and Bombi Points, was the first area of the sea bed to be given special protection in NSW.

Marie Byles was also an intrepid traveller throughout Southeast Asia and a founder member of the Buddhist Society of NSW. A lookout on the Scenic Rd that overlooks Bouddi is named in her honour.

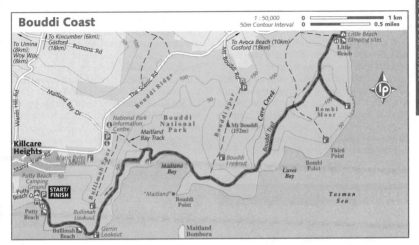

Bouddi Coast

Allfield Rd onto Blackwall Rd and continue for about 1.7km to a roundabout; here go left, cross over the Rip Bridge and follow Empire Bay Dr for almost 6km, and then drive south via Wards Hill Rd, which climbs very steeply up and over to the Scenic Rd. Turn right here, and then take the second road on the left, signposted to Putty Beach. This partly sealed, part-gravel road ends at the beach car park, 1.1km from the Scenic Rd.

Although private transport is the most practical option for this walk, it's possible to get to Bouddi National Park by train and bus. A good train service runs to the Central Coast, and **Busways** (☎ 4368 2277; www .busways.com.au) runs infrequent services (none on Sundays) to Killcare from Woy Woy ($4.20) and Gosford ($5.80). The one-way train fare to either station is $8.

THE WALK

From the car park, go east along Putty Beach to the steps at the eastern end of the sand. Climb to an open expanse of fretted and crumbling sandstone, which leads to a long boardwalk above a fine shoreline rock platform. Soon you come to a junction where a short track leads down to small **Bullimah Beach**, which is safe only for paddling (treacherous rocks lurk just below the surface). Back on the main track, shady steps take you up to **Gerrin Lookout** and fine views of Maitland Bay, the offshore rocks known as Maitland Bombora and the tall city buildings of the southern skyline. Continue

through eucalyptus woodland, interspersed with some splendid burrawangs, to a track junction; turn right to go down to **Maitland Bay** (about 1¼ hours from Putty Beach).

There's a pit toilet near the track at the western end of the beach, which is safe enough for swimming on a calm day. Go along to the eastern end and up the steep steps to a shallow gap on the spur leading towards Bouddi Point. There are good views of the coastal cliffs a short distance to the right; at low tide you might be able to make out the remaining fragment of the coastal paddle steamer *Maitland,* which foundered here in 1898 with the loss of about 27 lives, on the western side of Bouddi Point.

Continue along the main track up to a junction (the Mt Bouddi turn-off) and turn right towards Little Beach, with spectacular views of the Hawkesbury River estuary. The cliff-edge track, eroded in places, crosses a couple of gullies, separated by she-oak and banksia thickets, then descends to cross Cave Creek (about 45 minutes from Maitland Bay).

After this the way is up, via the many steps overlooking Caves Bay, to a small clearing. Turn left along a sandy 4WD track and continue climbing. Bear right at a fork and you soon come to the turn-off to Third Point on the right. There are good views of the cliffs from near the end of this track, but the next one to **Bombi Moor**, another 500m along the main track, is even more rewarding. The 1.5km return walk along a fire trail passes through heathland rich with wildflowers in spring; it ends right on the cliff edge, from where there are magnificent views southwards of Sydney's northern beaches and the city skyscrapers.

Back on the main track, continue steadily down through varied eucalyptus woodland to a T-junction and turn right to reach **Little Beach**, a small rocky cove (about 45 minutes from Cave Creek). There are toilets and barbecues here but no fresh water.

The return to Putty Beach is simply a matter of retracing your steps.

THE COAST TRACK

Duration	2 days
Distance	26km
Difficulty	moderate
Start	Bundeena
Finish	Otford
Nearest Town	Sydney (p51)
Transport	train, ferry

Summary This path crosses varied terrain along the cliffs and beaches in Royal National Park. Coastal views from atop eroded sandstone ramparts, heathland alive with birds, beautiful stretches of sand and shady palm forest combine to ensure a memorable walk.

Declared in 1879, Royal National Park is Australia's oldest (and the world's second-oldest) national park, and also a long-time haunt of Sydney bushwalkers. Within its 15,080 hectares is a wide-ranging network of walking tracks; the Coast Track is reputedly NSW's busiest walk. The route traverses traditional lands of the Dharawal Aboriginal people and there are several important Dharawal sites along the route or nearby, including rock engravings at Jibbon Point, near Bundeena, and a huge midden at North Era. Severe fires in 1994 (which flattened 90% of the park's vegetation) and 2001 (60% destroyed) have left little trace today but did prompt the realignment of (and improvements to) sections of the track.

ENVIRONMENT

Royal National Park covers a sloping sandstone plateau that rises from sea level in the park's north to about 300m in the south. Various sandstone features – cliffs

and caves – and dune systems created by changing sea levels and erosion dominate the landscape. Several plant communities feature. The most prominent is the coastal heath of banksias, boronias, tea-trees and hakeas that dominates the northern part of the Coast Track. Various types of eucalyptus woodland and pockets of remnant rainforest, such as the Palm Jungle, feature on the track's southern part. A healthy variety of frog, reptile and mammal species inhabits the park, and during winter whales are frequent visitors along its 19km coastline. Birds are the animals most visitors will see; more than 270 bird species have been recorded here. In the heath, various types of honeyeater, and wattlebirds, fairy-wrens and thornbills add colour. It's also fairly common to see yellow-tailed black-cockatoos travelling in sizable flocks – an awesome, and noisy, sight.

PLANNING

National Parks authorities advise Coast Track walkers to carry in all water. There are several creeks (usually running) along the way and creek water in the toilet/shower facilities at Wattamolla, but any water you collect must be boiled or treated before drinking. Many people walk the Coast Track in low-cut shoes, but boots are advisable – the track is stony and uneven in places.

Maps

The LPINSW 1:35,0000 *Royal National Park Tourist Map* covers the park in one sheet, accurately shows tracks and facilities, and is more than adequate for Coast Track walkers. The LPINSW 1:25,000 topographic maps *Port Hacking* and *Otford* show greater topographic detail.

Information Sources

The **Royal National Park visitor information centre** (☎ 9542 0648; Farnell Ave, Audley Heights; ◷ daily) is signposted from the Princes Hwy between Loftus and Engadine.

Permits & Regulations

All walkers staying at either the North Era or Providential Point sites must have a **bush camping permit** (per 2 people $6). The numbers of people using each site are strictly limited and you must book ahead; the visitor information centre takes bookings and accepts payments. Sites may be closed at times of high fire danger or to allow vegetation to recover. Wood fires are prohibited, so bring a portable stove for cooking. It's $9 per day to bring a car into the park.

GETTING TO/FROM THE WALK

CityRail trains run every 30 minutes from Central to Cronulla ($4.40 single, 47 minutes). The **Bundeena ferry** (☎ 9523 2990) leaves Cronulla hourly from 8.30am ($4.50, 20 to 25 minutes). The last ferry departs Cronulla at 6.30pm from November to March, and 5.30pm April to October. The ferry wharf is off Tonkin St, just west of Cronulla CityRail station and well signposted.

From the Bundeena ferry wharf, walk straight up Brighton St, past the shops and continue south. About 20m from the end of Brighton St, go left onto the pathway through to Rymill Place. Follow, then go right into Bournemouth St, left into Reef St, right into Beachcomber Ave and continue past the locked gate. The Coast Track starts on the left about 200m beyond the gate.

THE WALK
Day 1: Bundeena to North Era
6–7 hours, 17km, 150m ascent, 140m descent

From the start the track rolls for about 700m down to low cliffs and the ocean. There it turns sharply right (south), and there's a real sense of leaving Sydney behind. The first wide views of the coastline appear and the track ahead beckons, snaking through cliff-side heath.

The track stays close to the eroded cliff top for about 15 minutes then cuts inland and drops steeply down to a watercourse draining **The Waterrun**, an area of wet heathland. After rising back to cliff height, continue for 2km through the heath to Marley Head, crossing cliff top dunes that were deposited when sea levels started rising about 10,000 years ago. There's a profusion of eroded old tracks near Marley Head, but the track is well marked and it's no problem picking the way down to **Marley Beach**, with its striking backdrop of wind-scoured dunes. Cross the lagoon outlet at the northern end then continue towards the sign at the southern end of the beach. Marley is too frequently visited to be a genuine 'wild' beach, but it has that flavour, especially on a winter's day.

About 250m south of Marley take the left-hand fork and follow it to **Little Marley Beach.** It's reasonably safe to swim here, although like Marley it's unpatrolled. South of Little Marley the track hugs a stretch of majestic cliffs about 35m above the ocean, crossing sandstone shelves sculpted into weird shapes and dazzling yellow, red and orange hues. About 20 minutes past Little Marley and amid heath, the route jags sharply inland and runs straight for about 800m to a T-junction. Go left; soon after, the first sight of **Wattamolla** picnic area appears. It will likely be packed on any weekend there's not a hurricane forecast – winter or summer.

The track crosses Wattamolla Creek and its artificial swimming hole about 500m before lovely **Wattamolla Falls** and the picnic grounds. Continue across the main picnic area past the kiosk (open in summer) and main information sign to the parking bays. (To reach Providential Point bush camp site, take a left turn just past the toilets and walk east for about 200m.) Continue up to the fourth parking bay and walk along it to the fire trail gate. Turn left at the gate and continue. Go right at the water tank about 300m up the track and follow right at the 'Curracurrang' sign about 50m further along. The track winds around as it descends to the cliff line, which it follows to Curracurrang Gully and a creek crossing. Beyond the steel-grid section south of the creek, various track braids lead to the new steel bridge over a tributary stream. About 25m past the bridge the track goes right and loops up and behind a knoll dominated by low eucalypts. Another section of raised steel-grid track leads to a nice rolling downhill to **Curracurrong**, where a cliff waterfall and nearby **Eagle Rock** – a cliff formation that appears as its name suggests – provide an excuse to rest.

The track climbs away and slightly inland then crosses heath for about 2km. At Garie North Head the first views of **Garie Beach** appear and loom larger throughout the steep, zigzagging descent to the sand. Once at Garie, the walk enters its distinctly different second part. The low heath, sandstone and relatively flat going mostly disappear and are replaced by shale soils, pockets of coastal (littoral) rainforest and a series of climbs over headlands. Go south along

NEW SOUTH WALES

The Coast Track

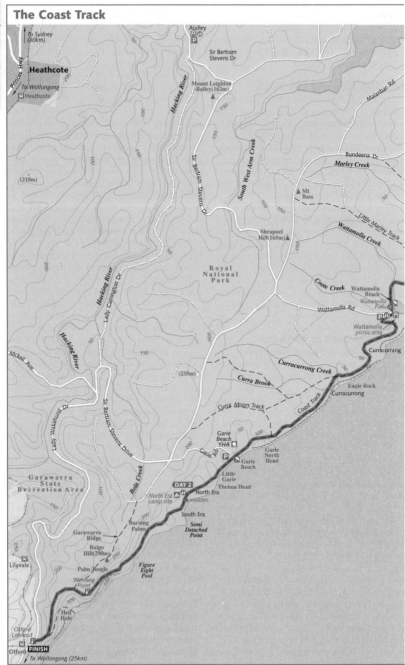

To Sydney (30km)

Heathcote

To Wollongong
Heathcote

Princes Hwy

Audley
P

Sir Bertram Stevens Dr

Hacking River

Mount Leighton -Bailey (162m)

Sir Bertram Stevens Dr

South West Arm Creek

Malabar Rd

Bundeena Dr
Marley Creek

(210m)

Mt Bass

Little Marley Track

Wattamolla Creek

Shrapnel Hill (165m)

R o y a l
N a t i o n a l
P a r k

Coote Creek

Wattamolla Beach
Wattamolla Falls

Wattamolla Rd

Hacking River

Wattamolla picnic area

Currarong

Mckell Ave

Hacking River

Lady Carrington Dr

Sir Bertram Stevens Dr

(235m)

Curra Brook

Curracurrong Creek

Eagle Rock
Currarong

Coast Track

Curra Moors Track

Garie Beach YHA
P

Garie North Head

Garie Beach

Bola Creek

G a r a w a r r a
S t a t e
R e c r e a t i o n   A r e a

Garie Rd

Little Garie
Thelma Head

DAY 2
North Era camp site
North Era midden

South Era

Semi Detached Point

Burning Palms

Garawarra Ridge

Lady Wakehurst Dr

Bulgo Hill (290m)
Palm Jungle

Lilyvale

Werrong Point

Figure Eight Pool

Hell Hole

Otford Lookout
Otford

FINISH

To Wollongong (25km)

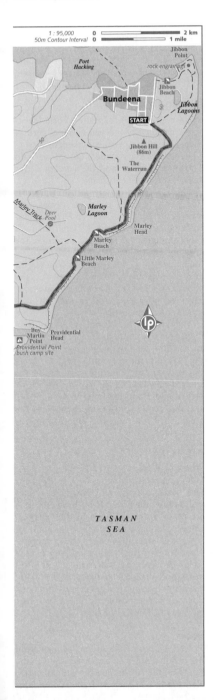

Garie; just uphill from the car park near the surf club is the small and basic (no electricity or phone) **Garie YHA** (bookings ☎ 9261 1111; bed $14), a good overnight alternative if you're walking with a group (you can book the hostel for $140). Traverse the rock platform in front of Little Garie Point then, at Little Garie, go to the right of the first shack and follow the markers through the other shacks to the stairs. Follow up and over the ridge. The **North Era camp site** is about 300m downhill, set in a wide, grassed area behind the football-pitch-sized midden.

Day 2: North Era to Otford

3–4 hours, 9km, 530m ascent, 450m descent

Spend some time checking out the huge midden before shouldering packs to continue south. Walk to the east of the midden then go up and over the rise to South Era. There, skirt around the front of the dune and pick up the track again just beyond the lagoon. The climb among the shacks is sandy and tiring at first, then breaks into the clear on a firm track with fine views of the ocean. Burgh Ridge rises to the right, and further west lies the 70m cliffs of **Garawarra Ridge**. After about 10 minutes, the track winds down through more shacks and cabbage tree palms to **Burning Palms**, the last chance on the walk for a swim. The track descends to within a few metres of the beach then climbs away, passing behind the beach through coastal rainforest.

For about 15 minutes after passing the old ranger shack the going is open and the views wide, then the track plunges into the **Palm Jungle** and palms, figs and lianas provide a dense canopy. For about 30 to 45 minutes there's a steady uphill – with a couple of steeper sections – towards the top of which the rainforest starts to open and other plant species hold sway, including striking gymea lilies and various types of taller eucalypt. Just before the walk's highest point, near **Werrong Point**, two lookouts about 50m apart provide spectacular views south. After another 10–15 minutes, the track meets the fire-trail-sized Cliff Track. Go right, and follow for about 800m, where the walking track continues. About 1km remains – an easy rise followed by an initially steep descent – before the track's end at the **Otford Lookout**. To reach Otford Station, go left and follow Lady Wakehurst Dr for

150m to Fanshawe Rd. Go right, and follow the signs for 400m to the station.

THE BLUE MOUNTAINS

The Blue Mountains have some truly fantastic scenery, excellent bushwalks and all the gorges, gum trees and cliffs you could ask for. For more than a century, the area has been a popular getaway for people seeking to escape the summer heat of Sydney. Despite the intensive tourist development, much of the area is so precipitous that it's still only open to bushwalkers.

The foothills begin 65km west of Sydney and rise to 1100m; the mountains are really a gently rising (east to west) sandstone plateau dissected by spectacular gorges formed over millennia by erosion. The blue haze that gave the mountains their name is a result of the fine mist of volatile oil given off by eucalyptus trees – which is also why eucalyptus forests can explode into firestorms. Blue Mountains National Park offers bushwalkers enough opportunities to fill a month's solid walking. The walks described lead to shady eucalyptus forest, Aboriginal rock art, remote rivers, renowned caves and spectacular sandstone ramparts.

In 2000, the Greater Blue Mountains was inscribed on the World Heritage list. It covers more than 10,000 sq km of wild, mostly forested landscape that begins just 60km inland from the Sydney CBD. Worldwide, few natural World Heritage Areas are as close to major population centres as the Greater Blue Mountains is to Sydney.

HISTORY
Established in 1959, Blue Mountains National Park now protects 2678 sq km of forested sandstone ridges and deep, rugged valleys. The vision for the park came from one of the most famous figures in Australian bushwalking, Myles Dunphy (1891–1985). An important tool in the campaign for the park was the NSW Lands Department's 1932 'Special Walking Clubs Issue' Blue Mountains map – inspired, and largely drawn, by Dunphy. Myles's son Milo (1929–1996) took to bushwalking and conservation with the same zeal as his dad. Between the mid-1980s and mid-1990s,

Milo played a pivotal role in doubling the area of land in NSW dedicated to national parks. The Dunphys' vision for a Greater Blue Mountains reserve was fully realised with the area's World Heritage listing.

ENVIRONMENT
The Greater Blue Mountains World Heritage Area consists of seven national parks – Blue Mountains, Wollemi, Yengo, Nattai, Kanangra-Boyd, Gardens of Stone and Thirlmere Lakes – and the Jenolan Caves karst (limestone) landscape.

This area supports a significant proportion of the world's eucalypt species, and reveals the eucalypts' superb environmental adaptation. Australia's Department of Environment and Heritage describes the area as 'a natural laboratory for studying the evolution of the eucalypts. The largest area of high diversity of eucalypts on the continent is located in southeast Australia. The Greater Blue Mountains Area includes much of this eucalypt diversity.'

The Greater Blue Mountains World Heritage Area also contains ancient relict plants such as the famous Wollemi pine, one of the world's rarest plant species; many threatened or rare marsupials, including the spotted-tailed quoll, the koala, the yellow-bellied glider and the long-nosed potoroo; and rare reptiles including the green-and-golden bell frog and the Blue Mountains water skink.

PLANNING
When to Walk
With none of the summer haze or problems with water scarcity and bushfires, winter can be the best time for bushwalks – days are often clear and down in the valleys it can be comparatively warm. But beware of sudden changes in weather and come prepared for freezing conditions; snow is possible between June and August. Autumn's mists and drizzle can make bushwalking less attractive, but the mountains in a thick mist are an atmospheric place. Summer days can be hot (in the high 20s).

Books
The NPA's *Bushwalks in the Sydney Region* has detailed notes on nearly 60 walks in the Blue Mountains and nearby national parks. Neil Paton's *Sydney and Blue Mountains*

The Blue Mountains

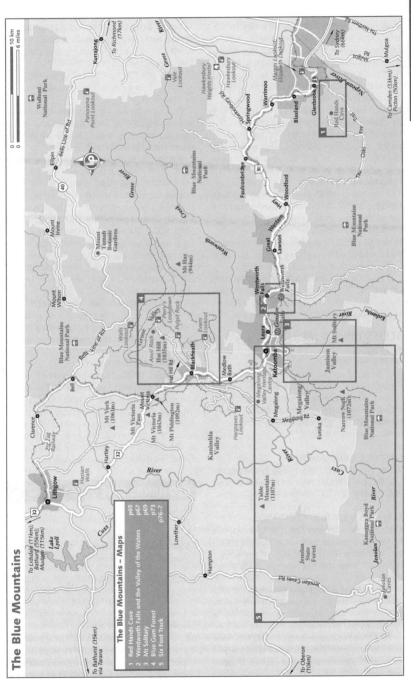

The Blue Mountains – Maps

1 Red Hands Cave	p65
2 Wentworth Falls and the Valley of the Waters	p67
3 Mt Solitary	p69
4 Blue Gum Forest	p73
5 Six Foot Track	p76–7

10 km
6 miles

To Lidsdale (11km);
Bathurst (55km);
Mudgee (115km)

To Bathurst (35km)
via Tarana

To Oberon
(10km)

To Camden (33km);
Picton (50km)

To Sydney
(66km)

To Richmond
(17km)

Kurrajong

Wollemi
National Park

Panorama
Point Lookout

Elpin

Bells Line of Rd

Grose   River

Mount
Irvine

Mount
Tomah
Botanic
Gardens

Mount
Wilson

Blue Mountains
National Park

Bells Line of Rd

Walls
Lookout

Bell

Mt York
(1061m)

Clarence

Zig Zag
Railway

Hartley

Lithgow

Lake
Lyell

Hassan
Walls

Coxs

River

Lowther

Hampton

Mt Victoria
Pass

Mt Victoria
(1043m)

Mount
Victoria

Mt Piddington
(1092m)

Kanimbla
Valley

Hargraves
Lookout

Blackheath

Medlow
Bath

Hat Hill Rd

Anvil Rock

Hat Hill
(1035m)

Perry's
Lookdown

Pulpit Rock

Evans
Lookout

Grose
Valley

Grose

Mt Hay
(944m)

Heathcote Creek

Blue Mountains
National Park

Faulconbridge

Springwood

Hawkesbury Rd

Hawkesbury
Lookout

Hawkesbury
Heights Hostel

Vale
Lookout

Grose   River

Warrimoo

Marges Lookout;
Elizabeth Lookout

Blaxland

Glenbrook

Red Hands
Cave

Nepean   River

Mulgoa
Rd

The Northern Rd

Woodford

Lawson

Great   Western   Hwy

Wentworth
Falls

Wentworth
Falls

Leura

Katoomba

Gordon
Falls

Mt Solitary

Jamison
Valley

Redjumba   River

Megalong
Valley Heritage
Centre

Megalong

Megalong Rd

Megalong
Valley

Narrow Neck
(1072m)

Euroka

Blue Mountains
National Park

Table
Mountain
(1107m)

Coxs   River

Jenolan
State
Forest

Kanangra Boyd
National Park

Jenolan   River

Jenolan Caves Rd

Jenolan
Caves

1

2

3

4

5

40

32

32

NEW SOUTH WALES

Bushwalks contains scores of walks in the area – mainly day walks, but several stretching over longer periods. *Blue Mountains Best Bushwalks,* by Veechi Stuart, is also a fine source of day walk ideas. John and Lyn Daly's *Take a Walk in Blue Mountains National Park* contains 40 walks.

National Park Explorer, Around Sydney by Alan Fairley is a readable guide to the Blue Mountains and other Sydney national parks; it includes information on geology, flora and fauna as well as suggested walks.

Information Sources

The excellent **NPWS Blue Mountains Heritage Centre** (☎ 4787 8877; bluemountains.heritagecentre @environment.nsw.gov.au; Govetts Leap Rd) is near Blackheath, about 3km east of the highway. It has all the information, maps and books you could need for walking in the area, plus a small selection of snacks and drinks.

There are **Blue Mountains visitor information centres** (☎ 1300 653 408; www.australiabluemountains .com.au) at Glenbrook, on the Great Western Hwy, and at Echo Point in Katoomba.

ACCESS TOWN & FACILITIES
Katoomba
☎ 02 / pop 17,900

The best all-round base is Katoomba, although there are accommodation options throughout the Blue Mountains. There's a free Blue Mountains **accommodation booking service** (☎ 4782 2857; info@bmbookings.com.au; 157 Lurline St), also open daily.

SUPPLIES & EQUIPMENT

There's a full range of walking gear at **Mountain Designs** (☎ 4782 5999; 190 Katoomba St) and **Paddy Pallin** (☎ 4782 4466; 166B Katoomba St).

SLEEPING & EATING

Katoomba Falls Caravan Park (☎ 4782 1835; Falls Rd; unpowered/powered sites for 2 $24/31, cabins $74-85) is close to walks and views, right across the road from the Mt Solitary walk starting point.

Katoomba (Blue Mountain) YHA Hostel (☎ 4782 1416; 207 Katoomba St; dm member/non-member $24/28, d $79) is comfortable, welcoming and just a hop from the main shops.

VIP Flying Fox Backpackers (☎ 4782 4226; www .vipbackpackers.com; 190 Bathurst Rd; dm $22, d & tw $60) receives consistently good reviews from travellers.

Central Backpackers (☎ 4782 9630; 144 Bathurst Rd; www.centralblue.com.au; dm $22, d without/with ensuite $65/75), close to the station and shops, is well appointed.

No 14 (☎ 4782 7104; 14 Lovel St; d & tw $59) is a peaceful and homely guesthouse run by ex-travellers.

Cecil Guesthouse (☎ 4782 1411; 108 Katoomba St; s/d from $55/85) has the style of the grand guesthouses, but with a lower tariff than many – and it includes breakfast.

Katoomba St has many, many good places to eat. The pleasant, reasonably priced **Savoy** (☎ 4782 5050; 26-28 Katoomba St; ☺ lunch & dinner) has an interesting menu of focaccia, pasta and Asian-inspired variety. Also part of the old Art-Deco Savoy Theatre is quirky **Avalon** (☎ 4782 5532; 18 Katoomba St; ☺ lunch Wed-Sun, dinner daily), one of the town's best restaurants with plenty of tempting meals.

The eternally popular **Blues Cafe** (☎ 4782 2347; 57 Katoomba St; ☺ lunch) serves mostly vegetarian and vegan food, while the moderately priced **Arjuna Indian** (☎ 4782 4662; 16 Valley Rd; ☺ dinner), is up the railway end of town, near Bathurst Rd. There's a **Coles supermarket** (cnr Parke & Waratah Sts) that's open seven days.

GETTING THERE & AWAY

Katoomba, 109km from Sydney's city centre, is almost a satellite suburb. CityRail trains run more or less hourly from Central ($11.40 one way, two hours). By car, exit the city via Parramatta Rd and detour onto the Western Motorway tollway ($2.20), known as the M4, at Strathfield. The motorway becomes the Great Western Hwy west of Penrith.

RED HANDS CAVE

Duration	4–4½ hours
Distance	11km
Difficulty	easy–moderate
Start/Finish	Glenbrook Causeway
Nearest Towns	Katoomba (left), Sydney (p51)
Transport	Train
Summary	A pleasant amble to an Aboriginal rock-art site, with the opportunity for an invigorating swim in a secluded creek pool.

This walk has two highlights: Red Hands Cave, a noted Aboriginal rock-art site; and secluded Crayfish Pool on Kanuka Brook,

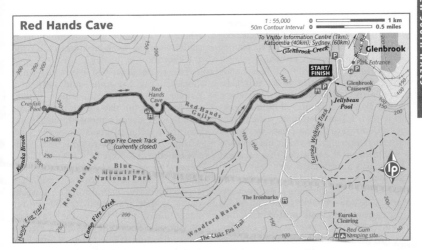

a beautiful place for a swim on a warm day. The rock shelter, 'discovered' in 1913, is decorated with numerous stencils and solid images of hands, created with coloured clays (ochre) by the Daruk (also spelt Dharug) Aboriginal people. The walk to the cave follows the well-used track beside Red Hands Gully, with some easy rock hopping to navigate. The walk down to the pool and back follows Red Hands Fire Trail and a steep track; it's rocky in places but generally easy to follow.

It used to be possible to complete a circuit walk from Glenbrook Causeway via Red Hands Cave, but bushfire damage has closed the lower part of the circuit, the Camp Fire Creek track.

PLANNING

Spring is the best time for Lower Blue Mountains walks. The water in Kanuka Brook may be safe to drink, but it's better to bring as much as you need for the day.

Maps & Books

The walks described in this section are covered by the LPINSW 1:25,000 *Penrith* map, which depicts all of the walking tracks except the final drop down to Kanuka Brook. The NPWS guide *Blue Mountains National Park Walking Track & Visitor Guide: Glenbrook & the Eastern Blue Mountains* has brief track notes along with information about picnic areas, lookouts and places of interest.

Permits & Regulations

The park entry fee is $7, payable at the entrance station 1.5km from Glenbrook (it's free to walk in). The park gates open at 8.30am and close at 7pm daily during summer (6pm in winter).

GETTING TO/FROM THE WALK

CityRail train services run at least hourly to Glenbrook from Sydney Central ($8, 1¼ hours) and Katoomba ($5.20, 45 mins). Exit the station to a footpath that parallels Burfitt Parade and Bruce Rd to the national park entrance. Walk down and across the causeway; the start of the Red Hands Track is a short distance to the right (about 1.8km from the station).

Glenbrook is 65km from Sydney via the Western Motorway and the Great Western Hwy. In Glenbrook, the turn-off from the Great Western Hwy to Blue Mountains National Park is clearly signposted. Follow Ross St to a T-junction and turn left along Burfitt Parade, which becomes Bruce Rd and leads to the park entrance.

THE WALK

From the junction of Red Hands Gully and Glenbrook Creek, Red Hands Track, which is rocky and sandy in places, follows the gully upstream to a junction (about 40 minutes from the start). Bear right and climb through mixed forest, including bloodwoods, she-oaks and turpentines (a tall tree with dark green, glossy leaves), to **Red**

Hands Cave (another 25 minutes). The cave is glassed in to protect the hand-stencils; detailed interpretive signs explain its history and how the hands were created.

A broad track leads to the Red Hands Cave car park (there are toilets nearby). To continue to **Crayfish Pool**, turn right along the Red Hands Fire Trail. Follow this generally west for 1.3km (15 minutes); the start of the track down to the pool leads westwards between two stringybark trees and opposite a small informal car park. This excellent track makes a tortuous descent, exploiting gaps and defiles in the craggy spur. The final steep section involves a slightly awkward move down boulders using footholds in a narrow slot. Walk upstream for five minutes: go up and over a large boulder, and then down through more boulders near a sheer wall on the left to deep Crayfish Pool, with its sandy beach and waterfall (30 minutes from the fire trail).

Return to Glenbrook Causeway via the outward route.

WENTWORTH FALLS & THE VALLEY OF THE WATERS

Duration	5½–7 hours
Distance	7km
Difficulty	easy–moderate
Start/Finish	Conservation Hut, Wentworth Falls
Nearest Town	Katoomba (p64)
Transport	train, bus
Summary	A classic Blue Mountains day walk, combining an edge-of-forever feel from cliff-top panoramas, numerous pools and waterfalls and a challenging side trip into the secluded, sylvan Valley of the Waters.

Adding to the pleasure of walking at Wentworth Falls is the convenience of its location (a day trip from Sydney is easily accomplished) and the wide range of trail variations on offer. The most popular route is the clockwise circuit from Conservation Hut following the Overcliff and Undercliff Tracks to Wentworth Falls and then back along the National Pass. This covers 5km and usually takes three to four hours. It's a spectacular route, coupling amazing views with refreshing waterfalls. It can get busy – especially at weekends – but that's balanced by the fact that National Pass track work (there's an ongoing upgrade program) is undertaken on weekdays, and closes the track for most of the day.

The route described here goes anti-clockwise on that circuit and adds on a couple of challenging side trips to extend the walk to a full day (seven hours maximum), with several options for picnics and swims in secluded pools along the way. Although most of the route is very clear, the trail down to Vera Falls is more tricky; hence the easy–moderate grading. The reward of making the trip to Vera Falls – especially if you walk during on a weekday – is that apart from wildlife you're likely to have the Valley of the Waters all to yourself. The route can be tackled in either direction; it's best to go to Vera Falls first, though, so as not to be faced with the 450m vertical slog back up to the Conservation Hut at the end of the day.

HISTORY

There have been walking tracks at Wentworth Falls since the 1830s; Charles Darwin was a visitor in 1837 and a walk here is named after him. So popular did the area become that the National Pass – a remarkable route cut into the side of the cliff over 100m above the valley floor – was started in the 1890s and finished by 1908. Wentworth Pass, which runs below the National Pass, was completed between 1901 and 1902, and was extended to join with Vera Falls in 1913. Slacks Stairs, down to the base of Wentworth Falls, were added in 1932.

PLANNING
Maps

The Lands 1:25,000 topographic map *Katoomba* covers the Wentworth Falls area and shows all tracks.

GETTING TO/FROM THE WALK

The **Blue Mountains Bus Company** (☎ 4751 1077; www.mountainlink.com.au) runs regular services from outside the Carrington Hotel on Katoomba St, Katoomba, to Fletcher St, Wentworth Falls (routes 685 and 690; $4.70, 15 minutes); get off where the road turns into Valley Rd and walk less than 100m to the Conservation Hut.

Cityrail trains run regularly from Katoomba to Wentworth Falls station ($2.80,

10 minutes), from where the Conservation Hut is about 20 minutes' walk. Turn left after crossing the bridge out of the station and pass the short parade of shops to reach the Great Western Hwy. Cross and walk to the right to Falls Rd (there's a short cut through Wilson Park). Keep heading down Falls Rd to Fletcher St then turn right; the Conservation Hut is at the end of this road.

If driving you can park either at the Wentworth Falls Picnic Area, within 30 minutes' walk of the falls, or at the Conservation Hut – the Short Cut Track links the two

THE WALK

From Conservation Hut take the right-hand track due west, heading downhill towards the Valley of the Waters. It'll take less than 10 minutes to reach **Queen Victoria Lookout** – the first of many view points along the walk – and views of Valley of the Waters way below. Sandwiched between sheer ruddy cliffs, a creek winds its way through the dense temperate rainforest of coachwood, sassafras and lilly pilly. A

minute later, the **Empress Lookout** provides a balcony view above the Empress Falls.

Two flights of steep metal stairs take you down into the valley towards the base of the falls. At the next junction take the left-hand National Pass route, following the stone steps down to the crossing at the base of **Empress Falls**, where the atmosphere is damp, lush and dark; in wet weather you'll need to watch your footing. The route shadows the creek as it twists and drops in tiny cataracts over the rocks.

Just after the point where you cross the creek again, the track to Vera Falls veers off to the right. This is a narrower, less well-defined track, with some junctions where you need to take care that you're going the right way. A return journey to the top of the falls takes around two hours. Initially, there's a steep zigzag down to **Flat Rock Falls**. Negotiate your way across rocks in the creek to the west side (true right). The route then heads steeply downhill.

After 15 minutes, you'll reach the junction for the Wentworth Pass track, which crosses the creek again at Red Rock Falls

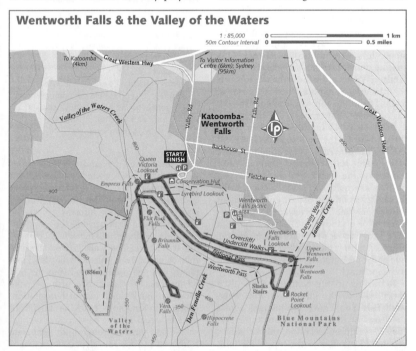

Wentworth Falls & the Valley of the Waters

and runs through the forest along the base of the cliffs towards the Lower Wentworth Falls. Our route sticks to the west bank of the creek. You'll need to be careful here; there are two turn-offs to the right that you should ignore. The second is clearly marked as the Roberts Pass track – don't take this but look for the tree marked with a red arrow and continue to head downstream. Here the trees twist into fantastic shapes to reach the light above, and stealthy creepers wait to trip up walkers.

The track crosses the creek one last time – there are pools to soak in, if you're getting warm – and then continues for around 15 minutes sharply downhill to the top of Vera Falls. There are actually two tracks, both ends of a loop to the falls – you can take either. There's a lovely vista of the valley and cliffs from **Vera Falls** and some more pools that are perfect for bathing in. You're likely to see flocks of white cockatoos and need to keep alert for snakes. To return the way you came to the National Pass junction takes around one hour.

From this junction, the views along the next couple of kilometres of the **National Pass** are some of the most remarkable of the whole walk – indeed, of the entire Blue Mountains. The track is cut into the sandstone cliffs, with multicoloured rock faces soaring above and the vast expanse of the Jamison Valley spread out below towards the distant Kanangra-Boyd wilderness. Runoff from the cliff tops provides the occasional cool shower.

After 30 to 45 minutes you'll arrive at the turn-off on the right to **Slacks Stairs** and the Wentworth Pass. These nine flights of steep metal stairs (named after an early trustee of the park), and the rocks you have to scramble over at the bottom, make this a diversion for the fit and confident bushwalker only. The reward at the base, though, of a sandy beach before the 48m drop of the **Lower Wentworth Falls** makes the effort of getting there well worthwhile. It's one of the best spots on the walk for a swim or picnic lunch.

Returning to the National Pass, it's a short walk to the glittering 110m **Wentworth Falls**. You'll have to hopscotch across the ledge of the falls to rejoin the track. It's a very stiff but relatively short climb of around 15 minutes to the top of the falls,

where you can also make a five-minute side trip to **Rocket Point**, another photographic vantage point.

From the falls follow the Overcliff and Undercliff Tracks back to Conservation Hut – around one hour's walk. The track's name becomes obvious as soon as you have to squat to negotiate the undercliff: a Lilliputian world of ferns, flowering heaths and stunted eucalypts clinging to the rocks.

There are several more view points, none far from the main track and all worthwhile side trips. Along the more exposed overcliff section of the track you're likely to scatter mountain dragons and skinks basking in the afternoon sun. **Lyrebird Lookout** provides a final panorama of the valley before the last 10-minute steady climb back to **Conservation Hut** (☎ 4757 3827; ✆ breakfast & lunch). It's a fine place to stop for breakfast, lunch or an afternoon tea of fresh scones, especially out on the deck with views over the valley.

MT SOLITARY

Duration	2 days
Distance	22km
Difficulty	moderate
Start/Finish	Katoomba Falls Kiosk
Nearest Town	Katoomba (p64)
Transport	bus

Summary Natural beauty and human history combine in this accessible out-and-back from the Blue Mountains' principal township. Stunning views and a sense of isolation are the reward for Mt Solitary campers.

Peer south over the Jamison Valley from Katoomba's most visited lookout, Echo Point, and a single visual reference point commands attention: Mt Solitary. Jutting above rippling, thickly forested valleys, the plateau-topped peak has delicious, middle-of-nowhere allure, making a walk to it all but irresistible. The walk is a manageable mix of descents, climbs and flat-tracking; plenty of easy-to-follow trail (but the odd navigational twist) and – of course, given the location – bucketloads of visual inspiration. It begins in Katoomba, takes in remnants of the area's coal-mining past, crosses rockfall rubble and passes through both temperate rainforest and open eucalypt country. High-

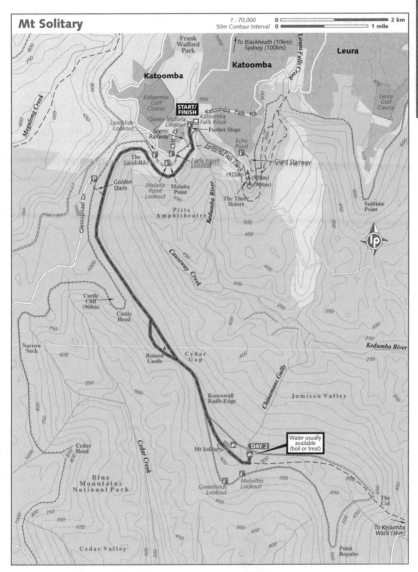

lights are the view from Ruined Castle (a favourite of many Blue Mountains walkers) and the peace of a night at Mt Solitary.

Solid uphills – including some scrambling – also make this an excellent training walk for more difficult challenges in the Blue Mountains and Kanangra-Boyd National Parks.

PLANNING

NPWS recommends you carry in all water, although there's usually water in Chinamans Gully on Mt Solitary, which you should boil before drinking. The Lands/LPINSW 1:25,000 *Katoomba* and *Jamison* maps cover the Jamison Valley area and show tracks in good detail.

NEW SOUTH WALES

GETTING TO/FROM THE WALK

The **Blue Mountains Bus Company** (☎ 4751 1077; www.mountainlink.com.au) runs regular services from Katoomba station past Katoomba Falls Kiosk (routes 686 and 696; $2.60, 15 minutes).

From Katoomba station it's about a 2km walk – mostly downhill – to the kiosk. Head straight down Katoomba St for about 1.3km then veer right into Katoomba Falls Rd. The kiosk is on the left, opposite Katoomba Park.

THE WALK
Day 1: Katoomba Falls Kiosk to Mt Solitary via Ruined Castle
4–5 hours, 11km, 390m ascent, 510m descent

Start at the stairs to the right (west) of the kiosk. Descend to the first junction (of three tracks) and go right, following the Katoomba Falls Track. Follow to the Round Walk junction and go left, following signs to the Furber Steps; these wind past several lookouts (from the **Queen Victoria lookout** there are great views of Mt Solitary and the tourist-magnet sandstone pillars, **Three Sisters**) and sidetracks, under sandstone shelves and through damp forest to the Federal Pass Track. Turn right here and continue to the bottom station of the **Scenic Railway**, built in the late-19th century to transport miners into (and shale and coal out of) the valley, but now established as one of Katoomba's main tourist draws. The precinct surrounding the railway (privately owned) has a network of boardwalks through the forest and a good many interpretive signs that provide glimpses of the past, especially of mining, which began here in 1878. It's worth wandering around for a while.

Stay to the right where the track forks just south of the Scenic Railway, and continue beneath soaring **Malaita Point** to the **Landslide**. This huge and rather scary rubble field was created by a series of rockfalls (probably triggered by earlier coal mining) during 1931. The first part of the track across it is indistinct in parts; steel poles and a few arrows show the way across the rocky and eroded gullies. The second part is easier to follow and shows vigorous signs of revegetation: blooming heath plants with small eucalypts and cedar wattle rising above.

Through rainforest west of the Landslide the track is wide and mostly flat. From here to the Ruined Castle turn-off it follows the course of the old horse-drawn mining tramway. The track passes a junction with the Golden Stairs (which descend steeply from a car park above on Narrow Neck) and walkers enjoy several changes in surrounding forest. In the cool rainforest tracts coachwood and sassafras shade the track; there's every chance you'll see a lyrebird, or at least their scratchings in forest litter. Blue gums and other eucalypt species stretch skywards in other parts. There are a number of well-used camp sites on either side of the track, some of which date back to mining days.

About 3km past the Golden Stairs, take the right turn at the sign to the **Ruined Castle**. After an abrupt climb the track turns southeast and follows the ridge. The crags for which Ruined Castle is named are about 500m from the turn-off below. Drop packs and scramble to the top of the southernmost crag to drink in the lush views (on a clear day anyway): all around the Jamison Valley, down precipitous Cedar Valley and as far as Lake Burragorang, the dwindling source of Sydney's fresh water supply. To the southeast, the route up Mt Solitary looks steep and intimidating.

After shouldering packs continue southeast on the track, which drops steeply back down to another junction. Go right to continue to Mt Solitary. Initially the going is down, to Cedar Gap, and then increasingly up, with the track often rocky and uneven. The way up Solitary follows a narrow ridge charmingly named the **Koorowall Knife-Edge** (sometimes spelt 'Koorawall'). The solid scrambling starts about 1.5km beyond the eastern Ruined Castle junction. It's not well marked; you need to stick to the ridge as much as possible by following the worn rocks (easier than it sounds) and looking for arrows. There's a critical left-turn arrow at a point where the track appears to go straight and dip down below the western cliff-line. The arrow is worn and near your feet, and points left and uphill – taking this turn will get you to the summit faster (if you miss the arrow you'll still get to the summit, via a scramble up a steep, tree-lined gully).

The **Mt Solitary summit** (c 960m) is a shady and soft casuarina grove with several tent sites. Views back to Katoomba from here are wonderful, but there's no water nearby. Continue east on the track, level at first and then descending, for about 1km to **Chinamans Gully**. There are some large camping caves at the point first reached, but it's better to turn left and follow the creek north for about 250m. The camp sites here are close to the most reliable water on the mountain. Just north at the cliff edge are wonderful views.

Day 2: Mt Solitary to Katoomba Falls Kiosk

4–5 hours, 11km, 460m ascent, 330m descent

The easy way home is to mostly retrace your outward journey, except you should go straight ahead at the Ruined Castle junctions – this cuts only a little distance, but a good deal of climbing, from the return. It's worth considering some variations to the return route. Climbing the **Golden Stairs** will carve about 3km off the journey. The hitch is you'll need a mobile phone to call **Katoomba-Leura Radio Cabs** (☎ 4782 1311) to come and fetch you; the fare back to Katoomba station is about $17. Another option is to catch the Scenic Railway back to the cliff top (which avoids the climb up Furber Steps). Trains leave every 10 minutes, the fare is $8 (last train 4.55pm). If you're feeling especially energetic you could continue along the Federal Pass Track, below Echo Point and the Three Sisters, then veer onto the Dardanelles Pass Track and finally climb back to Echo Point on the Giant Stairway. The last option will make the return a tiring but exhilarating 14km-plus journey.

BLUE GUM FOREST

Duration	2 days
Distance	19km
Difficulty	moderate
Start	Neates Glen car park
Finish	Evans Lookout
Nearest Towns	Katoomba (p64), Blackheath (p72)
Transport	train, bus

Summary A series of beautiful secluded worlds are revealed on this circuit walk through the Upper Grose Valley, starting with the dramatic Grand Canyon and culminating in the serene Blue Gum Forest.

The panorama at the end of Govetts Leap Rd, overlooking the yawning expanse of the Grose Valley, is one of the most breathtaking in the Blue Mountains – a sea of greenery stretching to the horizon, constrained by sheer cliffs of rippling sandstone. This walk takes you into the depths of the Grose to the atmospheric Blue Gum Forest. Although the route is generally easy to follow and reasonably well signed, we've graded it moderate because of the difficulty of climbing into and out of the Grose Valley, especially if you're carrying a heavy overnight pack. The effort is rewarded by the beauty of the valley and the many excellent vantage points that overlook it.

HISTORY

Govetts Leap ('leap' is a Gaelic word for waterfall) takes its name from surveyor William Govett, who came across the cascades dropping 170m into the Grose Valley in June 1831. From the end of the 19th century the area began to be managed and developed for sightseeing and walkers, with the local railway master, Tomas Rodriguez, achieving the seemingly impossible task of building a track (that bears his name) down the cliff face into the valley in 1899. The route along the Grand Canyon was opened in 1907.

It was the fight to save the Blue Gum Forest that helped to secure national park status for the Grose Valley and other parts of the Blue Mountains region. In 1932 a group from the Sydney Bushwalkers Club discovered that the forest was about to be cut down. The club members managed to raise the cash to buy out the lease for the land and thus preserve the Blue Gum Forest for the enjoyment of future generations of walkers. Their campaign also raised public awareness about protecting the natural environment.

Bushfires in 1994 damaged large areas of the Grose Valley, but the Blue Gum Forest escaped intact, and much of the rest of the bush has now regenerated.

PLANNING

The Lands/LPINSW 1:25,000 topographic maps *Katoomba* and *Mount Wilson* cover the Grose Valley area. Water is available along the route, but you'll need to boil it before drinking. The numerous 'unofficial' campsites you see in the Grose Valley should be used only in emergencies. The official sites are Acacia Flat and Burra Ko-rain Flat (near the confluence of the Grose River and Victoria Falls Creek). Both are fuel-stove-only sites – no fires.

NEAREST TOWNS

See Katoomba (p64).

Blackheath

☎ 02 / pop 4200

Blackheath, 10km west of Katoomba on the Great Western Hwy, has several quintes-sential but pricey Blue Mountains B&Bs, a couple of grocery stores and plenty of cafés. For budget accommodation, Katoomba is a better option.

There are tent sites at **Blackheath Caravan Park** (☎ 4787 8101; blkheath@tpg.com.au; Prince Edward St; sites for 2 $22-26), just off Govetts Leap Rd. The historic **Gardners Inn** (☎ 4787 8347; 255 Great Western Hwy; s $32-45, d $59-80) is opposite the train station; room tariffs include continen-tal breakfast.

GETTING THERE & AWAY

CityRail trains run regularly from Ka-toomba ($3, 15 minutes). The Blue Mountains Bus Company (☎ 4751 1077; www.mountainlink.com .au) runs services from outside Katoomba's Carrington Hotel to Blackheath (route 698; $6, 25 minutes) – regularly on weekdays and less frequently on weekends.

GETTING TO/FROM THE WALK

It's around a 4km walk (or a short taxi ride) from the Blackheath train station on the Great Western Hwy to the Neates Glen car park. A taxi from Katoomba to Neates Glen car park will cost around $20. If you're driv-ing and plan to leave your car overnight, the NPWS recommends you use the Grand Canyon Loop car park (which has toilets and water), further down Evans Lookout Rd, rather than the Neates Glen car park. Walking tracks link the Loop car park with both the start of the walk at Neates Glen and the finish point at Evans Lookout. Don't forget to lock your car and don't leave any valuables in it.

The Blue Mountains Bus Company route 698 service stops at St Andrews Rd, about halfway up Evans Lookout Rd (and at the Blue Mountains Heritage Centre on Gov-etts Leap Rd, if you're considering an alter-native finish point).

THE WALK
Day 1: Neates Glen to Acacia Flat

6–7 hours, 8km, 690m descent

From Neates Glen car park, a clear, mod-erately steep track winds its way down into a narrow gully, a shrouded, dripping world of mosses and ferns, many towering like verdant parasols. Take care, since it can be slippy here. To reach the bottom of the can-yon takes around half an hour; have a rest and soak up the otherworldly atmosphere of this rocky enclosure before continu-ing through a short tunnel and along the track shadowing Greaves Creek, way below. Amazing views of the **Grand Canyon**, in places 30m deep and a few metres wide, open up from this point and the route makes some thrilling passes under waterfalls and cliff overhangs before dropping to the creek. This is a truly magical spot, with the re-flected light from the water dappling the umber cliffs and lush vegetation. With time spent dallying, you'll probably be about two hours in the canyon.

The track hopscotches across the creek several times before reaching a junction. A track up to Evans Lookout lies across the creek to the left; our route follows the sign to Rodriguez Pass and Beauchamp Falls. In around half an hour – half of it on the creek's right bank, half on its left – you'll come to **Beauchamp Falls**. There are several spots from which to admire the falls, but take care since this is the trickiest part of the track to follow, with the route across boul-ders being far from clear. Keep an eye out for steps in the rocks to know you're head-ing in the right direction. Eventually, this steep route will bring you to a broad plateau in the cascades, a good spot for lunch and to bathe in one of the pools. Cross the creek at this point and go left, the opposite direction from the white arrow on the rock, which points to a dead end further up.

After an hour's walking you'll have reached the valley floor and will be fol-lowing the Rodriguez Pass to **Junction Rock**, at the confluence of Govetts Leap Brook and Govetts Creek. This is another fine spot for a cooling dip and you're likely to en-counter many cat-sized eastern water drag-ons guarding the rocks. Day walkers often peel off here, and take **Rodriguez Pass** uphill from here to Govetts Leap Lookout – the last section a tough haul up metal ladders.

The track to **Acacia Flat** (around one hour's walk) continues across Govetts Creek and along the stream's left bank, initially passing through an unofficial camp site. The going can get a bit jungly, and at one point you'll wade through a sea of knee-high ferns. It's generally flat, but there's one short climb just after the old Fortress Creek Flat camp site (closed for regeneration – no camping). At the crest of the hill, take the track to the right heading back down to the creek; Acacia Flat is less than a half-hour's walk from here.

The extensive camp site has a toilet and several paths leading down to the creek where you can get water (that must be boiled). After downing your pack, take time to enjoy the calm, cool atmosphere of the nearby Blue Gum Forest.

Day 2: Acacia Flat to Evans Lookout
6–7 hours, 11km, 680m ascent

In warm weather, an early start to climb the **Docker Buttress** – one of the steepest ways out of the Grose Valley – is recommended. From Blue Gum Forest, take the left-hand route up the hill, which starts climbing sharply almost immediately. (The track straight ahead eventually leads to Victoria Falls, 12km northwest – an alternative way out of the valley, if you've arranged transport to meet you at Victoria Falls Rd.) There are a few short flat sections between the uphill slogs, which get steeper and steeper until

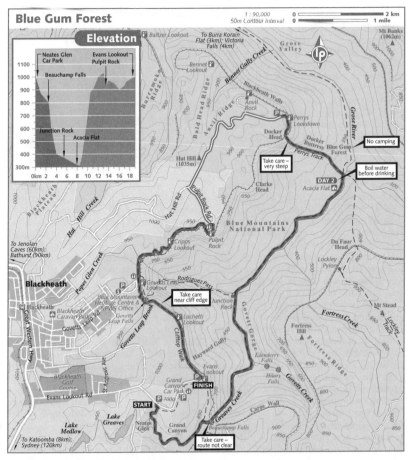

Blue Gum Forest

you're virtually rock climbing. Depending on your level of fitness, the 2km route, which rises 600m from the valley floor, takes between 1½ and three hours.

Docker Head is the first view point you'll reach on the cliff edge, but **Perrys Lookdown**, a bit further on, is the better vantage point. From the nearby car park (no water available), follow Hat Hill Rd for around 4km, an unshaded trudge enlivened by glimpses across the expanse of the valley and the flashing blue-and-red plumage of crimson rosellas. After around 45 minutes take the left-hand turning down Pulpit Rock Rd to the lookout, 10 minutes away. There are toilets and shelter here, but no water, so make sure you've brought plenty with you from the valley.

Pulpit Rock provides a magnificent view of the Grose Valley and an opportunity to study the layer-cake effect of the different types of vegetation, from the open forest of black ash and peppermint gums on the cliff tops via patches of swamp and woodland to the coachwood and sassafras in the valley below. On the northeast horizon is 944m Mt Hay, while southwest there's a view of **Govetts Leap Falls**, a slender ribbon of white water looking like a length of billowing muslin, hence the alternative name of Bridal Veil Falls.

Returning from the lookout point, take the left turn along Pulpit Rock Track, a route that meanders pretty much on the level around the cliff top towards Horseshoe Falls, a name that's self-evident once you see the concave recess the water has carved into the rock.

The track drops shortly before the falls to Popes Glen Creek, then climbs again towards **Govetts Leap Lookout**. On the way up you'll pass the turn-off for the Popes Glen Track, leading to Blackheath via woodlands and swamp, in around one hour.

If you haven't already paused for lunch already, Govetts Leap Lookout is a good spot to do so before tackling the final one- to 1½-hour leg to Evans Lookout; if you've had enough (and don't have a car to retrieve), the Blue Mountains Heritage Centre is a 500m walk up Govetts Leap Rd.

The route drops down to and crosses Govetts Leap Brook (there's a short track to the right here along the brook, called the Braeside Walk) and then climbs again to the cliff edge, affording eye-catching vistas of the Grose Valley most of the way. The track then shadows the Griffith Taylor Wall of rock, shooting down some 600m to the valley floor, and crosses a minor depression at Hayward Gully, before rising to the car park at Evans Lookout, which has toilets, water and a barbecue area. The actual lookout is a brief walk from here, but worth making the effort for one last look across Govetts Gorge towards the imposing bluff of Fortress Hill.

SIX FOOT TRACK

Duration	3 days
Distance	42km
Difficulty	moderate–demanding
Start	Explorers Tree, Great Western Hwy
Finish	Jenolan Caves
Nearest Towns	Katoomba (p64), Jenolan (p76)
Transport	bus

Summary Traversing the full range of Blue Mountains landscapes, from lush rainforest glens to open woodland, this heritage track follows the original route taken by late 19th-century travellers from Katoomba to the spectacular Jenolan Caves.

The appeal of the Six Foot Track (claimed to be the second-most popular overnight bushwalk in Australia, after Tasmania's Overland Track) derives from a combination of historical associations and gorgeous, constantly changing scenery. It's far from the most ambitious walk you can take in the Blue Mountains, although its difficulty shouldn't be underestimated. It's certainly among one of the prettiest trails, particularly in spring when wildflowers bloom in profusion.

Starting from the Explorers Tree just outside Katoomba, the track drops down through the rainforest of Nellies Glen, crosses the rolling meadows of the Megalong Valley and fords Coxs River. It then climbs over both the Mini Mini Saddle and Black Range to reach the Gothic splendour of Jenolan Caves, as awe-inspiring a climax today as it was a century ago.

Although it's possible to cover the route in less time (the record is an incredible three hours, 12 minutes, set during the annual marathon run), the best way to fully appreciate the landscape is to take three days, camping at Coxs River and on the Black Range. If you're a fast, strong walker and have arranged transport back from Jenolan (or an overnight stay there), a two-day itinerary is possible, camping at Alum Creek, roughly halfway along.

We have rated this walk as moderate–demanding, more in line with the Six Foot Track Heritage Trust's 'hard' grading. While the route is clear and well signposted, its length and two sustained climbs on Day 2 make it a challenge, especially with a heavy pack. On weekends and during holidays you're sure to encounter several walking parties along the way; plan a midweek trip for a quieter experience. The track can be walked in either direction, but it's easier to go from Katoomba to Jenolan, to avoid finishing with the climb up Nellies Glen.

HISTORY

The lure of Jenolan Caves as a tourism hot spot prompted the government to survey a route across the Megalong Valley in 1884. The first recorded trip along the whole track was by the NSW governor, Lord Carrington, and his wife in 1887. Although built as a bridle trail, the route quickly became popular with walkers. The Six Foot Track gained its present name in 1937 – by which time the 6ft-wide bridle trail was already close to impassable. The rise of motor transport caused the track to decline even more after WWII, reaching a nadir in the 1960s when an ill-conceived and later abandoned scheme to build a road down Nellies Glen scarred the landscape almost irreparably.

However, 100 years after it was first blazed, the track was remarked and reopened by the Department of Lands. Although fire trails now cover large sections of the original route, the route retains much of the fascination of its earlier years. The track is now managed by the Six Foot Track Heritage Trust, a non-profit, community-based organisation. The trust is administered through the Lands office in Orange.

PLANNING

The Lands/LIC 1:25,0000 topographical maps *Katoomba, Hampton* and *Jenolan* cover the route in the most detail. The Lands map/information sheet *Six Foot Track* should be considered essential – it shows all the important detail, including gradients, and its sales help to fund track maintenance. It's available at good map shops (p49) and in Blue Mountains visitor information centres (p64). The lack of reliable water sources are one of the main difficulties of walking the track. There are rainwater tanks at the Coxs River and Black Range camp sites. Boil any water taken from watercourses.

Guided Walks

The Six Foot Track Heritage Trust licences guiding companies to conduct walks along the track and can refer interested parties to

---

LIMESTONE LANDSCAPES

Dramatic and often hidden realms, limestone landscapes are marked by steep-walled gorges, sinkholes and extensive cave systems with underground rivers – in short, a speleologist's dream. On the surface, limestone country can be hard to pick. It's often characterised by barren, rocky ground in otherwise fertile country. As well as the Six Foot Track walk, which ends at Jenolan Caves, two other walks in this chapter traverse limestone country: Cooleman Plain (See Gorges, Plains & Caves, p94) and Bungonia & the Shoalhaven River (p107).

Limestone landscapes occur in areas where there are dense, well-jointed pockets of limestone near the surface, fed by rainfall and circulating groundwater. In a process called carbonation, the limestone reacts with the acid from rainwater as it seeps through the soil, then dissolves and is carried away. The water flows through existing joints in the limestone and enlarges them to form passages, caves and other features.

Caves are extremely varied, ranging from vertical shafts or narrow passages to soaring Gothic caverns decorated with stalactites (limestone pendants that hang from a cave ceiling, formed by deposits of calcite in dripping water) and stalagmites (cave-floor pinnacles formed as water drips from stalactites). Gorges generally form when a series of caverns collapse.

these licensed operators. The trust is currently administered through an office in the **Department of Lands** (☎ 6391 4321) in Orange, west of Bathurst, but administration will eventually pass back to the community and this phone number will change.

NEAREST TOWNS

See Katoomba (p64).

Jenolan

☎ 02

At track's end, there are several sleeping options at Jenolan Caves, which is administered by the **Jenolan Caves Trust** (☎ 6359 3911; www.jenolancaves.org.au). The **Jenolan Caves Resort** (☎ 6359 3322) includes up-market Jenolan

Caves House, with shared-facility rooms from $65, and bunk beds at a backpacker lodge, the Gatehouse, from $25. Room rates increase on weekends and public holidays.

Meals are available in Caves House at Trails Bistro and at Chisholm's Restaurant (mains $23).

GETTING THERE & AWAY

Jenolan is 72km from Katoomba. If you can't arrange a pick-up from Jenolan, Katoomba-based **Fantastic Aussie Tours** (☎ 1300 300 915) runs a daily transfer service to/from the caves for $35, departing from the caves at 3.45pm. If you plan to come out on a Sunday check ahead with them – low passenger numbers sometimes lead to cancellation.

Six Foot Track

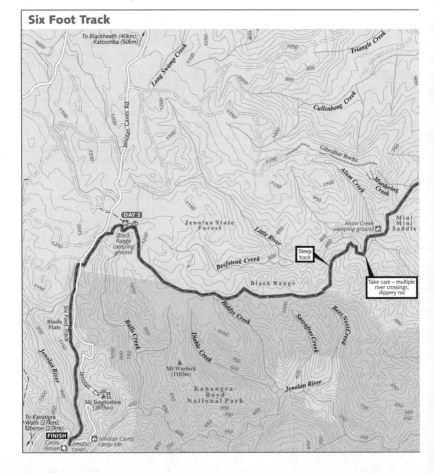

Blue Mountains Trolley Tours (☎ 1800 801 577; www.trolleytours.com.au; $35), also in Katoomba, has a Jenolan service that departs the caves around 3pm to 3.30pm each day.

GETTING TO/FROM THE WALK

The start of the Six Foot Track, at the Explorers Tree, is 2km west of Katoomba, just off the Great Western Hwy; a taxi to here costs about $7 to $8.

THE WALK
Day 1: Katoomba to Coxs River
6–7 hours, 15.5km, 750m descent

From the Explorers Tree head down the track to the start of the route into Nellies Glen. After 10 minutes, the track turns sharply right and descends into the glen along a series of uneven steps. To reach the bottom takes around 45 minutes, by which time your knees are likely to be rather wobbly.

The old track snaked in a more leisurely fashion through this beautiful enclave of warm temperate rainforest. Through the trees you'll hear, if not clearly see, Bonnie Doon Falls. The glen is named after a 19th-century mine operator's daughter – looking ahead you can see **Narrow Neck Plateau**, a knobbly finger of rock soaring out of the Megalong Valley, under which the coal and shale mines were once located.

At the bottom of the glen, the vegetation abruptly changes to drier woodland dominated by scribbly gum and smooth-barked

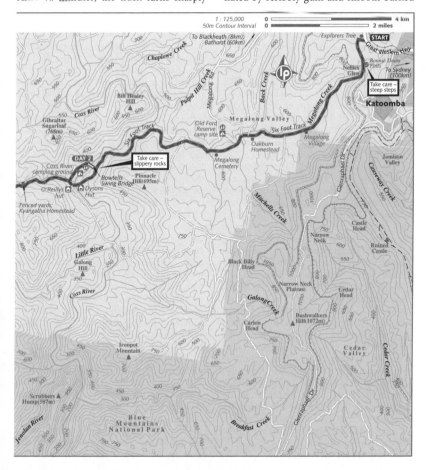

apple, which is neither smooth-barked nor an apple tree. The narrow route widens into an access road, which you follow as it shadows Narrow Neck on the left-hand side. Where you pass a paddock is the site of the long-abandoned **Megalong Village**, an early 20th-century community for workers at the nearby shale mine.

Ahead there are several locked gates to go through, all with stiles over them. Just after the **Oakburn homestead**, which was the early Megalong Post Office, the track continues through woods en route to the **Megalong Cemetery**, just across Megalong Valley Rd. At the entrance to the overgrown cemetery, a cairn lists those known to be buried here; only two marked graves remain, one fenced in by ornate ironwork.

Descending the track as it follows Megalong Creek, watch out for sharp-edged bits of pale stone on the ground. This is chert, brought by Aboriginal people to this area for use as cutting tools. The track undulates gently across open meadows, which is very English in feel until you look back towards the towering sandstone cliffs and take in the gum trees. One particularly fine old river gum marks the spot where you'll cross a small creek before climbing a hill that affords a beautiful panorama of the valley.

Approaching the Coxs River valley, the track drops back into woodland, punctuated by huge lichen-splashed granite boulders. Look out for one particularly large one known as Toad Rock, and for an enchanting glen of giant split boulders. This is one of the prettiest sections of the walk, sticking to the track's original route and dimensions. Below, the Coxs River can be heard and eventually the track will reach its side.

As long as the river isn't in full flood, there's a choice of crossings. The most thrilling is by the 90m-long **Bowtells Swing Bridge**. Only one person at a time is allowed to cross this metal suspension bridge, which is 30m above the rocky river bed. The best way to negotiate the bridge, if you take fright, is to look straight ahead and sing/whistle a tune.

If the water is low, it's usually possible to cross by the rocks below the bridge, or follow the track down the true left bank of the river for 1km to a narrow, shallow section at the confluence with Murdering Creek. Take care when crossing the river bed as the granite rocks are very slippery.

The official Coxs River camping ground (with toilets) is around 15 minutes' walk from the bridge.

Day 2: Coxs River to Black Range
7½–8½ hours, 20.5km, 900m ascent

This is the toughest, longest day of the walk so an early start and a steady pace are recommended. Also make sure you have sufficient water, especially as there are no sources at all once you start the long climb up and along the Black Range.

As a warm-up for the day ahead there's a one-hour climb of around 300 vertical metres along the fire trail beside Murdering Creek. At the top, the land opens up beside the fenced yards of the old **Kyangatha homestead**. A pear tree stands in the paddock and you're likely to encounter several ponies and horses, plus some cattle further along.

Enjoy the view before climbing another 200m over undulating fields across the Mini Mini Saddle. At the top, a forest of smooth-barked apple begins again as you drop down sharply towards **Alum Creek**, an official camp site, with no facilities and no guarantee of water in the creek either. Here you may want to remove your boots as the route crosses the river three times, but take care not to slip in the water. This is a good spot for lunch before the sustained steep climb up the Black Range. You may also be fortunate enough to spot grey kangaroos here.

At a steady trudge, it takes between 1½ and 2½ hours to reach the 1000m-high ridge of the Black Range. About halfway up, there's a track heading downhill to the right that you should ignore. The best view back is just before the summit, beside a cluster of spiky-headed grass trees. From here, with good eyesight – or binoculars – you'll be able to see the Hydro Majestic Hotel at Medlow Bath. A sign marks the start of the Kanangra-Boyd National Park on the left side of the track, while to the right is Jenolan State Forest.

The track twists for a leisurely 10.5km along the ridge towards the official camping ground. On the way, you'll pass several striking termite mounds. It's also high enough here for subalpine snow gums. After a couple of hours you should reach the junction with another fire trail, where the forest has been cleared; turn left and walk for 500m to the next left turn-off to the Black Range camp site, which has a toilet and shelter.

Day 3: Black Range to Jenolan Caves
4–4 ½ hours, 9km, 350m descent
The Black Range camping ground is on a marked deviation from the original Six Foot Track, which for a large part of this day's walk has long since been covered by Jenolan Rd. From the camp to the road via the deviation is 3km, around a one-hour walk through shaded woods of brown barrel eucalyptus and radiata pine (spreading from a nearby plantation). There's one short steep section to negotiate before reaching Jenolan Rd. Cross this and follow the adjacent track for another hour to Binda Flats.

The cleared grassy area of **Binda Flats** was once used to grow vegetables to feed residents at Jenolan Caves. Now, particularly in the late afternoon, it's possible to see grey kangaroos and wallabies grazing here. The route continues behind the cabins and down towards the caves in a more or less straight line for 4km. At times it's rocky, steep and rather narrow, but affords lovely views of the plunging wooded valley near the limestone caves.

You'll eventually arrive at a gap in the rock that acts as a window on a blue-tinged lake not far below, its luminous colour caused by the dissolved limestone. From here you can either reach Caves House, the end of the walk, by the direct right-hand route, or along the left-hand trail that goes via the looming cavern known as the Devil's Coachhouse.

Since this is really only a half-day walk, you'll have plenty of time to enjoy exploring **Jenolan Caves**. Regular tours are run through nine show caves, and if you've still got some energy, there are several short walks in the vicinity. For details of cave tours contact the **Jenolan Caves Trust** (☎ 6359 3911; www.jenolan caves.org.au).

KANANGRA-BOYD NATIONAL PARK

Kanangra-Boyd National Park and its eponymous wilderness have rich associations with NSW bushwalking and conservation, and have long been popular destinations for independent walkers and adventure-seekers. Although not as widely known as Blue Mountains National Park, its neighbour to the east and south, Kanangra-Boyd arguably outstrips 'the Blueys' for scenery and isolation. Those undertaking walks in the Blue Mountains enjoy the sense of being on the fringe of civilization; a Kanangra-Boyd walk feels like a journey into the wild. The entire park is one of seven included in the 10,000 sq km Blue Mountains World Heritage Area, declared in 2000.

ENVIRONMENT
The 68,000-hectare park contains some of the Greater Blue Mountains World Heritage Area's most remarkable landscapes and scenery – no mean boast. In a region dominated by grand sandstone cliffs and valleys, vast Kanangra Gorge (overlooked by Thurat Spires, Kanangra Walls and with Mt Cloudmaker in the distance) is the visual champion for pure majesty.

With so much of it a declared wilderness, the park and its habitats are an important reserve for rare plant communities and animals. It covers an extensive plateau deeply eroded by a network of creeks and rivers. Its highest point is 1334m Mt Emperor, about 10km northwest of Kanangra Walls, and it plunges to less than 200m in some creek and river gorges. Remnant rainforest is found on the plateau escarpments and there is extensive subalpine habitat of snow gums, swamps and bogs. The park protects the headwaters of the Kowmung, Kanangra and Jenolan Rivers, which are major contributors to Sydney's fresh water supply. In 2005, the Kowmung was given special protection as a NSW 'Wild River', which will ensure it remains free of threat from mining or forestry.

PLANNING
When to Walk
Conditions in Kanangra-Boyd closely resemble those in the Blue Mountains. Summer days can be warm, hazy and marred by bushfire danger and water scarcity, which makes autumn through spring the best time for walking. Mid-winter days are clear and cool; snowfalls can occur between June and August. Throughout the cool months, the valleys are often warmer than the high, exposed plateaus.

Information Sources

The **Blue Mountains Heritage Centre** (☎ 4787 8877; bluemountains.heritagecentre@environment.nsw .gov.au; Govetts Leap Rd), near Blackheath, has all the requisite maps, guides and information to Kanangra-Boyd. The park is administered from the **NPWS Oberon office** (☎ 6336 1972; 38 Ross St).

Permits & Regulations

The park entry fee (really, more like a parking fee) is $7. Bring $1 and $2 coins for the ticket machines.

ACCESS TOWN

See Katoomba (p64).

KANANGRA WALLS TO THE KOWMUNG RIVER

Duration	2 days
Distance	24km
Difficulty	moderate–demanding
Start/Finish	Kanangra Walls car park
Nearest Towns	Katoomba (p64), Oberon (pright)
Transport	private

Summary A challenging jaunt from one of NSW's most spectacular natural features – the plunging wilds of Kanangra Deep – to one of the state's iconic wilderness rivers.

Kanangra-Boyd National Park's best known attractions (Kanangra Walls, Kanangra Deep and Thurat Spires) derive a major benefit from being an extra few hours' drive from Sydney. Compared with similar natural monuments in the Blue Mountains, Kanangra-Boyd's highlights don't suffer from overcrowding: it's touch too far for the average day visitor. This effect is amplified in the case of the park's walks. On all but the most popular of holidays, as soon as one ventures away from the tracks near Kanangra Walls it begins to feel like very isolated country. A peaceful night near the banks of the Kowmung River is all one needs to understand why conservationists spent so much energy protecting this region.

PLANNING

Away from the Kanangra Walls area, any of the tracks in Kanangra-Boyd National Park aren't well marked, so maps and com-

pass are essential. Morong Creek at Boyd River camping ground is the nearest water supply to the track head (boil before use). Water availability between the Kanangra Walls car park and the Kowmung will depend on weather conditions. It's safest to carry all you'll need for the journey. NPWS recommends that walkers boil water taken from the Kowmung. The walk is covered by two LPINSW 1:25,000 topographic maps, *Kanangra* and *Yerranderie*. Both accurately show tracks and pads. The NPA's *Bushwalks in the Sydney Region* has notes on several walks in Kanangra-Boyd National Park.

NEAREST TOWN & FACILITIES

See Katoomba (p64).

Oberon

☎ 02 / population 2200

Quiet Oberon sits at 1113m, making it the Blue Mountains region's highest town and the one closest to Kanangra-Boyd National Park. The **Oberon visitor information centre** (☎ 6336 0666; www.oberonaustralia.com; cnr Ross St & Edith Rd) is open daily.

SLEEPING & EATING

Jenolan Caravan Park (☎ 6336 0344; www.jenolan caravanpark.com.au; 7 Cunynghame St; unpowered sites for 2 $14-18, powered $22-26, cabins $72-94) is a short walk from the Oberon shopping strip.

Big Trout Motor Inn (☎ 6336 2100; www.bluemts .com.au/bigtrout; Oberon St; s/d $89/99) is on the eastern end of the main street with 33 plain but comfy rooms. It has a Chinese restaurant (closed Monday).

Highlands Motor Inn (☎ 6336 1866; www.high landsmotorinn.com.au; cnr Dart & Fleming Sts; s/d $89/99) has classic motel rooms a touch closer to the town shops.

There's two bakeries and several cafés on the main street, plus an IGA supermarket that opens 9am to 5pm weekdays (shorter hours on weekends). The **Royal Hotel bistro** (☎ 6336 1011; mains from $17; ☾ lunch & dinner daily) offers reliable meals. **Oberon RSL** (☎ 6336 1607; cnr Oberon & Dudley Sts; ☾ lunch & dinner Tue-Sun) has a restaurant that also serves takeaways.

GETTING THERE & AWAY

A coach service runs between Mt Victoria and Oberon on Tuesday mornings and Friday and Sunday evenings. The one-way fare is $6.60; book through **Countrylink** (☎ 13 22 32;

www.countrylink.info). CityRail trains run regularly to Mt Victoria from Sydney Central (one way $13, 2¼ hours) and Katoomba ($3.60, 20 minutes).

Boyd River camping ground

The nearest sites to Kanangra Walls are at Boyd River camping ground, 7km southwest of the walk starting point. The site has pit/composting toilets and wood barbecues (bring your own wood). Sites are free.

GETTING TO/FROM THE WALK

Take the Great Western Hwy west from Katoomba and to Hartley. Go left onto Jenolan Caves Rd and follow for 45km to Jenolan Caves. Go through the arch and climb steeply for 7km to the Kanangra Walls turnoff (left). From Oberon, take the Edith Rd towards Jenolan Caves. The Kanangra Walls turn is about 23km out of town. Boyd River camping ground is 21km south of the turn and Walls car park another 7km.

Misty Mountains 4WD Tours (☎ 4757 2278; info@4wdtours.net.au) will do shuttles for walkers from the Katoomba area to/from Kanangra Walls for $400 (one way for $250). The vehicle fits up to six walkers.

THE WALK
Day 1: Kanangra Walls car park to Kowmung River
4–5 hours, 12.2km, 840m descent

Go east from Kanangra Walls car park, past the locked gate and continue along the track. About 300m along is the first of two junctions (about 50m apart) for the plateau walk leading to **Kanangra Walls**. Before taking the turn, go on 150m to Echo Head and Kanangra Walls lookout for an inspiring view of the soaring cliffs and plunging gorge that define the area. Return to the first track junction and set off (left) downhill, past some sedimentary cliffs and, just before the track rises, the turn to **Dance Floor Cave** (70m to 80m off to the right), named because it once contained – what else – a dance floor where local workers kicked up their heels. After a climb up some steps the track continues, following the Walls northeast; here and there are small tracks leading to the cliff edge. About 1.2km past Dance Floor Cave the track reaches a wide, upward-sloping rock platform; here take the narrow track off to the right that's obscured by heath. (To the left, there are brilliant views of Kanangra Gorge, Thurat Walls and Thurat Spires. If there's been rain, Kanangra Falls and Kalang Falls will be flowing, adding to the spectacle).

After running flat and passing the turn to the Kanangra Walls trig, the track starts to fall away. It's heavily eroded in places and overgrown with heath. After about 45 minutes it opens up into scrubby eucalypt forest, before a steep, short drop down the cliff line of Murrarang Top near Storm Stallion Point. Continue left (east) at the base of the descent, passing the camping-friendly **Coal Seam Cave**. There's often a container here,

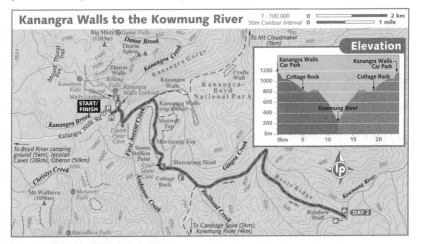

Kanangra Walls to the Kowmung River

collecting fresh water seeping from Murrarang Head through the overhang. Beyond Coal Seam Cave are a couple of hard-to-spot track junctions. The first, to the right about 300m to 350m along, leads to **Cottage Rock**, from which there are views of wild Arabanoo Creek and Canyon (allow 30 minutes for the side trip). Past here the track undulates (mostly descending) along the spine of the Gingra Range, mostly through open eucalypt country and with wonderful filtered views north and south. About 4km past Coal Seam Cave a marked tree (hard to spot) and tent site marks the turn-off down Roots Ridge and the Kowmung.

Go across the little clearing and veer right. From here the track is more a well-worn pad, easy to follow as it sticks closely to the ridge while dropping 600 vertical metres in a little over 3.5km. The first glimpses of the Kowmung come about 1km from the camp sites; there's a particularly fine view upriver from **Rainbow Bluff**, about 700m to 800m from the end of the day.

There are tent sites among the beautiful casuarinas on both sides of the river, some of the better ones on the eastern (opposite) bank and just upstream from the bottom of the track. The river and its surrounds are an enchanting place, and well worth a two-night stay to allow time to explore.

Day 2: Kowmung River to Kanangra Walls car park

5–6 hours, 12km, 840m ascent

This is a straightforward return on the outward route, to the extent that 800m-plus vertical ascents are straightforward. Take your time, have frequent breaks and savour the peace and quiet.

KOSCIUSZKO NATIONAL PARK

In southeast NSW, about 150km inland from the coast, is an area of high peaks, deep valleys, plateaus and plains collectively known as the Snowy Mountains, or 'Snowies'. Within this area Australia's highest summits are found, including Mt Kosciuszko (2228m), the highest peak on the continent – and the only direct evidence on the Australian mainland of glaciation

dating from the last ice age. Fortunately, this region is protected within Kosciuszko National Park, a huge reserve about 150km long and between 20km and 50km wide, encompassing an area of 690,000 hectares. The park contains a rich variety of flora and fauna, and all of NSW's ski resorts; it's also the backbone of the Snowy Mountains Hydroelectric Scheme, arguably Australia's greatest engineering feat.

Kosciuszko National Park is ideal for bushwalking. The gently rounded summits of the Main Range, including Mt Kosciuszko and Mt Twynam, are easily climbed without the need for long, arduous walks, although there is certainly enough space within the park to keep a walker busy for weeks.

The most popular area for walking is the Main Range between Thredbo and Charlotte Pass, containing Australia's highest peaks (p88). But other areas are definitely worth a visit, too. The southern region of the park has some wild and rarely visited localities, including the Chimneys (p92), while in the north are lower-altitude frost plains, limestone caves and gorges of the Cooleman Plain area. The three walks described here give a good introduction to these very different areas.

It's actually possible to complete a marathon walk through the mountains of Victoria, NSW and the ACT, and thus achieve a full traverse of the Australian Alps, though admittedly few walkers actually walk this route in one journey. The path, known as the Australian Alps Walking Track (p157), enters Kosciuszko National Park south of Dead Horse Gap, meanders over high peaks of the Snowy Mountains, and exits the park at the ACT border.

HISTORY

The earliest evidence of an Aboriginal presence in the region dates from at least 5000 years ago, when various tribes travelled to the mountains in summer to feast on the protein- and fat-rich Bogong moths.

The timing of the first visit to Australia's highest peaks by white settlers is a little unsure. While it's probable that stockmen from pastoral properties in the Monaro region ventured into the high country in the 1820s and '30s, it was not until 1840 that Paul Edmund Strzelecki climbed to the Main Range by way of Hannels Spur and summited the highest peak, which he named Mt Kosciuszko. Following 'discovery', the mountains were gradually settled by local stockmen who brought their livestock to graze on the plains during summer.

In 1859 word of gold discoveries in the Kiandra area spread and inspired a gold rush, and by 1860 Kiandra boasted a population of more than 15,000. As with many such booms, however, gold deposits were rapidly depleted and within a matter of years the town had only a few hundred residents. By about 1905 the area was virtually deserted.

From the 1920s, skiers and bushwalkers gradually discovered this impressive area. Hotel Kosciusko was built near Perisher Valley in 1909, but the ski resorts as we now know them did not develop until after WWII. Work started in 1949 on the massive Snowy Mountains Hydroelectric Scheme, and was finally completed in 1972. This huge scheme diverts water in tunnels through the mountains and produces electricity at many power stations on the steeper west side of the ranges. Much of the track network across the park was cut during this construction period.

ENVIRONMENT

It is not surprising in an area with terrain as mountainous and varied as Kosciuszko National Park that there is such a diverse range of flora and fauna. The park is home

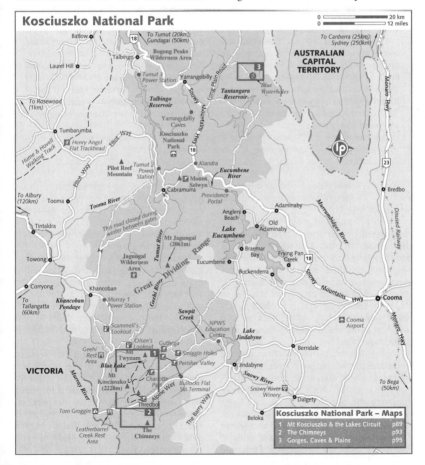

Kosciuszko National Park

Kosciuszko National Park – Maps	
1 Mt Kosciuszko & the Lakes Circuit	p89
2 The Chimneys	p93
3 Gorges, Caves & Plains	p95

NEW SOUTH WALES

CAPITAL WALKS IN THE ACT

Australia's national capital and its surrounding territory is one of the best places in the country to live if you're a dedicated walker. The vast spaces of Kosciuszko National Park (p82) extend so far north that they skirt the ACT's western border, while the rugged wilderness of the Budawangs (p97) and dramatic limestone landscape of Bungonia Gorge (p105) are closer to Canberra than any other city. But really, one needn't even leave the well-ordered confines of the ACT to find a score of decent walks.

The main walking lure for Canberrans is **Namadgi National Park** (www.environment.act.gov.au /bushparksandreserves/namadgi.html), the 1060-sq-km bushland haven that adjoins Kosciuszko and is the northernmost of several Australian Alps national parks, a chain of which extend northwards from the high country east of Melbourne. Namadgi is renowned for grasslands (and the large kangaroo population it supports), eucalypt forest and some tall peaks – several over 1800m. Popular Namadgi walks include the 16km return track from the **Naas Valley to Horse Gully Hut**, which starts just off the Boboyan Rd in the park's south. It's easy going and there's a good chance of seeing plenty of kangaroos. The area – like a lot of bushland around the ACT – was damaged in the disastrous 2003 fires, but it's recovering at a startling pace. Further north off the Boboyan Rd, the **Yankee Hat Walking Trail** is a mere stroll at 6km; it leads through more grasslands to some striking Aboriginal rock art on a granite boulder. For more information contact the **Namadgi visitor information centre** (☎ 6207 2900; namadginationalpark@act.gov.au; Naas Rd, Tharwa).

Closer to central Canberra, **Tidbinbilla Nature Reserve** (www.environment.act.gov.au/bushparksand reserves/parksandreserves/tidbinbilla) bills itself as the ACT's best place to see wildlife in a natural setting – which is a pretty fair assessment. In addition to several easy tourist walks, the reserve has a handful of more challenging day walks (ranging from 5km to nearly 20km) that provide access to some of the better views and taller peaks. Views from the **Gibraltar Trail** and **Camel Back Trail** are probably the most impressive. The **Tidbinbilla visitor information centre** (☎ 6205 1233), near the reserve entrance off Paddys River Rd, can assist with information on longer walks and more remote tracks.

The **Environment ACT** (www.environment.act.gov.au) website is an excellent starting point for more information on these and other ACT parks and reserves.

---

to about 200 species of birds, 30 species of reptiles, 30 species of mammals and 200 species of insects.

The lower and mid-mountain slopes are dominated by tall and slender mountain ash, mountain gum and alpine ash. This forest is home to eastern grey kangaroos, wombats, echidnas, ringtail and brushtail possums, native bush rats and marsupial mice. Higher up, in the region just below the snow line, the forest is predominantly snow gum, which is often buckled and weathered into weird shapes by heavy snow and strong wind. In some areas, the forest is coated in a thick understorey of tussock grass and shrubs, purple hoveas, royal grevilleas, yellow kunzeas and pink grass trigger plants, all of which flower delightfully in spring and summer.

Above 1800m is the alpine zone, where the climate is generally too cold and severe for any tree growth at all. Heaths, grasses, herbs and snowpatch vegetation dominate

here, as well as the rare feldmark, a low, ground-hugging migratory plant that grows on the most exposed (and often damaged) sites. Sphagnum bogs develop on wet sites, absorbing water and releasing it slowly throughout the year.

Birds species that frequent the alpine region include gang-gang and yellow-tailed black cockatoos, wedge-tailed eagles, pied currawongs, colourful flame robins and, in alpine ash forest, elusive lyrebirds. However, it's the common raven that you may see the most. In some areas, with luck, you may even espy an emu or two!

Lizards and skinks are common reptiles, but there are also some species which you do not want to see, such as black, brown and tiger snakes. Other undesirables which now, unfortunately, inhabit the park include feral animals, such as pigs, brumbies (wild horses), rabbits, hares, foxes and even cats. Some of these you're likely to spot, even if only as road-kill.

CLIMATE

As you'd expect of a mountainous region, there is a wide range of weather phenomena influencing the park's climate.

Temperature drops at a rate of about 1°C for every 150m of altitude gained, making the mountain tops over 10°C cooler than the lowlands. Average daily maximums at about 2000m range from 15°C in summer to 0°C in winter, but strong variations are common. Summer can still get quite hot at times and temperatures in autumn and spring can be anything from comfortably mild to cold, and frosts are common during these times. Winter is cold everywhere in the park.

Precipitation is heavy all year, but in summer is usually more erratic; torrential thunderstorms are common in the mountains during summer. Snowfalls are frequent in winter and snow covers most of the terrain above 1400m during this time. In the most elevated areas and on the western slopes of the ranges, rainfall can exceed 2000mm a year, tapering to less than 1000mm in the far northeastern sector of the park.

PLANNING

It's essential that you're well prepared with the right gear for a walk in the mountains, as weather conditions can be severe at times, even in summer. For further information on what to bring, see the boxed text p39.

When to Walk

Winter is really the only season when walking is out of the question, either because of the deep snow that covers the walking areas described here, or because of seasonal road closures that affect access. In most areas of the park you can walk any time between October and April, although in the highest areas, such as the Main Range, large areas are under snow until mid-November. The most popular bushwalking months are January to March, when weather is warm and generally stable, frosts are least likely and wildflowers are at their best.

Maps & Books

There are many good general maps of the park, most of which are available at the larger visitor information centres (p85), some local newsagents and bookshops. CMA's *Snowy-Kosciuszko – The Snowy Mountains* at 1:250,000 and the *Australian Alps Tourist Map* by Ausmap at 1:500,000 provide a good overview of the park and feature some town maps as well.

Both *Snowy Mountain Walks* by the Geehi Bushwalking Club and *Bushwalking in Kosciuszko National Park* by Charles Warner (primarily a guide for experienced walkers) are handy walking guides to the region. *Australian Alps – Kosciuszko, Alpine & Namadgi National Parks* by Deirdre Slattery has some track notes, but also contains loads of other information on the environment, flora and fauna, history and the development of the Snowy Mountains region. For historical background on the Snowy Mountains have a look at *Huts of the High Country* by Klaus Hueneke and *Kosciusko – The Mountain in History* by Alan EJ Andrews.

Information Sources

The best source of park information (including accommodation, transport, maps and books) is at the major Snowy Region visitor information centre at Jindabyne (p86). Other towns surrounding Kosciuszko National Park also provide information on the park. To the east, the **Cooma visitor information centre** (☎ 1800 636 525, 6450 1742; www.visitcooma .com.au; 119 Sharp St; ☼ closed Sun), in Cooma, has a large selection of maps and brochures, and a helpful inquiries desk. In Tumut, close to the northern end of the park, you'll find the **Tumut Region visitor information centre** (☎ 6947 7025; www.tumut.nsw.gov.au/trvc/trvc.html; 5 Adelong Rd) in the Old Butter Factory.

If approaching the park from Victoria, the **Khancoban Information Centre** (☎ 6076 9373; Scott St; ☼ 9am-noon & 1-4pm) sells a range of maps, books and park visitor permits. When the office is closed, you can purchase permits at the nearby **Khancoban Roadhouse** (☎ 6076 9400).

On the Internet, the **Australian Alps National Parks** (www.australianalps.deh.gov.au) website is an excellent source of general background information on the High Country.

Permits & Regulations

There are no camping fees but a fee is required for every car entering the park. The permit costs $16 a day in summer or $190 for an annual pass (which also gives you unlimited entry to every national park in NSW). Permits can be obtained at the visitor information centres (p85) or at the

NEW SOUTH WALES

toll booth on the Alpine Way just east of Thredbo. There are also some restrictions applying to bushwalkers (and skiers). No camping is permitted within the water catchments of the five glacial lakes on the Main Range and no campfires are permitted above the tree line.

Guided Walks

If you're not confident in tackling a walk on your own, there are a number of guided walks – from short day strolls to longer two-day walks – on offer from Thredbo. Contact Thredbo Sports (opposite) for details.

GETTING AROUND

There's little in the way of public transport within Kosciuszko National Park, except between the centres of Jindabyne and Thredbo. There are, however, several private transport companies that operate to locations within the park. The **Adaminaby Bus Service** (☎ 6454 2620) specialises in bushwalker transport and can provide a charter service to most areas. The Jindabyne-based **Snowy Mountains Taxi Services** (☎ 6457 2444) and John at **Jindabyne Motors** (☎ 6456 7340) also can be worth contacting for your local transport needs.

On the Victorian side of the park, if you require transport from either Corryong or Khancoban, try contacting **Bob Wilkinson** (☎ 6076 1418). He operates taxis and minibuses into the park from his base in Corryong, and will even provide coffee and sandwiches!

ACCESS TOWNS
Jindabyne
☎ 02 / pop 4400

As the main access town for snow skiing in New South Wales, Jindabyne is a busy, bustling place in winter. In summer, when 'Jindy' takes on a more relaxed pose, it becomes a good jump-off point for walks in the Kosciuszko National Park, particularly the southern sector. The town hugs the southern shore of Lake Jindabyne, a large water storage created as part of the huge Snowy Mountains Hydroelectric Scheme, and makes a good base for water sports.

INFORMATION

The **Snowy Region visitor information centre** (☎ 6450 5600; www.snowymountains.com.au; Kosciuszko

Rd; ☺ 8.30am-5pm), beside the main road in town, provides plenty of information on Kosciuszko National Park, offers a transport booking service and hires out EPIRBs for a flat fee of $10 (with a refundable $20 deposit). The centre houses numerous displays and the handy Sublime Café n Bar (opposite).

SUPPLIES & EQUIPMENT

At **Nuggets Crossing Shopping Centre** (Kosciuszko Rd) you'll find a chemist, banks and a large number of food and retail shops, including **Wilderness Sports** (☎ 6456 2966), which sells a wide range of outdoor gear. Camping equipment can also be purchased at **Paddy Pallin** (☎ 6456 2922; www.paddypallin.com.au; cnr Kosciuszko Rd & Alpine Way) a few kilometres west of town at the Thredbo turn-off. Behind the Nuggets Crossing complex is a **post office** (Gippsland St), while there's also a smaller collection of retail shops at the **Town Centre Plaza** (off Kosciuszko Rd) 300m east of Nuggets.

SLEEPING & EATING

Just west of town, at the Thredbo turn-off, is the **Snowline Holiday Park** (☎ 1800 248 148, 6456 2099; www.snowline.com.au; Kosciuszko Rd; unpowered/powered sites for 2 from $22/26, dm/cabin from $15/50) while right in town is **Jindabyne Holiday Park** (☎ 6456 2249; www.jindabyneholidaypark.com.au; Kosciuszko Rd; unpowered/powered sites for 2 from $21/25, cabins from $60). Both parks have shady positions and front the waters of Lake Jindabyne.

Hostel-style accommodation can be found at the handy **Snowy Mountains Backpackers** (☎ 1800 333 468; www.snowybackpackers.com.au; 7-8 Gippsland St; dm/d from $20/50; 🖳) close to the Nuggets Crossing shops.

Other establishments in the centre of town include the good-value **Jindy Inn** (☎ 6456 1957; www.jindyinn.com; 18 Clyde St; s/d from $35/55) and the **Lake Jindabyne Hotel/Motel** (☎ 1800 646 818, 6456 2203; lakejindabyne@bigpond.com; Kosciuszko Rd; s/d with breakfast $70/80; 🍴) on the shore of the lake and offering a spa, hotel pool and sauna.

Further accommodation options can be gleaned from **Snowy Mountains Reservation Centre** (☎ 1800 020 622), **Kosciuszko Accommodation Centre** (☎ 1800 026 354) and **Alpine Resorts & Travel Centre** (☎ 1800 802 315).

Note that accommodation prices rise more steeply than the ski lifts in winter.

While many restaurants close during summer, there are still a few cafés and takeaway outlets open all year at the

Nuggets Crossing and Town Centre shopping areas, including two supermarkets.

Adjoining the visitor information centre is **Sublime Café n Bar** (☎ 6457 1130; Kosciuszko Rd; mains $14; breakfast & lunch), a modern eatery catering for hungry information gatherers. Pastries and other goodies can be bought at the **Sundance Bakehouse & Tea Rooms** (Nuggets Crossing; pies $5, pastries $2.50; breakfast & lunch).

Cafe Susu (☎ 6456 1503; 7-8 Gippsland St; meals $8-15; 10am-9pm Mon-Fri, 8am-2pm Sun), good for a quick coffee or something more hearty, is a popular venue for both backpackers drifting through from the hostel next door and the more affluent. It is closed on Saturdays.

For a good carbo-load before or after a bushwalk, try **Il Lago** (☎ 6456 1171; 19 Nuggets Crossing; mains $22-27; dinner Tue-Sat), an Italian-style eatery serving pasta and pizza.

For wholesome pub-grub at a good price, head down to the **Lake Jindabyne Hotel/Motel** (☎ 1800 646 818; Kosciuszko Rd; mains $8-14; lunch & dinner), which is particularly popular on Tuesday and Thursday, when discounted schnitzels ($6) are on offer.

GETTING THERE & AWAY
See the Snowy Region visitor information centre (opposite) for transport bookings.

Transborder Alpine Express (☎ 6241 0033; www.transborder.com.au) runs Alpine Express buses between Canberra and Jindabyne (adult/child $45/22.50, three hours), via Cooma. **Summit Coaches** (☎ 1800 608 008, 6297 2588; www.summitcoaches.com.au) operates services on Monday, Wednesday, Friday and Sunday to/from Canberra (adult/child $43/19, 2¼ hours).

If you're driving, Jindabyne is about 468km from Sydney by way of Goulburn, Canberra and Cooma. From Cooma, follow the Snowy Mountains Hwy, then the Kosciuszko Rd west for 65km to Jindabyne.

There are two routes – both long trips – from Melbourne to Jindabyne: the first (560km) is via Wodonga, Corryong, Khancoban and Thredbo; and the second (535km) is through Gippsland and the towns of Traralgon, Bairnsdale, Bruthen and Buchan. Much of Barry Way between Buchan and Jindabyne is unsealed.

Thredbo
☎ 02 / pop 2900
The pretty ski village of Thredbo (1370m) has the most alpine charm of all Australia's ski resorts, and makes a convenient base for walks in the Mt Kosciuszko area. In winter it's a frenzied place offering great skiing with long runs, while in summer Thredbo is a less-hectic centre for outdoor pursuits with walks, cycling, bobsledding and other sports on offer.

The **Thredbo Information Centre** (☎ 1300 020 589; www.thredbo.com.au; Friday Dr; 8.30am-5pm), on the main street through town, provides helpful information on activities and can organise accommodation bookings.

Near the Thredbo Alpine Hotel is the **Village Square** where you'll find useful services, including a chemist, newsagent, supermarket, ATM and outdoor shop. Across the footbridge, near the base of the chairlifts, is **Thredbo Sports** (☎ 6459 4119; Valley Terminal; 8am-5pm), which sells outdoor equipment and lift tickets for the Crackenback chairlift, and also organises guided walks.

SLEEPING & EATING
Thredbo has various levels of accommodation even in the quieter summer period, with many establishments offering breakfast and dinner. To make an inquiry or booking, contact **Thredbo Accommodation Services** (☎ 1800 801 982) or the Thredbo Information Centre.

Thredbo YHA (☎ 6457 6376; thredbo@yhansw.org.au; 8 Jack Adams Pathway; dm/d from $24/$56;) offers budget accommodation and includes a good kitchen and balcony.

For more up-market accommodation try **Kasees Apartments** (☎ 6457 6370; www.kasees.com.au; 4 Banjo Dr; d from $100). There are self-contained units with mountain views and a sauna. Also of good value is **Candlelight Lodge** (☎ 1800 020 900; www.candlelightlodge.com.au; Banjo Dr; s/d $75/110), providing B&B accommodation, with the bonus of a licensed restaurant and bar on the premises.

Like nearby Jindabyne, many eateries are closed during summer, but lots are still open to cater for hungry outdoor enthusiasts. For self-caterers, there's a supermarket at the eastern end of the Village Square.

Altitude 1380 (☎ 6457 6190; Village Square; mains from $10; breakfast & lunch) is a good place for a morning coffee and cake before hitting the hills.

In the Thredbo Alpine Hotel complex, between Friday Dr and the Village Square, you'll find the popular **Pub Bar &**

Bistro (☎ 6459 4200; mains $10-20; ✪ lunch & dinner) with typical hotel meals. Opposite the pub is **Cascades Café & Bar** (☎ 6459 4200; mains $25-30; ✪ breakfast & dinner) with sunny window tables overlooking a large deck and ski slopes.

GETTING THERE & AWAY

Transborder Alpine Express (☎ 6241 0033; www .transborder.com.au) operates buses between Canberra and Thredbo (adult/child $64/32, 3½ hours), via Jindabyne. **Summit Coaches** (☎ 1800 608 008, 6297 2588; www.summitcoaches.com.au) runs services on Monday, Wednesday, Friday and Sunday to/from Canberra (adult/child $60/29, 2¾ hours).

If you just want to travel between Jindabyne and Thredbo, and you don't want to wait for a bus, contact one of the shuttle services listed under Getting Around (p86).

Transport inquiries and bookings can be made through the Thredbo Information Centre (p87) or the Snowy Region visitor information centre (p86).

Thredbo is an easy 33km drive west of Jindabyne on the Alpine Way. You can leave your vehicle in one of the designated overnight car parks east of the chairlift terminal.

MT KOSCIUSZKO & THE LAKES CIRCUIT

Duration	3 days
Distance	38km
Standard	easy–moderate
Start/Finish	Thredbo (p87)
Transport	bus, shuttle service

Summary A relatively easy stroll across Australia's highest mountains with uninterrupted views all the way. You'll encounter rocky peaks, broad plains, striking granite tors and mainland Australia's only glacial lakes.

The mountainous region from the peaks of the Rams Head Range to the Rolling Ground (including Australia's tallest peak, Mt Kosciuszko) is affectionately known as the Main Range. Within this area you'll find Australia's largest tract of truly alpine country. Mostly above the limit of tree growth, it incorporates Australia's highest peaks and five glacial lakes, including Blue Lake, possibly Kosciuszko National Park's most precious jewel. While snow gums can survive

in a few isolated localities, the vegetation is predominantly snow grass, herb fields, shrubs and sphagnum bogs. Numerous granite outcrops, some forming spectacular and gravity-defying tors, are scattered across the exposed mountaintops and plains, providing fantastic vantage points.

In the past, grazing (particularly by sheep) had such a severe effect on the ground cover protecting the fragile soil that whole mountain slopes were literally washed away. In the 1950s grazing was banned from the highest areas and erosion control programs were instigated. Evidence of drainage works can be seen in many areas of the Main Range, particularly around Carruthers Peak and Mt Twynam, where discreet retaining walls have been erected to slow runoff and encourage plant regrowth.

The large number of walkers heading to Mt Kosciuszko only adds to the erosion problem; so heavily trampled and damaged was the popular route from Thredbo that there is now a 6km paved path and raised metal walkway from the top of the Crackenback chairlift. Other sections of walking track on the Main Range have also been paved, camping has been banned within the watersheds of the glacial lakes to protect water quality and maintenance works are ongoing.

But don't let these environmental problems deter you. The exceptional views and ascents of Australia's three highest peaks are all major drawcards of this walk. And even the hordes of day walkers heading to Mt Kosciuszko from Thredbo in the height of summer won't bother you…there's plenty of room for everyone on the summit, and you'll be leaving them behind as you progress beyond Mt Kosciuszko in any case.

As a bonus, two short side-trips have been thrown in. They explore the boulderstrewn outcrop of North Rams Head and Mt Twynam, Australia's third-highest peak. Three days allows plenty of time to take in the sights of the walk, including the side trips.

PLANNING

It must be emphasised that this is a very exposed walk, so you must have a strong weather-proof tent, wet-weather gear, good sleeping bag, warm clothes and a fuel stove for cooking.

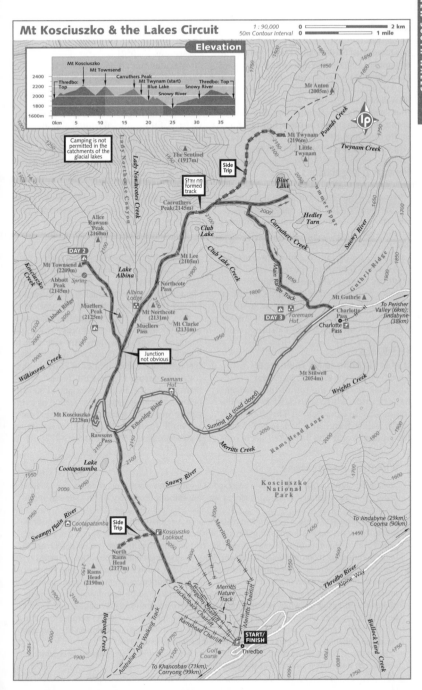

Mt Kosciuszko & the Lakes Circuit

1 : 90,000
50m Contour Interval

0 — 2 km
0 — 1 mile

Elevation

NEW SOUTH WALES

Maps

There are two excellent topographic maps covering the whole walk. The Department of Lands' 1:25,000 *Perisher Valley* map (one of a new series of maps) and SutMap's 1:40,000 *Mount Kosciuszko, Perisher & Thredbo* map are both good choices, and there's not much between them. They cover about the same area, but the SutMap sheet is smaller due to the difference in scale, which makes it a little easier to use.

Permits & Regulations

While no permits are required for this walk, there are some restrictions that apply to bushwalking on the Main Range. No camping is permitted within the water catchments of the five glacial lakes and all campsites should be hidden from roads and tracks. No campfires are permitted above the tree line.

As well, following the extensive 2003 bushfires, there are some areas where walking is prohibited. Check with the visitor information centres in Jindabyne (p86) or Thredbo (p88), before setting out, to see which areas are affected by closure.

THE WALK
Day 1: Thredbo to Mt Townsend
3 hours, 11km, 535m ascent, 255m descent

The walk starts at the top of the Crackenback chairlift, which whisks up walkers up the mountainside from behind Thredbo Sports in the Valley Terminal. The fare is $22 ($11 for children) and you'll need to keep your ticket for the return ride. If Crackenback is closed for maintenance, the adjacent Snowgums chairlift will run. The ride takes 10 minutes (or 20 minutes on the slower Snowgums lift) and it operates between 9am and 4.30pm daily. If you'd prefer not to pay for a ride on the chairlift you could walk up the Merritts Nature Track, which starts a little east of the Valley Terminal and joins the main route at the top station of the chairlift. Allow 1.5 hours for the climb.

The paved track begins right at the top of the Crackenback lift and heads north, soon crossing a creek, which is a good place to collect water. The path and metal walkway, raised above the snow grass, provides easy walking. From here on nearly the entire walk is above the tree line and, when temperatures climb and the sun beats down, you'll be praying for an alpine zephyr.

Aesthetically, the walkway is not particularly attractive. However, built to protect the plant life alongside the track that had been so heavily trampled, it serves its purpose well.

The track climbs to **Kosciuszko Lookout** – where you have your first glimpse of Kossy's rounded dome and where the side trip to North Rams Head departs – then reaches **Cootapatamba Lookout** in a saddle nearly 4km (one hour) from the chairlift. Lake Cootapatamba, Australia's highest glacial lake, sits below you to the west, often backed by a lingering snow-patch until well into summer.

You'll soon reach the old car park at Rawsons Pass. **Mt Kosciuszko** (2228m) is

---

WRAGGE'S OBSERVATORY

Something always close to a walker's heart is the weather. It's interesting, then, to ponder that many years ago Australia's highest building was a weather observatory on the summit of Mt Kosciuszko.

When Clement Wragge, a government meteorologist, began recording weather data here, little did he know what he was letting himself in for. Initially a collection of tents, 'Wragge's Observatory' suffered from buffeting by incessant winds. One tent and much of the measuring equipment it housed ended up 1600m below in the Geehi Gorge during one violent storm. Out of necessity, the observatory became a permanent structure in May 1898, when a wooden hut, with chimney access as one of the allowances for deep snow, was built. Horrendous tempests were common; on occasions the air was so electrically charged that sparks could be seen flying off any metal object waved in the air, while at other times winds were so strong that Wragge's staff had to be secured by rope when venturing outside to check the instruments. It's no surprise that the meteorologist earned the nickname 'Inclement Wragge'. By 1900 Australia's highest building was closed and abandoned, and was finally destroyed by lightning in 1914.

Regrettably, there are no remains…any that were left have either been pilfered or blown into oblivion by cumulative storms over the past 100 years.

only a short climb away to the west, but due to revegetation works you must follow the Summit Rd – which almost circles the mountain – for 1.5km to the top. As you'd expect, the views here are extensive, and encompass the highest peaks in the land. You may have to share the views with others, but hey, where else can you stand atop a hill and claim you are higher than anyone else in the country?

Head back down the Summit Rd for 750m to a signpost indicating a foot track that bears north. Follow this track as it gradually descends to a saddle south of Muellers Peak (8.5km and two hours from the start). Below you to the west of the saddle is the Wilkinsons Creek valley, which provides some camp sites. (In bad weather, or very dry conditions, this is a better camping option for the first night as the site is more protected than the Mt Townsend Plateau and water is plentiful.) The route to Mt Townsend leaves the main track at this saddle and heads northwest (not obvious for about the first 50m), skirting the western flank of Muellers Peak. It crosses a boulder field, then climbs gradually to a small plateau east of Mt Townsend. In fine weather this area makes a pleasant camp site – there are often small streams draining the plateau – and you can find shelter from the prevailing winds by choosing a site protected by boulders. A short rock scramble from the plateau leads to the summit of **Mt Townsend** (2209m), providing more dramatic views than those from Mt Kosciuszko. Of all the summits on this walk, Mt Townsend – Australia's second-highest mountain – is the pick of the bunch, yielding uninterrupted views across the Alps, especially to the northwest where the lowlands can be seen over a mile below.

SIDE TRIP: NORTH RAMS HEAD
1 hour, 2km return, 100m ascent

A highly worthwhile side trip, particularly in fine weather, is the short stroll to North Rams Head, a rocky prominence left behind as the glaciers retreated and melted away. In midsummer, the plains surrounding the mountain are carpeted in swathes of wildflowers, including billy buttons and snow daisies.

From Kosciuszko Lookout, bear west and climb the rocky slope. There is no track,

but please spread out if you're in a large group to help minimise damage to fragile alpine plants and soils. Within 10 minutes you'll reach a plateau where you can see the peak dominating your westerly view. The ascent of **North Rams Head** (2177m) requires some easy rock scrambling, but a birds-eye panorama unfolds as you reach the top. In an area where bizarre boulder formations abound, the sculpture-like tor just below and to the east of North Rams Head is a classic. Can you see the face?

Day 2: Mt Townsend to Snowy River
4 hours, 14km, 170m ascent, 640m descent

Retrace your steps to the saddle south of Muellers Peak, then follow the main track generally north to Muellers Pass. Alternatively, you could walk over the summit of **Muellers Peak** (2125m) – there is no track and the route requires some boulder hopping – then drop down steeply east over grassy slopes to Muellers Pass.

At the pass you'll see Lake Albina to the north, the headwaters of Lady Northcotes Canyon. As you continue along the track the ruins of Albina Lodge lie just below you. The hut was originally constructed for use by skiers, but the environmental problems it caused led to it being dismantled. The track skirts the western fall of Mt Northcote (2131m), joins the main divide again at Northcote Pass and continues just to the west of Mt Lee (2105m). Along this section information boards highlight areas of feldmark, which grow on damaged points along the exposed crest. All along this high spine of the Main Range you'll enjoy near endless views over the headwaters of the Snowy River and beyond to the dry plains of the Monaro region.

From the saddle beyond Mt Lee you get your first good look at the small, shallow Club Lake. The track then climbs north, zigzagging steeply to the summit of **Carruthers Peak** (2145m), two hours from camp. There are great views from here, particularly southwest to Mt Townsend and northeast to the distant Mt Jagungal (2061m) over the pyramid-like Sentinel (1917m) and Watsons Crags (2022m).

As the track descends from the summit you will notice the preventive measures (stone walls and drains) taken against soil erosion and vegetation loss on the eastern slopes of Carruthers Peak (2145m). Soon you reach a **saddle** where the main route swings east, while an old, faint 4WD track climbs northeast for the side trip to Mt Twynam (below). The saddle is covered with fragile feldmark and walkers are encouraged not to stray off the track.

Follow the main route east for 1km as it gently descends to a paved area in a shallow saddle. Leave your rucksacks here and follow the track for 1km to Blue Lake, which is tucked in at the base of cliffs on Mt Twynam's southern slopes.

In a country where the effects of glaciation are few and far between, **Blue Lake** is not to be missed. Of the five glacial lakes, Blue Lake is not only the finest but also the deepest, coldest and most dramatic. In winter, the crags on the north side are hidden beneath a thick layer of ice and frozen waterfalls, and provide one of the few training grounds in Australia for budding ice climbers. Even on a hot summer's day, the dark waters look cold and forbidding.

Gather your packs and follow the heavily used path down to cross Carruthers Creek. The track climbs a little to the crest of a spur – where you can catch the occasional glimpse of **Hedley Tarn** to the east, the last of the five lakes – then descends for about 2.5km to the valley. Here there are two large watercourses to cross; Club Lake Creek and the Snowy River. Both can be waded or crossed on stepping stones unless the water levels are high, in which case it's best to walk upstream to find a suitable crossing, or wait. A camp site exists between the two rivers a short distance upstream, near a lonely chimney stack, the last vestige of Foremans Hut. Make sure you camp at least 100m away from either watercourse.

SIDE TRIP: MT TWYNAM
1½ hours, 5km return, 150m ascent

The walk to Mt Twynam yields yet more wonderful vistas, including close-up views of the Sentinel (1917m) and Watsons Crags (2022m). If nothing else, you can bag the third highest peak in the country.

From the saddle east of Carruthers peak, follow the faint 4WD track up the slope to the northeast. The track remains close to the crest of the ridge until you reach the highest point near **Mt Twynam**. The summit (2196m), littered with small boulders, is

200m south from here across open grassland. Needless to say, the grandstand scene is unrestricted in all directions.

Day 3: Snowy River to Thredbo
3½–4 hours, 13km, 450m ascent, 260m descent

After you've negotiated the river crossing, take the path steeply east to rejoin the Summit Rd at Charlotte Pass. Summit Rd provides easy walking as it skirts the slopes of Mt Stilwell (2054m) and the Rams Head Range, with the broad plains of the upper Snowy River area dominating the scene. Just over 4km from Charlotte Pass the trail crosses a bridge over Merritts Creek; soon after you cross the Snowy River before climbing to **Seamans Hut**. This solid stone hut was built in 1929 in memory of Laurie Seaman and Evan Hayes, who perished on the slopes of Mt Kosciuszko in the winter of 1928.

Summit Rd continues on for 1.7km to Rawsons Pass, 2¼ hours from the Snowy River, from where you retrace your steps of the first day to the top of the Thredbo chairlifts.

THE CHIMNEYS

Duration	5–6 hours
Distance	17km
Standard	easy–moderate
Start/Finish	Dead Horse Gap
Nearest Town	Thredbo (p87)
Transport	shuttle service

Summary A generally easy walk across the attractive Boggy Plain culminates with a scramble to the rocky summit of the Chimneys. Some route finding is required, but there are great views into vast wild areas.

While most of the popular walks in Kosciuszko National Park lie in the area between Thredbo and the ghost town of Kiandra, some particularly interesting country can be found south of the Alpine Way in the southern section of the park. The Chimneys are a high, rocky outcrop providing an elevated post from which to view the surrounding mountains and plains. Dominating the Chimneys Ridge a few kilometres south of Thredbo, the peaks provide an unusual view of the Rams Head and Mt Kosciuszko area to the north. Other than Cascade Trail, the only tracks in the area are those formed by wildlife, including emus and brumbies. Although most of this route is off formed trails, the open Boggy Plain (also known as the 'Big Boggy') provides easy walking, and the upper reaches of the Thredbo River provide reliable guidance in a trackless landscape.

Starting near Dead Horse Gap the walk follows the north bank of the Thredbo River, then climbs gradually to the base of the Chimneys, though the last section is a little scrubby. The final ascent is a rock scramble – not too difficult – to the twin rocky prominences of the Chimneys. You could easily fill two days in this wild and scenic region.

PLANNING
Maps
Look no further than the Department of Lands' 1:25,000 *Chimneys Ridge* map.

GETTING TO/FROM THE WALK
The walk begins a few hundred metres east of Dead Horse Gap, where the Alpine Way crosses the Thredbo River. This point is also 4km west of Thredbo and 37km west of Jindabyne.

For information on transport to and from the trailhead, contact one of the shuttle services listed under Getting Around (p86) in the introduction to Kosciuszko National Park. Alternatively, you could walk from Thredbo to Dead Horse Gap, adding an additional 8km to the total length of the walk.

> **WARNING**
>
> Though the walk is rated easy–moderate, sound navigational skills are essential as much of the walking is off-track and, with the lack of prominent features, finding your way can be difficult in poor weather. You must carry a compass and a good topographic map, and, above all, be able to use them.

THE WALK
Cascade Trail climbs southeast away from the Alpine Way above the Thredbo River. After 2km Cascade Trail fords the river – there's also a footbridge – but the route to follow doesn't, and instead follows the north (true right) bank generally east. A brumby pad begins here and heads upstream into pretty **Boggy Plain**, providing views across the grasslands of the Thredbo River valley. About 2.5km from the ford the river veers briefly to the south; cross the river on some rocks where it begins to turn back eastwards and walk a little way uphill to locate some more brumby pads. Follow these east across the plain – or walk cross-country if you don't find them – but after about 1km from the river crossing you will need to bear southeast and ascend away from the river. There are faint pads in places, but it may be more convenient to make your own way. There are often emus grazing in the upper reaches of Boggy Plain and you

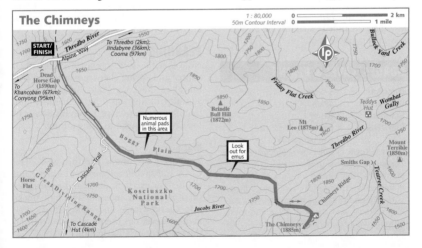

The Chimneys   1 : 80,000   0 ——— 2 km
50m Contour Interval   0 ——— 1 mile

will no doubt have noticed the huge piles of brumby droppings along the route.

You will soon be able to see the rocky outcrop of the Chimneys in the distance through a gap in the Chimneys Ridge; walk towards this prominent saddle. As you get closer to the saddle and gain height you'll need to cross a small stream and climb south up a little valley; the best route is about 50m east of the stream on an animal pad. Once on the saddle climb east – there is no pad – and ascend the Chimneys Ridge. There is some scrub at first but it's not unduly thick and the best route seems to be slightly on the north side of the ridge. Avoid the temptation to head directly for the Chimneys as the scrub is thicker on the south side and there are some boulders that hinder walking.

At a point directly north of the Chimneys, walk south onto a snow plain 200m west of a saddle. There are some camp sites in the trees at the base of the Chimneys and water can usually be found in the gully west of the snow plain. A rock scramble through stunted, gnarled snow gums is required to reach the top of these inviting little peaks; there is no marked route, so pick the best way you can. The highest point of the **Chimneys** (1885m) is marked by a cairn and dilapidated trigonometric point. There are excellent views of the Main Range to the north and the Jacobs River valley far below you to the south. The dry, yellow Monaro region can be seen on the eastern horizon.

Return to the start via the outward route, but take your time to soak up the pleasantness as you amble back.

GORGES, CAVES & PLAINS

Duration	5–6 hours
Distance	18km
Standard	easy
Start/Finish	Cooleman Mountain Camping Area
Nearest Town	Adaminaby (opposite)
Transport	shuttle service

Summary This circuit walk passes through dramatically varied terrain, including a pretty gorge, limestone caves, a waterhole and a curious sinkhole, and also includes a visit to an historic rural homestead.

Blue Waterholes and Cooleman Plain, tucked into the far northeastern sector of Kosciuszko National Park, are unusual and captivating for a number of reasons. The area around Blue Waterholes consists predominantly of tree-covered hills and broad grassy plains – the largest known as Cooleman Plain – providing delightful walking. At times, the area seems so benign that you'd hardly believe you were in the Kosciuszko National Park at all!

What is also surprising is the lack of running water above Blue Waterholes, a result of the plain's underlying limestone geology. Limestone is readily dissolved by carbon dioxide and water, as found in rainwater. The result is that streams draining the surrounding hills seep underground on reaching the plains, surfacing again at a few locations, most prominently at the Blue Waterholes where Cave Creek bubbles out from underground. The area is also riddled with caves and sinkholes, and the picturesque Clarke Gorge and the restored Coolamine Homestead are further attractions. If you've a keen eye you may see kangaroos, brumbies and even feral pigs in the area.

Unlike the southern areas of the park, which were torched by disastrous bushfires in 2003, the Cooleman region has fortunately remained unscathed.

The Blue Waterholes Fire Trail, a popular 4WD route, continues beyond the start of the walk to the camping areas at Blue Waterholes. The trail is quite passable to 2WD vehicles in dry conditions, but you may have difficulty negotiating the track after heavy rain.

PLANNING

Note that this walk cannot be accessed in winter and spring (between June and October) as the Long Plain Rd is closed to all traffic during this time. Remember, too, that if you wish to have a peep inside any of the caves, you need to bring a torch.

Maps

You need two maps for this walk. The CMA 1:25,000 *Peppercorn* and *Rules Point* maps show excellent detail and have a useful 10m contour interval. The foot tracks into Clarke Gorge and along Cave Creek aren't shown, but there's enough detail on the maps for easy navigation.

NEAREST TOWN & FACILITIES
Adaminaby

☎ 02 / pop 460

Popular as a base for fishing in the nearby streams and Lake Eucumbene, Adaminaby also makes a handy base for walks in the central and northern areas of Kosciuszko National Park. It's only a small town – and there's little to do – but it has good amenities for bushwalkers. Limited information about the region can be obtained from within the **Bake House** (Denison St), just off the highway.

SLEEPING & EATING

At the western end of Adaminaby, though not far from Denison St, is the **Alpine Tourist Park** (☎ 6454 2438; www.alpinetouristpark.com.au; cnr Lett St & Snowy Mountains Hwy; unpowered/powered sites for 2 $18/20, cabins from $42).

Tanderra Lodge (☎ 6454 2470; www.tanderra.com; 21 Denison St; s & d from $65) is in the main street right near the shops. Also on the main drag, offering both food and accommodation, is the **Snow Goose Hotel/Motel** (☎ 6454 2202; cnr Denison & Baker Sts; hotel s/d $40/60, motel s/d $55/65). The Snow Goose offers hearty lunch and dinner meals. Denison Street also has a number of takeaway outlets and a small supermarket.

GETTING THERE & AWAY

Adaminaby is on the Snowy Mountains Hwy, 51km from Cooma or 80km from Jindabyne (via Berridale). **Adaminaby Bus Service** (☎ 6454 2620) can shuttle walkers between Jindabyne and Adaminaby.

Cooleman Mountain Camping Area

While a long way from any of the nearest towns, this is a good camping ground equipped with toilets and tables, and plenty of space for cars.

GETTING TO/FROM THE WALK

From Adaminaby, drive west for 55km along the Snowy Mountains Hwy to the Long Plain Rd turn-off to the right (on a sweeping bend, about 20km north of Kiandra). Take this dirt road north for 17km to the Blue Waterholes Fire Trail turn-off to the east; 2.3km along this side trail brings you to the camping area.

Adaminaby Bus Service (☎ 6454 2620) is the best bet for a ride to the start of the walk, but you should call a few days in advance of your transport need. For other shuttle services see Getting Around (p86).

THE WALK

The route heads east and within 15 minutes reaches the open meadows of Cooleman Plain.

A further 2km leads to **Coolamine Homestead** (see the boxed text p96), just off the trail to your left. Wandering among the old cattle yards and machinery, and reading the old newspapers which adorn the walls of the main building, is like stepping back to yesteryear. You may feel that you are in a time warp, if even just for a moment. Information boards in the area give further insight into the history of this mountain outpost.

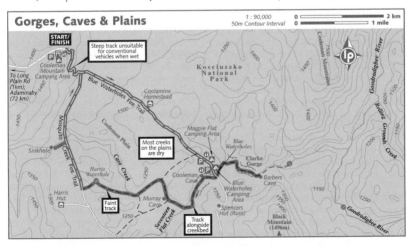

Gorges, Caves & Plains

1 : 90,000
50m Contour Interval
0 — 2 km
0 — 1 mile

COOLAMINE HOMESTEAD

The isolated mountain property of Coolamine Homestead dates from 1839 when a Canberra pioneer, Sir Terence Murray, stumbled upon the lush grasslands of Cooleman Plain and wasted no time in staking his claim. He built a slab hut and named the property Coolalamine Station, although it was soon known by its present name, Coolamine.

Over time a collection of buildings were added using building practices of the time, including horse hair for roof insulation and newspaper as lining for the internal walls. As the station prospered the homestead was extended and in 1889 even a cheese hut – a structure made out of grass thatch and clay to store cheeses while they matured – was built. By 1907 the main house (the one that you see today) was erected. Over time, further rooms were added to accommodate more employees; one particular room was used as a Sunday post office when mail was being delivered from Berridale, west of Jindabyne.

During the first half of the 1900s occupation of Coolamine declined and the buildings were gradually abandoned. The homestead deteriorated over the years to a state of virtual ruin, and by the late 1960s only four buildings remained. After 1975, when the land was finally passed from freehold to Kosciuszko National Park, the Kosciuszko Huts Association saw the historical value and importance of the homestead and began restoration works in 1977. The result of their handiwork, persistence and vision can clearly be seen today.

The trail crosses a low hill then descends steadily to the Blue Waterholes camping area, where it's common to see kangaroos grazing. At the end of the track, the cool and enticing waters of **Blue Waterholes** rise from beneath the plains like an oasis beneath the limestone crags. If it's hot, a refreshing dip may be in order.

At Blue Waterholes, which form the major headwater of Cave Creek, a trail heads downstream on the left bank. This soon crosses a broad stream, then immediately crosses over Cave Creek itself on stepping stones before continuing downstream on the right bank. It is worth following this track downstream for about 1km from the Blue Waterholes (or more if you wish) to gain access into the scenic **Clarke Gorge**. Here, the creek has carved a spectacular route through the rock, creating a narrow canyon hemmed in by 30m cliffs. It is possible to venture much further downstream, eventually reaching some waterfalls and cascades about 2.5km from the Blue Waterholes.

Return to Blue Waterholes, fill your drink bottles and locate Blue Waterholes Fire Trail where it crosses the dry creek bed just above the waterhole. Follow the trail for a few hundred metres before leaving it to follow a walking track up the Cave Creek valley, or walk up the bed of the creek itself. In summer, the rusty golden hues of 'he mountain grasses contrast vividly with the barren crags of the gorge beside the dry Cave Creek.

Along this section, the route follows part of the marked 'Nicole Gorge & Murray Cave Walk', and the track is easy to follow. Heading upstream, you soon pass Cooleman Cave (worth a cursory look) and, about 1.5km further on, **Murray Cave**, one of the most impressive of all the caves in the Cooleman Plain area. The entrance to Murray Cave is a narrow slot, but once inside the cave opens into a large chamber, which is refreshingly cool in summer. To the left as you enter, the cave continues for a further 200m, although it is often quite wet and not recommended without protective equipment, such as a hard-hat.

The **Nicole Gorge** walk climbs steeply up above the cave to the left of the entrance, but the better route is to follow another track which continues up the Cave Creek valley.

Not far beyond Murray Cave the valley broadens, and the track turns away from the creek bed and heads north to join the Blue Waterholes Fire Trail. Do not follow this track; instead, stay in the valley, cross Cave Creek to the north (true left) bank about 1km past Murray Cave – there is usually water running here – and locate a faint foot track heading west. This stays north of the creek for 750m then crosses the creek again before heading gently up a side valley to **Harris Waterhole**. This waterhole is an anomaly on these plains, being one of the few places where you'll find surface water.

Climb up the grassy slope southwest from the waterhole and you'll locate a obscure 4WD track. This soon meets another faint 4WD track, the Mosquito Creek Fire Trail, which you follow north. It descends into a shallow valley and climbs a low spur before dropping to another shallow valley, 1.5km from Harris Waterhole. Leave the track here – there are no signs to point the way – and walk southwest up this valley for 300m to an interesting phenomenon. Here, two small creeks flow down the hillside only to plummet underground into a limestone sinkhole. Peering into the sinkhole, you may feel as if you're being sucked towards the centre of the Earth.

Return to the faint track and continue north to rejoin the Blue Waterholes Fire Trail 1km east of Cooleman Mountain Camping Area. It's a 25-minute climb back up the trail to the end of the walk.

THE BUDAWANGS

The Budawangs form a complex maze of deep valleys and heavily forested canyons, presided over by towering cliffs and flat-topped sandstone peaks: this is some of the most spectacular bushwalking country in NSW. The walks described here lie mostly within the borders of the 162,000-hectare Morton National Park. The wild, densely timbered escarpment of Budawang National Park continues south of here, with Yadboro Creek forming the boundary between the two regions.

Despite the encroachment of farmers, prospectors and loggers into the valleys, and continuing conflict between conservationists and logging interests, the Budawangs still have a primordial, rugged feel, and give us an inkling of what untouched Australian wilderness might have been like before European settlement.

HISTORY

Visits by walkers to the Budawangs in the early years of the 20th century led to significant conservation efforts. In 1934 Australia's first wilderness area – the 3100-hectare Tallowa Primitive Reserve – was gazetted, primarily as a result of the work of Myles Dunphy (see p62). Mark Morton, a local member of the NSW parliament at the time, provided significant support and vision, and the national park today bears his name.

ENVIRONMENT

The Budawangs' high rainfall and significant altitude variation support a rich and varied flora and fauna. Rainforest thrives in the valleys and canyons where moist sheltered conditions prevail (trees present include the highly prized red cedar, used in making furniture, and brown beech). Coachwood forest exists further south towards Yadboro Creek, while eucalyptus forest, on the dry slopes, and mallee species eke out an existence on high rocky plateaus and exposed sandstone platforms. Heath and some alpine species dominate the higher altitude areas and windswept mountain tops.

Wildlife includes the usual Australian species (kangaroos, wallabies, koalas and dingos), with platypuses and native water

---

WARNINGS

Topographic maps and a compass are mandatory for walks in this area. Since the NPWS made the decision to let this area regenerate back into wilderness, some areas have become increasingly overgrown, and route-finding can be tricky. To further complicate matters, the high ridges and plateaus attract fog and low cloud that may obscure all visible landmarks. Be especially mindful of this when walking in the Monolith Valley area. Allow plenty of daylight hours for slower-than-usual travel and always set out with sufficient food, water and gear for an unplanned bivouac.

Due to the difficult nature of the terrain and the lack of surface water in summer, when streams and creeks often dry up, there is little protection for Budawangs walkers caught out in a bushfire. Prevention is better than cure, so keep a look out for signs of trouble, such as smoke, and plan on changing your route early to avoid being swallowed by a fire front. It's best to avoid the region in very hot, dry weather, especially if a northly or westerly wind is blowing. Check with one of the district NPWS offices (p98) for current fire-risk status before entering the park in danger periods.

rats common. Black-cockatoos are often seen, and the superb lyrebird can frequently be heard mimicking the calls of other birds as it scratches around the leaf litter on the forest floor.

PLANNING

Budawangs walks feature prolonged sections of track overgrown with dense scrub. Gaiters and long trousers are recommended. If you have inexperienced walkers in the party, a 10m length of 9mm rope will assist in scaling the route to the summit of The Castle.

While water tanks and creeks exist in many of the camping and picnic areas, they may be dry in summer, so it's best to carry sufficient water to the start of your walk. Check with NPWS on the availability of surface water before setting out.

When to Walk

Spring and autumn are the best times for Budawangs walks. The short daylight hours of midwinter add unnecessary veneers of haste and concern to walks in the Monolith Valley area. Cool periods in summer can be good if recent rains leave plenty of surface water and dampen the bushfire risk.

Maps & Books

Produced by the Budawang Committee (Coast and Mountain Walkers Club), the 1:50,000 *The Northern Budawang Range and the Upper Clyde River Valley Sketch Map* is essential for Budawangs walks. It includes some historical notes and handy walk summaries and much detail – such as locations of camping caves – that is not shown on the CMA 1:25,000 topographic maps *Corang* and *Milton*, which cover the area but are sadly out of date.

Pigeon House and Beyond produced by the Budawang Committee is the definitive reference to the history, geography, wildlife and bushwalks in this area. It's available throughout Australia from outdoor gear suppliers and bookshops, and includes extensive walk notes. Ron Doughton's *Bushwalking in the Budawangs*, despite its sometimes obtuse language, is the most extensive work on the area and is useful for planning. John and Lyn Daly's *Take a Walk in a New South Wales National Park South-Eastern Zone* has notes on Monolith Valley, Pigeon House, The Castle and other tracks in the area.

Information Sources

The **NPWS** (☎ 4423 2170; 55 Graham St) has a district office in Nowra, a subdistrict park office in **Ulladulla** (☎ 4454 9500); and a visitor information centre at **Fitzroy Falls** (☎ 4887 7270), on the park's northern boundary. The Ulladulla office is responsible for the areas covered by these walks, but you'll have more luck making contact with Fitzroy Falls or Nowra.

Permits & Regulations

NPWS asks walkers to fill in a journey intention form and return it to the office in **Ulladulla** (fax 4455 1850) before setting off on overnight trips (not necessary for the Pigeon House walk).

Bush camping is permitted everywhere except Monolith Valley, where overuse has damaged this fragile area.

ACCESS TOWN
Ulladulla
☎ 02 / pop 9500

Ulladulla, a holiday town on the NSW south coast, about 225km from Sydney, is the only sizable settlement relatively close to the park that provides accommodation and walk supplies. **Ulladulla visitor information centre** (☎ 4455 1269; shoalhaven.nsw.gov.au) is in the Civic Centre opposite the harbour.

SUPPLIES & EQUIPMENT
Boots Great Outdoors (☎ 4455 2526; 9/44 Deering St), is one block west of the Princes Hwy and has a full range of gear and fuel.

SLEEPING & EATING
Ulladulla Headland Tourist Park (☎ 1300 733 021; ulladullapark@shoalhaven.nsw.gov.au; South St; unpowered sites for 2 $20-30, powered $30-40, cabins $60-225) is close to town and within earshot of the surf; it's quiet outside of school holidays.

Travellers Rest Backpackers (☎ 4454 0500; 63 Princes Hwy; www.southcoasttravellersrest.com; dm $25, d & tw $50) is a small, friendly, homely place with just five rooms.

There are several motels in Ulladulla, although vacancies can be scarce in summer and school holiday periods. **Motel Harbour Royal** (☎ 4455 5444; 29 Burrill St; d $120-140) has a good off-highway location, while **Colonial Palms** (☎ 4455 1777; 13 Princes Hwy; d $135) and **Mollymook Seascape** (☎ 4455 5777; d $135) are opposite one another north of town.

Various restaurants, cafés and small eateries line Ulladulla's main street (the Princes Hwy). Down at the harbour, **Fisherman's Wharf Seafood** (☎ 4455 3906; Wason St; ◷ daytime) is the place to buy fresh fish, and it serves fish and chips during the day. Across the road, **Tory's Seafood Restaurant** (☎ 4455 0888; ◷ lunch & dinner) is a licensed restaurant with good views and fresh food.

The **Marlin Hotel Bistro** (Princes Hwy; mains around $20; ◷ lunch & dinner daily), serves pub fare, or for self-caterers the **Coles supermarket** (Boree St), one street west of the main drag, is open late daily.

GETTING THERE & AWAY

If driving from Sydney, take the Princes Hwy straight down the south coast – the highway runs directly through Ulladulla (225km from Sydney). **Premier Motor Service** (☎ 133 410) has a twice-daily south coast service from Central Station, Sydney, to Ulladulla (one way $31).

HEART OF THE BUDAWANGS

Duration	4 days
Distance	52km
Difficulty	moderate–demanding
Start/Finish	Wog Wog picnic area
Nearest Towns	Ulladulla (opposte)
Transport	private

Summary An extremely varied walk among some of Australia's most spectacular sandstone escarpment country. Monolith Valley, The Castle and Mt Owen are highlights, but there is much else to see besides.

This is breathtaking country. The views across the heavily forested valleys and ridges are dramatic, and the walker's gaze constantly alights on something new. The craggy rock walls of the lower sandstone plateaus are capped by dark, brooding sandstone peaks, such as The Castle. Monolith Valley is a highlight, dissected as it is by a maze of clefts and canyons scoured into its rocky battlements.

Tackling this walk in four days (it's possible to complete in three) allows more time to enjoy the Wog Wog to Burrumbeet section, including Corang Peak and Corang Arch, and more energy for the demanding Monolith Valley/The Castle/Mt Owen circuit.

NEAREST TOWN & FACILITIES

See Ulladulla (opposite).

Wog Wog picnic area

NPWS allows camping at the Wog Wog picnic area, the starting point of this walk. There's a pit toilet at the site but no other facilities. No tank water is available. Wog Wog Creek is about 300m downhill from the picnic area; boil water before drinking.

GETTING TO/FROM THE WALK

From Ulladulla you can circle north or south to reach the Wog Wog area. Heading north, take the Princes Hwy 54km to Tomerong then go left on Turpentine Rd. Continue for about 56km (most of it on the gravel Braidwood–Nowra road) to Nerriga. Continue south for 17km, then turn left onto the Mongarlowe Rd. Wog Wog picnic area is 5km on, after a creek ford. From the south, take the Princes Hwy for 50km and turn west on to the Kings Hwy just north of Batemans Bay. Follow for 43km, up Clyde Mountain, then go right and follow for 7km to Mongarlowe. Continue towards Charleys Forest and Nerriga; Wog Wog picnic area is 21km past Mongarlowe.

Travellers Rest Backpackers (☎ 4454 0500; www .southcoasttravellersrest.com) provides a shuttle to the Budawangs for guests. Discuss your requirements when booking a bed.

South Coast Nature Tours (☎ 4454 0072; www .southcoastnaturetours.com.au) will collect walkers from accommodation in the Ulladulla area to Wog Wog picnic area for $200 per person return. The owner offers discounts to larger parties, brings after-walk refreshments and he'll supply maps and compass for the walk if they're required.

THE WALK

Day 1: Wog Wog picnic area to Burrumbeet Brook valley

4–4½hours, 12.5km, 350m ascent, 270m descent

The walk starts from the area just behind the national park information board. Take the walking track to Wog Wog Creek, a short distance down the hill. Head upstream and along the track, crossing Wog Wog Creek and continuing up the hill for about half an hour. The track is wide and well marked; about 2km past the creek it crosses an old fence line. In the next few hundred metres the track passes two sandstone formations

Heart of the Budawangs – Wog Wog Creek to Burrumbeet

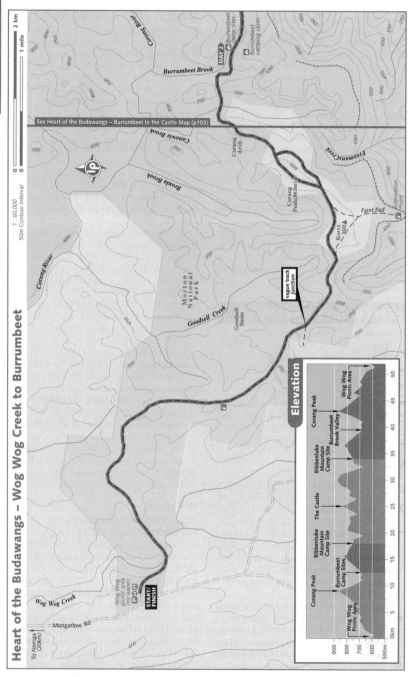

1 : 60,000
50m Contour Interval

2 km
1 mile

Conang River

Burrumbeet Camp sites

Burrumbeet camping caves

Burrumbeet Brook

DAY 2

See Heart of the Budawangs – Burrumbeet to the Castle Map (p103)

Canowie Brook

Corang Arch

Freemans Creek

Corang Peak (863m)

Faint Pad

Admiration Point

Korra Hill

Broula Brook

Morton National Park

Goodsell Creek

Goodsell Basin

vague track junction

Corang River

Wog Wog Creek

Mongarlow Rd

To Nerriga (20km)

Wog Wog picnic area (no water)

START/FINISH

Elevation

Corang Peak

Bibbenluke Mountain Camp Site

The Castle

Bibbenluke Mountain Camp Site

Burrumbeet Camp Sites

Wog Wog Picnic Area

Corang Peak

Bibbenluke Mountain Camp Site

Burrumbeet Brook Valley

Wog Wog Picnic Area

(the first to the right, the second on the left). Continue along the top of the next rise and descend to cross a saddle, before climbing again, heading in a southerly direction. Continue to follow the track through a gully, then climb again to a gap between large conglomerate outcrops.

The track continues southeast, crossing an exposed rocky area for a few hundred metres, then passes a barely discernible track junction about 6.5km from the start; the track veers left here. Continue, traversing the northern side of Korra Hill, part of the way on boardwalks, and reaching another track junction at the flat saddle. From here, an indistinct track can be taken south along the ridge to **Admiration Point** (1.8km return), which has excellent views across the Yadboro River to Currockbilly Mountain and east to the ramparts of The Castle and Mt Owen.

Just past the Admiration Point junction, take the left fork to the summit of **Corang Peak** (a 70m altitude gain to the 863m summit), from where great views of all the surrounding peaks and heavily forested valleys unfold (about three hours from the Wog Wog picnic area). Continue off the summit of Corang Peak to the northeast, passing **Corang Arch** about 15 to 20 minutes further along. This remnant of a collapsed sandstone overhang lies about 50m to the left of the main track; you need to be near the cliff edge to see it. From here the route descends indistinctly down a sloping conglomerate ramp, turns east and drops down steps to Canowie Brook. Continue across the Canowie Brook swamp, over the rise, and follow the track right (south) and down to cross a tributary of Burrumbeet Brook. A few hundred metres east near the brook there are good camp sites, while numerous small tracks lead off (to the right) to camping caves just south of the main track.

Day 2: Burrumbeet Brook valley to Bibbenluke Mountain camp site
2–2½ hours, 5.5km, 90m ascent, 80m descent

This is a short day so there's plenty of time to dawdle over breakfast. Continue up the Burrumbeet Brook valley northeast. About halfway up the climb to the head of the valley there's a right turn to **Yurnga Lookout**, which is worth the detour on a clear day for its views into the plunging deep below

Bibbenluke Mountain. The track climbs steadily for another 400m then follows a scenic ridge crest (with some fairly solid scrub-bashing) to the west and north of Bibbenluke Mountain. The track descends gently through more heath on boardwalks to a couple of creek crossings. There are some camp sites either side of the track 50m to 60m past the second creek, but it's better to continue for a few hundred metres and take the left (north) turn to the sites near the upper reaches of the Corang River. You can pass the afternoon with a jaunt up **Mt Tarn** (887m) – the pad is vague in places, but quite manageable – or drinking in the view of Mt Cole (877m), Mt Owen (876m) and Donjon Mountain that unfolds east of the Bibbenluke Mountain saddle.

Day 3: Bibbenluke Mountain camp site to Monolith Valley & The Castle return
8½ hours, 16km, 620m ascent, 590m descent

This section is strenuous and involves significant height gains and descents, so an early start is necessary to ensure you won't be finishing in the dark (be especially mindful of this on short winter days). Return south from camp and go left when you reach the main track. Follow this to the next junction and turn right (the left branch goes to Mt Tarn), fairly soon after entering light forest. The track meanders over fallen trees for about 500m to 600m to a creek crossing, climbs a little and then veers east and down to the saddle. From here it's all uphill to cliffs of Mt Cole.

Upon reaching the cliffs, go left and continue around Mt Cole's base to the north, following the rubble-strewn track and passing three camping caves before surmounting the saddle between Mt Cole and Donjon Mountain. Signs here indicate that you're entering the protected region surrounding Monolith Valley. Within this area, camping and fires are not permitted.

From here the track continues east, then veers south at the saddle between Mt Cole and Seven Gods Pinnacle. Continue down the small ravine along the course of the creek into the narrowest part of **Monolith Valley**. As the canyon widens, an arch of rock appears on the right, and is worth exploring. The canyon is all moss, ferns and shade, a magical and unexpectedly soft world after the heath-bashing that's come before. Continue on the track to the small wooden bridge. The trip from Bibbenluke Mountain camp site to here should take two hours. You'll need another three to four hours to reach and climb The Castle and return to this point.

To climb The Castle, cross the bridge and head up and east, following a creek-side track around and into the saddle between Mt Mooryan and Mt Nibelung, where several track braids lead through the tall grass. The track drops into a narrow defile down to the right, but it's best to avoid this by following cairns along the rock shelves to the left, then dropping to the base of the gully via a fixed chain. The track continues southeast and east, and descends beside a creek to the sign indicating the end of the protected area. Cross the creek and continue south, skirting the base of the cliffs of **Mt Nibelung** and finally dropping southeast into The Castle saddle. There's evidence of old camp sites here (camping's banned; a left turn leads to Cooyoyo Creek camp site, a steep 20- to 30-minute walk downhill).

Go straight ahead to reach The Castle, following the now less-distinct pad as it climbs slightly before heading along the eastern base of the cliffs past some camping caves and, up to the right, 'the tunnel', which can be ignored. (This constricted slot, marked by scratched arrows, provides access to the western side of The Castle, where there are great views of Mt Owen and the **Oaky Creek valley**; keep an eye on the time if you decide to take a look.)

About 100m past the tunnel the track rises to the start of the climb up the 'tail' of **The Castle**. From this point you'll need to patiently follow arrows scratched on the rock and wear marks, sometimes stopping to carefully review the options – there are quite a few false leads and wrong turns can get nasty. For the most part the climb is quite manageable for experienced walkers. There's an exposed section very low down that might be unnerving, otherwise the hardest sections are towards the top. Once you're on the ridge of the tail, the track undulates between outcrops and boulders, finally passing east of a prominent tower then continuing along a ledge for about 40m to the last major obstacle, a chimney. Here you may want to use the rope (mentioned in Planning p98) to assist less

confident members of your group (there is sometimes a length of rope hanging here, left by previous parties). Above, traverse out and round the bulge to the right, before bridging the final two short chimneys. This brings you out on the summit plateau, where the views are spectacular, particularly to the south and southeast. There's a logbook in a container about 15 minutes' bus trip south from the top of the climb (again, check timing before committing to an extra half-hour up here).

Return to Monolith Valley on the outward route and cross back over the small bridge. Go left for 20m to 30m then climb the steep, rocky track through a small slot and down into a boulder-strewn valley. Follow the vague line of cairns across the boulders of this for about 150m then go south and up a very steep track along a series of ledges. The final part of the ascent follows a gully up the eastern side of Mt Owen plateau, after which a line of cairns marks the path west for about 700m to 800m, to large cairns directly south of the saddle between Mt Owen and Mt Cole.

From here, a strenuous return detour (about 2.8km, up to 1½ hours) leads to the southern end of **Mt Owen plateau**; you should only attempt it if you have sufficient time (you'll need one to 1½ hours to get back to camp from the large cairns). Follow the vague but cairned route southwest. There are magnificent views across to The Castle from the south point. Follow the same route back to the large cairns.

The track is vague past the large cairns. You need to head north to the rim of the plateau (following cairns, and occasionally being distracted by false turns) and drop down a narrow gully (with a small rock shelter at its top) into the saddle between Mt Owen and Mt Cole. Follow the cairns (again, they're vague) westwards down the gully. The going is steep and scrambly; you need to be particularly careful when descending the tricky rock slab on the gully's left side. Not far beyond it you'll pass the protected area signpost.

From the mouth of the gully, head to the right along the base of the cliffs, past two camping caves, to the junction with the track used earlier in the day. Return to Bibbenluke Mountain camp site, following the same route used on the outward journey.

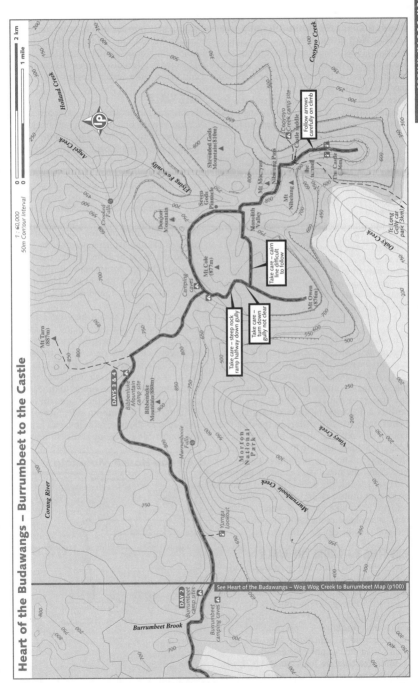

Heart of the Budawangs – Burrumbeet to the Castle

1 : 40,000
50m Contour Interval

0   2 km
0   1 mile

Holland Creek

Angel Creek

Canyoyo Creek

Crawford Falls

Shrouded Gods Mountain (810m)

Flying Fox Gully

Seven Gods Pinnacle

Donjon Mountain

Castle Saddle

Cooyoyo Creek camp site

Follow arrows carefully on climb

Mt Moollattoo

Nibelung Pass

Mt Nibelung

The Castle (830m)

Monolith Valley

To Long Gully car park (3km)

Oaky Creek

Mt Cole (877m)

Take care – cairn line difficult to follow

Take care – turn down gully not clear

Mt Owen (876m)

Camping caves

Take care – steep rock ramp halfway down gully

Mt Tarn (887m)

Bibbenluke Mountain camp site

Bibbenluke Mountain (880m)

DAYS 3 & 4

Murrumbooie Falls

Viney Creek

Morton National Park

Murrumbooie Creek

Corang River

Yurnga Lookout

DAY 2

See Heart of the Budawangs – Wog Wog Creek to Burrumbeet Map (p100)

Burrumbeet camp sites

Burrumbeet camping caves

Burrumbeet Brook

Day 4: Bibbenluke Mountain camp site to Wog Wog picnic area

6–7 hours, 18km, 350m ascent, 440m descent

Return to Wog Wog along the walk-in route. Expect to be tired from the previous day's exertions, so allow time for a slower pace and for rests. Unless you're keen for another look at the view from Corang Peak, take the lower track around its eastern flank. It's mostly level going on boardwalks.

PIGEON HOUSE MOUNTAIN

Duration	3 hours
Distance	5.9km
Standard	moderate
Start/Finish	Pigeon House Mountain car park
Nearest Town	Ulladulla (p98)
Transport	private

Summary A short but exhilarating walk via a series of ladders to the summit of Pigeon House Mountain, with sweeping views of the ocean and coastal plains.

This day walk provides magnificent 360-degree views of The Castle, Byangee Mountain and the rugged escarpments to the north and south of the park. The ocean is also visible, giving an interesting contrast between the dissected valleys of the Clyde River and its tributaries, and the distant coastal plains, from Mt Dromedary in the south to Point Perpendicular in the north. A series of metal ladders needs to be negotiated near the summit. These are very safe but quite exposed and the metal rungs may be slippery after rain. While the walk is short, it is fairly steep and quite hot and dry in summer – remember to take plenty of water. A water tank is available at the car park but is rain-fed and may be dry in summer.

GETTING TO/FROM THE WALK

From Ulladulla, go south (past Burill Lake) for 8km to Wheelbarrow Rd; go right and continue for 6km to a left turn at Woodburn Rd, then go right (after 3.2km) up Clyde Ridge Rd. Follow for 7km then go right into Yadboro Forest Rd. Veer left 4.3km ahead to reach the Pigeon House picnic area at the start of the walk.

South Coast Nature Tours (☎ 4454 0072; www .southcoastnaturetours.com.au) will collect you and your party from accommodation in the Ulladulla/Milton area and provide a shuttle to Pigeon House for $60 per person return. The owner offers discounts to larger parties and brings after-walk refreshments.

THE WALK

From the picnic area and car park, head straight up the hill on the obvious track past the interpretive NPWS sign. Continue for 800m until a small band of low cliffs and rocky outcrops is reached. Follow the track and eroded steps round to the left, up to the top of the bluffs, and across the national park boundary proper (the car park is actually in state forest). A small **lookout** here on the right, slightly off the track, gives great views to the south and tree-filtered glimpses of Pigeon House, which was named by James Cook in 1770 as he sailed up the east coast of Australia. The Murrumarang Aboriginal people knew it as Dithol or Did-Dell, meaning 'woman's breast', and it was a women's Dreaming area.

The track flattens out here on a lightly forested plateau, and the walking is easy and pleasant for 1km. Then the track steepens and keeps climbing right up to the rocky base of **Pigeon House Mountain** (720m). Take the track round to the left from here, up the metal steps, as it snakes round to the eastern and southern sides of the mountain below the cliff. On the southern side, more metal steps lead to the base of four metal ladders, which provide a route up some chimneys to

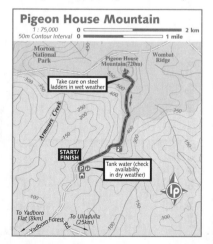

Pigeon House Mountain

1 : 75,000

50m Contour Interval

0 — 2 km

0 — 1 mile

Morton National Park

Pigeon House Mountain (720m)

Wombat Ridge

Take care on steel ladders in wet weather

Armours Creek

START/FINISH

Tank water (check availability in dry weather)

To Yadboro Flat (8km)

To Ulladulla (25km)

Yadboro Forest Rd

HUME & HOVELL WALKING TRACK

The Hume & Hovell Walking Track covers 440km between Yass and Albury on the route taken by Hamilton Hume and William Hovell on their expedition to Port Phillip in 1824–25.

Hume, one of the first children born in the new colony, played a part in the 'discovery' of the Goulburn Plains and Lake George. Hovell was an English sea captain who settled in the colony in 1813, but spent most of his time seeking adventure on the Southern Ocean.

The two set off from Hume's property near Lake George in October 1824 to strike a land route between the settled districts of NSW and the poorly known country on the continent's southern coast, 1000km away. After an eventful journey they reached the Yarra Ranges and gazed over the site of present-day Melbourne before high-tailing it back to Sydney via a more direct route (now followed by the Hume Fwy).

First proposed in 1925 on the centenary of the journey, the Hume & Hovell Walking Track was researched during the 1970s. About 300km of track had been marked and prepared by 1988 (with the aid of funding for that year's Australian Bicentennial), with a further 150km completed over the next decade. The track covers the NSW portion of Hume and Hovell's outward journey. It's fully signposted and can be taken in sections of various sizes – day walks, weekend walks or a total walk of about 24 days.

The track starts at Cooma Cottage on the outskirts of Yass and finishes at the Hovell Tree on the banks of the Murray River in Albury. Skirting the Australian Alps, much of the track is along forestry roads or through farmland. Camp sites, pit toilets and other facilities are provided along the way. The route has three track heads about 100km apart – James Fitzpatrick at Wee Jasper, Thomas Boyd on the Goobarragandra River (23km from Tumut) and Henry Angel on Burra Creek, near Tumbarumba. The route includes 17 bush camp sites, a great deal of improved track and three major bridges over rivers.

For more information call the **Department of Lands** (☎ 6937 2700). The Department's *Hume & Hovell Walking Track Brochure* kit has an index map, six sectional maps and information on walking distances, safety hints, facilities, transport and historical information. It's $22 and available from the Department and various tourist offices, map shops and outdoor gear suppliers.

---

the summit massif on the top. The ladders are reasonably exposed but solid and safe.

The views are fantastic from the top, although it's necessary to walk around to get the best vantage points. Byangee Mountain, The Castle and the craggy cliffs of the central Budawangs are all revealed in sharp relief from the summit. Return to the start along the same route.

BUNGONIA STATE CONSERVATION AREA

Bungonia Gorge and the Shoalhaven River valley area is a rugged and beautiful place. The towering cliff faces of the 300m-deep Bungonia Gorge make this the deepest limestone gorge in Australia. The area provides some of the most difficult long rock climbs in the country. It is also a major caving area, and speleology clubs flock here to explore the maze of caverns and tunnels, most of which can only be entered using fixed ropes and caving ladders.

The two-day walk described here starts in the Bungonia State Conservation Area, which at 4007 hectares is the largest of its kind in NSW. The reserve protects an area of the Southern Tablelands running from Bungonia Gorge to the south and up the steep west bank of the Shoalhaven River, where it borders nearby Morton National Park. The reserve has been protected since 1872; however, a reminder of the ugly march of progress – a gaping limestone quarry that produces ingredients used for making concrete, among other things – is visible from the start of the described route.

ENVIRONMENT

The low-nutrient limestone soils here leads to scrubby, stunted vegetation on the upper slopes and plateaus, with stringybark, yellow box, grey box and broad-leaved peppermint trees common. Many huge grass trees grow in the area. Along the lower reaches of the gorge, water exiting the caves system supports the growth of rainforest trees, including red cedars, giant stinging trees and sandpaper figs. At camp sites along the Shoalhaven River and the borders of Bungonia Creek, casuarinas or she-oaks provide a pretty canopy and ground cover of soft, pine-like leaves. Casuarinas make great windbreaks, and it's quite calming to lie back after a hard day's walking and listen to the gentle swish of breezes rustling through their foliage.

Bungonia's gorge is an ancient coral reef, which was crushed and compressed to form limestone about 400 million years ago. This limestone belt is one of the largest in NSW, and was once overlaid with less resistant shale. Water carved a swathe through this shale, exposing the three tilted limestone deposits and creating the deep, narrow canyon. The limestone deposits also provide a rich source of raw material for the quarry on the northern side of the gorge, visible from the Bungonia State Recreation Area. The quarry is due to be relocated north and out of sight of the lookouts by the year 2010.

PLANNING

It's best to boil or treat water as the Shoalhaven River and Bungonia Creek are fed in part by runoff from farmland.

When to Walk

If visiting in midsummer, NPWS recommends you plan to walk out of the gorge late in the day to avoid the worst of the heat.

WARNINGS

Falling Debris

The gorge is very narrow and high, and debris falling from above – including rocks and tree branches – can be a significant hazard along the boulder-choked bed of Bungonia Creek. This can be especially risky during storms and strong winds, when it may not be entirely obvious that stuff is getting blown around up top until it starts raining down on you. There is really nowhere to run if you're caught, so keep an eye out for windy weather before heading into the gorge.

Water Levels in the Gorge

Bungonia Creek can rise very quickly and without warning, and the gorge is a dicey place to be when the creek is up – the boulder choke at the eastern end of the gorge is particularly difficult to negotiate in such conditions. Check the weather forecast ahead of your visit and heed predictions for summer thunderstorms or heavy winter rains: the sort of events that drop rain on the catchment area upstream. Current conditions are available from the **Bungonia State Conservation Area visitor information centre** (☎ 4844 4277, infoline 4844 4341; Lookdown Rd, Bungonia). NPWS closes the gorge for safety reasons when the water level is up.

Quarry Blasting

A 700m-long restricted area is indicated by signs along the banks of Bungonia Creek, on the Red Track route used for the out-and-back into the Gorge on Day 1. This zone, on the north side of Bungonia Creek just beyond the boulder-choked eastern end of Bungonia Gorge, lies below a limestone quarry perched on the ridge high above. It is occasionally affected by rock falls triggered by blasting at the quarry.

Blasting occurs around 3pm on weekdays. Listen for several warning sirens preceding the blast. A continuous siren sounds from one minute before blasting until all is clear. A full explanation is given on the signs at each end of the affected area, so read these carefully. Remain outside the no-go area when blasting is taking place.

Maps

The CMA 1:25,000 *Caoura* map fully covers the area in the walk description but tracks aren't accurately marked. A useful NPWS visitor's leaflet, *Bungonia State Conservation Area*, is available from the visitor information centre. The leaflet indicates the location of all major tracks down to the junction of Bungonia Creek and the Shoalhaven River.

Useful books include *Fitzroy Falls and Beyond* published by the Budawang Committee, volume 2 of the NPA's *Bushwalks in the Sydney Region* (which has notes on Bungonia Gorge) and John & Lyn Daly's *Take a Walk in a New South Wales National Park South-Eastern Zone*, which includes notes on all the tracks in the area.

Information Sources

The **Bungonia State Conservation Area visitor information centre** (☎ 4844 4277, ☎ infoline 4844 4341; Lookdown Rd) is right near the park gate.

Park Fees & Regulations

Walkers should register their intended route and times of departure and return at the visitor information centre on entering the park. A book (with 24-hour access) is provided for this purpose. All camp sites along the Shoalhaven River and lower Bungonia Creek are fuel-stove only – no fires.

A car-entry fee of $7 per day is payable on entering the conservation area. Bring $1 and $2 coins for the ticket machines.

The park is closed twice a year for feral animal control. At this time, high-powered rifles are used within the confines of the gorge. Check with the visitor information centre for dates.

BUNGONIA GORGE

Duration	2 days
Distance	22km
Difficulty	moderate–demanding
Start/Finish	David Reid car park
Nearest Town	Goulburn (right)
Transport	private

Summary A fascinating walk through spectacular limestone gorge country, with some pretty camp sites along the banks of the Shoalhaven River. There are numerous opportunities for swimming in the heat of summer, in Bungonia Creek and the Shoalhaven River.

The variety of geographical features encountered here, along with the rugged nature of the limestone gorge country, make this an engrossing ramble. It involves a good deal of clambering over boulders, plus ascents and descents of steep gullies and ridges, so this walk receives a moderate–demanding rating, in spite of its relatively short length. It's possible to extend the walk significantly by adding in more of the country bordering the Shoalhaven River, both north and south of its junction with Bungonia Creek. However, the route as described presents a nice balance of the area's most interesting features.

NEAREST TOWN & FACILITIES
Goulburn

☎ 02 / pop 20,900

Goulburn is the nearest sizable town to the walk, making it the best place to stock up on supplies.

The **Goulburn visitor information centre** (☎ 4823 4492; www.igoulburn.com; 201 Sloane St), opposite Belmore Park, has regional information. There is no regular bus to Bungonia but the visitor information centre can supply phone numbers for local buses (for group charter) or taxis.

EATING & SLEEPING

Unless you pick a weekend when there's a special event on in town, you won't have too much trouble getting a bed in Goulburn.

Governor's Hill Carapark (☎ 4821 7373; 77-83 Sydney Rd; unpowered/powered sites for 2 $23/29, on-site vans/cabins from $70/84) is on the old highway near the town's northern fringe.

Sloane St (running parallel to the railway line) has a number of pubs offering basic accommodation, including the **Coolavin** (☎ 4821 2498; 188 Sloane St; s/d $30/60) and the **Carlton** (☎ 4821 3820; 285 Sloane St; r $50-60). The **Exchange Hotel** (☎ 4821 1566; 9 Bradley St; s/d $35/55) also offers a self-serve breakfast.

All the eating places are spread along the main drag (Auburn St), including some good old country bakeries and cafés, with the **Paragon** (174 Auburn St; ⏲ lunch & dinner daily) probably the pick of the bunch.

GETTING THERE & AWAY

Goulburn is 201km from Sydney, 659km from Melbourne and 89km from Canberra. **Greyhound Australia** (☎ 13 14 99), **Murrays**

(☎ 13 22 51) and **Fearnes** (☎ 1800 029 918) stop in Goulburn. Trains between Sydney and Melbourne also stop here daily. The one-way fare from Canberra is $9 and from Sydney $23; call **Countrylink** (☎ 13 22 32) for information and reservations.

Bungonia State Conservation Area

There is a convenient and well-equipped camping ground just behind the visitor information centre, near the park entrance gate. Hot showers, toilet facilities and a community kitchen are provided. Tent sites for two people are $10. It's recommended that walking parties stay at this camping ground on the night prior to the walk.

GETTING TO/FROM THE WALK

Driving from Sydney on the Hume Hwy, look for the signposted turn-off to Bungonia Gorge on the left, about 2km south of the Marulan exit (soon after passing the BP petrol stations). You take the same exit if coming from Goulburn (it's also possible to reach Bungonia from Goulburn on minor roads – follow the signs from Sloane St, next to the railway line).

From the Hume Hwy, follow the signs through the small township of Bungonia, turning left where indicated; the park gate is another 8km along a good sealed road. The gorge area and the trailhead are a little further along this road after the gate (the route to David Reid car park is well signposted).

THE WALK
Day 1: David Reid car park to Shoalhaven River Camp Site
5–6 hours, 12km, 420m descent

Although it's possible to enter Bungonia Gorge from the west, it's a much better experience to walk the gorge without a full pack, so our route does an out-and-back into the gorge from the east, before continuing on a circuit walk down to the Shoalhaven River.

Water is available from a tank near the car park, and it's advisable to stock up here if you're unsure of water availability in the gorge, particularly in summer. Leave the car here and pick up the start of the Red Track, heading east. All the walks in the recreation area are colour coded and well marked, with appropriately coloured arrows and squares appearing on geographical features and signposts along the trails. After 700m the track divides: follow the Red Track markers to the left and northeast.

The track drops past the top of a gully and through a saddle before descending sharply to a **lookout point** with views straight into the gorge. From here the track descends steeply on a ridge for about 500m to Bungonia Creek. Cross to the north bank, where the first of the quarry blasting signs stands. Turn left (west) and proceed (assuming that the hour and absence of sirens indicate that it's safe to do so) up the creek towards the gorge for about 700m, where another sign marks the end of the blasting-danger area.

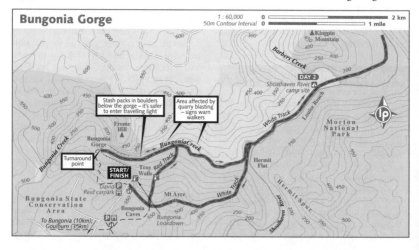

Bungonia Gorge

1 : 60,000
50m Contour Interval

BUNGONIA CAVES

Bungonia is an area containing predominantly vertical caves, created by water and dissolved acid from the atmosphere carving through the limestone bedrock to form deep underground ravines. Because of their vertical nature, descent into the chambers requires ropes and caving ladders, making exploration possible only by experienced cavers. The limestone belt here is about 4km long, 670m wide and 300m deep. Over 170 caves are recorded within the conservation area, and the region contains some of the deepest caverns on mainland Australia, including Blowfly Cave (152m), Odyssey Cave (142m) and Fossil Cave (131m).

The first cave was recorded in Bungonia around 1824; in 1872, a reserve titled Water Reserve No 27 was set up both to protect the caves and provide an area for public recreation. This was very likely the first reserve established for the purpose of public recreation in Australia, and perhaps the world. In 1892 the Skull Cave was discovered, and so named because it contained the skull of an Aboriginal child.

As limestone is very porous, water tends to permeate it quickly, draining through the soil and leaving little surface moisture. This is the reason for the rugged, stunted appearance of most of the vegetation in the Bungonia area.

The going gets tougher a short distance from here so this is a good place to stash packs. Continue, lightweight, into the gorge.

The gorge's eastern end is choked with large boulders, which take a lot of patient over-and-under negotiating; in times of high water in the creek it may be necessary to wade across sections here. Once you're past the boulder choke the going is easier. Towering above you, on either side of this deep, narrow defile, are limestone cliffs hundreds of metres high. The gorge is so constricted, however, that it feels as if you can touch both walls with outstretched hands. Follow the gorge up along the course of Bungonia Creek – the boulders gradually decrease in size. There is a risk of rock fall from the high walls here, so proceed with caution (see the boxed text p106). The logical turnaround point is the western end of the gorge. Follow your outward route back to the packs.

When you return to the point where the Red Track reaches the creek, keep following the vague track that continues downstream. You'll pass several deep-green waterholes and rocky sections of creek bed, crossing and recrossing the stream where necessary, before reaching a tight left-hand bend in the creek, about 2km from the quarry sign. Follow the creek left, passing a large flat camping area and another deep-green waterhole. This is a beautiful, shady swimming spot in summer.

Cross the creek to the south bank at the end of the pool and, a few hundred metres downstream, the confluence of Bungonia Creek and the **Shoalhaven River** is reached. Cross Bungonia Creek to the north and continue up the west bank of the Shoalhaven River, following the well-worn but unmarked track. Numerous camp sites are along here. Continue up to the crossing of Barbers Creek, and then follow the cairned track up and northeast over the low hill to a large flat area looking across to the saddle of **Rainbow Ridge**, just before a big horseshoe bend in the Shoalhaven River. A quick excursion down to the rapids of the Shoalhaven River (a 30-minute return trip) is well worthwhile.

It's possible to camp here, but there's a nicer camp site underneath shady casuarinas about 2km back along the outward route, near **Louise Reach** on the Shoalhaven River (about 500m southwest of Barbers Creek).

There are some excellent alternative camp sites around the junction of Bungonia Creek and the Shoalhaven River. Be sure to camp well above river level to ensure you stay dry if water levels rise overnight after rain.

Day 2: Shoalhaven River Camp Site to David Reid car park

4–5 hours, 10km

Leaving the casuarinas, continue southwest along the Shoalhaven River, following the outward route back to the Bungonia Creek/Shoalhaven River confluence. From here, pick up the **White Track**, which is indicated by a signpost on the south bank of Bungonia Creek, slightly up the hill. This track continues gently up and across a flat plateau for 500m, before climbing suddenly at a much greater angle. This track is steep! However, going up is easier than going down. Watch out for the slippery, loose shale that lies underfoot, as the path is so steep that falling is easy. On a hot day make sure you have plenty of water for the climb.

The track climbs steadily, with great views back across the Shoalhaven River valley from the previous day's walk. About 4.5km from Bungonia Creek you pass **Mt Ayre** – a good spot for a final look back at the Shoalhaven. Keep an eye out to the left (south) as you descend the western side of Mt Ayre for some brick chimney stacks way down on the Shoalhaven River banks – all that remains of the Tolwong copper smelter, which operated in the early years of the 20th century. The Red Track junction is just ahead. Don't forget to sign out of the activity register when you exit the park.

WARRUMBUNGLE NATIONAL PARK

The volcanic spires that define the skyline of the 21,000-hectare Warrumbungle National Park rise abruptly from the surrounding flat plains of western NSW like clusters of jagged, rocky teeth. These cliffs, domes and crags are visible for many kilometres before the approaching traveller reaches the park boundary. About 490km northwest of Sydney, this is an ancient landscape of imposing rocky buttresses, deep wooded valleys and primordial beauty, and is justifiably one of the state's most popular national parks, receiving up to 80,000 visitors per year.

The walk takes in some of the area's best features, including spectacular circuits of the Grand High Tops, Dows High Tops and the more remote Mt Exmouth, at 1206m the highest point in the park.

Before 1939, the Warrumbungle Range was known only to a core of hardy bushwalkers, climbers and local landowners. It came to national prominence when the renowned adventurer and photographer Frank Hurley made the Grand High Tops area the subject of an illustrated magazine article, turning the Breadknife into a widely recognised Australian icon.

HISTORY

Aboriginal people of the Wailwan and Gamilaroi (or Kamilaroi) language groups are the traditional custodians of this area. Signs of Aboriginal camp sites and fragments of stone implements, including quartz flakes used to fashion axes and cutting tools, are found all over the park. Explorer John Oxley was the first European into the region in 1818; settlers followed from about the late 1830s and quickly displaced the Aboriginal people.

Calls for the preservation of the Warrumbungles were first heard in 1936 and 3360 hectares were set aside as a national park in 1953. Further additions since have increased the park to its present-day size. The Warrumbungles' first ranger, Carl Dow, is credited with establishing the network of walking trails – cut by hand in difficult terrain.

ENVIRONMENT

About 17 million years ago, erupting volcanoes produced a thick layer of debris and molten lava on top of the area's sandstone base. Eons of erosion later removed the surrounding softer clays, exposing the harder volcanic plugs and dikes that form the jagged peaks and rugged buttresses seen today. Some of the park's well-known features, including the Breadknife, Belougery Spire and Crater Bluff, are the remnant cores of volcanoes long since eroded away.

The Warrumbungles form a boundary between the dry Western Plains and the more humid regions of coastal NSW. As a result, it is a meeting place for moist coastal species and plants of the dry inland regions. Remnant rainforest plants such as Port Jackson fig trees and maidenhair ferns exist side by side with hardy white cypress, prehistoric macrozamias, red gums – much loved by koalas – and striking white gums.

Due to the wide variety of habitats formed by the park's diverse geography, many different types of animal inhabit the area. Over 90 bird species have been recorded in the park, and goannas, eastern brown snakes, koalas, gliders, grey kangaroos, emus, wallaroos, and red-necked and swamp wallabies exist in large numbers. Sunset at the various grassy picnic and camping areas is usually the best time to view wildlife.

PLANNING
When to Walk

Walking is possible at any time of year, with autumn and spring providing the most pleasant conditions. In summer, temperatures in the high 30s and 40s are common, although nights can be cool. School holidays and long weekends can be very crowded. The quietest times to visit are in summer, winter and midweek, when it's quite likely you will have the trails to yourself.

What to Bring

A fuel stove is essential, as wood fires are banned on walking trails (there are fireplaces in the camping grounds.) At least 4L of water per person per day should be carried in the heat of summer – take adequate supplies with you from the valley. Creeks marked on topographic maps rarely flow, and aside from a small rainwater tank next to Balor Hut (which is often empty), there is no tap water on the higher walking trails. It's wise to boil or treat any tap water taken from within the park to make it safe to drink.

Maps & Books

The LPINSW 1:40,000 *Warrumbungle National Park Tourist Map* covers the entire park in good detail (including contour information). The park is also covered by four CMA 1:50,000 topographic maps: *Tenandra*, *Tooraweenah*, *Bugaldie* and *Coonabarabran*.

The NPWS guidebook *Warrumbungle National Park* by Peter Fox is an excellent resource and is small enough to take on the walk with you. It includes a useful *Walks Guide* booklet with some sketch maps, track notes and descriptions of major features in the park.

Information Sources

The park's **visitor information centre** (☎ 6825 4364) is inside its boundaries, about 300m off the John Renshaw Parkway (signposted on the right when driving from Coonabarabran). It stocks information booklets, topographic maps, gifts and snacks, and staff can organise hut bookings and accept payment for park use, hut and camping fees. Some information is also available at the Coonabarabran visitor information centre (p112).

ROCKIN' UP THE BUNGLES

The volcanic spires and imposing bluffs of the Warrumbungles offer some of the most atmospheric and challenging long rock climbs Australia has to offer. The area has been a mecca for climbers for many years, and enjoys a deserved reputation as a serious and scary place to touch rock. The history of climbing in the 'Bungles (as it's known to climbers) is a fascinating tale in itself, and starts in the early 1930s. A wild (some would say completely crazy) bunch of hardcore bushwalkers started pursuing rock climbing as an activity in itself at about this time, and formed a club known as the Blue Mountaineers. Their weekends were filled with horror ascents of iconic rock formations in the Blue Mountains, including the Three Sisters at Katoomba. With virtually no equipment, very poor quality ropes and incredible bravado, they achieved feats that would leave modern rock climbers, with their camming devices and strong harnesses, quaking in their grippy rubber boots. Two of the main crazies were the legendary Eric (Dr) Dark and Dot Butler, known as the 'Barefoot Bushwalker' – a name earned from the many wilderness walks she completed without shoes.

In 1932 Eric Dark and Osmar White made the first ascent of Belougery Spire after drinkers at the local pub proclaimed the ascent 'impossible'. In 1936 a party of three including Eric Dark and Dot Butler made the first ascent of Crater Bluff, an incredible achievement considering the technical nature of the climb, and the wildly exposed route they took. Take a moment to have a good look at Crater Bluff from the Grand High Tops track and you'll understand. Dot Butler, of course, completed the first ascent barefoot.

Today, the 'Bungles have lost none of their seriousness and awe-inspiring grandeur. As the rock routes are very long (up to 500m), climbing should only be attempted by very experienced parties who are familiar with long, multipitch climbs. Climbers must register at the visitor information centre before heading out; climbing is banned on the Breadknife and Chalkers Mountain.

NEW SOUTH WALES

Permits & Regulations

Park entry costs $7 per vehicle per day. Tent sites for two people are $10 at Camps Blackman and Wambelong, and $6 at Camp Pincham. Bush camping along trails is free. All fees should be paid at the visitor information centre, where you can also book overnight stays at Balor Hut ($4 per person per night). After hut fees are paid you'll be handed a key that must be returned upon completion of your walk.

If you're planning to go rock climbing in the park you must register at the visitor information centre.

Guided Walks

The national park's Discovery Program arranges Aboriginal cultural heritage walks that can be specially tailored to suit specific interests, such as traditional lifestyles or bush tucker. These are not overnight walks and, at $55 per hour, are a better deal for groups than individuals. The visitor information centre can provide more information and make bookings.

GETTING THERE & AWAY

The park lies 35km west of Coonabarabran and 490km northwest of Sydney. Driving from Sydney, it takes six hours to reach the park via Mudgee and about seven hours via Dubbo (via the Oxley and Newell Hwys). It's also possible to enter the park from the west, from the Castlereagh Hwy via Gulargambone and Coonamble. **Countrylink** (☎ 132 232) runs a daily train/bus service to Coonabarabran Monday to Friday; the one-way adult fare is $51.

This wonderful walk takes in all of the major sights and formations visible in the national park's central region. This includes the Grand High Tops, a walk across Dows High Tops with fantastic views of Bluff Mountain's massive west face, and a visit to Mt Exmouth, the park's highest peak. The walk could be done in two days; completing it in three allows for a more relaxed pace over the steep terrain, and time for the numerous possible detours.

NEAREST TOWN & FACILITIES
Coonabarabran
☎ 02 / pop 3000
Coonabarabran is 35km east of the park entrance and the logical place to stock up on any last-minute requirements. If driving from Sydney, it may be wise to stop in Mudgee or Dubbo for a major resupply of food and stove fuel as you will probably hit Coonabarabran late in the evening when the shops are shut.

The **Coonabarabran visitor information centre** (☎ 6842 1441; www.coonabarabran.com), on the Newell Hwy (John St), has some park information and walking books.

Petrol and kerosene are available from the service stations in town. Bring Shellite with you to be on the safe side; methylated spirits for stoves is available from the supermarkets.

EATING & SLEEPING
Several pubs in town have accommodation and cheap pub meals, and the road into the town centre is lined with motels.

The **Imperial Hotel** (☎ 6842 1023; d/B&B $35/51), opposite the town clock tower on the main street, is basic but convenient.

Acacia Motor Lodge (☎ 6842 1922; 10 John St; r $110) is slightly more up-market.

Wagon Wheels (☎ 6842 1860; Newell Hwy; d/cabin $70/50) is cheap and cheerful.

The **Warrumbungle Holiday Camp** (☎ 6842 3400; dm/cabin $14/50) is 12km from Coonabarabran on the national park road.

The **Jolli Cauli Cafe** (John St; ☯ lunch), opposite the Royal Hotel, is a pleasant café with a good selection of light food, cakes and coffee, and also provides Internet access for email. For self-caterers, the IGA and BiLo supermarkets, centrally located in Dalgarno St near the intersection with John St, are open daily.

WARRUMBUNGLES GRAND HIGH TOPS	
Duration	3 days
Distance	34km
Difficulty	moderate
Start/Finish	Pincham car park
Nearest Town	Coonabarabran (right)
Transport	private
Summary	Explore one of Australia's most spectacular volcanic landscapes on challenging and well-marked trails. While extremely steep in places, the walk affords wide views across the park's rocky features, and beyond to empty spaces of western NSW.

Warrumbungle National Park

Camping areas closest to the walk are at **Camp Pincham** (sites for 2 $6), south of the John Renshaw Parkway, and **Camps Wambelong** and **Blackman** (sites for 2 $10), which are west and east of Canyon Picnic Area. Camp Blackman also has hot showers. The visitor information centre can assist with bookings and payments.

GETTING TO/FROM THE WALK

Drive into the park on the John Renshaw Parkway and follow signs to the visitor information centre. After organising camping fees, continue to the trailhead at Pincham car park. Leave your vehicle here. (All access roads within the park are sealed, making wet weather access easy.)

THE WALK
Day 1: Pincham to Balor Hut via Bress Peak

4–5 hours, 10km, 760m ascent, 460m descent

From Pincham car park, follow the well-defined and clearly signposted walking track through Camp Pincham and continue south for about 3km over several wooden bridges to the Bress Peak track junction on the right (do not take the right-hand turn along West Spirey Creek to Ogma Saddle, or the left-hand turn to Goulds Circuit passed on the way).

Drop packs at the track junction and take the steep side trip up to **Bress Peak**, a 1.1km return walk via **Bridget Peak**. The track is amazingly steep with loose footing in sections, and walkers often pass it by, but the view from the summit across to the Grand High Tops from an unusual angle is well worth the effort. If climbing up in warmer weather, take plenty of water.

Returning to your packs, continue south along the track towards the Grand High Tops for 500m to a junction with the end of the Goulds Circuit track on the left. Drop packs again and complete the circuit (about 3.5km of steep ups and downs) as it heads back north over the rocky outcrops of **Macha Tor** and **Febar Tor**. When you meet the Grand High Tops track once again, follow it back up to the packs. Although this involves some doubling back, the views in all directions are worth the effort.

From the intersection of Goulds Circuit and Grand High Tops tracks, continue south towards the High Tops. The track begins to climb up towards the base of the **Breadknife**, and a bizarre section of paved track, looking like a back-yard barbecue area, continues steeply up for several hundred metres (this is known affectionately by track workers as the 'Yellow Brick Rd'). Just below the towering wall of the Breadknife is a track junction; turn right to reach Balor Hut. From the Pincham car park to here, the route described covers just over 10km.

Balor Hut was built in 1967 by ranger Colin Dow to house track workers. Coonabarabran Bushwalking Club maintains the hut, and it can sleep six people in reasonable comfort. It's often used as a base by climbers in the park. Beware the resident hut rat! He or she is a particularly voracious eater and the little wire hooks dangling from the roof are for hanging food out of harm's way. Bookings for the hut are essential.

ALTERNATIVE CAMP SITES

If you set out a bit later and do all the detours recommended, you'll probably want to stay in Balor Hut. If, however, you're feeling fit and have plenty of daylight, continue to the camp sites at **Nuada Saddle** (2.4km on, at the Bluff Mountain turn-off) or **Ogma Saddle** (4.6km on, at the junction of the Western High Tops and West Spirey Creek tracks).

Day 2: Balor Hut to Danu Saddle

7–8 hours, 15.5km, 930m ascent, 930m descent

Leaving Balor Hut you have two options. You can return to the track junction, continuing along the Grand High Tops track on the eastern side of the Breadknife. The track heads south then turns right (west) at Lughs Wall before passing **Lughs Throne lookout** – from which there are fine views of soaring **Crater Bluff** (1094m) – and continuing to Dagda Saddle. Alternatively, continue southwest down the track behind the hut and along the western side of the Breadknife. The tracks join at Dagda Saddle after about 600m. Doing a complete circuit of both tracks is worthwhile for the views if you have good weather.

From Dagda Saddle, continue west along the Grand High Tops track to Nuada Saddle (1.2km). Dump your packs at the track junction and take the 2.6km return detour to **Bluff Mountain**. This trip is not to be missed;

NEW SOUTH WALES

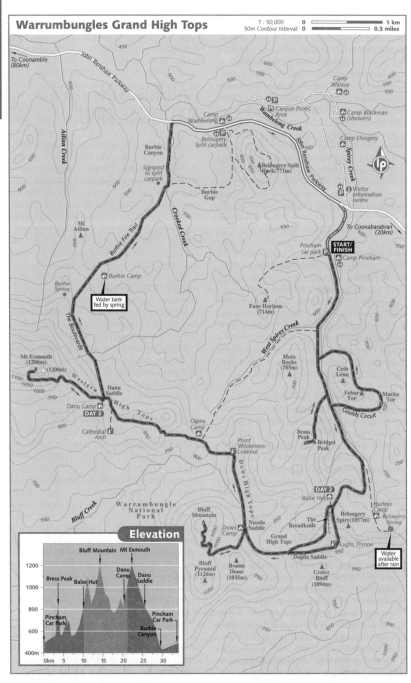

Warrumbungles Grand High Tops

1 : 50,000
50m Contour Interval

0 —————— 1 km
0 —————— 0.5 miles

Elevation

Bluff Mountain   Mt Exmouth

Bress Peak   Balor Hut   Danu Camp   Danu Saddle

Pincham Car Park   Pincham Car Park

Burbie Canyon

1200
1000
800
600
400m

0km   5   10   15   20   25   30

the 360-degree views from the 1200m summit are breathtaking. Further views are to be had by following an indistinct track north a few hundred metres from the summit cairn. Take warm clothes in winter as the summit may be cold and windy. Returning to the packs, head to Ogma Saddle via the Dows High Tops track. The saddle is reached after about 1.5km. The tracks from here to below **Danu Saddle** are not as well defined and maintained as those in the rest of the park.

From Ogma Saddle, continue along the Western High Tops track to Danu Saddle; (do not take the right-hand turn from Ogma, which heads northwest back to Camp Pincham). On the way to Danu Saddle a long section of loose scree and boulders is crossed, as well as a track to Cathedral Arch – a worthwhile side trip giving good views of Bluff Mountain.

At Danu Saddle, several tracks meet. Drop your packs here and take the signposted walk to **Mt Exmouth** (1206m), the park's highest point, about two hours return. The track passes over rocky scree slopes on the north side of the peak, before doubling back to meet the summit and spectacular views across the park and over to the plains in the west. Return to the camp site at Danu Saddle (total distance just over 5km).

Day 3: Danu Saddle to Pincham car park via Burbie Canyon
2½–3 hours, 8.5km, 100m ascent, 400m descent

Pick up the old 4WD track from Danu Saddle and head north for 2.4km to Burbie Camp, where spring water may be available from a tank. Head northeast along the sandy 4WD track to the signposted walking track to **Burbie Canyon**. Walk through the pleasant narrow canyon, where kangaroos

and emus are commonly seen, to the sealed road just west of Camp Wambelong. Turn right and head on to Pincham car park (about 4km further).

BARRINGTON TOPS NATIONAL PARK

Home to some of NSW's highest and wildest country, Barrington Tops National Park is the centrepiece of a complex of parks, reserves and state forests that cover more than 1000 sq km between the upper Hunter Valley and the mid north coast. The Barrington Tops Plateau, part of which this walk explores, is a 100-sq-km area entirely above 1400m elevation. Walkers are attracted to the plateau's peaceful snow gum woodland, intriguing subalpine swamps and its seemingly endless views: the Barrington country rises dramatically from surrounding farmland and its highest peak, Brumlow Top, crowns the park at 1586m. Predictably, given this altitude, the plateau is subject to rapidly changing weather. Damp, misty days, high rainfall, heavy frost and snowfalls are all part of the package.

The park is in the southernmost component of the 3665 sq km Central Eastern Rainforest Reserves of Australia (CERRA) World Heritage Area, declared in 1986 and extended in 1994.

ENVIRONMENT
The Barrington Plateau is a remnant of the vast lava sheet created in the millions of years after the break-up of the southern supercontinent Gondwana. It's one of only a few examples of these lava flows remaining;

BARRINGTON BADDIES

Barrington Plateau walkers can't help but notice the overbearing presence of Scotch broom, a heavily seeding weed that's spread by park visitors both desirable (outdoor-loving humans) and undesirable (feral pigs). Broom is regularly seen in dense thickets, which provides shelter to pigs. Park authorities are doing their best to control both: the pigs through trapping and other measures; the broom through trackside spraying and various biological controls. The casual observer would judge that the broom is winning the battle.

The discovery of the root-rot fungus *Phytophthora cinnamomi*, scourge of conservation managers in several Australian states, has prompted the closure of a large portion of the plateau, including two of the area's better walking tracks – the Watergauge Trail and Brumlow Creek Track. It's expected that the *Phytophthora* exclusion zone will be in place for some time.

the others – including the Dorrigo Plateau (p119) – form the main parts of the CERRA World Heritage Area. This is the highest region of NSW outside of Kosciuszko National Park, and much closer to the coast.

The steep eastern escarpment of the Barrington country forces moist easterlies to drop more than 1500mm rain each year in this area, which in combination with rich volcanic (basalt) soils provides excellent conditions for the subtropical, warm temperate and cool temperate rainforest found in damp areas throughout the park. Tall eucalyptus forests fill in the gaps at all altitudes, with subalpine grasslands and swamps a feature of the high plateau.

PLANNING

Many – not all – of the plateau's walks are on 4WD tracks and, especially on weekends and during summer and Easter school holidays, you can expect to see a few cars. Plateau tracks are closed to 4WDs from 1 June through 30 September and, while midwinter is the coolest time for walking, with heavy frosts and snowfalls fairly commonplace, the absence of cars is a bonus. If walking through the cold months you must bring a full suite of winter clothing and shelter. Even in summer, cool changes can bring very low temperatures to the park.

When to Walk

While walking in the Barrington presents no real difficulties, inexperienced walkers should be careful to check the weather forecast before setting out, especially during midwinter.

Maps

The CMA 1:25.000 topographic maps *Moonan Brook* and *Barrington Tops* cover the area of the walk. Both are somewhat out of date, particularly the Barrington sheet. The LPINSW/NPWS 1:100,000 *Barrington Tops National Park Tourist Map* is useful for planning. The NPWS free visitor guide *Barrington Tops National Park and adjacent reserves* has an overview map and information; NPWS's *Barrington Tops National Park Guidebook* ($10) provides greater depth in all aspects. John and Lyn Daly's *Take a Walk in a New South Wales National Park Sydney to Port Macquarie* includes notes on several walks in the area.

Information Sources

The **NPWS Gloucester office** (☎ 6538 5300; 59 Church St) is open during business hours and has a small selection of guides and brochures. Rangers will usually have a good idea of track conditions in the Tops.

BARRINGTON TOPS PLATEAU EXPLORER

Duration	3 days
Distance	39km
Difficulty	easy–moderate
Start/Finish	Barrington Tops Forest Rd near Polblue Swamp
Nearest Town	Gloucester (below)
Transport	private

Summary Easy tracks lead walkers past snow grass plains, subalpine forests, sphagnum swamps and stunning views.

Easy walking and blissful peace and quiet await walkers traversing the Barrington Tops Plateau. Tracks are wide and well marked, and there are several flat and comfortable camping areas with lots of space for larger-than-usual groups. Crisp mornings, swirling mountain mists and a subalpine landscape combine to provide a very different NSW north-coast walking experience.

NEAREST TOWN & FACILITIES
Gloucester
☎ 02 / pop 2650

Gloucester lies just east of the Bucketts, a range of rocky hills that are said to derive their name from the Aboriginal word 'buccans', meaning 'big rocks'. This is a fertile valley and Gloucester has long been a centre for beef, dairying and logging. The **Gloucester visitor information centre** (☎ 6558 1408; 27 Denison St) is open seven days.

SUPPLIES & EQUIPMENT
Basecamp Warehouse (☎ 6558 1444; 36 Church St), in Gloucester has a very limited range of gear. If you're driving up from Sydney, **Raymond Terrace Camping World** (☎ 4983 1910; Pacific Hwy), about 100km south of Gloucester, has a full range of fuels and gear.

SLEEPING & EATING
Gloucester Holiday Park (☎ 6558 1720; www.gloucesterholidaypark.com; Denison St; unpowered/powered sites

for 2 $8/19, bunkroom $15, cabins $40-64), has loads of choices and is an easy walk from the town centre.

The **Roundabout Inn** (☎ 6558 1816; Church St; s/d $50-60) has small and tidy rooms and a brasserie on location.

Bucketts Way Motel (☎ 6558 2588; www.bucketts .com; 19-21 Church St; d $81) at the north end of the main street has larger comfortable rooms and a restaurant (mains $20 to $30).

The eating choices in town are limited, with the Broadaxe bistro in the **Avon Valley Inn** (☎ 6558 1016; 82 Church St; ☽ dinner Tue-Sun) and the **United Chinese Restaurant** (☎ 6658 2222; 32 Denison St; ☽ dinner Tue-Sun) towards the top of the list.

Foodworks (☎ 6558 1405; cnr Church & King Sts) is the better of the town's two supermarkets.

GETTING THERE & AWAY

Gloucester is about 330km from Sydney. Go north on the freeway and, at its northern end, continue on the Pacific Hwy, following signs to Hexham and Raymond Terrace. Turn right onto Bucketts Way about 20km north of Raymond Terrace and follow for 80km to Gloucester.

Countrylink (☎ 132 232) runs three rail services daily through Gloucester; the one-way fare is $28.

Polblue Camping Ground

These are the nearest sites to the start of the walk, just 2km west on the Barrington Tops Forest Rd. Polblue has toilets and fireplaces; an easy circuit walk around Polblue Swamp begins at the camping area. There are no fees.

GETTING TO/FROM THE WALK

From Gloucester, go north on Thunderbolts Way to Barrington. Just west of the Barrington River, continue straight ahead on the Scone Rd when Thunderbolts Way goes right to Walcha. Continue for 59km on Scone Rd/Barrington Tops Forest Rd (just over 40km on gravel) to the Barrington Trail turn-off, to the left. Park down near the sign and picnic table.

Barrington Outdoor Adventure Centre (☎ 6558 2093; www.boac.com.au) will collect walkers from Gloucester station and provide a shuttle to the Polblue area for $250 return. The vehicle fits up to 10 walkers. If you arrive late, you can camp at Adventure Centre, about 1km

north of Gloucester; sites for two people are $20, with access to showers, toilets and kitchen facilities.

THE WALK
Day 1: Barrington Tops Forest Rd to Junction Pools Camp Site

3–4 hours, 13km, 185m ascent, 260m descent

Go past the gate (locked June–September) and continue downhill on the Barrington Trail. It's wide and easy going in pleasant, shady forest. If any 4WDs do come along (on this day or any other) you'll hear them many minutes in advance. Pass the turnoffs to Mt Carson and Mistake Ridge and, at about 3.6km, the Polblue Trail (another route to the Barrington Tops Forest Rd). By now you'll have grown accustomed to the mix of woodland and subalpine grasses, and have seen the first large groves of Scotch broom. There's every chance of seeing brumbies, or at least dodging the remains of their digestive processes.

After a steady climb alongside Polblue Mountain the track descends to a junction. About 800m ahead is Little Murray camp site – quite popular with the 4WD set – while to the right, the Barrington Trail continues towards Junction Pools and Mt Barrington. The track descends for a time before commencing another climb, this time around the western flank of Brumlow Top (1586m). Along the way you'll pass a junction with the walking track that links with Little Murray camp site. There's a long descent and some very pleasant winding through eucalypt forest before the left turn to **Junction Pools camp site** is reached. The last section of the walk passes the first good views of the plateau's open swamplands, birthplace of the Barrington River. Junction Pools camp site is 2km from the turn, set above the river with wonderful views of Edwards Swamp.

Day 2: Junction Pools Camp Site to Careys Peak & Edwards Swamp Return

3½–4½ hours, 13.3km, 255m ascent, 255m descent

This is an easy day, weather depending, to allow plenty of time to explore the Barrington Plateau and (again, weather permitting) some outstanding views. There's also quite a lot to see around Junction Pools and the upper Barrington River, so you'll probably find yourself dawdling through

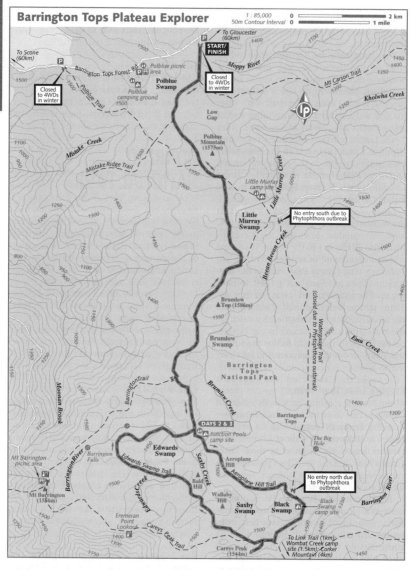

Barrington Tops Plateau Explorer

1 : 85,000

50m Contour Interval

the early part of the day. When you set out, head downhill from the camp site towards the main pool to the south, and about halfway down veer left and rock-hop across the Barrington River (with care if the water is up) to join the Aeroplane Hill trail. The wide track rises steeply at first then smoothly, continuing upwards through peaceful eucalypt forest, usually ringing with bird calls, for about 800m to the summit of **Aeroplane Hill**.

The track descends steadily, passing through some dense stands of dead Scotch broom, then undulates, before eventually giving way to the sedges and sphagnum of **Black Swamp**. On a misty day this is a very atmospheric place, with clouds swirling around surrounding peaks and through the trees lining the swamp. Continue to the junction with the Big Hole trail and go right (just to the left is a gate marking the border of the Phytophthora exclusion zone). The Black Swamp camp site is a short distance along the even wider trail – it's side-by-side walking all the way. About 1.6km along there's a big junction, with the Corker Trail, Link Trail (to Gloucester Tops) and Wombat Creek camp site all straight ahead. Our route is uphill to the right, signposted to Careys Peak. Just 500m on go left at the junction to reach **Careys Peak Hut** (a former walkers' shelter that's now collapsing) and, another 300m on, **Careys Peak** (1544m). If the weather's clear, you'll get one of the best views imaginable, down the steep escarpment and all the way to the ocean. It's a view you can spend a lot of time enjoying.

Return past Careys Peak Hut to the Barrington Trail junction and go left to continue. The track drops away steeply for 300m to the well-disguised junction with the Edwards Swamp trail (there's a cairn on the right and a sign, tucked in the bushes, on the left). Go right, and follow the single-track path down through a snowgrass clearing to another junction about 300m along. (The vague track to the left here leads back to the Careys Peak Trail. If you've plenty of time and are feeling up for an extended walk, you can do an out-and-back from here to either **Eremeran Lookout** – about 6km return – or **Mt Barrington** – about 12km return. Neither has views as good as those from Careys Peak, but the walk does pass through some pleasant forest). Continue from the junction on the Edwards Swamp trail.

The 6km back to Junction Pools provide the best look at the plateau's renowned sub-alpine swamps. The trail passes first **Saxby Swamp** and then **Edwards Swamp**, winding along beside the swamps, climbing forested hills and crossing several small watercourses on the way to the Barrington River upstream of Junction Pools. This was seasonal grazing country in the past and the remains of fence lines and gates attest to the human presence.

Once across the Barrington River, follow the signs to the right and continue along to the Junction Pools track. It's a short walk downhill back to camp from here.

Day 3: Junction Pools Camp Site to Barrington Tops Forest Rd

3–4 hours, 13km, 260m ascent, 185m descent

Return to Barrington Tops Forest Rd via the Day 1 route. For a variation, veer right at the walking track to Little Murray camp site, passed on the way in, which follows the old alignment of the Barrington Trail. This will add just a few hundred metres and less than half an hour to the journey.

DORRIGO NATIONAL PARK

Dorrigo National Park, which protects almost 12,000 hectares of rainforest and tall, moist eucalypt forest, is 600km north of Sydney. Straddling the Great Escarpment on the eastern edge of the Dorrigo Plateau and overlooking the lush Bellinger River valley, the park was added to the World Heritage list in 1986, as part of the Central Eastern Rainforest Reserves of Australia. The region's high rainfall ensures that its main creeks continue to flow throughout the year, with myriad waterfalls cascading through glades of rainforest trees with buttressed trunks and thick hanging vines.

ENVIRONMENT

The park protects a number of different rainforest types. On rich red volcanic soils, a dense subtropical rainforest canopy of strangler figs, black booyongs, yellow carabeens, giant stinging trees and a host of other species blocks out most of the light, leaving the forest floor relatively open. Hanging gardens of climbers, lianas and epiphytic ferns and orchids use the large trees for support to reach the life-giving light in the upper canopy.

On the poorer soils, a simpler but no less beautiful warm temperate rainforest is dominated by coachwood, crabapple, sassafras, soft corkwood and Dorrigo plum. It's this rainforest type that's seen on the Rosewood Creek Circuit. In the highest and coolest northeastern parts of the park a cool temperate rainforest occurs, with Antarctic beech growing in association with coachwood and hoop pine.

Over 120 species of bird have been recorded in the park. Avid bird-watchers come from afar to spot paradise riflebird, regent bowerbird, noisy pitta and green catbird. Brush turkeys and lace monitors cruise around the picnic areas with little fear of visitors. In the late afternoon red-necked pademelons come out to graze the lawn at the Dorrigo Rainforest Centre (below). Later in the evening ringtail and brushtail possums and grey-headed flying-fox feed in the rainforest canopy. Less often seen are sugar gliders, echidnas, potoroos and quolls. In late spring fire-flies and glow-worms make for a magical evening experience while in late summer and early autumn it's possible to see luminescent rainforest fungi.

PLANNING
When to Walk

Any time of the year is suitable for walking in Dorrigo National Park. The region's highest rainfall period is January–March, so summer days are often warm and humid. Due to the altitude, winters can be a little cold in the early morning and at dusk, but the days are usually clear and sunny; the driest months are July–September. It's wise to carry a light waterproof jacket at all times. Insect repellent is useful in the warmer months when mosquitoes and leeches can be a hassle.

Maps & Books

The Rosewood Creek Circuit is covered by the CMA 1:25,000 *Brooklana* map, but it's not really necessary. Maps for the tracks around the Dorrigo Rainforest Centre and the Never Never Picnic Area are available at the Dorrigo Rainforest Centre (see below). Tyrone Thomas's *50 Walks: Coffs Harbour and Gold Coast Hinterland* and John and Lyn Daly's *Take A Walk in a National Park Port Macquarie to Brisbane* include route descriptions of day walks in the park.

Information Sources

The **Dorrigo Rainforest Centre** (☎ 6657 2309; Dome Rd), which doubles as the NPWS Dorrigo Plateau area office, has excellent displays about the natural and cultural heritage of the rainforest. Staff can advise you of track conditions, weather reports and answer questions about the rainforest. The Centre sells various books and souvenirs and includes a café.

Permits & Regulations

Stay on the tracks to avoid erosion and damage to the ground vegetation. Dorrigo National Park has no camp sites (although bush camping is allowed in the more remote parts of the park).

Guided Walks

During school holiday periods NPWS rangers conduct short guided walks, including informational jaunts such as spotlight tours and bird-watching from the Dorrigo Rainforest Centre. **Hinterland Tours** (☎ 6655 2957; www.hinterlandtour.com.au), a local tour company with Ecotourism Australia accreditation, conducts guided day walks in the park and extended walking tours in more remote national parks in the region.

ROSEWOOD CREEK CIRCUIT

Duration	4 hours
Distance	7.5km
Difficulty	moderate
Start/Finish	Never Never Picnic Area
Nearest Town	Coffs Harbour (below)
Transport	private
Summary	A relatively easy circuit walk through the Never Never section of the World Heritage–listed Dorrigo National Park, through warm temperate rainforest and moist eucalypt forest.

The walk follows a well-maintained circuit through the subtropical rainforest. The forest here is dominated by coachwood trees. It's a relatively easy walk, but a steep section near the pretty Cedar and Coachwood Falls gives it a moderate grading.

NEAREST TOWNS & FACILITIES
Coffs Harbour

☎ 02 / pop 60,000

Coffs Harbour is the biggest town between Newcastle and the Gold Coast, and the nearest access point to Dorrigo National Park with good transport connections – it has excellent bus and train links and an airport with several flights daily from Brisbane and Sydney. Coffs has a good range of shops, supermarkets and plenty of accommodation. The **Coffs Harbour visitor information centre** (☎ 1300 369 070, 6652 1522; www.coffscoast.com.au; cnr Grafton & McLean Sts) is near the town centre.

SUPPLIES & EQUIPMENT
Coffs Harbour Camping World (☎ 6651 9088; 73 Grafton St) is central and stocks a wide range of camping fuels and other necessaries.

SLEEPING & EATING
The visitor information centre can assist with accommodation inquiries and bookings. Coffs is a big holiday centre and, outside school holiday periods, finding a site or a bed is not a problem.

Park Beach Holiday Park (☎ 6648 4888; www .parkbeachholidaypark.com au; Ocean Pde; unpowered/ powered sites for 2 $32/40, cabins $94-190) is close to the ocean and has plenty of sites.

Coffs Harbour YHA (☎ 6652 6462; coffsharbour@ yhansw.org.au; 51 Collingwood St; dm/d from $25/60) has sparkling clean rooms plus bike and surfboard hire.

Aussitel Backpackers Hostel (☎ 6651 1871; www .aussitel.com; 312 Harbour Dr; dm/d $22/55) offers free canoes and an Internet café.

Ocean Palms Motel (☎ 6652 1264; www.ocean palmsmotel.com.au; cnr Park Beach Rd & Ocean Pde; s/d from $65/69) has a pool and a charming South Seas feel.

The Jetty on Harbour Dr is Coffs' best destination for alfresco evening meals; the city centre is fine during the day for coffee and lunch.

Foreshores Café (☎ 6652 3127; 394 Harbour Dr; mains $6-20; ☻ breakfast & lunch) does huge breakfasts (including snazzy French toast) on its terrace.

Maria's Italian Restaurant (☎ 6651 3000; 368 Harbour Dr; mains $9-15; ☻ lunch & dinner) is an old-fashioned Italian place with a family-friendly menu featuring pizza and spaghetti bolognaise.

Fisherman's Co-op (☎ 6652 2811; 69 Marina Dr; ☻ daytime) at the nearby marina, sells fresh fish right off the boats. Home-made gelato is available and there's a nice picnic area.

GETTING THERE & AWAY
Coffs Harbour Airport is just south of town. **Virgin Blue** (☎ 13 67 89; www.virginblue.com.au) and **QantasLink** (☎ 13 13 13; www.qantas.com.au) operate flights between Coffs and several state capital cities. **Sunshine Express** (☎ 13 13 13; www.sunshineexpress.com.au) flies to Brisbane.

Buses leave from a shelter adjacent to the information centre. **Greyhound Australia** (☎ 13 14 99; www.greyhound.com.au) runs several services a day to Sydney, Brisbane and

points beyond. **Premier Motor Service** (☎ 13 34 10; www.premierms.com.au) has similar runs. Local operator **Kean's** (☎ 1800 625 587) runs to Bellingen, Dorrigo and inland cities such as Tamworth and Armidale.

Countrylink (☎ 13 22 32; www.countrylink.info) goes north to Casino (where the train used to branch off to Byron Bay) and Brisbane ($75, 5½ hours), and south to Sydney ($84, nine hours).

Hostel shuttles meet all long-distance buses and trains. Major car-rental companies are at the airport, or try the 24-hour **Coffs District Taxi Network** (☎ 13 10 08, 6658 5922).

GETTING TO/FROM THE WALK
Turn off the Pacific Hwy onto Waterfall Way south of Coffs Harbour, just north of Urunga. Drive through Bellingen and continue west along Waterfall Way, climbing the Great Escarpment and onto the Dorrigo Plateau. About 2km before Dorrigo township turn right onto Dome Rd and follow the signs to Dorrigo Rainforest Centre – there, check the track conditions. Continue along Dome Rd to the Never Never Picnic Area. The walk starts from the picnic area.

THE WALK
The Rosewood Creek Track starts at the southern end of the picnic area, just past a shelter. The track initially follows an old logging road through tall, moist eucalypt forest. Although this area was logged up to the early 1970s there are plenty of magnificent

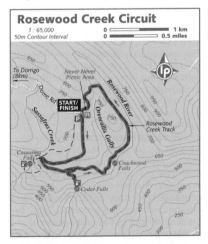

Rosewood Creek Circuit

old-growth eucalypt trees above the regenerating forest. After 1km, at the T-junction, go left and continue for about 800m to the intersection with the side track to **Cedar Falls**. Follow this side track as it descends steeply in a series of switchbacks to a point with a good view of the falls. Continue downwards, past an interesting type of dry rainforest growing on scree. It's possible to have a dip at the base of the falls but take care as the rocks can be slippery.

Retrace your steps back to the main Rosewood Creek Track. Turn right and continue along for another 1km to **Coachwood Falls**. You are now in warm temperate rainforest dominated by coachwood. A deep pool above the falls offers another chance for a swim. Again, take care if approaching the top of the falls.

Continue along the track as it climbs away from Rosewood Creek. After about 2.5km of pleasant walking through warm temperate rainforest, the track returns to the Never Never Picnic Area.

MORE WALKS

BLUE MOUNTAINS NATIONAL PARK
Grose River
The Blue Gum Forest walk (p71) can be extended for another three to four days (about 65km) through this moderate to demanding bush-bash, which follows the Grose River downstream from Blue Gum. It's a challenging but richly rewarding journey through the Grose Wilderness to the Nepean River, finishing near Richmond. There's no track, but navigation is easy because you follow the river. Once in the Grose Valley, the walk beside the river to Richmond is more or less on the flat – actually, slightly downhill. Take the LPINSW 1:25,000 topographic maps *Mount Wilson* and *Kurrajong*.

Katoomba to Kanangra Walls
This scenic four-day (45km) trek starts at the Narrow Neck Plateau and crosses the Wild Dog Mountains to end at spectacular Kanangra Walls (p80) in Kanangra-Boyd National Park. Advanced bushwalking and navigational skills are necessary. The distance and climbing involved make this a tough route. The ascent from Coxs River

to Gangerang Plateau and Mt Cloudmaker is around 700 vertical metres. Take the LPINSW 1:25,000 topographic maps *Katoomba, Jenolan* and *Kanangra*.

Katoomba to Mittagong
This four- to six-day (120km) walk for experienced bushwalkers starts at Narrow Neck and continues to the Coxs River. It's a long and not always terribly interesting haul on Scotts Main Range Rd (a fire trail) to the historic silver-mining town of Yerranderie, and then continues via the Wollondilly and Nattai Rivers to Mittagong. You'll need a swag of maps and a lot of advice: Volume 2 of the NPA's *Bushwalks in the Sydney Region* is a fine starting point. Ask the **NPWS** (☎ 4787 8877; www.nationalparks.nsw.gov.au) about track conditions and surface-water availability before starting.

The Three Peaks
This classic three- or four-day (80km) circuit starts at Katoomba, travels via Narrow Neck and the Wild Dog Mountains to Coxs River, then skirts the Krungle Bungle Range and traverses Mt Guouogang (1291m), Mt Paralyser (1155m) and Mt Cloudmaker (1164m) to finish at Kanangra Walls. It's difficult and you'll need to be fit and have complete confidence in your bushwalking and navigational skills. Take the LPINSW 1:25,000 topographic maps *Katoomba, Jenolan* and *Kanangra*.

KOSCIUSZKO NATIONAL PARK
Mt Jagungal Circuit
A popular and scenic southern route to Mt Jagungal, over five to six days, starts at Guthega Power Station – about 37km from Jindabyne along the Kosciuszko and Island Bend Rds). The route heads north up the Munyang River valley and heads past Schlink Pass and Valentines Hut to climb the prominent summit of Mt Jagungal (2061m). The return route crosses the heads of the Geehi and Valentine Rivers to Mawsons Hut, then traverses the Kerries – some of the most picturesque walking in the Australian Alps – before climbing Gungartan (2061m). Use the Department of Lands 1:25,000 *Geehi Dam* and *Jagungal* maps. Jindabyne is a handy base for this walk, where bushwalker shuttle services can be organised (see Getting Around, p86).

Cascade Hut

This 20km out-and-back walk (five to six hours) passes through a diverse range of scenic mountain country, from open plains to forested glades, highlighted by a visit to an old mountain hut. The walk begins at a point 300m east of Dead Horse Gap on the Alpine Way. Cascade Trail climbs through the lower reaches of Boggy Plain to reach the crest of the Great Dividing Range 4km from the start. The trail then dips into the western end of a long snow plain, from where Cascade Hut can be found 1km up the valley. The best map is the Department of Lands' 1:25,000 *Chimney Ridge*. Thredbo, 4km east of the starting point, is the nearest town. A shuttle can be organised to get you to the trailhead (see Getting Around, p86).

THE BUDAWANGS
The Castle via Kalianna Ridge

It's possible to climb The Castle (p99) in a tough day walk from Kalianna Ridge. Access is via the Yadboro Rd. Continue west from the Pigeon House turn-off (p104) and go right onto the Long Gully Rd past Yadboro Flat. Start and finish at the Long Gully car park, and carry sufficient water and plenty of food. The 10km to 11km return walk takes about 10 hours and includes nearly 800m of climbing – expect to come back pretty tired.

Take either the Budawang Committee 1:50,000 *The Northern Budawang Range and the Upper Clyde River Valley Sketch Map* or CMA 1:25,000 topographic map *Corang* – preferably both. For more information contact the NPWS **Nowra office** (☎ 4423 2170) or **Ulladulla office** (☎ 4454 9500).

DEUA NATIONAL PARK
Big Hole and Marble Arch walk

Deua is 1220 sq km of rugged NSW south coast escarpment and tablelands. About a third of the park is included in two large wilderness areas. The northwestern section of the park is a karst (limestone) landscape with 400-million-year-old caves, and walkers can see the Big Hole and Marble Arch without venturing underground.

The walk starts at Berlang camp site and goes first to Big Hole. From Big Hole, follow the track below the viewing platform downhill. From the base of the hill the walk is undulating and easy until the sharp

descent into the Marble Arch. There are bands of marble in the canyon walls, which are beautifully decorated with ferns in shadier parts. The return walk is 13km and takes about five to six hours. Berlang camp site is 35km south of Braidwood, on Krawarree Rd. For more information contact the NPWS **Narooma office** (☎ 4476 2888; cnr Field St & Princes Hwy).

MUTAWINTJI NATIONAL PARK
Homestead Gorge Trail

People visit Mutawintji, in far western NSW near Broken Hill, and come away changed. The park covers much of the Byngango Range and the lands around Mt Wright Creek. Custodians of these lands are the Malyankapa and Pandjikali Aboriginal people. The park was returned to its traditional owners in 1998. The land, waterways and resident plants and animals are associated with Dreaming stories and a cultural heritage that survives to the present day. Mutawintji visitors usually go with Aboriginal guides to see rock art and other sites. The park office in **Broken Hill** (☎ 08-8080 3200) has more details. The Homestead Gorge Trail is one of several walks in the parks. It covers 8km and usually takes about three hours, passing the cliffs of Homestead Creek before entering the Homestead Gorge.

LORD HOWE ISLAND
Mt Gower

Inscribed on the World Heritage list in 1982 for its remarkable plants, birds, marine life and exceptional natural beauty, Lord Howe Island is a remnant volcano off the NSW coast and unquestionably a unique destination. Once you've paid for the flight to the island and your accommodation (see www.lordhoweisland.info), tackle the eight-hour return trek up 875m Mt Gower. There's no other walk like it in Australia and few in the world. You'll see magnificent rainforest, take in dizzying views – the mountain rises literally straight out of the ocean – and can top it off (if visiting during cooler months) by calling out to get providence petrels to land at your feet. You must walk with a guide. It'll be a trifling charge compared to what you'll have already spent. And whatever you spend, it'll be worth it.

OXLEY WILD RIVERS NATIONAL PARK
Long Point to Wollomombi

Oxley Wild Rivers covers a spectacular wilderness area on the fringe of the New England Plateau. This is an unmarked route, which most walkers take two to three days to cover in the north of the park. It begins on the park's Michaeliana Walk at Long Point then descends to the Chandler River and follows the gorge upstream. You leave the river and follow the steep Chandler Track back up to the Wollomombi visitor area – a 33km trip. Private vehicle drop-off and pick-up needs to be arranged. Contact the NPWS **Armidale office** (☎ 6776 0000) for information on topographic maps and basic track notes.

Along Kunderang Brook

This tough, five-day walk follows the Bicentennial National Trail from Cedar Creek in Werrikimbe National Park to Georges Junction on the Armidale–Kempsey road. Most of the 75km route is unmarked; it follows Kunderang Brook as it descends to the Macleay River beyond Kunderang East Homestead in Oxley Wild Rivers National Park. This is beautiful and isolated country. The walk includes several watercourse crossings, and steep climbs and descents. Private vehicle drop-off and pick-up needs to be arranged. The CMA 1:25,000 topographic maps *Kemps Pinnacle, Green Gully, Kunderang, Big Hill* and *Carrai* cover the route. Basic track notes are available from NPWS **Armidale office** (☎ 6776 0000).

ROYAL NATIONAL PARK
Waterfall to Heathcote

This station-to-station walk takes in a high sandstone plateau and a creek with fine swimming pools. From Waterfall head down the Uloola Track (a fire trail), which descends to Blue Pools and Uloola Falls. Continue to Heathcote via Uloola Turrets (sandstone boulders) then Karloo Pool. From here follow the Karloo Track up to Heathcote, turning left near the fire station and right at the next two junctions to the train station. Allow four to five hours for this 11km walk. The 1:35,000 *Royal National Park Tourist Map* accurately shows the tracks.

WOLLEMI NATIONAL PARK
Wolgan Valley & Glow Worm Tunnel

For experienced independent walkers, the Wollemi is the place for genuine adventure. NSW's largest wilderness area, it's a spectacular patchwork of winding rivers, gorges and undisturbed forest. Less adventurous walkers can get a taste of Wollemi on a 10km loop from the Wolgan Valley to the Glow Worm Tunnel. You'll need private transport. Drive to Lithgow, head for Mudgee, then take the turn off for Newnes and travel on for just over 27km. The walk follows the old railway corridor from Wolgan Valley colliery to the Glow Worm Tunnel (you'll need a torch and, yes, there are plenty of glow-worms) then returns via the Pagoda Track and Old Coach Rd. The CMA 1:25,000 topographic map *Ben Bullen* map covers the area.

Victoria

Australia's smallest mainland state covers just 3% of the country but it is the proverbial good thing in a small package. Whatever your walking mood, Victoria will almost certainly cater to it: alpine experiences, razorback ridges, peachy-postcard beaches, moody cliffs and forests both thick and thin. You can camp alone on alpine summits or you can snuggle into the freshly pressed bed sheets of a B&B at the end of a day. About the only thing you can't do is suggest that Victoria lacks a diversity of walking experiences.

The Great Dividing Range ends its east-coast journey in Victoria, and though you won't find the range's highest peaks here, you will find its greatest array of walks. At the very tail of the range, rising from the agricultural plains of the Wimmera, there is the rocky heaven of the Grampians, standing like a sandstone wave.

Along the coast, the Great Ocean Road is only now burgeoning into the sort of walking destination such beauty demands. And while you might expect the coast between Australia's two largest cities – Sydney and Melbourne – to be a sprawling mass of humanity, it is as green on the ground as it is on a map. This coast is lined with national parks, including a pair of Victorian parks that are among the country's finest coastal showpieces: Wilsons Promontory and Croajingolong National Parks offer wilderness and wildlife on tap.

Even close to Melbourne you will find surprisingly dramatic landscapes: Werribee Gorge cut deep into the land, Mornington Peninsula bays battered by Bass Strait, and the sharp-ened ridge of the Cathedral Range.

HIGHLIGHTS

- Witnessing nature's resilience as **Wilsons Promontory** (p175) sprouts anew from the ashes of a bushfire
- Balancing atop the knife-sharp ridge of the **Cathedral Range** (p135) as you head for the lyrebird-inspired Farmyard
- Emerging from farmland and bush onto castaway **Milanesia Beach** (p143) on the Great Ocean Walk Highlight
- Watching sunset light from atop **Mt Difficult** (p152) in the Grampians
- Conquer the highest mountains in the **Victorian Alps** (p155) with their exposed peaks, pretty snow plains, rocky crags and tall forests
- Seeing wildlife and a wild coast as you walk the beaches of **Croajingolong National Park** (p180)

■ TELEPHONE CODE: 03 ■ www.parkweb.vic.gov.au ■ www.visitvictoria.com

ENVIRONMENT

Victoria is like greater Australia in microcosm, with desert-like landscapes in its west, extensive stands of temperate rainforest in the east, mountains in between and strings of beaches along the length of the coast. The southern reaches of the Great Dividing Range, which runs east to west through Victoria, buffer the north of the state from rain and cold southerly winds, producing drier and warmer conditions and places such as Big Desert and Little Desert.

Sixteen landform and vegetation regions are recognised in Victoria, ranging from the semiarid mallee in the northwest, to grassy woodlands on the western plains, to tall, wet forests with pockets of temperate rainforest in the highlands and eastern coastal areas. The wetter forests of the south contain the tallest hardwoods in the world – a tree on the Watts River, a tributary of the Yarra, was measured at 132.6m in 1872, and is still listed by Guinness as the tallest tree ever recorded (the area is now closed as catchment, so the tree may still be standing).

Victoria has a decent share of the national wildlife, with pretty much all of the pin-up creatures found here. Koalas are common in some of the heavily wooded areas of the south, while platypuses and wombats are widespread throughout the state. Grey kangaroos are common in cleared lands adjacent to bushland, and especially around the Grampians, though red kangaroos are

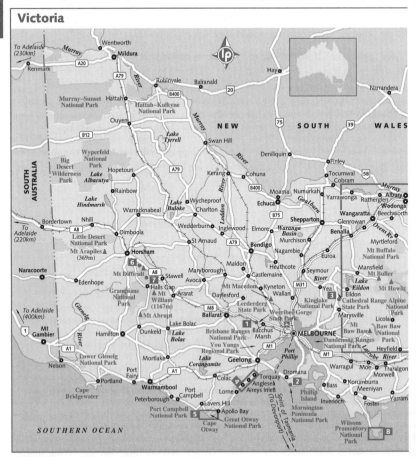

Victoria

found only in the mallee country, outside of the areas covered in this chapter.

INFORMATION
When to Walk
Like much of southern Australia, the most comfortable walking times are spring and autumn, though Victoria is a perennial – there is a walking track somewhere here that beckons at any time of year. In summer the Victorian Alps are at their best, yet it is almost too hot in the state's other great range, the Grampians. In winter the rugged coast is at its most powerfully impressive, with storms in Bass Strait lashing the coast. You might get wet, and it might be windy, but it will be a scene worth witnessing.

Maps
State-wide road maps are easily obtained at specialist map shops, bookshops and news-agents. Topographical maps for walkers are published by the state government's mapping agency, Geospatial Information, in the Vicmap series. All but the far northwest corner is covered at 1:25,000, while several Outdoor Leisure Map sheets (also Vicmap) focus on popular areas (at various scales) such as the Grampians, Wilsons Promontory, Cathedral Range and the Great Ocean Road. These usually contain some natural history and walking information.

For details of maps covering individual walks, see the Planning section in the introduction to each walk.

Books
Lonely Planet's *Victoria* will be a handy guide as you skip between walks. *Victoria's National Parks*, published by See Australia Guides, makes for good planning material, with sections on each national and state park in Victoria.

State walking guides include *Take a Walk in Victoria's National Parks* by John and Lyn Daly, which contains more than 200 walks in 35 national parks; Tyrone Thomas' *120 Walks in Victoria*; *Weekend Walks Around Melbourne* and *Day Walks Around Melbourne* by Glenn Tempest; and *Day Walks Victoria* and *Day Walks Melbourne* by John and Monica Chapman and John Siseman.

Information Sources
For general information on Victoria, its parks and its walks, the following will be of some assistance:

Federation of Victorian Walking Clubs (☎ 9455 1876; http://home.vicnet.net.au/~vicwalk) Peak body for more than 70 walking clubs in Victoria.

Parks Victoria (☎ 13 19 63; www.parkweb.vic.gov.au) Manages Victoria's parks; the website has details of all parks in the state, with links to printable park notes. Phone queries about any park in the state should be directed here first.

Tourism Victoria (☎ 13 28 42; www.tourism.vic.gov.au) Information on general travel around the state.

Victorian National Parks Association (☎ 9347 5188; www.vnpa.org.au) A leading conservation organisation with a very active walks program.

Park Fees & Regulations
Entry fees apply only to three national parks featured in this chapter – Mornington

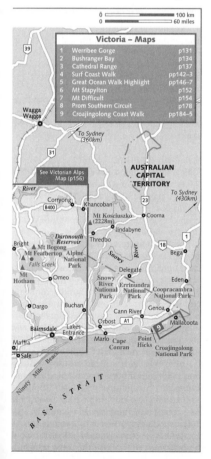

Peninsula, Wilsons Promontory and Mt Buffalo – which makes the National Park Pass ($67.60) useful only if you are planning to visit these particular parks a few times. Annual passes are also available for each of these three parks.

See the Planning sections of individual walks for details of fire restrictions; for information of Total Fire Bans, see the boxed text p24.

Guided Walks

Anaconda Adventures (☎ 03-8720 4013; www .anacondaadventures.com.au) Walks at Wilsons Promontory, the Victorian Alps and the Great Ocean Walk.

Auswalk (☎ 03-5356 4971; www.auswalk.com.au) A selection of walks along the Great Ocean Road, Grampians, Mornington Peninsula, Croajingolong and the Victorian Alps.

Bothfeet (☎ 1300 767 416; www.bothfeet.com.au) Walking tours along the Great Ocean Walk and around Daylesford.

Epicurious (☎ 0407 261 510; www.epicurioustravel.com .au) Sections of the Great Ocean Walk and Great South West Walk.

Parktrek (☎ 03-9486 7070; www.parktrek.com) Walks in Croajingolong, Wilsons Promontory, the Victorian Alps, Great Ocean Road and Grampians.

Walk 91 (☎ 03-5237 1189; info@walk91.com.au) Two-and three-day guided and self-guided walks on the Great Ocean Walk.

GATEWAY
Melbourne

☎ 03 / pop 3.6 million

Australia's second-largest city prides itself, among other things, as being the nation's sporting capital, which usually means sitting and watching somebody else compete. It helps keep the numbers down on walking tracks, at least. Food is the city's other passion, making it an oasis if you have been out on the track eating dried stodge for a few days.

INFORMATION

Information Victoria (☎ 1300 366 356; 356 Collins St) State government bookshop with a good section of bushwalking titles and topographic maps of Victoria and Australia (with laminator). Upstairs, there is a computer for printing out park notes on national parks around the state.

Map Land (☎ 9670 4383; www.mapland.com.au; 372 Little Bourke St) Set among the outdoor stores, with maps of all Victorian walking areas.

Melbourne Visitor Centre (☎ 9658 9658; www.visit melbourne.com; Federation Sq) Good source of information about the city and has a 'Greeter Service', matching visitors to volunteer guides for a half-day walking tour of the city. There is also an information booth (Bourke St Mall) in the city centre.

SUPPLIES & EQUIPMENT

Most of Melbourne's outdoor equipment stores are clustered on Little Bourke St, between Elizabeth and Queen Sts, where boots briefly replace briefcases. In this small stretch you will find **Paddy Pallin** (☎ 9670 4845), **Mountain Designs** (☎ 9670 3354), **Snowgum** (☎ 9600 0099), **Bogong Equipment** (☎ 9600 0599), **Platypus Outdoors** (☎ 9602 3933) and **Pinnacle Outdoors** (☎ 9642 2955). **Kathmandu** (☎ 9642 1942; cnr Bourke & Elizabeth St) is nearby. If you are in a thrifty mood there are clearance stores for **Kathmandu** (421A Smith St) and **Mountain Designs** (412 Smith St) in the inner suburb of Collingwood. Mountain Designs also has a clearance centre upstairs from its Little Bourke St store.

Coles (Melbourne Central, 203-245 La Trobe St) and **Safeway** (cnr Lonsdale & Swanston Sts) supermarkets are both central, while it is almost compulsory to rummage through the produce section at the **Queen Victoria Market** (513 Elizabeth St; ☽ 6am-2pm Tue & Thu, to 6pm Fri, to 3pm Sat, 9am-4pm Sun).

SLEEPING & EATING

Ashley Gardens Big 4 Holiday Village (☎ 1800 061 444; www.big4ashleygardens.com.au; 129 Ashley St, Braybrook; camp site $31-37, cabins $70-146; ☒) has a spacious area 9km northwest of the city. It is reached by bus No 220 from Queen St in the city; get off at stop 33.

Friendly Backpacker (☎ 9670 1111; www.friendly group.com.au; 197 King St; dm $28, d & tw $78; ☐) is large but far from institutional, and is a good place for a hungry walker – there is free breakfast, free pancakes on Sunday morning and free dinner on Tuesday night. Each bed has a locker and individual reading light.

Greenhouse Backpacker (☎ 9639 6400; www .friendlygroup.com.au; 228 Flinders Lane; dm/s/d $29/65/78; ☐) is nearer to the city centre with similar offerings. It has a large, open rooftop area; there are no views but there are sun lounges.

If you want something without any frills or pretensions (and prices to match), try **Kingsgate Hotel** (☎ 9629 4171; www.kingsgatehotel .com.au; 131 King St; economy/standard d $99/129). You'll find discounted rates on the website.

Victoria Hotel (☎ 9653 0441; www.victoriahotel .com.au; 215 Little Collins St; s $50-95, d $70-120; 🐾 💻 🍴) is a Melbourne institution and remarkably good value for the location, just off Swanston St. Rooms have shared or private bathroom.

Hotel Y (☎ 8327 2777; www.hotely.com.au; 489 Elizabeth St; d from $119; 🐾 💻) could redefine your image of the YWCA. Newly renovated, each floor has a different (very bright) colour. It is comfortable and chic and one of the best midrange options in the city. Guests get free use of the gym and pool at the Melbourne City Baths.

Atlantis Hotel (☎ 9600 2900; www.atlantishotel .com.au; 300 Spencer St; d from $140; 🐾) has smart rooms on the west side of the city. There is a coffee bar at reception, and deluxe rooms ($160) have great views over Docklands.

Melbourne's ethnic diversity is reflected in the exhaustive variety of its cuisines. Food is a local obsession and there are people who believe that Melbourne is one of world's great eating cities. Because Melbourne revolves around its CBD less than most other cities, some of the best options are away from the centre, but there are also some excellent choices inside the city.

Hardware Lane, near the outdoor stores, is full of good little eateries: **Invita** (32 Hardware Lane; mains $9-12) specialises in organic vegetarian, and is the spot for nibbling on brown rice balls and vegetarian lasagne; while **aloi na!** (59 Hardware Lane; mains $10-21; 🕑 lunch Mon-Fri, dinner Mon-Sat) ostensibly serves rich Thai food but dabbles in other Asian favourites such as tandoori and nasi goreng.

To sample Melbourne's Middle East you should conversely head west, to the new Docklands precinct and **mecca bah** (55a Newquay Promenade; mains $16-20; 🕑 lunch & dinner) for warming tagines and the house speciality of Turkish pizzas. If you want to glam up a little, head for the sister restaurant **mecca** (☎ 9682 2999; mid-level, Southgate; mains $28-40; 🕑 lunch & dinner).

Chocolate Buddha (Federation Sq; mains $15-20; 🕑 lunch & dinner) specialises in noodles not chocolate (alas) and appeals for its communal Japanese-style dining room.

GETTING THERE & AWAY
Air
Melbourne airport (☎ 9297 1600; www.melair.com.au) is 22km northwest of the city, with some Jetstar interstate flights also arriving at **Avalon airport** (☎ 5227 9100; www.avalonairport .com.au), about 55km from Melbourne. **Qantas** (☎ 13 13 13; www.qantas.com.au), **Virgin Blue** (☎ 13 67 89; www.virginblue.com.au) and **Jetstar** (☎ 13 15 38; www.jetstar.com.au) operate flights between Melbourne and cities across the country.

Skybus (☎ 9335 2811; www.skybus.com.au) operates a 24-hour shuttle service between the city and Melbourne airport ($15, 20 minutes). **Sunbus** (☎ 9689 6888; www.sunbusaustralia .com.au) runs between the city and Avalon airport ($16, one hour).

Bus
Greyhound Australia (☎ 13 14 99; www.greyhound .com.au) buses leave from the **Melbourne Transit Centre** (58 Franklin St) for Adelaide ($55, nine hours), Sydney ($70, 12 hours) and Brisbane ($180, 22 hours). **Firefly Express** (☎ 1300 730 740; www.fireflyexpress.com.au; 261 Spencer St) buses depart from its offices and travel to/ from Sydney ($65, 12 hours) and Adelaide ($55, 10 hours). Buses leave from the Firefly Express office. **V/Line** (☎ 13 61 96; www.vline .com.au) is the main operator for destinations within Victoria. V/line buses depart from **Southern Cross Station** (Spencer St).

Car
Airport Rent-A-Car (☎ 1800 331 033; www.airportrent acar.com.au) is based at Melbourne airport. The following companies, except Apex and Rent-a-Bomb, also have offices at the airport.

Apex (☎ 1800 777 779; www.apexrentacar.com.au; 11 Mareno Rd, Tullamarine) Five kilometres from the airport.
Avis (☎ 9663 6366; www.avis.com.au; 2/8 Franklin St)
Budget (☎ 9203 4844; www.budget.com.au; 398 Elizabeth St)
Europcar (☎ 8633 0000; www.deltaeuropcar.com.au; 89 Franklin St)
Hertz (☎ 9663 6244; www.hertz.com.au; 97 Franklin St)
Rent-a-Bomb (☎ 9335 6777; www.rentabomb.com.au; cnr Mickleham & Freight Rd, Tullamarine) Near the airport.
Thrifty (☎ 8661 6000; www.thrifty.com.au; 390 Elizabeth St)

Train
Long-distance trains operate out of **Southern Cross Station** (Spencer St). **Great Southern Railway** (☎ 13 21 47; www.gsr.com.au) runs the *Overland* to/from Adelaide (seat/sleeper $65/149, 10½ hours) three times a week. **CountryLink** (☎ 13 22 32; www.countrylink.info) connects Melbourne

to Sydney (economy/first class $75/105, 11½ hours, two daily). Victoria's rail network is operated by **V/Line** (☎ 13 61 96; www.vline.com.au). Services are of limited use to walkers, but they can get you near some walks.

MELBOURNE REGION

The High Country, Grampians and Wilsons Promontory may be Victoria's walking diamonds, but you don't need to go far from Melbourne to find a few fantastic walking options. Within 100km of the city you will find a beach that can only be accessed by walkers, a deep, rugged gorge and a knife-point range more akin to something in the Victorian Alps. Public transport links to walking destinations around the city are not great so you had best plan on driving.

WERRIBEE GORGE

Duration	2½–3 hours
Distance	8km
Difficulty	easy–moderate
Start/Finish	Quarry car park
Nearest Town	Melbourne (p128)
Transport	private

Summary Dip into one of the most rugged bits of country near to Melbourne, following a dry ridge down to swimming holes and some easy scrambling along the river.

If you are driving west from Melbourne towards the Grampians, you will notice a gash of rock to the left of the highway just beyond Bacchus Marsh. Hidden beneath is Werribee Gorge, which is up to 200m deep and is one of the most dramatic land features near to the city. The major walk in 575-hectare Werribee Gorge State Park crosses a dry ridge to then meander back through the gorge. The route through the gorge involves some rock hopping and rudimentary scrambling, though a recently installed hand cable has made it a more simple passage. The name 'Werribee' is believed to be derived from an Aboriginal word meaning 'swimming place' and it is a fitting title, with a number of swimming holes to be found along the walk's river stretch. You will find it welcome in a place where the heat can seem greatly magnified.

ENVIRONMENT

The oldest rocks exposed in the gorge are sediments deposited in a sea bed about 450 million years ago. These were folded and bent by upheavals in the earth's crust, evident in the anticlines (arch-shaped fold in rock in which rock layers are upwardly convex) and synclines (basin-shaped fold in rock in which rock layers are downwardly convex) you will see along the route. About three to four million years ago, lava from nearby volcanoes spread across the surrounding lands, creating basalt plains. Unrest along a fault in the earth's crust opened the way for the Werribee River to slice through.

Stringybarks and box gums are the dominant trees of the 250 native species found in the park. Along the river you will find manna gums, with smooth grey-white bark – look out for koalas. The cliffs provide ideal nesting sites for wedge-tailed eagles and peregrine falcons, most likely to be seen during the August to November breeding season. Platypuses also inhabit quiet pools in the river.

PLANNING
When to Walk
The spring display of wildflowers, especially wattles, makes this the best season for this park. Throughout summer, the pools in the gorge are just right for refreshing swims. Camping is not allowed within the park.

Maps & Books
Meridian Productions' 1:35,000 topographic map *Lerderderg & Werribee Gorges* also has a selection of background information.

NEAREST TOWN
See Melbourne (p128).

GETTING TO/FROM THE WALK
Werribee Gorge is around 60km west of Melbourne. Leave the Western Fwy at the Pentland Hills Rd exit, 5km west of Bacchus Marsh, andS turn right at a T-junction along the Pentland Hills Rd, which goes under the freeway. Turn left immediately beyond the overpass. Follow this road for about 2km to another underpass (Werribee Gorge is visible to your left), turning left along sealed Myers Rd and continuing steeply downhill past the park entrance to the Quarry car park (6km from the freeway).

THE WALK

Begin north (past the toilet) from the information shelter, climbing through an old quarry to a disused vehicle track. Turn right here and walk up to the car park at the park entrance.

Go along the sealed road for about 25m and then turn left through a small gate. Follow the clearly defined track through open woodland, climbing onto a ridge and passing the turn-off to the Short Circuit walk. About 100m on, there is a turning to the right to **Eastern Viewpoint**. This lookout gives expansive views across the brown hills to the north, and east towards distant Melbourne. Back on the main track, continue through open forest before swinging left into ridge-top grassland (the You Yangs are visible to the east). From here the ridge begins to fall away to the west; follow it down to the turn-off to **Western Viewpoint** for a peep into the gorge entrance.

Return to the main track and turn right, descending along a narrow spur. Veer left around a rocky point and continue descending. Nearing the river, the track U-turns left, continuing above the **Werribee River** for about 10 minutes before descending to its bank (one hour from the start). High on the right you will see the Falcons Lookout cliffs, a popular climbing wall.

Follow the bank, first through rock fall and then along narrow rock ledges, to the second river bend. Rounding this, you come to sandy **Needles Beach**, the best swimming hole along the river. At the next bend there is a low bluff to negotiate before the river meanders past **Lion's Head Beach**, where there is the prospect of another swim if the one 15 minutes ago hasn't satisfied you.

Past the beach you come to a trickier scramble around a bluff, though a hand cable has eliminated much of its challenge. After this it is a stroll beside (and in) a water channel that was built in 1926–29 to supply water to Bacchus Marsh. After about 15 minutes, pass the Short Circuit walk turn-off to the left and bear right down some steps to **Meikles Point picnic area** (45 minutes from Needles Beach). Go through to the far end of the picnic ground, then left up some steps, walking to the right of the toilets to

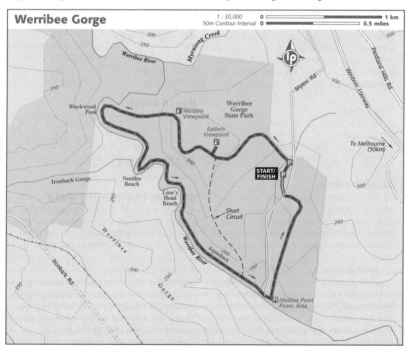

Werribee Gorge

1 : 30,000
50m Contour Interval

0 _____ 1 km
0 _____ 0.5 miles

VICTORIA

MELBOURNE MEANDERS

Melbourne is blessed with good walking almost all the way along its edges. Werribee Gorge, Bushrangers Bay and the Cathedral Range are the pick of the walks, but they are in no way the only options. If you wish to do a bit more walking near to the city, consider the following areas.

Dandenong Ranges

Only 35km from the city, the Dandenong Ranges are one of Melbourne's most popular escapes, cherished for their magnificent forests of towering eucalypts and luxuriant fern gullies. Five areas make up the 3215-hectare Dandenong Ranges National Park – Sherbrooke Forest, on the southern slopes, is the best of them, with its mountain ash forest, fern gullies and plenty of lyrebirds; it can be accessed on foot from Belgrave train station, on the suburban train network.

Macedon Ranges

Block-like Mt Macedon is one of the more striking mountain vistas from Melbourne, and also a good walking drawcard. For one of the longest day outings near the city you can stride out on the Macedon Ranges Walking Trail, which begins in the town of Macedon and makes a 30km loop over Mt Macedon, the Camels Hump and Mt Towrong, easing off in the middle to make a gentle loop around Sanatorium Lake. Macedon can be reached from Melbourne by train.

Woodlands Historic Park

Plane spotters and bushwalkers unite in this area of eponymous woodland and grassland at Melbourne airport's edge. Walks here can take in Woodlands Homestead, city views from Gellibrand Hill and mobs of grazing eastern grey kangaroos. A full circuit of the main features will take about half a day, and you will need your own transport.

Brisbane Ranges

One of the few opportunities close to the city to set out for a few days of walking, the Burchell Walk extends for 39km through the dry bushland of the Brisbane Ranges. The walk begins in the former gold-rush township of Steiglitz and meanders north for three days to Boar Gully. Koalas are prolific in the ranges. A shorter option is to walk into Anakie Gorge on the ranges' eastern side. There is no public transport to the ranges. Fires in February 2006 burned 7000ha around the national park. You'll see much evidence of this as you walk.

You Yangs

An iconic landmark on the city's western horizon, the granite humps of the You Yangs top out at Flinders Peak (348m). The best walk circuits this peak, starting at Turntable car park and swinging around a saddle before looping back. Conclude your walk by taking the track up to the summit of Flinders Peak. The circuit route is 4.5km in length, with the summit climb adding another 3km.

Cape Woolamai

At the southeastern tip of Phillip Island, Cape Woolamai is noteworthy for two things: the pink granite that forms the rugged point, and the migratory mutton birds (short-tailed shearwaters) that arrive here in September each year. To see the best of the cape you can walk a 10km circuit, beginning on Woolamai Surf Beach, and passing the Pinnacles sea cliffs to the cape. The return route crosses inland through the mutton-bird rookeries to Safety Beach. Allow three or four hours.

Coastal Art Trail

The walk you can have without leaving Melbourne, following the shore of the city's exclusive bayside suburbs. The Coastal Art Trail extends for 17km between Brighton and Beaumaris, and is showcased by signboards highlighting the coast's influence on Heidelberg School painters such as Arthur Streeton, Tom Roberts and Frederick McCubbin. The trail can be reached on the suburban train network; stations near the trail are Middle Brighton, Brighton Beach, Hampton and Sandringham.

join a marked track that angles steeply up a spur. Bear left on the crest, then left again to cross a gully and continue on to a sharp road bend. Follow the road for 100m into Quarry car park (30 minutes from the river).

BUSHRANGERS BAY

Duration	3½–4 hours
Distance	13.7km
Difficulty	easy
Start	Baldry Crossing
Finish	Cape Schanck (right)
Nearest Town	Melbourne (p128)
Transport	private

Summary Combines much that is great about Morninqton Peninsula: a secluded beach, Cape Schanck lighthouse and remnants of native bush.

The Mornington Peninsula National Park covers a narrow strip of coast between Point Nepean and the town of Flinders. Along Main Creek it also arrows inland to incorporate Greens Bush, one of the few remaining sections of native vegetation on the peninsula. The walk described here combines these two features of the park – bush and beach – into a great day trip.

For most of the walk's length you follow the Two Bays Walking Track. This coast-to-coast route stretches 26km from Dromana to Cape Schanck, crossing Arthur's Seat en route. Its best section is described here.

If you can't organise a vehicle shuttle at each end of the track, an alternative to the route described here is to begin at Boneo Rd and walk into, and back out from, Cape Schanck. Compensation for the out-and-back nature of this walk is that you get to see its best feature – Bushrangers Bay – twice.

Dieback (see p47) is a problem in Greens Bush, so keep to the defined walking tracks.

PLANNING
When to Walk

Just about any time of the year is suitable for this walk; if you strike a hot summer day you can always cool your feet at Bushrangers Bay (while heeding the swimming warnings). Camping is not permitted in the national park. There are no reliable sources of fresh water along the walk, so carry all you will need for the day.

Maps

Vicmap's 1:25,000 topographic map, *Cape Schanck*, covers the area of the walk and shows most walking tracks. The *Melway* street directory also shows most of the route, barring the final wander into Cape Schanck, and is sufficient for such a well-marked track.

Permits & Regulations

Though there is a $4.10 vehicle entry fee to Mornington Peninsula National Park it io not payable if you park at Baldry Croos ing or Boneo Rd. If you leave a vehicle at Cape Schanck you will need to pay the fee (disguised as a parking fee).

NEAREST TOWN & FACILITIES

See Melbourne (p128).

Cape Schanck

For some moody pre- or post-walk accommodation you can stay in former lighthouse-keeper cottages at **Cape Schanck lighthouse** (☎ 03-5988 6251; www.austpacinns.com.au; d/cottage $120/165), with the lighthouse as your bed lamp and Bass Strait as your backyard pond. The motel-style Inspector's Room is the most modern option, while the oldest cottage, built in 1859, has an open fireplace.

To reach Cape Schanck, turn left at the end of the Mornington Peninsula Fwy and follow Boneo Rd for 12km to Cape Schanck Rd. The car park is 4km along this road.

GETTING TO/FROM THE WALK

The most direct approach from Melbourne to Baldry Crossing is along Mornington Peninsula Fwy. Near its end, take the Jetty Rd exit and continue south to Browns Rd, then Baldrys Rd. Baldry Crossing is about 2km along Baldry Rd, 9km from the freeway.

If driving from Cape Schanck to Baldry Crossing, turn right at Boneo Rd, then left onto Meakins Rd shortly after passing the car park for the walk into Bushrangers Bay. Turn left at the road's end, then quickly left again into Baldrys Rd. The car park is about 2km ahead.

THE WALK

Cross Baldrys Rd from the car park and follow the walking track into the open eucalyptus bushland of **Greens Bush**. Walk beside Main Creek for five minutes, then begin

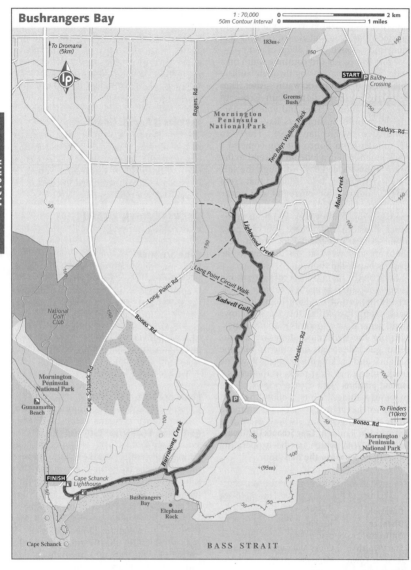

Bushrangers Bay

1 : 70,000
50m Contour Interval

climbing above it. Pass a track junction to the right, cross a bracken-filled side creek on a boardwalk and continue the climb away from Main Creek. Nearing the ridge top, turn left onto Two Bays Walking Track.

Beyond a ridge-top swathe of bracken the track heads back into woodland and some dense clusters of grass trees. Follow the ridge down to ferny **Lightwood Creek** (one hour from the start). Pass a track junction (out to Rogers Rd) on the right, then round a gully and amble above Lightwood Creek and the deeper Main Creek valley once again. Cross the two ends of the Long Point Circuit Walk and pass through a stand of banksias to **Kadwell Gully**. About 1km beyond the gully, with the track crisscrossed by kangaroo superhighways, you emerge onto an open, grassed ridge. You will almost certainly see kangaroos. Boneo Rd is 800m ahead.

Cross Boneo Rd and continue south on a wide, sandy track, passing through banksia thickets and clumps of wattle. After 1km there are glimpses along Main Creek to the ocean; another 1km and you are staring down onto Bushrangers Bay, which is dominated by Elephant Rock. Thirty to 45 minutes from Boneo Rd you come to a track junction. Turn left and descend to the beach at **Bushrangers Bay**. Although the surf may look inviting, bear in mind that cross rips (undertows or currents) can make swimming hazardous. To see the best of the bay, cross Main Creek and head to the beach's eastern end, where you can poke about beneath **Elephant Rock**. From here there are also views across the bay to the Cape Schanck lighthouse.

Back on the main track, cross Burrabong Creek and climb beneath a canopy of tea-tree to the top of the 80m-high cliffs. Set back from the cliffs, the track follows their general line towards Cape Schanck. Nearing the lighthouse there are a couple of good **viewpoints** onto the tip of Cape Schanck and back to Bushrangers Bay. The track emerges at a car park; to the left is a **lookout platform** with clearer views of the previous vantage points. Follow the road down to the main car park (45 minutes from Bushrangers Bay), where there is a basic kiosk. Tours of **Cape Schanck Lighthouse** (adult/child $12/10), which has been operating since 1859, leave on the half-hour.

CATHEDRAL RANGE

Duration	2 days
Distance	18.6km
Difficulty	demanding
Start/Finish	Cooks Mill camp site (p136)
Nearest Town	Marysville (p136)
Transport	private

Summary Discover an isolated walking wonder as you pick along the narrow and rocky ridge of the Cathedral Range, where there is always a view and a few superb lyrebirds.

The Cathedral Range State Park offers the most rugged and rewarding walking near Melbourne, although it doesn't come without some effort. To walk the circuit that is described here, you must be confident about scrambling on rock while carrying a backpack. If you are in any doubt about your ability, consider abbreviating the walk to a circuit of the range's northern end, following the Jawbone Creek Track west from Cooks Mill to the Farmyard, and then following the Day 2 description here. Jawbone Creek Track is steep but it's in no way technical.

The walk described here can be tackled in either direction, though walking clockwise is recommended since the descent from Sugarloaf Peak is more problematic than the ascent.

PLANNING
When to Walk
Avoid midsummer as you will be in the full glare of sun all the way across the ridge. Because of this, you will invariably need to drink more water than you expect, and there may be no resupply at Jawbone Creek, so ensure you have adequate supplies. Spring and autumn are both excellent times to walk, while the Cathedrals can also be a good place on which to break the chill of winter – avoid the ridge, however, if there is the likelihood of rain or mist.

Maps & Books
Vicmap's 1:25,000 topographic map *Cathedral Range* contains some basic walk notes and is a good resource, though the trail from Cooks Mill to Jawbones car park is incorrectly marked. Pick up also the park notes from the Marysville visitor information centre (p136); these show the new trail.

Federation Day Walks, produced by Maroondah Bushwalking Club, may be difficult to find but it contains more than 20 walks in the area, including a couple in the Cathedrals.

Permits & Regulations
Access to the ridge is not allowed on days of Total Fire Ban. Fires are not permitted at the Farmyard (or anywhere along the range), so carry a fuel stove. If you are camping at either Cooks Mill or Neds Gully, firewood collection is banned, so bring any firewood with you.

VICTORIA

NEAREST TOWN & FACILITIES

Buxton and Taggerty are marginally nearer the trailhead, but Marysville offers a far better range of services.

Marysville

☎ 03 / pop 625

If you have been to the Cathedrals isn't the obvious next stop Victoria's one-time honeymoon capital? Marysville is still very much a place people come to swing hands with a loved one. If not that, then for the abundance of king parrots.

The **visitor information centre** (☎ 5963 4567; www.marysvilletourism.com; Murchison St) can supply you with maps and park notes. You will find basic camping supplies at **Marysville Hardware & Auto** (Murchison St).

SLEEPING & EATING

Marysville Caravan & Holiday Park (☎ 5963 3443; 1130 Buxton Rd; unpowered sites for 2 $27-31, powered sites for 2 $29-33, cabins $60-105) is in the centre of town, with the Steavenson River running right through it.

Blackwood Cottages (☎ 5963 3333; www.blackwoodcottages.com.au; 38 Falls Rd; cottages $125-145, spa cottages $160-180) come complete with washing machine, dishwasher and park notes on all the walking options around the area. Ask the helpful and knowledgeable owners for a look at the house copy of *Federation Day Walks*. There are tennis courts also, if you still have some puff left.

Maryton Park B&B Country Cottages (☎ 5963 3242; maryton@bigpond.com; 36 Maryton Lane; d $135) are 5km out of town (towards the Cathedral Range) and overlook a berry garden, nut grove and a lake from which you can pluck your own trout for dinner. There is complimentary port and home-made chocolates in each cottage. The attached **Cumquat Tree Tearooms** (mains $18-30; ☿ lunch Sat & Sun, dinner Fri, Sat, Mon & Tue) draws on the best of local produce, including rib-eye steaks as high as a Cathedral Range escarpment.

Foodworks (Murchison St) has sufficient supplies for a night out on the track, while **Marysville Country Bakery Cafe** (cnr Murchison St & Pack Rd; ☿ 7am-5.30pm) is parrot central and an institution worth walking up an appetite for.

Fraga's café (19 Murchison St; mains $17-25; ☿ lunch Thu-Tue, dinner Fri-Sun) has no parrots and no olde-worlde gimmickry, just a modern menu to be enjoyed in the art-filled dining room or at the outside tables (where you probably will be among the parrots).

Crossways Country Inn (4 Woods Point Rd; mains $18-25; ☿ lunch Sat & Sun, dinner Fri-Sun) picks up the yesteryear slack with fine-china displays, framed Hollywood starlets and candle lighting; a chintzy way to enjoy a chicken parma or roast-of-the-day.

GETTING THERE & AWAY

Marysville is 95km from Melbourne along the Maroondah Hwy (across the magnificent Black Spur). **McKenzie's Tourist Services** (☎ 9853 6264; www.mckenzies.com.au) has a daily bus to/from Melbourne's Southern Cross station ($14, 2½ hours).

Cooks Mill Camp Site

Set among manna gums (keep an eye out for koalas) on the banks of Little River, **Cooks Mill camp site** (per vehicle $11.50) is a large, well-spaced area central to everything in the park. There are two approaches – the shortest is to take Buxton Rd 8km from Marysville (or 3km from Buxton), turning right into Mt Margaret Rd, then forking left onto Cerberus Rd (Cooks Mill is 10km on). This road might not be suitable to 2WD at all times. Otherwise, head north from Buxton on Maroondah Hwy, turning right into Cathedral Lane. Turn right again after 3km into Little River Rd and follow this south to Cooks Mill.

THE WALK

Day 1: Cooks Mill Camp Site to Farmyard

3–4 hours, 8.3km, 520m ascent, 170m descent

Head off from the walking track at the western end of the camp site, winding up St Bernards Track until it enters Jawbones car park (about 30 minutes from Cooks Mill). Turn left and begin the road slog, and a climb of 300m, towards Sugarloaf Saddle (45 minutes to one hour from the car park).

WARNING

The spring below the camp site at the Farmyard is unreliable, especially in late summer and autumn. You should carry enough water for the full two days. If this makes your pack uncomfortably heavy, avoid the section of the walk from Sugarloaf Peak across the Razorback to the Farmyard.

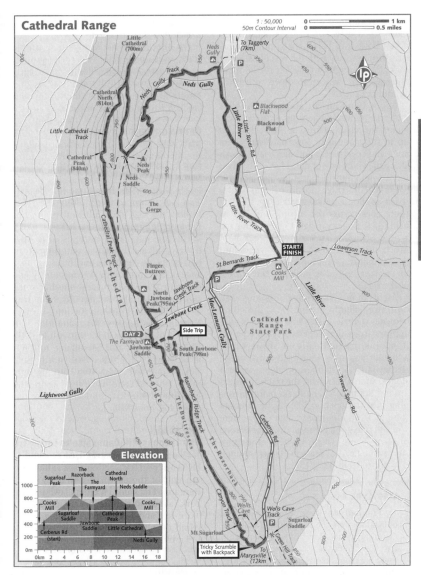

There are good views of the Jawbone peaks early on.

At **Sugarloaf Saddle** turn right onto the walking track, forking almost immediately left onto the Canyon Track. (The right trail ascends through Wells Cave, a more technical route than the Canyon Track, making the final climb along a flake of rock. Wells Cave itself becomes extremely narrow and you won't fit through wearing a backpack.) Skirt a rock outcrop and ascend along the spur, which steepens as you climb. Scramble up through the next fractured line of rock, then continue to the left of the main line of rock. Cut across this below the point at which the rock becomes cliff, and funnel up a narrow break in the rock. This is the most exposed section of the walk, though if you hold your balance it is not particularly difficult. Stay with the weak line in the rock until it angles to the left of the main outcrop. Here, you drop down to a track behind the rock.

About 100m on, an orange arrow on a gum tree points you back up onto the rock. Follow the reliable arrows as the track angles up to the summit of **Sugarloaf Peak**. There are some spectacular and airy views north along the spiky line of the ridge – what you see is what you will have to walk.

Follow the ridge north – it's as knife-sharp as the name **Razorback** suggests. The route goes across the top of, and just in behind, the rocky ridge top, making for a slow, scrambly and enjoyable rock hop. Much of the way there are good views into the agricultural Acheron Valley and, ahead, to the two Jawbones peaks in the middle of the ridge.

After about 30 minutes, as the trail dips away slightly to the west, the going becomes a little easier and the rock disappears from the ridge top. Don't panic; it returns intermittently in about 400m, although you now walk below it through stringybark forest on the ridge's western slopes. Soon afterwards, the track contours around South Jawbone Peak, before dropping into the open saddle of the **Farmyard** (one to 1½ hours from Sugarloaf), where you will find good camp sites, either shaded or open. There is a spring below the camp site, at the head of Jawbone Creek, though it is not reliable (see p136).

SIDE TRIP: SOUTH JAWBONE PEAK
20 minutes, 800m, 70m ascent

From the centre of Farmyard a simple track eases up the hill to the rocky summit of **South Jawbone Peak** (798m). From here, all of the principal features of the ridge – Sugarloaf Peak, North Jawbone Peak and Cathedral Peak – look close. You can also look down on the road you trudged up first thing this morning; it looks much better from afar.

Day 2: Farmyard to Cooks Mill Camp Site
3½–4½ hours, 10.3km, 270m ascent, 620m descent

You can continue north along the ridge (follow the sign for Cathedral Peak), but the more interesting route is to begin along Jawbone Creek Track (signposted to Jawbones car park). After about 100m turn left, crossing the creek and heading up a small gully. In roughly five minutes you'll come to a T-junction (and another small camp site). Dump your pack here and take the right-hand track, crossing through a small clearing and then climbing 50m (steeply at the end) to the summit of **North Jawbone Peak** (795m), about 15 minutes from Farmyard. Drop down to the obvious ledge below the summit for the best views you will get of South Jawbone and Sugarloaf Peaks.

Return to your pack and continue straight ahead, climbing back to the ridge top, where you turn right. About 100m on, a trail drops away to the right towards Neds Saddle – stay on the ridge. At this end of the range the ridge is more gentle than near

---

LIAR, LYRE *Andrew Bain*

The Farmyard takes its name for the resident superb lyrebirds that have taken to imitating the calls of surrounding farmlands. Around this camp site, especially beside Jawbone Creek and on the slopes of North and South Jawbone Peak, the lyrebirds are as visible as they are showy. In five or six walking trips to the Cathedral Range, I have never failed to see one of these gregarious birds. Occasionally, such as one morning on the trail to North Jawbone Peak, there has even been the treat of the ultimate mating display.

This day I heard the lyrebird well before I saw it, mistaking it at first for a whipbird – it was, after all, making the unmistakable cracking call of a whipbird. By the time I spotted it, the male lyrebird was mimicking a kookaburra, strutting about with its gorgeous tail up over its back and head like the fan of a society lady. A few metres away a seemingly uninterested female wandered about the bush. Slowly the male employed every noise it knew – cicadas, cattle, currawongs, other birds. When I left it, the lyrebird had become the ultimate conservationists' nightmare – a bird that knew the sound of a chainsaw. Hardly the thing to impress the ladies, you would think.

Sugarloaf but it still makes for an interesting rock hop.

After crossing a run of high knolls, pass by a second turning to Neds Saddle (about 45 minutes from North Jawbone Peak). Climb on for five minutes to the summit of **Cathedral Peak** (840m). Here, the track drops away on the eastern side of the ridge, although it continues to follow its general line down and to the north. Just before a saddle you come to a third track junction (roughly 30 minutes from Cathedral Peak). Drop your pack again and make the short climb onto **Little Cathedral** (700m), the end of the line so far as tracks go in the Cathedral Range. The view north along the ridge will confirm the knowledge that you have been walking in rugged terrain.

Return to your pack and take the left fork, which contours across the ridge and into Neds Saddle. Take a hard left, onto the track that is signposted 'Neds Gully' (the track to Neds Peak leads to a viewless summit), and descend across the slopes of Neds Peak. After about five minutes the track begins a switchbacking descent. About one hour from Little Cathedral, the track crosses Neds Gully, recrossing its various streams several more times until you reach a T-junction. Turn right – the left turn heads a short distance into **Neds Gully camp site** (per vehicle $11.50) – following the track along the bank of Little River. The valley will seem positively lush (except for the short section of pines) after your hours on the ridge. Around thirty minutes away from the junction, you will arrive back at Cooks Mill.

GREAT OCEAN ROAD

The aptly named Great Ocean Road, stretching between Torquay and Warrnambool, is the popular choice as Australia's most scenic drive. With two very different stretches of coast divided by the death throes of the Otway Ranges, it attracts motorists in herds, but there are a number of walking trails delightfully removed from the heavy tread of this holiday migration.

We have chosen the two prime coastal walks in the region – the Surf Coast Walk and the Great Ocean Walk. For a taste of the damp and lush hinterland there's good walking among the waterfalls behind Lorne (see p186).

HISTORY

The idea for the Great Ocean Road was suggested in 1917 as a way to employ soldiers returning from WWI. A trust was established the following year and the first surveys completed. Construction began near Lorne in September 1919, though it would take 13 years to complete the road and require the labour of around 3000 workers. The road was officially opened on 26 November 1932.

ENVIRONMENT

The Great Ocean Road is a tale of two coasts. Along the Otway Range, at its eastern end, the hillsides are blanketed in thick forest and drained by waterfalls. At its western end, the road concludes in grassy agricultural land and limestone cliffs and stacks such as the Twelve Apostles. The difference is evidenced by rainfall figures – Lorne receives around 200mm more rain per year than Port Campbell. The two walks in this section are on the different sides of the divide.

In December 2005, the former Otway National Park and the Angahook-Lorne, Carlisle and Melba Gully State Parks, as well as some areas of state forest, were incorporated into the new 103,000-hectare Great Otway National Park, increasing the national park area by around 60,000 hectares, and making it the largest coastal national park in the state.

PLANNING

Information Sources

The **Great Ocean Road visitor information centre** (☎ 5237 6529; www.greatoceanrd.org.au; Great Ocean Road, Apollo Bay) is a good starting point. If you are driving along the road from Melbourne to the Great Ocean Walk you will pass right by it. The website has a heap of basic, downloadable maps, including 15 walking maps (the Surf Coast Walk among them).

Guided Walks

Each of the companies listed on p128 offers walking tours along the Great Ocean Road: Auswalk on the Surf Coast Walk and all others on the Great Ocean Walk.

VICTORIA

SURF COAST WALK

Duration	2 days
Distance	32km
Difficulty	easy
Start	Torquay
Finish	Fairhaven
Nearest Towns	Torquay (below), Aireys Inlet (right)
Transport	bus
Summary	Discover the cliffs, beaches and lighthouse at the end of Australia's most famous scenic drive – it's even better on foot.

At the Great Ocean Road's eastern end, the Surf Coast Walk is unlike most other Australian walks because it can be done in comparative comfort. Skipping between holiday towns, it is a great chance to walk without the need to hump your home on your back. Passing over and across some of Australia's most attractive cliffs and beaches, and taking in bushland the Great Ocean Road largely ignores, there is much to recommend the walk over the drive.

The route described here varies slightly from the Surf Coast Walk proper, but is more scenic and more practical to public transport. Gone is the largely uninspiring climb from Fairhaven into Moggs Creek at its end; added as a taster of the coast to come is the section between Torquay and Jan Juc.

PLANNING
When to Walk
This route can be walked at any time. Summer is most popular, with the mixed blessings of warm weather and cooling crowds.

Maps
Though the trail isn't marked, the 1:50,000 Royal Australian Survey Corps' topographic maps titled *Anglesea* and *Torquay* cover the length of the walk. The free *Surf Coast Official Touring Map*, available at the Torquay visitors centre (below), is a necessary complement. It shows a basic outline of the walk and has inset maps of Torquay, Anglesea and Aireys Inlet.

NEAREST TOWNS
Torquay
☎ 03 / pop 8000
The Surf Coast's major town is, shall we say, a little obsessive about its surfing. Here, you will find what is billed as the world's largest surf museum and an entire plaza filled with surf shops. Set into the Surfworld Australia Surfing Museum is the **Torquay visitors centre** (☎ 5261 4219; Beach Rd).

Of the three caravan parks, **Torquay Public Reserve** (☎ 5261 2496; Bell St; unpowered/powered sites for 2 $10/25, cabins $65-120) is nearest to the start of the walk.

Bells Beach Lodge (☎ 5261 7070; www.bellsbeach lodge.com.au; 51-53 Surfcoast Hwy; dm $20-25, d $50-65; 🖳), with its *faux* bathing boxes, hires surfboards if you fancy strutting the waves as well as the coast.

Norfolk Cottage B&B (☎ 5264 8182; 22 Island Dr; d $90-150; 🐾) has stepped from the pages of *B&B Weekly*, with its English country garden, home-made biscuits and plump quilts. The attic is all yours, including the large spa.

Growlers (23 The Esplanade; mains $15-26; 🍴 breakfast, lunch & dinner) has an inventive menu and proximity to the beach. Near the Torquay Surf Beach, **Café Splash** (2/15 Bell St; burgers $9) does all-day breakfasts and a variety of burgers, sandwiches and cakes.

V/Line (☎ 13 99 36; www.vline.com.au) has five daily buses – two on weekends – from Geelong's Transport Mall to Torquay ($5.40, 40 minutes). Return buses run four times a day (twice on weekends).

Aireys Inlet
☎ 03 / pop 1000
Fairhaven, at walk's end, is a residential extension of Aireys Inlet, a town as earthy – at least by Great Ocean Road standards – as its unsealed roads. Pinned to the ground by the Split Point Lighthouse, it is not a place to come on a budget. The cheapest accommodation is at **Aireys Inlet Holiday Park** (☎ 5389 6230; www.aicp.com.au; 19-25 Great Ocean Road; unpowered/powered sites for 2 from $20/22, cabins $65-165; 🐾 🖳).

In Fairhaven itself there is quirky **Ocean Inlet at Fairhaven** (☎ 5289 7313; oceaninlet@bigpond .com; 34 Wybellenna Dr; d $200-250) with a gazebo-style bed-sit with floor-to-ceiling windows overlooking native gardens. A tiny cabin next door contains your kitchenette and bathroom.

On the walk, you will pass two B&Bs: **Cimarron** (☎ 5289 7044; www.cimarron.com.au; 105 Gilbert St; d $125-175, garden flat $150-200; 🐾 🖳), 1km east of Boundary Rd, with a free library of 1000 movies and 3000 books; and **Aireys by the Light** (☎ 5289 6134; 2 Federal St; d $165-265; ⚇), located – surprise, surprise – by the lighthouse. All rooms have ocean view and there's a central spa.

Aireys Inlet Hotel (☎ 5289 6279; 45 Great Ocean Road; mains $15-22) has a beer garden and bistro meals, while **A La Grecque** (☎ 5289 6922; 17 Beach Rd; mains around $25; ⚇ breakfast, lunch & dinner Wed-Sun) is the creation of famed Lorne restaurateur Kosta Talihmanidis, offering fine but informal dining to celebrate the end of a fine walk.

The V/Line buses that serve Torquay (see opposite) continue to Aireys Inlet ($10.40, 1¼ hours from Geelong), also stopping at the Fairhaven Surf Club.

THE WALK
Day 1: Torquay to Anglesea
4–5 hours, 18km

Begin by walking southwest along **Torquay Surf Beach**, at the town's southern end. Past the surf club, turn upstream on the true left (north) bank of Spring Creek to the footbridge, crossing it and following the wide path to the tip of **Rocky Point**, where a set of wooden steps leads down onto **Jan Juc beach**.

Head west along the beach for about 15 minutes, leaving it at the third set of steps, marked 77W. (Avoid the temptation to continue to the steps at the beach's end; these have been partly destroyed by land slips.) Despite the lack of signage, the head of these steps marks the official start of the Surf Coast Walk.

TIME & TIDE

Given perpetual low tide it would be possible to walk almost the full length of the Surf Coast Walk along the beaches. Though this isn't feasible, it is worth coordinating your walk so that a part of each day corresponds with low tide. The best places to aim for low tide are Bells Beach/Southside (Day 1), making it possible to walk below the cliffs from Bells to Point Addis; and Split Point (Day 2), granting you close-up views of Table Rock and its spread of rock pools. Tide times can be checked at www.bom .gov.au/oceanography/tides – Anglesea tides are 30 minutes earlier than at Port Phillip Heads.

From the steps, an obvious trail heads southwest along the cliff tops, climbing slowly with the cliffs and offering views ahead of sloping sandstone headlands. After 20 minutes the trail leaves Jan Juc, swinging inland through heath to meet Bells Blvd at a white, wave-shaped marker denoting the entrance to the Bells Beach Surfing Recreation Reserve.

The path now stays beside the road into the car park, reached about 45 minutes from Rocky Point. Take the first set of steps to **Bells Beach**, which surfers know as a nirvana, and others might know for its starring role in the movie *Point Break,* though for a beach with enormous raps in is surprisingly small.

At low tide you can walk to the beach's end and simply round the headland on its rocky platform. Away from low tide, this route should not be attempted – you could get more than wet, as this section of coast has a wrath that has claimed at least 19 ships. Instead, take the path (not the road) at the obvious gully, crossing the footbridge and climbing back on to the cliffs.

At the Southside car park, five minutes from Bells, you will strike two paths. The sealed path heads down to Southside Beach. Follow instead the gravel track, which eventually meets Jarosite Rd near the crest. Walk on the road verge for about 200m, until just past a sign for Ironbark Basin, and turn left at the narrow path into the heath.

Soon you will come to a vehicle track and a confusing web of paths. Go virtually straight on, beside the sign for the Jarosite Track, and drop to an unexpected **dam**, its waters as brown and viscous as liquid chocolate. This is followed by another mess of signs; stay with the Jarosite Track as it heads uphill and inland.

Near the top of the hill, through grass trees as prolific as lawn, you reach a T-junction. Turn left, following the 'Car Park' sign. Here, the vegetation thins, opening up views across the top of the Ironbark Basin to pencil-sharp Point Addis.

Twenty minutes from the dam, and 100m before the Ironbark Basin car park, turn left on to Ironbark Track, descending back to the cliff tops through the eponymous ironbarks with their furrowed bark. At the cliff edge (a tiger snake breeding ground) turn right, staying on Ironbark

VICTORIA

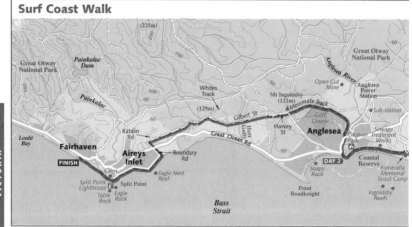

Surf Coast Walk

Track and coming almost immediately to a lookout across unstable cliffs that resemble melted wax.

The track ascends behind these cliffs, veering right at the Koori Cultural Walk, then left again after about 200m. This path ends at Point Addis Rd; turn left and follow the road to the point (45 minutes from the start of the Ironbark Track).

Point Addis offers views the virtual length of the walk, back to Jan Juc and west to Split Point Lighthouse. Take the track at the car park's western edge, winding down to the beach, which is cleaved by a rocky spit. At the spit, turn up the creek to a set of steps, walking up and away from the coast and into a stand of she-oaks. Follow the cliff tops past the Eumeralla Scout Camp to the Anglesea River in **Anglesea** (1¼ hours from Point Addis).

ANGLESEA
☎ 03 / pop 2200

The first point at which the Great Ocean Road actually touches the coast, Anglesea stakes much of its celebrity on the kangaroos that famously graze its golf course.

The **Anglesea Beachfront Family Holiday Park** (☎ 5263 1583; www.angleseafcp.com.au; Cameron Rd; sites $26-35, cabins $76-152; 💻) offers the most practical camping – it is the first thing (after the sewage works) you come to in town. **Anglesea Backpackers** (☎ 5263 2664; angleseabackpacker@iprimus.com.au; 40 Noble St; dm $20-23, d $60-70; 💻) is run by a surfer but welcomes walkers.

The **Anglesea Motor Inn** (☎ 5263 3888; www.angleseaoz.com; 109 Great Ocean Road; d $110-240; ❌ 🐾), overlooking the river, is only a few metres off the trail, while you need only cross the river to find **Anglesea Rivergums B&B** (☎ 5263 3066; anglesearivergums@bigpond.com; 10 Bingley Pde; d $100-140; ❌), with river views and a cloud-soft bed to prepare you for another day of walking.

Angahook Cafe & Stores (119 Great Ocean Road) is a combination restaurant/gourmet deli/grocer that will fit most catering needs. The salmon steaks at the **Surfing Albatross** (89 Great Ocean Road; mains $16-21; 🕐 breakfast, lunch & dinner) will make you forget you are supposed to be doing it rough, while the menu at **Rose Chinese Restaurant** (65 Great Ocean Road; mains $17-25) resembles an electoral roll.

Day 2: Anglesea to Aireys Inlet
3½–4 hours, 14km

Finding the path out of Anglesea is about the Surf Coast Walk's greatest difficulty. Head upstream on the Anglesea River's true right (west) bank, crossing the Great Ocean Road and continuing into Coogoorah Park. When you draw level with the playground's wrecked ship, go left up the embankment (it won't feel right, but it is) to meet an unsealed road. Take the sandy foot track straight ahead, following the power lines. A wire fence will gradually separate you from the lines, but at the break in the fence, head through and back to the rubbly road under the lines.

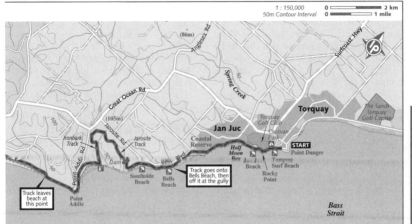

After about 500m, the lines kink to the right. Take the smaller track to the left, then turn immediately right to join a narrow path contouring above Anglesea. This is one of the walk's best stretches: ahead, you will see the road to Mt Ingoldsby – your guiding line – and below, you might snatch glimpses of the golf course's kangaroos.

After 10 minutes you ascend to the Messmate Track, turning left amid less inspiring views of an open-cut coal mine. The Messmate Track climbs in ever-steeper steps to **Mt Ingoldsby** (121m), one hour from Anglesea, from where you will have a view of Anglesea that is blotted by the mine and the belching substation.

Turn right at the summit onto unmarked Harvey St, veering left after 10 minutes onto (also unmarked) Gilbert St, rejoining the power lines – grow to like them, they are with you until Aireys Inlet.

Gilbert St drops steeply into and out of reedy **Hutt Gully**, then meanders towards Aireys. At Boundary Rd, 1¼ hours from Mt Ingoldsby, turn left, crossing the Great Ocean Road and continuing to the car park at Boundary Rd's end.

From the car park, you have a choice between spectaculars. At low tide, you can descend to the beach and round Split Point from below, threading between the headland and fez-shaped **Table Rock**. Otherwise, follow the cliff path, with its frequent views, to reach **Split Point Lighthouse** in about 30 minutes. Built in 1891, the 'White Queen',

as the lighthouse became known, is open to visitors just one day a year.

Round the lighthouse and follow the path signed 'Inlet & Beach', passing a **cairn** that marks the graves of two settlers. Joining the beach where it blocks Painkalac Creek, the final sandy stroll to the surf club at Fairhaven takes about 15 minutes.

GREAT OCEAN WALK HIGHLIGHT

Duration	3 days
Distance	43km
Difficulty	moderate
Start	Johanna Beach car park
Finish	Glenample Homestead
Nearest Towns	Lavers Hill (p144), Princetown (p145)
Transport	shuttle service

Summary Sample the country's newest long-distance trail, seeing some of the Great Ocean Road's little-known beauties and ending beside its showstopper, the Twelve Apostles.

By its very name, the Great Ocean Walk makes clear its intention to become one of the most famous names among Australian walking tracks, coupling itself to the fame of the Great Ocean Road.

Completed in January 2006, the full trail extends from Apollo Bay to Glenample Homestead, adjacent to the Twelve Apostles, a distance of 91km. The section described here covers the most remote and dramatic piece of the track, along beaches and cliffs that most people don't know exist since they can't be seen from the Great Ocean Road. It is a section that the track's creators have dubbed the 'wild side', in comparison to the eastern end of the walk, known as the 'mild side'.

The walk begins on roads that loop inland, but the coastal sections thereafter more than compensate. You will wander gorgeous Milanesia Beach and climb almost continuously across coastal ridges for the first two days (on Day 1 alone your ascents total more than 800m) each with a subtle variation on the view. As an alternative, you can begin on Milanesia Track, parking by the large gate near its end. While this does cut out the first section of road, you will also miss some good early views of Johanna Beach.

PLANNING
When to Walk

It is quite feasible to walk this track at any time of year. Winters can be fierce – it is not called the Shipwreck Coast for nothing – but also show this rugged coast at its most dramatic, if you can put up with the extra discomfort. This is also the season when you might spot southern rights whales on their annual migration.

Maps

Vicmap's 1:50,000 topographic map *The Otways & Shipwreck Coast* covers the area of the described route (and of the entire Great Ocean Walk), though it doesn't show the track. Use it with Parks Victoria's *Great Ocean Walk Information and Map Guide* brochure for the most complete resource.

Information Sources

Being the newest walking trail in the country, it is not surprising that the Great Ocean Walk has its own website – www .greatoceanwalk.com.au. You will find most details you might need on the site, or check with Parks Victoria (p127). The Great Ocean Road visitor information centre (p139) is also well schooled in details about the new walk.

Permits & Regulations

Parks Victoria requests that all walkers go east to west along the track – Johanna Beach

to Glenample Homestead in this case. You must register your walking and camping intentions – registration forms are available on the Great Ocean Walk website (www .greatoceanwalk.com.au). Great interest in the walk is anticipated and you should try to register around six weeks ahead.

Fires are banned along the track, so carry a fuel stove.

NEAREST TOWNS & FACILITIES

A number of accommodation providers along the Great Ocean Walk will transport you to and from the trail each day. For a selection of recommended places, log on to www.greatoceanwalk.com.au/search _accomm.asp.

Lavers Hill
☎ 03

Lavers Hill is the high point of the Great Ocean Road, at least geographically. Despite the general feeling of abandonment, there are a couple of good sleeping and eating options.

Lavers Hill Roadhouse (☎ 5237 3251; Great Ocean Road; unpowered/powered sites for 2 $12/17, d without bath $48) is as basic as Lavers Hill itself. Hope for the unlikely – a log-truck-free night – as it is right by the road.

The decor in the tiny rooms at **Otway Junction Motor Inn** (☎ 5237 3295; Great Ocean Road; d $89-140) fancies that it is in Italy but the views are all Otways. The attached **Otway Junction Bistro** (mains $18-30; ☺ breakfast, lunch & dinner) does pub-style meals in a Tuscan setting. As a bonus, there is a great selection of biscuits.

Southern Heights B&B (☎ 5237 3131; Great Ocean Road; www.southernheights.com.au; d $115-149) is 4km west of town and by far the pick of the litter. Perched on an open hilltop, there are two modern rooms – the better one has a view along the coast to Point Flinders, near Cape Otway. Adults only.

Foggy Hill Bistro (lunch $11.50, mains $15-23; ☺ lunch & dinner) is attached to the roadhouse and worth seeking out for a traditional bistro menu and an inventive specials list.

GETTING THERE & AWAY

Lavers Hill is around 240km from Melbourne along the Great Ocean Road, or along Hwy 1 to Colac, then across the range through Gellibrand River. **V/Line** (☎ 13 61 96;

www.vline.com.au) runs a Friday service between Melbourne and Warrnambool that stops at Lavers Hill ($45, 5¾ hours).

Johanna
☎ 03

Set behind the dunes of one of the state's fiercest surf beaches, and right next to the trailhead, Johanna camping ground has grassy areas and toilets. At the time of writing it was free to camp here, but this is likely to change. There are a few self-contained cottages tucked along the Red and Blue Johanna Rds. Of these, the **Boomerangs** (☎ 5237 4213; www.theboomerangs.com; 3815 Great Ocean Road; d $200) wins on novelty value for its shape (boomerang) design (jarrah floors and vaulted ceilings) and views (the Southern Ocean). Closer to the beach are **Johanna Seaside Cottages** (☎ 5237 4242; www.johannaseaside.com .au; 395 Red Johanna Rd; d $185-200; 🖳), each with spa and wood fires, though there's a minimum two-night stay.

Princetown
☎ 03

Bypassed by the Great Ocean Road, tiny Princetown is princely only in name. With the air of a roadhouse stop, it can be a nice antidote to the frills and frenzy of other Great Ocean Road towns.

Apostles Camping Park (☎ 5598 8119; www .apostlescampingpark.com; unpowered/powered sites for 2 $18/22, cabins $50; 🖳) is grass disguised as a camping ground but has great views over the lower Gellibrand River. The office is the general store, as is **Do Duck in Café** (mains $5-7), serving sandwiches, baked potatoes, nachos and the like.

There's also camping at the Princetown camping reserve (p148).

Talk of the Town (☎ 5598 8288; talkofthetown tavern@bigpond.com; motel r & cabins $100) wears more hats than a milliner, being a **tavern** (mains $14-21; 🕒 lunch & dinner), motel, greasy spoon and **pizzeria** (pizzas $7-17; 🕒 dinner). There are two tiny motel rooms and a dorm-style cabin overlooking the river wetlands.

Clifton Lodge (☎ 5598 8128; cliftonlodge@big pond.com; 1450 Great Ocean Road; d $60-100) is 3km west of town – just 2km from Glenample Homestead – with spacious and quiet, two-bedroom pine cottages.

Glenample Farmstay (☎ 55988237; www.glenample .com.au; 2621 Great Ocean Road; d $100-120) is a 2000-acre property surrounding the Glenample Homestead. It has a self-contained cottage sleeping up to eight people. Access is from Simpson Rd, east of the homestead.

GETTING THERE & AWAY
Princetown is 30km west of Lavers Hill, just off the Great Ocean Road. The Friday **V/Line** (☎ 13 61 96; www.vline.com.au) service from Melbourne to Warrnambool stops at the Princetown turnoff on the Great Ocean Road ($50, 6¼ hours). The general-store owners can also arrange transport to Melbourne ($20).

GETTING TO/FROM THE WALK
Johanna Beach car park is reached along either sealed Red Johanna Rd (10km east of Lavers Hill) or unsealed Blue Johanna Rd (4km east of Lavers Hill) – the car park is at the end of the roads. Glenample Homestead is on the Great Ocean Road, 5km west of Princetown.

Timboon Taxi Service (☎ 0438 407 777) will transport you from Glenample Homestead to Johanna Beach (or vice-versa) for around $50. **Walk 91** (☎ 03-5237 1189) also offers a shuttle for around $65. Both can transport you between all accessible points along the Great Ocean Walk.

THE WALK
Day 1: Johanna Beach Car Park to Ryans Den Camp Site
4–5 hours, 14.4km, 850m ascent, 750m descent

At the northern end of the car park begin west, through two farm gates. The farm track climbs high onto the coastal hills, with surprisingly good views of the farmland below. In about 10 minutes you round the first hill, coming to a small **saddle** with views back along Johanna Beach, invariably being assaulted by surf. If you turn back left and walk for 200m you will find the Johanna Beach walkers' camp site.

Stay high on the hillsides, ignoring gates to the left signposted 'Management Vehicles & Walkers Only' – there is a good view west along the coast from the first gate. Coming to a fence-line the track turns inland, crossing through a final gate and joining Old Coach Rd. Climb on through intermittent bush to a junction with Milanesia Track (1¼ to 1½ hours from the start). Turn left, skirting a pine forest.

VICTORIA

After about 45 minutes – as the road swings south again – cross through a large gate into a private property. The track here descends through some beautiful eucalypt woodland before making a final, steep drop onto **Milanesia Beach**. The impressive white headland to the east is Lion Headland.

Walk west along the beach for 300m to a prominent spur. If it is high tide or large seas you will need to take the track below the spur, climbing steeply away from the beach onto the cliffs (this track rejoins the main walk at the next creek). Look for the 'decision point' signs on the beach.

Outside of high tide and large seas, continue along the beach, below cliffs so pitted with rounded rocks they resemble an indoor climbing wall. At the beach's end, beside a deeply cut creek, take the set of steps inland. Fork left after 30 metres (the right turn is the end of the high-tide track above Milanesia Beach) and cross the creek, climbing through vegetation for 800m to an old vehicle track. Turn left and after 100m branch right (the left track leads down to sea-edge rock platforms and is overgrown

with blackberries), heading up the hill to ascend across the high ridge of Bowker Point – there are fantastic views east to Cape Otway lighthouse as you climb.

After crossing through a small saddle, the track parallels the coast, swinging in and out of small gullies and climbing across another ridge to reach the junction with the Ryans Den Track (the Side Trip, below, turns left here).

Contour above Ryans Den (the small cove to your left) for 500m and begin a steep climb on steps to round a ridge. Ryans Den camp site is visible among the trees on the adjacent ridge. In about 10 minutes turn left at a junction and walk 150m into the camp site (1¼ to 1½ hours from Milanesia Beach). There are eight tent sites clinging to the narrow ridge.

SIDE TRIP: RYANS DEN
15–30 minutes, 800m

At Ryans Den Track turn left and descend along the wide track, which is steep and sometimes slippery. At its end it narrows to a foot track, burrowing through paper-

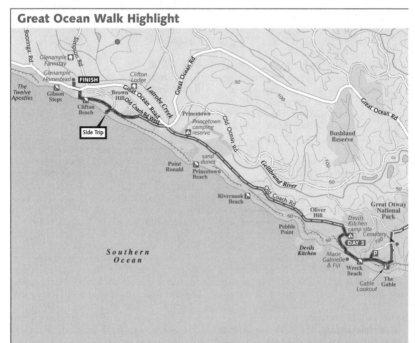

Great Ocean Walk Highlight

barks to emerge at **Ryans Den**. Cross carefully over the creek's slippery rock to reach the shore with its rocks smoothly rounded by time and the ocean. There are also some fantastically eroded, knobbly boulders at the mouth of the creek. Return along the same path.

Day 2: Ryans Den Camp Site to Devils Kitchen Camp Site
5–6 hours, 15.2km, 500m ascent, 500m descent
Return to the main track, turn left (west) and descend to a seasonal creek before switchbacking up the slope of the next ridge. The climb ends steeply, following a line of fence poles, but it does offer among the best views of the walk, down onto Cape Volney and back beyond Johanna Beach.

The track follows the fence poles around the coast for 400m, leaving them to head across to an old vehicle track (30 to 45 minutes from camp). Descend and climb steeply as the track rounds **Cape Volney** – nearing the point of the cape there is a great **viewpoint** just off the track, looking east along the coast.

The vehicle track follows ridge lines past Point Reginald – a nice stretch of walking without being spectacular. After 20 to 30 minutes the road rounds the top of a point for a good **view** across to Moonlight Head. At a track junction soon after, veer right, descending into a gully and then climbing onto a low spur, which you follow inland. Look out for a narrow pillar of remnant rock to the left of the track; just beyond here, the track steepens considerably, turning back on itself above Moonlight Head to join a road (1½ to two hours from camp).

Follow the road inland, passing **Moonlight Retreat** (☎ 03-5237 5277; www.moonlightretreat.com; d $155-295), where the B&B rooms look out to the distant Twelve Apostles – bring binoculars if you really want to see them. Dinner service is available. A few minutes beyond, you come to a junction with Moonlight Head Rd. Turn left, returning towards the coast.

Veer left at the next two intersections (if you are heading towards a high tide on Wreck Beach, turn right at the first intersection to follow the high-water alternative)

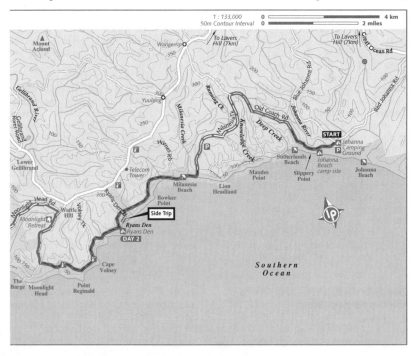

GREAT OCEAN WALK

The idea for a Great Ocean Walk was born over a bottle of port in the early 1990s among accommodation providers in the region, though it would be more than a decade before the dream became reality in 2006.

The 91km walk begins in Apollo Bay and ends beside the famed Twelve Apostles, running mostly through the newly created Great Otway National Park. Unlike the Great Ocean Road, it adheres to the coast for most of its length, and offers tremendous variety: beaches, cliffs, rainforest, lighthouse and farmland, with the Twelve Apostles as a finishing post.

It can be walked in five days, though it's promoted as an eight-day walk, which allows you to settle into the slow rhythm of the coast. Seven walker camp sites have been created along the trail's length (as well as four drive-in sites), each positioned at points of great beauty. Each camp site has a composting toilet, and all but Blanket Bay have a shelter and table. There are also water tanks at each site – be sure to treat the water before drinking. Tent sites are spaced throughout the bush to create a sense of removal.

The trailhead in Apollo Bay can be accessed by a **V/Line** (☎ 13 99 36; www.vline.com.au) bus service from Melbourne, and there are dedicated shuttle services (see p145) to return you to Apollo Bay or in between.

and pass an old **cemetery** on your left. After 45 minutes you come to the Gable Lookout car park. Find the signposted walking track at its southern end and wander out to the **Gable Lookout**, passing a turn-off to Wreck Beach. The lookout is atop 130m-high cliffs, among the highest in mainland Australia. Return to the Wreck Beach junction and turn left (west), descending through she-oaks, grass trees and heath into a gully.

Beyond the gully, the track parallels the coast to a T-junction. Turn left and descend a seemingly endless set of steps to **Wreck Beach**. Walk west (right) along the beach for about 500m and you will come to the **rusted anchors** of the *Marie Gabrielle* resting in a series of rock pools – at high tide they may be underwater. About 300m further west is the upturned (and less evocative) anchor of the *Fiji*, embedded in cement.

Pick around the rust-coloured boulders at the next point and, five minutes on (midway to the next point), turn up a flight of stone steps, leaving the beach. Climb through paperbarks, continuing west along a ledge to begin with, then doubling back to climb to a track junction. Turn right; the Devils Kitchen camp site is five minutes' walk east.

Day 3: Devils Kitchen Camp Site to Glenample Homestead

3¼–4½ hours, 13.4km, 200m ascent, 250m descent
Return to the track junction and continue straight on (west), turning left along a 4WD

track in about 50m. The tracks hairpins almost immediately (this road can have some very boggy sections), heading inland. In five minutes you come to Old Coach Rd (and the high-tide track above Wreck Beach). Turn left (west), walking through heath and scrubland – keep an eye out for echidnas, which are common along this section. As you follow the sandy road west, along the park fence-line much of the way, there are occasional views into the agricultural Gellibrand Valley.

After about one hour, as you bottom out beside the Gellibrand Valley, merge with another 4WD track and continue west along the fence-line. Fifteen minutes on, the road swings inland, dropping again toward the Gellibrand River and then climbing through the vegetated dunes behind Princetown beach. Circuit a roundabout (a trail to the left heads down to Princetown Beach) and follow the road out, past **Princetown camping reserve** (unpowered/powered sites $14/18) and across Gellibrand River (1¾ to 2½ hours from camp). Princetown (p145) is on the hill to the right – a boardwalk across the wetlands into town begins just beyond the bridge.

Follow the road on for another 500m to the Great Ocean Road, but take the sharper left turn into Old Coach Rd West. Stay with the road as it bends right (ignoring a foot track that goes straight on) and, 15 minutes from the Great Ocean Road, break away left onto a foot track (signposted to Clifton Beach). Continue through dense tea-tree scrub, climbing to views ahead that culminate in the Twelve Apostles. The track now winds along the cliff top, crossing a wire fence and a rough road. Walk straight on (the Side Trip, below, goes left), joining a boardwalk across the sandy cliff tops.

The track stays atop the cliffs until just before the beach at Gibson Steps, and the first of the Apostles. Here, the track veers inland, descending to the Great Ocean Road. Turn left along the road, then right after about 100m, following the entrance road up to **Glenample Homestead** (10am–5.30pm). The entrance gate on the Great Ocean Road will be closed outside of the homestead opening hours.

SIDE TRIP: CLIFTON BEACH
20–30 minutes, 1km
For an eye-level look at the most famous section of the Great Ocean Road, turn left at the Clifton Beach road and then right at the grassed parking area at its end. Follow a narrow track through a break in the cliffs and down to **Clifton Beach**. The stacks of the Twelve Apostles look very close from here.

GRAMPIANS NATIONAL PARK

The Grampians are a series of mountain ranges clustered together to form one of Victoria's most outstanding natural features, with sandstone escarpments that rise above the Wimmera Plain like petrified waves. Cradled inside is a host of wildlife, rock art, waterfalls, fantastic rock formations, wildflowers and myriad bushwalking opportunities along more than 150km of tracks.

In January 2006 a lightning strike on Mt Lubra, 15km south of Halls Gap, started a bushfire that burned around 130,000 hectares, including almost half of the national park. The two areas covered in this section were not burned, though it could be years before other popular walking areas such as the Wonderland Range and Major Mitchell Plateau (p187) make a full recovery.

ENVIRONMENT
The Grampians extend for about 100km north–south and 50km east–west at the western extremity of the Great Dividing Range. They comprise a long central, almost continuous spine of peaks through the Mt Difficult, Serra, Victoria and Mt William Ranges. Mt William (1167m) is the highest summit in the Grampians.

The greater part of the ranges is made up of hard, quartz-rich, western-leaning sandstone beds, or 'cuesta' landforms – rocky ridges with one side steeper than the other, which are the result of differing rates of erosion of hard and softer rock. Outcrops of granite in the Grampians are most obvious as narrow bands in the Wonderland area, where vegetation is taller and relatively luxuriant.

The Grampians is renowned for its flora, especially wildflowers. More than 85 flowering plant species exist in the Grampians, and there are 18 endemic plant species. The diversity of the vegetation means a great array of habitats, ranging from wet heathlands to woodlands on rocky outcrops, and a corresponding range of animal communities. Mammals are particularly easy to spot in the Grampians, though it will be some time before the full effect of the January 2006 bushfires is known. The most easily seen animals are the eastern grey kangaroo, which is abundant, and the swamp wallaby. Echidnas are often seen in healthy woodlands throughout the park.

PLANNING
When to Walk
The Grampians' season is almost year-round, influenced by two factors: hot summers and prolific spring wildflowers. You'll probably want to avoid too much walking in the former but will welcome it during the latter. Rainfall is not excessive at any time of year – nearby Stawell averages around 580mm annually – though most falls between May and October.

Maps & Books
The Grampians are covered by two Vicmap 1:50,000 topographic maps in the Outdoor Leisure series: *Northern Grampians* and *Southern Grampians*. Both walks in this section are covered by *Northern Grampians*, though it's a little outdated – it doesn't show all of the Mt Stapylton track or Stapylton camping ground, but is accurate for the Mt Difficult walk.

VICTORIA

Parks Victoria has produced a series of three walking brochures: *Northern Walks, Southern Walks* and *Wonderland Walks.* Tyrone Thomas' *80 Walks in the Grampians* covers exactly what the title promises, while *Discovering Grampians Gariwerd* by Alistair and Bruce Paton is an all-round resource, featuring colour plates of wildflowers and details of 48 walks.

The Grampians in Flower by IR McCann will help you pick one petal from another. The last two books can be ordered from the **Victorian National Parks Association** (www .vnpa.org.au).

Information Sources

For the most detailed information about the Grampians pay a visit to Brambuk (right). **Friends of Grampians Gariwerd** (http://home.vicnet .net.au/~gariwerd; annual membership $5) Works to conserve the park, and runs regular bushwalks. **Grampians Marketing** (www.visitgrampians.com.au) Regional tourism body. The site is most useful as a link to accommodation around the area.

Permits & Regulations

There are no entry fees to the park, and sites at the 13 campgrounds dotted around the park cost $11 for two people. Bush camping is permitted anywhere except in the Wonderland Range, around Lake Wartook and in parts of the Serra, Mt William and Victoria Ranges.

Guided Walks

Grampians Personalised Tours & Adventures (☎ 03-5356 4653; www.grampianstours.com.au) operates a selection of bushwalks in the Grampians, ranging from half-day to four days.

ACCESS TOWN
Halls Gap

☎ 03 / population 300

The small town of Halls Gap is pinched between the Wonderland Range and the northern tail of the Mt William Range. A singular tourist town, it is unobtrusive and likeable and a good base for all walks in the national park.

The **visitor information centre** (☎ 1800 065 599; Centenary Hall, Grampians Tourist Rd) has a free accommodation booking service and can also book tours and activities. **Brambuk the National Park and Cultural Centre** (☎ 5356 4452; www.brambuk.com.au; Dunkeld Rd) is 2.5km south of town and has park displays, Aboriginal cultural displays and activities, and rangers are available for walking information. There's also a good bookshop with some bushwalking titles.

GARIWERD

The Grampians' original inhabitants were two Koori (Aboriginal) peoples, the Djab wurrung and Jandwardjali, for whom the mountains were known as Gariwerd. In 1991 the national park was even renamed Gariwerd, but was changed back to Grampians National Park the next year when a new state government came to power.

The importance of the mountains as a Koori cultural site is evident in the number of art sites among the escarpments. There are more than 100 rock-art sites in the Grampians – or about 80% of all rock-art sites in Victoria. Five of these are promoted as tourist sites, two of which are located near Mt Stapylton. The small rock overhang of Ngamadjidj is reached along a 300m loop walk out of Stapylton camping ground and features a line of white human figures (Ngamadjidj means 'white person'). It is thought to be a place where people camped and repaired tools. A short drive away, reached on a 700m walk from the Hollow Mountain car park, is Gulgurn Manja, which features hand prints of Koori children around eight to 12 years old.

The most evident sign of Koori cultural influence is the presence of Brambuk the National Park and Cultural Centre (above). The building is designed to reflect the contours of the Grampians' mountains and a cockatoo – the totemic symbol of both the Djab wurrung and Jandwardjali people – in flight.

Brambuk means 'belonging to the Bram brothers', key figures in the legendary creation of the mountains. For the Kooris, Brambuk symbolises their renewal after nearly two centuries under European domination. Here, Kooris teach visitors about their cultural practices, stories, beliefs and management of the land. You can also sample some bush food at the Brambuk Bush Tucker Cafe (opposite).

SLEEPING & EATING

Halls Gap Caravan Park (☎ 5356 4251; www.hallsgap caravanpark.com.au; Grampians Tourist Rd; unpowered sites for 2 $19-23, powered sites for 2 $22-26, on-site caravans $47-68, cabins $71-130) is as central as a GPO but a little spartan. **Parkgate Resort** (☎ 1800 810 781; www.parkgateresort.com.au; Grampians Rd; unpowered sites for 2 $25-31, powered sites for 2 $27-36, cabins $80-175; ▣ ▣) has more razzle-dazzle with tennis courts, games room and nine different types of cabin. There's also a large grassy area to camp among the kangaroos.

Of the hostels in town, **Grampians YHA Eco-Hostel** (☎ 5356 4544; www.yha.com.au; cnr Grampians Tourist Rd & Buckler St; dm/s/d $24/54/60; ▣) leaves the smallest footprint, with solar water heating, grey-water toilets and scrap bins for the chooks and worms. There are fresh herbs and eggs in the kitchen each morning and pot-belly stoves in the two lounges.

The self-contained cottages at **D'Altons Resort** (☎ 5356 4666; www.daltonsresort.com.au; 48 Glen St; standard/deluxe/2br $100/120/140; ▣ ▣) are ringed around a grassed area popular with kangaroos. Deluxe rooms have spa, stereo and dishwasher.

Pinnacle Holiday Lodge (☎ 5356 4249; www .pinnacleholiday.com.au; Heath St; s & d from $89; as) has the wonderful knack of being both central and well hidden, tucked away behind Stony Creek Stores. The rooms are arranged to maximise views of the Wonderland Range.

Mountain View Motor Inn (☎ 5356 4364; www .mountainviewmotorinn.com.au; Ararat Rd; d $90-105, cottages $135-180; ▣) has a standard wing of motel rooms but well-spaced cottages for a camp-like sense of isolation.

The **general store** (Grampians Tourist Rd) has a good range of groceries and some camping gear; don't rely on it for anything useful.

Halls Gap Hotel (Grampians Rd; mains $14-23; ☯ lunch & dinner) has a fairly unimaginative menu (barring the half-dozen things it can do with a chicken schnitzel) but is about the best value in town. Fall into step with the 'Trekkers T-bone'.

Quarry (☎ 5356 4858; Stony Creek Stores, Grampians Tourist Rd; mains $22-30; ☯ lunch & dinner) overlooks Stony Creek and the tips of the Wonderland Range, and has a menu that ranges across the globe. Try the Razor Back Stack for the visual equivalent of a sandstone pinnacle. Bookings advised.

Brambuk Bush Tucker Cafe (Brambuk the National Park and Cultural Centre, Dunkeld Rd; mains $8-16; ☯ breakfast & lunch) is the place for kangaroo steak sandwiches, emu kebabs and other bush treats.

GETTING THERE & AWAY

Halls Gap is about 260km from Melbourne via the Western Hwy to Ararat and then via Moyston or Stawell. **V/Line** (☎ 13 61 96; www .vline.com.au) operates a daily train and coach service from Melbourne to Halls Gap ($48, four hours) via Ararat and Stawell.

MT STAPYLTON

Duration	4–4½ hours
Distance	12.2km
Difficulty	moderate–demanding
Start/Finish	Stapylton camping ground (below)
Nearest Town	Halls Gap (opposite)
Transport	private
Summary	An exciting and scenic walk, with plenty of rock hopping, to a fine mountain summit in the northern Grampians.

There are many higher peaks than Mt Stapylton in the Grampians, but few offer such exhilarating and rewarding climbs. Between sections of well-made walking track, there's plenty of rock hopping, some moderate scrambling and a close-up look at one of the most imposing and colourful cliffs in the country. If you've ever dreamed that you'd like to be a rock climber, this place might just inspire you to give it a go.

NEAREST TOWN & FACILITIES

See Halls Gap (opposite).

Stapylton Camping Ground

In view of the Mount of Olives, **Stapylton camping ground** ($11) has toilets, an untreated water source and a great location. There's room for caravans. To reach the camp from Halls Gap, turn west onto Grampians Rd, travelling 43km to Plantation Rd. Turn right; Stapylton camping ground is 5km along this road (the final 2km is unsealed). If travelling from the Western Hwy, Plantation Rd is 25km along Grampians Rd.

THE WALK

The walk starts at the western end of the camping ground and immediately crosses

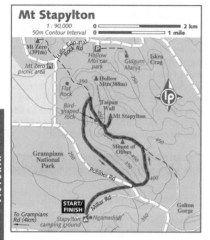

Mt Stapylton

1 : 90,000
50m Contour Interval

0 — 2 km
0 — 1 mile

over narrow, unsealed Millar Rd. Follow the track west through open bush – popular with eastern grey kangaroos – to Pohlner Rd. Cross straight over and follow a clear path through bushland for about 100m to a junction. Bear right towards a break in the ridge, climbing through it on a series of short flights of sandstone steps. The track reaches a broad ridge and swings north, climbing more gently through stringybark woodland.

Merge with a track coming in from the southeast, veering left and continuing along the ridge. Soon you emerge onto a rib of rock (one hour from the start) with good views of the rugged Mt Difficult Range to the south. Edge along the west side of the rock rib and descend back into woodland.

For the next 15 minutes or so, the route switches between the sandy track and seams of rock. At the edge of a deep cleft, descend steeply to a gully. The path soon heads back out onto rock; about 50m on, look up to the right to spot a red triangle, indicating the line upwards for a short but steep scramble. Turn left along a wide rock ramp, dropping away left again after about 50m. At the base of the rock turn left. Quickly the track swings back right, generally skirting the cliffs. Ascend to a track junction and turn right.

Climb back to the now-narrow ridge top, dropping off the eastern side to the base of the summit cliffs. The track turns up into a gorge-like break in the cliffs. Cross the gully above a rock fall and double back

left along a wide sandstone ramp, rounding the beautifully fretted sandstone cliffs. Then comes a slightly awkward scramble up a 2m chimney, an airy traverse and a final scramble up to the rocky summit of **Mt Stapylton**. The view takes in Mt Zero and Hollow Mountain nearby, the Victoria and Mt Difficult Ranges and, to the west, Mt Arapiles, looking like Uluru in miniature.

Return to the last track junction and bear right towards Mt Zero picnic area. In a couple of minutes you begin a great descent down a broad band of rock hundreds of metres long, with the colourful **Taipan Wall** soaring above. This striped wall is among the most challenging climbing walls in the country. For those not into harnesses and karabiners it's also one of the most attractive bits of rock architecture in the land. Soon you'll pass a large remnant of sandstone shaped like a bird.

Keep right of a deep ravine and re-enter woodland. A few minutes on (30 to 45 minutes from the summit), turn left. (If you have the time, it's worth wandering straight on for about 400m to **Flat Rock**, which offers the best views of Mt Stapylton and Taipan Wall). The main track heads through woodland below Mt Stapylton and the **Mount of Olives**, with good views of their classic Grampians cliffs. About 40 minutes along this track you arrive back at the track junction above Pohlner Rd. Turn right and retrace your steps to the camping ground.

MT DIFFICULT

Duration	2 days
Distance	22.6km
Difficulty	moderate–demanding
Start/Finish	Beehive Falls car park
Nearest Town	Halls Gap (p150)
Transport	private

Summary Climb through sandstone cliffs to the highest peak in the northern Grampians and arguably the ranges' best viewpoint; a sunset stunner.

True to its name, Mt Difficult doesn't yield easily but it's arguably the best long walk in the Grampians. Though its summit is just 806m above sea level, it's an indication of the terrain that you will climb more than 1000m on the first day to reach it.

The route described here can be varied in a couple of ways. For a long day outing you can beeline straight for the peak by following the Day 2 description in reverse. An equally popular approach is to climb Mt Difficult from Troopers Creek camping ground at its foot, spending the night in one of the camp sites near Deep Creek. Both these options can mean sacrificing sunset on Mt Difficult, which is the reward you want for a day of walking effort.

Mt Difficult was untouched by the bushfires of January 2006 but was burnt back in January 1999, when a bushfire burned more than 5000 hectares of the national park (as well as surrounding areas). There's little sign of fire damage now.

Navigation is fairly simple along this route with all track junctions marked by silver plaques showing tracks and distances.

PLANNING
What to Bring

There are no reliable water sources along the route of this walk so you will need to carry your entire supply; allow at least 6L.

Permits & Regulations

All walkers on this route are required to fill out a trip intention form at Brambuk (p150). You will be required to contact Brambuk when you finish walking or a search will be initiated. The walk is also through a fuel-stove-only area (despite all the heavy camp-fire scars you'll see), so no fires are allowed.

NEAREST TOWN
See Halls Gap (p150).

THE WALK
Day 1: Beehive Falls Car Park to Mt Difficult Saddle

4½–5½ hours, 14.9km, 1050m ascent, 500m descent

Begin south from the car park on a wide trail through open eucalypt woodland. The track soon comes to often-dry Mud Hut Creek, following it to a wooden bridge at the base of the escarpment. Cross the bridge and ascend on stone steps to the foot of **Beehive Falls** (20 to 30 minutes from the car park). You'll need to be here in winter or spring to see the falls at anything more than a dribble, though it's a beautiful and cool spot at any time.

Cross back over the creek and begin a steep, winding climb through the lower escarpment. Cut back across a small creek to a second line of rock, mottled here like the hide of an elephant. Briggs Bluff is the tall, pointed peak ahead. Begin ascending this next section on the rock before funnelling into a small, stony gully.

At the head of the gully the track swings south, climbing again to a wide ledge overlooking the cleft of **Mud Hut Creek**. Here, the track flattens, heading south atop the ledge (the trig point on Mt Difficult is visible ahead). Follow the obvious track across rock and sand for about 15 minutes before swinging east to cross a small gully and climb towards the cave-riddled cliffs. Passing between a pair of giant boulders the track veers north, following the foot of the cliffs to a track junction (one hour from Beehive Falls).

Turn right (the left turn goes to Briggs Bluff; see p155), walking east through eucalypt woodland. In about 200m you pass through a number of camp sites. Scramble through one line of rock and then edge around the base of the next to reach a track junction. Turn left, descending past some camp sites to cross one arm of **Deep Creek** (which will almost certainly be anything but deep) and then climbing steeply to the foot of the cliffs ahead. Swing first east and then west at their base, gradually climbing through the cliffs. At the last line of cliffs, the track breaks left through a narrow gap in the wall, and you are rewarded with a view south along the Mt Difficult Range and across the plains to Mt Langi Ghiran.

Cross two more inlets of Deep Creek (there is a good camp site at the first crossing) and continue on south through stringybark, banksias and grass trees. Soon, as you begin rounding Deep Creek Gorge, there are fleeting views of Lake Wartook, cradled in the centre of the Mt Difficult Range. Pass through another camp site, veering right at the large, worn boulder in the camp.

Soon after, you begin a gradual climb through bush all but air-brushed orange with lichen. Thirty minutes from the last camp site, turn right and descend through stringybark woodland to join a disused 4WD track. Veer left along the track (there is a decent camp site to the right) and, in

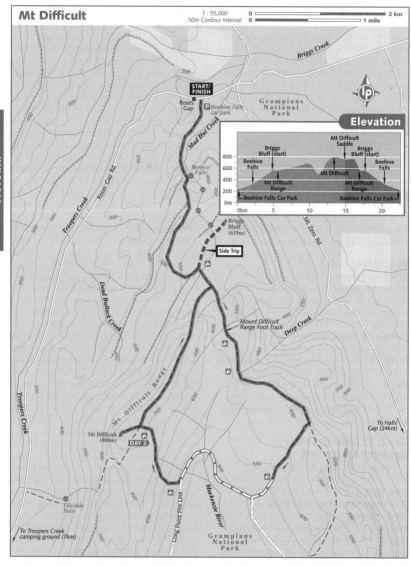

Mt Difficult

1 : 55,000
50m Contour Interval

Elevation

another 300m, turn right onto the Long Point Fire Line, a management vehicle track. Heading back north the track crosses two arms of the **Mackenzie River** (look for beautiful coral ferns at both crossings). These tiny streams flow on to become one of the Grampians' most impressive attractions: Mackenzie Falls.

A few minutes past the second crossing the track hairpins south, crossing three streams to a junction with a foot track. There's a camp site here that can be a good option as the stream beside it is the most likely of any along the walk to contain water.

Turn right and begin climbing beside the fern-lined creek. The switchbacking climb is relentless for about 20 to 30 minutes, but then flattens out, contouring north. Turning west the track squeezes between two boulders and climbs – more gently now – up to a small saddle just below the summit of Mt Difficult (about 45 minutes from the Long Point Fire Line). There are a few good camp sites here; set up your tent and then take the track north out of camp for about 100m. Turn left onto a path that turns in behind the first line of rock and then winds easily up to the summit of **Mt Difficult** (806m). The view from here is a what's-what of the Grampians: Mt Stapylton and Mt Zero to the north; and Mt Rosea, Mt William and its tower, and the trailing line of the Serra Range to the south. It's well worth getting here for sundown; on a good night it's one of the best sunset vantage points in the state.

SIDE TRIP: BRIGGS BLUFF
45 minutes–1 hour, 2.4km return, 80m ascent

At the Briggs Bluff junction turn left and head north. The route is marked by small cairns and the polished line of years of walking use. Generally descend for about 800m, until you cross a wooded gully. From here, ascend on bare rock to the summit of **Briggs Bluff** (619m). From the top, you'll see lumpy Mt Stapylton to the northwest, the distant bubble of Mt Arapiles to the west and the ramped summit of Mt Difficult to the south. Return to the junction along the same path.

Day 2: Mt Difficult Saddle to Beehive Falls Car Park
2–3 hours, 7.7km, 550m descent

Take the track north out of camp again, passing the turn-off to Mt Difficult, and heading out across sandstone slabs and into woodland. Passing through a camp site, after 600m the track climbs to the edge of a large seam of rock. Walk along its base, and then edge away to continue north across nicely smoothed slabs. After about 40 minutes you enter a beautifully sculpted section of rock, which is more reminiscent of the Wonderland Range than Mt Difficult. A few minutes on you come to a junction, turning left to rejoin your outward route. Swing left at the Briggs Bluff turning and descend back past Beehive Falls to the car park.

VICTORIAN ALPS

Rising about 100km northeast of Melbourne and stretching for 250km right to the New South Wales (NSW) border is a mountainous region of high ridges, plateaus and deep valleys collectively known as the Victorian Alps. The Alps are home to the highest mountains in the state; from the tallest peaks, the views are almost limitless as range after range fades towards the horizon. The Great Dividing Range, which parallels the east coast of Australia from western Victoria right up to Cape York in Queensland, forms the backbone of the Alps, rising to a height of 1986m at Mt Bogong.

Much of the region is contained within a number of national parks, the largest of which, at 646,000 hectares, is the Alpine National Park. (Other smaller but equally important High Country parks are Baw Baw National Park and Mt Buffalo National Park.) The Alpine National Park abuts Kosciuszko National Park, creating a massive zone protecting most of the country's alpine regions. Unfortunately, the boundaries of the Alpine National Park have been creatively routed so that pockets of alpine ash and other mountain hardwoods still see the frequent activity of timber getters. Another oddity is that cattle grazing has continued in some sectors of the park for many years, though this practice seems likely to cease beyond 2006 due to recent Victorian Government legislation.

The Victorian Alps are a tourist attraction year-round. Pretty towns can be found in the valleys around the area, each catering for the traveller and offering a good base from which to explore the mountains. In winter, downhill skiers flock in large numbers to the major ski resorts of Falls Creek, Mt Buller and Mt Hotham, and to smaller areas at Mt Baw Baw and Mt Buffalo. Rolling plains and rounded summits make cross-country skiing popular, while bush camping, 4WD driving and fishing are popular in the summer months.

But by far the best way to see the most attractive, captivating and isolated parts of the Victorian Alps is on foot. This huge area is well covered by a network of walking tracks and old 4WD roads, giving relatively easy access to most of the scenic country.

VICTORIA

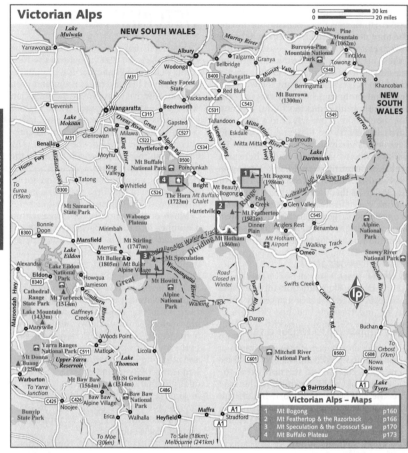

HISTORY

Evidence suggests that this region was first visited by Aboriginal people at least 5000 years ago, and even earlier in the surrounding lowlands. They gathered on the mountain plains during the summer months to feed on the protein-rich Bogong moths, which they found in cracks and fissures in rocks. But it was not until the mid-1800s when European Australians first reached the Alps. One of the first visits to the highest areas was made by two graziers, Jim Brown and Jack Wells, who traversed the Bogong High Plains in 1851. They named many of today's well-known features, including Mt Feathertop, Mt Fainter and Pretty Valley, and cut the area's first stock routes.

In the 1880s and 1890s, there was an influx of graziers and miners (after the discovery of gold deposits). Prospectors pushed far up the valleys, and some even high onto the mountains. While most sources of gold eventually ran dry, the Red Robin mine (near Mt Hotham), founded in 1941, remains a viable, small-time operation.

Locals, appreciating the scenic beauty of the mountains, began promoting the area with brochures and guided walks. Residents from the town of Bright formed the Bright Alpine Club in 1887 and members led excursions to the mountains in both summer and winter; Mts Buffalo (p171) and Feathertop (p164) being two of their most visited areas. Roads were gradually cut to the heads of the valleys, then over the Alps at Mt Hotham, so that a large section of the mountains became readily accessible to travellers. Bushwalking boomed in the 1920s – and was given further impetus by the Great Depression of the 1930s – and is still a most popular pastime today, while tourism has become one of the region's most prosperous industries.

ENVIRONMENT

The flora and fauna of the Victorian Alps varies little from what you can expect with Kosciuszko National Park; you're less likely to see emus and feral pigs on any of the walks in the Victorian High Country, though deer (feral in Australia) are common, particularly in the Mt Howitt area. More detailed information can be garnered from the Kosciuszko National Park's Environment section (p83).

CLIMATE

The Victorian Alps are part of the same mountain range that forms the heart of the Kosciuszko National Park in NSW, and experience a similar climate (see p85).

PLANNING

It's essential to be well prepared for a walk in the mountains, as weather conditions can be severe at times, even in summer. The Gearing up for the Mountains boxed text (p39) has further information.

When to Walk

Winter is unsuitable for walking, not only because of the deep snow that covers many parts of the walking areas described here, but also because seasonal road closures affect access to some places. For the most part, you can walk any time between October and April, though the most popular months are January to March when the days are usually warm, the weather is generally stable and wildflowers put on their best displays.

Maps & Books

There are many good general maps covering the Australian and Victorian Alps. One

---

AUSTRALIAN ALPS WALKING TRACK

This challenging, and at times spectacular, long-distance walk traverses about 680km of alpine country and summits Australia's highest peaks. Starting from the tiny historic village of Walhalla in Victoria, it ends at the Namadgi Visitor Centre on the southern outskirts of Canberra in the Australian Capital Territory (ACT).

When the original plan for a Victorian 'Alpine Walking Track' was mooted in the 1940s it was met with much disdain by walkers who wanted to keep the mountains free of marked trails. However, in the 1950s and 60s, with logging and tourist roads pushing further into the Victorian mountains and slowly eroding the wilderness value of popular walking destinations, the idea of an Alpine Walking Track became increasingly popular.

The 400km Alpine Walking Track was completed in 1976 and stretched from Walhalla to the Victorian border at Tom Groggin (near Thredbo), but it was not until the early 1990s that the track was extended through the high country of NSW and the ACT as well, creating the Australian Alps Walking Track.

The track, most of which is clearly marked, takes about eight weeks to walk in total, but most walkers tend to complete sections of the track as shorter, less demanding tours. If you are interested in walking the entire track remember that no major towns are passed (only a few ski villages), so it is necessary to store food caches at designated points beforehand.

The best source of information on the track is John Siseman's *Australian Alps Walking Track*. This excellent guide includes detailed track notes, as well as background information on history, environment, climate, flora and fauna, camping, and maps.

of the better maps is *High Country Victoria,* published by Hema Maps. It provides a good overview of the area at a scale of 1:300,000.

A few handy guidebooks with extensive walking notes include *Bushwalks in the Victorian Alps* by Glenn van der Knijff, a full-colour guide, and *Victoria's Alpine National Park* by John Siseman. Both guides include track notes to a number of walks and plenty of photographs, as well as ample background and planning information.

Australian Alps – Kosciuszko, Alpine & Namadgi National Parks by Deirdre Slattery has some track notes, but also contains loads of other information on the environment, history and development of the Victorian Alps and Snowy Mountains region.

Information Sources

The best places for information on the region, including accommodation, transport, maps and books, are visitor centres in Bright, Mt Beauty and Mansfield.

The **Australian Alps National Parks** (www .australianalps.deh.gov.au) website is a useful source of background information on the Alps region.

Permits & Regulations

There are no camping fees for bush camping in the Alpine National Park, although there is a charge for using a camp site at the established camping ground in Mt Buffalo National Park (p172). Mt Buffalo National Park also charges a vehicular entrance fee (p172).

One major restriction to be aware of is that no campfires are permitted in the areas surrounding the summits of Mts Bogong and Feathertop, as these are declared as fuel-stove-only areas.

ACCESS TOWN
Bright

☎ 03 / pop 1900

Within the upper reaches of the Ovens Valley, Bright is a pretty town that thrives on tourism and is increasingly a centre for adventure pursuits, including cycling, walking, skiing, rockclimbing and hang gliding. It has a wide range of facilities and services, and is an excellent springboard for bushwalking in the surrounding mountains.

INFORMATION

The **Bright Visitor Centre** (☎ 5755 2275; www .brightescapes.com.au; 119 Gavan St; ⏲ 9am-5pm) has plenty of information for travellers and has a helpful **accommodation booking service** (☎ 1300 551 117). There's also a **Parks Victoria office** (☎ 5755 0000; 46 Bakers Gully Rd), which can offer advice on the condition of roads in the surrounding mountains.

SUPPLIES & EQUIPMENT

The shopping strip is on Ireland St, where there are various shops, takeaway outlets, cafés, supermarkets and **Bright Disposals & Outdoor Centre** (☎ 5755 1818; 9 Ireland St) selling a variety of outdoor and camping equipment. There are a few banks and a post office on Gavan St, just uphill of the visitor centre.

SLEEPING & EATING

There is a plethora of caravan parks in and around Bright. The largest is **Bright Caravan Park** (☎ 5755 1141; www.brightcaravanpark.com.au; Cherry Lane; unpowered/powered sites for 2 from $20/24, cabins from $55), occupying a shady location beside Morses Creek and only a short walk from the town centre.

Bright Hikers Backpackers' Hostel (☎ 5750 1244; www.brighthikers.com.au; 4 Ireland St; dm/s/d $21/30/44; 💻) has a cosy atmosphere and a great veranda overlooking the main shopping street.

Elm Lodge Holiday Motel (☎ 5755 1144; www .elmlodge.com.au; 2 Wood St; s/d from $55/70; 🐾) sits amid pleasant gardens and is a popular place for backpackers. Nearby, the comfortable **John Bright Motor Inn** (☎ 5755 1400; www .albury.net.au/~jbmotel/; 10 Wood St; s/d from $85/90) has motel-style accommodation and is only a few minutes' walk from the shops.

Jackie's (☎ 5750 1303; 6 Ireland St; breakfasts $6-11, mains $5-12; ⏲ breakfast & lunch) offers a multitude of good pre-walk breakfasts, as well as a lunch menu including sandwiches, shepherd's pie and nachos.

Close to the tourist office is **Tin Dog Café & Pizzeria** (☎ 5755 1526; cnr Gavan & Barnard Sts; pizzas $14-20, mains $18-21; ⏲ breakfast, lunch & dinner), popular with outdoor enthusiasts at any time of year, but particularly in summer.

Opposite the clock tower is the **Liquid Am-Bar** (☎ 5755 2318; 8 Anderson St; mains $14-25; ⏲ dinner Thu-Tue), a restaurant-cum-bar that exudes a relaxed ambience and offers a wide variety of meals.

There's no shortage of takeaway food outlets in town, including two bakeries, one in Gavan St and one at the top end of Ireland St. For self-caterers, there are two supermarkets, both in Ireland St.

GETTING THERE & AWAY
Bright is 306km northeast of Melbourne by road, first along the Hume Fwy (M31), then along the Great Alpine Rd (B500).

V/Line (☎ 13 61 96; www.vline.com.au) operates a daily train/bus combination between Melbourne and Bright (adult/child $49.20/24.60, 4½ hours).

MT BOGONG

Duration	2 days
Distance	26.5km
Standard	moderate–demanding
Start/Finish	Mountain Creek Camping Area (p161)
Nearest Town	Mt Beauty & Tawonga South (right)
Transport	private

Summary A long ascent to Victoria's highest summit along good tracks, then a panoramic ridge walk to Camp Valley. As well as great views, the route passes an old stone hut and an isolated mountain waterfall.

A big brute of a mountain, accessible only by long, demanding climbs, Mt Bogong was for many years familiar only to local cattlemen. They drove their cattle to the mountain tops each summer to graze on the sweet herbs and grasses that grow in profusion. Over the years the cattlemen cut paths on which they drove their cattle. By the early 1900s Mt Bogong had been discovered by bushwalkers and cross-country skiers, and a series of huts slowly appeared on the mountain. Summit Hut (now destroyed) and Michell Hut were built as refuges on the two most popular access routes to the mountain, and the popular Cleve Cole Hut was built in memory of a pioneer skier of the region who died on the mountain (p161).

It's the views, though, not the huts that provide the highlights; from the sweeping upper slopes of Mt Bogong you can see to the horizon in some directions, while the nearby hills fill the scene in others. Admittedly, the climb is long, gaining 1400m in altitude, but it's gratifying nonetheless, and the scenery more than compensates for any effort. The two side trips, to West Peak and the cascading Howmans Falls, could easily be completed from a base camp at Cleve Cole Hut, extending the trip to three days.

PLANNING
It should be noted that this is a very exposed walk in sections and you must have a strong weatherproof tent, wet-weather gear, good sleeping bag, warm clothes and a fuel stove. Cleve Cole Hut does have a number of bunk beds, but it's often full and shouldn't be relied upon. As well, there's often no water available on the climb to Mt Bogong until you reach the camp site, so make sure you carry plenty of water (1.5L to 2L should suffice).

Maps
Vicmap's 1:50,000 topographic map *Bogong Alpine Area,* part of the Outdoor Leisure Map series, is the best choice. It shows a good level of track detail with a 20m contour interval.

Permits & Regulations
The walk falls within a fuel-stove-only area. No campfires are permitted, so you must carry a fuel stove for cooking.

NEAREST TOWN & FACILITIES
Mt Beauty & Tawonga South
☎ 03 / pop 1650
At the head of the Kiewa Valley, Mt Beauty (and its adjoining town of Tawonga South) is an excellent base for walks on Mt Bogong and the Bogong High Plains. Confusingly, Mt Beauty is not a mountain, but a small country town that survives on tourism and the nearby Kiewa Hydroelectric Scheme.

INFORMATION
On the left as you approach Mt Beauty from Tawonga South is the **Alpine Discovery Centre** (☎ 5754 1962; www.alpinediscoverycentre.com.au; 31 Bogong High Plains Rd; ☼ 9am-5pm). It is open daily and has an **accommodation booking line** (☎ 1800 033 079). Also on the highway, but a little further back in Tawonga South, is a **Parks Victoria office** (☎ 5754 4693). There are two banks in the shopping centre in Hollonds St, while the post office is located back down the highway in Tawonga South.

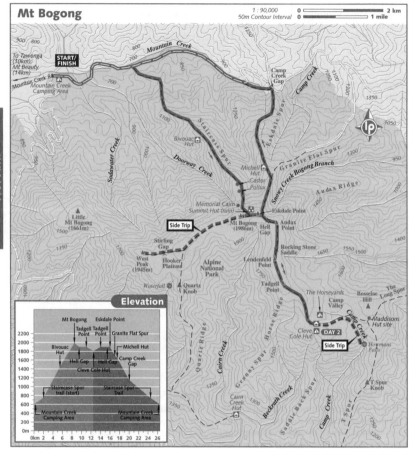

Mt Bogong

1 : 90,000
50m Contour Interval

Elevation

SLEEPING & EATING

Carver's Log Cabins (☎ 5754 4863; www.netstar.com .au/carvers; Buckland St; cabins from $100; ⌘) enjoys good views of Mt Bogong from the pleasant gardens and offers self-contained cabins sleeping up to six people.

The award-winning **Braeview** (☎ 5754 4756; www.braeview.com.au; 4 Stewarts Rd; B&B s & d from $120, studio apt s/d $205/225, cottage s/d $270; ⌘) has well-equipped rooms containing TVs and bar fridges, and desirable views of the nearby mountains (for free!). The cottage, and some of the B&B rooms, have spa tubs, and guests are provided with a complimentary food platter on arrival.

Popular with locals and tourists alike, the **Mt Beauty Bakery & Café** (☎ 5754 4870; Hollonds &

Kiewa Sts; meals $4-8; ⌚ 6.30am-6.30pm) serves the usual pastry fare – such as pies, sausage rolls and pasties – but also a selection of sandwiches, cakes and antipasti.

For a more upmarket meal try **Roi's Diner** (☎ 5754 4495; 177 Kiewa Valley Hwy; mains $18-25; ⌚ dinner Thu-Sun), on the uphill side of the road in Tawonga South, which serves a variety of excellent modern Italian dishes.

Good for a feed after the completion of the walk is the **Bogong Hotel** (☎ 5754 4482; 169 Kiewa Valley Hwy; mains $14-17; ⌚ lunch Sun, dinner Thu-Mon), in the small town of Tawonga, 4km north of Tawonga South. Here you can sit and admire the peak you've just climbed while enjoying a traditional counter meal. Just off the main road in Mt

Beauty is the shopping centre on Hollonds St, where you'll find a supermarket and a few cafés and takeaway outlets.

GETTING THERE & AWAY
Mt Beauty is 365km from Melbourne via Myrtleford, and just 25km from Bright (p158). From Albury, 95km away, drive through Wodonga then head along the Kiewa Valley Hwy.

V/Line (☎ 13 61 96; www.vline.com.au) operates a train/bus combination between Melbourne and Mt Beauty (adult/child $55.70/27.80, 5½ hours), also via Bright, on Monday and Friday. You could also take a train to Albury (on the Victoria–NSW border), from where you can catch a bus; **Pyles Coaches** (☎ 5754 4024; www.pyles.com.au) runs a service between Albury and Mt Beauty (adult/child $25/18, 1½ hours) Monday to Friday.

Tawonga Caravan Park
Closer to the trailhead is **Tawonga Caravan Park** (☎ 5754 4428; www.mtbeauty.com/tawonga caravanpark; Mountain Creek Rd; unpowered/powered sites for 2 from $16/22, cabins from $46), 1km east of the small town of Tawonga (not to be confused with Tawonga South, 4km away). The park provides shady sites and fronts the Kiewa River, a frequent destination for anglers.

Mountain Creek Camping Area
The closest camping option to the walk is at the Mountain Creek Camping Area, right at the trailhead. There are plenty of flat camp sites, a toilet and picnic tables, all beside a fresh mountain stream.

GETTING TO/FROM THE WALK
Mountain Creek Camping Area is 15km from Mt Beauty. Drive north for 4km from Mt Beauty to the small town of Tawonga. Turn east, opposite the Bogong Hotel, onto Mountain Creek Rd, which leads to the camping area.

If you require a ride from Mt Beauty, contact the **Mt Beauty Taxi Service** (☎ 5754 4739, 0409 573 909).

THE WALK
Day 1: Mountain Creek Camping Area to Cleve Cole Hut via Mt Bogong
5–7 hours, 12.5km, 1400m ascent, 200m descent

The route follows a 4WD track east into the forest from the camping area. Within 15 minutes you'll come to a grassy area and gate; it is possible to drive 2WDs to this point, so you could start the walk here. Continue along the track, negotiating five creek crossings, until you reach the sixth crossing. Fill your water bottles here as

---

THE DEATH OF CLEVE COLE

In 1937 Cleve Cole Hut was constructed on Mt Bogong at the head of Camp Valley in memory of Cleve Cole, who died after being stranded on the mountain during a blizzard in August 1936.

Cleveland 'Cleve' Cole and his companions Percy 'Mick' Hull and Howard Michell were nearing the end of a ski tour from Mt Hotham, some 50km away. While ascending Mt Bogong, they were greeted by driving snow and thick fog. Unable to find the summit, the route to Camp Valley, or even the spur they'd just ascended, they dug a snow cave. For the next two days they were held captive by the blizzard. On the fourth day, with little food remaining and with their general condition worsening – and having written farewell letters to their loved ones – they made a final attempt to reach the top. Astonishingly, they found the summit cairn and thought they could find their way to the Staircase Spur and, therefore, a relatively easy route off the mountain.

Unknowingly, they followed a course onto the southern side of the mountain instead of the north. They battled for hours, finally reaching Big River below the snow line, but civilization was miles away. They followed the Big River downstream for two days, unable to light a fire and sleeping inside hollow logs for shelter. A week after reaching Mt Bogong, Howard, the fittest member of the group, struggled on in search of help. Mick set up a rough camp and nursed Cleve, who could no longer walk and was suffering from hypothermia. Howard eventually stumbled into the small gold-mining town of Glen Valley, and a rescue party was soon on its way.

Mick and Cleve were rescued ten days after their ordeal began and were carried to the village of Glen Valley. Cleve's condition had deteriorated to such an extent that he later died from severe hypothermia and frostbite.

The solid hut, built in his honour, still stands today.

BOGONG HIGH PLAINS SHORT WALKS

The Bogong High Plains, 32km from Mt Beauty up the Bogong High Plains Rd, is a region of high rounded peaks, broad snow plains and shallow valleys, sporadically clothed in snow gum forest; and they're a walker's paradise. Below are a few short walks that will give you a taste of what the area has to offer.

The best take-off point for walks is Falls Creek, 30km from Mt Beauty and right on the edge of the plains. A thriving ski resort in winter, Falls Creek is quiet outside this time. Most of the village shuts down after the snow melts, although a handful of lodges, cafés and bars remain open.

All walks are covered by the Vicmap 1:50,000 topographic map *Bogong Alpine Area,* available from the Snowland Centre in Falls Creek.

Ropers Lookout

A short walk (4km) offering a good introduction to the region, the lookout provides expansive views of Falls Creek and the surrounding terrain.

Starting from the eastern end of the Rocky Valley Storage dam wall, follow a track alongside the Rocky Valley Aqueduct north for 25 minutes to where the aqueduct ends. A track climbs straight up the hill, then loops to the south to end at the interesting basalt outcrop of Ropers Lookout (1700m). Allow 1½ hours.

Mt Nelse

As one of the tallest peaks on the Bogong High Plains, Mt Nelse stands well above the tree line and offers unlimited views in all directions.

While not particularly 'short' (three hours, 11km), this walk is nonetheless quite easy with good tracks for most of the route. Big River Fire Track leaves the Bogong High Plains Rd 5km east of Falls Creek.

Follow the track northeast to the Park (a large snow plain), then generally north to where it levels off west of Mt Nelse. Leave the track here and walk across the grassy plain to the summit of Mt Nelse (1882m).

Wallaces & Cope Huts

These two huts are among the oldest and most interesting on the Bogong High Plains, and are the legacy of some of the region's pioneers. Wallaces Hut, originally used by cattlemen, is classified by the National Trust, while Cope Hut is the only hut on the plains built specifically for ski tourers.

This two-hour, 8km walk starts where a 4WD track heads east away from the Bogong High Plains Rd about 10km from Falls Creek. Follow this track east for 15 minutes to Wallaces Hut, the oldest hut on the Bogong High Plains. Continue down the main track (east) as it descends gently to meet Langford West Aqueduct. Turn right and you'll soon reach Rover Lodge, a large building used by the Rover Scouts, 25 minutes from Wallaces Hut.

Beyond Rover Lodge, the route follows the aqueduct, then veers briefly onto a foot track before joining a 4WD track that leads west to Cope Hut. Past the hut, the track soon rejoins the Bogong High Plains Rd, which you follow north for 800m. Take the snow pole line (and accompanying track) northeast, which soon brings you back to Wallaces Hut. Retrace your steps back to your vehicle.

Mt Cope

The prominent rocky summit of Mt Cope provides a great vantage point from which to admire the surrounding plains and, particularly, Pretty Valley.

The start of this 3km track is at a signpost ('Mt Cope') on the Bogong High Plains Rd, 13km beyond Falls Creek. This faint track heads southwest over the plains before climbing to the boulder-covered summit of Mt Cope (1837m).

this is the last reliable water supply until you reach Cleve Cole Hut.

Ten minutes later, the signposted track up the Staircase Spur leaves the main track on your right. The track climbs steeply over the series of flat sections that give the spur its name, until you reach **Bivouac Hut** at 1440m and about two hours (5.5km) from the start. It is possible to camp by Bivouac Hut, but you will have to rely on a rainwater tank for drinking water. The hut itself offers shelter and has a small potbelly stove, but there are no bunks.

Continuing, the track soon climbs steeply again. About an hour from the hut, the track unexpectedly climbs out of the forest and onto the windswept grassy moors of the upper mountain, where you get your first good distant views. Snow poles now accompany the route. At times, with a gentle breeze, these poles emit an eerie sound; in a misty storm, the noise can be quite unnerving. Further up you will pass a **memorial cairn** marking the place where three skiers died in a 1943 blizzard.

A while later you may notice the scattered ruins of Summit Hut. (There is a small semi-permanent spring a few metres above the ruins.) Another 300m brings you to a T-junction at the top of the high, treeless ridge that forms the summit plateau of Mt Bogong. At this point, marked by a snow pole and signpost, turn west and follow the track for five minutes to the huge cairn at the summit of **Mt Bogong** (1986m). It will take you about four to five hours to cover the 8.5km from the start of the walk.

Bogong, an Aboriginal name that loosely translates as 'big fella', befits the title of Victoria's highest peak; after the climb up, you'll understand why. Soak in the 360-degree panorama, including the Snowy Mountains (Australia's highest mountain range) on the northeast horizon, while enjoying a well-earned rest. West Peak, the obvious dome seen at the western end of the summit ridge, can be visited with an easy side trip (right).

Return to the T-junction mentioned above and follow the track east to **Hell Gap**. The route swings slowly round to the south then gradually east again as it passes over Rocking Stone Saddle, Lendenfeld Point and Tadgell Point; there are exceptional

views all along this high ridge. The track then descends into the forest before reaching the grassy camping area beside **Cleve Cole Hut**, 4km and one hour from the summit. With eight beds, a sink, running water and stove, the hut is luxurious compared with most mountain huts but is often full with walkers.

If the camping area is crowded, consider camping about 300m north of the hut at the Horseyards, visible across the shallow valley. The pleasant grassy camp sites, near some old yards, can be seen from the hut, and water can be obtained from a small creek 100m before reaching the camp site.

SIDE TRIP: WEST PEAK
1½ hours, 6km return, 40m descent

From Mt Bogong, a faint track leads west down the broad ridge and into a shallow saddle. Here the track is poorly defined, but walk slightly south of west to the top of Hooker Plateau. A few old snow poles are scattered along the route. From the western edge of Hooker Plateau, descend west into a saddle and locate a foot pad which will bring you to **West Peak** (1945m). The Kiewa River valley and ranges to the west look particularly impressive from here.

Return to the summit along the same route. Note that this trip is not advisable in foggy conditions, beacuase it is easy to become disoriented on the featureless Hooker Plateau.

Day 2: Cleve Cole Hut to Mountain Creek Camping Area
4–5 hours, 14km, 200m ascent, 1400m descent

From the hut, return along the track towards Mt Bogong. At Hell Gap, a track bears north and skirts the east side of Eskdale Point to join the Eskdale Spur, 500m away. The path heads down the spine of the narrow spur to a track junction where the spur flattens out. At the edge of the tree line, this is your last opportunity to savour the outstanding vista. The main track heads left (northwest) and soon arrives at **Michell Hut** – rebuilt in 2004 after being destroyed in 2003 by bushfire – which relies on a small tank for water.

Beyond the hut the route descends deeper into the forest, crossing a small stream that is reliable in all but the driest of times, and eventually leads to the prominent Camp

Creek Gap about 45 minutes from Michell Hut. Here there is a track junction; take the route heading west into a gully. After only 15 minutes you reach a scrub-free 4WD track. Providing pleasant walking through pretty forest, this track in turn leads in 6km to the end of the walk at the Mountain Creek Camping Area.

SIDE TRIP: HOWMANS FALLS
1 hour, 4km return, 150m descent

The short trip to Howmans Falls, cascading 50m over a series of three smaller falls, is highly recommended. From Cleve Cole Hut follow the walking track, and snow poles, east into the snow gum woodland. The track descends to the treeless Camp Valley, then heads alongside Camp Creek, crossing it twice before swinging round to the south. The path ends at the top of the **waterfall**. Of course, exercise caution when viewing the falls from the nearby (unprotected) cliffs.

If you have allocated a third day for your walk, this side trip can easily be made from the overnight camp near Cleve Cole Hut, combining it with the West Peak side trip for a long day walk.

MT FEATHERTOP & THE RAZORBACK

Duration	2 days
Distance	36km
Standard	demanding
Start/Finish	Harrietville (right)
Nearest Town	Harrietville (right)
Transport	private

Summary Mt Feathertop, Victoria's second-highest peak, rewards walkers with a superb all-round panorama. An unusual hut, excellent views along the impressive Razorback ridge and diverse eucalyptus forest are among the highlights.

Named for the appearance of lingering snowdrifts in spring and often dubbed the 'Queen of the Victorian Alps', Mt Feathertop has attracted walkers for decades. And for good reason: it's one of Victoria's most attractive and impressive mountains; it's cut off from the High Country to the east by the deep valley of the Kiewa River; it boasts commanding views; and it stands

aloof at the head of the Ovens Valley, dominating the skyline. Snaking away from Mt Feathertop to the south is the Razorback, a high bare ridge that's been a mecca for walkers and skiers since the 1930s and is one of Australia's most scenic ridge walks.

In winter, cross-country skiers and budding mountaineers are drawn to Feathertop's snowy slopes, ridges and crags. Built as a base for these activities, the peculiar MUMC Hut (p167) can easily be visited on a short side trip. While winter sees the region at its most dramatic, the slopes are prone to ice and Mt Feathertop has claimed several lives, but in summer the mountain is generally benign and makes for a perfect walking destination.

PLANNING

This is a very exposed walk in sections and you must have a strong weatherproof tent, wet-weather gear, good sleeping bag, warm clothes and a fuel stove. Be aware that there are few places to collect water, apart from the sources indicated, and the water tank at Federation Hut cannot be relied upon; so make sure you carry plenty on each day (2L should be enough). Federation Hut also has a number of sleeping benches, but it's popular and often full so you must be prepared to camp. For more details on clothing and equipment, see the boxed text p39.

Maps

The most useful map for this walk, with an excellent level of topographic and track detail, is the Vicmap 1:50,000 topographic map *Bogong Alpine Area*.

Permits & Regulations

Mt Feathertop and its immediate surrounds, including the Razorback, have been declared a fuel-stove-only area. This means no campfires are permitted, and you must carry a fuel stove for cooking.

NEAREST TOWN
Harrietville

☎ 03 / population 140

At the foot of Mt Feathertop is the village of Harrietville. There's not much to do, but it's a pretty spot and makes a good base for walks to Mt Feathertop. Some maps can be bought at the small general store, but you will need to buy groceries in Bright (p158).

You can gather further information from the **Harrietville Tourism Association** website (www.harrietville.com).

SLEEPING & EATING

The **Harrietville Cabins & Caravan Park** (☎ 5759 2523; hville_cpark@netc.net.au; Camping Park Rd; unpowered/powered sites for 2 $16/20, cabins from $80), backs onto the West Branch of the Ovens River south of the Snowline Hotel.

Shady Brook Cottages (☎ 5759 2741, 0438 050 475; www.shadybrook.com.au; 2 Mountain View Walk; d from $110; 🔀) occupies a bush setting at the foot of Mt Feathertop. There's a choice of B&B rooms or fully equipped cottages with spas and verandas.

CasBak on the Ovens Holiday Units (☎ 5759 2531, www.casbakalpineunits.com.au; 206 Great Alpine Rd; cabins from $95; 🔊) is in a pretty park-like setting dominated by European trees. The salt-water pool is ideal for easing post-walk pains and strains.

Motel-style accommodation can be found at the **Snowline Hotel** (☎ 5759 2524; www .snowlinehotel.com.au; Great Alpine Rd; s/d from $65/75) where you can also arrange for a cooked breakfast and, ahhh, a cold beer!

There's not much for foodies in Harrietville. However, the **Snowline Hotel** (mains $14-18, pizzas $7-15; 🕑 lunch & dinner), which has a sunny balcony where you can enjoy a refreshing drink and meal, is a popular place after a hard walk. The general store has a limited range of takeaway food.

GETTING THERE & AWAY

Harrietville is 24km south of Bright (p159) along the Great Alpine Rd (B500). Although there is no public transport, the **Bright Taxi Service** (☎ 0408 589 370) can take passengers to/from Harrietville.

GETTING TO/FROM THE WALK

From Harrietville, turn east onto Mt Feathertop Rd just north of the School Bridge (near the small general store and riverside park). Follow this road for 1km to where the bitumen ends at a small information board and car park.

THE WALK

Day 1: Harrietville to Federation Hut

5–6 hours, 13km, 1360m ascent, 210m descent

A broad track heads into the forest and crosses a small stream. Fill your drinking

bottles here as there may be no water at the trackside springs further up the mountain. The trail narrows and begins its steady ascent. After 2km you cross a major gully that, during spring, carries a good supply of water. Continue past the signposted Picture Point (although there is nothing to see here) and Tobias Gap, eventually reaching the top of the spur at Wombat Gap (two hours and 6km from the start).

Soon after entering alpine ash forest, you pass a small spring (which is generally reliable for most of the year). Thirty minutes further on you pass the ruins of the **Feathertop Bungalow** – a large structure built in the 1920s for use by skiers, but destroyed by wildfire in January 1939 – on your left; then within 200m you pass a side-track to a small creek a few hundred metres away to the east. This is the last reliable water point along the main track. There are some flat, grassy camp sites at the water-point turn-off.

About 10km from the start, the track breaks out from the forest to arrive at **Federation Hut**, where you get your first good views since starting out. There are sheltered camp sites among the trees near the hut.

The summit cannot be seen from the hut, but a short stroll of a few minutes to a small knoll south of the hut provides a fine view. There is a rainwater tank by the hut (although during dry periods this may be empty) and a spring 30 minutes to the east, though this is not as reliable as the one near the Feathertop Bungalow ruins. Another generally dependable water source is on the west side of Mt Feathertop; see the side trip to the MUMC Hut (p167).

It is worth making the two-hour return trip to the summit on the first day to shorten the walk on Day 2. The track leads northeast from the hut to a track junction in a saddle just to the east of Little Mt Feathertop. Take the left-hand track then, shortly afterwards where the track forks, the right-hand track (the track to the left leads to the MUMC Hut, an interesting side trip). A steep climb up the narrow ridge ends on reaching the summit of **Mt Feathertop** (1922m) where a sweeping panorama of the surrounding peaks and valleys is stunning. With steep slopes dropping away in most directions, you'll feel as though you're on top of the world.

VICTORIA

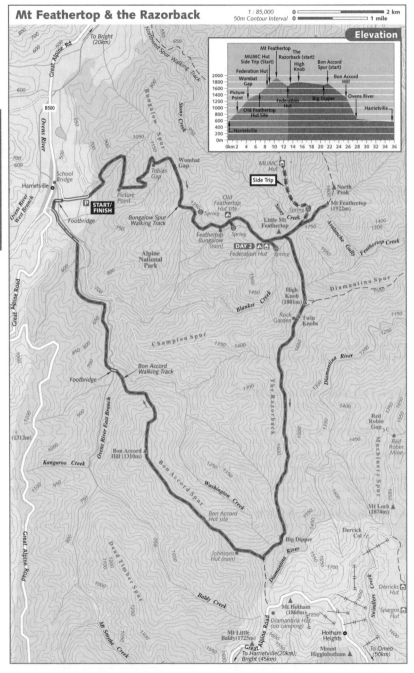

Mt Feathertop & the Razorback

1 : 85,000
50m Contour Interval

Elevation

MT FEATHERTOP UFO

The first geodesic structure of its kind built in Australia, the Melbourne University Mountaineering Club (MUMC) Hut was constructed in the 1960s by a group of active climbers keen to create a base from which they could practise their mountaineering skills in winter. Mt Feathertop was their ideal choice; its steep, snowy slopes are prone to ice (especially on the mountain's steep southeast face) and there is plenty of terrain to hone telemarking, snow camping, cramponing and self-arrest techniques.

Tragically, a car accident on the way to the mountain during construction claimed the lives of three club members, and memorial plaques can be seen in the hut. So prominent was the hut's shiny reflection that Ovens Valley residents, convinced it was distracting to drivers at certain times of day, insisted that the club paint it; every few years the dark green paint job is stripped away by the harsh alpine weather and must be renewed.

SIDE TRIP: MUMC HUT
2 hours, 6km return

A visit to MUMC Hut (see the boxed text above) makes for a pleasant return journey from the camp site. Walk along the track from Federation Hut towards Mt Feathertop, but then take the left-hand track where the trail forks 200m northeast of the saddle near Little Mt Feathertop.

The path initially cuts across the steep western face of Mt Feathertop (crossing a reliable spring) before joining the Northwest Spur for the final section to the hut, which stands beacon-like where the spur begins its headlong descent to the Ovens River valley below.

Day 2: Federation Hut to Harrietville
8–9 hours, 23km, 340m ascent, 1490m descent

Return to the first track junction above Federation Hut and follow the southeast track as it sidles round the west side of a hill to the join the Razorback, a high ridge separating the Ovens and Diamantina River valleys. You will come to yet another junction, where a track heading east leads to Diamantina Spur and a very steep descent to the Kiewa River West Branch. Take the right-hand track, skirting around the western side of High Knob, and bypassing the summit, to arrive at a magnificent **rock garden** that's wedged into the side of the Twin Knobs. During summer, this area is likely to be absolutely carpeted with wildflowers.

Beyond Twin Knobs, the track gains the ridge again and generally follows the spine of the Razorback, at times passing through forested glades, for another 7km to eventually pass into a deep saddle known as

the **Big Dipper**. A short but steep climb to the head of the Bon Accord Spur follows, where you'll be rewarded with extensive views and the comforting knowledge that the remainder of the walk is mostly downhill.

Bear west from the top of the hill and follow the Bon Accord Walking Track. It descends gently at first but then becomes more steep as it moves into tall alpine ash forest to reach the former site of Bon Accord Hut (torched in 2003 by bushfire) on a large flat area 40 minutes from the head of the spur.

The first 2km beyond the hut site is an easy ramble. Soon another descent begins, but the track is not unduly steep, and before long you reach the depths of the valley at the junction of the Ovens River East Branch and Washington Creek, about 7km from the Razorback. The river is crossed on a footbridge, and then a track heads downstream on the western side of the river, providing relaxed walking for a while. Not far from the river crossing, the track improves and follows a course just above an **old aqueduct** for a while. While it's not always obvious, the aqueduct was constructed by gold miners around the turn of the 20th century.

About 4km from the river crossing the track joins a dirt road and this is followed west for a short distance to join a minor sealed road on the fringe of Harrietville. Turn right, then right again after another 100m and follow a foot pad beside the river for 500m to a footbridge over the Ovens River. On the far side is Mt Feathertop Rd, which will lead you back east to the beginning of the walk.

VICTORIA

VICTORIA

MT SPECULATION & THE CROSSCUT SAW

Duration	2 days
Distance	31.5km
Standard	moderate–demanding
Start/Finish	Upper Howqua Camping Area (opposite)
Nearest Town	Mansfield (right)
Public Transport	private

Summary Climb up to the Crosscut Saw, a narrow ridge providing stupendous views, and spend the night at one of the best camp sites in the mountains. An ascent of Mt Howitt, and views of impressive cliffs and crags, completes a great weekend walk.

Since the 1920s the Wonnangatta Wilderness, which includes the peaks of the Mt Howitt area near the headwaters of the Wonnangatta River, has been one of the most sought-after walking areas in the Victorian Alps: the spectacular summits, ridges and spurs in the area have drawn walkers like moths to a flame. With such evocative names given to the geographical features of the area – Mts Buggery and Speculation, the Crosscut Saw and the Terrible Hollow, to name just a few – you can only wonder as to their origins. In 1982 the area was given the protection of national park status, but logging of the superb mountain forests in the lower areas hasn't helped the aesthetics of the once pristine river valleys. Fortunately, many of the old logging tracks are now being reclaimed by nature and are becoming increasingly overgrown, although paradoxically a few major tracks remain, giving relatively easy access for bushwalkers. In the 1980s many of the peaks in this area, including Mt Howitt, were used for horse-riding sequences in the popular Australian films, *The Man From Snowy River* and *The Man From Snowy River 2*.

This really is a beautiful region in which to spend a few days – or longer. As you walk, you'll be wondering what's over the next hill, or round the next bend, and unless fatigue gets the better of you, you may find it hard to stop walking. It's perhaps the most scenic region in the Victorian Alps.

PLANNING

It is essential that you carry enough drinking water for each day as few water points are

passed. There is, however, a reliable water source near the camp on Mt Speculation.

In addition, there are numerous seasonal road closures between the wetter months of June and October, and the access road to the trailhead is closed to traffic at Telephone Box Junction (near Mt Stirling). To check road conditions before you set forth, contact **Parks Victoria Information Centre** (☎ 13 19 63; www.parkweb.vic.gov.au).

Maps

Vicmap's 1:50,000 topographic map *Howitt-Selwyn* covers the entire walk and is the best choice for geographic and contour information. The Victorian Mountain Tramping Club (VMTC) 1:50,000 topographic map *Watersheds of the King, Howqua & Jamieson Rivers*, specially produced for bushwalkers, makes a useful additional reference.

NEAREST TOWN & FACILITIES
Mansfield
☎ 03 / pop 2500

A popular stopping-off point for campers, walkers and 4WD enthusiasts, Mansfield is a major gateway to the Alpine National Park. On weekends, Mansfield could well be regarded as the 4WD capital of Victoria, and you might feel feeble without one!

The **Mansfield visitor information centre** (☎ 5775 1464; www.mansfield-mtbuller.com.au; Maroondah Hwy; ⏰ 9am-5pm) offers an **accommodation booking service** (☎ 1800 039 049).

SUPPLIES & EQUIPMENT

The Maroondah Hwy, named High St in town, is the main road on which you will find an array of shops including banks, a chemist, a post office, food and retail shops, and **Outdoor Pleasure** (☎ 5755 2826; www.outdoorpleasure.com.au; 63 High St), a gear shop selling a wide range of camping, fishing and other outdoor equipment.

SLEEPING & EATING

The **High Country Holiday Park** (☎ 5775 2705; www.highcountryholidaypark.com.au; 1 Ultimo St; bunkhouse $12, unpowered/powered sites for 2 from $20/23, cabins from $63; ⚡)) has a wide range of facilities including a children's pool, games room and tennis courts, and occupies a shady location a short walk from the centre of town.

The **Mansfield Travellers Lodge** (☎ 5775 1800; www.mansfieldtravellodge.com; 116 High St; motel rooms s/d from $75/80; ▨) is in a handy location in the main street and can provide a continental breakfast. Part of the same complex is the **Mansfield Backpackers' Inn** (dm $25). There's a fully equipped kitchen, barbecue, laundry and drying room available for use by motel and inn guests.

In a beautifully restored bank building dating from 1866 is **Tavistock House** (☎ 5775 1024; www.tavistockhouse.com.au; cnr High & Highett Sts; d from $120) where all rooms have been charmingly decked out with Victorian-style furniture and decor. It's smack-bang in the middle of Mansfield, and the owners welcome you with a bottle of vino or bubbly.

The **Mansfield Hotel** (☎ 5775 2101; www.mansfieldhotel.com.au; 86 High St; mains $15-20; ☺ lunch & dinner) dates from 1862, although the fully renovated interior is definitely 21st century. The large courtyard is a pleasant place to enjoy a meal while finalising your walk plans.

The **Mansfield Regional Produce Store** (☎ 5779 1404; 68 High St; mains $7-15; ☺ breakfast & lunch daily, dinner Fri) sells delicious home-made foods for self-caterers, including breads, condiments, ice cream and crepes. If you want to eat in, or just relax with a coffee, grab a seat at the communal table.

The trendy **Sweet Potato** (☎ 5775 1955; 50 High St; mains $10-18; ☺ lunch & dinner Thu-Mon) is a licensed café offering good food with a relaxed ambience.

High St has numerous cafés, takeaway outlets and a supermarket. There's also a supermarket on Highett St.

GETTING THERE & AWAY

Mansfield is 192km northeast of Melbourne along the Melba Hwy (B300) to Yea, Goulburn Valley Hwy and Maroondah Hwy. If coming from the north, leave the Hume Fwy (M31) at the Midland Hwy exit near Benalla and travel south to Mansfield.

V/Line (☎ 13 61 96; www.vline.com.au) operates a daily bus between Melbourne and Mansfield (adult/child $34/17, three hours).

Upper Howqua Camping Area

A number of bush camp sites exist at the trailhead in the upper Howqua River valley. Water is handy, and this location is convenient if you want an early start in the morning.

GETTING TO/FROM THE WALK

There is no public transport from Mansfield to the trailhead, so your best option is to use a private vehicle.

From Mansfield, follow the Mt Buller Rd east for 40km (past the villages of Merrijig and Sawmill Settlement) to a road junction at Mirimbah. Turn left onto the Stirling Rd and this leads, in 8km, to Telephone Box Junction. Follow the right-hand road (Circuit Rd) from the junction for 19km (over Howqua Gap) to an intersection where Bindaree Rd leaves Circuit Rd on the south side.

Bindaree Rd zigzags its way down to meet the Howqua River, about 10km from the turn-off; avoid any minor side tracks that branch from the main road. In the valley, the road is blocked at the Upper Howqua Camping Area and vehicular access terminates here.

THE WALK
Day 1: Upper Howqua Camping Area to Mt Speculation via the Crosscut Saw
5–6 hours, 15.5km, 1310m ascent, 490m descent

Follow the closed road upstream for 3.5km, crossing the river a few times, to a track junction at the foot of Howitt Spur where the valley really starts to feel enclosed. There is a small camping area here.

Cross to the north side of the Howqua River and follow the continuation of Upper Howqua Rd, here called Queen Spur Rd, up the southern slopes of **Stanleys Name Spur**. The track provides easy walking as it climbs steadily for 3.5km (one hour) to a saddle on the crest of the spur. Turn right (east) at the saddle and follow an old, indistinct, 4WD track for 200m to where a yellow marker on a tree indicates the faint walking track on your right climbing to the crest of Stanleys Name Spur. The track undulates until it reaches a pleasant camp site in a **saddle** at the foot of the Crosscut Saw. There is usually water in a creek 100m to the north, except in the driest times. Ahead of you through the trees soars the jagged form of the Crosscut Saw, a narrow ridge lined on its upper slopes with layers of rock, buckled and folded over the ages to create the impressive outline we see today.

Continue east very steeply up the spur; there are a few rocky bluffs to negotiate that require a bit of scrambling and are not

VICTORIA

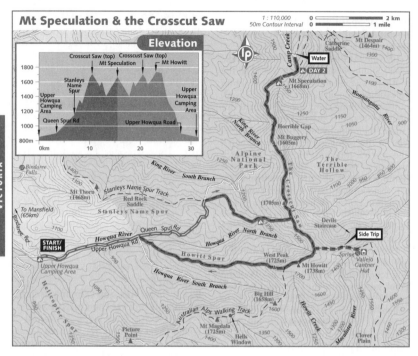

Mt Speculation & the Crosscut Saw
1 : 110,000
50m Contour Interval

for the faint-hearted. After about 1km, the track cuts to the left, sidling across the steep slope, and eventually tops out in a saddle at the southern end of the Crosscut Saw. Turn north here and follow the obvious path, the Australian Alps Walking Track, for about 15 minutes as it climbs to the highest summit of the **Crosscut Saw** (1705m). Spread around you are a number of stunning peaks, although your eyes will likely be drawn to the rugged outlines of the Razor and the Viking to the northeast. As you continue, slopes drop away steeply on both sides of the Crosscut Saw, into the tall forests of the Terrible Hollow on one side, and into craggy slopes on the other.

The track undulates generally northwards over many of the knolls that make up the teeth of the Crosscut Saw, then descends through a saddle before a short climb brings you to **Mt Buggery** (1605m). There are some pretty trees on the summit, although only restricted views. The route certainly falls away quickly from the top to Horrible Gap, although it's not nearly as bad as the names 'Buggery' or 'Horrible' would suggest.

Beyond Horrible Gap the track ascends through thick forest to more open country near Mt Speculation. Higher up the route climbs a few rocky bluffs before arriving at the summit of **Mt Speculation** (1668m) and one of Victoria's most spectacular camp sites. In a region where a surplus of striking peaks rise above the forests, Mt Speculation is one of the best. The view south from the summit, particularly in autumn when fog often fills the upper Wonnangatta Valley early in the morning, is wonderful. On the horizon, beyond the craggy summits of the Razor and Viking, you can even make out Mts Bogong and Feathertop and other peaks of the Bogong High Plains.

There are lots of flat, grassy camp sites on the summit ridge; if the weather is fine it's best to overnight here. Further to the east, and about 100m below the summit, there are more excellent camp sites (still with stunning views), which offer more shelter in adverse conditions. Water can be found at the head of **Camp Creek**, about 1km northeast of the summit, along a well-defined track. It's about a 45-minute return trip.

Day 2: Mt Speculation to the Upper Howqua Camping Area via Mt Howitt
5–6 hours, 16km, 580m ascent, 1400m descent

Return along yesterday's route to the saddle where Stanleys Name Spur track joins the southern end of the Crosscut Saw. From the saddle (2½ hours from Mt Speculation), continue walking along the Australian Alps Walking Track. It passes through another saddle, then climbs onto the exposed plateau northeast of Mt Howitt. Here you'll find a track junction, the left (east) track heading to Macalister Springs and Vallejo Gantner Hut, which can be visited on a side trip (below). Continue southwest over the plains for 1km to **Mt Howitt** (1738m). Here you're greeted by an outstanding panorama and one of the finest viewpoints in the Victorian Alps.

The route now heads west and is less obvious across the summit plateau. At a T-junction, the Australian Alps Walking Track heads south, but keep right and follow the minor track west as it descends to a slight saddle before climbing to the head of Howitt Spur at **West Peak** (1725m). This prominent knoll provides an excellent lookout from which to view the curious geology of the nearby peaks. Differential weathering and folding of sediments has produced dramatic bands of rock, and these tilted sedimentary layers can be seen to good effect on the escarpment running west from near West Peak all the way to the Bluff.

Howitt Spur plummets from West Peak; the track negotiates the very steep upper section by way of a series of short scrambles and zigzags. Once down in the forest, the route eases off considerably and becomes a pleasant ramble all the way to the Howqua River (about 1½ hours from West Peak). Continue along the outward route of Day 1 to the end of the walk.

SIDE TRIP: MACALISTER SPRINGS
1 hour, 3km return, 50m ascent, 140m descent

The short trip to Macalister Springs provides a different, and intriguing, perspective of the depths of Terrible Hollow and the Crosscut Saw. From the track junction 1km northeast of Mt Howitt, a well-defined foot track heads east along a narrow ridge, providing fine views to the north. Leaving the ridge the track contours round to a spring – the headwater of the Macalister

River – and to the slanted A-frame **Vallejo Gantner Hut**, with space for four on a sleeping platform.

There are three camping options in the vicinity of Macalister Springs. The most scenic (but also most exposed) sites are on the ridge a few hundred metres northeast of the spring, while more protected camp sites are just above the spring and near the hut.

MT BUFFALO PLATEAU

Duration	5–6 hours
Distance	16km
Standard	easy–moderate
Start/Finish	Camp Plain
Nearest Towns	Bright (p158)
Public Transport	private

Summary This is a wonderful day walk, with short climbs to three prominent lookouts, giving an excellent overview of Buffalo Plateau. Highlights include attractive snow plains, snow gum and alpine ash forests, and some shapely granite tors.

Mt Buffalo National Park, one of Australia's first national parks, celebrated its centenary in 1998. Named by early explorers Hume and Hovell in 1824 (see the boxed text p105) because of its distinctive shape when viewed from the west, Mt Buffalo has arguably some of the most varied and attractive scenery found anywhere in Australia.

Formed by a geological uplift of molten rock many millions of years ago, the plateau has since been eroded heavily along a series of weaknesses, or faults, leaving today's high plateau; and some of the most bizarre granite rock outcrops you're ever likely to see.

Historically, Mt Buffalo has been popular with nature lovers and bushwalkers since it was first climbed by local miners and farmers in the 1850s. So popular did the area become that in 1910 the Victorian government built the large, rambling, Chalet (p172), which has provided accommodation for thousands of visitors over the years. Australia's first ski lift was constructed on the plateau in 1936, creating an all-season resort.

Mt Buffalo's subalpine environment has a diverse range of flora and fauna, and some plants are endemic to the park, including the Buffalo sallee, Buffalo wattle and fern-leaf baeckea. Many creeks drain the plateau along a series of faults, before plummeting off the plateau's rim in a spectacular series of cascades and waterfalls. Best viewed from the lookouts and tracks near the Chalet (see the boxed text, p174), Crystal Brook and Eurobin Creek are two of these major watercourses.

The described walk – an easy day's outing for most people – encompasses many of the plateau's diverse variety of scenic highlights.

PLANNING

Mt Buffalo soils are extremely fragile and prone to erosion, so please be careful not to stray off the defined tracks. Remember, too, that many of the lookouts on the plateau are simply large boulders often perched precariously above formidable drops, and you'll need to exercise extreme caution in some instances.

Maps & Books

The Vicmap 1:25,000 topographic map *Eurobin* covers the entire walk. However, if you are interested in walking more of the park, you will need to get the 1:25,000 map *Buckland* and possibly the *Dandongadale* and *Nug Nug* maps as well.

Permits & Regulations

Walking permits are not required, but it is a good idea to book a camp site if you wish to camp on the plateau at the Lake Catani Camp Ground (below), which is usually full during holiday periods. There is also a park entry fee of $9.70 for a day, or $15.30 for two days, per car, payable at the Entrance Station.

NEAREST TOWNS & FACILITIES

Although the small town of Porepunkah is close to the base of Mt Buffalo National Park, Bright (p158), only 6km further away, has a wider variety of accommodation choices and loads of eateries.

Lake Catani Camping Ground

The most convenient place to stay near the trailhead for campers is on the plateau at the **Lake Catani Camping Ground** (sites for 2 $16.50). Bookings are essential during holiday times; contact the **Entrance Station** (☎ 03-5756 2328; Mt Buffalo Rd). The camping area is 2km from the start of the walk near the shore of Lake Catani.

Mt Buffalo Chalet

Dating from 1910 is the historic and rustic **Chalet** (☎ 03-5755 1500, 1800 037 038; www.mtbuffalo chalet.com.au; en suite s/d from $70/125, guestroom per person incl shared bathroom $35) where there is an array of outstandingly scenic short walks at your doorstep. Inside the large complex you'll find a cosy bar, a games room with a full-sized billiard table and lounges with open fires, still adorned with early 20th-century fittings. There's a variety of deals on offer; prices increase according to the standard of accommodation and some packages include breakfast, or both breakfast and dinner, in the charming old ballroom. The price also includes your park entrance fee.

GETTING TO/FROM THE WALK

There is no public transport from Bright to Mt Buffalo, except during the winter ski season. If you don't have private transport, you could take a taxi to the plateau; contact the **Bright Taxi Service** (☎ 0408 589 370).

From Bright, drive to Porepunkah along the Great Alpine Rd, then follow the Mt Buffalo Rd into Mt Buffalo National Park. Once on the plateau, 25km from Porepunkah, keep right at an intersection (the left-hand road leads to the Chalet) and continue for about 500m to Reservoir Rd and the start of the walk adjacent to a snow clearing depot.

THE WALK

Reservoir Rd leaves the Mt Buffalo Rd and crosses Camp Plain before following the pretty valley of Crystal Brook upstream. The walking is effortless, and the track almost flat, for a little over 3km (45 minutes) to an intersection. Turn right (west) and follow Mt McLeod Track up the slope for a few hundred metres to a signposted walking track on the left, which heads toward Og, Gog & Magog. The walking track leads above a small reservoir before climbing to a T-junction; turn left and walk 300m to the triple rock formations of **Og, Gog & Magog** (1490m) for fine views of the surrounding terrain and many of the high peaks of the Victorian Alps.

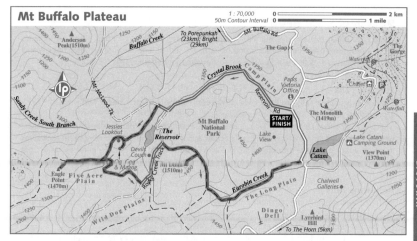

Return to the T-junction and proceed around the flanks of **Jessies Lookout**. Keen observers may notice wombats, or even the elusive lyrebird, in the forested sections of this walk. The track soon descends to the south and arrives at another T-junction. The described walk will return to this point later, but now follow the right-hand track as it skirts around the northern extremity of Five Acre Plain – attractively littered with boulders – which you can see sporadically through the trees. Twenty minutes' walking will bring you to an intersection and a signpost indicating the way 500m southwest to Eagle Point (two hours, 7.5km from the start). Like many other rocky lookouts in the park, **Eagle Point** (1470m) can only be ascended by climbing a series of ladders. The view south from the top includes Mts Cobbler, Howitt, Stirling and Buller. This is also a fine place to enjoy lunch.

Return to the T-junction south of Og, Gog & Magog and head along the walking track pointing to Rocky Creek Track. Initially you feel as if you're heading back towards Eagle Point but soon the track veers southeast past the grassy head of Five Acre Plain before looping around the north side of a hill to meet up with Rocky Creek Track on Wild Dog Plains. Turn left and follow the track north to cross the headwaters of **Crystal Brook**. Here, the tiny rivulet spits and coughs its way around boulders as it flows down the plain. Remarkably, just 4km down the valley, this stream reaches the plateau's

edge at the Gorge, where it dives in a fit of windblown spray over the lip creating a fine feathery waterfall; the tallest in the park.

Press on up the track, soon passing the side track to **Devils Couch**, which can be easily climbed if desired. A little further on, around 10 minutes from the Crystal Brook crossing, is the signposted turn-off (right) to Mt Dunn.

After strolling 1km southeast along this well-trodden path – passing drifts of alpine everlastings and pink trigger plants – you'll reach a T-junction just below Mt Dunn, barely visible through the alpine ash forest. The track climbs to **Mt Dunn** (1510m); again, ladders are required for the ascent. The return journey will take about 30 minutes, but is well worth the effort, particularly as Mt Dunn's central location on the plateau ensures extensive views in all directions. Allow plenty of time to savour the captivating scene from this rocky roost.

Backtrack to the T-junction east of Mt Dunn, turn right and follow the main route south towards Eurobin Creek and the Long Plain, keeping left when passing two signposted side tracks along the way. Once on the Long Plain the track swings to the northeast and stays close to Eurobin Creek, paralleling its south bank for a little over 1km before crossing to the north bank for the final section of track to the Mt Buffalo Rd. With the end in sight, though not visually, a 15-minute stroll north along the road brings you back to Camp Plain.

VICTORIA

MT BUFFALO SHORT WALKS

There is so much to see in Mt Buffalo National Park that you should try and allow a little extra time – you don't need much – for some of its finest sights; here are a few suggestions. You'll need the Vicmap 1:25,000 topographic maps *Buckland* and *Eurobin*.

Eurobin Falls

These two attractive falls are best seen in winter or spring – or after heavy rain – when there's a good flow of water.

Framed by trees, Ladies Bath Falls, just a short walk from the road, is particularly attractive, while Eurobin Falls are more visually spectacular as torrents of water pour over huge rock slabs in a frothy race down the mountainside. The 2km foot track starts about five minutes' drive from the Entrance Station and takes about 45 minutes return.

Rollasons Falls

Buffalo Creek, draining the northern portion of the plateau, rushes through a narrow gorge and has carved the twin Rollasons Falls, two separate falls just a short distance apart. On a hot day, the pool at the base of the lower falls makes a great swimming hole.

The 4km (return) foot track to Rollasons Falls starts about halfway to the plateau from the Entrance Station. As the trail approaches falls, the route divides: left to the upper fall and right to the lower fall, and it's worth visiting both. Allow 1¼ hours.

The Gorge

Immediately in front of the Chalet stupendous cliffs fall away towards the Ovens Valley far below. From the western edge of the car park a 3km (return) track leads to the point where Crystal Brook plummets over the rim of the Gorge. Nearby are numerous excellent lookouts that will keep you awestruck; the views of the falls and distant ranges are exceptional. All tracks are well marked and easy to follow. Allow one hour.

The Monolith

Opposite the Parks Victoria office on Mt Buffalo Rd, near the start of the Mt Buffalo Plateau walk (p171), is a 2km (return) track that ascends east to the balancing tor named the Monolith (1419m), from where a brilliant all-round panorama unfolds.

The trail itself is not difficult and takes about 45 minutes there and back. Although the final climb to the top is up a steep stairway, the perilous-looking tor is quite easily climbed.

The Hump

As the second-highest peak in the Park, the Hump provides a grandstand outlook over the peaks and plains of the plateau, and also affords a close-up view of the Cathedral, probably the plateau's most prominent granite outcrop.

At a high saddle about 1km north of the Cresta ski field, a track heads west away from Mt Buffalo Rd and climbs to another saddle between the Hump and the Cathedral. Follow this track south from the saddle to the Hump (1695m). Allow around 45 minutes for this 1.5km (return) walk.

The Horn

As you'd expect, the views from the Horn (1723m) – the highest point of Mt Buffalo – are not just impressive but also the most extensive of any seen from the plateau.

The 1.5km (return) track begins at the very end of the road across the plateau, about 3km south of the Cresta ski area, where there is a fine lookout. The prominent trail (45 minutes return) climbs round the western and northern edges of the Horn, getting steeper near the top, where the path is protected by wire fences.

WILSONS PROMONTORY NATIONAL PARK

Known affectionately as 'the Prom', 50,300-hectare Wilsons Promontory National Park is almost a byword for bushwalking in Victoria. Hanging from the coast like an afterthought, its granite mountains slope away into secluded, sandy bays. Once the start of a land bridge to Tasmania – you see the same lichen-smeared granite through the Furneaux Islands and the east coast of Tasmania – the Prom now forms the southernmost point of mainland Australia.

Wilsons Promontory is arguably the national park most cherished by Victorians, and certainly among the most used, receiving around 400,000 visitors a year. Great numbers of bushwalkers have had their introduction to overnight walking here, and the Prom's universal appeal means that it continues to attract an eclectic mix of walkers – the person in the tent beside you is just as likely to be carrying a guitar as they are gaiters.

Visitors to the park will find an extensive network of well-maintained walking trails. Walks vary from short nature trails out of Tidal River to overnight rambles to more remote areas. Sections of the Prom Southern Circuit described here are among the park's most popular walking areas, but a carefully managed permit system manages to control any sense of crowding. In 2005 a fire swept through the park, but the flora and fauna are on the road to recovery; see the boxed text p177.

HISTORY

The original inhabitants of the Prom area were the Aboriginal Brataualung people, who called it Yiruk or Woomom. It was a place to retreat to from attackers, though they also spent part of each year here.

The first European to sight the Prom was George Bass in 1798. Returning later with Matthew Flinders, Wilsons Promontory was named after a friend of Flinders. Sealers and whalers were the first to exploit its natural resources; loggers, pastoralists and tin miners followed. A timber mill was built at Sealers Cove (of which you will only notice the remnants of a pier).

In 1898, 36,800 hectares were set aside as a temporary national park. This was made permanent in 1905, though logging, grazing and tin mining all continued at various times.

ENVIRONMENT

Around 18,000 years ago, when ocean levels were far lower, the Prom was the beginning of a granite land bridge that connected Tasmania to the mainland. The Prom has more than 700 native plant species and 33 mammal species, while 230 bird species – about half Victoria's total – breed in or visit the area. If you come in spring, one of the great sights is from the lighthouse, with thousands of short-tailed shearwaters (mutton birds) skimming across Bass Strait. Commonly seen mammals include eastern grey kangaroos, swamp wallabies, echidnas and wombats, which are about as common as campers at Tidal River. Almost decimated by the 19th-century sealing trade, Australian fur seals are occasionally seen on the coast and around the cliffs below the lighthouse.

PLANNING
When to Walk

It is feasible to walk at the Prom year-round, though autumn (March to May) brings the most stable weather, and summer (December to February) the most hours of sunshine. In January the average maximum daily temperature is 20.7°C, but can reach into the high 30°Cs; by July it is a less appealing 11.8°C. The greatest concentration of rain is from May to August. Jutting into Bass Strait, the Prom can experience wild bursts of weather, with the prevailing westerlies dragging in storms – it's worth coming here just to see nature's fury.

The summer school holidays (from just before Christmas until about the end of January) can make the place very crowded, as can Easter.

Maps & Books

The Vicmap 1:50,000 topographic map *Wilsons Promontory National Park* covers all walking tracks in the park with accuracy. *Wilsons Promontory: Marine and National Park Victoria* by Geoff Westcott has detailed notes on the history, geology, and flora and fauna of the park. *Discovering the*

VICTORIA

Prom by the Victorian National Parks Association is a very useful, pocket-sized guide to the many walks around the promontory. *A Field Guide to Wilsons Promontory* by David Meagher and Michele Kohout will get you up to speed on the flora and fauna you will be wandering past.

Information Sources

The park **visitor centre** (☎ 1800 350 552; Tidal River) is 30km south of the park entrance along the access road. Walking-permit applications and accommodation bookings for the lighthouse should be made here.

Park Fees & Regulations

Entry to the Prom costs $9.50 per vehicle, though it is free if you have booked your permit. Overnight walks, such as that described here, require a permit. This can be obtained from the park visitor centre (p175); it is recommended that you book by phone as camp sites on the Prom Southern Circuit – and especially the cottage at the lighthouse – can fill well ahead of time, particularly during summer and Easter.

Fires are banned throughout the park, so carry a fuel stove.

PROM SOUTHERN CIRCUIT

Duration	3 days
Distance	57.6km
Difficulty	moderate
Start	Telegraph Saddle
Finish	Tidal River (p177)
Nearest Town	Foster (p176)
Transport	shuttle service

Summary Spend a night in a lighthouse cottage and wander the beaches and regenerating forests of one of Victoria's most popular walking tracks.

This wide-reaching circuit highlights the best of the Prom's east and west coasts, and throws in a bit of the rugged south as a bonus. You will head out through protected coves on the east coast, and wander back along wild and windswept beaches. In between you will see forests that have begun their rebirth from a major fire (see the boxed text (opposite).

This walk offers the opportunity for a bit of bush luxury. Accommodation on the second night is available in cottages at the lighthouse, and each one has a kitchen, heated lounge and – joy of joys – a hot shower. Bookings are essential.

Before setting out, check tide times at the Tidal River visitor centre; they are posted on a noticeboard outside. While never impassable, the Sealers Creek crossing can rise to a chilling waist height at high tide. Tide tables can be checked in advance at www.bom.gov.au/oceanography/tides – Port Welshpool is the closest listing.

If you want to visit South Point (p180), or just fancy a more leisurely return from the lighthouse, consider extending the walk to four days, with a night camped at Oberon Bay.

All camp sites have toilets and drinking water channelled from creeks.

NEAREST TOWN & FACILITIES
Foster
☎ 03 / pop 1000

The former gold-mining town of Foster, on the South Gippsland Hwy, is a convenient place to break the journey to the Prom and buy supplies. It is the kind of town dependent on its nearby national park – after the April 2005 bushfires, supermarkets recorded a 20% downturn in sales. **Parks Victoria** (☎ 13 19 63; 3a Main St) has an office in town.

Prom Central Caravan Park (☎ 5682 2440; 38 Nelson St; unpowered sites $18-26, powered sites $20-30; cabins $60-85) has free barbecues, a camp kitchen and laundry facilities.

Prom Coast Backpackers Hostel (☎ 5682 2171; 40 Station St; dm/d $25/60; 🖳) is in a converted and homely berry-coloured cottage with free use of bikes and the washing machine. Next door, comfortable **Warrawee Holiday Apartments** (r $90-110) are owned by the same family. Transport to Tidal River can also be arranged (see p177).

Foodworks (Main St) and **IGA** (Main St) supermarkets are about 50m apart.

Dining choices are limited. The **Exchange Hotel** (43 Main St; mains $15-27; ☺ lunch & dinner) is open every day – come Tuesday for a cheap chicken schnitzel – while the **Foster Golf Club** (Reserve St; ☺ dinner) has bistro-style meals and doubles as the local Chinese takeaway.

V/Line (☎ 13 61 96; www.vline.com.au) has a weekday bus service departing Melbourne's Southern Cross station at 4.30pm, arriv-

BLACK BEAUTY

In late March 2005, Wilsons Promontory park rangers conducted planned burns around Tidal River. Ten days later, on 1 April, a fire reignited, burning south to within metres of the lighthouse. Around 6200 hectares, or 13% of the national park, was burned, most of it in the area of the walk described here.

It was a publicity disaster, prompting a media rant against planned burns, but when the bulk of the walking tracks reopened six months later, spring had well and truly sprung from the ashes. Grass trees were thriving and wildflowers were making their return. Eucalypts were sprouting new growth and fresh wombat scat littered the paths.

The contrast that already existed between the Prom's east and west coasts had become a gulf. The east coast between Sealers Cove and North Waterloo Bay was untouched by fire, while the west coast – particularly behind Little Oberon Bay – burned so intensely it looked like a preview of the apocalypse. Other contrasts had been created anew, with slopes of burned forest ending in gullies still thick with rainforest.

It is these contrasts that are the new attraction of walking at the Prom. It is worth re-visiting this walking wonderland even if you have been here many times before.

ing in Foster at 7.15pm (the Saturday bus departs Melbourne at 6.50pm, and the Sunday bus leaves from Dandenong train station at 6.40pm). The return service leaves Foster at 7.49am daily except Sunday; the Sunday bus departs Foster at 3.25pm. An extra service departs Melbourne on Friday at 6.10pm. Tickets cost $27.

Tidal River

The popularity of **Tidal River camping ground** (☎ 1800 350 552; camp sites for 3 peak/off-peak $20/16.50, 4-bed hut peak/off-peak $56/54, 6-bed hut peak/off-peak $85/81, unit peak/off-peak from $106/93, cabin peak/off-peak from $147/134) has made it a virtual metropolis of Victorian camping. Such is the demand that a ballot system is used to allocate sites over the summer school holidays (from about Christmas until the end of January). Applications for huts and cabins during this period are accepted during May, with the draw taking place on 1 June. Applications for camp sites are accepted through June, with a 1 July draw. A minimum stay of one week is required at this time. There is a small shop with a limited range of groceries, camping supplies and takeaway food.

GETTING THERE & AWAY

To drive to Tidal River from Melbourne, join the South Gippsland Hwy in Dandenong and continue until the signed turn-off for Wilsons Promontory at Meeniyan (148km). Tidal River is 73km from Meeniyan via Fish Creek. Allow about three hours.

There is no public transport to Tidal River, but Prom Coast Backpackers Hostel (p176) will drop you off and pick you up from the Prom ($15 per passenger) with advance arrangement.

GETTING TO/FROM THE WALK

In the main walking season – November to Easter – the road to Telegraph Saddle is closed and a free shuttle bus operates between the Tidal River visitors' car park and Telegraph Saddle. If walking outside this season, the road is open, and you will either have to slog up it, a walk of around an hour, or leave a car at Telegraph Saddle and Tidal River.

THE WALK
Day 1: Telegraph Saddle Car Park to Refuge Cove
4–5½ hours, 16.5km, 280m ascent, 480m descent

From the car park's eastern end, follow the 'Sealers Cove' sign pointing east. The sandy track heads out through eucalyptus forest, contouring gently round Mt McAllister and up the southern slope of Titania Creek valley. As you near Windy Saddle (45 minutes from the car park) you leave the burned area and won't see it again until Waterloo Bay. A grassy circle in thick bush, Windy Saddle once had views but they are now blocked by trees.

From here the track continues roughly east for the next 7km, descending 300m through sassafras, myrtle and beech to Sealers Cove. The last 2km of the walk is

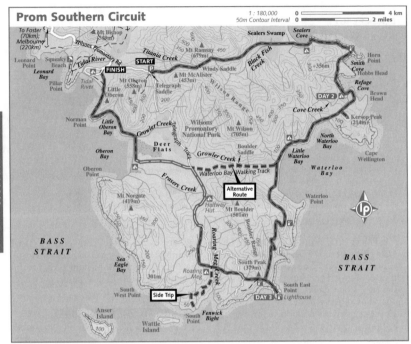

Prom Southern Circuit

through the primordial-looking Sealers Swamp, much of it along a boardwalk. The water in **Black Fish Creek** (and the drinking water at each of the camp sites) is rust-coloured from the tannin leached from the surrounding tea-trees.

Once you hit the beach at **Sealers Cove**, turn right and walk 500m to the Sealers Creek outlet for your first (and deepest) wade. The Sealers Cove camp site is just beyond, 1½ to two hours from Windy Saddle.

Walk directly through the camp site and onto the signposted track to Refuge Cove. Climb for 45 minutes up and around the headland to a lookout near **Horn Point** with uninterrupted views of Five Mile Beach (one of the destinations for the Prom Northern Circuit, p188) to the north and the Seal Islands to the east. As you round Horn Point there is a view ahead to Refuge Cove and, immediately behind it, Kersop Peak.

Turning southwest, the path angles around Smith Cove, cuts across the 'neck' of Hobbs Head and descends to North Refuge Beach. Turn right and plough along the

beach for 50m, turning back onto the track, which continues above the foreshore rocks to the next sandy bay at **Refuge Cove**. The immediate camp site is reserved for boat campers, so walk down onto the beach and along to its opposite end. Take the track back into the bush to reach the walkers' camp site on the true left bank of Cove Creek. This is arguably the best-set camp site at the Prom.

Day 2: Refuge Cove to Wilsons Promontory Lighthouse

5–6½ hours, 17.9km, 580m ascent, 530m descent
This day begins with a good heart-starter. Climb around the scrubby headland over slabs of exposed granite with good views back to Refuge Cove, turning south for a winding ascent to the side-track (on the left) to **Kersop Peak** (214m), 30 to 45 minutes from Refuge Cove. The summit (10 minutes return) is one of the best vantage points along the walk, with fantastic views south to Waterloo Bay, the lighthouse and sharp-tipped Rodondo Island, which is actually a part of Tasmania.

Back on the main path, descend to **North Waterloo Bay** through shady stringybark woodland. Walk southwest along the beach and, at its end, follow the track back above the rocks. This section of track has been rebuilt after the April 2005 bushfires; it now climbs up onto the hillside and soon through areas burned in the fires.

Descend onto the beach at **Little Waterloo Bay** and cross the tannin-stained creek. Turn up into the bush to the camp site (1¼ to 1¾ hours from Kersop Peak). From here the track continues behind the beach (there's no access to the track from the beach's southern end). Continue south round the headland, fording Freshwater Creek as you come out onto **Waterloo Bay beach**.

Almost immediately the alternative route (p180) turns west, but the main route continues south along the beach for 1.7km. Nearing the end of the beach, about 40 minutes from Little Waterloo Bay, the track turns up through the dunes and begins the steep 300m climb onto the slopes of Mt Boulder.

At the top of the climb you rise onto a ridge of secondary summits, following the ridgeline south for a short time until you come to a **lookout** on a large granite boulder. The lighthouse now looks near and North Waterloo Bay pleasantly far behind. From here the track swings west, cutting across the ridge and descending in indirect fashion into the adjacent valley. Cross the rainforested creek, then ascend the adjoining spur.

VICTORIA

WILSONS PROMONTORY DAY WALKS

As one of Victoria's prime weekend getaways, Wilsons Promontory has rightly acquired a network of short tracks that could extend your stay here beyond the three days it takes you to walk the Southern Circuit. The following trails are all easily accessed from Tidal River. Little Oberon Bay and Sealers Cove can also both be reached on day walks.

Mt Oberon

From Telegraph Saddle, climb west to the summit of Mt Oberon (558m), ascending about 350m. Though it is far from the Prom's highest peak it is regarded as the best viewpoint. Allow two hours for this 6.8km return walk.

Vereker Outlook

For a view of Corner Inlet – the bite in the Prom's northern edge – drive to the Five Mile car park, on Five Mile Rd, and climb past a rocky outcrop to this lookout at the northern end of the Vereker Range. It will take an hour to complete this one-hour, 3km return walk.

Tongue Point

From Darby Saddle (on the main park road) a 5.6km trail heads through eucalypt woodland and she-oaks, and past two minor summits with good views, to near the tip of narrow Tongue Point. Allow about 1½ hours. If you have two vehicles, you can leave one at the Darby River car park and walk to it from Tongue Point to vary the route.

Mt Bishop

Begin this 5.3km, two-hour route by climbing along the easy Lilly Pilly Gully walk (which can be accessed from the Tidal River camping ground), then ascend to the summit of Mt Bishop (319m) for a good look across Tidal River. Return part way along the ascent trail before turning off southwest for a shorter and steeper descent.

Picnic Bay & Whisky Bay

The small beaches of Picnic Bay and Whisky Bay, north of Tidal River, can be reached on short tracks from nearby car parks, but a more interesting approach is to begin from Squeaky Beach, crossing Leonard Point to Picnic Bay. Continue to this beach's northern end and cross Picnic Point to Whisky Bay. Return along the same route; the 4km return walk will take about 1½ hours.

Follow it south, with a few westerly veers, until finally contouring around South Peak to a track junction (two to three hours from Waterloo Bay). Turn left, and it's a 15-minute walk, past some wind-sculpted tors, to the **lighthouse cottages** (Sun-Fri $43-69, Sat $71-95). The concrete path to the lighthouse is the steepest climb of the day.

The managers offer **lighthouse tours** (☿2-4pm) but only to guests.

ALTERNATIVE ROUTE: WATERLOO BAY WALKING TRACK
1¼–1¾ hours, 4.8km

If you are short on time or energy you can slice off the southern half of this walk by turning inland at Waterloo Bay beach. Fifty metres past Freshwater Creek, turn west (right), making your way up through wetlands and hakea-studded heathland to the large boulders on Boulder Saddle. Mt Wilson (705m) rises to the north.

Beyond the saddle is a series of giant granite tors. The path contours beneath them and descends through banksias, tea-trees and gnarled she-oaks to the junction with Telegraph Track, rejoining the main route as it returns from the lighthouse.

Day 3: Wilsons Promontory Lighthouse to Tidal River
6¼–8 hours, 23.2km, 550m ascent, 600m descent

Return to the track junction 1km from the lighthouse, turning left and beginning the climb west. Within five minutes, a side track of just a few metres leads to a **lookout** back to the lighthouse. Continue climbing to reach Telegraph Track, a management-vehicle road, turning right. Follow this zigzagging road for 600m, watching for an unmarked foot track to the left. Take this track, which heads directly west to **Roaring Meg camp site**, cutting out the meanders of the road, though adding in a few steep pinches as you climb in and out of three creeks. Roaring Meg is reached 1½ to two hours from the lighthouse.

The side trip to South Point (p180) leaves from the southern end of the camp site, while the main track heads off west (left) about 20m before you reach the road. Quickly it veers north, through a sea of grass trees, before rejoining Telegraph Track.

Telegraph Track rounds Martins Hill and descends past **Halfway Hut camp site**, with glimpses west to Oberon Bay, to reach the junction with Waterloo Bay Walking Track (about two hours from Roaring Meg). Continue straight on for 100m, turning left onto the marked track to Oberon Bay.

Pass by the camp site, with its warren of sites, and out onto the beach at **Oberon Bay** (45 minutes to one hour from the track junction). Turn right onto the beach, which is 2km long and bordered by an extensive system of sand dunes. Cross Growler Creek and turn upstream for 100m to the heavily eroded track entrance. Contour around to **Little Oberon Bay**.

Round the headland to Norman Point lookout (its views will be pretty much obliterated once the bush regenerates) before descending the final 1km to **Norman Beach**. You can reach Tidal River on the path through the stand of tea-trees behind, or you can give your feet a final flogging on the concrete-hard beach to arrive at the camping ground two to three hours from Oberon Bay.

SIDE TRIP: SOUTH POINT
2 hours, 7.4km

The walk to South Point is one for the logbook: this is the southernmost point of mainland Australia. Take the track heading south from Roaring Meg camp site and contour round the hills before descending to the rocky point. Ahead is only Bass Strait – if you squint you still won't be able to see Tasmania.

CROAJINGOLONG NATIONAL PARK

Croajingolong…a difficult place to spell but a great place to walk. This national park is one of 12 biosphere reserves in Australia, and protects a magnificent stretch of rugged Victorian coastline, extending from Bemm River in the west to Cape Howe in the east, on the NSW state border. It is a wild, 87,500-hectare tangle of swamps, forests and heathlands, fringed by remote, windswept beaches and tidal estuaries, and is one of the last remaining untouched bits of coast in southeast Australia.

Despite being coated in magnificent bush, it is the coast that is Croajingolong's great attraction, and on the walk described here you will see the greater part of it. It is also something of a treasure chest of wildlife. On one visit here we encountered fur seals, snakes, sea-eagles, wedge-tailed eagles, bats, crabs, a ring-tailed possum, dolphin, lace monitor, wallaby and scorpions…all in one day.

HISTORY

Aboriginal occupation at Croajingolong dates back more than 40,000 years, and this area was a favoured residence of the Krautungulung people – the name Croajingolong is a corruption of their name. Evidence of their long occupation is visible in the many shell middens that occur at various points along the sandy coast – more than 60 are known to exist.

Point Hicks, about 2km west of Thurra River, was the first section of eastern Australian spotted by James Cook's *Endeavour* crew in 1770, and George Bass also sheltered in Wingan Inlet for 10 days in 1797. Sealers had arrived by 1820, and went on to all but wipe out the local Australian fur seal population (happily seals have since returned).

During WWII, the area that is now Mallacoota aerodrome was a strategic defence base from which Hudson bombers patrolled the waters of Bass Strait looking for Japanese submarines. The threat was taken so seriously that all shipping was generally routed away from the strait and round the coast of Tasmania. Japanese sub crews are known to have come ashore on the remote beaches to take on water supplies. The current Old Coast Rd, now used as part of the coast walking track, was once a military supply and telegraph line, connecting an observation post on Little Rame Head with the operations headquarters at Mallacoota.

ENVIRONMENT

The vegetation in Croajingolong is extremely diverse, ranging from subtropical vines, ferns, mosses, native orchids and stands of warm temperate forest, to banksia forest and heathland on the coastal fringe. Inland there are pockets of rainforest, as well as woodlands, plains and low-lying swamps.

The bird life is the park's most evident and prolific natural feature. More than one-third (or 306) of Australian bird species have been recorded here – more even than in Kakadu. Pelicans, lyrebirds, satin bowerbirds, parrots, cockatoos, oystercatchers, sea-eagles, hawks and migrating seabirds are all present. There are also 52 mammal and 26 reptile species, including the giant lace monitor, a regular sight along the walk, even on the beaches. The Skerries, a set of rock islands just off the coast at Wingan Inlet, support a colony of Australian fur seals. They can often be seen in the inlet or even on the beach beside the inlet – do not approach them. If you are lucky you may see migrating whales heading up and down the coast.

INFORMATION

When to Walk

Croajingolong is enjoyable at any time of the year, though severe storms and strong winds are common, so be prepared for all events, even in summer. Winter can be cold and wet (in June the average maximum at nearby Gabo Island is 14°, with more than 100mm of rain). That said, the number of clear sunny days on this coast varies little between summer and winter.

What to Bring

Carry a good stock of garbage bags as your pack may become immersed during a river crossing, or you may even need to float it across at Wingan Inlet. Weather conditions leading to flooded rivers and heavy seas can mean waiting at the source of the problem until conditions improve, so take an extra day or two of food for emergencies.

Maps & Books

Vicmap's 1:50,000 topographic maps *Cann-Point Hicks* and *Mallacoota* adequately cover the route. *Walking the Wilderness Coast* by Peter Cook and Chris Dowd is an excellent book, covering the coast from Lakes Entrance to Pambula (NSW) – about an 18-day walk if you are keen.

Permits & Regulations

A strict permit system applies to overnight walkers in Croajingolong National Park. Between Thurra River and Wingan Inlet, and again between Wingan Inlet and Shipwreck Creek, only 25 walkers are permitted to camp each night. You are allowed to camp a maximum of two nights in one spot, and the number of walkers in a group is limited to eight.

In busy times, especially over the Christmas holidays and Easter, the demand for permits exceeds the allotted number, so it is wise to book well ahead. Bookings for Easter open on 1 January, and for Christmas on 1 August. At other times of the year you can book permits up to three months ahead. Permits cost $5 per person per night.

Permit forms can be obtained from **Parks Victoria** (☎ 13 19 63) and should be sent to the **Mallacoota Parks Victoria office** (fax ☎ 03-5161 9540; PO Box 179, Mallacoota 3892).

CROAJINGOLONG COAST WALK

Duration	5 days
Distance	59km
Difficulty	moderate
Start	Thurra River camping ground (p183)
Finish	Mallacoota aerodrome
Nearest Towns	Mallacoota (opposite), Cann River (p183)
Transport	shuttle service

Summary Wander the wild, rugged coast of far-eastern Victoria, across some of the most unspoilt beaches in the state. Sweeping deserted stretches of sand, rocky headlands, coastal dunes and tidal inlets are all features.

The coast around and in Croajingolong National Park often goes under the stage name of the 'Wilderness Coast', and it is by far the wildest, most removed bit of coast in the state. This walk follows the coast almost unstintingly, wandering inland only when the coast becomes impassable, and features a variety of scenery ranging from wide, open beaches to small coves with rocky headlands, river estuaries and coastal heathlands.

Water can be an issue on this walk, particularly at the height of summer. High tides can inundate the river estuaries and make their water brackish and undrinkable for many kilometres upstream. In summer, water sources can dry up, so the nightly stops may need to be varied from those given here, depending on water supplies. Alternative water sources are detailed in the walk description, and you should always check with park authorities in Mallacoota

or Cann River as to the current water situation. Be certain to treat all drinking water.

Almost one-third of Croajingolong is designated as 'wilderness' area, meaning that it is being left to return to its natural state. This walk passes through some of that wilderness area, particularly across Sandpatch Point, and by its nature it is more wild and tangly than most tracks you will encounter. Already there are some grumbles among walkers that the signage on this route is not sufficient, making route-finding difficult. In light of this, walkers should be proficient in bush navigation.

While it is possible for a fit and gung-ho walking party to traverse this route in good weather in as little as three long days, it is worth taking the time to absorb and explore the region at a leisurely pace.

NEAREST TOWNS & FACILITIES
Mallacoota
☎ 03 / pop 1040
Abutting the NSW border, and completely surrounded by Croajingolong, Mallacoota is a one-road-in, one-road-out town with great access to remote ocean beaches, an extensive estuarine waterway system, an abundance of bird life, surf and, of course, the national park. **Mallacoota Information Shed** (☎ 5158 0800; Main Wharf, cnr Allan & Buckland Drs) is operated by friendly volunteers, while **Parks Victoria** (☎ 5161 9500; cnr Allan & Buckland Drs) has excellent outdoor displays and information on Croajingolong. **Mallacoota Bait & Tackle** (☎ 5158 0050; 14 Allan Dr) has some very basic camping gear.

SLEEPING & EATING
All prices here are off-peak; work some overtime if you are coming in Christmas holidays, because prices shoot up.

Mallacoota Foreshore Camp Park (☎ 5158 0300; camppark@bigpond.com; unpowered/powered sites for 2 $14/17.50, on-site caravans $35) has hundreds of grassy sites extending along the foreshore, with sublime views of the lake and its resident black swans and pelicans.

At **Mallacoota Hotel Motel & Backpackers** (☎ 5158 0455; inncoota@speedlink.com.au; 51-55 Maurice Ave; dm $22, motel s/d from $55/66; ❂ ❂) the backpacker rooms are a bit shabby but there is a good shared kitchen and it is conveniently located next to the pub (and you get use of the motel pool). Simple motel rooms overlook the lawn and pool.

The eco-friendly, creative and comfortable **Adobe Mudbrick Holiday Flats** (☎ 5159 0329; www .adobeholidayflats.com.au; 17-19 Karbeethong Ave; cabins $55-135) are about 5km from town, with plentiful wildlife and gorgeous inlet views. Linen costs extra and kayaks are available for hire.

The early-1900s timber **Karbeethong Lodge** (☎ 5158 0411; www.karbeethonglodge.com.au; d $75-180) has small bedrooms but wonderful serenity on the broad verandas overlooking the inlet. Rates include continental breakfast.

There are two supermarkets on Maurice Ave in the centre of town for any last-minute supplies. **Croajingolong Cafe** (Allan Dr; mains $6.50-11; ☺ breakfast & lunch Tue-Sun) overlooks the inlet and is a perfect place to linger and settle into walking speed. Great smoothies; no credit cards.

Tide Restaurant (☎ 5158 0100; 70 Maurice Ave; mains $15-25; ☺ dinner) has a prime lakeside location, and serves quality food and wine. The sunny outdoor deck is deservedly popular.

GETTING THERE & AWAY
Mallacoota is 23km off the Princes Hwy. **V/Line** (☎ 13 61 96; www.vline.com.au) services travel to/from Melbourne ($68, eight hours) on Tuesday, Thursday and Sunday. Be sure to inform V/Line that you are going to Mallacoota, as a shuttle bus meets passengers at Genoa, on the highway, for the transfer into town.

Cann River
☎ 03 / pop 250
A highway crossroads, small Cann River is 40km from the walk start at Thurra River. You will find basic food supplies but you should pick up your walking provisions elsewhere. The **Parks Victoria** (☎ 5158 6351; Princes Hwy) office is the main visitor information centre for Croajingolong – collect your permits here.

Toss a three-sided coin to choose between Cann River's motels. If you are weary you can plump for one of the two spa rooms at **Cann Valley Motel** (☎ 5158 6300; cannvalleymotel@bigpond .com.au; Princes Hwy; s&d $80-120).

The courtyard at **Pelican Point Coffee Lounge** (Princes Hwy) is great on a sunny day.

Thurra River Camping Ground
At the trailhead, **Thurra River camping ground** (sites off-peak/peak $13.50/15) has running water

and pit toilets. Advance bookings are required over summer and Easter school holidays.

If you want something a little more seductive, you can stay in former lighthouse-keeper cottages at nearby **Point Hicks Lighthouse** (☎ 03-5158 4268; www.pointhicks.com.au; up to 6 people $230-300), mainland Australia's tallest lighthouse. During the summer and Easter school holidays, there is a minimum seven-night stay; on long weekends it is a minimum of three nights. Bookings for the camping ground can be made through the lighthouse or Parks Victoria.

GETTING TO/FROM THE WALK
To drive to Thurra River camp site, take Tamboon Rd south from Cann River for 15km, turning left onto Point Hicks Rd and following it for 25km. Point Hicks Rd may be closed after heavy rain.

A car shuttle from Mallacoota to Thurra River can be arranged through **Tony Gray** (☎ 0408 516 482, 03-5158 0472). He charges $200 for up to six people. Your car is left at the Mallacoota aerodrome.

THE WALK
Day 1: Thurra River Camping Ground to Gale Hill Camp Site
4 hours, 10km
Follow the dirt road from the camping ground east, take a right turn at the fork and head out to the beach via several other camp sites. Head east along the beach and you will soon come to the outflow of the Thurra River. This crossing is usually a fairly straightforward wade, though heavy rains can increase the flow considerably. Occasionally, the flow will be blocked altogether by a sandbar.

Continue east along the beach for 1.5km to the mouth of the Mueller River – if you have waded the Thurra it is almost certain you will be getting wet again. Water can be found behind the dunes on the eastern side of the inlet, 300m up from the crossing.

Continue along the beach, which provides great swimming in summer but can be exposed to strong southerly winds in winter. Head for the visible rocky section of beach, cross this and a rocky prominence soon becomes visible on the beach: here lies the entrance between the dunes to Gale Hill. Follow this track over the dunes,

VICTORIA

across a small wooden bridge and into the tea-tree for five minutes to the camp site. Water is available from a small soak here, though it may dry up in hot weather.

Day 2: Gale Hill Camp Site to Wingan Inlet
4 hours, 12km

Return to the coast and continue east along the beach, heading towards rocky **Petrel Point**. Continue over the rocks around the point, keeping slightly inland towards the grassy patches in bad weather. If the wind is really strong and the sea is raging, there is a rough track through vegetation higher up the hill.

Drop down onto the second small beach when the end of the rocks is reached and head east, passing many small rocky outcrops for about 3km. A high dune here comes close to the sea, and can be an obstacle at high tide or in rough seas. Cross the rock bar and a signpost appears marked with red arrows, heading left up into the sand hills. This section of track cuts overland through melaleuca scrub to avoid the

cliffs of **Rame Head**. Rock hopping round Rame Head is not recommended as large waves and tides may prevent access, and rocks may be slippery or unstable.

In about one hour, a track junction to Ram Head (a peak not the point) is marked. A brief but quite steep walk gets you to a **lookout** here, and is worth visiting. Back on the track, which is marked by red arrows as it continues northeast, the forest becomes more dense and is very pretty. The track then drops into attractive **Fly Cove**, just before Wingan Inlet.

Head northeast along the sand and pick up the vague track visible on the lower section of sand dunes. This leads to the camp site, along a wooden boardwalk around the inlet lagoon. This camp site is accessible to car campers, but there is a designated camping area for wakers, along with a supply of water.

Day 3: Wingan Inlet to Benedore River
5–6 hours, 15km

Wingan Inlet is one of the larger estuaries on the coast and has a fast outflow. Only

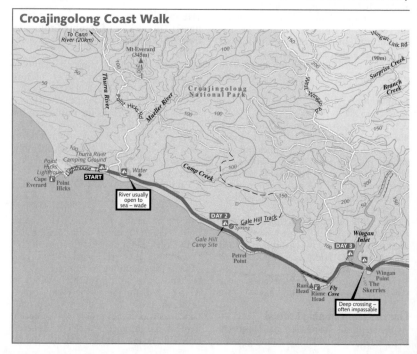

Croajingolong Coast Walk

attempt this crossing at low tide (see the boxed text p186); the current is strong, so be careful. If the inlet is deep in summer, ask around and you may be able to arrange a lift across in a boat with anglers camped here. In winter, however, the place is a little deserted, especially mid-week. If, as a last resort, you are forced to swim or wade across deep water, bag up your goods inside a garbage bag (don't bother with the pack itself), pop it inside your pack and watch out for deep holes.

A small track – the Easby Track – continues on the other side (another camp site is located here) and heads up the hill. After 15 minutes it drops back down to the beach. Head towards Easby Creek with a lot of rock hopping, passing a small soak on the way that is a good source of water. Water in Easby Creek in not suitable for drinking; there is a camp site here, however.

Continue rock hopping along the coast for about 4km, after which **Red River** is reached. The estuary here is wide and deep, but the crossing point near the sea is usually an easy wade across. Walk along the mouth of Red River across the beach. About 100m past the river entrance, follow the Red River Walking Track left into the dunes.

Climb steeply up and over the first and second dunes, descending wooden steps to the Red River camp site, perched above the beautiful estuary and nestled among tea-trees and banksias. The water here is brackish. An alternative water supply is about 30 minutes away along the overgrown 4WD track (turning left at a junction). If the weather is windy you may prefer to camp here than at Benedore River.

Follow the overgrown 4WD track, heading right at the junction and walking northeast up a hill through progressively thicker forest and sword grass to a second track junction. Take the right fork (signposted 'Sand Patch Track') and follow it through thick forest to where the track narrows and drops to the beach. Water can be found near where the track exits – fill up here if possible. Continue for 15 minutes along the beach to **Benedore River**. There are camp sites on both sides of the inlet, but the higher, less swampy west side is better.

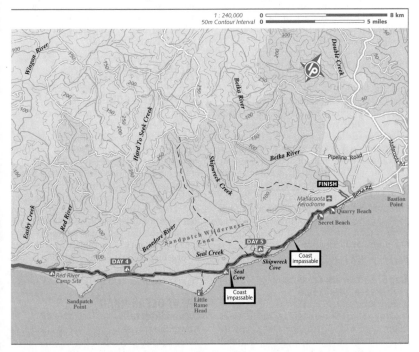

VICTORIA

WARNINGS

High seas, high tides and stormy, southerly weather can make walking over rocky points unsafe, and crossing the many inlets difficult. Fast-flowing water can sweep you off your feet, pack and all, and push you into the breakers. As a general rule, if you are in any doubt about the safety of a crossing, wait. Wingan Inlet can be particularly deep and difficult, and should only be tackled as close to low tide as possible. Check tide times at www.bom.gov.au/oceanography/tides before you set out – tides are listed for Eden (NSW), though Point Hicks tides are only eight minutes later. Check also with Parks Victoria for information on the status of crossings.

Snakes are very common throughout the park, so care is required (particularly near scrubby areas around water courses where they may be foraging for food). Wearing gaiters can provide a small measure of protection.

Paralysis ticks are extremely common in this area, and it is wise to check yourself and your companions each night for these tiny, unwelcome passengers – see p384 for information on removing ticks.

Day 4: Benedore River to Shipwreck Creek
3½ hours, 10km

Cross the inlet. It can be a little deep, but is generally easy to wade across. Pick up the track beside the lagoon that heads north for 150m to the camp site on this side. An old 4WD track continues inland from here and over the dunes behind Little Rame Head to Seal Cove (about two hours from Benedore River). Take the side track to the small **Little Ram Head** peak for an interesting diversion, though the junction can be hard to see.

Seal Cove has a pretty camp site right near the beach, and the swirling patterns in the pyramid-shaped rock at the beach's eastern end are worth a look. On the west side of Seal Creek, a track heads off into the scrub, continuing uphill through forest towards the west, then swinging east to cross Seal Creek. Head along an old 4WD track until a gate marked 'Walkers Only' is reached; pass through the gate and continue on the track through heathland bordered by forest. The trail crosses a section of boggy ground for about 30 minutes before descending through the trees to pretty **Shipwreck Cove**. Walk up the steps and continue 500m to the camp site in the forest, just to the south of the numbered car-camping spots. Water is available upstream in Shipwreck Creek.

Day 5: Shipwreck Creek to Mallacoota Aerodrome
4 hours, 12km

Pick up the track marked 'To Heath Track 200m' and follow it to the Old Coast Rd (it's been closed to vehicles for some time).

You leave the forest quickly and continue through heathland, skirting the cliffs of the rocky coastline, with glimpses of small coves emerging through the heath. Head along the track until you reach an intersection with Centre Track, which leads to **Secret Beach**; you are now outside the national park. Turn right and follow the road north as it turns to bitumen. Skirt Mallacoota aerodrome to pick up your car if it was left here during the car shuttle. If you came to Mallacoota by bus, just keep walking along the road; the town is about 5km ahead.

MORE WALKS

LERDERDERG GORGE

Across the highway from Werribee Gorge (p130), Lerderderg is deeper and longer and offers a more committing gorge walk. Beginning at O'Briens Crossing camping ground, the way is obvious (follow the bed of the Lerderderg River) even if the going is not; at times over the three days you will be bush-bashing through the vegetated river bed. There are no designated camp sites but there are some beautiful small beaches on which to roll out your mat. Ending at Mackenzies Flat picnic ground, you will need to organise a car shuttle. Meridian Maps' 1:35,000 topographic map *Lerderderg & Werribee Gorges* 1:35,000 covers the gorge.

GREAT OCEAN ROAD
Lorne Waterfalls

Above the tourist town of Lorne a series of waterfalls tumbles out of the Otway Range.

From Cumberland River in the west to Cora Lynn or Erskine Falls in the east, it is a simple task to piece together a walk that incorporates up to 13 waterfalls. Two days is a comfortable time to see all the waterfalls, and you can base yourself in Lorne or camp the night at a small site beside Sharps Rd. Plan your route by scanning Vicmap's 1:50,000 topographic map *The Otways & Shipwreck Coast*. Lorne is serviced by the daily **V/Line** (☎ 13 61 96; www.vline.com.au) bus between Melbourne and Apollo Bay.

GRAMPIANS NATIONAL PARK
Wonderland
The extraordinary Wonderland Range is deservedly the most popular walking area in the Grampians. The best (and longest) approach to the range winds its way past the Elephants Hide, through Grand Canyon and Silent Street and up to the protruding summit of the Pinnacle. Heading back, about 50m below the Pinnacle a track signposted to Halls Gap leads to the right along the cliff top for several hundred metres, then down the eastern flank of the Wonderland Range. Allow about four hours for this 9.6km walk. Vicmap's *Northern Grampians* map has a 1:25,000 inset of the Wonderland Range that shows the tracks. Beginning in Halls Gap itself, this is one of the few Grampians walks you can access without a vehicle.

Mt Rosea
Mt Rosea (1009m) is the most rewarding of the Grampians' high peaks. Mt William and the D'Alton Peaks are slightly higher, but the first is reached by walking along a sealed road, and the second is all but inaccessible. Mt Rosea, though, is reached along marked tracks after a climb of around 400m. The track begins at Rosea camping ground on Silverband Rd and ascends towards a stand of Grampians gums found nowhere else in the world. The view from the summit extends from the rock-climbing icon of Mt Arapiles in the west to the Langi Ghiran Range near Ararat in the east. Allow about three hours for the 7km return walk. Vicmap's 1:50,000 topographic map *Northern Grampians* covers the area.

Major Mitchell Plateau
Along with the Mt Difficult walk (p152), a traverse of the Major Mitchell Plateau

to Mt William, the highest peak in the Grampians, is the classic overnight outing in the Grampians. Major Mitchell Plateau sits below, and south of, Mt William. Ascending along Fyans Creek, you summit Mt William before descending to the plateau, where camp is made beside First Wannon Creek (usually a reliable water source) on the plateau. The next day, you descend to Jimmy Creek picnic area – a vehicle shuttle will be needed to get you back to Fyans Creek. The route is almost entirely covered by Vicmap's 1:50,000 topographic map *Southern Grampians*, though the first couple of kilometres along Fyans Creek are on the *Northern Grampians* map.

GREAT SOUTH WEST WALK
The Great South West Walk (GSWW), in the southwest of the state, is one of the finest long-distance walking tracks in Australia, featuring lovely eucalyptus forests, pockets of cool temperate rainforest, the limestone gorge along the Glenelg River and the nearly unbroken 60km-long beach of Discovery Bay. Although long, it is a fairly easy walk, and can be completed in 12 to 14 days. Beginning in Portland, the trail distance is 225km along the Discovery Bay beach route, or 247km by a more-popular inland route through Mt Richmond National Park. There are 16 camp sites, spaced 10km to 20km apart; you also pass through the small town of Nelson. *The Great South West Walk,* a booklet of 1:100,000 maps, provides practical information and a basic description of each stage. **Friends of the Great South West Walk** (www.greatsouthwestwalk.com) is a good first contact for walkers. Portland has air and bus connections to Melbourne.

VICTORIAN ALPS
Bogong High Plains Circuit
This six-day, 85km walk covers the best of the Bogong High Plains, including pretty plains surrounded by snow gum glades and easily accessible peaks. Mt Beauty (p159) is a handy base from where the walk, starting at Bogong Village, can be accessed. The route climbs to Mt Fainter and beyond to the Niggerheads, before looping over the plains to Mt Nelse and onto Mt Bogong (p159) via T-Spur. Crossing the mountain to the west side, the route passes Bogong Creek Saddle returning to Bogong Village.

The Vicmap 1:50,000 topographic map *Bogong Alpine Area* is an excellent reference. Regarded as moderate standard, this is an ideal 'longer' walk in the Bogong High Plains area.

The Bluff

This short (13km) but spectacular day walk traverses a panoramic craggy ridge high above the Howqua River. You will need a good map (see p168) to guide you to the start at the northern base of the Bluff, 60km southeast of Mansfield (p168), the nearest town. Drive towards Mt Buller, turn onto Howqua Track, then follow Brocks Rd and Bluff Link Rd to reach the Bluff car park. For the walk you need the Vicmap 1:50,000 topographic map *Howitt-Selwyn* and 1:25,000 topographic map *Buller South*. The route is steep for 1km, climbing up through broken crags which require a bit of scrambling. Once on the Bluff, the path is easily followed over Mt Eadley Stoney before reaching Bluff Hut. You can either retrace your steps, or circuit back to the starting point along Sixteen Mile and Bluff Link Rds.

Lake Tali Karng

Formed by a massive landslide a few thousand years ago, Lake Tali Karng has the appeal of a mountain oasis hidden deep within a narrow valley; it is an inviting and special place. Starting on the plains at McFarlane Saddle, 61km northeast of Licola, this moderate-grade two-day walk traverses the open Wellington Plains, passing Mt Wellington itself, before descending Riggalls Spur. Camp is made by the lake. Climb up the steep Gillios Track, and across the rocky Spion Kopje, to return to the car park. The walk is accessed through Traral-

gon, Heyfield and Licola (260km from Melbourne). The Vicmap 1:25,000 topographic map *Tali Karng* and 1:50,000 topographic map *Tamboritha-Moroka* show the route.

WILSONS PROMONTORY
Prom Northern Circuit

Infinitely less crowded than the Prom Southern Circuit, the circular, 57km walking track near the promontory's northeastern tip crosses swampland to remote Five Mile, Three Mile and Chinaman Long Beaches. There are five camp sites en route, though the most likely itinerary is a three-day walk, camping at Five Mile Beach (or Johnny Souey Cove) and Tin Mine Cove. The track from Tin Mine Cove back to the trailhead at Five Mile Rd car park is overgrown with prickly heath, poorly defined and with potentially deep creek crossings, making this a route for experienced walkers only. A self-assessment form confirming your proficiency in such skills as compass use and navigation must be completed before you walk. Vicmap's 1:50,000 topographic map *Wilsons Promontory National Park* shows the route.

MITCHELL RIVER NATIONAL PARK

The Mitchell River is well known among white-water paddlers but less so among bushwalkers, which means you will see few people as you wander the 18km stretch of its banks through this national park north of Bairnsdale. Beginning at Angusvale, the trail heads through the spectacular cliffs of the Amphitheatre to the Den of Nargun and Deadcock Den, gorges rich in scenery and Aboriginal legend. There is camping at Angusvale, or other accommodation in Bairnsdale. Carry Vicmap's 1:50,000 topographic map *Cobbannah-Tabberrabbera*.

Tasmania

Lying 240km south of Victoria across tempestuous Bass Strait, and the last significant outpost before Antarctica, the island state of Tasmania feels remote. But despite its compact size (68,332 sq km), Tasmania is home to some of the best walking in Australia. Promoted as 'the natural state' in tourist literature and even on local car number plates, it's an apt description. More than a third of the state lies within some form of conservation reserve, including 19 national parks, containing an awesome diversity of environments: highland lakes, windswept beaches, complex caves, wild rivers, dramatic coastline, wildlife-rich islands, rugged mountain ranges and dense temperate rainforest. Much of this is accessible via more than 2000km of walking tracks, ranging from easy rambles to the most adventurous and challenging walking in the country.

Despite a long history of bad environmental management, Tasmania is famous for its wilderness areas, among the least-disturbed temperate wild lands on earth. Both the air and water in parts of the state are claimed to be the purest on the planet, while the Tasmanian Wilderness World Heritage Area, which covers 20% of the island, is internationally renowned. Yet, ironically, the preservation of much of the environment Tasmania is now proud of has been achieved only by protracted environmental campaigns on rivers and in forests, and in the media, parliaments and courts.

Tasmania is a generally friendly, unhurried and safe holiday destination. Furthermore, the establishment of fast Bass Strait ferries and low-cost flights in recent years have made Tasmania more accessible than ever, so there is even less reason for walkers to leave this walking wonderland off any travel itinerary.

HIGHLIGHTS

- Exploring rugged peaks, waterfalls and temperate rainforests on the classic **Overland Track** (p214)
- Looking out across World Heritage–listed wilderness from the high summit of **Frenchmans Cap** (p229)
- Cooling off in the turquoise waters of **Wineglass Bay** (p242) after a hot morning's walk
- Trying not to get dizzy peering over Australia's highest sea cliffs at **Cape Pillar** (p200)
- Gazing across the surf towards Antarctica while walking the windswept sands of **Prion Beach** (p240)

ENVIRONMENT

Tasmania's coastline, a multitude of bays and estuaries often interspersed with bold headlands, resulted from river valleys and coastal plains being flooded by rising sea levels after the last ice age, 10,000 years ago. By contrast, the Central Plateau, which was covered by a single ice sheet, is a sometimes-bleak environment dotted with thousands of lakes. Most of the island's western half is a maze of mountainous ridges bearing signs of recent glaciation. The major environmental differences across the state are largely due to the interaction of prevailing moist westerly winds with these mountains; the rainforest valleys and sometimes-snow-capped western mountains contrasting with the mild climate of the eastern 'sun coast'.

The diverse flora ranges from the dry forests of the east, to the alpine moorlands of the centre and the rainforests of the west. Many of the state's plants are unlike those found in the rest of Australia and have ties with species that grew more than 50 million years ago, when the southern continents were joined as Gondwana (p25). Tasmania's eucalyptus trees range from the very tall swamp gum (*Eucalyptus regnans;* the tallest flowering plant in the world, which can grow to 100m) to the smallest, the shrubby alpine varnished gum (*E. vernicosa*).

Tasmania's fauna is not as varied as that of the rest of Australia and it has relatively few large mammals, with its largest marsupial, the Tasmanian tiger (thylacine), now extinct for some 70 years. Nevertheless, Tasmania is the final refuge for a number of species that have long disappeared from the mainland (the eastern quoll and pademelon, for example). The carnivorous Tasmanian devil is endemic (and under threat; see p28), while wallabies, wombats and possums are common, and there's a wide variety of seabirds, parrots, cockatoos, honeyeaters and wrens. Birds of prey such as falcons and eagles are also readily seen.

INFORMATION
When to Walk

Frequent wet weather is a fact of life when walking in Tasmania, at any time of year, especially in the west. But if suitably equipped, walking in the rain can be enjoyable, with the vegetation colours appearing more vivid and the mist focusing your attention on near details. Even so, winter days are cooler and more likely to be wet, especially in the west and the highlands, where snow is also likely. November to April is generally the best time to walk in Tasmania. Late summer (February to March) can be particularly pleasant, but there may be restricted availability of water in some eastern areas at this time.

Maps

The best maps for the walks described in this chapter are published by Tasmap (previously known as Land Information Services). Tasmap's 1:500,000 *Tasmania Visitor Map* is a good reference for planning your trip around the island; it shows the various national parks and features road maps of major towns on the reverse. For maps covering individual walks in this chapter, see the Planning section in the introduction to each walk. The maps can be purchased from various outlets in Hobart (see p193) or ordered direct from **Tasmap** (☎ 03-6233 7741; tasmapsales@dpiwe .tas.gov.au).

Books

Lonely Planet's *Tasmania* guide is an excellent in-depth supplement to the general travel information given in this chapter.

For information on national parks and many shorter walks throughout the state look for *A Visitor's Guide to Tasmania's National Parks* by Greg Buckman. Tyrone Thomas' *120 Walks in Tasmania* is also a useful reference, covering mostly day walks. Another guide to shorter walks is the glossy *Day Walks Tasmania* by John and Monica Chapman. John Chapman is also the author of *South West Tasmania* and, with John Siseman, *Cradle Mountain Lake St Clair and Walls of Jerusalem National Parks,* which describe a range of often more challenging overnight walks. At the time of research, the available editions of some of these guides were a bit dated. For other titles about walking in specific areas, see Maps and Books in each section.

The photogenic qualities of the Tasmanian wilderness and its unique flora and fauna have given rise to a plethora of pictorial and natural history books. For example, Peter Dombrovskis' *Wild Rivers* is an early classic whereas *Primal Places* by Chris Bell is a recent offering.

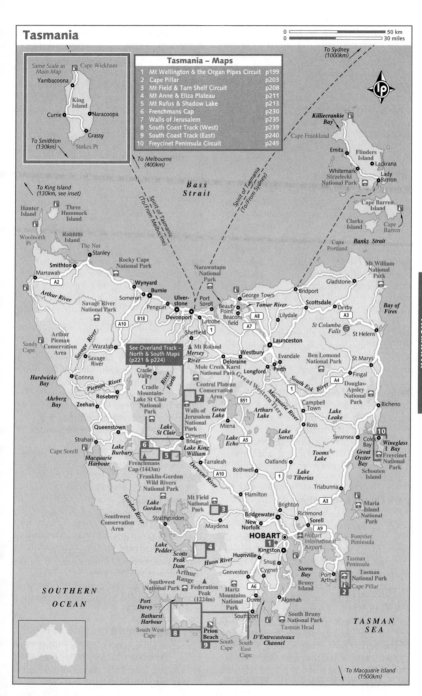

Tasmania

0 — 50 km
0 — 30 miles

To Sydney (1000km)

Tasmania – Maps

1	Mt Wellington & the Organ Pipes Circuit	p199
2	Cape Pillar	p203
3	Mt Field & Tarn Shelf Circuit	p208
4	Mt Anne & Eliza Plateau	p211
5	Mt Rufus & Shadow Lake	p213
6	Frenchmans Cap	p230
7	Walls of Jerusalem	p235
8	South Coast Track (West)	p239
9	South Coast Track (East)	p240
10	Freycinet Peninsula Circuit	p245

Same Scale as Main Map

Cape Wickham

Yambacoona

King Island

Currie   Naracoopa

Grassy

To Smithton (130km)   Stokes Pt

To Melbourne (400km)

Killiecrankie Bay

Cape Frankland

Emita   Flinders Island   Lackrana

Whitemark   Strzelecki National Park   Lady Barron

To King Island (130km, see inset)

B a s s   S t r a i t

Spirit of Tasmania (To/From Melbourne)

Spirit of Tasmania (To/From Sydney)

Cape Barren Island

Hunter Island   Three Hummock Island

Clarke Island   Cape Barren

Woolnorth Pt   Robbins Island   The Nut   Stanley

Cape Portland   Banks Strait

Sandy Cape

Marrawah   Smithton   Rocky Cape National Park   Narawntapu National Park   George Town   Bridport   Gladstone   Mt William National Park

A2   Arthur River   Wynyard   Burnie   Ulverstone   Port Sorell   Beauty Point   Tamar River   Scottsdale   Derby   Bay of Fires

Savage River National Park   Somerset   Penguin   Devonport   Latrobe   Beaconsfield   A8   Lilydale   A3

A10   B18   Sheffield   1   A7   St Columba Falls   St Helens

Arthur Pieman Conservation Area   Waratah   Mt Roland   Mersey   Westbury   Launceston   Ben Lomond National Park   St Marys

Savage River   Deloraine   Evandale   Fingal

Hardwicke Bay   Corinna   Pieman River   Cradle Valley   Mole Creek Karst National Park   Longford   Perth   A4   Douglas-Apsley National Park   Bicheno

Ahrberg Bay   Roseberry   Cradle Mountain-Lake St Clair National Park   Central Plateau Conservation Area   B51   Arthurs Tiers   Campbell Town   Lake Leake   10   Coles Bay   Wineglass Bay

Queenstown   Zeehan   Walls of Jerusalem National Park   Great Lake   Arthurs Lake   Ross   Swansea   Great Oyster Bay   Freycinet National Park

Strahan   Lake St Clair   Miena   Lake Sorell   Schouten Island

Cape Sorell   Lake Burbury   Frenchmans Cap (1443m)   Derwent Bridge   Lake King William   Lake Echo   Oatlands   Tooms Lake

Macquarie Harbour   Franklin-Gordon Wild Rivers National Park   Tarraleah   A5   Lake Sorell   Bothwell   Lake Tiberias   Triabunna

Southwest Conservation Area   Lake Gordon   Strathgordon   Mt Field National Park   A10   Hamilton   1   A3   Maria Island National Park

3   Bridgewater   Brighton   Richmond   Forestier Peninsula

Lake Pedder   Scotts Peak Dam   Maydena   New Norfolk   Sorell   A9

Southwest National Park   Arthur Range   Huonville   HOBART   Hobart International Airport   Tasman Peninsula

4   Huon River   Kingston   Snug   Port Arthur   Tasman National Park

Federation Peak (1224m)   Hartz Mountains National Park   Geeveston   Cygnet   Storm Bay   Bruny Island   Cape Pillar

Port Davey   Dover   Alonnah   2

Bathurst Harbour   Southport   South Bruny National Park   T A S M A N   S E A

South West Cape   8   Prion Beach   9   South Cape   South East Cape   Tasman Head   D'Entrecasteaux Channel

S O U T H E R N   O C E A N

To Macquarie Island (1500km)

TASMANIA

Alpine Tasmania by Jamie Kirkpatrick is an illustrated guide to the flora of the mountainous regions of the island. *Tasmanian Mammals* by wildlife photographer Dave Watts is an excellent field guide. You might also want to look at *The Fauna of Tasmania – Birds* and *The Fauna of Tasmania – Mammals,* both by RH Green.

Leatherwood Online (www.leatherwoodonline.com) is an online magazine with good articles and photography.

Information Sources

The **Parks & Wildlife Service** (PWS; www.parks.tas.gov.au) has an excellent website with information on Tasmania's national parks, World Heritage Area (WHA), environment, and basic information on some walks. Also available is **Tasmania's Essential Bushwalking Guide & Trip Planner** (www.parks.tas.gov.au/recreation/mib.html), with sections on the planning, minimal-impact bushwalking, first aid and what gear you need to cope with Tasmania's changeable weather.

Tourism Tasmania (☎ 03-6230 8235, 1800 806 846; www.discovertasmania.com) disseminates loads of information about Tasmania, and its website contains details of key destinations, festivals, tours and accommodation.

The website of the government-run **Tasmanian Travel Centres** (☎ 1300 655 145; www.tastravel.com.au) is good for planning a travel itinerary. There are privately run Tasmanian Travel & Information Centres (TTICs) in several Tasmanian cities and visitor information centres in some smaller towns. These are noted in Information sections in this chapter.

Park Fees & Regulations

Apart from the Overland Track (p214), no walks in Tasmania require permits or are otherwise regulated. However, entry fees do apply to all national parks and these encompass most of the walks described in this chapter. There are passes for pedestrians or vehicles, so make sure that your pass will cover your needs. For example, if you plan to visit the Walls of Jerusalem National Park by car you'll only need a pedestrian pass as the car park is just outside the boundary of the park. For visiting walkers, the most convenient option is the eight-week Holiday Pass ($30 per person or $50 per vehicle with up to eight seats), but see the **PWS website**

(www.parks.tas.gov.au) for the range of options. Application forms can be downloaded from the website. Passes can also be obtained from major park visitor information centres, Service Tasmania's state-wide offices, and on board the Spirit of Tasmania (during summer). Tasmanian Travel Centres in Melbourne and Sydney also sell passes.

Most popular tracks have a registration book at the start and finish, which walkers are encouraged to fill in to give the PWS more information about track use. The books are not used for safety purposes, so tell someone reliable where you're going, or register (and de-register) your trip with a local police station.

Many of Tasmania's national parks, including the entire Tasmanian Wilderness World Heritage Area, are fuel-stove-only areas in which campfires are either banned, or only permitted at a few designated sites. This is a good policy to adopt when walking anywhere in Tasmania. During days of Total Fire Ban (p25) all fires are forbidden, even fuel stoves.

Guided Walks

Several companies offer guided walks in Tasmania, including on some of the routes described in this book. For the Overland Track, a few options are available (p218). **Tarkine Trails** (☎ 03-6234 3931; www.tarkinetrails.com.au) For something different, you could try this small company focusing on walks among the forests and beaches of Tasmania's less-visited northwest.

Tasmanian Expeditions (☎ 03-6339 3999, 1300 666 856; www.tas-ex.com) Has the most extensive range of itineraries.

Leaving Luggage

Most hostels will let you leave gear for a few days while you are out on a walk. The Backpackers Barn & Wilderness Centre in Devonport (p195) has luggage storage in secure lockers for $10 per week. All of the track-transport bus services operated by Tassielink feature an option to have your luggage forwarded to your next destination and stored for $5.

GETTING AROUND

Buses run along most major highways year-round. **TassieLink** (☎ 1300 300 520; www.tassielink.com.au) runs from both Hobart and Launceston to the state's west, the east coast, from

Hobart to Port Arthur, and south from Hobart down the Huon Valley. **Redline** (☎ 1300 360 000; www.tasredline.com.au) services the Midland Hwy, Bass Hwy (north coast) and the east coast.

During summer, TassieLink buses also run along some minor roads to popular bushwalking destinations. Special fares that enable you to be dropped off at the start of a walk and picked up at the end are offered. Most track services will only run with a certain number of passengers, so the onus is on the walker to book in advance.

Tassielink also has discount Explorer passes for people planning to do a lot of bus travel. Used efficiently they can save you money, but they don't allow much time for getting out walking and they can't be used for routes specifically servicing walking tracks. The shortest pass gives seven days' travel in 10 days ($175) and the longest gives 21 days' travel in 30 days ($280). Redline offers its Tassie Pass, from $135 for seven days, but Redline's route network is not nearly as extensive as Tassielink's.

GATEWAYS
Hobart
☎ 03 / pop 200,000

Straddling the Derwent River and backed by the forested and sometimes-snow-capped bulk of Mt Wellington (1270m), Hobart is the second-oldest, smallest and most southerly of Australia's capital cities. It combines a rich colonial heritage with a splendid natural setting, a lively waterfront area and good access to the WHA and east coast.

INFORMATION
The **Hobart visitor information centre** (☎ 6230 8233; www.tasmaniasouth.com; tasbookings@tasvisinfo .com.au; cnr Davey & Elizabeth Sts) has loads of brochures, maps and information for travellers, plus a booking service covering the entire state ($3 booking fee).

Bushwalking advisory staff at the **Parks & Wildlife Service** (PWS; ☎ 1300 135 513; www.parks .tas.gov.au; 134 Macquarie St) are inside the Service Tasmania office from December to March. Information and fact sheets for all national parks are also available here.

Maps
A range of maps and some walking guide books can be purchased directly from **Serv-**

ice Tasmania (☎ 1300 135 513; www.service.tas.gov .au; 134 Macquarie St).

Tasmanian Map Centre (☎ 6231 9043; www.map -centre.com.au; 100 Elizabeth St) stocks a good range of walking maps and books.

Many outdoor equipment shops also stock relevant maps.

SUPPLIES & EQUIPMENT
You can buy stove fuel and lightweight freeze-dried meals, as well as outdoor equipment, at **Mountain Designs** (☎ 6234 3900; www.mountaindesigns.com; 111 Elizabeth St); **Paddy Pallin** (☎ 6231 0777; www.paddypallin.com.au; 119 Elizabeth St); **Snowgum** (☎ 6234 7877; www.snowgum.com .au; 104 Elizabeth St); **Jolly Swagman** (☎ 6234 3999; 107 Elizabeth St); and **Mountain Creek** (☎ 6234 4395; 75-77 Bathurst St). Paddy Pallin, Mountain Creek and Jolly Swagman also hire some walking gear.

Emergency Position Indicating Radio Beacons (EPIRBs; p388) can be hired from **Service Tasmania** (☎ 1300 135 513; www.parks.tas .gov.au/recreation/epirbs/epirbs.html; 134 Macquarie St; ☽ Mon-Fri), and also in Launceston, Burnie and Devonport, for $30 per week.

The most central option for self-caterers and those stocking up for walks is **City Supermarket** (148 Liverpool St). Otherwise Woolworths and Coles have large supermarkets just off Sandy Bay Rd, 2km south of the central business district (CBD).

SLEEPING & EATING
Hobart has a variety of accommodation catering to all tastes and price brackets. The most convenient for walkers are in and around the CBD and the older suburbs to the north and west.

There are no camping grounds anywhere near the city. Self-contained cabins are available at **Elwick Cabin & Tourist Park** (☎ 6272 7115; www.islandcabins.com.au; 19 Goodwood Rd, Glenorchy; $65-90 for 2), about 8km north of the city centre, but the nearest park with a camping option is **Barilla Holiday Park** (☎ 1800 465 453, 6248 5453; www.barilla.com.au; 75 Richmond Rd, Cambridge; unpowered/powered site for 2 $17/22, cabins for 2 from $75), 13km from town and near the airport. It has an on-site restaurant.

Central City Backpackers (☎ 6224 2404; www .centralbackpackers.com.au; 138 Collins St; dm $20-25, s/d $50/60), in the heart of the CBD, is a rambling hostel with loads of communal space, OK rooms, friendly staff and extras such as baggage storage. There is no parking, although it is possible to park on the street outside meter hours.

Travellers with a car might prefer to stay at **Adelphi Court YHA** (☎ 6228 4829; adelphi@yhatas .org.au; 17 Stoke St, New Town; dm $25, d $60, d without/with en suite $60/70), although Tasmanian Redline Coaches' airport shuttle provides a drop-off and pick-up service. The hostel is 3km from the CBD but reasonably close to the North Hobart restaurant strip.

The **Astor Private Hotel** (☎ 6234 6611; www .astorprivatehotel.com.au; 157 Macquarie St; s/d with shared bathroom $60/85, d with en suite from $130) is a large, central 1920s guesthouse that has retained much of its character. There are old-style rooms with shared bathrooms plus brand new and very appealing en suite rooms, and rates include breakfast.

Wellington Lodge (☎ 6231 0614; www.wwt.com .au/wellingtonlodge; 7 Scott St; s/d $90/130-140) is in the small suburb of Glebe, next to Queen's Domain. The four comfortable rooms are in a restored Victorian townhouse set in magnificent gardens and rates include breakfast.

Hobart Macquarie Motor Inn (☎ 6234 4422, 1800 060 954; www.leisureinns.com.au; 167 Macquarie St; r $90-125; P 🖦) is a large central motel that won't win any architectural awards but is well equipped. At the time of research, refurbishment was planned after which rates will increase by $15 to $30.

Hobart's CBD has some good spots for brunch and lunch, but evening options are generally better closer to the water or historic precincts. Salamanca Pl is a good choice for cafés and restaurants. For the most diverse selection of eateries, head to Elizabeth St in North Hobart, a cosmopolitan strip of pubs, cafés and restaurants.

Seafood is on offer everywhere you look near the waterfront. Constitution Dock has a number of permanently moored barges that serve as floating takeaway seafood stalls. Nearby, **Mures** (☎ 6231 2121; www.mures .com.au; Victoria Dock) offers a ground-level fishmonger and an inexpensive seafood bistro (meals $7-13; ☽ lunch & dinner), with an à la carte restaurant upstairs.

Jackman & McRoss (☎ 6223 3186; 57-59 Hampden Rd; ☽ breakfast & lunch) is a deservedly popular bakery-café in Battery Point.

The **New Sydney Hotel** (☎ 6234 4516; 87 Bathurst St; mains $9-19; ☽ lunch Mon-Sat, dinner nightly) is a cosy watering hole, popular for cheap, filling counter meals.

Sirens (☎ 6234 2634; 6 Victoria St; lunch $8-13, dinner mains $16-23; ☽ lunch Mon-Fri, dinner Tue-Sat) serves up creative vegetarian and vegan food in a warm, welcoming space.

GETTING THERE & AWAY

Hobart is within easy driving distance of most of the national parks and major towns in Tasmania.

Air

Several airlines service routes between Hobart and the Australian mainland. **Virgin Blue** (☎ 13 67 89; www.virginblue.com.au) and **Jetstar** (☎ 13 15 38; www.jetstar.com.au) have direct flights to/from Melbourne (from $70), Sydney (from $100), Brisbane (from $150) and Adelaide (from $130). **Qantas** (☎ 13 13 13; www .qantas.com.au) has direct flights to/from Sydney and Melbourne; usually they're more expensive than the budget airlines. The airport is 16km from the city centre; there's a **shuttle bus** (☎ 0419 382 240; $10) and a taxi should cost about $35.

Bus

Two main bus companies service other towns and, in summer, some walking tracks to/from Hobart; **TassieLink** (☎ 6271 7320, 1300 300 520; www.tassielink.com.au; 64 Brisbane St) and **Redline** (☎ 1300 360 000; www.tasredline.com.au; 199 Collins St).

There are multiple daily services on the major routes between Hobart and Launceston or Devonport (for the Spirit of Tasmania ferry) and fares are about $30 and $50, respectively. See p192 for more travel details.

Car

Most car-rental firms have representation at the airport. City offices include **AutoRent-Hertz** (☎ 6237 1111; www.autorent.com.au; cnr Bathurst & Harrington Sts), **Avis** (☎ 6234 4222; www.avis.com.au; 125 Bathurst St), **Budget** (☎ 6234 5222, 13 27 27; www .budget.com.au; 96 Harrington St), **Europcar** (☎ 6231 1077, 1800 030 118; www.europcar.com.au; 112 Harrington St) and **Thrifty** (☎ 6234 1341, 1800 030 730; www .tasvacations.com.au; 11-17 Argyle St).

Some of the cheaper local firms include **Lo-Cost Auto Rent** (☎ 6231 0550, 1800 647 060; www.rentforless.com.au; 105 Murray St), **Rent-a-Bug** (☎ 6231 0300, 1800 647 060; www.rentforless.com.au;

105 Murray St) and **Selective Car Rentals** (☎ 6234 3311, 1800 300 102; www.selectivecarrentals.com.au; 47 Bathurst St).

Devonport
☎ 03 / pop 25,000
The town of Devonport is a popular arrival point for travellers, being the Tasmanian port for the Spirit of Tasmania car-ferries that operate routes to/from Melbourne and Sydney. It is a convenient base for walkers heading for the Overland Track and the Walls of Jerusalem National Park.

INFORMATION
The waterfront **Devonport visitor information centre** (☎ 6424 4466; tourism@dcc.tas.gov.au; 92 Formby Rd; ☿ daily from 7.30am) is open for all Spirit of Tasmania ferry arrivals. It can make most travel and accommodation bookings, and also sells national parks passes.

For walking-related information (including travel and accommodation) head for the **Backpackers Barn & Wilderness Centre** (☎ 6424 3628; www.backpackersbarn.com.au; 10-12 Edward St; ☿ 9am-5pm Mon-Fri, 9am-2pm Sat). It can also organise a charter bus to areas not serviced by public transport.

SUPPLIES & EQUIPMENT
As well as a source of walking information, the Backpackers Barn & Wilderness Centre (above) is an excellent bushwalking shop with gear for sale or hire (including tents, sleeping bags and mats, backpacks and cooking sets). It also offers a day relaxation area, with a shower for those sprinting back to catch a ferry or plane post-walk.

Mountain Designs (☎ 6424 8699; www.mountaindesigns.com; 2 Rooke St) also stocks a full range of outdoor gear, including freeze-dried food and stove fuels.

EPIRBs (p388) can be hired from the **Service Tasmania shop** (☎ 1300 135 513; www.parks.tas.gov.au/recreation/epirbs/epirbs.html; 21 Oldaker St; ☿ Mon-Fri), and also in Hobart, Launceston and Burnie, for $30 per week.

For food supplies, head for the large **Coles/K-Mart** (cnr Gunn & Best Sts) or **Woolworths** (74 Best St) supermarkets, less than 10 minutes' walk from the city centre.

SLEEPING & EATING
Abel Tasman Caravan Park (☎ 6427 8794; 6 Wright St; unpowered/powered sites $17/23, on-site vans/cabins $45/95) offers very clean amenities and a good beachfront location in East Devonport, just five minutes' walk from the ferry terminal.

Tasman House (☎ 6423 2335; www.tasmanhouse.com; 114 Tasman St; dm $15, d without/with bathroom $35/40) is a large hostel with good facilities, 20 minutes' walk from town (or you can arrange transport when booking). The building was once part of Devonport hospital and looks it. Camping and hiking equipment is also available for hire, but the quality may not be great. Guided walks can also be arranged, but there are better operators around.

There's nothing fancy about centrally-located **Molly Malone's** (☎ 6424 1898; mollymalones@vantagegroup.com.au; 34 Best St; dm $15, d without/with bathroom $35/50), above Molly Malone's Irish pub, but it has clean, basic four-bed dorms and a comfy lounge. It can be noisy on Friday and Saturday nights.

The foreshore **River View Lodge** (☎ 6424 7357; www.riverviewlodge.com.au; 18 Victoria Pde; s without/with bathroom $75/90, d from $105/85) is a friendly, old-fashioned country-style place opposite a strip of picnic table–dotted greenery. The en suite rooms are good value and the rates include breakfast.

Rannoch House (☎ 6427 9818; www.rannochhouse.com.au; 5 Cedar Ct; s/d from $105/125) is a homestead set among relaxing landscaped grounds in East Devonport. All five rooms have en suites and rates include a cooked breakfast.

Located near the ferry terminal, **Alice Beside the Sea** (☎ /fax 6427 8605; www.alicebesidethesea.com; 1 Wright St; d $130) offers comfortable, self-contained units within cooee of the beach and a supermarket.

A wander along Rooke St will pass quite a wide selection of eateries. For example, **Bellas Café and Restaurant** (☎ 6424 7933; 157-159 Rooke St; mains $13-20; ☿ breakfast, lunch & dinner Tue-Sun) offers focaccias, Italian fare and some attractive desserts.

Next door, **Sharkies Seafood Restaurant and Takeaway** (☎ 6423 1911; 155 Rooke St; mains from $17; ☿ lunch Wed-Sun, dinner nightly) provides a completely different menu.

Rosehip Café (☎ 6424 1917; 12 Edward St; meals $6-10; ☿ breakfast & lunch Mon-Fri), at the Backpackers Barn & Wilderness Centre, does healthy burgers, salads, focaccias and soups.

The **Alexander Hotel** (☎ 6424 2252; 78 Formby Rd; mains $10-18; ☿ lunch & dinner) is a local favourite that churns out good counter meals with exotic panache.

GETTING THERE & AWAY

Devonport is 100km from Launceston along the Bass Hwy; Hobart is another 200km further south along the Midlands Hwy.

Air

There are regular flights to/from Melbourne with **Qantaslink** (☎ 13 13 13; www.qantas.com.au; fares from $110).

The airport is 5km east of town. A **shuttle bus** (☎ 0400 035 995) runs between the airport, ferry terminals, the visitor centre and your accommodation for $10 per person. The shuttle can meet all arrivals into Devonport. Bookings for departures are essential. A **taxi** (☎ 6424 1431) will cost $12 to $15.

Bus

TassieLink (☎ 1300 300 520; www.tassielink.com.au) operates an 'express' service that connects ferry arrivals/departures with Launceston ($18) and Hobart ($45). It also delivers embarking passengers from Strahan/Queenstown and Hobart. TassieLink also runs from Launceston to Devonport (drop-off only) and then via Sheffield to Cradle Mountain (and on to Queenstown and the west coast).

Redline (☎ 1300 360 000, 6336 1446; www.tasredline .com.au; 9 Edward St) operates a service from Launceston to Devonport and on to Burnie. Its terminal is opposite the Backpackers Barn & Wilderness Centre (p195) and will also stop at the ferry terminal when the ferry is in, while TassieLink coaches pull up outside the Devonport visitor information centre and the Spirit of Tasmania terminal.

If none of the scheduled services suit your particular bushwalking needs, charter a minibus from **Maxwells** (☎ 6492 1431, 0418 584 004) or through the Backpackers Barn & Wilderness Centre (p195).

Car

Devonport has several cheap car-rental firms, such as **Rent-a-Bug** (☎ 6427 9034; www .rentforless.com.au; 5 Murray St) and **Lo-Cost Auto Rent** (☎ 1800 802 724, 6424 9922; www.rentforless.com.au; 22 King St). **Budget** (☎ 13 27 27, 6427 0650; www.budget. com.au) and **Thrifty** (☎ 1800 030 730, 6427 9119; www.tasvacations.com.au) have representatives at the airport and ferry terminal.

Sea

There are three high-speed **Spirit of Tasmania vehicular ferries** (☎ 13 20 10; www.spiritoftasmania .com.au) operated by TT-Line. One ferry leaves nightly in each direction to/from Melbourne, with additional day sailings during summer; one-way fares (per adult) are up to $145 for a seat and $215 for the cheapest cabin option, depending on season; for an extra $60 you can take your car. The third ferry sails twice weekly to/from Sydney but at the time of writing the future of this service appeared uncertain; one-way fares are up to $190 for a hostel bunk and $270 for the cheapest cabin option, depending on season; cars are an extra $60. Terminal locations are in Devonport (Esplanade, East Devonport; ie across the river from the CBD), Melbourne (Station Pier, Port Melbourne) and Sydney (47-51 Hickson Rd, Gate D8N, Darling Harbour). For all ferry crossings there are limited, discounted advance purchase fares available – inquire when booking.

HOBART REGION & THE SOUTHEAST

Tasmania's capital city is well endowed with nearby natural areas and many contain a range of day and overnight walking options, from sea level to treeless mountain summits. Not the least of these is Mt Wellington, rising directly from Hobart's western suburbs. The cliffs and beaches of the Tasman Peninsula, the waterfalls and alpine lakes of Mt Field National Park (p206) and several other walking destinations (p246) are also within 100km of the city.

ACCESS TOWN

See Hobart (p193).

MT WELLINGTON & THE ORGAN PIPES CIRCUIT

Duration	5–7 hours
Distance	13km
Difficulty	moderate
Start/Finish	Fern Tree
Nearest Town	Hobart (p193)
Transport	bus

Summary Walk forest tracks past a waterfall and the impressive Organ Pipes, climb to the summit and return via the alpine plateau and some 19th-century ice-house ruins.

Mt Wellington's forested slopes rise directly west of Hobart, with the 1270m summit less than 10km from the wharfs, marinas and office blocks of the city. It holds a special place in the hearts of many Hobart residents and, for many Tasmanian walkers, the tracks on Mt Wellington are the first tackled. A trip up the mountain is a good way for walkers who have just arrived in Tasmania to get out and stretch.

On a clear day there are stunning all-round views from the top – the city, Derwent estuary and Storm Bay, with the World Heritage Area's rugged skyline to the west. Crossing the boulder-strewn summit plateau evokes a sense of wildness that contrasts with the proximity of the city centre. A network of tracks and paths wind their way through the bush picking out points of interest like O'Gradys Falls, Sphinx Rock, Myrtle Gully and the soaring dolerite columns of the Organ Pipes.

The ascent is more straightforward these days than in 1836, when Charles Darwin ascended the mountain during his now-famous round-the-world voyage on HMS *Beagle*; he found it 'a severe day's work'.

With your own transport, you could drive to the Springs and undertake a shorter circuit from there, starting along the Lenah Valley or Pinnacle Tracks. The extensive network of tracks provides many alternative options for those with less time, in a lazier mood or who wish to avoid the summit due to cloud or snow.

ENVIRONMENT

Mt Wellington's altitudinal range and fire history give rise to a wide variety of veg-

etation communities, many traversed on this walk. Various eucalyptus forest types occur on the lower slopes, with remnant rainforest in damp gullies. On the upper slopes, subalpine forest and shrubs give way to the prostrate alpine plants of the summit plateau.

Mt Wellington is the eastern focus of the 18,250-hectare Wellington Park. Sections of the mountain's slopes form part of Hobart's drinking water catchment area; walkers are asked to use toilets before entering the region.

PLANNING
When to Walk

There is somewhere to walk on Mt Wellington at any time of year. Even periodic winter snow can be enjoyable, on a fine day with appropriate gear, but ice can form on the summit tracks and white outs develop very quickly. Because of its height, Mt Wellington's summit can experience atrocious weather at any time of the year; if the summit is shrouded in cloud it is best to stick to the lower slopes. The walk described here is a high level circuit so is best tackled outside the winter months.

Maps & Books

Tasmap's 1:20,000 *Wellington Park Recreation Map* shows the entire Mt Wellington track network, including the route described here. It also has some good background information on the history and environment of the mountain.

The Hobart City Council's free booklet *Hobart Walks* describes a number of walks on the mountain as well as other areas of urban bushland. *Mt Wellington Walks* by Jan Hardy and Bert Elson might also be worth checking out.

Emily Stoddart's *The Mountain – A People's Perspective* provides just that, from the point of view of a range of those living on and around 'the mountain'.

On The Mountain is a classy large format book by photographer Peter Dombrovskis (who lived on the mountain's slopes), writer Richard Flanagan and ecologist Jamie Kirkpatrick.

Information Sources

The **Wellington Park website** (www.wellingtonpark .tas.gov.au) has a range of information on the

---

WELLINGTON WEEKENDERS

Hobartians have been escaping to 'the mountain' for a long time. Between 1888 and 1912 dozens of private weekend huts were constructed on the lower slopes. Generally of timber construction, many were substantial structures with verandas and rustic decoration, some so elaborate they featured on picture postcards. But by the late 1920s most of the timber huts had been burnt or fallen down, and subsequent bushfires have removed most evidence of their existence.

park, including some useful pre-visit information and a live weather update from the Mt Wellington summit. An information centre is planned at the Springs and may be constructed by the time you read this.

NEAREST TOWN

See Hobart (p193).

GETTING TO/FROM THE WALK

Metro bus numbers 48 and 49 from Franklin Square, opposite the Hobart GPO, take you to Fern Tree, where the tracks to Mt Wellington and the Organ Pipes begin.

THE WALK

The small suburb of **Fern Tree** has a general store, café and tavern. From the tavern walk 60m north down Huon Rd to a small car park and picnic area; the Fern Glade Track ascends stone steps into the trees here. Follow this track, ignoring all side tracks, as it ascends beside the fern-lined creek, crossing it several times, to reach **Radfords Monument** at a major track junction. The monument is dedicated to GH Radford who died in a snow storm descending from the Pinnacle during a 1903 race from the city to the summit and back. Cross Radfords Track and continue on for 10 minutes, crossing Finger Post Track, to Pinnacle Rd. Cross the road and descend Woods Track to the signed junction with Betts Vale Track. Turn left (west) here and stroll up to pretty **O'Gradys Falls** (30 to 45 minutes from Fern Tree).

Cross the bridge and continue on Betts Vale Track, ascending a damp gully to the junction with Circle Track. Turn right and then right again soon after, to follow Shoobridge Track north past the **Octopus Tree**, its

---

WARNING

Cold winds can strafe the summit plateau any time of year. Even leaving Hobart on a fine summer's day, it can be a bit of a shock to feel the need for gloves and fleece jackets on the summit of Mt Wellington. It will be at least 10°C cooler than downtown Hobart (without allowing for the wind). Bring everything you would normally bring on a day trip to an alpine area if you are going to the summit.

---

tentacle-like roots clasping a large boulder. Watch for the junction with Sawmill Track (the sign faces away from you), then turn left and follow this track uphill, past the overhang of Sphinx Rock. Continue on Sawmill Track, crossing the Lenah Valley Track and Pinnacle Rd, then angling up to join the Organ Pipes Track (45 to 60 minutes from O'Grady Falls). The views have opened up now, with Hobart and the Derwent estuary below and the towering **Organ Pipes** above, and only get better as you ascend further. It's worth walking north along the Organ Pipes Track for 10 to 15 minutes to take in the full extent of the cliffs and perhaps get a stiff neck watching the climbers who frequent these crags in summer.

Return along the Organ Pipes Track and continue contouring south on this track, rather than turning off back down the Sawmill Track. After 10-15 minutes it joins the Pinnacle Track at a rustic seat with a view of the Organ Pipes; if the weather is poor and the summit in cloud, bear left and follow this track down to the Springs (20 to 30 minutes). Otherwise, turn right uphill and climb ever more steeply. The Zig Zag Track emerges on the summit plateau just south of the huge communications tower. The summit itself, marked by a trig beacon and 2¾ to 3¾ hours from Fern Tree, is just beyond the tower in the middle of a parking area. Below the car park is a **viewing platform** from where you can take in the expansive views of Hobart, and the bays and islands beyond. It's also worth a wander across to the western side of the summit car park to a display that explains the significance of the mountain (known as Kunanyi) to the local Aboriginal community.

Return south past the communications tower and, ignoring Zig Zag Track, bear right and follow the South Wellington Track, a rough, marked route along the edge of the summit plateau. The alpine landscape on this section is wonderful, with odd jumbles of frost-weathered, egg-shaped dolerite boulders littering the plateau. In the gaps, hardy alpine plants find shelter to grow. After about 30 minutes, the track begins to descend gently, opening up new views to the south across Bruny Island and the Huon Valley, and passing a sign for the **Rocking Stone**, a perched boulder on the plateau edge 100m east of the track. The track enters

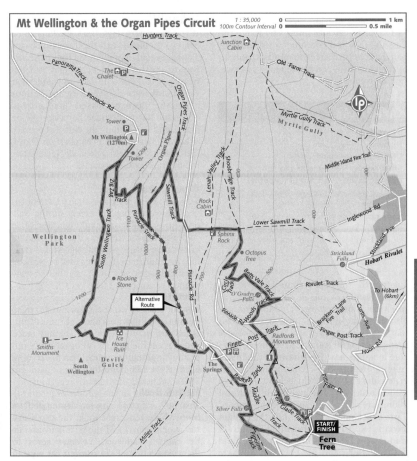

Mt Wellington & the Organ Pipes Circuit
1 : 35,000
100m Contour Interval

stunted trees and soon reaches the turn-off west to Smiths Monument; bear left (east) here. Dr John Smith died after becoming lost while descending from Mt Wellington in 1858. The route now becomes a well-defined stony track and leaves the plateau to begin its descent through bush. During the steep descent you'll pass several old **ice house ruins**, built to make ice in the days before refrigeration. Look out for a short side track on the right soon after starting the descent; it leads to the most obvious ruin. When in operation, the structures were packed with snow, which would become ice over winter, after which it was carved into blocks and carried down the mountain on ponies. Continue descending to the junction with Milles

Track, then turn left (north) and follow this contouring gravel path a short distance to a major signed track junction. Turn right here and descend stone steps to a road beside a grassy opening. Dream of the ale you might have enjoyed at the old Springs Hotel which stood here until destroyed in the bushfires that ravaged Mt Wellington in 1967. Cross the road and continue descending to the Springs picnic area (1½ to 2½ hours from the summit). Radfords Track enters the bush on the south side of the picnic area. Descend this track for a few minutes (this track section is shared with mountain bikers, so keep watch for them), then turn right downhill at the first junction, adjacent to a large drain. Follow the steep narrow track down to meet a major track just above **Silver Falls**, a small cascade framed by tree ferns. Pass the falls and continue down the wide path back to Fern Tree (45 minutes from the Springs), bearing left at the major intersection en route.

CAPE PILLAR

Duration	3 days
Distance	33km
Difficulty	moderate
Start/Finish	Fortescue Bay (p202)
Nearest Towns	Port Arthur (opposite), Eaglehawk Neck (p201)
Transport	private

Summary Walk along the edge of the highest sea cliffs in Australia, with bush and heath-cloaked hills above and the sea foaming around stacks below.

Visitors to the Port Arthur Historic Site on the Tasman Peninsula rarely realise that just a few kilometres away, hidden by bush-clad hills, are the highest and most spectacular sea cliffs in Australia. The impressive scenery on offer can be seen from roadside lookouts near Eaglehawk Neck, but to fully appreciate the vertigo-inducing dolerite cliffs and sea stacks below, a cliff-top walk is necessary. The highest cliffs (almost 300m) are at Cape Pillar, with the isolated Tasman Island opposite, while the slender Totem Pole (see boxed text, p204) lies off Cape Hauy. This walk links both these areas with a circuit via Mt Fortescue. If you have little time, a day trip to Cape Hauy provides a coastal landscape taster.

PLANNING

If you have extra days, the Cape Pillar walk can be combined with the Tasman Coastal Trail for a four-day extended walk. The best way to do this might be to first sort out transport to Fortescue Bay and undertake the circuit walk described here, continue along the Tasman Coastal Trail around Fortescue Bay to Bivouac Bay campsite on Day 3, and north along the cliff-girt coast to Waterfall Bay or Devils Kitchen on Day 4. This is just south of Eaglehawk Neck, where public transport is available.

When to Walk

You can walk this track at any time of the year. However, the few creeks on the walk only have small catchment areas and often stop flowing or dry up later in summer, after a few weeks without significant rainfall, so finding fresh water can be difficult during this period.

What to Bring

Drinking water can be scarce or brackish in the Cape Pillar area and you'll need containers to carry water to the recommended camp sites. It's best to fill up at every opportunity along the route. You'll also need a fuel stove (see opposite).

Maps & Books

Tasmap's 1:75,000 *Tasman National Park Map & Notes* covers the walk, and also shows the Tasman Coastal Trail and other walks on the Tasman Peninsula. *Peninsula Tracks* by Peter and Shirley Storey covers 35 popular walks in the area and is worth checking out if you plan to spend more time there.

DOLERITE

The dark massive rock known as dolerite is such a ubiquitous feature of the Tasmanian landscape, capping the highest peaks and backing many coasts, that few give it a second thought. But in both volume and form it is unlike such rocks in most other parts of the world.

As molten rock (magma), at a temperature of 1100°C, it flooded into the crust 175 million years ago during the initial phase of the Gondwana break-up (p25). The intrusive event lasted a geological blink-of-an-eye, perhaps less than one million years, during which 40,000 cu km of magma was emplaced, mostly as sheets 300m to 500m thick, termed sills. As the magma cooled and crystallised to form dolerite, the distinctive columnar joints developed.

The thick, massive sills and columnar structure of dolerite facilitate the development of tall, steep cliffs with separated towers or pinnacles. In coastal settings, the sea either obscures or removes the debris or talus aprons that would occur below such cliffs on land, steepening them. Nowhere are such cliffs better developed than in the Cape Pillar area.

Permits & Regulations

The area is a national park so you'll need a pass (p192).

Campfires are not permitted in the park, except at Fortescue Bay camping ground, so you'll need a fuel stove.

Phytophthora (p47) is not present in the southern part of the walk area; to maintain this situation and help prevent the spread of this fungus, clean mud and soil from boots and other gear at the Lunchtime Creek washdown station.

NEAREST TOWNS & FACILITIES
Port Arthur
☎ 03 / pop 170

As one of the biggest mainstream tourist draws in Tasmania, it is a surprise to discover that Port Arthur, the location of the infamous mid-19th century convict prison, is not much more than the historic site plus a scattering of motels and guesthouses. Just before the turn-off to the historic site is a general store and petrol station. Bring all your camping needs from Hobart.

SLEEPING & EATING

All accommodation options in Port Arthur can be heavily booked in summer.

The spacious and well-equipped **Port Arthur Caravan & Cabin Park** (☎ 6250 2340,1800 620 708; www.portarthurcaravan-cabinpark.com.au; Garden Point Rd; unpowered/powered sites $17/19, dm $16, cabins $85-95) is 2km north of Port Arthur, above Stewarts Bay Beach.

Roseview Youth Hostel (☎ 6250 2311; yhatas@ yhatas.org.au; Champ St, off Safety Cove Rd; dm/d $20/45) has OK facilities and crowded dorms but a great location at the edge of the historic site.

Port Arthur Villas (☎ 6250 2239, 1800 815 775; www.portarthurvillas.com.au; 52 Safety Cove Rd; d $130-

145) has older-style self-contained units sleeping up to four, and a nice garden and outdoor barbecue area.

Comfort Inn Port Arthur (☎ 6250 2101, 1800 030 747; www.portarthur-inn.com.au; 29 Safety Cove Rd; d $140-180) is a motel with flash views over the historic site and unremarkable accommodation. Dining options inside the pub are the **Convict Kitchen** (meals $12-18; ☻ lunch & dinner) and the more formal **Commandant's Table** (mains $17-28, ☻ dinner).

Daytime food options also include takeaways from the general store and a café inside the historic site visitor information centre.

GETTING THERE & AWAY

Public transport connections to the Port Arthur area are surprisingly poor. **TassieLink** (☎ 1300 300 520; www.tassielink.com.au) connects Hobart and the Tasman Peninsula, but the timetable is geared more to school students than to travellers. There's a weekday bus service between Hobart and Port Arthur ($22) during school terms, and a 4pm service from Hobart on Monday, Wednesday and Friday during school holidays. Buses stop at all the main towns on the peninsula.

Eaglehawk Neck
☎ 03 / pop 90

The small settlement of Eaglehawk Neck is on the isthmus that joins the Tasman Peninsula to the mainland. It is about 15 minutes' drive north (on the A9 Arthur Hwy) of the turn-off for Fortescue Bay (the start of the walk) and near the northern end of the Tasman Coastal Trail. It has a basic general store, but you'd be wise to bring all camping and walking needs from Hobart.

SLEEPING & EATING

Eaglehawk Neck Backpackers (☎ 6250 3248; 94 Old Jetty Rd; camp sites per person $7, dm $18) is a simple, endearing hostel, with a tiny camping area, in a peaceful location west of the isthmus.

Eaglehawk Café & Guesthouse (☎ 6250 3331; eaglehawkcafé@bigpond.com; 5131 Arthur Hwy; d $110-130; mains $7-15; ☻ breakfast & lunch) is a classy eatery and has three inviting B&B rooms above the dining area. Rates include breakfast.

Rooms at the **Lufra Hotel** (☎ 6250 3262; www .lufrahotel.com; Pirates Bay Dr; s/d $75/110), perched above Tessellated Pavement, are pretty standard but comfortable. There are good eating options downstairs: a **café** (☻ breakfast

TASMANIA

& lunch) and **restaurant** (mains $15-27; dinner) and a public bar with traditional pub grub.

Officers Mess (6250 3635; off Arthur Hwy; mains $10-22; breakfast, lunch & dinner) has a pretty basic general store and café, but it does serve hot food and takeaways, and there's an ATM here.

GETTING THERE & AWAY
Buses from Hobart to Port Arthur (p201) pass through Eaglehawk Neck.

Fortescue Bay
6250 3
Hidden down a gravel road off the highway and right at the start/finish of the walk, **Fortescue Bay camping ground** (6250 2433; sites for 2-6 people $11) sits behind a sweeping sandy beach backed by thick forests. It lacks powered sites, but firewood is available and there are fireplaces, gas barbecues, toilets and cold showers. Booking is advised during holiday periods. Fortescue Bay is part of the Tasman National Park so the usual park entry fees apply. There are no shops here so bring in all your own food.

GETTING TO/FROM THE WALK
With the start of the walk 12km off the main highway down a gravel road, the logistics of getting to and from the walk from Port Arthur or Eaglehawk Neck will not be easy for those relying on public transport. You can get to the turn-off from the main highway by bus, after which you'll be facing an unappealing two- to three-hour road bash to reach Fortescue Bay. Alternatively, you could try to hitch or negotiate a lift from the owners of wherever you are staying.

If you are driving, Fortescue Rd turns left (east) off the Arthur Hwy 13km south of Eaglehawk Neck. Follow the road past the beach camping area to the Mill Creek car park and picnic area at its end.

THE WALK
Day 1: Fortescue Bay to Bare Knoll
4½–5½ hours, 13km, 630m ascent, 400m descent
From the day-use car park, follow the foreshore path 150m east to Mill Creek camping area. The track to Cape Hauy and Mt Fortescue are signposted from the boat ramp.

The track initially follows the water's edge, but then swings east and climbs gently inland. The forest throughout this area

was burnt in a bushfire in 2003, but lots of green regrowth has softened the previously stark landscape. After a steep stony section, the track undulates over several rises, with planking across wetter sections, reaching the Cape Hauy Track junction, about one hour from Fortescue Bay. The side trip down to Cape Hauy (below), overlooking the Candlestick and slender Totem Pole (see p204) sea stacks is well worth the effort.

Take the rocky track to the right (south), signposted to Mt Fortescue. Vague at first, it rises gently for 10 minutes to emerge on the cliff top at **Monument Lookout**. To the south the sweep of Munro Bight is backed by bedded sandstone cliffs, giving way to dolerite (p200) towards distant Cape Pillar, with the white tower of Tasman Island lighthouse visible beyond. The track continues near the cliff edge, passing several other lookouts. You eventually leave the burnt area and traverse wetter forest, with tree ferns and mossy trunks and rocks, ascending steadily towards the wooded summit of **Mt Fortescue** (490m; 1¼ to 1¾ hours from the Cape Hauy Track junction). Nearby rocks provide a view towards Cape Pillar.

Continue beyond the summit and descend south, steeply in places; the leaf litter and mud underfoot can be very slippery. The track crosses Retakunna Creek just above **Wughallee Falls** (45 to 60 minutes from Mt Fortescue) and heads upstream for a few minutes to a track junction. There's a good camp site down the short side track to the right, on the creek bank among slender eucalypts and tree ferns. If continuing to the Bare Knoll camp site, which has no water, fill up your water containers here.

Follow the onward track southwest from Retakunna Creek, climbing steeply to a junction with the Cape Pillar Track on the side of Tornado Ridge (30 to 40 minutes). Turn left (south) and follow the Cape Pillar Track for 10 minutes to Bare Knoll and a sheltered camp site among wind-tossed trees.

SIDE TRIP: CAPE HAUY
1½–2 hours, 3km return, 130m ascent/descent
Head east from the track junction and follow the track down across rock slabs. The trees fade away and views south open out across the cliffs beneath Mt Fortescue and into the hazy distance to Cape Pillar itself. Climb across a steep rise and descend

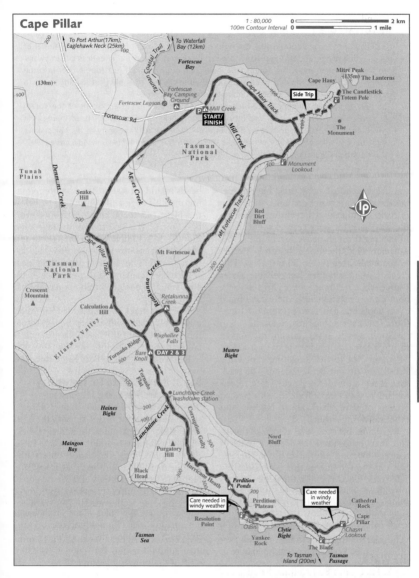

towards Cape Hauy where the track gradually deteriorates. Continue to follow the crest of the headland until you reach a warning sign. Just beyond this are dizzying views of the **Totem Pole** slotted in a turbulent chasm between the end of Cape Hauy and the sheer-sided island that marks the continuation of the headland into the ocean.

You can scramble down a little further to get a more impressive view, but the descent becomes more dangerous as you continue. Return via your outward route.

Day 2: Bare Knoll to Cape Pillar Return
4½–5½ hours, 12km return, 420m ascent/descent

Leaving your camp at Bare Knoll, head

THE TOTEM POLE

It is difficult not to be impressed by the sight of the Totem Pole, a 65m-high vertical finger of rock standing at the end of Cape Hauy in defiance of gravity and the relentless ocean swells. Seen from the right angle, the Totem Pole looks as though it might just topple over into the chasm it occupies. The thought of climbing it would terrify most people (just looking at it is a dizzying experience), but it has been climbed a number of times.

In 1997 top British climber Paul Pritchard almost died attempting an ascent of the Totem Pole. Low down on the route he was hit by a falling block, suffering serious head injuries. He survived an epic rescue to be told he'd never walk again. He tells the story of his painstaking journey back to relative mobility in his books *The Totem Pole and a Whole New Adventure* (1999) and *The Longest Climb: Back from the Abyss* (2005).

---

southeast with just a day pack, but remember to take some water containers with you in order to top up at Lunchtime Creek on the way back for your second night. After tunnelling through dense vegetation across Tornado Flat, the track descends steeply to **Lunchtime Creek** (20 to 30 minutes). This creek is generally the last reliable water source when heading south. There is also a boot-cleaning station here where you should clean boots and gaiters to prevent phytophthora (p47) spreading further south.

Climb south from Lunchtime Creek through low heath, with views west across Maingon Bay to the long finger of Cape Raoul and distant Bruny Island. The track then enters a wonderful patch of forest, contouring east of Purgatory Hill, with twisted crowns of stringybark above banksia and other flowering shrubs.

Swinging back to the southeast again you then cross **Hurricane Heath**, a mass of mauve-flowering tea-tree shrubs in November. On the far side of this area a narrow side track heads right (southwest) towards a patch of taller vegetation for 100m and a sheltered camp site (one to 1½ hours from Bare Knoll).

A 10 minute descent across an open wind-blasted area leads to the brackish Perdition Ponds. Walkers have camped here in the past, but this is not recommended; the site is exposed and the sandy soil prone to erosion. A narrow corridor through thick scrub leads up and across Perdition Plateau to a **cliff edge viewpoint**. The view along the cliffs of Clytie Bight to the Blade pinnacle and the inaccessible Tasman Island is nothing short of spectacular. The track continues along the cliff edge to a sandy area known as the Oasis, where the track

heads inland for a short time before rejoining the cliff edge and continuing to below the **Blade** (45 to 60 minutes from Perdition Ponds). If it isn't too windy, take a few minutes to scramble out to the end of this exposed promontory for airy views of Tasman Island. The white-stained slabs near sea level on Tasman Island are fur seal haulouts and, if the wind is right, you may hear them barking.

The main track continues for 15 minutes to **Chasm Lookout**, with a steep final climb to this highest point of Cape Pillar, the cliffs falling a sheer 280m into the sea.

Retrace your steps to Bare Knoll campsite.

Day 3: Bare Knoll to Fortescue Bay
2–3 hours, 8km, 90m ascent, 320m descent

The walk out to Fortescue Bay is an easy stroll. Retrace your Day 1 steps to the Tornado Ridge Track junction, and then bear left and continue to follow the Cape Pillar Track north. The track soon enters forest burnt in 2003, although, as elsewhere, regrowth is progressing. Traversing open buttongrass country, extended sections of planking ease wetter areas. The track re-renters forest near Snake Hill and eventually commences a steady descent, winding down to cross Agnes Creek. About 15 minutes later Fortescue Rd is reached, 150m west of the camping ground.

WEST & WORLD HERITAGE AREA

Tasmania's west really is wild. The most rugged region of Tasmania, formidable mountains, buttongrass plains, tranquil lakes, dense rainforests and a treacherous coast are all compelling features of this beautiful region. One of three southern temperate wilderness regions (the others are in New Zealand and Patagonia), this isn't the only link between these regions (see right).

A large part of Tasmania's western wilderness is World Heritage–listed on Unesco's register of natural and cultural places of world significance – see www .parks.tas.gov.au/wha. The World Heritage Area (WHA) was listed in 1982 and granted Australian legal status in 1983, following a failed attempt by the Tasmanian government to dam the Franklin River (below). When Unesco was asked to consider the nomination of the area for listing, it was accepted on the basis of satisfying a record seven out of a possible 10 criteria. After a number of significant additions, the Tasmanian Wilderness World Heritage Area today encompasses 1.38 million hectares, which is some 20% of Tasmania's land area.

This West & World Heritage Area section features many of the most difficult and strenuous walks in Tasmania, covering high and potentially dangerous terrain on rough tracks exposed to the worst weather. But their wildness and isolation are also what many walkers come to Tasmania to experience.

HISTORY

Arriving in Tasmania via a land bridge from the mainland at least 35,000 years ago, the Tasmanian Aboriginal people lived in the then-grassy valleys of western Tasmania through the last ice age, the southernmost humans on earth at that time. These valleys were abandoned by about 12,000 years ago as the forests expanded after the end of the ice age, but occupation continued mainly around the resource-rich coast until the 1830s, a few decades after the arrival of Europeans.

ENVIRONMENT

In the southwest, convoluted quartzite ranges rise from rolling buttongrass plains and are cut by deep gorges cloaked in dense rainforest. The dolerite-capped mountains and plateaus of the central highlands are often rimmed by columnar cliffs, a dramatic backdrop to the many lakes. The WHA was covered by ice during several ice ages over the last two million years (to current sea level at one point) and these glaciers have sculpted many highland landforms.

While the most extensive temperate rainforest lies in the northwest Tarkine region, rainforest is also well developed in and characteristic of western Tasmania and the WHA. Tasmania's rainforest and alpine areas contain a distinctive suite of plants that evolved on the supercontinent

TASMANIA

THE WORLD HERITAGE AREA – THE FIGHT FOR PROTECTION

Few World Heritage Areas (WHAs) have been embroiled in as much contentious environmental debate as the Tasmanian Wilderness WHA. The flooding of Lake Pedder, then part of Southwest National Park, by the HEC (Hydro Electric Commission) in 1972 prompted concern over the levels of protection afforded by national park status.

The Tasmanian Wilderness Society (now The Wilderness Society) was founded in 1976 to provide organised opposition to the HEC's planned damming of the Gordon and Franklin Rivers. The Society was instrumental in having the area World Heritage–listed by Unesco in 1982. But that, and a change in state government, did not prevent the beginning of dam construction on the lower Gordon. In the summer of 1982–83 the issue burst onto the national arena with the 'Franklin River Blockade' and the arrest of 1400 protesters. In the 1983 Federal election, the Australian Labor Party was elected on a promise to enforce the WHA's protection. Despite a legal challenge by the Tasmanian government, the Franklin River scheme was abandoned. This was a landmark decision, further clarifying the constitutional powers of the federal government over state governments.

After further controversy, many protests and a government inquiry, this time over forestry, the WHA was enlarged in 1989 and now covers 20% of Tasmania. Despite this, the scale of industrial forestry has expanded dramatically and the Wilderness Society and others continue to argue for appropriate protection for additional areas.

Gondwana (p25). Many animals, especially invertebrates, also display a Gondwanan heritage. Subsequent evolution has produced many species unique to Tasmania. Such species include conifers like King Billy, pencil and Huon pine, and invertebrates like the mountain shrimp inhabiting highland tarns or velvet worms found in rotting logs. Nor are Gondwanan affinities restricted to plants and animals; Tasmania has more geological similarities with Antarctica than with much of mainland Australia.

Forests dominated by tall – sometimes very tall – eucalyptus trees also exist in the west, the wet climate contributing to a rainforest understorey in many areas. If the area remains free of bushfires for 300 years or so, this understorey may eventually supplant the eucalypts as they die.

In some alpine areas, the arrangement of dwarf shrubs, small tarns and rich green cushion plants brings to mind a landscaped rock garden. In the southwest, many broad valleys are blanketed by peat soils with buttongrass, their seed 'buttons' waving on long stalks.

PLANNING
When to Walk

The summer months (November to April) are generally the best time for walking in Tasmania's western areas. The days are longer and the prevalence of cool and wet weather is generally somewhat less. However, the weather can be fickle and changeable at any time of the year, so be prepared for the worst.

WARNING

The walking in western Tasmania and the WHA is often at significant altitudes, and the weather can be very changeable. This brings with it the potential difficulties of low temperatures, high winds, poor visibility and heavy rain or snow. Snow is a possibility in the alpine areas of Tasmania at any time of the year. Although the Overland Track is now quite well constructed, many of the other tracks can be rough and muddy in places. Even if just heading off for a day walk, walkers considering walking in the West & WHA should be well equipped for mountain weather.

What to Bring

Many walks in western Tasmania traverse highland areas, so it's essential to be properly prepared (see Gearing Up For the Mountains, p39). As the entire WHA is a fuel-stove-only area (p192), fuel stoves are required for all overnight walks.

Books

The thin booklet *Tasmania World Heritage* includes work by some of Tasmania's best photographers and provides an excellent overview of the WHA and its values. For scientific detail you could seek out *Tasmanian Wilderness World Heritage Values,* published by the Royal Society of Tasmania.

MT FIELD & TARN SHELF CIRCUIT

Duration	5–6 hours
Distance	12km
Difficulty	moderate
Start/Finish	Lake Dobson
Nearest Town	National Park (opposite)
Transport	private

Summary Explore the glaciated uplands of Mt Field National Park, traversing snow gum woodland, alpine vegetation and bouldery crests, returning along the beautiful Tarn Shelf.

Mt Field National Park lies adjacent to the eastern fringes of the WHA and only an hour's drive from Hobart. From the towering swamp gums and tree ferns around Russell Falls and the park entrance, a dirt road winds up to Lake Dobson and the start of several fine walking tracks exploring the alpine forests, moors and boulder fields.

The one-day walk described here makes a beautiful alpine circuit across the Rodway Range, returning along Tarn Shelf. While there are no tough ascents or large gains in altitude, parts of the route can still be quite arduous. Scrambling and hopping across jumbles of boulders is the order of the day on the ascent to Rodway Range. Fit walkers can consider visiting Mt Field West, but adding this side trip makes for a long day, with a more demanding level of difficulty; start early from Lake Dobson (see p208). Given clear weather, the views from the high sections of this walk are absolutely tremendous, but the exposed alpine environment is unforgiving in poor conditions.

HISTORY

Mt Field National Park was created in 1916. It was an expansion of a reserve created around Russell Falls in 1885, making it (along with Freycinet) one of Tasmania's oldest parks. At this time, the park area was a mere 2000 hectares and it has subsequently increased to 16,756 hectares. However, in 1949 timber interests managed to excise 1472 hectares for logging, much of which was tall swamp gum, with 1500 hectares of mixed forest added in return. Logging continues in the Florentine Valley, in uncomfortable proximity to both Mt Field and the eastern fringes of the WHA. The operations in the Florentine Valley are readily viewed from the summit of Mt Field West.

ENVIRONMENT

The upper reaches of the park show plenty of evidence of past glaciation; U-shaped valleys, cirques, tarns and jumbles of moraine debris. Lake Seal lies within an impressive glacial trough, and ice that accumulated on Tarn Shelf, in the lee of the Rodway Range, fed a glacier that flowed down the Broad River valley during the last ice age.

Few other national parks in Australia offer Mt Field's diversity of vegetation; tall swamp gum forests with tree ferns near the park entrance, temperate rainforest along the Lake Dobson road, then alpine woodland and moorland at higher elevations.

PLANNING

The national park contains a number of other walking options, both alpine and lowland. At the very least, before going up to Lake Dobson, it's worth taking the short stroll to Russell Falls from the visitor information centre, not just to view the waterfall, but also to see the huge swamp gums and tree ferns along the way. The Tall Trees circuit a short distance up the Lake Dobson road is also worth a look.

If cloud hides the tops of the Rodway Range you might consider a lower level circuit along Tarn Shelf to Twilight Tarn, returning via Lake Webster, instead of the route described here.

When to Walk

Walking in the alpine regions of Mt Field is normally feasible from October to April, but the high ridges are very exposed to bad weather, low cloud can render visibility poor and the track is not always well defined, so err on the side of caution when deciding on suitable weather for this walk. See also the Warning boxed text on p210.

Maps

Tasmap's 1:50,000 *Mt Field National Park Map & Notes* shows this and other walks in the national park.

Information Sources

The **national park visitor information centre** (☎ 6288 1149), at the park entrance, has lots of information on the area's walks, can provide updates on weather and snow conditions, sells park passes, and contains a café and a good, small interpretive display.

NEAREST TOWN

National Park

☎ 03 / pop 170

National Park consists of only a few houses and a pub just outside the park entrance. It is, however, a convenient base for both the Mt Field and Mt Anne (p209) walks. Russell Falls is only a short stroll away, and if viewing marsupials is your thing, then a visit to the open lawns at the park entrance at dusk will reward you with plenty of possums and pademelons.

SLEEPING & EATING

Land of the Giants Campground (unpowered/powered sites for 2 $20/25) is a privately run, self-registration camping ground with good facilities (toilets, showers, laundry, free barbecues) just inside the park. Bookings not required. Site fees are in addition to national park entry fees.

The **Lake Dobson Cabins** (☎ 6288 1149; s & d $22) are three simple six-bed cabins located near the lake and make a good base for exploring the highland parts of the park. They are equipped with mattresses, cold water and wood stoves, but lack power. Book at the visitor information centre.

National Park Hotel (☎ 6288 1103; Gordon River Rd; s/d $40/80) is a laid-back pub offering reasonable rooms with shared facilities, plus counter meals most nights. Rates include breakfast.

Russell Falls Holiday Cottages (☎ 6288 1198; Lake Dobson Hwy; d $120) are conveniently located next to the park's entrance. These spotless cottages have rather dated furnishings, but are roomy and well equipped.

Waterfalls Café (☎ 6288 1516; meals $7-15; 🕑 lunch) is a simple eatery inside the visitor information centre.

Groceries are available from small stores at Westerway (8km east on the B61) and Maydena (13km west on the B61). However, it is best to bring fuel and walk-food supplies from Hobart.

GETTING THERE & AWAY

Public transport connections to Mt Field National Park are not regular. From December through March, **TassieLink** (☎ 1300 300 520; www.tassielink.com.au; 64 Brisbane St, Hobart) runs one bus on Tuesday, Thursday and Saturday from Hobart to Mt Field ($28); bookings are essential.

Unfortunately the service does not run to the top car park so to undertake the alpine walks you really need your own transport. If driving, Mt Field National Park is 75km northwest of Hobart along the Brooker Hwy, B62 and then the Gordon River Rd.

GETTING TO/FROM THE WALK

From the national park visitor information centre, drive up the narrow, winding gravel road to the car park at Lake Dobson. In winter this road is sometimes snow-covered and may be closed.

THE WALK

Leave the Lake Dobson car park and follow the path around the southern shores of the lake. Just after the end of the boardwalk, bear left uphill onto Urquart Track and follow this to meet the ski field access road. Alternatively you might take a longer route straight ahead around the lake, traversing **Pandani Grove**, to meet the ski field road lower down. Pandanis grow only in Tasmania and, despite their palm-like appearance, are actually a giant heath.

Turn onto the road and climb through several hairpin bends to reach a cluster of ski lodges. Follow the 'Alpine Tracks' signposts along the front of the buildings, where the road deteriorates into a rocky walking track. Views across the eastern section of the park are fairly unobstructed as you sidle

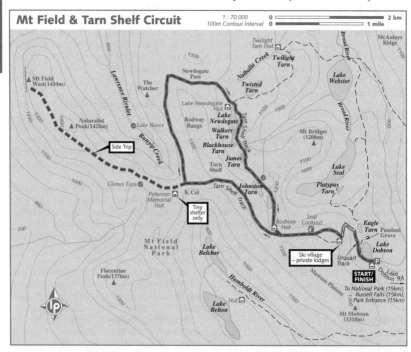

through stands of beautiful snow gums. The track is rough and rocky in places before it emerges onto a broad shoulder 15 minutes from the ski lodges. Extensive duckboards carry you across wet flat ground towards Rodway Hut. Along the way the **Seal Lookout** provides views across the impressive glacial trough containing Lake Seal. Ten minutes of easy walking on the duckboards brings you to a track junction just above Rodway Hut (day shelter and emergency use only), about one hour from Lake Dobson. The Tarn Shelf Track descends to the north past the hut (a snow pole line climbs in the opposite direction onto the Mawson Plateau). Continue straight ahead (west) on a third track signposted for the Rodway Range. The track quickly deteriorates into a route marked with snow poles and splashes of red paint. The going is arduous, hopping between boulders, but the dolerite provides excellent friction.

After a short climb the route traverses northwest along the crest of the **Rodway Range**. In clear conditions views extend right across the Southwest National Park, and north across the Central Plateau towards the distant peaks of Cradle Mountain–Lake St Clair National Park. More immediately, Mt Field West (1434m) is the highest point on the impressive ridge stretching 3km to the northwest from K Col.

Descend to K Col (45 to 60 minutes from Rodway Hut), where the boulders give way to wet ground carpeted with alpine flora. Fitter walkers with time and good conditions on their side can now make the side trip to Mt Field West (right). Otherwise follow the muddy, marked track north, rising towards the bluff of The Watcher and Newdegate Pass (30 minutes from K Col). The track is vague in the area of Newdegate Pass and is very easy to lose – it's best to look carefully for markers as the route swings sharply to the east. If you do lose the route, climb to higher ground and look for a section of duckboard. **Newdegate Pass** is also carpeted with alpine flora, including bright green cushion plants, in places forming dams to tiered series of small tarns.

The route descends steeply east from Newdegate Pass, on a defined track, to reach Lake Newdegate Hut (day shelter and emergency only) at the northern end of Lake Newdegate. After crossing the lake outlet, turn right onto the Tarn Shelf Track. This track skirts the eastern shores of **Lake Newdegate**, passing through the stark dead trunks of numerous native pines, killed by a bushfire that started in logging areas below Mt Field West in 1966. The southern end of Tarn Shelf escaped this fire and living pencil pines protrude from thickets of deciduous beech, which turn golden before losing their leaves in autumn.

Continue following the track generally southeast along Tarn Shelf, passing lakes and tarns and crossing glacier-scoured ridges to Rodway Hut (one hour from Lake Newdegate). Turn left at the junction above the hut and retrace your steps back to Lake Dobson car park (45 minutes).

SIDE TRIP: MT FIELD WEST
3–3½ hours, 6.5km return, 240m ascent/descent
Mt Field West (1434m) is the highest summit in the national park. It offers great views on a clear day but makes for a long outing if combined with the full circuit described above. Cross the boggy flats of K Col, past the small stone Peterson Memorial Hut (day shelter and emergency use only) and climb steadily past Clemes Tarn, then northwest up the spur towards Naturalist Peak (1428m). Passing this peak, a generally level walk of 1km or so crosses a beautiful alpine plateau with many small tarns to the summit of Mt Field West. The views across the heavily logged Florentine Valley into the WHA present a stark juxtaposition of wilderness lost and wilderness protected. Return to K Col by the route of ascent.

MT ANNE & ELIZA PLATEAU

Duration	7–8½ hours
Distance	15km
Difficulty	moderate–demanding
Start/Finish	Condominium Creek
Nearest Towns	National Park (p207)
Transport	bus (summer only)
Summary	Climb the highest peak in the southwest on an exposed alpine walk with stunning mountain scenery.

From most angles, Mt Anne (1423m) looks like improbable terrain for walkers. It rises to the east of Lake Pedder, a towering fang of dolerite with sheer faces on all sides,

TASMANIA

connected to the more rounded peak of Mt Eliza (1289m) by a rolling plateau carpeted by alpine vegetation. Parts of this walk offer incredible views across much of the southwest wilderness, and also of the tremendous glacial scenery of the Anne Range itself.

PLANNING

This description describes a there-and-back visit to Mt Anne. This is a fairly long one-day effort, involving some 1400m of total ascent, so start early (there is a good camp site beside Condominium Creek at the start of the track that may facilitate this). Or you could make the walk a more leisurely 1½-day outing by staying overnight at High Camp Memorial Hut. Even if you don't make it to the summit, the views of both Mt Anne and the WHA from Mt Eliza are well worth the effort.

It is possible to continue beyond Mt Anne, but walkers attempting the demanding three-day Anne Circuit should be fit, well equipped and very comfortable on steep, exposed ground, as well as with scrambling over boulders, all with a full pack.

When to Walk

The summer months (November to April) are generally the best time for walking in Tasmania's western mountains. See also the Warning boxed text below.

High and isolated, Mt Anne can experience particularly awful weather. Given the exposed nature of Eliza Plateau (where the track is not always well-defined) and the extent of steep and dangerous ground around the ridges, the walk should only be attempted in clear and stable weather. Snow and ice build-up in winter can make the summit a realm for mountaineers only.

Maps

Tasmap's 1:25,000 topographic map *Anne* is the most suitable for this walk.

WARNING

A good head for heights and confidence on steep ground is required for the final summit ascent, but the views are good and extensive from many parts of the walk even if you don't proceed to the actual summit.

NEAREST TOWN

See National Park (p207).

GETTING TO/FROM THE WALK

TassieLink (☎ 1300 300 520; www.tassielink.com.au; 64 Brisbane St, Hobart) runs a summer-only service from Hobart to Scotts Peak, passing the start of the walk, three days per week. The bus departs the Hobart bus terminal (at the address listed here) at 8am Tuesday, Thursday and Saturday, passing the Mt Anne track at around 12.45pm, and returns the same day. The one-way fare is $68 and booking is recommended.

For those with their own transport, simply follow the B61 Hwy (Gordon River Rd) towards Strathgordon and turn left onto the unsealed C607 (Scotts Peak Rd), signposted for Mt Anne and Scotts Peak. The trailhead at Condominium Creek is signposted on the left about 20km to the south.

THE WALK

A well-constructed track leaves the car park at Condominium Creek and crosses a buttongrass plain for a few hundred metres to reach the foot of Mt Eliza's long west ridge. The track climbs steep steps onto the ridge, and magnificent views begin to open out behind. The steps can seem very strenuous with a heavy pack, but some relief is gained after 30 minutes. A level section of track, muddy in places, leads into a dip from where the track climbs steeply again for 10 minutes to gain the crest of Mt Eliza's west ridge. From here a steady ascent leads to **High Camp Memorial Hut** (1½ to two hours from the car park), tucked among stunted gum trees on the bouldery slopes of Mt Eliza. The small hut has a water tank at the back and a toilet just below. There are a few small tent sites below the hut.

Beyond High Camp Memorial Hut the track becomes much rougher and is marked with cairns. It swings to the northeast and climbs steeply over boulders and rock steps, then trends back to the east following a ridge to the summit of **Mt Eliza** (1289m). The strenuous climb from High Camp Hut takes 45 minutes to one hour and is rewarded (in clear weather) by spectacular views of the Frankland Range across Lake Pedder. This vantage point is a worthwhile destination itself and many walkers venture no further.

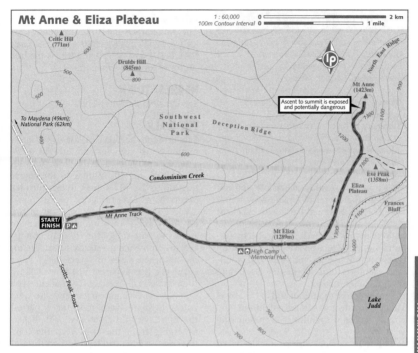

Mt Anne & Eliza Plateau

1 : 60,000
100m Contour Interval

Celtic Hill (771m)

Druids Hill (845m)

To Maydena (49km); National Park (62km)

South west National Park

Deception Ridge

Mt Anne (1423m)

Ascent to summit is exposed and potentially dangerous

North East Ridge

Condominium Creek

Eve Peak (1358m)

Eliza Plateau

Frances Bluff

START/ FINISH

Mt Anne Track

Mt Eliza (1289m)

High Camp Memorial Hut

Scotts Peak Road

Lake Judd

TASMANIA

Descend slightly and then rise gently to a broad rounded crest. The precipitous drop to **Lake Judd** is now before you and it is well worth detouring 100m or so to the east to view the lake. Another gentle descent and ascent leads northwards to a broad col dotted with an assortment of tarns. Cushion-plant communities abound on this col and are complemented by clusters of stunted pandani. From the col, a short climb leads round the western shoulder of **Eve Peak** (1358m). Descend awkwardly across large boulders to reach a broad col beneath Mt Anne (one to 1½ hours from Mt Eliza). The route leading right (east) here is the difficult, three-day Anne Circuit. The route to the summit of Mt Anne (1423m) is the marked route continuing straight ahead (north).

Follow the marked track across the col and climb around to the left of an outcrop. The track drops down to an extensive boulder field beneath the cliffed south face of Mt Anne. The most difficult section on the final summit tower above requires confidence on steep ground so you may wish to reassess the situation now, remembering

that the descent will likely be more awkward than the ascent.

The route is cairned diagonally left across the boulder slope to a square-cut corner close to the eastern extent of the cliffs. Once at the foot of the corner you'll need to use your hands and exercise great care, and if the rock is wet or icy you are advised not to attempt this section. Climb directly up for a few metres to reach a ramp, which can be followed to the left (as you face the cliff) and upwards to a sloping platform on a blunt and very exposed ridge. Make a slightly awkward move off this to another ledge (you may need a short rope here; if you feel nervous at this point, don't proceed further) and then walk carefully back to the right on a wide and sloping ledge. Now climb through a small notch onto the eastern side of the mountain and walk along a wide ledge to where cairns show the way up the last scramble to the **summit** (45 to 60 minutes from the col). The views and sense of achievement are considerable. Follow your route of ascent to return to the Eliza Plateau and back down to the car park.

MT RUFUS & SHADOW LAKE

Duration	6–8 hours
Distance	18.5km
Difficulty	moderate
Start/Finish	Cynthia Bay (Lake St Clair; p219)
Nearest Town	Derwent Bridge (p219)
Transport	bus

Summary Traverse a wide variety of vegetation to and from a grand mountain viewpoint, relaxing beside a tranquil lake on your return.

Mt Rufus is a readily accessible summit at the southern end of Cradle Mountain–Lake St Clair National Park, with excellent views in all directions, especially of the high peaks in the park itself. The mountain's slopes feature a variety of vegetation types, including eucalypt forest and woodland, rainforest and alpine moorland, and several tranquil lakes.

Tracks on the mountain and in the Hugel Valley provide for a range of in-out and circuit walks, depending on mood and weather.

The full-day clockwise circuit described here involves a 680m ascent to Mt Rufus, followed by a more leisurely return descent via Shadow Lake and the Hugel Valley (although the walk could readily be completed in the reverse direction).

PLANNING
When to Walk
The summer months (November to April) are generally the best time for walking in Tasmania's western mountains. See also the Warning boxed text on p210.

If the weather or mountain visibility is poor, consider the alternative Shadow Lake Circuit (see opposite).

Maps
Tasmap's 1:25,000 topographic map *Rufus* and 1:50,000 *Lake St Clair Day Walk Map & Notes* both show the walk. However, the Tasmap 1:100,000 *Cradle Mountain-Lake St Clair Map & Notes* also shows the route, and walkers completing the Overland Track may already have this. This map is also the only publication showing the new Shadow Lake Link Track, albeit at a less useful scale.

Information Sources
The walk starts at the Parks & Wildlife Service's **visitor information centre** at Lake St Clair (☎ 6289 1172; fax 6289 1227) and this is the best source of local information.

NEAREST TOWN
See Derwent Bridge (p219).

THE WALK
Pass through the Lake St Clair visitor information centre complex and turn left, at the sign. All walking tracks'. Follow the wide gravel path for 10 minutes to the signed turn-off to the 'Mt Rufus Circuit'; turn left (west) here. A buttongrass plain, then a tea-tree swamp, give way to eucalypt forest and a good track undulating over low stony moraine ridges for 15 to 20 minutes before commencing a steady climb. Passing the upturned bases of several large fallen eucalypts, it is apparent just how shallow-rooted these tall trees are. The tall eucalypts become increasingly sparse and the track enters highland rainforest for a period, the myrtle trunks festooned with lichen. Emerging from the rainforest, the track traverses an extended level section through subalpine forest, spindly eucalypts above wiry shrubs.

Towards the end of this section is a signed track junction, 1½ to two hours from the visitor information centre. The summit ridge of **Mt Rufus** should be visible ahead; if it's shrouded in cloud it may be best to turn right (north) here and complete the Shadow Lake Circuit (see opposite). Otherwise, follow the rocky track straight ahead (west).

The track climbs steeply onto a stony moraine crest and follows this up to an open alpine basin; there are now good views back down to Lake St Clair. The profusion of emergent dead eucalypts on the slopes below resulted from bushfire several decades ago.

The track now heads south, skirting the lip of the basin, then ascends steeply to Mt Rufus' east ridge, a broad crest with alpine grass and shrubs dotted with rocks. Recline on the grass and take in the expansive view. Follow the ridge crest, first northwest and then southwest to the large **summit** cairn (around 2½ to 3½ hours from the visitor information centre; the route is

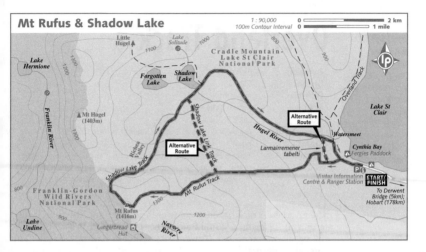

Mt Rufus & Shadow Lake

marked by snow poles). From here there is a wonderful view: the Franklin headwaters and Frenchmans Cap to the west, the serried peaks of the Du Cane Range beyond Mt Hugel to the north, and the Shadow and Forgotten Lakes in a basin to the northeast.

Head northwest from the summit, descending a broad open ridge towards the saddle between Mts Rufus and Hugel, and pass a group of sandstone outcrops sculpted by aeons of wind and rain. The track swings east and an extended boardwalk section leads to **Richea Valley**, named for the botanical genus of the pandani and scoparia growing there. These heaths are Tasmanian endemics with a Gondwanan heritage (p206), and can produce a spectacular floral display in early summer. There is a beautiful grove of snow gums and pandania at the valley's lower end.

Entering rainforest as the slope steepens, the track winds down to emerge onto an open plain, covered with more Richea shrubs. Soon after re-entering forest on the far side of the plain, the track reaches the junction with the Shadow Lake Link Track (right). Bear left and follow the track over a stony rise. **Shadow Lake** appears through the trees ahead. The track skirts the eastern shore to another track junction, 1½ to two hours from Mt Rufus. A few pencil pines fringe the lake and platypus are occasionally seen. You could try your luck fishing for introduced trout here, if you have a

fishing licence. Continue straight ahead at the Shadow Lake Track junction. The track traverses buttongrass openings and subalpine woodland, before commencing a steady descent. Eucalypt forest and rainforest alternate, and the rushing Hugel River is heard, but not seen, for a while. After paralleling the river for some time, the track descends into rainforest again and crosses to the south bank on a massive bridge.

There are two options here. Turn left and follow the river bank downstream to Watersmeet, there joining the broad gravel path leading right (south) back to the visitor information centre (1½ to two hours from Shadow Lake). Or turn right off the bridge and follow the Larmairremener tabelti Aboriginal cultural walk; this loop is slightly longer and joins the Mt Rufus Track which is then followed, left, to the path back to the visitor information centre.

ALTERNATIVE ROUTE: SHADOW LAKE CIRCUIT

The main route in the previous section is known as the Mt Rufus Circuit. The Shadow Lake Circuit is a shorter (four to five hours, 13km), lower-altitude option utilising the well-constructed Shadow Lake Link Track. The junctions with this track are noted in the previous description. This circuit is a good alternative if the mountain weather is poor, or if you're feeling less energetic.

(Continued on page 229)

TASMANIA

Overland Track

Duration	6–7 days
Distance	80km
Difficulty	moderate
Start	Cradle Valley (p218)
Finish	Lake St Clair
Nearest Towns	Cradle Valley (p218) and Derwent Bridge (p219)
Transport	bus
Summary	Traverse the highest ground in Tasmania, taking in wild alpine moors, craggy peaks and swathes of luxuriant rainforest on the most famous multi-day walk in Australia.

The Overland Track traverses some of the highest and most spectacular terrain in Tasmania. Monolithic ranges of shattered peaks rise above rolling alpine moorland. Towards its southern end at Lake St Clair, Australia's deepest lake, the track descends into valleys cloaked in wet eucalyptus and haunting myrtle rainforest. Beyond the already diverse main route, side tracks visit roaring waterfalls, tannin-stained lakes and craggy summits.

The track is arguably the best multi-day walk in Australia and justifiably popular, so much so that a booking system has been introduced in recent years, aiming to limit crowding and environmental damage. The volume of walkers traversing the sensitive alpine terrain has created a problem with track erosion similar to the difficulties on other popular tracks in the World Heritage Area (WHA). Over recent years a good deal of the track has been 'hardened', with boardwalks, parallel planks and log paths replacing the once infamous mires of knee-deep mud. In addition, and unusually for Tasmanian walks, there are basic but comfortable bushwalkers' huts at overnight stops along the track (although carrying a tent is still strongly recommended). Despite these improvements, the environment remains wild and the weather often unpredictable, so the walk remains the challenging experience it has always been.

HISTORY

Cradle Mountain and Lake St Clair were first visited by European explorers in the 1820s, and prospectors and hunters searched the region well into the 20th century. But it was Austrian immigrant Gustav Weindorfer and his wife Kate who were instrumental in the process of recognition that led to the Cradle Mountain area becoming a national park (opposite). In 1931 fur trapper Bert Nichols blazed the Overland Track and by 1935 it was consolidated and being used by independent walking parties.

ENVIRONMENT

Many of the attributes of the Tasmanian Wilderness World Heritage Area (p205) are contained within Cradle Mountain–Lake St Clair National Park. Of particular prominence to walkers is the rainforest and alpine vegetation. The endemic conifers (King Billy pine, pencil pine) and southern beeches (myrtle, deciduous beech) all have relatives in other southern continents – links to the ancient supercontinent Gondwana (p25).

A distinctive feature of the park is the columnar dolerite that forms most of the peaks, and this also has a Gondwana connection. This rock intruded into the crust in a molten state 175 million years ago and is solidified evidence of magma from the initial break-up of Gondwana (p200).

The park's present topography is largely the result of the cumulative effect of at least four ice ages during the last two million years. Even during the most recent, which ended just 10,000 years ago, only the high peaks protruded above an ice cap and glaciers flowed down valleys like the Forth and filled the trough now occupied by Lake St Clair. Glacial erosion smoothed the landscape and gouged out pre-existing river valleys, depositing moraine debris where the ice melted, while the higher peaks exposed above the ice were shattered by frost action.

You stand a good chance of seeing several of Tasmania's native marsupials along the track. Bennett's wallabies are common around Waterfall Valley and New Pelion Hut, while the smaller pademelon is happier in the thick bush around Windy Ridge Hut. Dusk strolls by torchlight (flashlight) should reveal sightings of ringtail or brushtail possums and possibly a wombat, quoll or Tasmanian devil. The call of the currawong is ubiquitous the length of the track and these cheeky raven-like birds have even learnt how to open pack zips and clips to seek tasty treats – beware!

PLANNING

During summer, the track must be walked from north to south (see Park Fees & Regulations, p217), but can be traversed in the other direction outside this period.

THE WEINDORFERS' LEGACY

In 1910 Gustav Weindorfer climbed to the top of Cradle Mountain, looked across the rugged terrain and announced, 'This must be a national park for all the people for all time. This is magnificent, and people must know about it and enjoy it'.

Born in Austria in 1874, Gustav Weindorfer is most famous for building the alpine chalet, Waldheim (German for 'Forest Home') at Cradle Valley in 1912. He came to Australia in 1900 where he met Kate Cowle (b 1864). They were married in 1906 and spent their honeymoon on Mt Roland (p38).

What has captured the imagination of generations is the fact that Gustav had the foresight to identify the area's natural significance a century ago, and together with the help of friends began to lobby successive governments to have the area preserved. What is less well known is that his wife, Kate, also played a key role in the preservation of this area. Her passion extended to botany and by becoming a member of a field naturalists club she learned about the uniqueness of the mountain's bushland, encouraging Gustav's appreciation of the landscape. The Weindorfers shared their time between Cradle Mountain and their farm at Kindred (near Devonport). Their spirit was tenacious – in those days a horse and cart could only get within 15km of Cradle Mountain, and from there it was a choice between pack horse or walking in order to carry in supplies. It was Kate who purchased some 60 acres of land in 1912, covering the present entrance to the park, where Gustav was able to build his alpine chalet Waldheim. Gustav and Kate encouraged visitors to come to their remote home to share in the marvels of Cradle Mountain. In 1916 Kate died after a long illness, and Gustav lived at Waldheim permanently, devoting his life to preserving the mountain he loved. A reserve at Cradle Mountain was declared in 1922 but Gustav, who died in 1932, didn't live to see the proclamation of a much larger national park in 1940. Half a century after Weindorfer's death Cradle Mountain–Lake St Clair National Park formed part of the area recognised and listed as World Heritage by Unesco (see p209).

The original Waldheim chalet burnt down in 1974, but it was rebuilt using traditional bush carpentry techniques and stands proudly as a humble legacy to potent insight. Just inside the doorway Gustav inscribed 'This is Waldheim/Where there is no time/And nothing matters'.

There are basic, usually unstaffed, huts the length of the Overland Track but, despite the summer season booking system (opposite), sleeping spaces in huts are not allocated and hut space for everyone is not guaranteed, so periods of poor weather can still result in crowded huts.

Depending on how much time and energy you have, how fit you are and how much you want to see, the Overland Track can be walked in as little as four days, or you can spend eight or even 10 days. A straight-through walk skipping side trips will take five days for an average group. Taking in most of the side trips will require about eight days, including ascents of Cradle Mountain, Mt Ossa, and perhaps the chance to wander through the tarns and snow gums of the Labyrinth. But it's best to take an opportunistic approach to the side trip options, avoiding rigid plans and being mindful of the weather on the day.

Most walkers walk from Cradle Mountain to Narcissus Hut (65km) then utilise the Lake St Clair ferry to complete their journey. But the full Overland Track includes the additional 17km section along the western shore of Lake St Clair. The walk could also be extended at the northern end; if staying in the Cradle Mountain area the night before starting your walk, you might consider starting your walk at the Visitor Centre and following the scenic 5.5km Cradle Valley Boardwalk to Ronny Creek.

When to Walk

December to March has generally better weather and more daylight than other periods. Late summer can have some of the most settled weather of the year, and autumn (late April) features the colours of the deciduous beech ('fagus'), popular with local walkers. But despite these general conditions, rapid weather changes are possible at any time, including the onset of high winds, rain, snow, sleet and poor visibility. Such poor weather is much more likely during the winter months, and the track can become snowbound; only very experienced and well-prepared walkers tackle the Overland Track in winter conditions. Spring (September to November) weather can be very unsettled and, while calm days occur, winter conditions still blast the area regularly.

Flowers of the Richea scoparia heath are abundant along the Overland Track during summer
GRANT DIXON

What to Bring

Given this is a highland walk, it's essential to be properly prepared (see Gearing up for the Mountains, p39).

As with all of the WHA, campfires are not permitted in the national park, and the hut stoves are not suitable for cooking, so you'll need a fuel stove. Stove fuel can be bought at the Cradle Mountain Visitor Centre if you haven't brought it with you.

The walkers' huts are basic; they are not equipped with mattresses, for example. Hut space for everyone cannot be guaranteed, so even if you're planning on using the huts for sleeping, you should nevertheless consider the walk a tent-based outing. Walkers are strongly advised to carry some form of shelter, at any time of the year, for both safety and comfort.

Only limited supplies are available locally; you should plan to bring everything for the walk with you from a major town like Devonport or Launceston.

Maps & Books

The Tasmap 1:100,000 *Cradle Mountain-Lake St Clair Map & Notes* is published specifically for the Overland Track, and has notes on history, the environment and the walk itself. *The Overland Track – One Walk, Many Journeys,* published by the Parks & Wildlife Service (PWS), is a compact reference that can be carried on the walk. It has lots more detail than the Tasmap map notes and is a particularly good on flora and fauna. Both these publications form part of an Overland Track information kit that can be posted to you ($25) when booking a walk on the track.

Walkers contemplating shorter excursions at either end of the Overland Track will find Tasmap's 1:20,000 *Cradle Mountain Day Walk Map & Notes* and 1:50,000 *Lake St Clair Day Walk Map & Notes* useful.

Chris Bell's book *Beyond the Reach* contains stunning photographic imagery of the national park. *A View to Cradle* by Nic Haygarth details the European history of the region now partly encompassed by the national park.

Information Sources

The excellent Overland Track **website** (www.overlandtrack.com.au) covers all aspects of walking the track. The **Cradle Mountain Visitor Centre** (☎ 03-6492 1133; cradle@parks.tas.gov.au) at the park entrance about 3km from the junction with the main highway, is open all year. Here you can discuss your walking plans with the staff and this is where you must collect your Overland Track Pass. There is also the small **Cradle Information Centre** (☎ 03-6492 1110) at the shuttle bus terminal, 2km outside the park.

At the southern end of the walk, the **Lake St Clair visitor information centre** (☎ 03-6289 1172; fax 03-6289 1227), at Cynthia Bay, has good interpretive displays.

Park Fees & Regulations

A booking system and fees for Overland Track walkers were introduced in 2005, part of a package of management changes aiming to both limit environmental impacts and to maintain the quality of the walker experience. Bookings can be made and availability checked via the website (www.overlandtrack.com), by phone (☎ 03-6233 6047) or in person at Tasmania's major national park visitor information centres; book early if planning to visit during the popular Christmas–New Year period. The booking system only operates during the main walking season (1 November to 30 April), and only applies to those walking the entire Overland

Track in a single journey. A booking gives a fixed departure date, but after departure walkers can spend as many days as they like on the track and choose their own itinerary. During the booking period all Overland Track walkers are required to travel north to south (Cradle Mountain to Lake St Clair) and pay a fee of $100 per walker, regardless of whether the walkers' huts or camping areas are utilised. This fee is in addition to the entry fee (Park Pass) required for all Tasmanian national parks. Refer to the website for further details on the booking system and lots of other information for Overland Track walkers.

All of the national parks within the WHA are fuel-stove-only areas; campfires are prohibited.

Camping is forbidden in the Cradle Mountain day walk area, between Cradle Valley and Waterfall Valley. Elsewhere, camping is permitted throughout, except where signs indicate otherwise. However, walkers are generally encouraged to limit their environmental footprint and utilise the worn or hardened camping grounds, with associated toilets, in the hut precincts.

> 'Walkers are generally encouraged to limit their environmental footprint and utilise the worn or hardened camping grounds'

Guided Walks

Several companies offer guided walks on the Overland Track, including **Tasmanian Expeditions** (☎ 03-6339 3999, 1300 666 856; www.tas-ex.com) and **Craclair Tours** (☎ 03-6339 4488; www.craclair.com.au). The trips are six to eight days in duration, cost up to $1500 and include supply of equipment and protective clothing in many cases. The most luxurious guided trip is operated by **Cradle Mountain Huts** (☎ 03-6391 9339; www.cradlehuts.com.au). The six-day walk costs $2200, but you travel with a light pack staying in unobtrusive private huts stocked with food and wine.

NEAREST TOWNS & FACILITIES
Cradle Valley
☎ 03

Cradle Valley, near the north end of the track, isn't so much a town or village as a collection of tourist facilities strung along the length of the Cradle Mountain access road.

SLEEPING & EATING

Waldheim Cabins (☎ 6492 1110; cabins from $70) are a bunch of basic four-, six- and eight-bunk huts in Cradle Valley, fantastically located for walking in the area. Bookings are handled by Cradle Mountain Visitor Centre.

All other accommodation and eating options at Cradle Mountain lie adjacent to Cradle Mountain Rd, outside the national park but within 3km of the park boundary.

Cradle Mountain Tourist Park (☎ 6492 1395, 1800 068 574; www.cosycabins.com/cradle; unpowered/powered sites for 2 $30/35, dm $30, cabins for 2 $125-165) is a bushland complex with a camping ground, bunkhouse and self-contained cabins situated 2.5km outside the national park. The camping ground includes large camp kitchens and shelters for drying out wet gear.

Cradle Mountain Highlanders Cottages (☎ 6492 1116; www.cradlehighlander.com.au; cabins for 2 $110-180) is a genuinely hospitable place with a rustic collection of self-contained timber cottages.

Cradle Mountain Lodge (☎ 6492 1303, 1800 737 678; www.cradlemountainlodge.com; d from $230) should by all rights be designated a township, as there are around 100 well-appointed cabins surrounding the main lodge. In the lodge proper, you can eat in the informal **Tavern Bar** (mains $12-19; ⓧ lunch & dinner) or more formal **Highland Restaurant** (mains $19-26; ⓧ dinner).

Cradle Mountain Chateau (☎ 6492 1404, 1800 282 020; www.federalresorts.com.au; standard r from $240) is comfortable, and some of the more standard rooms have terrific views of the car park. There's a fine-dining restaurant and bistro, and the impressive **Wilderness Gallery** (☎ 6492 1404; www.wildernessgallery.com.au; admission $5) showcasing incredible environmental photography.

There is a very limited general store near Cradle Mountain Lodge; it's best to bring all supplies with you from a major town.

GETTING THERE & AWAY

TassieLink (☎ 03-6271 7320, 1300 300 520; www.tassielink.com.au) operates scheduled bus services between Launceston, Devonport and the west-coast towns of Strahan and Queenstown via Cradle Mountain on Tuesday, Thursday and Saturday. From November to March there are additional services between Launceston and Cradle Mountain on all other days, but the bus only travels via Devonport on the return journey from Queenstown to Launceston. The one-way fare from Devonport is $33 and from Launceston it's $47. Tassielink also offers a range of package fares for Overland Track walkers; for example, Devonport–Cradle Mountain/Lake St Clair–Hobart for $65, or Hobart–Cradle Mountain/Lake St Clair–Hobart for $105.

There are a number of operators who can provide charter services direct to the track start or finish. **Tiger Wilderness Day Tours** (☎ 03-6394 3212; www.tigerwilderness.com.au/bush) and **Maxwells** (☎ /fax 03-6492 1431) run services on demand to both ends of the Overland Track, while in Devonport, **Backpackers Barn & Wilderness Centre** (☎ 03-6424 3628; www.backpackersbarn.com.au; 10-12 Edward St) can also arrange charters.

Cynthia Bay

☎ 03

Occupying the eastern wing of the visitor information centre building, **Lake St Clair Wilderness Park** (☎ 6289 1137; www.lakestclairwildernessholidays.com.au; unpowered/powered sites for 2 $12/15, dm $25; cabins $195; mains $5-10; ☒ breakfast, lunch & dinner) manages most of the options at Cynthia Bay, at the southern end of Lake St Clair. This includes campsites, bunks in a budget lodge, self-contained alpine cabins and a café/bistro.

If you wish to camp free of charge, Fergy's Paddock, about 10 minutes north along the Overland Track, has tent sites and toilets.

Maxwells (☎ 6289 1141, 0428-308 813) runs an on-demand shuttle between Cynthia Bay and Derwent Bridge. The one-way fare is $10 per person.

Derwent Bridge

☎ 03

Derwent Bridge is a small settlement on the Lyell Hwy, 5km south of Lake St Clair.

SLEEPING & EATING

Derwent Bridge Wilderness Hotel (☎ 6289 1144; dm $25, d without/with bathroom $95/115; mains $13-25; ☒ breakfast, lunch & dinner) is a chalet-style pub with an impressive high-beamed roof in the warm bar. The hostel and hotel accommodation is plain but comfortable and there's reasonable food at its restaurant.

Derwent Bridge Chalets and **Travellers Rest Cabins** (☎ 6289 1000; www.derwent -bridge.com; d $120-210) offer a range of comfortable self-contained cabins and chalets run by the same people.

Hungry Wombat Café (☎ 6289 1125; mains $8; ☒ breakfast & lunch), part of the Caltex service station, is a well-managed, friendly and clean café well placed to feed the famished.

GETTING THERE & AWAY
Tassielink (☎ 03-6271 7320, 1300 300 520; www.tassielink.com.au) operates scheduled bus services between Hobart and the west coast towns of Strahan and Queenstown via Derwent Bridge and Lake St Clair (Cynthia Bay), daily except Monday and Wednesday ($41). From November to March there are additional services between Hobart and Lake St Clair on Monday and Wednesday.

If you need to return to Cradle Mountain from Lake St Clair after walking the Overland Track, to pick up your car perhaps, this is possible utilising Tassielink services via Queenstown on Tuesday, Thursday and Saturday ($49).

For details of charter services see Getting There & Away under Cradle Valley (p219).

GETTING TO/FROM THE WALK
A free shuttle bus runs between the Visitor Centre, visitor information centre and start of the Overland Track at Ronny Creek, 5km into the park, continuing to Lake Dove. During the busy season the shuttle runs as often as every 20 minutes. If walking during the booking season (November to April), remember to check in and collect your Overland Track Pass from the Visitor Centre before heading to the start of the walk.

Most Overland Track walkers finish their trek at the northern end of Lake St Clair, rather than continuing along the Lakeside Track. **Lake St Clair Wilderness Park** (☎ 03-6289 1137; www.lakestclairwildernessholidays.com .au) operates a ferry service the length of Lake St Clair, between Narcissus Hut and the visitor information centre at Cynthia Bay ($22 one way). During summer the ferry leaves Cynthia Bay at 9am, 12.30pm and 3pm, arriving at the Narcissus Hut 30 minutes later, and booking is generally necessary. There may be additional services at busy times. There is a radio in Narcissus Hut for contacting the ferry operator to confirm your arrival.

THE WALK
Day 1: Ronny Creek to Waterfall Valley
3¼–5 hours, 10km, 380m ascent, 250m descent

The Overland Track starts as a boardwalk heading southwest up a grassy valley from opposite the Ronny Creek car park. Bear right after crossing the creek and follow the Overland Track signs, ascending through lush rainforest past Crater Falls, up onto an exposed ridge above Crater Lake, then more steeply to **Marions Lookout** (1¼–1¾ hours from Ronny Creek). The ascent to Marions Lookout is the largest single height gain on the Overland Track (excluding side tracks), so you can easily justify taking a breather to appreciate the jagged form of Cradle Mountain ahead, and the view back down into the cirque of Crater Lake.

The track climbs gently south onto Cradle Plateau; covered in cushion plants and prostrate vegetation this is one of the most exposed sections of the entire walk and it can be pretty bleak up here in poor weather. After crossing Plateau Creek, the imposing summit of **Barn Bluff** (1559m) comes into view ahead, and 30 to 40 minutes' walk from Marions Lookout brings you to the small, shingle-clad Kitchen Hut, an emergency shelter set at a track junction.

From this junction the Overland Track continues south, initially ascending to the Cradle Mountain summit track turn-off (see Side Trip: Cradle Mountain, p222), then descending and traversing the western side of Cradle Mountain, below a slope that becomes a golden swathe

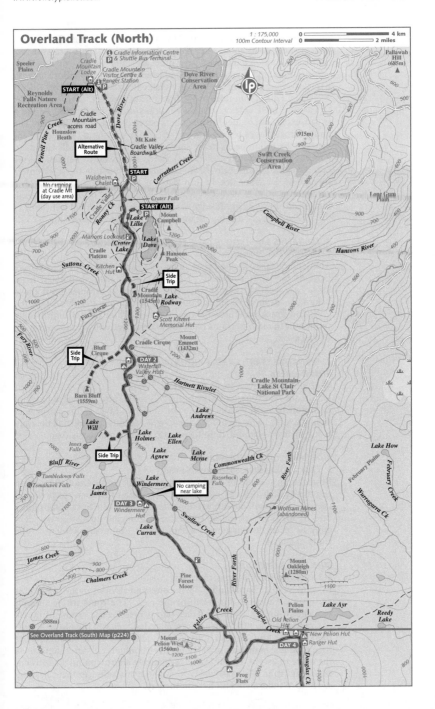

Overland Track (North)

1 : 175,000
100m Contour Interval

0   4 km
0   2 miles

Speeler Plains

Cradle Mountain Lodge

Cradle Information Centre & Shuttle Bus Terminal

Cradle Mountain Visitor Centre & Ranger Station

START (Alt)

Dove River Conservation Area

Pallawah Hill (685m)

Reynolds Falls Nature Recreation Area

Cradle Mountain access road

Pencil Pine Creek

Dove River

Hounslow Heath

Mt Kate

Cradle Valley Boardwalk

Carruthers Creek

Alternative Route

(915m)

Swift Creek Conservation Area

Waldheim Chalet

START

No camping at Cradle Mt (day use area)

Crater Falls

Cradle Valley

Ronny Ck

Lone Gum Plain

Campbell River

Hansons River

START (Alt)

Lake Lilla

Mount Campbell

Marions Lookout

Crater Lake

Lake Dove

Cradle Plateau

Suttons Creek

Kitchen Hut

Hansons Peak

Side Trip

Cradle Mountain (1545m)

Lake Rodway

Furz Gorge

Furz River

Scott Kilvert Memorial Hut

Bluff Cirque

Cradle Cirque

Mount Emmett (1432m)

Side Trip

DAY 2

Waterfall Valley Huts

Barn Bluff (1559m)

Hartnett Rivulet

Cradle Mountain– Lake St Clair National Park

Lake Will

Innes Falls

Lake Holmes

Lake Andrews

Lake Ellen

Lake How

February Plains

February Creek

Side Trip

Lake Agnew

Lake Mcrae

Commonwealth Ck

River Forth

Wurragurra Ck

Bluff River

Tumbledown Falls

Tomahawk Falls

Lake James

Lake Windermere

Razorback Falls

No camping near lake

DAY 3

Windermere Hut

Wolfram Mines (abandoned)

Lake Curran

Swallow Creek

James Creek

Chalmers Creek

Mount Oakleigh (1280m)

Pine Forest Moor

River Forth

Pelion Plains

Lake Ayr

Reedy Lake

(888m)

See Overland Track (South) Map (p224)

Pelion Creek

Douglas Creek

Old Pelion Hut

New Pelion Hut

Ranger Hut

Mount Pelion West (1560m)

DAY 4

Douglas Ck

Frog Flats

of deciduous beech in autumn. Almost immediately after entering an area of snow gums above Fury Gorge the going becomes more arduous. Small sections of duckboard and mud are interspersed with sections across large angular boulders, beyond which you'll reach a junction with a track coming up from the east, from Lake Rodway and the Scott Kilvert Memorial Hut (45 minutes to 1¼ hours from Kitchen Hut).

The Overland Track continues southwest from this junction across a broad, exposed shoulder forming the western bounds of **Cradle Cirque**. The going across planks is easy and on a clear day you should have excellent views of the Pelion peaks to the south. Continue round Cradle Cirque to another junction where a side track heads southwest to Barn Bluff (see Side Trip: Barn Bluff, below). Shortly after this junction the track enters forest and descends steeply into **Waterfall Valley**. Beyond the imposing composting toilet (a necessary feature at all the huts) is the new 20-bunk hut. A little beyond, at the edge of the trees, is the small old hut (built in the 1950s) with good camping on the adjacent open grassy area.

ALTERNATIVE START: DOVE LAKE TO MARIONS LOOKOUT
1–1¼ hours, 2km, 280m ascent
This option takes in the classic view of Cradle Mountain across Lake Dove as you start your walk. Follow the path rising southwest from Dove Lake, bearing right at a junction and passing through forest above Lake Lilla. Beyond Wombat Pool, the track climbs steeply to join the Overland Track on a broad shoulder above Crater Lake. Climb steeply south now to reach Marions Lookout, as described above (one hour from Dove Lake).

ALTERNATIVE START: CRADLE MOUNTAIN VISITOR CENTRE TO RONNY CREEK
1½–2 hours, 5.5km, 100m ascent, 40m descent
Follow the wide boardwalk from the Visitor Centre through a patch of rainforest then up the open valley of the Dove River to the car park at Ronny Creek. There are glimpses of Cradle Mountain ahead and the walk is surprisingly peaceful, despite the proximity of the access road.

SIDE TRIP: CRADLE MOUNTAIN
2–3 hours, 2.5km return, 340m ascent/descent
Branching just south of Kitchen Hut, the track to the Cradle Mountain summit (1545m) climbs relatively gently at first but soon steepens and cuts across the boulder-strewn slopes to the right. The track climbs more directly for the final section to the top, zigzagging up a steep bouldery gully to reach the shattered crest of Cradle Mountain. Return via the route of ascent.

SIDE TRIP: BARN BLUFF
2–3 hours, 5km return, 360m ascent/descent
In good weather Barn Bluff (1559m) offers great views of the moorlands and glacial valleys in the north of the park. The route to the summit branches from the Overland Track part way along the exposed traverse of Cradle Cirque, 30 minutes before Waterfall Valley to the south. A well-marked track leads around Bluff Cirque to the base of the mountain. The final scramble to the summit ascends steep boulders and scree. Return via the route of ascent. Given Day 2 is relatively short, you might consider returning from Waterfall Valley to attempt this side trip then, heading south to Windermere Hut later in the day.

Day 2: Waterfall Valley to Windermere
2–3 hours, 8km, 80m ascent, 100m descent

Returning to the main track from Waterfall Valley Huts, a short descent brings you to a bridge over Hartnett Rivulet. After climbing gently away from the rivulet, the track follows the edge of a sandstone scarp above a couple of the waterfalls for which the valley is named, then rises and rounds a wooded spur coming down from Barn Bluff. A section of gentle climbing, much on duckboards, leads to an open alpine moor looking down on **Lake Holmes** (one hour from Waterfall Valley Huts). From here you can see the track descending past the western shore of Lake Holmes before climbing again to another treeless crest. Near Lake Holmes, a side track heads west to Lake Will (see Side Trip: Lake Will, below).

Beyond Lake Holmes, the Overland Track traverses a very exposed plateau with views across the myriad lakes and tarns to the west. At a rocky crest, Lake Windermere comes into view nestled among patches of eucalyptus. Beyond, to the south, the bulk of Mt Pelion West rises starkly above Pine Forest Moor. Descend steeply on a rocky track for 20 to 30 minutes to reach the shores of Lake Windermere. Camping is not permitted here, but another 10 minutes of walking will bring you to the 16-bunk Windermere Hut set in the shelter of some myrtle. There are a number of wooden tent platforms in openings near and beyond the hut, constructed to limit the environmental impact of camping in the area.

SIDE TRIP: LAKE WILL
1½ hours, 3km return, 50m ascent/descent

A boardwalked track leads to the shores of Lake Will from the signposted turn-off on the Overland Track near Lake Holmes. The pencil pine–fringed lake is quite beautiful and the views to Barn Bluff dramatic.

Day 3: Windermere to Pelion Plains
5–7 hours, 17km, 150m ascent, 240m descent

The longest day on the Overland Track starts with a pleasant 15 to 20 minute walk through scattered eucalyptus forest to a buttongrass plain at the eastern end of Lake Curran. There is a short, steep ascent onto an open top and then two more small rises are crossed to reach the northern edge of **Pine Forest Moor**. This waterlogged terrain is crossed dry-shod and fairly effortlessly on duckboard and parallel planks to a track junction just before a forested hill. Here a stretch of duckboard nips off to the left (east)

Mt Oakleigh overlooks the gentle gradients of the Pelion Plains, traversed on Day 3
GRANT DIXON

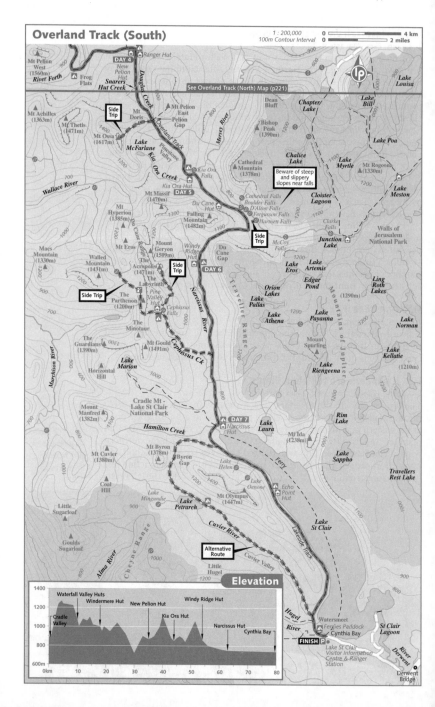

Overland Track (South)

1 : 200,000
100m Contour Interval

See Overland Track (North) Map (p221)

Beware of steep and slippery slopes near falls

DAY 4
DAY 5
DAY 6
DAY 7

Side Trip

Alternative Route

Elevation

Waterfall Valley Huts
Windermere Hut
New Pelion Hut
Windy Ridge Hut
Cradle Valley
Kia Ora Hut
Narcissus Hut
Cynthia Bay

FINISH

to a **lookout** (one minute return). Pelion Plains, Day 3's destination, are perched across the valley, below the crags of Mt Oakleigh, itself towering above the U-shaped glacial valley of the River Forth.

The Overland Track enters thick low tea-tree and myrtle forest and climbs steadily on a boulder-strewn path. Descending the southern slopes of the hill, the towering pandani make a fairytale scene. After emerging from the trees, the track crosses a small creek lined with copses of pencil pines, the bulk of Mt Pelion West now looming close ahead. Thirty minutes of relatively level walking through broken forest brings you to **Pelion Creek**, a good spot for a break (2½ to 3½ hours from Windermere).

Beyond Pelion Creek the track traverses thick dark myrtle forest and becomes quite rough in places, with tree roots prevalent, as it sidles then steadily descends around the eastern slopes of Mt Pelion West. Emerging into the open again at **Frog Flats**, the track descends a little further to cross the River Forth on a wooden bridge; at 720m above sea level it's the lowest point on the Overland Track (one to 1½ hours from Pelion Creek). There are poor campsites here, and leeches and mosquitoes are often prevalent; continuing on to camp near the New Pelion Hut area is a better option.

After traversing another opening, the track re-enters the forest. Parts of this section have the roughest terrain on the entire walk, but planned works may address this. The track climbs through rainforest before entering woodland on the fringe of Pelion Plains. A side track leads north across wet buttongrass to Old Pelion Hut (five to 10 minutes), which was built back in 1895 following the discovery of copper nearby. On a warm day there is a good swimming hole in **Douglas Creek** below the hut.

The spacious New Pelion Hut is situated another 10 minutes' walk beyond the Old Pelion turn-off. This new hut is the largest in the park, with bunks for 36, and its all-round veranda has great views over Pelion Plains to Mt Oakleigh (1280m). There is good camping beside the Overland Track just above the hut.

Day 4: Pelion Plains to Kia Ora Creek
3 hours, 9km, 280m ascent/descent

The track climbs gently away from New Pelion Hut, heading south towards Pelion Gap through mixed forest. After 20 minutes the track crosses Snarers Hut Creek and in another 20 minutes climbs past a small waterfall on Douglas Creek. The track begins to climb in small, steep sections, interspersed by flatter stretches through dense myrtle forest. Finally the gradient steepens consistently and the trees begin to thin as you reach **Pelion Gap** (1126m) and a world of new views (1½ to two hours from New Pelion Hut). To the west a side track leads towards Mt Ossa (1617m), the highest summit in Tasmania (see Side Trip: Mt Ossa, p226). Prickly scoparia carpets Pelion Gap and can produce a colourful wildflower display in early summer.

South of Pelion Gap the slopes are scattered with small snow gums among the bleached, dead trunks of pencil pines, burnt in a past bushfire (see the boxed text, p227). The Overland Track heads southeast, here hardened with wooden cord and duckboard, descending gently into the mixed light forest and open moor of **Pinestone Valley**. The imposing wall of Cathedral Mountain lies across the Mersey valley ahead. Steeper descents follow, leading to the mixture of forest and open buttongrass that surround Kia Ora Hut (one hour from Pelion Gap). The hut has bunk space for 20 and many wooden camping platforms secreted in the trees nearby. If you look around the hut you may well see the nests of welcome swallows under the eaves. These small blue-and-orange birds flit tirelessly around the hut in spring and summer. Look out also for the yellow wattlebird with its curious neck flaps. This bird is the largest of Australia's honeyeaters.

SIDE TRIP: MT OSSA
2½–3½ hours, 5km return, 500m ascent/descent

Heading west from Pelion Gap, the track to Mt Ossa (1617m) ascends towards then contours around the southern slopes of Mt Doris to reveal the tremendously steep northeast ridge of Mt Ossa rising beyond a col. A rough trail leads up into a gully, from where a steep rock scramble leads up to the summit plateau, carpeted with cushion plants, and a short walk to the summit itself. Views are extensive, covering half of Tasmania on a clear day, and the Du Cane Range to the south is particularly impressive. Return to Pelion Gap via the route of ascent. Mt Ossa is best avoided if the weather looks threatening or if the summit is in cloud.

Day 5: Kia Ora Creek to Windy Ridge
3–4 hours, 10km, 240m ascent, 200m descent

The track crosses Kia Ora Creek on a wooden bridge and large boulder and continues southeast through thick eucalyptus and myrtle scrub. It climbs gently for 30 minutes and then descends very slightly before making a final short ascent to historic **Du Cane Hut**, set in a small clearing. Now an emergency shelter only, the earliest part of the hut was built in about 1910 by snarer, prospector and guide Paddy Harnett. With his wife and young child, he lived here for several winters, trapping local wildlife for its thick winter fur. The surrounding forest can be a mass of white leatherwood flowers in December and January.

Beyond Du Cane Hut are some of the most beautiful swathes of rainforest on the Overland Track. Some 30 to 40 minutes of gentle undulations through dark myrtle forest brings you to a junction with a track to the left (east) to Fergusson and D'Alton Falls. Beyond this junction, the Overland Track climbs steadily to the Hartnett Falls turn-off and the myrtle gives way to fairly open eucalyptus forest. At their best after heavy rain, at least one of these Mersey River waterfalls should be visited (see opposite).

Spectacular views of Du Cane Range are the payoff for scaling 1617m high Mt Ossa
GRANT DIXON

DEAD STAGS

Native conifers are badly affected by fire. Unlike eucalyptus they do not regenerate quickly and you'll see large stands of dead 'stags' in several upland areas (eg Pelion Gap on the Overland Track). Over a third of Tasmania's King Billy pines have been lost to bushfires in just 100 years, and many areas of other conifers and deciduous beech have also been lost. Many of these fires have been human-caused and it is largely because of this that the WHA is a fuel-stove-only area.

Glimpses of Falling Mountain (1482m) to the west and the Traveller Range to the south can be had through the trees as you climb the stony trail to Du Cane Gap (45 minutes from the Hartnett Falls turn-off). From Du Cane Gap the track descends steeply into a beautiful stand of Tasmanian alpine yellow gums, spread among moss cloaked myrtle. In rain the mustard colour of the gum bark has to be seen to be believed, contrasting wonderfully with the deep greens of the myrtle and the luminous greens of mosses.

Leaving the yellow gums behind, the trail descends steeply again, reaching Windy Ridge Hut in 30 to 45 minutes from Du Cane Gap. The hut has bunk space for 16 people and is set into a thickly wooded hillside, with views to the precipitous eastern aspect of the Du Cane Range. Secluded camping platforms are scattered beside the track to the north and south of the hut.

SIDE TRIP: D'ALTON & FERGUSSON FALLS
1½ hours, 2km return each, 120m ascent/descent

A steep, roughly-marked track descends northeast through open myrtle forest from the signposted turn-off on the Overland Track, leading to another signed junction. Branch left (northwest) to D'Alton Falls; branch right (northeast) to the upstream Fergusson Falls. There is an impressive narrow gorge just below Fergusson Falls. The riverbank near the falls is steep and very greasy when wet; take care, there have been serious accidents here.

SIDE TRIP: HARTNETT FALLS
1 hour, 2km return, 80m ascent/descent

The track leading down to Hartnett Falls branches from the Overland Track about 10 minutes towards Windy Ridge Hut from the D'Alton and Fergusson Falls turn-off. Descending through mixed forest, the track leads through an open buttongrass area to the top of the falls.

Day 6: Windy Ridge to Narcissus River
3 hours, 9km, 150m descent

The track descends very gently for the first 30 minutes from Windy Ridge Hut. Dense thickets of myrtle give way to open eucalyptus forest (mostly whitetop stringybark) as the track flattens out. Here and there the track skirts the fringes of buttongrass plains. Beyond the Pine Valley turn-off (1½ to two hours from Windy Ridge; see Side Trip: Pine Valley, the Labyrinth & Acropolis, p228), the Overland Track continues along the flat bottom of the valley, the gums gradually thinning out to be replaced by stretches of buttongrass spanned by boardwalks. The view of the valley holding Lake St Clair opens out and within another few minutes you arrive at Narcissus Hut (one hour from the Pine Valley junction). The lake is visible just a little way to the southeast and a track leads down to the jetty where the ferry docks.

SIDE TRIP: PINE VALLEY, THE LABYRINTH & ACROPOLIS

The signposted turn-off to **Pine Valley** is about 1½ to two hours (5km) south of Windy Ridge Hut. A good track crosses bridges over Narcissus River and Cephissus Creek (twice), traversing short plains and rainforest to Pine Valley Hut (one to 1½ hours and 4km from the Overland Track). If planning onward side trips to either the Acropolis or the Labyrinth, it is best to overnight at Pine Valley.

The walk to the summit of the **Acropolis** (1471m) involves a 630m ascent and is a return trip of four to five hours from Pine Valley Hut. Continue beyond the hut, through rainforest north past Cephissus Falls. After crossing the creek, the track climbs steeply to a broad, open shoulder. The Acropolis' southern bluff rears ahead. A clear track heads towards it, but the final scramble through the upper bluffs can be difficult in places, and is best avoided under snow or ice. There are up-close views of the slender dolerite spires comprising the Acropolis' distinctive skyline, and a spectacular vista of Mt Geryon's east face, from the summit. Return via the route of ascent.

The **Labyrinth** is a lake-studded plateau surrounded by high peaks. The access track branches west just beyond Pine Valley Hut, climbing steeply 300m through forest to a saddle. It then sidles west of the Parthenon (1200m) to a good lookout over the Labyrinth and towards the precipitous Mt Geryon (1509m), 1½ hours from the hut. Beyond here the track descends somewhat, then ascends again to another good lookout, or you can continue around Lake Ophion and on to the shores of Lake Elysia (two to 2½ hours from Pine Valley). Return to the hut via your outward route.

Day 7: Narcissus River to Cynthia Bay
5 hours, 17km, 60m ascent/descent

Lake St Clair was known as Leeawuleena ('sleeping water') by the local Aboriginal people, and is Australia's deepest lake at 167m. The traverse of the Lakeside Track, around the western shores of the 14km-long lake, has a reputation for being a little dull in comparison to the rest of the walk, and many walkers drop it in favour of taking the ferry, especially if they're tired or the weather is poor. But in reality the track just offers a different perspective to the expansive views of the northern Overland Track; enclosed rainforest, glimpsed water views and several small beaches.

Perusal of the map may suggest a longer alternative route crossing Byron Gap and traversing the Cuvier Valley. However, this rough and poorly marked route is not maintained to the same standard as the Lakeside Track and should be attempted by experienced walkers only.

From Narcissus Hut the track heads southwest and crosses a swamp on an elevated boardwalk. Once across the plains the track enters the forest, reaching the small Echo Point Hut in two hours. The camping area around it is poor. Continue through forest for another three hours, mostly near the lake shore, with plenty of tree roots and an interesting mix of trees and ferns. After crossing the Cuvier River bridge at Watersmeet, a broad path leads to the visitor information centre at Cynthia Bay.

(Continued from page 213)

FRENCHMANS CAP

Duration	4 days
Distance	47km
Difficulty	moderate–demanding
Start/Finish	Lyell Hwy
Nearest Town	Derwent Bridge (p219)
Transport	bus

Summary Trek across muddy plains and through tangled rainforest to a convoluted quartzite massif cradling dark lakes and dominated by the most distinctive mountain in the west.

Along with Federation Peak and Cradle Mountain, Frenchmans Cap (1446m) must be one of the most inspiring mountains in Australia. It's certainly the most prominent peak in the Franklin-Gordon Wild Rivers National Park. The peak's south and east faces have been carved into vertical cliffs up to 400m high, giving it a tremendous profile when viewed from the Lyell Hwy, and it is surrounded by jagged ridges cradling a series of glacial lakes. The walk is rather more arduous than the nearby Overland Track. The track is rough in places, there are a number of steep climbs, including the long ascent to Barron Pass and the side trip to the summit of Frenchmans Cap itself, and the Loddon Plains (the 'sodden Loddons') have a justifiable reputation for deep mud.

ENVIRONMENT

At least 700 million years separate the two events primarily responsible for the landscape you see today. The quartzite bedrock began life as layers of sand and silt on the floor of an ancient sea. After deep burial, multiple episodes of recrystallisation and folding, and aeons of erosion the quartzite was exposed at the surface. Today's awesome topography is largely the result of glacial sculpting over two million years.

Avoidable, human-caused fires have caused considerable damage to the area. In 1966 an extensive bushfire burnt the area around Lake Tahune and Artichoke Valley. Decades later there are still no King Billy pine seedlings in places where all the parent trees were killed. In 1980, an escaped walker's campfire at Lake Vera incinerated 6000 hectares of forest and buttongrass plains.

PLANNING

Frenchmans Cap can be attempted as either a three or four-day walk. Many walkers choose the former option, visiting the peak as a long return daytrip from Lake Vera, and thereby humping only a day pack up Barron Pass.

The alternative is to spend a night at Lake Tahune, which is arguably the most stunningly located hut in all of Tasmania. This allows more time in the Frenchmans Cap area for taking in the surroundings and a leisurely ascent, and is the option described here.

When to Walk

The warmer temperatures of the summer months (December to March) is generally the best time for walking in Tasmania's western mountains. See also the Warning boxed text on p210.

What to Bring

As with all of the WHA, campfires are not permitted in the Frenchmans Cap area, and the hut stoves are not suitable for cooking, so you'll need a fuel stove. Despite the huts, carrying a tent or some form of shelter is strongly advised for safety reasons.

Tahune Hut is fitted with a small methylated spirit–burning stove for heating; if planning on using this you're encouraged to carry your own fuel (one litre will burn for six or seven hours).

Maps

Tasmap's 1:50,000 *Frenchmans Cap Walk Map & Notes* is the best map for this walk and its notes provide a good outline of the area's history and environment.

Permits & Regulations

As a WHA national park, the usual park fees apply and no campfires are permitted (p192).

Phytophthora (p47) is not present in much of the area traversed by the track; however, to maintain this situation and to help prevent the spread of this fungus, clean the mud from your boots and gaiters at the washdown station at the base of Mt Mullens.

NEAREST TOWN AND FACILITIES

See Derwent Bridge (p219).

TASMANIA

GETTING TO/FROM THE WALK

Tassielink operates Lyell Hwy bus services between Hobart and the west coast towns of Queenstown and Strahan, passing the start of the track (daily except Monday and Wednesday, $43).

If travelling by car, note that the roadside car park is quite remote; you could consider parking your car at Lake St Clair and catching the bus to the start of the track.

THE WALK
Day 1: Lyell Hwy to Lake Vera
4¼–6¼ hours, 16km, 450m ascent, 280m descent

A few minutes' descent into forest leads to the Franklin River suspension bridge. Beyond the river the track traverses heathland and rainforest, then climbs steeply before it takes a short sidle to the crest of Mt Mullens (662m; one to 1½ hours from Lyell Hwy). In clear weather, the distinctive profile of Frenchmans Cap rises dramatically to the west.

A good gravel track descends steadily southwest from Mt Mullens, then two short muddy plains (mostly boardwalked) are

crossed to enter the band of forest around the Loddon River (1¾ to 2½ hours from Lyell Hwy). A suspension bridge spans the river, and there is good riverbank camping just downstream on the far (west) bank.

Turn left off the bridge and soon the track heads out onto the **Loddon Plains**. The track across the 'sodden Loddons' is wide, braided and very muddy in many places. Getting muddy to your knees is almost inevitable. Try to avoid walking on the track margins and promoting further widening. A section of boardwalk, then a gravelly rise, provide some respite from the mud midway across the plains.

One to 1½ hours from the Loddon River the track enters a wide band of scrub and forest, and crosses two wooden bridges in quick succession –branches of Philps Creek. There are camp sites here, the best just beyond the second bridge.

Swinging southwest up Philps Lead, the track heads directly for the crags of **Philps Peak**; both features are named for JE Philp, who cut the original track in 1910. Very muddy at first, the track becomes merely

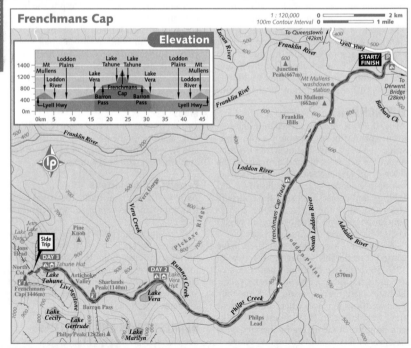

Frenchmans Cap

1 : 120,000
100m Contour Interval

Elevation

THE FRANKLIN ADVENTURE

The Franklin River provides another type of wilderness journey – sensational but hazardous rafting. Experienced rafters can tackle it if they're fully equipped and prepared. For the inexperienced (who make up about 90% of all Franklin rafters), there are tour companies offering complete rafting packages.

Either way, if you're thinking about it, check out the Franklin rafting notes on the PWS website (www.parks.tas.gov.au/recreation/boating/frankl.html). Several companies offer complete rafting packages: **Rafting Tasmania** (☎ 03-6239 1080; raftingtas@ozemail.com.au), **Tasmanian Expeditions** (☎ 03-6334 3477, 1800 030 230; www.tas-ex.com) and **Water By Nature** (☎ 1800 111 142; www.franklin rivertasmania.com).

To get the feel of the place pick up a copy of Richard Flanagan's award-winning novel *Death of a River Guide* (1995), which weaves together Tasmanian history and myths in a story set on the Franklin River. Or Johnson Dean's exciting narrative, *Shooting the Franklin* (2002), describing early Tasmanian canoeing and the first descent of the Franklin in 1959.

wet and eroded later. After following the lead for 45 to 60 minutes, you re-enter scrub and re-cross Philps Creek on a log. Climbing steeply northwest into beautiful myrtle and sassafras rainforest, you might ease the effort of this climb by reflecting that there are no more extended muddy sections before Frenchmans Cap. A short descent, crossing the Rumney Creek plain, another short, steep descent and then a scrubby plain bring you to Lake Vera hut, beside Vera Creek (45 minutes to 1¼ hours from upper Philps Creek). Enclosed in a steep-sided glacial basin cloaked in rainforest, Lake Vera is hidden by scrub from the hut.

The light and airy Lake Vera hut accommodates about 20 people on large platform bunks. To camp, continue for a few minutes across the bridge over Vera Creek to several trackside openings in scrub above the northeast end of the lake.

Day 2: Lake Vera to Lake Tahune
2½–4½ hours, 6km, 560m ascent, 160m descent

Cross Vera Creek and continue into dense tea-tree scrub past the camp site openings. Innovative track log ladders make relatively light work of the 20 minute traverse of Lake Vera's steep western shore. Huon pine grows here (see the boxed text, p232) and, just after leaving the lake shore, the track passes between the sawn halves of a large long-fallen Huon pine log. Note the pale yellow colour of the wood, the distinctive smell (take a sniff close to the wood) and the apparent lack of rot.

The 400m climb to **Barron Pass** takes one to two hours, but there's plenty to look at

on the way; tangled rainforest, cascading streams and soaring white cliffs. The crest appears suddenly and the panoramic view is dominated by Frenchmans Cap, its stupendous southeast face rising beyond a forested spur. Imagine the valley below filled by glacial ice 20,000 years ago.

The track briefly descends back into rainforest west of Barron Pass, then sidles below the ramparts of Sharlands Peak, before rising to traverse a rocky skyline ridge. A short, steep descent leads to green Artichoke Valley. After climbing a series of steep steps beneath twin rock knobs, the surfaced track rises slightly further and crosses the slope westwards towards the gleaming Frenchman. It then descends steep flights of steps before contouring around to **Lake Tahune** hut (one to 1¾ hours from Barron Pass), the lake basin remaining hidden until the last minute. Myrtle regrowth surrounds the hut and screens it from the lake, cupped beneath Frenchmans' east face.

The hut has sleeping space for 16, on bunks with mattresses! There is a small camp site overlooking the lake, 30m from the hut, but the best camping is on or near the helipad, 100m north of the hut, down a track past the toilet. Note that the helipad may need to be used without warning so tents can't be left erected here during the day.

SIDE TRIP: FRENCHMANS CAP SUMMIT
1½–2 hours, 3km return, 480m ascent/descent

Continue past Lake Tahune hut, cross the dry lake outlet, then climb steeply west towards North Col. Before reaching the col the track swings south, rising across a shelf on Frenchmans' east face, then switchbacks north along a higher shelf. Approaching North Col, a sign indicates the route to the summit, left and up a short rock wall. (The route straight ahead leads to Irenabyss, on the Franklin River, a long and demanding side trip.) As the track winds its way towards the summit there are several short rock walls to scramble up, and climb down again on your return, requiring a head for heights. Keep an eye out for rock cairns marking the route in some sections. The final plod up a stony slope brings you abruptly to the edge of Frenchmans' precipitous southeast face and, as befitting a high and isolated peak, all-encompassing views. Cradle Mountain is prominent to the northeast, Macquarie Harbour and the Southern Ocean gleam westward, Hobart's Mt Wellington lies among the folds of mountains to the southeast, and directly below a string of dark lakes is cradled by dense forest.

Days 3 & 4: Lake Tahune to Lyell Hwy
6–9½ hours, 22km, 440m ascent, 1000m descent
Retrace your inward route back to the Lyell Hwy from Lake Tahune. Fit walkers might consider walking back all the way to the highway in a day, for others there are a number of camp-site options en route, noted in the previous description of the inward route.

HUON PINE

Huon pine grows only in Tasmania, mostly in wet areas along the western rivers, its light-green foliage often dangling from branches overhanging the water. It is one of the longest-living organisms on earth; trees dated at over 3000 years old have been found.

Huon pine has been sought and cut since the 1820s, by convicts from the short-lived penal colony on Sarah Island and subsequently the tough 'piners' who explored the western rivers. Its resistance to rot made it a fine boat-building timber, and its fine grain and easy working properties were desirable for crafting fine furniture. Many areas of Huon pine are now protected in national parks, and harvesting elsewhere is carefully managed.

WALLS OF JERUSALEM

Duration	3 days
Distance	23km
Difficulty	easy–moderate
Start/Finish	Walls of Jerusalem car park
Nearest Town	Deloraine (opposite)
Transport	bus (charter)

Summary Visit a compact alpine area littered with biblical names, walking beneath extensive cliffs, past glacial tarns and through quiet pencil pine forests.

Bordered to the west by the mountains of Cradle Mountain–Lake St Clair National Park, and to the east by the moors and lakes of the Central Plateau Conservation Area, the Walls of Jerusalem National Park brings combines these features in a compact and intimate area. The 'Walls' are a group of cliff-ringed summits sheltering several small and very beautiful valleys linked by low cols and dotted with lakes and groves of pencil pines. The circuit route described here can be done in two days, but the area is worth a leisurely exploration over three days.

HISTORY
The surveyor James Scott applied the name 'Walls of Jerusalem' to the area in 1848 and the biblical theme has been maintained in subsequent nomenclature. He noted some good grazing for stock and it was used for this purpose to some degree well into the 20th century, both before and since, and for fur trapping into the 1960s. The Walls area became a national park in 1981 and was incorporated into the enlarged WHA in 1989 (see p205).

ENVIRONMENT
Even during the Last Glacial, when glaciers were the least extensive of any recent ice age, an icecap nevertheless lay astride the western Central Plateau. The landscape of the Walls of Jerusalem has thus been heavily influenced by glaciation. Most of the walls were glacially carved, with gouging by the ice along fault lines creating the valleys. Depressions in the valleys, either scoured by ice or dammed by moraines, have filled with water, resulting in a scattering of lakes and tarns of all sizes throughout the area.

One of the most significant features of the Walls area are the pencil pines, especially the large swathe growing south of the Temple. These trees grow at altitudes in excess of 800m and can live for more than 1200 years. Elsewhere on the Central Plateau such extensive forests have been largely destroyed by human-caused bushfires. The pines are complemented by stunted snow gums growing on the exposed hillsides, and large bolster plants and sphagnum mounds on the valley floors. These latter plants are very sensitive to trampling, taking years to recover from the impact of an ill-placed boot; watch where you plant your feet if wandering off the hardened tracks.

Bennett's wallabies are very common in the area, and you may well see an eastern quoll scampering around your camp site at dusk. And if you don't glimpse a grazing wombat, you'll certainly notice their large burrows and cube-shaped droppings.

HIGHLAND FILM SET

Snaring (trapping) of local wildlife in winter, when their fur coats are thickest, was undertaken by high-country shepherds and by manual workers attempting to supplement their meagre income. Dramatising this life and filmed in the Walls area, Roger Scholes' 1987 film *Highland Winter* tells the story of a woman brought up in harsh isolation who has to come to terms with her marriage to a reclusive trapper. Dixon's Kingdom hut was refurbished for the filming, and another temporary hut was constructed below the West Wall.

PLANNING

To undertake the complete circuit described here walkers should have some navigation competency, as tracks become less distinct beyond Dixon's Kingdom hut and Mt Jerusalem. An alternative option, both more leisurely and staying to formal tracks, is to camp two nights at Wild Dog Creek and explore the Walls on the second day with just a day pack, returning to the car park directly on Day 3.

When to Walk

The summer months (November to April) are generally the best time for walking in Tasmania's western mountains. See also the Warning boxed text on p210.

The Walls can be very beautiful under winter snow, but this is a time for well-prepared and very experienced walkers when route finding can be arduous and difficult.

What to Bring

While there are huts in the Walls of Jerusalem area, these are maintained as a reminder of the trapping heritage of the park and are really only suitable as emergency shelters. As with elsewhere in the Tasmanian highlands, a good tent is essential. And you'll need a fuel stove as campfires are not permitted.

Maps & Books

The Tasmap 1:25,000 *Walls of Jerusalem Walk Map & Notes* is very useful, and there are notes on the back of the map on the area's history and environment. *Cradle Mountain Lake St Clair and Walls of Jerusalem National Parks* by John Chapman and John Siseman is worth a look if you'd like to explore more remote routes in the park.

Permits & Regulations

As a WHA national park, the usual park fees apply and no campfires are permitted (p192).

Camping is forbidden within 200m of the Pool of Siloam to allow plant regeneration. Apart from this there are no restrictions on camping in the Walls area. However, the PWS has constructed a hardened camping ground, with a toilet, at Wild Dog Creek. Walkers are encouraged to camp here, rather than within the nearby central Walls area, to limit the impact on this popular and sensitive area.

The PWS generally discourages walking off the hardened tracks within the Walls area, and has explicitly closed the steep and unstable gullies cutting the West Wall; if you must climb King Davids Peak, do so from Herods Gate.

NEAREST TOWN
Deloraine
☎ 03 / pop 2170

This regional centre is on the main highway and also provides a good base if planning other walks in the region (eg Great Western Tiers). The **visitor information centre** (☎ 6362 3471; www.greatwesterntiers.org.au; 98 Emu Bay Rd) has information on regional attractions.

SLEEPING & EATING

Deloraine Apex Caravan Park (☎ 6362 2345; West Pde; unpowered/powered sites for 2 $16/19) has a picturesque location beside the Meander River.

Highview Lodge Youth Hostel (☎ 6362 2996; 8 Blake St; dm/d from $22/45) has warm, timber-floored confines, friendly staff and great views of the Great Western Tiers, even from the toilets!

Originally a coaching inn, **Bonney's Inn** (☎ 6362 2974; www.bonneys-inn.com; 19 West Pde; s/d $130/175) has comfortably upgraded colonial-style en suite rooms with full breakfasts.

Deloraine Delicatessen & Gourmet Foods (☎ 6362 2127; 36 Emu Bay Rd; mains $5-10; ☷ breakfast & lunch Mon-Sat) is a fine place for late-morning baguettes, bagels and focaccias with a variety of tasty fillings.

Empire Brasserie (☎ 6362 2075; 19 Emu Bay Rd; mains $10-20; ☷ breakfast, lunch & dinner), has a selection of à la carte dishes.

Scooters (☎ 6362 3882; 53-55 Emu Bay Rd; mains $15-18; ☷ breakfast, lunch & dinner) is a licensed restaurant with contemporary cuisine and excellent seasonal dishes.

GETTING THERE & AWAY

Both **Redline** (☎ 1300 360 000; www.tasredline.com .au) and **TassieLink** (☎ 1300 300 520; www.tassielink .com.au) travel past Deloraine on their bus services between Launceston and Devonport (p195) and beyond, but bookings are required for stops.

GETTING TO/FROM THE WALK

There is no regular public transport to the Walls of Jerusalem track and many walkers opt to access the walk direct from Devonport or Launceston, rather than Deloraine. **Tiger Wilderness Day Tours** (☎ 03-6394 3212; www .tigerwilderness.com.au/bush) will take you to the Walls track from Devonport or Launceston (from $180 return for two people), and can also organise fuel and gear hire. **Deloraine Radio Cabs** (☎ 03-6362 3432; 3/15 East Westbury Pl) will drop or collect walkers for up to $110 per person from Deloraine. Both operators will also quote for drop-offs at other walking tracks.

If driving from Deloraine, take the B12 through Mole Creek, then the C138 and finally the C171 (Mersey Forest Rd) to Lake Rowallan; remain on this road, following 'Walls of Jerusalem' signs to the car park at the trailhead.

THE WALK
Day 1: Walls of Jerusalem Car Park to Wild Dog Creek

2½–3 hours, 6km, 600m ascent, 60m descent

A good track climbs from the car park, past a registration booth, then continues more steeply, emerging after 10 to 15 minutes onto flatter ground amid towering gum trees. The rest of the climb to **Trappers Hut**, a restored 1940s fur trapper's hut, is in stages; steep sections interspersed by flat sections, which allow you to grab a breather. The final haul to the hut is steep and bouldery and most walkers will need about an hour to reach the hut from the car park.

Beyond the hut the track continues to climb, soon reaching a fork junction; bear left (southeast) here. The right-hand fork leads to Lake Adelaide, your return route. The trees become thinner and stunted and, 20 to 30 minutes beyond Trappers Hut, the track descends to cross a creek above a small lake. The track then undulates across a wonderful landscape of rocky outcrops and small lakes, known as Solomons Jewels, surrounded by stunted snow gum and pencil pine. In the distance King Davids Peak is visible, its precipitous eastern face dropping abruptly to **Herods Gate**. After descending gently to cross the marshy valley of Wild Dog Creek on boardwalks, a short climb leads to the camping ground, a series of wooden tent platforms and associated toilet and water supply.

Day 2: Wild Dog Creek to Lake Adelaide

3–4 hours, 9km, 120m ascent, 290m descent

A short climb from the camping ground brings you to Herods Gate and the entrance to the Walls of Jerusalem. The high peaks that line the Overland Track (p214) form the western skyline. Continuing southeast past a small lake, the track then contours along slopes to the southwest of Lake Salome. On your right, high cliffs and boulder slopes come down from the summit of King Davids Peak. The track rises across a low ridge from where you can survey the cliffs of the West Wall and King Davids Peak. Continuing from the ridge the track passes some pencil pines on the left and reaches a junction. The left-hand track leads to a flat camping area just 100m away, set above the **Pool of Bethesda**. Meanwhile, the main track climbs on parallel planks towards the prominent pass known as **Damascus Gate**, from where side trips are possible (see p236). Beyond Damascus Gate the track descends for 15 minutes through a wonderful grove of pencil pines that extends all the way to **Dixon's Kingdom hut** (one hour from Herods Gate; emergency shelter only). Reg Dixon began to visit the Walls in the 1930s and built this hut as a base for fur trapping. Mt Jerusalem can be climbed as a side trip (see p236).

There is no formed track between Dixon's Kingdom Hut and the eastern end of Lake Ball. However, navigating your own course down through Jaffa Vale is easy and provides wonderful walking, albeit a little wet underfoot. It is probably best to bear

off towards Mt Moriah and then drop down to meet the Lake Ball track directly, rather than crossing the swampy flat ground at the east end of Lake Ball. A pole set on a prominent hummock indicates the beginning of the track west around **Lake Ball**.

For the first 30 minutes the track winds through beautiful myrtle forest and then crosses an awkward boulder slope before reaching Lake Ball hut (emergency shelter only), an old trappers' hut. Towards the western end of the lake, views across the water open out and stunted snow gums are dominant. A small creek is crossed just before you drop down to the water's edge at the very western end of the lake (1½ to two hours from Dixon's Kingdom Hut).

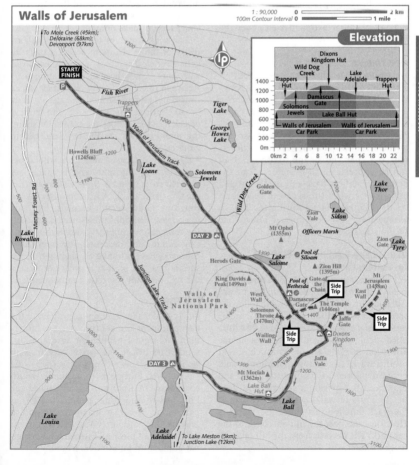

The route then crosses low-lying flat ground and fords a sizable creek (which is difficult to cross in flood) to reach a small saddle. The track then descends steeply through eucalyptus forest to meet the Junction Lake Track on the shore of **Lake Adelaide**. There are some good flat camping areas at this junction. Turn right (north) to find good camping around the northern end of the lake.

SIDE TRIPS: THE TEMPLE & SOLOMONS THRONE
30–40 minutes each, 1km return each, 110–130m ascent/descent

From Damascus Gate, constructed rock tracks ascend east to the Temple (1446m) and southwest, up a steep gully through the cliffs, to Solomons Throne (1470m). Both places offer excellent views over the Walls area.

SIDE TRIP: MT JERUSALEM
1½–2 hours, 4km return, 200m ascent/descent

The route heads north from Dixon's Kingdom Hut, rising beside grassy pencil pine forest to Jaffa Gate. It then swings east and climbs onto the southern shoulder of Mt Jerusalem, from where a rocky track ascends northeast to the summit (1459m). The extent and character of the Central Plateau can be appreciated from here, as can the damage bushfires have caused (fire wiped out a vast area of fire-sensitive vegetation on the Central Plateau during the 1960s), emphasising just how special forests like Dixon's Kingdom are.

Day 3: Lake Adelaide to Walls of Jerusalem Car Park
2½–3½ hours, 8km, 60m ascent, 420m descent

Follow the rough track north from Lake Adelaide for the next 5km as it follows a series of broad treeless valleys. The going is muddy in places and the track can be a little bit difficult to follow around Lake Loane. Direction markers are pretty much absent on this track, so in snow conditions you'll be hard pushed to stay on the track and may need to navigate a general line. Two to 2½ hours of walking should see you at the track junction just above the Trappers Hut. Descend past the hut and back to the car park. The descent from the hut takes 30 to 45 minutes.

SOUTH COAST TRACK

Duration	6–7 days
Distance	86km
Difficulty	moderate–demanding
Start	Melaleuca (p238)
Finish	Cockle Creek
Nearest Town	Dover (p238)
Transport	plane, bus (summer only)
Summary	Traverse remote beaches, buttongrass plains and rainforest in the remote southwest wilderness, with spectacular scenery and views of the inland mountains.

The South Coast Track is, after the Overland Track, the most popular long-distance walk in the WHA. However, it has quite a different character to that of the Overland Track in terms of both landscape and a lesser level of development.

The walk traverses the remote southern fringe of the WHA, with access usually by light aircraft. The coast is deeply embayed with long, sandy beaches alternating with steep and rocky headlands. Hills, their slopes sometimes thickly forested, rise steeply from broad buttongrass plains. Scrub-fringed creeks meander across the plains. Offshore, the many islands are the last land before Antarctica.

The South Coast Track is a wilderness walk, lacking any huts, and is much less extensively hardened than walks such as the Overland Track. A number of extensive rough or muddy sections remain. Depending on your level of fitness and the weather, the walk can be quite arduous with significant ascents and descents. The track does, however, have a range of sheltered camp sites at beaches, so that if sufficient food is carried, pleasant rest days can be planned.

HISTORY
Shell middens in several places attest to the occupation of the south coast by Tasmanian Aboriginal people for several thousand years before the arrival of European settlers.

The first European to walk the south coast was GA Robinson, who reached the Port Davey Aboriginal people in 1830 as part of his five-year Friendly Mission, a scheme that ultimately resulted in the incarceration of most of Tasmania's Aboriginal population on Flinders Island.

Tin was discovered at Cox Bight in 1891, and Charles King commenced tin mining at Melaleuca in the 1930s. His son Deny and his family lived there after WWII, becoming the sole residents of southwest Tasmania. Deny built the first walkers' hut at Melaleuca in 1955.

Light aircraft, engaged in aerial survey work, commonly landed on Cox Bight beach during the 1940s. A rough airstrip was cleared at Melaleuca in 1947. Deny King constructed the present airstrip in 1956, facilitating today's frequent scenic and walker flights into the area.

ENVIRONMENT

The many rocky headlands and shore platforms on the South Coast provide an opportunity to walk through some major parts of Tasmania's billion-year geological history, with generally progressively younger rocks exposed as you walk east. They include ancient folded metamorphic rocks at Cox Bight, 500-million-year-old sandstone and siltstone on the Ironbound Range, colourful conglomerate at Osmiridium Beach, sharply eroded limestone strata at Surprise Bay, once-molten columnar dolerite at Granite Beach, and sandstone deposited on an ancient floodplain at South Cape Rivulet.

The soils of the buttongrass plains are peats, composed of decayed plant remains, and can be two or more metres thick. The small yabbie (freshwater crayfish) is common on the plains and lives in burrows visible at the surface as small round holes or mud chimneys.

The rare orange-bellied parrot can be seen around Melaleuca (below), and you may flush the secretive ground parrot as you walk through buttongrass areas. Seabirds likely to be seen along the coast include terns, fairy prions (whalebirds) and short-tailed shearwaters (mutton birds). Offshore, you may sight the shy albatross or Australasian gannet.

Much of the fauna is nocturnal, but you will certainly come across the wombat's characteristic square droppings.

PLANNING

The South Coast Track can be walked in either direction. However, access to Melaleuca, the western end of the track, is generally by light plane and so subject to weather conditions. To avoid the possibility of being stranded at Melaleuca by poor weather, it is recommended that the track be walked west to east (from Melaleuca to Cockle Creek).

While seven days is the recommended duration of the walk, it is worthwhile allowing more time to explore the beaches and as a precaution against flood delays.

It is possible to have a food cache stored at Melaleuca (which you must arrange to have flown in prior to your walk). This may be useful if you wish to extend the walk by also walking the four-day, 70km Port Davey Track and start or finish at Scotts Peak Rd, or undertake other walks in the area.

When to Walk

The South Coast Track can be walked at any time of the year, although the weather is likely to be better and flooded streams less of a potential problem in summer (December to March). Also, regular public transport from the walk's finish and more frequent flights to the start are only available from December to March.

THE RAREST PARROT

The orange-bellied parrot *(Neophema chrysogaster)* is among the rarest and most endangered of the world's wildlife. It is a colourful bird, slightly larger than a budgerigar, with a bright-green back and distinctive orange patch between its legs. There are no more than 200 individuals in the wild and most of these breed at Melaleuca in summer.

The bird migrates to spend winter in coastal southeast mainland Australia, where habitat reduction since European settlement has been blamed for the bird's declining numbers. A captive breeding program, with periodic release of young birds, aims to improve the outlook of the species.

In summer, the parrots can be observed from a hide, named in memory of Deny King, 100m east of the Melaleuca airstrip.

Maps & Books

The Tasmap 1:100,000 *South Coast Walk Map & Notes* covers the walk and includes environmental information and brief track notes.

The South Coast Track and other regional walks are described in John Chapman's *South West Tasmania* and Ken Collins' *South-west Tasmania – A Natural History and Visitors Guide*. The latter includes much information on flora, fauna and geology.

Christobel Mattingley's *King of the Wilderness: The Life of Deny King* (2001) provides plenty of insights into the area in describing the life of a man who lived most of his life at Melaleuca (see p236).

Permits & Regulations

The usual park fees and fuel-stove-only regulations apply (p192). However, campfires are allowed at two camp sites – Surprise Bay and Deadmans Bay – but only within the designated fire sites.

There are no restrictions on camping on the South Coast Track, but to avoid the continually increasing impact on the track from walkers, you are encouraged to use the major established camp sites at the various beaches and rivers along the route.

STOVE FUEL

Stove fuels (gas, methylated spirits or Shellite) are classified as dangerous goods and so cannot be carried on the light planes that fly to Melaleuca. However, the two flight operators (Tasair and Par Avion) both maintain a fuel store at Melaleuca, so if flying in to start your walk at Melaleuca, you can arrange to buy fuel on arrival.

NEAREST TOWN & FACILITIES
Dover

☎ 03 / pop 570

Dover is a picturesque fishing port overlooked by the conical Adamsons Peak. If starting the South Coast Track from Cockle Creek, Dover (21km south of Geeveston on the Huon Hwy) has a supermarket and is the last chance to buy any food items you haven't brought from Hobart (p193).

If passing through Dover at the end of your walk, the excellent **Gingerbread House bakery** (☎ 6298 1502; ☺ lunch), on the corner of Main and Station Rds, is well worth a visit.

> **WARNING**
>
> Few of the rivers and streams crossed by the South Coast Track are bridged and most must be forded. Heavy rain can cause rivers to rise quickly and some can become difficult or impossible to cross safely, particularly Louisa River.
>
> High tides combined with storm swells can render coastal traverses at the bases of cliffs at Cox Bight, Granite Beach and near Lion Rock hazardous; there is a real risk of being washed away by a misjudged wave.

Melaleuca

If you fly in late in the day, or choose to spend time at Melaleuca (the start of the walk), a short track heads north from the airstrip to two walkers' huts, or you can camp in the open tea-tree forest nearby, on the shore of Melaleuca Lagoon. Drinking water is only available from tanks, so use it frugally. When wandering around Melaleuca, be aware that an area (denoted with signs) around the home and garden of the late Deny King remains under private leasehold to his family. Please respect it as such.

GETTING TO/FROM THE WALK

There is no road access to the start of the South Coast Track at Melaleuca – the only options are to fly or walk in. Small (two- to five-passenger) single-engine planes fly on demand from Hobart to Melaleuca, subject to weather conditions, and are run by **Tasair** (☎ 03-6248 5288; www.tasair.com.au) and **Par Avion** (☎ 03-6248 5390; www.paravion.com.au), both based at Cambridge airport. The fare is $140 per person. A minimum of two is required, but the carriers generally try to fill planes by combining groups where possible. Bookings are essential. In the peak summer months there are generally several flights per day, so even solo walkers can usually make it to Melaleuca on their preferred day.

Melaleuca can also be reached by a four-day walk along the Port Davey Track from Huon River camping ground at the end of Scotts Peak Rd. **TassieLink** (☎ 1300 300 520; www.tassielink.com.au; 64 Brisbane St, Hobart) has a minibus service along this track during summer.

Cockle Creek is serviced by a summer-only (December to March) TassieLink minibus three days per week. The bus departs its Hobart bus terminal, 64 Brisbane St, at 8.30am Monday, Wednesday and Friday, and returns from Cockle Creek at 1.45pm on the same day. The one-way fare is $65 and booking is recommended.

THE WALK
Day 1: Melaleuca to Cox Bight
3–4 hours, 13km, 110m ascent/descent

The Track starts on the western side of the Melaleuca airstrip and passes through old mine workings before crossing Moth Creek on a log bridge. Cox Bight is a 10km level walk on a well-defined track south down the broad valley from the Melaleuca airstrip.

Walk eastwards along the first of Cox Bight's broad beaches. There is a sheltered camp site at the outlet stream of freshwater **Freney Lagoon** (1km along the beach). Beyond the end of the beach, another 2km along, Point Eric is crossed on a marked inland track. There is sheltered camping on the eastern side of **Point Eric**, with water from Goring Creek, just a few hundred metres east along the beach.

Light aircraft can actually land on the flat white sand at the western end of Cox Bight beach (subject to tides and weather) and this is an alternative access point for the start of the walk.

Day 2: Cox Bight to Louisa River
5–7 hours, 18km, 280m ascent, 250m descent

Despite its name, the South Coast Track partly traverses country some distance inland. The most lengthy inland section commences at Buoy Creek, at the eastern end of Cox Bight. From here, a level section precedes the very sharp ascent of the **Red Point Hills**, the first of a number of high points on the track providing extensive views. A gradual descent to Faraway Creek follows, and the sheltered camp site at Louisa Creek is only a short distance further east (2½ to 3½ hours from Cox Bight).

The track then sidles round the Spica Hills before crossing the extensive buttongrass **Louisa Plains** on a lengthy section of planking. The easy mud-free walking afforded by the planking allows you to take your eyes off your feet and take in the surrounding landscape, including the broad expanse of the plains and the ominously steep slopes of the Ironbound Range ahead.

The Louisa Plains are bounded to the east by forest along the meandering **Louisa River**. The river is the largest crossed by the track and must be forded – there is a rope in situ to assist your balance. There are camp sites in the forest on both banks of Louisa River. If it is raining and the river appears crossable when you arrive, it may be prudent to camp on the far bank to avoid being held up by any overnight flooding.

Day 3: Louisa River to Deadmans Bay
6–10 hours, 12km, 900m ascent, 920m descent

Most walkers consider the crossing of the Ironbound Range the most physically demanding part of the South Coast Track,

TASMANIA

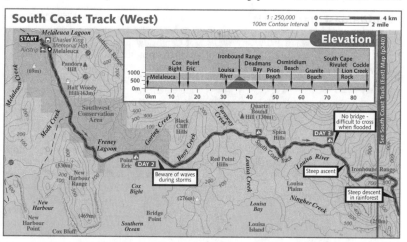

and with good reason. The 900m climb up the western slope of the range is steep and largely without respite. Given the open nature of the country, if it looks like being a hot day an early start on the climb is recommended. This open terrain does allow you to stop almost anywhere to take in the extensive views while you catch your breath. On a more cautionary note, the range is also very exposed, and freezing wind-driven rain is possible at any time of the year. If the weather is poor and the range shrouded in cloud, it may be more pleasant passing a rest day exploring the rainforest along the banks of Louisa River.

The track traverses the only alpine country of the walk on the top of the **Ironbound Range** (2½ to five hours from Louisa River) with, in clear weather, views along the entire south coast and out to various offshore islands. Water can be obtained from the small creek crossed several hundred metres east of the crest (about 950m) of the range.

After this creek, the track enters forest for the long descent of the southeastern side of the range. Some sections are thick with tree roots and require care with foot placement, and you may have rather rubbery knees by the time you complete the long descent. After winding through coastal forest and scrub, with glimpses of the sea, the track reaches Deadmans Bay. There is good camping here beside the large creek where the track reaches the coast.

Day 4: Deadmans Bay to Osmiridium Beach

4½–6 hours, 13km, 150m ascent/descent

Walk 100m east along the rocky foreshore to where the track again heads inland through buttongrass and then forest before emerging on **Turua Beach**. Walk east along the sand and round the small headland to the second beach. From the eastern end of Turua Beach the track follows the coast around Menzies Bluff towards Prion Beach with some fine views through openings in the coastal forest and scrub. Note that the small stream crossed at the far western end of Prion Beach may be the last good water before Osmiridium Beach.

The route now traverses **Prion Beach**, probably the most spectacular beach on the south coast, a long stretch of sand receding into the sea-spray haze with the distinctive form of Precipitous Bluff rising inland beyond the dunes. Remove your boots and give your feet the pleasure of unconstrained walking along the 4km of sand, with the roar and foam of the Southern Ocean your constant companion.

The outlet of **New River Lagoon**, deep and wide, must be crossed from Prion Beach and two dinghies are provided for you to row across it. Please ensure one boat (with its oars) is left upside down and tied up well out of reach of tides and floods on each bank for subsequent walkers, after you have completed your crossing (follow the instructions posted at the boat crossing).

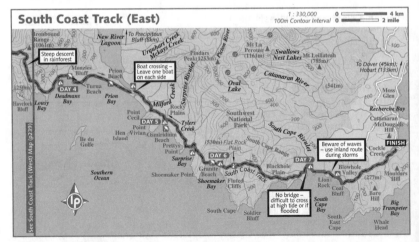

MOBILE SANDS

The Prion Beach area provides a dramatic example of the dynamic nature of coastal environments. The long spit that impounds New River Lagoon, of which Prion Beach is the seaward side, has grown westwards and stabilised since the sea reached its present level 6000 years ago.

Rafts of slumped vegetation and root mats can be seen on the dune faces behind Prion Beach. These attest to periodic erosion during large storms, with the sand mined from the dunes probably distributed eastwards.

The position of the mouth of New River Lagoon moves periodically, sometimes quite rapidly. Storms during February 1999, and the resultant backing up of the lagoon waters, resulted in the break-out of the lagoon outlet near the boat crossing, 2km west of its previous position against the rocks of Point Cecil. It has subsequently migrated eastwards again.

If your party is large, several crossings will be required, as the boats will safely hold no more than three people and gear.

There is a sheltered camp site on the northern side of the Prion Beach boat crossing (2½ to 3½ hours from Deadmans Bay camp site). Water can be taken from a small creek five to 10 minutes' walk northwest of the camp site, but it can often be brackish.

From the camp site, the track traverses the crest of vegetated dunes east to **Milford Creek**. The waters of this creek are particularly dark, stained by buttongrass, and the ford of the creek can appear much deeper than it actually is. From Milford Creek cross the expanse of sand to the eastern end of Prion Beach, where steps climb the steep scrub-covered dune face.

The track heads cross-country through low forest behind Point Cecil to the open **Rocky Plains**. Tylers Creek is reached after crossing a low hill. A spacious and sheltered camp site lies on its banks a short distance downstream, accessed by a side route branching left from the main track a short distance before the creek. Osmiridium Beach is a short distance further downstream.

Day 5: Osmiridium Beach to Granite Beach

3–4 hours, 8km, 320m ascent, 300m descent

Return to the main track from the Tylers Creek camp site. The track leaves Rocky Plains soon afterwards and climbs into forest. From here eastwards the landscape through which the trail passes changes character from the open plains and beaches of the west to lengthy forest sections inland. However, the track does return to the coast at several large bays, the first being **Surprise Bay** (1½ to two hours from Tylers Creek).

The spacious camp site here lies in coastal forest above the dark limestone strata at the eastern end of the beach. Surprise Rivulet must be forded to reach it, requiring care if it is in flood or the tide is high.

Soon after leaving Surprise Bay camp site, the track ascends steeply before descending rather more gently to Granite Beach. Traverse the dark sand and rounded dolerite boulders, with views of the spectacular Fluted Cliffs, to the waterfall at the eastern end of the beach. Scramble up beside the waterfall and follow the track 100m east to another spacious and sheltered camp site.

During storms with high tides, waves can break against the cliffs at the eastern end of Granite Beach, making access to the ascent next to the waterfall potentially hazardous. In these conditions spend time watching the waves to decide if it is safe to proceed, and then time your sprint with care.

Day 6: Granite Beach to South Cape Rivulet

5½–7 hours, 10km, 580m ascent, 600m descent

You can take some of the sting out of the steep climb of the South Cape Range from Granite Beach camp site by telling yourself it is the last major ascent of the walk. **Flat Rock Plain**, an opening near the summit, is a great place to recline and take in the final view back along the coast and across the various islands.

There are some rather muddy areas to be traversed across the forested top of the South Cape Range before descending to a small creek, which is the only reliable water on the range (2½ to 3½ hours from Granite Beach). The track then climbs again, briefly, before beginning the long forested descent to the buttongrass opening of Blackhole

Plain. The forest on this section is magnificent, with many of the trunks sheathed in climbing heath.

Beyond Blackhole Plain, another short climb and forested descent and you will suddenly emerge into the open on the bank of South Cape Rivulet. The rivulet must be crossed, which can be difficult at high tide or after heavy rain. The best camp site is on the east bank adjacent to the lagoon, but there is also a site on the west bank that can be used if the rivulet cannot be crossed.

ALTERNATIVE CAMP SITE

If you still feel energetic you might walk still further to the camp site near Lion Rock (another one to 1½ hours east). The sheltered camp site is atop the dune above the second creek east of Lion Rock, accessed by the obvious steps constructed to prevent erosion of the dune face. Water is obtained from the creek flowing out onto the beach.

Day 7: South Cape Rivulet to Cockle Creek

3–4½ hours, 12km, 150m ascent/descent

Continue eastwards along the beach, over a small headland and then along another beach. Here there are two options. A signposted track climbs high over Coal Bluff, with good views in places. Alternatively, you can scramble over the boulders strewn below the coastal cliffs to **Lion Rock**, a vaguely sphinx-like rocky island just offshore. If the tide is high or a storm swell is running, the inland route is definitely the better option to choose.

Just past Lion Rock the track reaches the last beach on the South Coast Track. This beach is a popular day-trip or overnight destination from Cockle Creek and the track from here on is well constructed and obvious. From the eastern end of the beach, climb the steps up and round the rocky headland, with its expansive view across South Cape Bay, then traverse the coastal scrub and heath of Blowhole Valley to the road head at Cockle Creek.

EAST COAST

Tasmania's scenic east coast is known as the 'sun coast' because of its mild climate and above-average exposure (by Tasmanian standards) to the great yellow orb. So when you've had enough of western deluges, or just wish to avoid them, the east coast is a good spot for drying out your pack and soaking up some sunshine. And the drier climate and hardier terrain means that the walking is generally easier than in the west. Freycinet National Park is one of the most scenic areas and its beaches and granite peaks are the prime walking destination on the east coast, but there are a number of other options (p247).

FREYCINET PENINSULA CIRCUIT

Duration	2 days
Distance	31km
Difficulty	easy–moderate
Start/Finish	Walking tracks car park
Nearest Town	Coles Bay (opposite)
Transport	bus
Summary Experience beautiful coastal walking featuring sandy beaches and granite peaks, then lounge on one of the most scenic beaches in Australia.	

The dramatic granite peaks of the Hazards and the turquoise waters and pristine white sand of Wineglass Bay are the postcard images of Freycinet National Park. But there is much more to the park, which encompasses the entire Freycinet Peninsula, and a network of walking tracks provides access to the best bays, beaches and peaks. About four hours is ample time to take in Wineglass Bay and return via Hazards Beach. The overnight walk described here makes a circuit of the whole peninsula, but if you're in a leisurely mood you might consider taking three days, with more opportunities for exploration and swimming, camping at Wineglass Bay on the second night.

HISTORY

The scenic and other values of the Freycinet Peninsula were recognised early on and a national park was declared in 1916, among the first in Australia. French names are prominent on Tasmania's east coast, especially around Freycinet Peninsula. They result from the 1802 survey and scientific expedition led by Nicolas Baudin. Freycinet is named in honour of a sub-lieutenant on the *Géographe*, one of Baudin's ships.

ENVIRONMENT

The Freycinet Peninsula's distinctive reddish-pink granite was injected into the crust during the Devonian period, approximately 400 million years ago, and is related to the granites of Flinders Island and Victoria's Wilsons Promontory.

Due to the drier climate and well-drained soils, Freycinet's vegetation is dominated by eucalypt woodland, heathland and groves of she-oaks, often carpeted with their needle-like leaves. Springtime boasts the attraction of wildflowers, especially in the heathland areas.

Local fauna includes the superb white-bellied sea-eagles, black cockatoos, yellow wattlebirds, yellow-throated honeyeaters, brush-tailed possums, echidnas, Bennett's wallabies and all three of Tasmania's snake species. The latter may curl up on tracks during summer, but usually slither away if disturbed.

PLANNING

There are a number of streams along the route, details of which are given in the walk notes, but these should not be relied upon. Towards the end of summer, or after a long dry spell, there may be little fresh water at all. Contact the **national park visitor information centre** (☎ 03-6256 7000) for the current drinking water situation or consider a day walk via Wineglass Bay and Hazards Beach.

There is a hut at Cooks Beach with bunks to sleep about eight people, although it is fairly run-down and most walkers will find a tent more comfortable.

Some camp sites are located among mature old she-oak and eucalyptus trees. Cast your eyes upwards when selecting a tent site; old trees can readily shed limbs or even fall over.

When to Walk

Any time of year can be good for walking at Freycinet, but there may be more water around in spring, with the added bonus of wildflowers.

What to Bring

You will need a fuel stove (see p243) and, while the Coles Bay stores have a reasonable selection of groceries, you should aim to bring stove fuel with you from Hobart or Launceston.

Given the sporadic availability of water (see Planning, left) you should plan to carry one litre or more with you each day. If the water tanks at Cooks Beach hut are empty, you will need to carry several litres of water for the night also.

Maps & Books

The best map to use is Tasmap's 1:50,000 *Freycinet National Park Map & Notes*. For a virtual introduction or souvenir of the park, look for Rob Blakers' photographic book, *Freycinet*. Both are available at the park visitor information centre.

Information Sources

Park and walking information is available from the helpful **national park visitor information centre** (☎ 03-6256 7000; freycinet@parks.tas.gov .au) at the park entrance, just to the south of Coles Bay.

Permits & Regulations

You'll need a national parks pass for this walk (p192), available locally at the park visitor centre and at Iluka supermarket (p244). Campfires are not permitted in the national park; you'll need a fuel stove.

Much of the area's vegetation is sensitive to Phytophthora (p47). The PWS asks that walkers help prevent the spread of this fungus by cleaning mud and soil from boots and other gear at camp sites before moving on to the next section of the walk.

There are no formal restrictions on camping but the PWS encourages walkers to use the major established camping grounds, all equipped with toilets.

NEAREST TOWN
Coles Bay

☎ 03 / pop 120

This small coastal town is both dominated and sheltered by the spectacular 300m-high pink granite range known as the Hazards.

SLEEPING & EATING

Accommodation is at a premium at Christmas, January and Easter; book well ahead for these periods.

Richardsons Beach at the national park entrance is the main **camping ground** (☎ 6256 7000; fax 6256 7090; freycinet@parks.tas.gov.au; unpowered/powered site $11/14). Camping here is basic, but extremely popular, and sites for

TASMANIA

the busy period are determined by a ballot drawn on 1 October. However, during the peak period there is very limited, first-come-first-served tent space available in a small designated backpacker camping area, for those without cars who are unable to drive elsewhere.

Iluka Holiday Centre (☎ 6257 0115, 1800 786 512; www.ilukaholidaycentre.com.au; Coles Bay Esplanade; unpowered/powered site for 2 $20/25, on-site van for 2 $50-65, cabins & units for 2 $80-130) is a large, busy and well-maintained park with good amenities, plus a shop (with an ATM), tavern and bakery next door. Also here is the popular **Iluka Backpackers** (dm/d $24/55), a YHA hostel that's light on character but very clean, with a large kitchen.

Coles Bay Youth Hostel (dm $10, r $45-50) is another YHA facility, at the Fisheries, in the national park just beyond the walking tracks car park. It comprises two very basic five-person cabins. Book through Tasmania's **YHA head office** (☎ 03-6234 9617; www.yha.com.au; 1st fl, 28 Criterion St, Hobart); a ballot system operates for the busy summer and Easter periods.

Freycinet Rentals (☎ 6257 0320; www.freycinet rentals.com; 5 Garnet Ave, Coles Bay) has 14 houses/units on its books, of varying sizes (sleeping up to six). Summer prices range from $130 to $180.

For self-catering, there is the small Iluka Supermarket or the Coles Bay Trading Company store, in Garnet St. The latter also does takeaway food and has a small snack and sandwich bar overlooking Richardsons Bay and the Hazards.

Madge Molloy's (☎ 6257 0102; ⏰ dinner Tue-Sun), next door, is a licensed, smoke-free, café-restaurant specialising in fresh seafood.

The Iluka Tavern has counter meals and dinners daily.

GETTING THERE & AWAY

Coles Bay is 31km down the sealed C302 side road from the Tasman Hwy and neither Redline nor TassieLink buses service this route. You must rely on **Bicheno Coach Service** (☎ 03-6257 0293), which runs from Bicheno to Coles Bay ($10), connecting with both Redline and TassieLink services at the Coles Bay turn-off. Bookings are advised; Redline and Tassielink drivers will call ahead if you book through these companies to ensure there will be a seat on the smaller bus to Coles Bay.

Redline (☎ 03-6336 1446, 1300 360 000; www.tas redline.com.au) operates weekday services passing the Coles Bay turn-off from Launceston ($32) and Hobart ($28), via the Midland Hwy and the inland B34 linking road. **TassieLink** (☎ 03-6271 7320, 1300 300 520; www.tassie link.com.au) has services passing the Coles Bay turn-off three times per week to/from Hobart via the Tasman Hwy ($27) and twice per week to/from Launceston ($29).

GETTING TO/FROM THE WALK

It is 5km along a fairly uninteresting sealed road from Coles Bay to the walking tracks car park, but you can follow the shoreline on foot via Honeymoon Bay (1½ hours). Alternatively, Bicheno Coach Services runs shuttle services to/from the car park up to two or three times daily Monday to Saturday, depending on demand. A single fare costs $5.

THE WALK
Day 1: Walking Tracks Car Park to Cooks Beach via Hazards Beach
4–5 hours, 13km, 80m ascent, 120m descent

The track begins just beyond the walker registration booth in the car park. Follow the signposts for Wineglass Bay for a few minutes to reach a junction. The track to the left, which you'll return along, leads to Wineglass Bay. The good track continuing straight ahead is signposted for Hazards Beach. Follow this as it contours round the base of Mt Mayson (415m). The first 30 minutes are flat and easy with occasional views out of the scrubby bush across Great Oyster Bay. The track then climbs across rock slabs to negotiate a spur. After crossing several more small spurs and dry creeks you enter a dense thicket of she-oaks, and another few minutes of flat walking brings you out onto **Hazards Beach**, a 3km sweep of sand backed by **Mt Freycinet** (620m).

Walk south along the beach. After 15 minutes a sand ladder climbs the dune. This track leads inland across the narrow isthmus that separates Hazards Beach from Wineglass Bay and 30 minutes of walking will take you there if you are doing a one-day circuit. On the peninsula circuit, continue along the length of the beach (45 minutes to one hour) to Lagunta Creek and a large camping area with toilet (about two hours from the car park). The creek

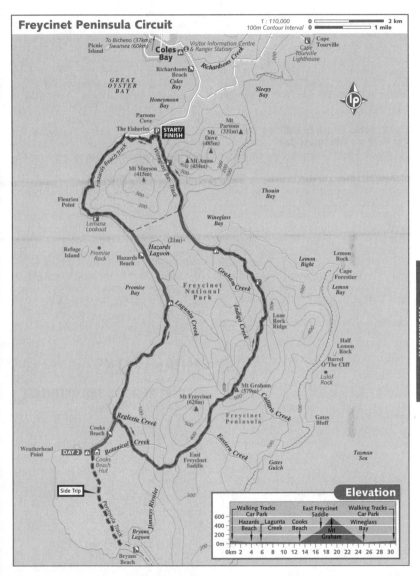

Freycinet Peninsula Circuit

is brackish beside the camping area, but a small trail leads upstream 100m or so to where better water is available.

A signpost directs you out of the camping area and south through open eucalyptus forest towards **Cooks Beach**. Don't expect to find water in the creeks here. About two hours of mainly flat walking brings you to the north end of Cooks Beach. The track swings inland here, headed for Mt Graham, tomorrow's route. To reach the camping area at Cooks Beach walk to the south end of the beach (20 to 30 minutes) where there are good sites set in the shelter of she-oaks behind the beach. The toilet, hut and water tanks are a little further back inland.

SIDE TRIP: BRYANS BEACH
2 hours, 6km, 70m ascent, 70m descent
For views of Schouten Island, just off the tip of Freycinet Peninsula, a trip to Bryans Beach is worthwhile. Follow the relatively level track from Cooks Beach hut through heathy forest to the west end of the long arcuate beach.

Day 2: Cooks Beach to Walking Tracks Car Park via Wineglass Bay
5½–7 hours, 18km, 760m ascent, 720m descent
Leave the camping area and retrace your steps of the previous day back along Cooks Beach. At the northern end of the beach, at Regleeta Creek, take the track inland signposted for Wineglass Bay. It climbs gently to the southeast for a little more than 1km through light blue gum forest to reach Botanical Creek. At most times of the year you can find water here. The track continues in a southeasterly direction and steepens considerably for the next 500m to cross a ridge. Swinging to the northeast the track rises gently and the ground becomes increasingly boulder-strewn towards East Freycinet Saddle (just over 300m). Continue from the saddle for 20 minutes to reach a broad gully just below the col between Mt Freycinet and Mt Graham. The creek here is not permanent. The track steepens and becomes rougher during the steep ascent to the summit of **Mt Graham** (579m; 30 minutes from the creek; three to four hours from Cooks Beach). The weather can be surprisingly bleak up here at times, and even snow has been recorded. Dump packs at the track's high point and walk across rock slabs to get excellent views of the peninsula, including the northern reaches of Wineglass Bay and the rock walls of Mt Dove dropping almost sheer into the startling blue water. You should also be able to make out the onward track below, running northeast across a scrubby plateau before disappearing into a woody gully. Buttongrass, more familiar in Tasmania's western peatlands, occurs on the wetter parts of this plateau.

The far edge of this plateau is reached in about 30 minutes from the summit of Mt Graham and the track becomes rough and steep as it descends into the gully containing Graham Creek (another ephemeral creek). The track climbs onto the east wall

of the gully and in one very short section skirts a vertical drop, which might give vertigo sufferers a hard time. Shortly after this point the track swings out of the gully and follows the lower extension of Lone Rock Ridge down to **Wineglass Bay** (45 to 60 minutes from Graham Creek; four to 5½ hours from Cooks Beach), a crescentic white beach in a beautiful setting.

At the southern end of Wineglass Bay is a large well-shaded camping area. Any water found here is often of poor quality, but may be better a little upstream. Despite this, you could choose to spend a second night here and lounge away the afternoon on this beautiful beach.

Wineglass Bay beach takes 30 minutes to skirt, and above the northern end there is a track junction. To the left, a track leads across the isthmus to Hazards Beach, while to the right a well-constructed track begins the steady climb to the saddle between Mt Mayson and Mt Amos. A viewing platform 100m to the right of the saddle gives a final panorama of Wineglass Bay before the track descends steadily back to the car park (one hour from Wineglass Bay).

MORE WALKS

HOBART REGION & THE SOUTHEAST
Labillardiere Peninsula
Quiet and rural Bruny Island is just one hour's drive and 20 minutes by ferry from Hobart. As well as having some beautiful white-sand beaches, penguin colonies and bush-clad hills, the southern coastline of the island has been incorporated into South Bruny National Park. The best walking in the park follows good tracks round the Labillardiere Peninsula, giving fine coastal views. This easy-to-medium circuit starts at the Jetty Beach camping ground and takes around six hours. Tasmap's 1:75,000 *Bruny Island Walks Map & Notes* shows this and other walks on the island.

Hartz Peak
Only 84km southwest of Hobart, Hartz Mountains National Park is within the boundaries of the WHA. Following signposts from Geeveston, an access road climbs high up on Hartz Mountain, leaving a five-hour moderate return walk across

alpine terrain to reach Hartz Peak (1255m). In clear weather there are good views of the southwest mountains, including Federation Peak, but also the scars of industrial forestry in the Picton valley below. Due to its proximity to Hobart the walk can be popular on weekends, although it is not served by public transport. Tasmap's 1:50,000 *Hartz Mountains Day Walk Map & Notes* covers this and other walks in the area.

WEST & WORLD HERITAGE AREA
Western Arthurs Traverse

For many serious walkers, the traverse of the Western Arthurs is the finest walk in Tasmania, but it should not be underestimated. While the start/finish point is accessible by public transport in summer, the walk is remote, strenuous and potentially dangerous and normally takes more than seven days. From near Scotts Peak Dam, the route traverses the Western Arthur Range before returning along the adjacent Arthur Plains. The range has a rugged crest of steep quartzite ridges exposed to the full brunt of westerly weather. A high level of fitness, self- reliance and good route-finding skills are basic requirements for this walk, which repels many walkers who attempt it. For more details on the route see *South West Tasmania* by John Chapman and consult Tasmap's 1:100,000 topographic map *Old River*.

Federation Peak & Eastern Arthurs

The distinctive fang-like summit of Federation Peak (1224m) is an icon of the Tasmanian wilderness. This is another very demanding eight- to 10-day walk. The return trip is along the crest of the Eastern Arthur Range, which like the Western Arthur Range features spectacular, although very difficult, terrain. The most difficult section of the entire walk is reaching the summit of Federation Peak itself, and two walkers have been killed attempting its steep, exposed scramble.

Only well-prepared, experienced and fit walkers should consider this route. As for the Western Arthurs Traverse (above), the route starts and finishes near Scotts Peak Dam. John Chapman's *South West Tasmania* has more details and Tasmap's 1:100,000 *Old River* topographic map shows the route.

EAST COAST
Leeaberra Track

This two- to three-day easy–moderate walk traverses the fine eucalypt forest of the Douglas-Apsley National Park. This is the largest dry forest in Tasmania, a significant remnant of the forests that once covered all of eastern Tasmania. From the start at Thompsons Marshes, dry and reasonably easy walking leads for 25km south to the Apsley Waterhole, passing below the dolerite spire of Nicholls Cap en route. The walk is designed to be done in this direction so as to prevent the spread of phytophthora (p47). Bus services run within 7km of the start and finish. The walk is covered by Tasmap's 1:50,000 *Douglas-Apsley National Park Map & Notes*.

Maria Island

Located 10km off the east coast of Tasmania, and accessible by bus from Hobart then ferry from Triabunna, Maria Island has a significant place in the history of the European settlement of Tasmania. The 19km-long island is a national park and is dominated by the summits of Mts Maria (709m), Bishop and Clerk. The last two summits are good moderate out-and-back day-walk destinations with expansive views, but Mt Maria is somewhat longer. Or you can ramble around the old settlement of Darlington, or visit the aptly-named Fossil Cliffs or Painted Cliffs. Tasmap's 1:50,000 *Maria Island National Park Map & Notes* details all these options.

THE NORTH
Meander Falls & the Great Western Tiers

The dramatic escarpment of the Great Western Tiers rises beyond Deloraine (p233) and a number of tracks provide day-walk opportunities on the forested slopes, as well as access to the sometimes-bleak Central Plateau beyond. One option within the Meander Falls Forest Reserve, 28km from Deloraine (no public transport) is an easy–moderate out-and-back walk through rainforest along the Meander River to the base of the falls, which descend the escarpment in two tiers and are at their best after rain. Another option is a more demanding return circuit via Split Rock. You'll need four of Tasmap's 1:25,000 maps (*Quamby Bluff, Pillans, Lake Mackenzie, Breona*) or both

TASMANIA

the 1:100,000 *Meander* and *Mersey* sheets to cover the area, but neither show the complete track network. John and Monica Chapman's *Day Walks in Tasmania* describes the walk.

Mt Roland

Rising boldly beyond rolling farmland near Sheffield, the imposing face of Mt Roland is as much a local icon as the more famous Cradle Mountain. A track from O'Neils Rd, near Gowrie Park, provides easy–moderate access to the alpine plateau and summit of Mt Roland, or there is a more demanding circuit via Mt Vandyke. Both day walks are shown on Tasmap's 1:50,000 *Mt Roland Day Walk Map;* if this is unavailable the 1:25,000 topographic map *Cethana* covers the area, but doesn't show all tracks. Tassielink's West Coast bus service from Launceston via Devonport passes through Gowrie Park three days per week, returning later the same day. John and Monica Chapman's *Day Walks in Tasmania* describes the walk.

South Australia

The driest state on the driest continent on earth: it's a maxim all but implanted into the minds of every South Australian. The capital, Adelaide, receives an average of just 565mm of rain a year, and it is lush compared to most of the state. Appropriately, South Australia (SA) has some of the country's finest semiarid walking.

The state's showcase walking feature is the Flinders Ranges, with its ever-changing colours creating one of the country's most enticing walking destinations. To many people the Flinders begin and end inside Wilpena Pound, a circle of peaks that serves as a tourist bull's-eye, but venture outside the Pound and you quickly discover that it is just a small piece of a grand line of mountains. Alligator Gorge brings the outback nearer to Adelaide than you might otherwise have imagined, while the Heysen Highlight will convince you that the best views of Wilpena are not from within, but from the outside.

Once you have brushed the Flinders dust from your clothes you will find something a little greener in the Mt Lofty Ranges, at Adelaide's edge. On a map, the Yurrebilla Trail is an amble through suburbia but in reality you will find a corridor of wildlife-rich greenery that constitutes the city's true parklands.

Continue south, across the Investigator Strait, and a totally different walking experience beckons. On Kangaroo Island's west coast, limestone cliffs form a dramatic border to a wilderness crowded with wildlife. Toss a few Southern right whales into the sea and you could be standing atop the Great Australian Bight's celebrated cliffs.

SOUTH AUSTRALIA

HIGHLIGHTS

- Enjoying dawn views across Wilpena Pound and Bunyeroo Valley as you set out from **Yanyanna Hut** (p272) on the Heysen Highlight
- Watching tiny Fourth Creek morph into the high waterfalls of the **Morialta Conservation Park** (p257)
- Splashing through **Alligator Gorge** (p265) as the cliffs close around you.
- Wandering track-free and carefree across the high cliffs of **Kangaroo Island's west coast** (p258)
- Discovering Wilpena Pound's underworld as you descend into **Edeowie Gorge** (p268)

| ■ TELEPHONE CODE: 08 | ■ www.parks.sa.gov.au | ■ www.southaustraliantrails.com |

ENVIRONMENT

South Australian lands are the most pro-tected in the country – more than 20% of the state is covered by conservation parks of some sort. The Great Victoria, Simpson, Strzelecki and Sturt Stony Deserts form a cap across the north and west of the state, seemingly held aloft by a mountain range that runs from the Strzelecki Desert south to Cape Jervis – all the mainland walks in this chapter are within this range.

As you walk you will see plenty of SA's bird emblem, the magpie, but not its mam-mal emblem, the southern hairy-nosed wombat. The state is home to four species of kangaroo: red, western grey, eastern grey and the euro, while koalas are easily sighted along the Yurrebilla Trail and all but own Kangaroo Island.

The landscape is dominated by fire- and drought-tolerant plants, inlcuding acacias (wattles), eucalypts and saltbush. Most ob-vious are the larger eucalypts, especially the river red gums that grow along water-courses throughout the state (especially along the Heysen Highlight, p269, and in Edeowie Gorge, p267), the blue gums and candlebarks of the Mt Lofty Ranges, and the sugar gums of Kangaroo Island. There is a distinct boundary between the eucalypt-dominated communities of the south and the acacia communities further north – Mt Remarkable National Park (p263) is a good place to see this crossover.

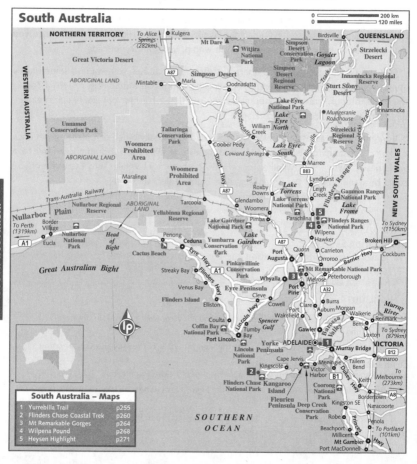

South Australia – Maps	
1 Yurrebilla Trail	p255
2 Flinders Chase Coastal Trek	p260
3 Mt Remarkable Gorges	p264
4 Wilpena Pound	p268
5 Heysen Highlight	p271

INFORMATION
Maps
Decent maps of the state are not difficult to find, and a useful complement to any of them is Fullers *Adelaide & SA Country Towns*, with street maps of more than 80 SA towns.

Landsmap publishes a 1:50,000 map series that covers areas from the Gammon Ranges south to Mt Gambier and west to Head of Bight – all walking areas in this chapter are covered by the series. For details of maps covering individual walks, see the Planning sections in the introductions to each walk.

The Map Shop (right) in Adelaide is the best place to purchase maps.

Books
Lonely Planet's *Adelaide & South Australia* is an excellent supplement to the information provided in this chapter.

For a thumbnail look at most of the walking options around the state pick up a copy of the *South Australian Trails* brochure from the South Australian Visitor and Travel Centre (below). For a scaled-down version, grab *40 Great South Australian Short Walks*, which can also be downloaded from www .southaustraliantrails.com. Jim Crinion's *40 Adelaide and Country Walks* focuses on walks around and south of the capital, while *50 Real Bushwalks around Adelaide* by George Driscoll has brief descriptions and mud maps (basic sketch maps) of walks between the Barossa Valley and Cape Jervis.

Information Sources
For general state-wide information there are several good starting points:

Bed & Breakfast Booking Service South Australia (☎ 1800 227 677; www.bnbbookings.com) Online booking service for about 100 B&Bs around the state.

Department for Environment and Heritage (DEH; ☎ 08-8204 1910; www.parks.sa.gov.au) The national parks authority; the website contains pages on all national parks in this chapter.

South Australian Visitor and Travel Centre (☎ 1300 655 276; www.southaustralia.com)

Trails SA (www.southaustraliantrails.com) Government-run website to promote walking (and other) trails around the state.

Walking Federation of South Australia (☎ 08-8361 2491; www.walkingsa.org.au) Peak body for 40 bushwalking clubs; the website contains a number of walk suggestions.

Park Fees & Regulations
Entry fees apply for most of the parks in this chapter. You can pay the fee on arrival, or, if you are going to be around for a while, there are three park passes to consider. Only the Kangaroo Island passes (p259) will get you into Flinders Chase National Park, but the Multi Park Pass ($63/99 per vehicle without/with camping) covers all other parks in this chapter, allowing you entry for 12 months. The two-month Holiday Pass ($28/44 per vehicle without/with camping), covering the same parks, is the most useful for visiting walkers. Passes can be obtained online at www.parks.sa.gov.au/parks/visitors/pass/index.htm.

See the Planning sections of individual walks for details of fire restrictions; for information on Total Fire Bans, see p24.

Guided Walks
Ecotrek (☎ 08-8346 4155; www.ecotrek.com.au) Walks in Wilpena Pound, Kangaroo Island, the Heysen Trail and Gammon Ranges.

Parktrek (☎ 03-9486 7070; www.parktrek.com) A nine-day walking tour that includes snippets of each of the Flinders Ranges' walks in this chapter, plus a Kangaroo Island walking tour.

World Expeditions (☎ 1300 720 000; www.worldexpeditions.com.au) Seven-day walking trip in the Flinders and Gammon Ranges.

GATEWAY
Adelaide
☎ 08 / pop 1.4 million
Until recently, Adelaide felt like a small town disguised as a city. Fuelled now by coffee and juice bars, and with one of Australia's busiest cultural calendars, SA's capital gives the impression of being a whole lot more grown-up.

INFORMATION
Friends of the Heysen Trail (☎ 8212 6299; www .heysentrail.asn.au; 10 Pitt St; ☷ 10.30am-2.30pm Tue & Thu, 10.30am-1.30pm Wed & Fri) Stocks maps, brochures and books on the Heysen Trail and many other paths and parks throughout SA.

Map Shop (☎ 8231 2033; www.mapshop.net.au; 6-10 Peel St) All the books and maps you will need for walks in SA.

South Australian Visitor and Travel Centre (☎ 1300 655 276; www.southaustralia.com; 18-20 King William St) Useful for general enquiries but not flush with walking information.

SUPPLIES & EQUIPMENT

There is a gaggle of equipment stores – **Paddy Pallin** (☎ 8232 3155), **Mountain Designs** (☎ 8232 3155), **Annapurna** (☎ 8232 3155), **Scout Outdoor Centre** (☎ 8223 5544) and **Flinders Camping** (☎ 8223 1913) – at the western end of Rundle St. **Woolworths** (86 Rundle Mall) is the most central supermarket, while you can pick up scroggin (trail mix of snacks, often consisting of fruit, nuts and chocolate) items from the **Central Market** (btwn Grote & Gouger Sts; ☺ 7am-5.30pm Mon-Thu, 7am-9pm Fri, 7am-3pm Sat).

SLEEPING & EATING

Adelaide Caravan Park (☎ 8363 1566; www.adelaide caravanpark.com.au/adelaide.html; 46 Richmond St, Hackney; powered sites for 2 $27, cabins $80-95, units $100-130; ▣) is on the banks of the River Torrens, 2km northeast of the city centre. It has plenty of grass but not for camping on; that's what the gravel is for.

My Place (☎ 8221 5299; www.adelaidehostel.com .au; 257 Waymouth St; dm $21, d & tw with TV $55; ▣) is as welcoming as the name suggests, with the luxury of inner-spring mattresses, free use of bikes, a DVD library and a selection of video games. There is a sauna in which to sweat out those walking aches and a weekly city tour if you are new in town.

With 245 beds, the **Adelaide Central YHA** (☎ 8414 3010; www.yha.com.au; 135 Waymouth St; dm/d from $23/60; ▨ ▣) can sleep a population larger than many SA towns. It has a large communal area with table-tennis and pool tables and views over Light Sq, plus, an industrial-sized kitchen, free DVDs in the cosy TV room and an attached travel agency.

The rooms at **Festival City Motel** (☎ 8212 7877; ecfestival@chariot.net.au; cnr North Tce & Bank St; s/d/tw incl breakfast $90/110/115; ▨) are furnished a little like a retirement home, but they are immaculately clean and directly across from the train station. Ask about standby rates. Also across from the train station is the **Strathmore Hotel** (☎ 8238 2900; www.strath .com.au; 129 North Tce; d incl breakfast from $115; ▨), a one-stop travellers' shop with an attached café, restaurant, bar, and attractive renovated rooms with all the mod cons.

Director's Studios (☎ 8213 2500; www.savillesuites .com.au; 259 Gouger St; d/studio from $100/120; ▨) has unfussy but spacious rooms handy to the central bus station. Studios have kitchenette with microwave and toaster. The associated Director's Hotel has slightly cheaper rooms.

If you have come to town with your walking appetite already fitted, the **Cumberland Arms** (205 Waymouth St; mains $9-16; ☎ lunch & dinner Mon-Fri) is among your best bets – plate-sized schnitzels are at the cheapest end of the menu.

If the Adelaide plain has you craving mountains, the Himalayan theme at **Everest** (187 Rundle St; mains $13-18; ☺ breakfast, lunch & dinner), set among the equipment stores, will appeal. The pastas and risottos are good.

At **Amalfi Pizzeria Ristorante** (29 Frome St; pizzas $11-20, mains $15-22; ☺ lunch Mon-Fri, dinner Mon-Sat) you can join the city suits for superior pizza and pasta in the fashionable East End dining strip.

GETTING THERE & AWAY

Air

Adelaide airport (☎ 8308 9211; www.aal.com.au) is 7km west of the city.

Qantas (☎ 13 13 13; www.qantas.com.au), **Virgin Blue** (☎ 13 67 89; www.virginblue.com.au) and **Jetstar** (☎ 13 15 38; www.jetstar.com.au) operate flights between Adelaide and other capital cities as well as major centres such as Alice Springs, the Gold Coast, Cairns and Canberra. **Skylink** (☎ 8332 0528; www.skylinkadelaide.com; adult/child $7.50/2.50) runs shuttles between the city and the airport (via the Keswick interstate train terminal).

Bus

Adelaide's **central bus station** (101-111 Franklin St) contains terminals and ticket offices for all major interstate and statewide services. For bus timetables see www.bussa.com.au. **Greyhound Australia** (☎ 13 14 99; www.greyhound.com.au) has direct services to Melbourne ($55, 10 hours), Sydney ($125, 24 hours) and Alice Springs ($235, 19½ hours), while **Firefly Express** (☎ 1300 730 740; www.fireflyexpress.com.au) operates services to/from Melbourne ($55, 10 hours) and Sydney ($110, 23½ hours). **Premier Stateliner** (☎ 8415 5555; www.premierstate liner.com.au) is the main operator for destinations within SA.

Car

The following companies can provide you with a hire car. Avis, Budget, Delta Europcar, Hertz, Rent-a-Bomb and Thrifty also have offices at the airport.

Airport Rent-A-Car (☎ 1800 331 033; www.airport rentacar.com.au; Adelaide airport)

Apex (☎ 1800 777 779; www.apexrentacar.com.au; 969 Port Rd, Cheltenham)

Avis (☎ 8410 5727; www.avis.com.au; 136 North Tce)

Budget (☎ 8418 7300; www.budget.com.au; 274 North Tce)

Delta Europcar (☎ 8114 6350; www.deltaeuropcar .com.au; 142 North Tce)

Hertz (☎ 8231 2856; www.hertz.com.au; 233 Morphett St)

Rent-a-Bomb (☎ 13 15 53; www.rentabomb.com.au) Offices in New South Wales, Victoria & Queensland.

Thrifty (☎ 8410 8977; www.thrifty.com.au; 23 Hindley St)

Train

The **interstate train terminal** (Railway Tce, Keswick) is southwest of the city centre. From Adelaide, trains travel to Melbourne, Perth, Sydney, Alice Springs and Darwin, with all services operated by **Great Southern Railway** (☎ 13 21 47; www.gsr.com.au).

ADELAIDE REGION

YURREBILLA TRAIL

Duration	3 days
Distance	54km
Difficulty	easy–moderate
Start	Belair railway station
Finish	Ambers Gully
Nearest Town	Adelaide (p251)
Transport	train, bus
Summary	Discover Adelaide's truly wild side as you walk between a series of national and conservation parks overlooking the city.

Completed in 2003, the Yurrebilla Trail provides Adelaide with an asset possessed by few other major cities: a multiday walking track on its very doorstep. As you wander through Waite Conservation Reserve on Day 2 of this walk you will be just 10km from the city, yet you are more likely to see kangaroos than people. The trail traces the line of the Mt Lofty Ranges – the bump in the ironed shirt of Adelaide – linking seven national and conservation parks, including arguably Adelaide's greatest natural asset, Morialta Conservation Park. You can walk the trail's entirety or use the suburban bus network to sample it in sections. There are trail markers (and distances) every 500m along the route.

Accommodation can be tricky if you vary your stops from those described here (see the boxed text on p254). Accommodation in the Adelaide Hills is a fluid thing, however, so it is worth checking with the South Australian Visitor and Travel Centre (p251) to see if any new options spring up.

PLANNING
When to Walk

As it is so near to Adelaide, this is the sort of walk that allows you to sit back and wait for a decent burst of weather, whatever the time of year. To catch Morialta's waterfalls at their finest, you will want to come shortly after a decent rain, which is most likely between May and October.

Maps

DEH's brochure-like 1:20,000 *Yurrebilla Trail Bushwalking Map* is purpose-designed for this walking route. Landsmap's 1:50,000 topographic maps *Adelaide* and *Noarlunga* cover the area but do not show the trail.

NEAREST TOWN & FACILITIES

See Adelaide (p251).

Belair National Park

Just 1.5km from the Belair railway station, the **Belair National Park Caravan Park** (☎ 08-8278 3540; Upper Sturt Rd, Belair; unpowered/powered sites for 2 $18/24, cabins $55-85) has a bush setting enjoyed by campers as well as possums, roos and koalas. The kiosk is good for a starting snack but little more.

GETTING TO/FROM THE WALK

Suburban trains depart the Adelaide railway station every 30 minutes or so (hourly on weekends) for Belair (35 to 50 minutes). To return to the city from Ambers Gully, walk west for 1km along Gorge Rd to the corner of Coulls Rd and take bus Nos 178 or 578 (30 minutes).

THE WALK
Day 1: Belair Railway Station to Brownhill Creek Caravan Park
2¼–3 hours, 9.5km

The trail begins on the southern side of the railway station, passing beneath the large 'The National Park' archway to enter **Belair National Park**, SA's first national park.

At the information board, follow the path east along the fence-line, through a stand of sugar gums and across Sir Edwin

Ave. Take the path straight ahead and descend to Perroomba Creek, turning right onto Brady Gully Track. Veer right again after 100m to recross Sir Edwin Ave, turning left onto a path that rounds **Playford Lake**, which is rimmed with gums and populated by ducks. Cross the small inlet stream to a road junction. Turn left along the road, then almost immediately right at the next road junction, turning left again onto a foot track that winds east alongside Workanda Creek. Ignore the first track junction and continue over the bridge, turning right straight after. Walk about 100m to a set of signboards and take the path to the right. Turn right again after 100m (getting dizzy yet?) – you are now paralleling the main Echo Track, which you should see just a few metres to your left.

At the foot track's end, turn left and immediately right onto the Echo Track – after making more turns than a populist politician to here, the route straightens out for a while. At **Echo Tunnel** the track burrows through a hillside beneath the Adelaide–Melbourne railway. Detouring around a side gully, you return to Workanda Creek beside its lower **waterfall**. It is an impressive bit of rock, though you need to be here soon after rain to see of water. Ignore the path across the top of the falls and continue southeast along Echo Track to a junction with the wider Workanda Track. Turn left, contouring around the hills and ignoring side trails to merge into the Wilyawa Tack. Follow this to the park boundary at Sheoak Rd (one to 1¾ hours from the railway station).

Walk west on Sheoak Rd for 50m, turning right into Pony Ridge Rd. At the road's end, continue straight along the walking track, and descend steeply to a road beside Brownhill Creek. Turn left, walking along the road for 1km. At the entrance to **Brownhill Creek Recreation Park** a narrow track leaves the road to the right, crossing the creek and following its true left bank. At the charmingly named **Manure Pits** – once used to store fertiliser to try to prevent pollution of the river – recross the creek, following the road briefly before returning to a track that switches to and fro between banks. One hour from Sheoak Rd you rejoin the road (by a picnic area), crossing a bridge and walking 500m to grassy **Brownhill Creek Caravan Park** (☎ 08-8271 4824; www.brownhillcreekcaravanpark.com.au; Brownhill Rd, Mitcham; unpowered/powered sites for 2 $20/25, cabins $80-130), strung out along the creek.

Day 2: Brownhill Creek Caravan Park to Crystal Hill Sanctuary
6¾–7½ hours, 26km

From the caravan park entrance veer right up the Peter Nelson Walking Trail, taking the wooden steps up to **McElligott's Quarry**, for

YURREBILLA'S ACCOMMODATION CURSE

When the Yurrebilla Trail opened in September 2003, it seemed a masterly piece of accommodation planning. On the first day you walked 17.5km to Eagle on the Hill Hotel for a bed with a view. Day 2 was an easy 16km into any one of three B&Bs in ever-so-cute Norton Summit, leaving a neat 20.5km to conclude the trail on Day 3. Within two years, Eagle on the Hill Hotel and all three Norton Summit B&Bs had closed. Suddenly, the user-friendly Yurrebilla Trail was as much an exercise in logistics as walking, committing walkers to at least one long walking day.

There are now few ways to vary the itinerary described here. The main alternative is to stay in the YHA cottages below Mt Lofty Summit and outside Morialta Conservation Park.

A couple of off-track B&Bs provide another option. If you turn right at Greenhill Rd on Day 2, it is about 1km into Summertown, where you will find **Summertown Homestead** (☎ 08-8390 0497; www.summertownbnb.com.au; 4 Cummins Dr; d $240). On reaching Lobethal Rd near the end of Day 2, you can also turn right and walk for 2km to the **Chapel B&B** (☎ 08-8390 1792; www.thechapel.com .au; Lobethal Rd, Ashton; d $210), in a converted chapel. The walk along Lobethal Rd, however, will be neither pleasant nor particularly safe because the road is narrow and heavily trafficked.

It is also quite possible to base yourself in Adelaide and commute by bus each morning. Buses run between the city and Eagle on the Hill (bus Nos 163 to 166), Summertown (bus 820) and Morialta Conservation Park (bus 102 stops within 1km of the main car park). Travel times are around 30 to 40 minutes. There is also a connector bus into Cleland Wildlife Park (bus No 163 or 165, changing to bus 823 at Crafers).

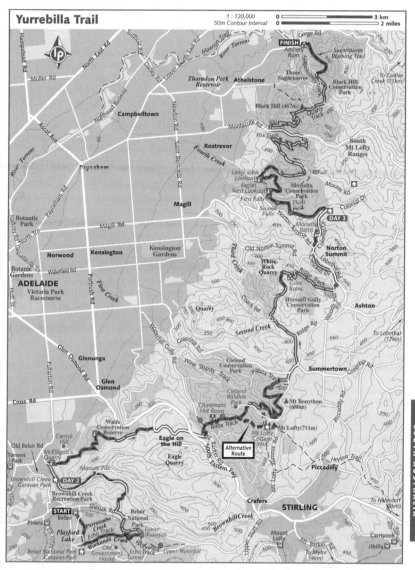

Yurrebilla Trail

1 : 120,000
50m Contour Interval

0 — 3 km
0 — 2 miles

views over the city and the coast at Glenelg. The trail continues north from beside the quarry, along an unsealed road.

At the entrance to Brownhill Reserve turn left through a gate. Below, you will see the mottled roof of Carrick Hill mansion. Cross through a stile into **Waite Conservation Reserve**, the nearest point to the city at which kangaroos exist in their natural habitat. Inside the reserve the trail swings onto a rough vehicle track and into a hollow below a large water tank. Turn right and head upvalley before zigzagging back west to a **viewpoint** beyond a few she-oaks (one hour from the caravan park). The view incorporates almost the entire Adelaide plain.

The trail now turns its back on the city, heading east through grey box woodland and olive trees. Turn right onto a faint vehicle track, making a short climb to exit the reserve. Take the track to the left and you will soon see Mt Lofty Summit's white obelisk and its three ugly sisters: the TV towers that are one of Adelaide's less attractive landmarks. Pass through a gate and, about 200m on, turn left through another gate to re-enter Waite Conservation Reserve. It's a fleeting return, as the trail soon heads back out through a gate. Follow the trail towards the farmhouse. Turn left onto the driveway and walk up to Mt Barker Rd, turning right and walking 30 to 45 minutes along the road's bike lane: this was once the main road into Adelaide, now it's a ghost road virtually ceded to cyclists, motorbikers and walkers.

About 100m past the abandoned Eagle on the Hill Hotel, turn left through a stile into **Cleland Conservation Park**. Turn left in another 200m onto a narrower track that winds down through stringybark forest. Continue straight on at the next junction, heading upvalley past the ruins of **Chinamans Hut** and following the signs for Mt Lofty Summit. Watch for some finger-like coral ferns in a rock face beside the track, then cross over the footbridge to reach a track junction.

The Yurrebilla Trail follows the path signposted 'Wildlife Park' for 500m to the park entrance road (the alternative route turns right, see right). If you fancy cuddling a koala, turn left and follow the road into **Cleland Wildlife Park** (adult/child $13/8); if you can survive without it, turn right, then left at the water tanks. Turn immediately right again onto Wine Shanty Track. In 500m an eroded track comes down from the right; you have now joined the mighty Heysen Trail.

For the next hour the Wine Shanty Track winds through gullies below Mt Bonython, ignoring all tracks to the right. Finally, you do turn right at Pillbox Track, climbing and leaving Cleland Conservation Park onto Mt Lofty Summit Rd. Turn left, walking beside the road to Greenhill Rd. Cross this busy road and pick up the track again at the bus stop, walking what feels like a full circle to meet Ridge Rd.

Follow Ridge Rd north (left), leaving it to briefly wind in behind a radar tower. About 500m on, turn left into Coach Rd, following it up to **Horsnell Gully Conservation Park**.

After rounding the first bend in the road, take the track to the right. Turn right again immediately after the phytophthora station and continue through stringybark forest. When you come to a track junction 500m on, turn right and descend towards the visible tiers of White Rock Quarry, passing through some of the thickest bushland of the walk.

Cross a blackberry-choked stream and turn right, heading upvalley to **Giles Ruins** (one to 1½ hours from Greenhill Rd). The first building was a workers' quarters, the second was the homestead. Here, the trail begins climbing away from the creek, ascending to a ridge, where it turns right. In 15 minutes the trail peels away left onto a lesser track to reach Woods Hill Rd. Turn left, then right onto a narrow sealed road after 50m. Look for a faint foot track that heads away right, doubling back to again meet Woods Hill Rd. Here, the trail turns back on itself, descending to Lobethal Rd. (This last section of trail is through private property and is closed from December through March and on days of Total Fire Ban. At these times, walk along Woods Hill Rd to Lobethal Rd, where you rejoin the trail.)

Turn left and walk along the road, turning into the second road on the left (Crescent Dr) for a quieter and safer entry into Norton Summit (one hour from Giles Ruins), which is basically a pub masquerading as a town – the **Scenic Hotel** (pub meals $11-17, restaurant meals $21-30; ☑ breakfast Sat & Sun, lunch & dinner daily) is an Adelaide institution, its balcony famed for its city views.

Turn right onto Colonial Dr, branching right onto a track that climbs above and away from the road to the stone **Morialta Barns**, once part of an estate belonging to a state premier. The track swings back to Colonial Dr, following it for 1.3km to **Crystal Hill Sanctuary** (☎ 08-8390 1111; partnerz@bigpond .net.au; dm from $25, cabins $80), which has farm cabins on one side of the road and a renovated stone cottage on the other.

ALTERNATIVE ROUTE: MT LOFTY SUMMIT
1 hour, 3km

Mt Lofty Summit is Adelaide's lookout of lookouts, and it is a worthwhile (if steep) diversion from the main trail. At the Bilba Track junction, turn right along a stream, following it to a small waterfall. Turning

---

TRAILBLAZER

For one weekend each October, the Yurrebilla Trail hosts not the usual few hikers but hundreds of runners and walkers competing in the **Trailblazer Challenge** (www.recreationsa.org). Modelled on the successful Oxfam Trailwalker events, which began in Hong King as a training program for Gurkha soldiers, competitors walk or run 18km, 25km, 50km or 100km. The 50km event has a cut-off time of 20 hours, with the 100km event to be completed within 40 hours – winning teams complete the 100km in around 16 hours.

The course begins in the Adelaide parklands and follows the River Torrens to Ambers Gully, swinging onto the Yurrebilla Trail and following it for 25km into Cleland Conservation Park. It then strikes out through Mylor and the Kuitpo Forest.

---

onto a spur, you begin a 250m climb to Mt Lofty Summit. About 400m below the summit you pass the **Mt Lofty Cottage YHA** (☎ 08-8414 3000; www.yha.com.au; cottage $50-70). Turn left at the junction here, then up the narrower track to the right to reach **Mt Lofty Summit**, where there is a **restaurant** (mains $25-30; ☽ dinner Wed-Sun), **café** (mains $8-16), gift shop and views across the Adelaide plain and Fleurieu Peninsula.

Retrace your steps past the YHA cottage to a track junction 650m (and signposted as such) from the summit. Turn right and follow this track through a gate, crossing the sealed road and descending to meet the main trail on the Wine Shanty Track.

Day 3: Crystal Hill Sanctuary to Ambers Gully

4¼–5¾ hours, 18.5km

A few metres beyond the sanctuary, turn left and cross through a series of stiles. Across the creek, turn left onto the old vehicle track, walking along the boundary of **Morialta Conservation Park**, the most impressive and rugged of the Mt Lofty Ranges' parks. At the junction with Third Falls Track, turn left and then immediately right, dropping steeply to the creek (30 to 45 minutes from Crystal Hill). **Third Falls** are 50m upstream, tumbling over a 20m-high rock platform.

Continuing downstream, stay left at a junction to head through she-oaks and beneath rock walls that offer Adelaide's best rock climbing. Pass by (but not across) the bridge over **Second Falls**. Continue for 300m to **Eagles Nest Lookout**, peering down onto First Falls, which looks like a stray piece of Kimberley country. From the final lookout point take the higher tack that heads away right, winding around the escarpment to **Deep View Lookout** (45 minutes from Third

Falls) and a scene that includes the drudg ery of the Adelaide suburbs in one direction and wonderful First and Second Falls in the other.

Turn up the hill (through the phytophthora station), rounding the ridge and climbing to a smooth track. About 2km from Deep View Lookout, you reach a track junction. If you take a hard right here and follow Moores Rd for 2.5km you come to **Morialta Walks YHA** (☎ 08-8414 3000; www.yha.com .au; cottage $50-70). Take the trail to the left, leaving the Heysen Trail and descending (steeply at times) along a spur. U-turning back past Fox Dam, the track makes an undulating 1.5km descent to Montacute Rd. Turn left and walk 1.5km along the road to Quarry Track (1¼ to 1¾ hours from Deep View Lookout).

Turn right onto Quarry Track, entering **Black Hill Conservation Park**, and begin to climb. One short section is the steepest ground you will have encountered for the past three days – cheer yourself up by enjoying the final **view** back to Adelaide. The trail ascends to a short side track leading away left to the viewless summit of Black Hill (one to 1½ hours from Montacute Rd). Continue northeast on the main trail to a green tank, where you turn left onto Sugarloaves Track. Stay on this track as it contours above Ghost Tree Gully and up into a grassy saddle between the knolls of the **Three Sugarloaves**.

Turn left atop the saddle, staying with Sugarloaves Track. In a few minutes turn right at Sugarloaves Walking Trail and descend into Ambers Gully. Pass a usually dry waterfall to meet Main Ridge Track, turning left before **Ambers Ruin** to re-enter suburbia and the trail's end (45 minutes to one hour from Black Hill).

SOUTH AUSTRALIA

KANGAROO ISLAND

Australia's second-largest island (4416 sq km) has plenty to offer walkers, including some of the best wildlife encounters in the country. The showpiece for anyone on foot is Flinders Chase National Park, gazetted in 1919 and now covering around 17% of the island. Here, you can walk for a few minutes to view platypuses or you can amble for a few days in the company of kangaroos, koalas and goannas. It quickly becomes apparent why Matthew Flinders named the place after a resident marsupial (even if only because his crew killed and ate 31 of the things).

ENVIRONMENT

Connected to the mainland at various times, Kangaroo Island's land bridge last submerged around 9500 years ago, creating an isolation that has led to much species variation between the island and the mainland. The island has 14 endemic bird subspecies, one endemic mammal species (Kangaroo Island dunnart) and 46 endemic plant species. The Kangaroo Island kangaroo is a subspecies of the western grey kangaroo, and is smaller and more solid; tiger snakes here can be entirely black; and even a bird as common and widespread as the New Holland honeyeater has different wing and beak sizes to mainland birds. As you walk, keep particular watch for glossy black-cockatoos, Australia's rarest cockatoo, with only an estimated 250 existing in the world – it is possible, though not likely, that you may spot one around Ravine des Casoars.

PLANNING
Books

Kangaroo Island on Foot by former Flinders Chase ranger Jody Gates describes 23 walks throughout the island. *Natural History of Kangaroo Island,* edited by Margaret Davies, Charles Twidale and Michael Tyler, is a good resource for delving further into the island's natural nuts and bolts.

Information Sources
Kangaroo Island Gateway visitor information centre (☎ 08-8553 1185; www.tourkangarooisland.com .au) is just outside Penneshaw. The DEH office in Kingscote (opposite) can supply information on walks around the island, though queries about Flinders Chase are better directed to the **Flinders Chase visitor information centre** (☎ 08-8559 7235; www.environment.sa.gov .au/parks/flinderschase; Rocky River).

GETTING THERE & AWAY
Rex (☎ 13 17 13; www.regionalexpress.com.au) and **QantasLink** (☎ 13 13 13; www.qantas.com.au) fly daily between Adelaide and Kangaroo Island ($70, 30 minutes). QantasLink also flies direct from Melbourne to Kangaroo Island on Saturday and Sunday ($230, two hours).

SeaLink (☎ 13 13 01; www.sealink.com.au) operates a ferry service across the Backstairs Passage between Cape Jervis and Penneshaw (45 minutes) up to eight times daily. Cars cost $65 to $80, with each passenger (including driver) an extra $40.

GETTING AROUND
Budget (☎ 08-8555 3133; www.budget.com.au) and **Hertz** (☎ 08-8553 2390; www.hertz.com.au) have cars available at the airport; the latter also has cars available at the Penneshaw ferry terminal.

FLINDERS CHASE COASTAL TREK

Duration	2 days
Distance	35km
Difficulty	moderate
Start/Finish	Ravine des Casoars car park
Nearest Town	Kingscote (opposite)
Transport	private
Summary	Wander the isolated cliffs of Kangaroo Island's west coast, where the dramatic geography is tempered by the tropical colouring of the ocean.

Following Kangaroo Island's westernmost coast, this walk heads across limestone cliffs that rise up to 100m above the sea, passing isolated rocky coves to the welcoming beach at West Bay.

Though the walk is rated moderate, it is very much an outing in two parts. Day 1, along the cliffs, is moderate–demanding, crossing ankle-twisting, fractured limestone, while Day 2 is no more than a stroll along a closed vehicle track. The bush along this track is pleasant, though it is shaded by the memories of the exhilarating previous day.

If you have two cars and an extra day, you can avoid the inland walk by continuing south along the coast to the lighthouse at Cape de Couedic. On the second day, walk to Snake Lagoon camping ground (20km), then to Cape de Couedic (16km) on the third day.

PLANNING
When to Walk
The island's climate is milder than the mainland – in January and February the average maximum temperature is around 23.5°C (compared to 28.5°C in Adelaide), making summer walking more feasible. Rainfall is slightly lower than in Adelaide and is concentrated between about May and August. Couple this with biting winds and the west coast can be unpleasant in winter. Numerous wildflowers bloom from late July to November, while March, April, October and November offer the best combinations of comfortable temperatures and low rainfall.

Maps
Landsmap's 1:50,000 topographic maps *Borda* and *Vennachar* cover the area – the walk along the cliffs isn't shown since it is not on marked trails. The Day 2 route is marked on the maps.

Permits & Regulations
Overnight walkers in Flinders Chase National Park must obtain a trip intentions form and discuss their plans with a ranger. Forms can be downloaded from www.environment.sa.gov.au/parks/flinderschase/visit/index.htm, or picked up at the Flinders Chase visitor information centre.

Entry to the park is $7.50 per person and walkers' camping is $4 per night. There are also two Kangaroo Island park passes to consider: the **Kangaroo Island Tour Pass** (adult/child $43/25) gives unlimited entry to Flinders Chase for a year, plus tours at Seal Bay, Kelly Hill Caves, and Cape Borda and Cape Willoughby lighthouses; the **South Coast Ticket** (adult/child $28/17) allows entry into the park, plus tours at Seal Bay and Kelly Hill Caves.

Camping along the described route is only permitted at West Bay, and bookings are required. Fires are prohibited, so fuel stoves must be used.

NEAREST TOWN & FACILITIES
Kingscote
☎ 08 / pop 1400

SA's first settlement may be Kangaroo Island's main town but it is still a sleepy seaside place. It is also the closest town to this walk, despite being more than 100km away. It is the place to pick up supplies, even if it is more practical to stay nearer to Flinders Chase. The useful brochure *Bushwalking in Kangaroo Island Parks* can be picked up at the **DEH office** (☎ 8553 2381; 37 Dauncey St).

Grassy **Kingscote Nepean Bay Tourist Park** (☎ 8553 2394; www.kingscotetouristpark.com.au; First St; unpowered/powered sites for 2 $20/23, cabins without/with bathroom from $50/85) is in Brownlow, roughly 3km from town, one street inland from a seaweed-carpeted beach.

KI Central Accommodation (☎ 8553 2787; 19 Murray St; dm/d $20/50) looks a bit like a doss house and is a good place to prepare for or relax from a walk.

Seaview Motel (☎ 8553 2030; www.seaview.net .au; 51 Chapman Tce; guesthouse s/d $65/75, motel s/d $125/135) has great bay views, with rooms that range from boarding school–style to the classically furnished spa suite. There is a **restaurant** (mains $17-33; ☙ dinner) on site.

Bella (54 Dauncey St; lunch $8-15, dinner $15-24; ☙ lunch & dinner) offers a rare mix of fine dining and greasy take-out. You can dine on pan-fried King George whiting or carry home a barbecued chook.

Ozone Hotel (Kingscote Tce; breakfast $8, mains $13-30; ☙ breakfast, lunch & dinner) has a typical pub menu brightened with local produce such as marron and garfish.

Foodland (Commercial St) is the best of the supermarket options.

Flinders Chase National Park
☎ 08

The closest accommodation to the trailhead is at **Harvey's Return camping ground** (sites for vehicle $8), which has toilets and a water tank. Cape Borda Lighthouse, 3km west, has three cottages: **Flinders Light Lodge** ($125), **Hartley Hut** ($80) and **Woodward Hut** (per person $16). Rocky River camping ground offers showers but is by the visitor information centre, around 50km from the trailhead.

There are a couple of private options at the park's edge. **Flinders Chase Farm** (☎ 8559 7223; chillers@internode.on.net; West End Hwy; dm/cabins $20/50, r $70) has a wing of motel-style rooms, two tiny cabins and an attractive hostel with a woolshed theme. The open-air kitchen has a vinyl collection that ranges from Meatloaf to Mouskouri. **Kangaroo Island Wilderness Retreat** (☎ 8559 7275; www.kiwr.com; South Coast Rd; eco lodge r $140, d $200; mains $28-33; ✖ 🖳) is set in 113 hectares, and has resident wallabies, rooms set around a native garden and its own 30-minute bushwalk through sugar gums, banksias and tea-trees.

Food options at this end of the island are as rare as the glossy black-cockatoo. **Chasers Cafe** (Flinders Chase visitor information centre; burgers $13; ◷ 9am-5pm) will see you through the day, but the restaurant at Kangaroo Island Wilderness Retreat is only for guests.

GETTING TO/FROM THE WALK

From Kingscote drive 75km along Playford Hwy to the junction with West End Hwy. Continue straight along Playford Hwy (unsealed now) for another 27km. Turn left just beyond Harvey's Return camping ground and drive 6km to the road end at the Ravine des Casoars car park. From Rocky River join West End Hwy, turning west onto the unsealed section of Playford Hwy after 23km.

THE WALK
Day 1: Ravine des Casoars to West Bay
5–6½ hours, 19km

From the southern end of the car park, past the phytophthora station, fork left onto a sandy track that winds down into the **Ravine des Casoars**. This 'Ravine of the Cassowaries' was named by French explorer Nicolas Baudin in 1803 because it contained great numbers of dwarf emus – they were extinct by the time of settlement just 33 years later.

After 20 minutes the track turns west and descends slowly through sugar gums to the tannin-stained creek. Follow the creek downstream, entering mallee forest just before reaching a track junction 1km from the coast. Continue straight on, walking now along the bank of the creek, to a wooden footbridge (one to 1¼ hours from the start). Cross the bridge and walk beneath the dunes to the small **beach**. In the limestone cliffs on the opposite bank you will see a series of **caves**, but avoid the temptation to enter them as they are important wildlife refuges.

From the beach, climb steeply onto the southern hillside to the cliff top. West Bay

is 15km away to the south. There is no set trail, simply follow the cliffs all the way, across fractured limestone, keeping within about 15m of the cliff edge where the mallee scrub is thinnest. You will often find a trodden path of sorts as a guide. It is slow, undulating walking but the coastal views are such that you won't want to hurry anyway. Feral goats and the small Rosenberg's goanna are commonly seen.

After two to three hours the cliffs swing southwest, forming a large headland. Continue close to the cliff edge, avoiding the thickening scrub. Within 45 minutes you round the headland and begin south again, passing through a surreal patch of eroded limestone – you will see brittle platforms of rock and stalagmites rising from the earth.

Continue along the cliffs, rounding a series of small coves on ever-rougher limestone to **Vennachar Point**. Below here, the Glasgow-bound *Loch Vennachar* was wrecked in 1905, though such was the spread of the wreckage it wasn't located until 1976. Turn east and follow the granite and limestone cliffs into sandy **West Bay**.

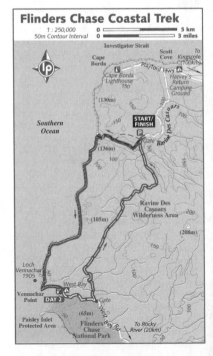

Flinders Chase Coastal Trek

1 : 250,000
50m Contour Interval

0 ⸺ 5 km
0 ⸺ 3 miles

Investigator Strait

Cape Borda
Scott Cove
To Kingscote (100km)
Playford Hwy
Harvey's Return Camping Ground
Cape Borda Lighthouse 150
(130m)

Southern Ocean

START/FINISH 🅿
Gate
Ravine Des Casoars

(136m)
100

Ravine Des Casoars Wilderness Area
(208m)

(105m)
150

Loch Vennachar 1905
West Bay
Vennachar Point
DAY 2
Gate
(65m)
To Rocky River (20km)
Paisley Inlet Protected Area
Flinders Chase National Park

A HOME AMONG THE GUM TREES

It is not by accident that Flinders Chase National Park can feel like an unfenced zoo. Cape Barren geese and kangaroos graze the lawns at Rocky River, koalas have been called a plague and tammar wallabies, virtually extinct on the mainland, flourish. Many of the animals were placed here not by nature's hand, but by human hands.

Isolated even from the settlements on Kangaroo Island, Flinders Chase was chosen early last century as a haven to preserve threatened wildlife. Between 1911 and 1957, 16 bird, six mammal and two reptile species were introduced around the island's western edge. Some, such as the emu, hairy-nosed wombat, shingle-back lizard and magpie goose, failed to colonise, but others thrived, including the koala, platypus, Cape Barren goose and ringtail possum.

Thirty minutes from the point, descend to the beach. The camping ground is at the southern end, behind the dunes and the anchor from the *Loch Vennachar*. The camping ground has a water tank and toilet.

Day 2: West Bay to Ravine des Casoars
4–5 hours, 16km

Follow the road out of camp and east through low-growing yacca, casuarina and eucalyptus scrub. After 30 to 40 minutes, turn left through a gate onto a wide 4WD track (vehicles are prohibited) and into an area of regeneration. This obvious track leads north through attractive scrub. After two to three hours of gradual climbs and descents, green fields and a long ridge become visible to the north. The track then turns northwest, dropping back to the **Ravine des Casoars**, where the gums will look like forest giants after the past two days of scrub. Scan the canopy for koalas as you climb through tall woodland to the car park.

FLINDERS RANGES

Described by Sir Hans Heysen as 'nature's bones laid bare', the Flinders Ranges are a continuation of the Mt Lofty Ranges, beginning near Crystal Brook and running north to Mt Hopeless before petering out in the Strzelecki Desert. For walkers the Flinders contain two major areas of interest: the Flinders Ranges National Park (Wilpena Pound and Heysen Highlight walks) and the Mt Remarkable National Park (Mt Remarkable Gorges walk). If you wish to spread your walking wings a little wider, head for Dutchmans Stern (p273) or Mt Brown.

Much of the Flinders average less than 400mm of annual rain, which puts it on the cusp of the desert but without the associated deprivations – this is a great place to flirt with the outback without placing yourself at peril. The country may be harsh but the walking usually isn't. Water is easily obtainable on all three walks described here, and Wilpena Pound may contain the best-marked trails you have ever walked.

ENVIRONMENT

About 800 million years ago the earth's crust thinned and formed a long trough called the Adelaide Geosyncline. Submerged under the ocean, it reached from Kangaroo Island in the south to Mt Hopeless in the north. Over the next 300 million years it filled with sediment. Around 500 million years ago the Geosyncline was squeezed and pushed up to form a long mountain chain. Mudstone, shale and siltstone around what is now the Flinders Ranges eroded away, leaving the stronger quartzite that forms today's sharp ridges.

More than 450 native plant species have been recorded in the Flinders Ranges National Park alone, though just a few will dominate your thoughts. Primary among these is the river red gum, which towers from the Flinders' dry creek beds. Porcupine grass, a spinifex, coats the hillsides in the north, softening them visually even if the grass is like a hedgehog to the touch. Cypress pines are also a common sight on all of the walks.

The real mammal-of-the-day in the Flinders is the yellow-footed rock wallaby. Most visible in Brachina Gorge – away from the walking routes described here – it also inhabits the Mt Remarkable Gorges and the Wilcolo Valley, which you walk through on the final day of the Heysen Highlight. If you don't see this iconic creature, take

SOUTH AUSTRALIA

compensation from the many kangaroos that crowd the ranges – kangaroos may outnumber trees inside Wilpena Pound. Of the reptiles, it probably won't be the snakes you will need to worry about – on the Heysen Highlight you will be hard pressed not to step on the shingle-back lizards.

PLANNING
Maps & Books

Hema Maps' 1:500,000 map *Flinders Ranges* is a good resource for getting around the ranges. Walking trails are marked, and there are inset maps of the Flinders Ranges and Mt Remarkable National Parks.

To whet your walking appetite seek out a copy of *Walking in the Flinders Ranges* by CW Bonython, one of the classic Australian adventure yarns, recounting a 1000km walk along the length of the ranges. *Flinders Ranges Walks,* edited by Peter Beer, has a selection of walks (and mud maps) throughout the Flinders.

Permits & Regulations

Park entry to the Mt Remarkable and Flinders Ranges National Parks is $7 per car ($4.50 per motorbike). Walker bush camping is $4 per night. Fires are not permitted along any of the walks, so you will need to carry a fuel stove.

ACCESS TOWN
Port Augusta

☎ 08 / pop 13,194

Port Augusta is the so-called 'crossroads of Australia', with highways radiating from this town to Perth, Darwin, Adelaide and Sydney. As such, it has an overriding feeling of functionality, and for walkers it is indeed functional, with Wilpena Pound and the Mt Remarkable National Park a short drive away. The **visitor information centre** (☎ 1800 633 060; www.portaugusta.sa.gov.au; 41 Flinders Tce) is in the Wadlata Outback Centre, while the **DEH** (☎ 8648 5020; upstairs, 9 Mackay St) has a few brochures on the Flinders Ranges and bushwalking (as well as a resident jungle python).

Better Homes Supplies (☎ 8642 3033; 16-22 Woodstock St) has a selection of camping gear.

SLEEPING & EATING

Leafy and large, the **Port Augusta Big 4 Holiday Park** (☎ 1800 833 444; www.portaugustabig4.com.au;

unpowered/powered sites for 2 $25/27, cabins $55-110; ☒ ☒) is laid out in lines as straight as the Adelaide CBD and has a camp kitchen and laundry.

Poinsettia Motel (☎ 8642 2411; 24 Burgoyne St; s/d $55/65) is the pick of the motel litter lining the highway north of town, with prices reduced by competition but facilities improved by new microwaves and TVs. It is just a stroll across the bridge to the city centre. On the highway south, **Comfort Inn Port Augusta** (☎ 8642 2755; www.comfortpa.com.au; Hwy 1; d $75-145; ☒ ☒) was Comfort Inn of the Year in 2004 and is well shielded from the highway traffic noise. The attached **Gallery Restaurant** (mains $18-26; ☾ dinner) gives the usual suspects an unusual twist – *wasabi* oysters, emu satays and a shared Drover's Tucker Platter ($56), consisting of emu satays, kangaroo fillet, camel ragout and crocodile steak with bush tomato relish and quandong glaze.

Northern & Exchange Hotel (4 Tassie St; ☾ lunch & dinner) is two conjoined pubs melded into a dining conglomerate.

Maxi's Pizza Bar (pizzas $6-14) brings the Flinders Ranges to town with standard pizzas renamed into features such as Wilpena Cheese and Brachina Gorge Hawaiian, while **Wharfie's Bistro** (mains $10-17) does oysters, steaks and hickory chicken. Or you can just plump for a counter meal.

For a change from the hotels and motels that dominate Port Augusta's dining scene, graze at popular **Hot Peppers Café** (34 Commercial Rd; breakfast $8, burgers $9), where the coffee menu is like an honour roll.

Coles (Jervois St) and **Woolworths** (Tassie St) are both central.

GETTING THERE & AWAY

O'Connor Airlines (☎ 8723 0666; www.oconnor-airlines .com.au) flies between Adelaide and Port Augusta ($185, 35 minutes) on weekdays.

The **bus terminal** (☎ 8642 5055; 23 Mackay St) is in the city centre. **Premier Stateliner** (☎ 8415 5555; www.premierstateliner.com.au) travels to Adelaide ($41, four hours, four to six per day), while **Greyhound Australia** (☎ 13 14 99; www .greyhound.com.au) runs to Alice Springs ($225, 14½ hours, daily). Only Premier Stateliner tickets can be purchased at the terminal.

The **train station** (Stirling Rd) is at the city centre's southeastern edge. Through **Great Southern Railway** (☎ 13 21 47; www.gsr.com.au)

you can take the *Ghan* from Port Augusta to Alice Springs (seat/sleeper/gold-class sleeper $171/542/710, 14½ hours), Darwin (seat/sleeper/gold-class sleeper $403/1277/1680, 43 hours) or Adelaide (seat/sleeper/gold-class sleeper $37/113/300, four hours) on Friday and Sunday. The *Indian Pacific* travels to Perth (seat/sleeper/gold-class sleeper $272/844/1100, 34 hours) on Sunday and Thursday, and to Adelaide (seat/sleeper/gold-class sleeper $37/113/300, four hours) and Sydney (seat/sleeper/gold-class sleeper $266/591/770, 31 hours) on Tuesday and Friday.

Rental cars are available from **Budget** (☎ 8642 6040; www.budget.com.au; 14 Young St) and **Avis** (☎ 8641 1010; www.avis.com.au; 35 Victoria Pde).

MT REMARKABLE GORGES

Duration	2 days
Distance	40km
Difficulty	moderate
Start/Finish	Mambray Creek (p264)
Nearest Town	Port Germein (right)
Transport	private
Summary	Wander a high ridge to link two superb gorges in the less-heralded Southern Flinders Ranges.

Mt Remarkable National Park might well be described as the forgotten Flinders – it is the place everybody drives past in their hurry to get to Wilpena Pound. But stop and walk for a while and you will discover that there is much to recommend it, especially in and around beautiful Alligator Gorge.

The 16,000-hectare national park is divided into two sections: Mt Remarkable and Mambray Creek. The walk described here is the major outing in the Mambray Creek section, beginning near the park headquarters and ranging out to the park's most striking feature: narrow, brick-red Alligator Gorge. The circular route can be comfortably completed in two days, although variations can string it out to a third day. If you have the time it is worth allowing an extra day to enjoy around the area around Alligator Gorge.

Water tanks are plentiful along the route – check with rangers at Mambray Creek as to water levels.

PLANNING
When to Walk
Early spring (September to mid-October) is the ideal time for this walk, with creeks still flowing and wildflowers colouring the hillsides. It also makes a good winter walk, with the average July maximum temperature at nearby Port Pirie being a comfortable 16.4°C (1.5°C higher than Adelaide) and monthly rainfall averaging little more than 40mm. Bush camping in the park is prohibited between 1 November and 30 April. If you want to walk this route between those dates your best option is to begin at Alligator Gorge, camping the night at Mambray Creek.

Maps
Landsmap's 1:50,000 topographic maps *Melrose* and *Wilmington* cover the walk. Buy them in Adelaide.

Information Sources
Any questions about the park and its walks can be answered by rangers at the **Mambray Creek park office** (☎ 08-8643 7068; www.environment .sa.gov.au/parks/mt_remarkable).

Permits & Regulations
Camping is prohibited in Alligator Gorge, Hidden Gorge and within 2.5km of the junction of Alligator and Mambray Creeks. Bush camping in the park is prohibited between 1 November and 30 April.

NEAREST TOWN & FACILITIES
Port Germein
☎ 08 / pop 279
Port Germein's big claim to fame is that it supposedly has Australia's longest wooden jetty (a gong also claimed by Busselton in Western Australia), at 1283m, and when the tide is out it needs just about every metre. It is a likeable slow-paced town unless you are a crustacean – crabbing is Port Germein's prime recreation.

Port Germein Caravan Park (☎ 8634 5266; Esplanade; unpowered/powered sites for 2 $14/20, cabins $50-65) is basic but has the best jetty views in town. The advertised 'grassed camping areas' are the exception not the norm.

Go easy on the alcohol if you are sleeping at the **Port Germein Hotel** (☎ 8634 8244; High St; s/d $30/60; mains $9-16; ☾ lunch Fri-Sun, dinner daily), where the floors of the generous-sized rooms

SOUTH AUSTRALIA

have more slopes than a ski resort. The counter meals are the old-fashioned sort that still believe in coleslaw and beetroot.

The **general store** (High St) only has survival-level supplies, so stock up in Adelaide or Port Augusta.

Port Germein is 240km from Adelaide along Hwy 1. **Premier Stateliner** (☎ 08-8415 5555; www.premierstateliner.com.au) buses from Adelaide ($45, 3¼ hours, one to three daily) and Port Augusta ($18, 45 minutes, two daily excluding Saturday) stop at Port Germein.

Mambray Creek

Inside Mt Remarkable National Park, and set among magnificent river red gums, **Mambray Creek camping ground** (per car/motorbike $8/5) has hot showers, a cavalcade of wildlife and is just metres from the trailhead. **Mambray Cabin** ($35-40) is within the camping ground, with a gas stove and four beds (linen not supplied).

If driving to Mambray Creek, follow Hwy 1 north from Port Germein for 20km (or 48km south from Port Augusta), turning right at the signposted Mambray Creek turn-off. The camping ground is 6km from the highway. **Premier Stateliner** (☎ 08-8415 5555; www.premierstateliner.com.au) operates a service from Adelaide ($45, 3½ hours) or Port Augusta ($18, 30 minutes) and will drop you at the turn-off (you will have to walk the 6km to Mambray Creek).

THE WALK
Day 1: Mambray Creek to Longhill Camp
3–4 hours, 13km

From the day-visitor car park (as popular with emus as people), begin east along the 4WD track. You can stay with the track as it makes a series of fords along Mambray Creek, or you can avoid the fords by following a couple of alternative walking trails. The route is through a wooded floodplain where euros are plentiful and kookaburras and galahs provide the entertainment. After 45 minutes you reach a water tank at the junction of Mambray and Alligator Creeks.

Turn left off the 4WD track, cross Mambray Creek and head generally north along the banks of **Alligator Creek**. This is a beautiful stretch of walking, a classic Flinders' scene of river red gums, stony creek bed and rust-red cliffs. You will cross the creek numerous times as the cliffs close in first on

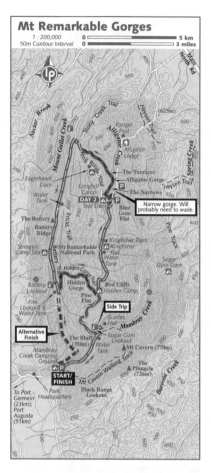

one side and then the other. After 40 minutes the track turns northeast, with the valley widening and filling with cypress pines. At Pine Flat swing southwest between darkening cliffs, and in 500m you come to the junction with Hidden Gorge Trail.

Continue straight ahead through Hidden Camp (no facilities), which sits below beautiful ochre cliffs, to join a rough valley track. This fords the creek a few more times to **Red Cliffs**. Here, the track climbs out of the valley through bottlebrush and mallee scrub. You will catch an occasional glimpse of the valley before you pass the junction with Fricks Trail (with water tank). Just ahead is grassy Kingfisher Flat camping ground (with toilet and water tank).

The track climbs on gradually to Teal Dam. Turn left here, following a narrow path through the bush to a vehicle track. Turn left again and cross Alligator Creek to reach Longhill Camp (1½ to two hours from Hidden Camp). The camp has no facilities but Blue Gum Flat, with toilets, gas barbecues and tap water, is just 300m away. It is worth exploring Alligator Gorge in the evening.

SIDE TRIP: SUGAR GUM LOOKOUT
30–40 minutes, 2km return
At the junction of Mambray and Alligator Creeks continue northeast on the 4WD track, crossing Mambray Creek to stone Scarfes Hut (no camping). Here, the track turns uphill to a ridge and overgrown **Sugar Gum Lookout**, set among native pines and large sugar gums. Follow the cairns to a lower ledge for the best view of the cliffs above Alligator Creek.

Day 2: Longhill Camp to Mambray Creek
6½–8 hours, 27km
Return along the vehicle track, past the trail to Teal Dam, into Blue Gum Flat. At the information board turn left, forking immediately left again to descend into **Alligator Gorge**, named not for the presence of any reptiles, but supposedly after an Aboriginal shepherd called Alli. Head upstream (north), crossing the creek several times until the closing walls force you to simply wade through the **Narrows**, where the red quartzite cliffs clamp almost shut. Continue through the gorge, passing a set of steps up to Alligator Gorge car park.

At the next fork in the creek, turn left to the **Terraces**, which are slabs of rock rippled like sand from a time when this was ocean-front real estate. Walk up the slabs and continue upstream, beginning a 250m climb to Battery Ridge. At first the track can be vague, but stay beside the creek and it will always turn up. The gorge walls soon close in again spectacularly and you will be splashing once more along the creek bed.

Fork left again at the next split in the creek. The gorge soon shallows and the path becomes more distinct, switching from bank to bank. At the next fork in the creek (45 minutes to one hour from the Terraces) continue straight on, following the path that climbs steeply between the

creeks. This grass tree-covered hillside becomes a canvas of wildflowers in spring and has great views back over the bush to Mt Remarkable.

At a junction of 4WD tracks continue straight ahead, through a stand of sugar gums, to a junction before a saddle. Turn left across the saddle and up to Battery Track. Straight ahead is a narrow path to a **viewpoint** overlooking Spencer Gulf and Port Augusta. On a clear day, Whyalla can be seen across the gulf to the southwest.

Turn left along Battery Track, which you follow for two hours, passing a water tank at the junction with Fricks Trail. There are great views of a parallel escarpment to the east, at least until the she-oaks take over the bush beyond Fricks Trail. Watch for emus, wedge-tailed eagles and sunning snakes. After 1½ hours you come to Stringers camp site (no facilities), which is little more than a cleared area of dirt beside the track, though it does have an ocean view.

From here Battery Track slowly descends, reaching a side track to **Battery Lookout** for the clearest view yet of Spencer Gulf. Port Pirie is visible to the south, framed by grass trees. Five minutes on, by a water tank and fire lookout tower, turn left onto Hidden Gorge Trail for a gradual 20-minute descent north before rounding the spur (and a meat-ant metropolis) into **Hidden Gorge**. The gorge walls flicker between steep, pine-covered slopes and towering, ever-more-impressive quartzite cliffs. Where the creek turns briefly south there is a beauty, with the cliffs worn back to reveal lilac-coloured rock in the jagged face.

Take the inside corner at the next bend for a simple scramble down through a rock fall. Ten minutes later, past large rock falls on both slopes, the gorge narrows dramatically before opening out towards the junction with the trail along Alligator Creek (1¼ to 1¾ hours from Battery Ridge). Turn right and retrace your steps to Mambray Creek.

ALTERNATIVE FINISH: OVER THE BLUFF
1½ hours, 5km
If the thought of a long second day doesn't appeal, continue along the Battery Track for 1km past the fire lookout tower, then turn left where the 4WD track makes a sharp right turn. This trail heads southeast down

a long spur to the **Bluff** (350m), reached after a short climb. There are some good views over the plains. The trail then turns southwest down into more open terrain before descending steeply to Mambray Creek. Turn right and head back to the car park.

WILPENA POUND

Duration	2 days
Distance	28.8km
Difficulty	easy–moderate
Start/Finish	Wilpena Pound Resort (opposite)
Nearest Town	Hawker (right)
Transport	bus

Summary A highlights package incorporating the Pound's best tracks into an easy circuit capturing the best of this natural amphitheatre.

Wilpena Pound is a circular beauty spot on the face of the outback. Fifteen kilometres long and 8km wide, it is one of the most striking landmarks in the country, and to many people it is *the* Flinders Ranges. All of the marked trails in and around the Pound are manageable as day-walks, but the route described here combines the best tracks into a single circuit walk, with the added allure of spending a night inside the Pound. You also have the opportunity to walk much of it without your pack. Trail marking through the Pound is unequalled, with distance markers every 200m and regular directional markers.

PLANNING
When to Walk
Walking is best between May and October, when temperatures average between 13°C and 25°C and there is usually water in the creeks and the rockhole near Cooinda Camp. Prepare for cold nights – freezing dawns are not unusual in winter. Avoid summer, when temperatures frequently rise to 45°C.

Maps
Landsmap's 1:50,000 topographic map *Wilpena* covers the whole Pound. Buy it in Adelaide if possible.

Permits & Regulations
Cooinda is the only permitted camp site inside the Pound. Walks listed on the trailhead

bushwalkers' register as either 'medium' or 'difficult' (such as the walk described here) should be entered into the register.

NEAREST TOWN & FACILITIES
Hawker
☎ 08 / pop 298
Hawker is 55km south from, and in sight of, Wilpena Pound. You can whet your appetite for the Pound by checking out the **Wilpena Panorama** (cnr Wilpena & Craddock Rds; adult/child $5/2), a stunning landscape painting depicting the 360-degree view from atop St Mary Peak. It shows most of the terrain you will cover in the Wilpena Pound and Heysen Highlight walks.

Teague Hawker Motors (☎ 8648 4014; cnr Wilpena & Craddock Rds) has that bush knack for being all things to all people: petrol station, knowledgeable visitor information centre, seismograph station and the **Flinders Ranges Accommodation Booking Service** (☎ 1800 777 880; www.frabs.com.au), which offers stays at six stations, mostly around Hawker. It also has the largest selection of books on the Flinders you are ever likely to find.

SLEEPING & EATING
Hawker Caravan Park (☎ 8648 4006; www.hawkersa.info/hcpark.htm; unpowered/powered sites for 2 $23-25/24-33, cabins $80-125) has an open area featuring drive-through sites, including the outback rarity of grassy tent sites.

Hawker Hotel-Motel (☎ 8648 4102; hawhotmot@internode.on.net; cnr Elder & Wonoka Tces; s/tw/d with shared bathroom $35/50/55, motel s/d $70/80, meals $11-19) has no-frills hotel rooms and self-contained motel rooms on the edge of town. Lunch and dinner are from a standard pub-grub menu with the addition of items such as salmon salad and 'cold collation'.

The spacious rooms at the **Outback Chapmanton Motel** (☎ 8648 4100; www.hawkersa.info/biz/outback.htm; 1 Wilpena Rd; s/d $85/95) are the best in town. The associated **Chapmanton Holiday Units** (Arkaba St; s/d $90/100) are about 500m away and are plainer and a bit frayed but offer two bedrooms and a kitchen. Shared reception is at the motel.

Hawker General Store (cnr Wilpena & Craddock Rds; sandwiches $4-7) has supplies enough if your walking palette is undemanding. The attached café does sandwiches and hot dogs, with cameos by such notables as celery juice and zucchini and leek soup.

SAINT OR SERPENT?

St Mary Peak (1171m) is the highest mountain in the Flinders Ranges and a place of great significance to the Adnyamathana (or Hill People), who prefer that visitors don't climb it. In the Adnyamathana dreaming, two serpents travelling south camped at a waterhole near Edeowie Gorge. That night, a group of people held an initiation ceremony in the Pound. The serpents twined together around the ceremony, surrounding its participants and eating all but two of them. The serpents' bodies now form the walls of the Pound, as they lay here still watching the escape of the two initiates. St Mary Peak is the head of the male serpent (Beatrice Hill is the head of the female).

To respect the wishes of the Adnyamathana, you should not climb onto St Mary Peak beyond Tandera Saddle.

Old Ghan Restaurant (☎ 8648 4176; Leigh Creek Rd; lunch $10-16, dinner $17-24; lunch Wed, dinner Thu-Sat) is set in the old stone railway station at the western end of town, and has an eclectic menu that ranges from crumbed camembert with quandong chutney, to barramundi reared at the local school, to nachos.

GETTING THERE & AWAY

Gulf Getaways (☎ 1800 170 170) runs buses between Port Augusta and Wilpena, stopping at Hawker. Buses depart Port Augusta ($40, one hour 20 minutes) at 3.30pm Friday and noon Sunday, and make the return from Wilpena ($20, 45 minutes) 2½ hours later.

Wilpena Pound Resort

The **Wilpena Pound visitor information centre** (☎ 08-8648 0048; www.environment.sa.gov.au/parks/ flinders_ranges) is an excellent source of walking info.

Beautifully set just outside Pound Gap, **Wilpena Pound Resort** (☎ 1800 805 802; www .wilpenapound.com.au; dm $30, s $115-185, d $125-199;   ) has four room types with localised names – Brachina, Aroona, Heysen and Edeowie – but generic motel features. For top dollar you get a kitchen and a bigger TV. The resort also manages the adjoining **camping ground** (unpowered/powered sites for 2 $16/22, permanent tent $50), where your neighbours will be feathered and furred as well as human. Permanent tents have power and a fridge.

The resort store has a wide range of supplies, though it is mostly items (frozen pizzas, cheesecake etc) you won't want to stuff into a backpack. At **Captain Starlight's Bistro** (mains $14-23; breakfast & dinner) you can watch Skippy graze metres away as you eat one of his mates. **Poddy Dodgers Bar** (mains $13-17; lunch) offers a pub atmosphere next door.

Gulf Getaways (☎ 1800 170 170) buses leave Port Augusta for Wilpena ($50, 2¼ hours) at 3.30pm Friday and noon Sunday, stopping at Hawker en route. They return from Wilpena 2½ hours later.

THE WALK
Day 1: Wilpena Pound Resort to Cooinda Camp via Edeowie Gorge
4¾–5¼ hours, 15.3km

From the bushwalkers' register beside the store begin along the bank of **Wilpena Creek**. Cross the creek at the second bridge (look out for a giant, hollowed river red gum on your right), then turn left, walk 100m and turn right. Follow the 'St Mary Peak Outside Trail' posts through open woodland to a junction where the Heysen Trail peels away right into the camping ground.

Continue straight ahead as the path undulates northwest, crisscrossed by dry gullies and kangaroo trails. You get your first glimpse of St Mary Peak's ramp-like summit at the 1.8km marker, but it is another 30 minutes before the first decent view.

Soon after, the 300m climb to Tandera Saddle begins in earnest, ascending west through several rocky outcrops – some of the climbing involves basic scrambling. There are regular views north across the arched back of the Heysen Range.

At the final outcrop, after 45 minutes to one hour of climbing, veer left (following the blue reflectors) to rise onto **Tandera Saddle**. The view includes St Mary Peak to the northwest, Mt Boorong to the southeast and the mogul-like peaks of the Pound's opposite wall in between. If you are intent on climbing St Mary Peak (see the boxed text, above), note that it involves more scrambling and can be treacherous if wet.

SOUTH AUSTRALIA

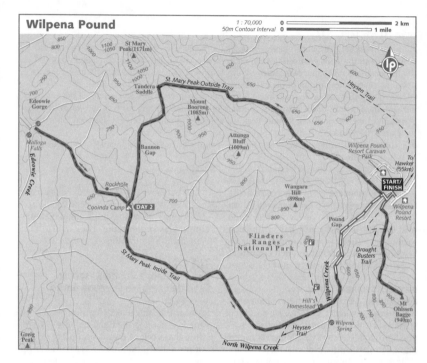

Wilpena Pound

1 : 70,000
50m Contour Interval

It should not be attempted if the summit is covered by cloud.

The old walking track straight down into the Pound is now closed (though still very visible). Instead, turn left along the ridge, descending across the slope of Mt Boorong, officially entering the Pound as you leave the ridge. If it seems like a shorter descent than the climb, it is – the floor of the Pound is around 180m higher than the surrounding land. As you descend you will get glimpses across the scrub that reveal the Pound's circular shape.

Passing through Bannon Gap, you come to stony **North Wilpena Creek** (one to 1¼ hours from Tandera Saddle). Cross it to reach Cooinda Camp (no facilities), set among low mallees. Water is available at a rockhole (marked on the *Wilpena* map) about 500m from camp. To find the hole, follow the Edeowie Gorge trail until just beyond the 9.0km marker, looking for a small rock ledge on your right. The rockhole is below here; it is an easy scramble down.

Store your pack in camp and take the Edeowie Gorge trail, which leads northwest

from camp. It is a well-formed track but you will still be pushing through casuarinas much of the time. Pass the **rockhole** and cross North Wilpena Creek twice (there may be water at the first crossing) before climbing to some rock shelves with good views north to Tandera Saddle and the ribbed back of St Mary Peak. Pass another gully – look to your right and you will see a set of rock steps masquerading as a waterfall – and 10 minutes later you come to a large cairn and a glimpse into Edeowie's depths.

The trail descends into **Edeowie Gorge** and the end of the marked track. Follow the creek bed west for five minutes, edging around the left side of a waterfall. **Malloga Falls** are 20m on, inside the narrow slot of an orange side canyon.

Retrace your steps back to camp.

Day 2: Cooinda Camp to Wilpena Pound Resort

3½–4½ hours, 13.7km
Get an early start this morning and you will be mingling with kangaroos most of the way to Hill's Homestead.

Head south out of camp on a path that soon becomes a wider track, passing from stands of cypress pine and young eucalyptuses into open woodland dotted with large, unruly gums. Twenty minutes after passing through a large clearing, popular with kangaroos, the trail reaches a junction with the Heysen Trail. Continue straight on to **Hill's Homestead**, a stone settlers' home built in the early 1900s. There is a water tank and toilet here and the beginning of the trail to Wangara Lookouts, set on a gentle ridge running north from the homestead.

Cross the footbridge and join the road, passing a beautiful pool where Wilpena Creek briefly widens. Walk through **Pound Gap** to the 0.8km marker, where the track to Mt Ohlssen Bagge breaks away right. Take this track, crossing Wilpena Creek and continuing straight ahead into open country.

Avoid the right turns to the Drought Buster Trail and climb gradually through porcupine grass, casuarinas and grass trees. The trail zigzags round a series of weathered outcrops, working its way southeast along a wide shelf to a break in the summit escarpment, where it turns west. Once through the escarpment it doubles back to follow the cliff edge to the summit of **Mt Ohlssen Bagge** (940m), which has a great view into the Pound, including Edeowie Gorge and the upturned nose of St Mary Peak. To the north, directly below, you will see the resort and its solar power station.

Retrace your steps to the road, turn right and follow it into the resort.

HEYSEN HIGHLIGHT

Duration	3 days
Distance	61.5km
Difficulty	moderate
Start	Parachilna Gorge
Finish	Wilpena Pound Resort (p267)
Nearest Town	Hawker (p266)
Transport	shuttle service

Summary Follow the northern end of the Heysen Trail to discover the Heysen and ABC Ranges and the best views of Wilpena Pound.

If you don't have a spare two months to walk the entire Heysen Trail (below), consider walking this northernmost section instead. This is where the trail is arguably at its most magnificent, following the curling Heysen and ABC Ranges, which run north from Wilpena Pound. It is also the section most fitting to a Heysen Trail experience – it was around here, particularly around the Aroona Valley, that Sir Hans Heysen, the painter for whom the trail is named, took much of his artistic inspiration.

There are reliable water sources at Aroona and Yanyanna Hut and usually at the vehicle camp sites near the trail. For information on water levels at other locations, check with rangers at Wilpena.

PLANNING
When to Walk

The best season is around August to mid-October when you can expect fine, warm

HEYSEN TRAIL

Named after Sir Hans Heysen (1877–1968), a renowned painter of the Flinders Ranges and Mt Lofty areas, the Heysen Trail stretches for 1200km from Cape Jervis on the Fleurieu Peninsula to Parachilna Gorge in the Northern Flinders Ranges. It is one of the most daunting long-distance walks in the country. Even if you are able to walk 30km per day, you will be on the trail for 40 days, much of the time through semiarid country. Most people take around 60 days to walk the trail.

Sections of the trail that run through private property are closed from about November through to March, while trails through national and other parks close on days of Total Fire Ban. This is not a walk you want to tackle in summer anyhow – average January maximums in Hawker are around 34°C.

The Friends of the Heysen Trail (see p251) should be your first stop if considering a walk along the Heysen Trail – its website has some excellent planning material. Pick up also the two dedicated guidebooks to the trail, *Heysen Trail – Northern Guide* and *Heysen Trail – Southern Guide*. They feature brief descriptions of each section, have excellent maps and are ring-bound for ease of use on the trail.

conditions and a decent mat of wildflowers. Day 1 of the walk runs through private property and is closed between 1 November and 15 April and on days of Total Fire Ban.

Maps & Books
The series of maps dedicated to the Heysen Trail have been phased out and replaced by two books. *Heysen Trail – Northern Guide* covers the described route and includes accurate maps and mostly accurate elevation profiles. The alternative is to buy the Landsmap 1:50,000 topographic maps *Wilpena, Oraparinna* and *Blinman,* though they don't show the trail.

NEAREST TOWN & FACILITIES
See Hawker (p266) and Wilpena Pound Resort (p267).

Angorichina Tourist Village
Near the head of Parachilna Gorge, **Angorichina Tourist Village** (☎ 08-8648 4842; unpowered/powered sites per person $9/10, dm from $14, cabins $70; 🅿 🖳) is in the literal middle of nowhere, which is handy since that places it very near to the trailhead. Camp sites are shaly but have great views onto the ABC and Heysen Ranges. Mountain bikes can also be hired ($45 per day) if you need to ride back to Wilpena to pick up your car.

GETTING TO/FROM THE WALK
The trailhead is at a car park inside Parachilna Gorge, 3.7km west from Angorichina Tourist Village.

Alpana Station (☎ 08-8648 4864; www.alpana-station.netfirms.com) operates a shuttle service for walkers between Wilpena Pound and Parachilna ($140).

THE WALK
Day 1: Parachilna Gorge to Aroona Valley
4–4½ hours, 16.3km

From the car park, cross the stile and the wide bed of Parachilna Creek to a tributary threading south between the Heysen Range on your right (west) and the ABC Range on your left (east). After five minutes cross another stile, turning up the far (easternmost) stream of the creek; the closest stream leads to a fenced dead-end.

The trail switches between the soft creek bed and a vehicle track, but always follows the general course of the creek. Ringneck

> **WARNING**
> River red gums (which are ominously known as widow-makers) can unload branches without warning, so choose your tent site carefully, well clear of these large trees.

parrots are common here, as are shingle-back lizards.

After 45 minutes to one hour, climb above the creek, following a fence to a small saddle. Round the spur into Wild Dog Valley and a plain covered in cypress pine, dotted with wattle. Continuing south, views open out of the Heysen Range and Mt Bell, with its red escarpment and lush gorges.

The trail dips into Wild Dog Creek a couple of times but mostly stays on the vehicle track. About one hour from the saddle you reach a fence. Walk beside this, crossing the creek and climbing steeply onto the opposite bank. Crossing a stile, you will get a glimpse west into Crisp Gorge.

Descend back to the creek, crossing it several times on a narrow and faint (but well-marked) path before rejoining a vehicle track. This continues faithfully south, beside and along the creek to Taring Saddle (45 minutes from the stile). You have now climbed around 320m since leaving Parachilna Gorge, though it should have been almost imperceptible.

Begin an equally gentle descent into the Aroona Valley, pass the windmill at **Pigeon Bore** (where you can pump iron-tasting water) and head through open woodland for 1½ hours to an old farm gate. Cross a stile and turn east, walking 100m to **Aroona Lookout**, with views across the valley to Mt Hayward and Walkandi Peak. Also here are the foundations of **Aroona Homestead**, built in 1854 for the first pastoralist in the area, John Hayward.

Over the rise is the pug-and-pine **Aroona Hut**, where Hans Heysen stayed a number of times. The Aroona Valley camping ground, a fantastic, sprawling site at the foot of the ABC Range, is 100m east of the hut. It has toilets, drinking water and bins.

Day 2: Aroona Valley to Yanyanna Hut
6–7½ hours, 24km

Head east from the camping ground on a 4WD track, climbing into the ABC Range.

It is a gentle ascent mostly, though there is a steep pinch after about 800m. The track descends east from here to reach a junction with a walking trail. Take this path southeast (the 4WD track continues straight on for 1.8km to Red Hill Lookout, which has carbon-copy views to that ahead at Brachina Lookout).

Cross a wide creek, then begin a sustained climb into the Brachina Formation. After 10 minutes you reach Yuluna Hike junction. Turn left, heading east along the spur to **Brachina Lookout**. From this fantastic vantage point you can see Wilpena Pound to the south and the long lines of the Heysen and ABC Ranges.

The trail drops off the back of the range, crosses a 4WD track and continues southeast. Crossing Brachina Creek several times you reach the ruins of **Morela Hut**, an outstation of Hayward's Aroona property, though now just a fireplace. Below the ruins you will see the Trezona Bore windmill but it has no accessible water supply.

Take the faint path (not the 4WD track) south, rounding the hillocks and then following Brachina Creek. After about 40 minutes you break from the creek, veering into open country that only becomes more open and hard-baked as you walk. As the pines disappear and the elegant wattles (looking most inelegant) become more predominant there are more good views of the Pound. The way can be confused by the many animal tracks that intersect the path – stay at a fairly constant height; the trails that head up the hills are the critters'.

Two hours from Brachina Lookout you come to a track junction with the Trezona Hike. Turn right and cross back towards Brachina Creek, which is now winding up to become one of the Flinders' most famous gorges. Within 30 minutes you reach a road. Turn right and walk 100m to the Trezona Trailhead (with water tank). If you fancy an early finish, Trezona camping ground stretches out ahead of you.

Turn left (south) at the trailhead and cross through grasslands and over Brachina Gorge Rd. Cutting southeast across the bends of a creek you reach Middlesight Water Hut in 30 minutes. The hut has four bunks, a water tank and the appearance of a power substation. In the creek beside the hut there is a permanent **spring**.

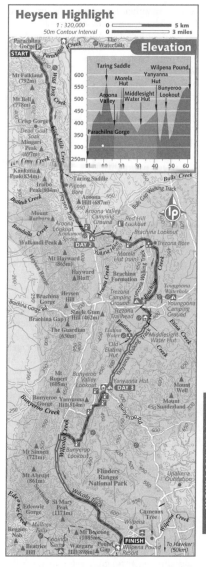

Turn right onto Yanyanna Walking Track (joining here the Mawson Trail, an 800km mountain-biking route from Adelaide to Blinman), swinging southwest. As the track zigzags through a few creeks you will see the forlorn ruin of **Old Elatina Hut** (1¼ to 1½ hours from Trezona Trailhead) to the west. Just beyond, and betrayed by the greenery, there is another **spring**, slightly upstream from where it is marked on maps.

After another 1¼ to 1½ hours you reach Bunyeroo Rd. Turn left and, 400m on, turn right into **Yanyanna Hut**, a corrugated-iron shelter with a water tank, floor space for mattresses and room outside to throw a few tents.

Day 3: Yanyanna Hut to Wilpena Pound Resort
5½–6¼ hours, 21.2km

The first 7km of this day is the most rugged of the walk, but it is a doddle thereafter. Start early and you will witness one of the Flinders' signature scenes: dawn over Bunyeroo Valley.

The trail leaves Yanyanna Hut from the western end of the stockyards. It is an ill-defined path at first but the markers are always visible as you climb the round peak south of the hut for a spectacular view of the Pound: St Mary Peak is central, with the Sawtooth running off its western shoulder, and Mt Abrupt as stark as its name suggests. Climb onto the next peak south (for an equally good view), then drop steeply west down a spur to **Bunyeroo Creek**. Turn left along the creek bed, which soon narrows to a crevice. As the valley widens again, stay in the creek bed until a sweeping S-bend. Here the trail takes to the right bank, climbing away and west onto a shelf above the creek. Follow the shelf to a creek confluence, crossing straight over to a track junction (1¼ to 1½ hours from Yanyanna Hut). Turn left and join a 4WD track after 100m.

Climb for 30 minutes along the flanks of some low hills, then veer right onto a foot track. This climbs more steeply for 400m to a crest where a side track to the left climbs further along the ridge to **Bunyeroo Lookout** for your closest look yet at the Pound.

Return to the crest, where the trail descends northwest, switching across ridges and slipping through a **gorge** in the ABC Range to emerge into the beautiful Wilcolo Valley (30 minutes from the lookout). Cross the Wilcolo Creek and continue straight on (ignoring a track to the right) to meet the Wilcolo Track. Turn left and follow the track for two to 2½ hours, passing beneath Mt Abrupt, St Mary Peak and Mt Boorong. At a gate (and a billboard-sized sign) turn

right onto a foot track, descending to a creek and then winding into a low run of hills.

The trail swings east, passing between several knolls. As the trail turns south again you get final views of the Pound, with Mt Ohlssen Bagge most prominent, and soon the trail intersects with a 4WD track. Turn left and walk 500m into the Wilpena Pound camping ground.

MORE WALKS

KANGAROO ISLAND
Hanson Bay
The white-sand beach at Hanson Bay is one of the more idyllic locations on the rugged Kangaroo Island coast, and can be accessed along a walking trail from Kelly Hill Caves. The trail winds past Grassdale Lagoon and along South West River to emerge at the beach's eastern end. Return the same way to complete the 18km walk.

For information on the walk, see the DEH office in Kingscote or the Kelly Hill Caves visitor information centre. Carry Landsmap's 1:50,000 topographic map *Grainger*.

Rocky River
For an enjoyable day walk encapsulating much that is great about Flinders Chase National Park, a circuit route out of Snake Lagoon is recommended. Walk to the cliff tops immediately south of the lagoon, then follow the coast north through Sandy Bay and around Cape Bedout to Breakneck River. Follow this inland to West Bay Track, returning along it to Snake Lagoon. Landsmap's 1:50,000 topographic map *Vennachar* covers the area.

FLINDERS RANGES
Mt Remarkable
The walk to the summit of the Southern Flinders' standout peak used to begin from the Melrose showgrounds, but this track has been closed due to rock fall. The route now follows the Heysen Trail from the war memorial above Melrose (accessed from the road to the caravan park). The 12.2km return walk makes for a good day out, though a more appealing, two-day approach can be made from Mambray Creek, at the start of

the Mt Remarkable Gorges walk (p263). Following that route to Sugar Gum Lookout, it continues east on fire trails across the Black Range and onto the western slopes of Mt Remarkable. You can return to Mambray Creek the same way or, if you have spare wheels, you can make the shorter descent to Melrose. Landsmap's 1:50,000 topographic map *Melrose* covers both routes, though the trail from the war memorial isn't marked. The *Mount Remarkable National Park Summit Hike* brochure, obtainable from the Melrose Caravan Park, has a map sufficient for the first walk.

Dutchmans Stern

A prominent bluff 10km west of Quorn, named for its resemblance to an early Dutch sailing ship, the Dutchmans Stern's most striking feature is its quartzite escarpments. A half-day, 10.5km walk heads through she-oaks and sugar gums, and past the escarpments, to views that include Wilpena Pound and Mt Remarkable. You can rent out the old **homestead** (Sun-Thu $70, Fri & Sat $80) at the foot of the bluff; it sleeps up to 15 people. Landsmap's 1:50,000 topographic map *Port Augusta* covers the walk. Gulf Getaways buses from Port Augusta or Wilpena stop in Quorn but you will have to make your own way out to the peak.

Blinman Pools

Beginning at Angorichina Tourist Village (p270), a 12km return walk heads through cypress pines and river red gums to a pair of pools, and seasonal waterfalls, on Parachilna Creek (or Blinman Creek, depending on which side of Parachilna Gorge you live). Landsmap's 1:50,000 topographic map *Blinman* covers the area, though the trail isn't marked.

DEEP CREEK CONSERVATION PARK

Deep Creek is one of the most enticing walking destinations in easy reach of Adelaide. The 4500-hectare park runs along Fleurieu Peninsula's south coast, staring across to Kangaroo Island, and includes 20km of the Heysen Trail. From Aaron Creek picnic area you can follow the creek to the coast (11km) or connect to the Blowhole Beach track along the Heysen Trail. Trig Campground is the other major trailhead, offering short, challenging walks to Deep Creek Waterfall and Deep Creek Cove, or a circuit (10.4km) taking in both. Information is available at **park headquarters** (☎ 08-8598 0263). Landsmap's 1:50,000 topographic maps *Cape Jervis* and *Torrens Vale* cover the park. It is is easily accessed from Adelaide, though Cape Jervis or Yankalilla make closer bases.

LINCOLN NATIONAL PARK
Investigator Trail

A place of quiet coves, sheltered beaches and sheer cliffs, Lincoln National Park, 20km south of Port Lincoln, is also the location of one of South Australia's few viable long-distance trails. The Investigator Trail, named after Matthew Flinders' boat, winds 93km through the park, making a figure-eight loop that includes Pillie Lake, Cape Donington and Taylors Landing. Allow about five days. Information can be obtained at the Port Lincoln **DEH office** (☎ 8688 3111) or **visitor information centre** (☎ 1300 788 378; www .visitportlincoln.net). Pack the Landsmap 1:50,000 topographic map *Jussieu*. There are air and bus connections to Port Lincoln from Adelaide. Air connection is by **Regional Express** (Rex; ☎ 13 17 13; www.regionalexpress.com.au). Bus connection is by **Premier Stateliner** (☎ 8415 5555; www.premierstateliner.com.au).

Western Australia

Australia's largest state is often smallest in the minds of walkers but it shouldn't be. In the southwest corner of Western Australia (WA), and in isolated pockets around the rest of the state, there are walking opportunities that rival anything in the rest of the country.

A day on a West Australian walking track is never dull. On the Bibbulmun Karri and Coast walk, you will wander through karri forest that seems to touch the sky and past enormous tingle trees, endemic to just a tiny area around Walpole. Hours later you will be walking along a rock-strewn coast with barely a tree in sight. On the Cape to Cape Track you can look out across the Indian Ocean and hope – often not in vain – to witness a breaching humpback whale. And everywhere you walk there are wildflowers, with spring in the west heralding the finest floral display in the country.

Mountain walkers are better served in eastern Australia or Tasmania, though there are a couple of notable exceptions. The Stirling Range covers just a small area but it offers knife-sharp ridge lines and unexpectedly rugged terrain – the scramble up Toolbrunup Peak will dispel any notion that small doesn't equal challenging. The adjacent Porongurup Range is the geometric opposite, with rounded domes and boulders that balance atop smooth sheets of granite.

This chapter concentrates on WA's southwest region, between Albany and Bunbury, with a few suggestions for walks elsewhere in the state on p301.

HIGHLIGHTS

- Catching a first glimpse of bone-white **Boranup Beach** (p288), before realising you are going to have to walk its sandy length
- Being dwarfed by one of the country's great forests on the **Bibbulmun Karri and Coast** (p290) walk
- Admiring the Devil's Slide from a boulder-top vantage point on **Nancy Peak** (p296)
- Scrambling your way to the summit of **Toolbrunup Peak** (p300)
- Scaling the highest peak in southern WA, **Bluff Knoll** (p299)

| ■ TELEPHONE CODE: 08 | ■ www.naturebase.net | ■ www.westernaustralia.com |

WESTERN AUSTRALIA

ENVIRONMENT

By any definition WA is large – 10 times the size of the UK, and almost as large as Argentina. It has more than one-third of the Australian coastline, nearly half its islands and, more even than the rest of the country, settlement here is pressed hard against the coast by the large deserts at its back.

For all that, even just the small pocket that is southwest WA boasts remarkable environmental diversity. Behind the heath-lined coast and the thousands of wild-flower species (see below) are forests of a type found nowhere else on earth, with the magnificent karri, jarrah and tingle trees endemic to this part of the state. Each of these trees is worth seeing – you can see all of them on the Bibbulmun Karri and Coast walk (p290) – with the karri tree among the most beautiful eucalyptuses in the country, right up there with the snow and ghost gums. For more detailed information about karri and tingle trees, see p295.

While trees and wildflowers are the natural stars of WA's southwest, there is also plenty of wildlife. You won't see the state's more iconic critters (such as the quokka and bilby) on the walks in this chapter, but the tall forests around Walpole do support the state's highest diversity of marsupials. If you're lucky you might spot a honey possum, a remarkable creature in several ways. This tiny marsupial (not actually a possum) somehow gets all its dietary requirements from nectar and pollen, and in the southwest there are always enough flowers for it to survive. The male's sperm is larger than that of the blue whale, and it has the largest testicles (relative to body size) of any mammal: if men were so well endowed they'd have the equivalent of a 4kg bag of potatoes between their legs.

The heath and its wildflowers are also good for a field guide worth of birds.

INFORMATION

When to Walk

All the walks in this chapter are at their very best in spring, when wildflowers cover much of the state's south. For other factors influencing individual walks, see the relevant When to Walk sections.

Maps

If you are travelling just in the area covered by the walks in this chapter you won't need a complete state map – Quality Publishing Australia's 1:926,000 *South West Western Australia* map is a better option, with a bonus blow-by-blow description of tourist

---

WILDFLOWERS

The initials WA might just as easily stand for Wildflowers Abound, this state being one of the best places in the world to witness a seasonal native flower show. There are more than 12,000 recorded types of wildflower in WA, including around 4000 in the southwest. And though the marketing machines have chosen an area north of Perth to be a designated 'Wildflower Way', some of the best displays are in walking areas covered in this chapter.

The Stirling and Porongurup Ranges are particularly noted for flowers – more than 1000 flowering plants have been recorded in the Stirlings, including about 80 that are found nowhere else. The Stirling Range is noted for its Darwinias, or mountain bells, which have clusters of bell-shaped flowers enclosed by brightly coloured leaves (or bracts). There are 10 known species of mountain bell, and nine are endemic to the Stirling Range. They grow on slopes above 300m; Bluff Knoll is a great spot to see them.

Another flower with plenty of character, and easily found, is the sundew. These beautiful carnivorous plants have given up on the soil supplying their nutritional needs and have turned instead to trapping insects with sweet globs of moisture on their leaves, and digesting them to obtain nitrogen and phosphorous. On bright days these gluelike globs can be seen glowing in the sun.

If you have come to WA especially to walk among wildflowers, you might also want to check out one of the annual wildflower shows. In late September you'll strike the Albany Wildflower Festival and Walpole Native Orchid Show, while the Porongurup Wildflower Walks are in October.

A couple of good wildflower websites are CALM's **FloraBase** (http://florabase.calm.wa.gov.au) and the **Wildflower Society of Western Australia** (http://members.ozemail.com.au/~wildflowers/manydays.htm).

features, plus details of camp sites, climate and driving distances. The Bibbulmun Track and its camp sites are also marked. Strip maps for driving routes can be downloaded from the **RACWA** (www.rac.com.au) website.

Most of the maps you will need for walks in this chapter are either in the NATMAP 1:100,000 series or CALM's 1:50,000 series. Special track maps exist for the Bibbulmun and Cape to Cape Tracks. For details of maps covering individual walks, see the Planning section under each walk.

Pick up your maps at the Perth Map Centre (p278) or call ahead to order them from the Albany Map Centre (p289).

Books

A copy of Lonely Planet's *Western Australia* will enhance your travel experience around the state.

Wild Places Quiet Places, published by CALM, is a good and colourful guide to the national parks south of Perth, and it includes all the parks mentioned in this chapter. CALM's two-volume *Family Walks in Perth Outdoors* series describes 104 walks near the capital, most of them less than 10km long. *Bushwalks in the South-West* details 49 walks through WA's forests, along the coast past Esperance, and into the mountains; the background information is excellent.

CALM has also produced what it calls a Bush Books series. Titles of particular interest to walkers include *Common Wildflowers of the South-West Forests, Geology & Landforms of the South-West, Common Trees of the South-West Forests* and *Common Birds of the South-West Forests,* while *Bush Tucker Plants of the South-West* might help supplement your walking diet.

A Long Walk in the Australian Bush by William Lines offers an account of a walk along the Bibbulmun Track, looking at the much-debated and vexed issue of forestry in Western Australia.

Information Sources

Get started on your visit to WA by checking out the following agencies:

CALM (☎ 08-9334 0333; www.naturebase.net) Website contains details of individual parks, and the online Nature-Base Bookshop.

Discover West Holidays (☎ 1800 999 2435; www .discoverwest.com.au) Offers a state-wide hotel booking service.

Western Australian Visitor Centre (☎ 1300 361 351; www.westernaustralia.net)

Park Fees & Regulations

A day pass (car/motorcycle $9/3) is required for Porongurup and Stirling Range National Parks, but entry is free to all other parks in this chapter. The All Parks Annual Pass ($51 per vehicle) gives you access to all WA parks for a year, while the Holiday Pass (per vehicle $22.50) offers the same benefit for four weeks. Passes can be purchased at CALM Outdoors (p278) or other CALM offices.

See the Planning sections of individual walks for details of fire restrictions; for information on Total Fire Bans, see p24.

Guided Walks

Bibbulmun Track Foundation (☎ 08-9481 0551; www.bibbulmuntrack.org.au) A selection of walks along the Bibbulmun Track; can also arrange private guided walks for groups.

Environmental Encounters (☎ 08-9306 1810; www .environmentalencounters.com.au) Walks on the Cape to Cape Track and in the Stirling and Porongurup Ranges.

Inspiration Outdoors (☎ 08-9378 2523; www .inspirationoutdoors.com.au) Seven-day Cape to Cape Track walk and a variety of walks along sections of the Bibbulmun Track.

Leeuwin Naturaliste Treks (☎ 08-9757 1021; www .mronline.com.au/treks) One- to four-day treks along the Cape to Cape Track.

Wildside Walks (☎ 08-9844 8091; www.wildsidewalks .com.au) Albany-based company offering short walks along the Bibbulmun Track.

World Expeditions (☎ 1300 720 000; www.world expeditions.com.au) Seven-day Bibbulmun Track (including a day in the Stirling Range) and four-day Cape to Cape Track walks.

GATEWAY
Perth

☎ 08 / pop 1.4 million

With its nearest large city, Adelaide, being around 2700km away, Perth is often called the world's most isolated city, and it is a place of beaches and bush as much as buildings. It is also within a day's drive of the five major walks described in this chapter.

INFORMATION

Bibbulmun Track Foundation (☎ 9481 0551; www .bibbulmuntrack.org.au; 1st fl, 862 Hay St) Make a stop here (above Mountain Designs) if heading out on the Bibbulmun Track.

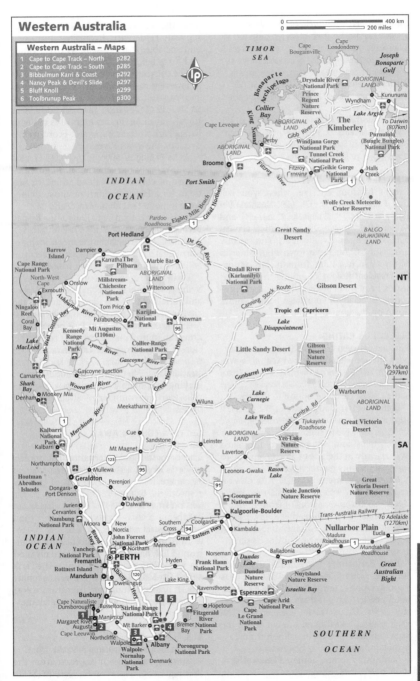

CALM Outdoors (☎ 9399 9746; 40 Jull St, Armadale; ☺ 9am-2pm Mon, Tue, Thu & Fri) Buy park passes here and gather literature on parks and walks. It's convenient if you are heading out to Albany or the Stirling Range but less so (25km from the city) if you are getting organised in Perth.

Perth Map Centre (☎ 9322 5733; 900 Hay St) Call ahead to be sure maps will be in stock (and you are better off folding your own).

Western Australian Visitor Centre (☎ 1300 361 351; www.westernaustralia.net; Albert Facey House, cnr Forrest Pl & Wellington St) Books tours and you can flick through brochures over a coffee in the café attached.

SUPPLIES & EQUIPMENT

Perth's outdoor enclave, where you will find **Paddy Pallin** (☎ 9321 2666), **Mountain Designs** (☎ 9322 4774), **Mainpeak** (☎ 9322 9044) and **Kathmandu** (☎ 9226 0562), is on central Hay St, between King and Milligan Sts. You can buy groceries as you leave town at **Woolworths** (Murray St Mall), just 100m from the bus station. **City Provisions** (868 Hay St), among the outdoor stores, has a small but excellent range of groceries, especially if your bush palette comes down on the gourmet side.

SLEEPING & EATING

Pinched between the Swan River and the airport, the somewhat cramped **Central Caravan Park** (☎ 9277 1704; www.perthcentral.com.au; 34 Central Ave, Ascot; powered sites for 2 $30, cabins from $88; 🅿 🅡) is the closest camping option to the city.

Grand Central Backpackers (☎ 9421 1123; grandcentralbp@hotmail.com; 379 Wellington St; dm/s/d $20/38/52, d with bathroom $60) has rooms fit for battery hens, and was seemingly furnished by the early settlers, but is convenient to everything as its name suggests.

Governor Robinsons (☎ 9328 3200; www.govrobinsons.com.au; 7 Robinson Ave, Northbridge; dm/d/tr $20/55/75, d with bathroom $65; 🅡) is more like a communal B&B, with leather sofas, a large dining table and a cottage-style kitchen, quietly removed from Northbridge's scruffier edges.

Hotel Northbridge (☎ 9328 5254; 210 Lake St, Northbridge; budget s/d $45/55, d $120-170; 🅿 🅡) has a country-pub exterior, but is like a boutique hotel inside. The guest veranda has perfect city views. The **restaurant** (lunch $10, mains $20-30; ☺ breakfast, lunch & dinner) is a cut above the usual pub fare, getting its salmon from Tasmania and cheese from Gorgonzola.

Settle into a second home at **Pension of Perth** (☎ 9228 9049; www.pensionperth.com.au; 3 Throssell St,

Northbridge; s/d $115/135; 🅿 🅡 🅢), overlooking leafy Hyde Park. Exquisitely furnished and sociable, it has discounts over winter and for extended stays.

The converted, self-contained apartments at **Riverview on Mount Street** (☎ 9321 8963; www .riverview.au.com; 42 Mount St; ste Sun-Thu $85-99, Fri & Sat $105-115; 🅿 🅡) have the best address in town, eyeballing the city high-rises but with Kings Park as their backyard. Front rooms overlook the Swan River.

At **No 44 King St** (44 King St; breakfast $9-15, mains $18-32; ☺ 7am-late) you can sift through a global list of coffees, cakes and wines, or settle in for a large breakfast or classy dinner from a menu that changes weekly.

Expect more than lager louts at the **Belgian Beer Café Westende** (cnr Murray & King Sts; mains $23-32; ☺ lunch & dinner), where the menu includes warm goat's cheese and slipper lobster; you will love the food even if you hate Brussels.

Perth is closer to parts of Asia than it is to Sydney, and this is reflected in the number and variety of Asian restaurants around the city. **Sparrow** (434a Williams St, Northbridge; mains $4-7.50; ☺ lunch & dinner Mon-Sat) is a popular Indonesian joint with the cheapest prices this side of Denpasar, while **Lido Restaurant** (416 William St, Northbridge; mains $8-15; ☺ lunch & dinner) straddles the Vietnam/China food border, making it possible to follow rice-paper rolls with any number of sweet-and-sour dishes.

GETTING THERE & AWAY
Air

The domestic and international terminals of **Perth Airport** (☎ 9478 8888; www.perthairport .net.au) are 10km and 13km east of the city respectively. **Qantas** (☎ 13 13 13; www.qantas.com .au) and **Virgin Blue** (☎ 13 67 89; www.virginblue .au) operate regular flights between Perth and other Australian cities. **Skywest** (☎ 1300 660 088; www.skywest.com.au) flies from Perth to Albany ($120, one hour, one to four daily) and Darwin ($260, three hours, daily). The **Perth Airport City Shuttle** (☎ 9277 7958; www.perthshuttle .com.au) provides transport from the airport to the city centre, hotels and hostels (domestic/international terminal $12/15).

Bus

For masochists, **Greyhound Australia** (☎ 13 14 99; www.greyhound.com.au) buses leave from the Wellington St bus station for Darwin ($680,

60 hours, one daily). The intrastate bus services of use to walkers are **Transwa** (☎ 1300 662 205; www.transwa.wa.gov.au) and **South West Coach Lines** (☎ 9324 2333); the latter departs from a bus terminal on Mounts Bay Rd.

Car

It is mostly the usual suspects of car-rental agencies, except for local company Bayswater. All of the following, except Bayswater and Apex, also have an airport office.

Airport Rent-A-Car (☎ 1800 331 033; www.airport rentacar.com.au) is at the airport.
Apex Rent-A-Car(☎ 1800 777 779; www.apexrentacar .com.au; 141-151 Adelaide Tce)
Avis (☎ 9325 7677; www.avis.com.au; 46 Hill St)
Bayswater Car Rental (☎ 9325 1000; www.bayswater carrental.com.au; 160 Adelaide Tce)
Budget (☎ 9480 3111; www.budget.com.au; 960 Hay St)
Europcar (☎ 9226 0026; www.deltaeuropcar.com.au; 3-5 Gordon St, West Perth)
Hertz (☎ 9321 7777; www.hertz.com.au; 39 Milligan St)
Thrifty (☎ 9464 7444; www.thrifty.com.au; 198 Adelaide Tce)

Train

Great Southern Railway (☎ 13 21 47; www.gsr.com .au) operates the *Indian Pacific* between Perth and Adelaide (seat/sleeper/gold-class sleeper $310/960/1250, 43½ hours) and Sydney (seat/sleeper/gold-class sleeper $515/1250/1640, 70 hours) twice a week. Trains are of no use to walkers for getting around the areas covered in this chapter.

LEEUWIN–NATURALISTE NATIONAL PARK

CAPE TO CAPE TRACK

Duration	7 days
Distance	133.5km
Difficulty	moderate
Start	Cape Naturaliste
Finish	Cape Leeuwin
Nearest Towns	Dunsborough (p280), Augusta (p281)
Transport	private

Summary WA's premier coastal walk, with a tantalising mix of walking, waves and whales, and a pair of lighthouses at the start and finish posts.

WA has the longest coastline in Australia, so it is only right that you should take the time to explore it. For walkers, the Cape to Cape Track is the showpiece coastal walk in the state, connecting Cape Naturaliste and Cape Leeuwin (and lighthouses) in the state's far southwest. You will pass over high cliffs, through a variety of bush, across long, isolated beaches and through the westernmost stand of karri forest in the country.

Most of the walk falls within Leeuwin–Naturaliste National Park, which runs the length of this coast – sometimes it is nearly as narrow as the path, other times it butterflies inland for up to 5km.

Facilities are good along the track: you can throw down your tent in dedicated walker camp sites or break it up with stops in towns such as Yallingup and Prevelly Park. All the camp sites along the track have toilets and picnic tables. And all except Point Rd also have water tanks, though you shouldn't rely on them entirely – there have been instances of tanks being stolen.

There are additional accommodation options to those listed here if you are prepared to do some extra walking (or can arrange a pick-up from an accommodation provider). All places listed in the walk description are within about 1km of the track.

ENVIRONMENT

The dominant feature of the Capes region is the Leeuwin–Naturaliste Ridge, composed of 600-million-year-old granite overlaid with relatively new limestone (about two million years old). The ridge parallels the coast, rising up to 200m, and is a constant sight as you walk the Cape to Cape Track; there are around 300 caves along the ridge.

On the windswept western slope of the ridge, the two main vegetation types are woodlands of aromatic peppermint gums and colourful banksias, and low heathland with wattles, honey-myrtles (bottlebrush), coastal daisy bushes, pimelias and other natives. On the eastern side, which you venture across to on Day 6, there are small areas of jarrah and marri eucalyptus forest and, at Boranup, the westernmost occurrence of karri forest. This forest, less than 100 years old, is secondary regrowth after clear-felling occurred here from the 1880s and 1913.

Birds are a feature of the coast – expect to see splendid fairy-wrens, western rosellas and '28' parrots. Snakes, of which this coast has three species, are also fairly common. Tiger snakes (black) and dugites (brown) should be given a wide berth – tiger snakes can be aggressive – while a more welcome sight is the mottled and nonvenomous carpet snake. Walk brochures describe the latter as a 'rare treat', though during our research they were abundant, including a nest of six large carpet pythons beside the track near Willyabrup Cliffs. Play safe, and give all snakes a wide berth.

PLANNING
When to Walk

The track can be walked year-round, though one of the best times is during the whale migration: humpback whales frequent the area from around October to December (which coincides with a great wildflower display); southern right whales can be seen between June and September. The presence of the warm Leeuwin Current offshore makes winters here relatively mild and feasible for walking, though river crossings may be tricky. This coast, particularly Dunsborough and Prevelly Park, is a party favourite among school leavers so, unless you find drunk 17-year-olds charming, you might want to avoid late November and early December.

Maps & Books

The Cape to Cape Track is covered by two NATMAP 1:100,000 topographic maps – *Busselton* and *Leeuwin* – though neither shows walking tracks. In mid-2006 CALM issued a new two-part waterproof map covering the length of the track. These are available at the online **NatureBase Bookshop** (www.naturebase.net), operated by CALM. Another option is to buy the *Cape to Cape Track Guidebook* by Jane Scott and Ray Forma, which has copious track information and 19 detailed maps.

Information Sources

For information on Leeuwin–Naturaliste National Park and the Cape to Cape Track, contact the **CALM Busselton office** (☎ 08-9752 5555; 14 Queen St). **Friends of the Cape to Cape Track** (www.capetocapetrack.com.au) maintains an excellent website, with details of accommodation options, guided walks, a general map of the track and a FAQ section filled with useful titbits.

Permits & Regulations

Campfires are not allowed along the track, so carry a fuel stove.

NEAREST TOWNS
Dunsborough

☎ 08 / pop 1600

With its beaches protected by Cape Naturaliste, Dunsborough is one of southern WA's top holiday spots, even though it feels a bit like a beachside suburb. The **visitor information centre** (☎ 9755 3299; Naturaliste Tce) has a free accommodation booking service.

SLEEPING & EATING

Dunsborough Lakes Holiday Resort (☎ 9756 8300; Commonage Rd; unpowered/powered sites for 2 $20/24, cabins $65-175; ☒) is a large, cabin-dominated park on the town's eastern edge – the only things small here are the golf (mini) and tennis (half-court).

The dorms at **Dunsborough Inn** (☎ 9756 7277; www.dunsboroughinn.com; 50 Dunn Bay Rd; dm $23, s/d $25/50; ☐) are a bit cell-like but it is a case of location, location, location, with the hostel smack-dab in the centre of town.

Dunsborough Rail Carriages & Farm Cottages (☎ 9755 3865; www.dunsborough.com; Commonage Rd; carriages $90-100, cottages $125-160; ☒) is set among red gums on a 104-acre property just east of town. There are resident, free-ranging roos, and lemon trees and herb gardens to help spruce up your meals in the self-contained cottages.

If you want some pre- or post-walk pampering (or the nearest access to Cape Naturaliste), try the Capes' newest slice of luxury, **Quay West Resort Bunker Bay** (☎ 9756 9100; www.mirvachotels.com.au; Bunker Bay Rd; studio from $210, 1-bedroom villa from $280; ☒ ☐ ☒), 12km west of Dunsborough. There is a day spa and wildflower gardens, and it is a 3km walk along the coast to Cape Naturaliste lighthouse.

Stock up for the walk at **Coles** (Dunsborough Centrepoint, Dunn Bay Rd) or **Dewsons** (cnr Dunn Bay Rd & Naturaliste Tce).

Groovy **artèzen** (234 Naturaliste Tce; breakfast $9-17, mains $14-30; ☺ breakfast & lunch daily, dinner Wed-Sat), on the main shopping strip, has a wide-ranging menu, from *pannini* to local venison and fish, all cooked to perfection.

If you (literally) have a healthy appetite, **Sonja's** (2/1 Naturaliste Tce; salads $5-10, burgers $8-9) is for you, with tofu and tempeh burgers, free-range chicken rolls and a range of salads.

GETTING THERE & AWAY

Dunsborough is 260km south of Perth and 24km west of Busselton. **South West Coach Lines** (☎ 9324 2333) and **Transwa** (☎ 1300 662 205; www .transwa.wa.gov.au) have daily services between Perth and Dunsborough ($31, 4½ hours).

Augusta

☎ 08

Australia's most southwesterly town is the literal end-of-the-road, which seems to isolate it from the hype of nearby Margaret River. The **visitor information centre** (☎ 9758 0166; cnr Blackwood Ave & Ellis St) has a range of brochures, including a free walking trail guide of the town.

SLEEPING & EATING

Grassy and shaded by melaleucas, **Turner Caravan Park** (☎ 9758 1593; turnerpark@westnet .com.au; 1 Blackwood Ave; unpowered/powered sites for 2 $20/23) has good views across to the mouth of the Blackwood River.

Baywatch Manor Resort (☎ 9758 1290; www.bay watchmanor.com.au; 88 Blackwood Ave; dm $23-25, s $45-80, d $55-80; 🖳) is faultlessly clean and the staff are particularly helpful – two reasons it has been named YHA Australian hostel of the year for most of the last decade. Walkers can request foot spas. Two doors down, **Georgiana Molloy Motel** (☎ 9758 1255; www.augusta accommodation.com.au; 84 Blackwood Ave; s $85-105, d $89-115) is just as neat, with larger-than-average, self-contained rooms.

SupaValu (Blackwood Ave), opposite the hotel, has sufficient supplies for a week on the trail, while **Squirrels** (Blackwood Ave) is that unlikely mix of fish 'n' chippery-cum health-food store, with pasta, rice, couscous, nuts and dried fruit lined up in bulk bins.

At the **Augusta Hotel** (Blackwood Ave) there is a trio of eating options: **Café Cumberland** (mains $22-29; ⌚ lunch Tue-Sun, dinner Tue-Sat), grill-your-own **Jimmy's Bar & Grill** (mains $14-18; ⌚ dinner Fri-Mon) and counter meals with a grandstand view of the wide Blackwood River.

You had better go hard on the steaks, pastas and couscous veggie stacks at **Colourpatch Café** (98 Albany Tce; mains $19-28), since it is billed as the 'last eating house before the Antarctic'. Service can be suitably glacial.

GETTING THERE & AWAY

Augusta is 325km south of Perth, along the Bussell Hwy. **South West Coach Lines** (☎ 9324 2333) and **Transwa** (☎ 1300 662 205; www.transwa .wa.gov.au) have daily services between Perth and Augusta ($40, six hours).

GETTING TO/FROM THE WALK

Cape Leeuwin lighthouse is 8km from Augusta, along Leeuwin Rd. Cape Naturaliste lighthouse is around 13km from Dunsborough, along Cape Naturaliste Rd. **Augusta Taxis** (☎ 0417 914 694) will transport you between Augusta and Cape Leeuwin for around $15. **Dunsborough Taxis** (☎ 9756 8688) can take you to Cape Naturaliste from Dunsborough for around $20. If you want to shuttle between the two towns to use the taxi services, Transwa buses run twice daily (once on Saturday) between Augusta and Dunsborough ($13).

If you've some excess energy at the start, you can walk to Naturaliste lighthouse from Dunsborough, following the 13.5km Meelup Trail through Meelup Beach Eagle Bay and Bunker Bay. You could walk this and reach Mt Duckworth camp site in a day.

THE WALK
Day 1: Cape Naturaliste to Yallingup
3½–4 hours, 13.7km

From the lighthouse car park, begin along the sealed path southwest to a track junction. The track turns left but if you are walking in winter or spring, it is worth first checking out the track to the right, which leads 600m to a cliff-top **whale lookout**. You can dump your pack at the track junction (there is a good hiding tree a few steps south of the junction). After turning left, cross West Coast Rd. The track here is wide and sandy, passing through low heathland (at the time of research this section was being upgraded to allow wheelchair access through to Sugarloaf Rd).

After 45 minutes the track turns west, paralleling and then crossing Sugarloaf Rd. As you walk on, there are good views back along the coast you have just walked but barely seen. In about five minutes you reach a junction. The track heads left but it is worth dumping your pack and taking the short side track to the right to **Sugarloaf Rock lookout**. The rock itself is home to the most southerly breeding colony of red-tailed tropicbirds in Australia – the bird is distinguished by its two long, red tail streamers that are almost twice its body length.

WESTERN AUSTRALIA

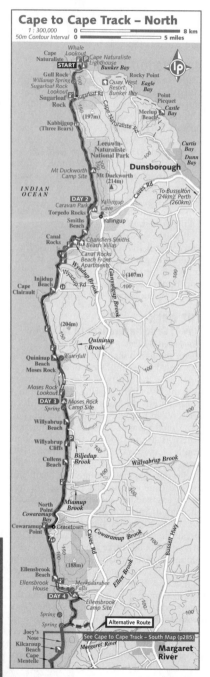

Cape to Cape Track – North

Back on the track, long vistas soon open up to Yallingup, spilling down the Leeuwin–Naturaliste Ridge, and the sandy tip of Cape Clairault. The track generally follows the weathered edge of the low limestone cliff until Kabbijup Beach (better known to surfers as Three Bears) comes into view. Near the Kabbijup car park (with toilet), take the steps down onto **Three Bears** (45 minutes from Sugarloaf Rd), ploughing through the soft sand until near the beach's end. Here, the track climbs to the cliff top, following it for around 30 minutes before joining a 4WD management track.

About 1¼ to 1½ hours from Kabbijup car park, with the knee-high heath having yielded to thick tea-tree, you pass Mt Duckworth camp site, set back from the track. Continue along the sandy track, taking the path straight ahead where the track turns inland. Cross a gully and ignore a sandy track to the right, climbing and following the coastline to Rabbits car park. Take the steps down onto the beach and grind your way to its southern end. Cross the limestone outcrops to a second small beach, where you climb the stone steps up into **Yallingup** (45 minutes from Mt Duckworth camp site).

YALLINGUP

☎ 08 / pop 300

Better known as 'Yals', Yallingup is more famous for its waves than its walks, but it is a convenient stop to ease you into the track. For a town that occupies a fair chunk of the ridge, there is little actually here.

Yallingup Beach Holiday Park (☎ 1800 220 002; www.yallingupbeach.com.au; cnr Yallingup Beach & Valley Rds; sites for 2 $20-29, cabins $50-125), on the foreshore, claims itself as the 'best located park in Western Australia', which is only a minor exaggeration. Prices go silly (sites $45, cabins up to $225) during school holidays and long weekends.

Seashells Caves House (☎ 9755 2131; www.seashells.com.au; Yallingup Beach Rd; d $175-495, mains $18-35) is about 800m inland and was completely refurbished in 2005. All (but one) rooms have a spa, and there is a restaurant and bar.

Step from the surf to surf 'n' turf at **Surfside Café** (Valley Rd; lunch $10-21, dinner $16-30; ☼ breakfast & lunch daily, dinner Thu-Mon) – the only dining option by the beach. It also does battered takeaways in another part of the building.

SURF TALK

You are going to see more surfers than walkers on the Cape to Cape Track, so it is handy to know a little about the local waves. There are more than 20 noted surf breaks between Cape Naturaliste and Redgate Beach, while Contos and Boranup Beaches offer good waves further south. The following is a rundown of some of the major breaks you will walk past:

- Three Bears – One of the best, with three waves (Papa Bear, Mama Bear and Baby Bear) offering left and right breaks.
- Yallingup – Its long breaking lefts are a favourite among Malibu riders, while the right break offers consistent barrels.
- Supertubes – Fast right-hand tubes over a shallow reef at the northern end of Smiths Beach.
- Guillotine – Fast-breaking lefts and rights over a shallow onshore reef at the southern end of Cullens Beach.
- North Point – World-class right hander that is only for the brave: the entry is by leaping off the North Point headland. If the swell is up you will see some amazing waves as you round this point near Gracetown.
- Lefthanders – As the name suggests, a left break over a shallow reef. Very popular.
- Margaret River Mouth – One for the beginners, offering a gentle beach break. Popular spot for surf schools.
- Margaret's Main Break – The wave that put Margaret River on the surf map, with an ever-reliable left break.

For a more comprehensive rundown on the surf, find yourself a copy of the *Yallingup-Margaret River Surf Map*, usually available at Yallingup Beach Holiday Park.

The **general store** (Caves Rd) is about 1km from the track, with a rudimentary selection of supplies – OK if you don't mind carrying tins.

Day 2: Yallingup to Moses Rock Camp Site

5–6½ hours, 20.3km

Return to the top of the stone steps, turning south along the sealed path, which in turn swings right at the road, following beside it to a car park. Take the signposted Torpedo Trail, passing Torpedo Rocks below. Soon after, look for a stepped path to the right, which leads down onto **Smiths Beach**. Walk the length of the beach, then climb to a sealed road (45 minutes to one hour from Yallingup). The mustard-coloured buildings here are the **Canal Rocks Beach Front Apartments** (☎ 08-9755 2166; www.canalrocks.com.au; Smiths Beach Rd; studio $195-220, 2br unit $210-305), where all apartments have a spa, and the front ones have terrific beach views – you can wake to the sight of surfers on Supertubes. About 300m east, and staggered up the hill, all units at **Chandlers Smiths Beach Villas** (☎ 08-9755 2062; www.chandlerssmithsbeach.com.au;

Smiths Beach Rd; 2br units $110-180) have views along the coast to Sugarloaf Rock. At the time of research a new resort was being constructed next door to the Beach Front Apartments. It was expected to open in late 2006 and plans included a few camp sites.

Turn right at the road above the beach and walk to its end. From here the track snakes through some large granite boulders to a short, stiff climb skirting a rocky outcrop. Resume the snaking course, this time through heathland, to a **lookout** with a view across to Canal Rocks. Five minutes on, a signposted side track to the right leads 100m to a permanent **spring** seeping from a limestone outcrop.

Cross Canal Rocks Rd, contouring and then climbing above it to **Rotary Lookout** (30 minutes from Smiths Beach), which stares down onto Canal Rocks and back to Sugarloaf Rock. A short way past the lookout, the trail descends again towards the coast, with great views of Cape Clairault and Injidup Beach ahead. Cross Wyadup Brook and follow a fence around the point. Cross Wyadup Rd and wander through grassland and heath to drop onto **Injidup Beach** either just before or just after Mitchell Rocks (45 minutes to one hour from Rotary Lookout).

Leave the beach soon after you pass below a lookout platform, turning up a vehicle track and then immediately right onto a path that tunnels through the tea-trees. At the head of a long flight of steps, turn right (ignoring a set of long steps that continue up southeast into private property) and later right again onto a sandy 4WD track. Rounding the crest of Cape Clairault, you come to a set of gates. Take the track to the left (with the darker sand) to be greeted by a new view: Gracetown and Point Cowaramup away on the southern horizon.

As the track continues along the cliffs, ignore a pair of roads heading inland. Fifty metres past the second road, turn right onto an overgrown walking track (it quickly gets better). This wanders atop the cliffs, rounding a headland with several **lookouts** back onto the weathered coast. At the next track junction, circle what looks like a tea-tree roundabout and continue straight on. Soon you rejoin the main vehicle track, turning right to enter a hollow behind the dunes.

At the car park, walk west down a track to **Quininup Beach** (1½ to two hours from Injidup Beach). Crossing Quininup Brook (or its sandbar), look upstream and you will see the red walls of a **waterfall**. A track of sorts goes up the south side of the brook to the falls, though try to stay off the darker sand, which is sacred to local Aboriginal people.

Around 100m past the brook, the track turns up into the dunes (including one steep sand climb that will shred your calves) and onto solid ground atop the cliffs. The national park is very narrow at this point (note the house just away to the east).

Round a couple of gullies and pass through Moses North car park (with toilet) to begin a gentle climb. Switching across to an old vehicle track you soon turn inland, leaving the track and joining a walking trail. Cross a couple of 4WD tracks to ascend to the platform at **Moses Rock Lookout** (45 minutes to one hour from Quininup Beach). Over the ridge to the south are the grooved Willyabrup Cliffs, popular with climbers, and a closer-looking Gracetown.

Climb on, before descending gradually into a thick archway of tea-trees. Just beyond the next road is Moses Rock camp site, with tent areas burrowed into the tea-trees.

Day 3: Moses Rock Camp Site to Ellensbrook Camp Site
5½–6 hours, 21.5km

Begin west from the camp site, turning south after 100m to descend to a small permanent spring. About 200m on, as the 4WD track swings inland, take the faint path that continues along the coast to **Willyabrup Beach** (30 minutes from camp). Cross Willyabrup Brook on the large stepping stones, turning off the beach 100m beyond. Climb to a car park and turn right along a 4WD track. At the next road junction, turn right and walk 200m to where a set of wheel tracks heads away south through the long grass – this short section can get very overgrown so be wary of snakes.

Skirting the park boundary fence, you begin to get good, close views of **Willyabrup Cliffs**. Descend steeply to cross Biljedup Brook, with an equally steep climb back out, crossing a road to reach a lookout platform. (If you turn right at the road you will come to Willyabrup car park with toilet and water tank; the tank is used by climbers also, so don't rely on it for water.) Continue south through the heath for about 25 minutes, descending a set of log steps to **Cullens Beach**. The marked track runs behind the foreshore dunes but you can just as easily wander along the beach.

Near the beach's end, follow the signs back up through the dunes to pass a lookout at the encouragingly named surf break, **Guillotine** (Gallows is just behind you). Ten minutes on, turn right onto a sandy vehicle track, continuing south beside the coast. Just past the first stream, turn left onto a sandy road and cross Miamup Brook (a reliable water source). As the road swings inland around another stream, turn right onto a faint path and wander south, just a few metres in from the rocky shore. Near North Point you will almost have to bullock your way through the thickening scrub, emerging onto a wide, sandy track.

Cross a sandy clearing to join a track that heads to the exposed edge of **North Point** (1½ hours from Cullens Beach). Follow the track markers down off the edge of the point to a lower shelf of rock. Round the point and pick up the track as it drops into a thicket of tea-trees. Descend to the boat ramp and follow the soft beach (and a scramble across a rock outcrop) into **Gracetown**. For a feed or a bed there's **Sea Star Café** (☎ 08-9755 5000; 4 Bayview Dr; r $95; baguettes $10-15, mains $24-27). Rooms are in a house at the back of the café; the upstairs double has a bed with a view, looking across the bay to North Point. Next door, **Bay Store** (2 Bayview Dr) sells a basic range of groceries and a better selection of alcohol. There is also a caravan park in town but it is 3km off the track.

Walk 50m past the café, along the main road, and turn right into Percy St. At its end, follow the short footpath to a second road and car park. From the car park, take the wide track (not the steps) southwest through the overreaching tea-trees. As the track swings west, climb the steps to the right. Just before the lookout platform (with your last view of Cape Clairault), the track steps off the boardwalk into an open area of limestone. Cross Point Cowaramup (better known as South Point) and momentarily re-enter heath before traversing another barren patch of limestone and sand. Pass a set of wooden steps and a car park before entering the large Left Hander's car park (with toilet). For the next hour it's steady as she goes: a southerly bearing through heath, tea-trees and a lookout platform at **Ellensbrook Beach**. The first 1km is through sand, which slows things down, but it then gets firmer underfoot.

After skirting around Ellensbrook Beach, turn up the true right bank of Ellen Brook, watching for another turn to the right after about 300m. Squelch across a small swamp to enter the grounds of **Ellensbrook House**, built by settler Alfred Bussell in the 1850s. Go around the homestead and inland along the creek to climb onto a boardwalk. It is a paved path from here to Meekadarabee Falls, 800m away. Passing the first grotto, the track leaves the pavers, heading away southeast (**Meekadarabee Falls** are 50m further along the sealed track at a mossy grotto). Five minutes on, the track forks – either path will deliver you to Ellensbrook camp site.

Day 4: Ellensbrook Camp Site to Prevelly Park

3–3¾ hours, 11.5km

This short day should freshen you up for longer to come. You can walk past Prevelly Park today but the next site is 18.5km on.

From Ellensbrook camp site, climb southeast into tall forest. Stay with the road

WESTERN AUSTRALIA

as it swings south along the park boundary. Ignoring a track to the east, the road turns back west, passing by some large grass trees (blackboys). Coming to a T-junction, turn left and walk along the crest of the ridge for a while (a stretch of land popular with white-tailed black-cockatoos). Turning right at the next T-junction, you begin your return to the coast. As the forest slips away there are good views south to Cape Mentelle and Kilcarnup Beach. Over the next rise the track turns south and, after a steep descent, crosses a couple of low ridges to merge with another road. Turn right at the next junction – turn left if you are taking the Alternative Route (below). This road swings south as it comes in behind the foreshore dunes of Kilcarnup Beach. Drop onto **Kilcarnup Beach** 50m before a protruding limestone cliff known as **Joey's Nose** (1½ to 1¾ hours from camp). This beach is generally firmer (and whiter) than those you have previously walked, which is a good thing since you will be on it for 2km.

Towards the end of the beach, near the tip of Cape Mentelle, turn up the vehicle track and then swing right onto a walking track after 50m. About 200m on, turn left onto a sandy road. Turn off again at the second track to the right to go through a gate labelled 'Emergency Access' – you qualify as an emergency. Fork left at the next junction. This track skirts the edge of three small bays cut into the cape, heads through a sand blow and descends to the mouth of **Margaret River** (one to 1½ hours from Joey's Nose). Wade through the river (or cross the sandbar in summer) and climb to the car park. Follow the road out for 100m, turning left onto a walking track that ascends in behind the Wallcliffe Cliffs. After about 15 minutes the track comes to a bike path. The Cape to Cape turns left but Prevelly Park is to the right.

ALTERNATIVE ROUTE: MARGARET RIVER WINTER CROSSING
1½ hours, 6km
If Margaret River is high (you can check by ringing CALM at Busselton), it can be a deep and fast-flowing crossing. To avoid this, turn left instead of right as you come over the low ridges on the southbound road about 1¼ hours from Ellensbrook camp site – there is a sign and map posted at

the junction. Turn left again at the next junction and follow this track to Caves Rd. Turn right and cross Margaret River, turning right again onto the bike path beside Wallcliffe Rd about 2km on. You rejoin the main track above Prevelly Park.

PREVELLY PARK
☎ 08
Prevelly Park is an unobtrusive holiday town by the mouth of the Margaret River – if you don't make the turn into town, you won't even notice it is here.

About 400m off the track, **Prevelly Park Beach Resort** (☎ 9757 2374; 99 Mitchell Dr; sites per person $11-17, on-site vans $50-90, cabins $70-120) is a sprawling, open caravan park. Across the road, **Prevelly Villas** (☎ 9757 2277; www.prevelly villas.com.au; 30 Pearce Rd; 3br villa $125-250) offers a beach-house kind of experience. If you crane your neck, you might be able to see the ocean.

The general store is in the caravan park office, with a noodles-and-pasta range of supplies. **Sea Gardens Café** (Mitchell Dr; pizzas $13-23, mains $23-27; ☺ breakfast, lunch & dinner), beside the caravan park, has a stepped outdoor patio so that everybody gets a view of the dunes and the surfers' point breaks.

Day 5: Prevelly Park to Contos Camping Ground
5–6 hours, 18.5km
Return to the bike path, following it up and across busy Wallcliffe Rd. The path then parallels the road for a few hundred metres. Turn off it at an old vehicle track to the right. As this track swings east, cross straight over another 4WD track onto a faint trail. At the top of the hill, turn back south onto a more defined path. At its end, turn left and then right to swing around a communications tower (45 minutes from Prevelly).

Walk south along the 4WD track for 15 minutes (in spring look for kangaroo paw flowers at the road side) turning left at its end. This track skirts **Blackboy Hollow**, so named for the number (and size) of blackboys (grass trees) in the fringing scrub. As the road curls away north, turn right (south) onto a narrower track, which meanders past a couple of enormous grass trees.

Climb gently for 20 minutes to cross a road. Ten metres beyond the road, turn right and pass through a gate. At the top of a short climb, turn left to begin a 120m descent to **Boodjidup Brook** (one to 1½ hours from the tower). Cross the creek on a metal footbridge and climb out through a mini-forest of arum lilies. Walk above the creek, following it all the way to the beach – much of this section is through long grass so watch out for snakes.

Turn south along the beach – ahead is another 2km of sand walking, far softer and slower than the last. Round the rocky point and at the end of the next small beach, below the calcified cliffs, climb up to a car park (1¼ to 1¾ hours from the Boodjidup Bridge).

From the car park's southern edge, head straight back to the sand of **Redgate Beach**. The better news is that it is firm and white again. Exit the beach at the far end, climbing through heath and then into a dense, skeletal stand of tea-trees. Turn left at a 4WD track, then fork right as the road splits.

Across the headland known as 'the Ledges', there is a maze of vehicle tracks. Follow the well-placed track markers, generally bearing south until you emerge at a sandy road. In about 500m turn right and then fork immediately right again. In 50m the track swings right and narrows through a jumble of limestone. In a couple of minutes there is a good view north across Bob's Hollow Bay. From this point, scramble down through the limestone escarpment (there is a tiny castaway beach to your right if you are after some R&R) and wander along the base of the cliff to a set of steps. These lead up past a series of **grottoes** (and a spring) to the top of the cliffs (one hour from Redgate Beach car park), the highest of the walk so far.

For the next 3km, the track ambles along the cliff top with great views down onto the coast and ahead to Cape Freycinet. As the cliffs veer briefly inland you are rewarded with the best view of all, straight down onto the white crescent of Contos Beach.

Walk east, turning right at Conto Rd and then quickly left. About 300m on, turn right onto a narrow track, brushing through grass trees to a T-junction (one hour from the grottoes). Turn left and enter **Contos camping ground** (sites $6).

Day 6: Contos Camping Ground to Hamelin Bay
5½–6½ hours, 21.5km

Return to the T-junction just outside the camping ground, and walk straight on (south), descending steeply. Follow the ruler-straight road for 15 minutes, dipping into marri woodland. Pass through a gate and turn left into **Point Rd camping ground** (sites $6). Continue straight on, entering a stand of karri trees and turning right onto Georgette Rd. Climb steadily to intersect with Brozie Rd. Turn left and then right into Davies Rd (signposted throughout as Daves Rd), 30 to 40 minutes from Point Rd camping ground. For the next one to 1½ hours this road will be your guiding line through some of the Capes' most impressive forest: grass trees, banksias, marri and the country's most westerly karri trees, isolated from other areas of karri growth.

Turn right at Trig Rd and ascend through a hollow blanketed in grass trees to the crest of the Leeuwin–Naturaliste Ridge. After re-crossing Georgette Rd and coming to the top

---

ONE-DAY WONDERS

If you haven't the time to commit to a week on the Cape to Cape Track but fancy a glimpse, there are some good sections that can be walked out and back in a day. The following is our pick of the options – each has vehicle access and can be walked. Distances given are one way.

- Yallingup to Wyadup Rd (Day 2, 6.8km) – Pick through the rocky outcrops on Smiths Beach before an extended look at Canal Rocks; a great section for whale watching in spring.
- Willyabrup Cliffs to Gracetown (Day 3, 8.5km) – Check out the climbers' cliffs, then the surfers' breaks before rounding exposed North Point into Gracetown.
- Redgate Beach to Contos Beach (Day 5, 6.5km) – Wander past the grottoes at Bob's Hollow Bay, then climb to cliff-top views – the equal of any along the track.
- Hamelin Bay to Deepdene Beach (Day 7, 9km) – Climb to Foul Bay lighthouse, then discover the wonderful limestone platforms beside Cosy Corner Beach before rounding Cape Hamelin.

of the ridge, an unmarked track to the right leads to Boranup (Trig) Hill (see the Side Trip, below). Walk straight on, turning left at a T-junction and heading south until you intersect with Boranup Rd.

Turn right here, heading west. After the road swings briefly south, take a walking track straight on at the next road bend. Descend towards the coast, turning left when you join a road at a hairpin bend. Follow the road's spiralling course onto spectacular **Boranup Beach** (1½ to two hours from Davies Rd). Soak it in; it is yours for the next 6km and it is not often firm.

About two hours later, at the very end of the beach, climb up the steps before the boat ramp into **Hamelin Bay Eco Holiday Park** (☎ 9758 5540; www.augusta-resorts.com.au/hamelin .html; unpowered/powered sites for 2 $18/22, cabins $70-125). It is the sort of park where you might stand out, not because you are walking but because you don't have a boat. The beauty of the location, however, might just have Yallingup's boastful caravan park trumped. The kiosk stock suggests sauce and vinegar and little else gets eaten here, so carry your own provisions for this night.

SIDE TRIP: BORANUP (TRIG) HILL
15 minutes, 800m return

From atop the ridge the unmarked trail heads north along the crest (stomp around as you walk – it sounds as though there is a cave beneath at one point) before curling back south to a lookout tower atop **Trig Hill**. There is a view across the forested slopes of the ridge and a peep of the ocean, but it is slowly being overgrown. Return on the same path.

Day 7: Hamelin Bay to Cape Leeuwin
7–8 hours, 26.5km

From the boat ramp, climb the wooden steps to the west, which lead up onto White Cliff Point. Just before the **lookout platform** at the tip of the headland, drop away south through sand onto a wild stretch of beach – it is soft enough here that snowshoes could be an asset. As you approach the first lot of rocks the track turns steeply east into the dunes to join a 4WD track. Follow this for 10 minutes, until a walking track peels away left, wandering up and down some steep sand ridges to **Foul Bay lighthouse** (1¼ to 1½ hours from Hamelin Bay), perched

on a hilltop 90m above the sea. From here, there is a good view back to White Cliff Point and Hamelin Island, with its WWII radar station.

Turn right to arc around the lighthouse and follow a gravelly track down to Cosy Corner Rd. Turn right, then left onto a 4WD track in about 100m. Fork right about 100m after the track begins descending, and follow this road to the coast. The road turns south, away from popular Cosy Corner Beach, and crosses a line of **limestone platforms** that have been weathered into a series of pillars and potholes – the potholes can turn into blowholes in heavy seas so care needs to be taken. Peer into them and you will see the ocean coming and going.

At the end of the platforms the track crosses behind the rocky point. Pass through a makeshift car park and back down onto a small beach on the point's northern side. Near the beach's end, turn off into the heath, the track adhering to the edge of the lichen-smeared boulders (and sometimes on them) that form the point of **Cape Hamelin**. Dropping off the boulders, it winds through heath to a small, shelly beach. Cross through the first of the rock outcrops and then take the path back into the heath to avoid the next, larger outcrop. Cross two small beaches, join a 4WD track and veer right onto **Deepdene Beach** (one to 1¼ hours from the lighthouse). This is pretty much the track's final beach, and also its longest – 8km, depending on conditions around the rock platforms ahead – and among the softest. All the beach walking of previous days has been training for this one.

If you are planning to stay at Deepdene camp site (or need water), turn up into the third (and widest) sand blow in the dunes, about 10 minutes along the beach. There is an old vehicle track on the southern side of the blow; the camp site is about five minutes inland.

After about 1½ hours of beachcombing you come to a line of **rock platforms**, similar to those at Cosy Corner Beach. Conditions here fluctuate. Some seasons you can continue along the beach at their base, but if the beach has been washed away (as it regularly is), walk along at the back edge of the platforms, where there is a path of sorts. As the platforms become more stable (and flat), drop down and walk across their tops. Scramble around the rocky point beyond the platforms and continue along the beach – Cape Leeuwin lighthouse looks a lot closer now.

At the beach's end (one hour from the start of the rock platforms), climb up onto more platforms and follow the track through the dunes, paralleling the coast beneath an assortment of **limestone pillars**. Climb above a sandy cove and turn left along a 4WD track (the right turn leads 100m to a lookout). The road climbs sharply inland for five minutes, turning right onto a walking track. Follow this path (constructed in 2005 to move the route closer to the cliffs) for 25 minutes, merging with another track and continuing south. Wander through heavy scrub for about 40 minutes to a lookout (set just off the track to the right) for a view back to Deepdene Beach's southern end.

Descend more steeply now to Skippy Rock Rd, turning left and then immediately right, ducking beneath some overhanging peppermint trees to reach the coast. Walk across the granite slabs, cutting across the point to the small beach at **Quarry Bay**, where you will find a number of seeps and a remarkable set of orange **tufa cliffs**, created by a combination of spring water, algae and bacteria. Go up the wooden steps to find a path heading south from the car park. The track follows the coast, first through long grass and then across granite slabs to a small cove with a water wheel, once used to supply water to lighthouse keepers. From the water wheel car park, take the sealed path and then the road to **Cape Leeuwin lighthouse** (40 minutes from the lookout).

You can purchase an end-to-end walkers' certificate at the lighthouse if you want documented proof of your week.

SOUTH COAST

The south coast defies simple categorisation. From flat, treeless coasts it rises to the forests of Walpole–Nornalup National Park, where you can forget about not being able to see the forest for the trees – in few other places in Australia will you be so overwhelmed by a walk through a forest. Even far from the karri trees of Walpole–Nornalup, 100km away in the Porongurup Range you will find an island of karris, but the main attractions here are wildflowers and granite.

ACCESS TOWN
Albany
☎ 08 / pop 22,400
Set on large King George Sound, Albany is WA's oldest settlement. When the sun comes out, the action moves east to the suburb of Middleton Beach. Within 120km of the Stirling and Porongurup Ranges and Walpole, it is a feasible base for all south-coast walks.

INFORMATION
Albany Map Centre (☎ 9841 1179; 126 York St) A small collection of walking maps.
Albany visitor information centre (☎ 1800 644 088; www.albanytourist.com.au; Proudlove Pde) Beside a

---

THE LONG WALK

If a day of walking out and about around Albany has you tired, consider the experience of the first non-Aboriginal walkers in the area, James Newell and James Manning. In 1835 the cutter *Mountaineer*, with Newell (and his sister Dorothea) aboard, was wrecked in Thistle Cove, inside what is now Cape Le Grand National Park (p302). The survivors sought refuge on Middle Island, in the camp of a sealer-turned-pirate, the notoriously violent John 'Black Jack' Anderson.

Newell and Manning – who had travelled as a passenger on Anderson's boat from Kangaroo Island – were later put ashore by Black Jack near Cape Arid, west of Esperance. They were left without food and given no guns with which to hunt. Albany, the outlier of civilisation, was about 650km away. They began walking. Months later they arrived, supposedly having survived on tree roots and limpets. They were almost too weak to talk, their bodies like skeletons.

As a postscript to the walk, Anderson was charged with theft, an accusation made against him by Manning. Anderson was acquitted on the evidence of Dorothea Newell, who had become Black Jack's mistress.

For a fictionalised account of Newell and Manning's journey, pick up a copy of Sarah Hay's Vogel Award-winning book *Skins*.

WESTERN AUSTRALIA

lean-to that serves as the Bibbulmun Track's southern trail-head, and stocking a *Walking Naturally in Albany* booklet.

CALM (☎ 9842 4500; 120 Albany Hwy) The main contact point for the Stirling Range and Porongurup Range National Parks. It also has a display on each park in the area.

SUPPLIES & EQUIPMENT

For camping or walking supplies, try **Trail-blazers** (☎ 9841 7859; 184 Albany Hwy). Take your supermarket pick from **Coles** (cnr Albany Hwy & Lockyer Ave) or **Woolworths** (Lockyer Ave); they are metres apart.

SLEEPING & EATING

Middleton Beach Holiday Park (☎ 9841 3593; www .holidayalbany.com.au; unpowered sites for 2 $26-31, pow-ered sites for 2 $27-32, cabins $93-200; 🖳) has prime real estate, just a dune from the ocean, and prices to match.

Albany Bayview (☎ 9842 3388; albanyyha@westnet .com.au; 49 Duke St; dm $20, d from $50; 🖳) is a ram-bling and comfortable YHA hostel, 400m from town. There are bikes for hire and a free barbecue on Wednesday nights. Take an upstairs room if you want bay views.

Vancouver House (☎ 9842 1071; www.vancouver housebnb.com.au; 86 Stirling Tce; d without/with bathroom $100/125; 🖳) is a B&B to stay at after, not before, a walk to reacquaint yourself with a few charms and civilities. There is port and chocolates in the lounge each evening, a different breakfast menu every day of the week and bathrobes and a foot spa in each room.

Just a salt shake from the beach, **Norfolk Sands** (☎ 9841 3585; 18 Adelaide Cres, Middleton Beach; s/d incl breakfast $55/80) has tidy, simple rooms furnished in Asian style. There is a common room for self-caterers. The same owner runs **Bay Merchants** (18b Adelaide Cres, Middleton Beach; sandwiches $8-11, breakfast $5-15), a quality café-cum-provedore with fantastically fresh sandwiches.

For a relaxing read and feed, try **Stirling Terrace Bookcafé** (168 Stirling Tce), where the fare includes such items as coconut salad and pan-fried sardines. For more of a splurge, dine next door at **Ristorante Leonardos** (☎ 9841 1732; 164 Stirling Tce; mains $29-32; 🕒 dinner Mon-Sat), where you will find local produce prepared in European style.

GETTING THERE & AWAY

Skywest (☎ 1300 660 088; www.skywest.com.au) flies daily between Albany and Perth ($120, one hour). **Transwa** (☎ 1300 662 205; www.transwa.wa .gov.au) runs a Perth–Albany bus service ($40, six hours) via Mt Barker, and a longer route ($60, eight to nine hours) through Walpole. The fare between Walpole and Albany is $18 (1½ hours).

You can rent a vehicle from **Albany Car Rentals** (☎ 9841 7077; 386 Albany Hwy), **Avis** (☎ 9842 2833; 557 Albany Hwy) or **Budget** (☎ 9841 7799; 360 Albany Hwy). The latter two also have offices at the airport.

BIBBULMUN KARRI & COAST

Duration	4 days
Distance	61.4km
Difficulty	moderate
Start	Walpole (opposite),
Finish	Peaceful Bay (opposite)
Transport	private
Summary	See some of Australia's finest forest and a remote slice of coast as you sample part of the great Bibbulmun Track.

More than any other part of the Bibbulmun Track, it is the section between Walpole and Peaceful Bay that highlights the track's *raison d'être* – to showcase southern WA's forest and coast. Out of Walpole the track heads into forests of tall karri and stout tingle trees, exiting a couple of days later to wander along an isolated and beautiful section of coast.

For most of the walk, you will be in-side the Walpole–Nornalup National Park, established in 1911 and encompassing around 18,100 hectares of forest, heathland and coast. Nornalup is an Aboriginal word for 'place of the tiger snake', and it is pretty fair to assume that you will see a few; give them a wide berth.

The track is marked throughout with yel-low triangles and a black Waugal, or rain-bow serpent, and it is quite feasible to walk it without a tent. The Bibbulmun Track's three-sided shelters – the site of each night's stop – have raised platforms for sleeping. You can also complete the walk in three days by 'double hutting', combining Days 3 and 4, though if you want to rush through this country you should probably question why you are here.

Carry a bit of cash so you can stop in at the Tree Top Walk (p295).

PLANNING
When to Walk
You can't have a great forest without great rain, and Walpole is regularly the wettest place in WA, averaging more than 1000mm annually. If you want to witness Walpole–Nornalup's great show of wildflowers, November is the driest of the spring months. September and October receive around 100mm.

Maps & Books
Map 7 *Walpole* of CALM's 1:50,000 *Dibbulmun Track* series covers the route in topographic detail, with the helpful addition of elevation profiles and distance tables. The pocket-sized *A Guide to the Bibbulmun Track: Southern Half* is a handy reference that won't take up much room in your backpack.

The Bibbulmun Track has become something of a publishing industry, and you can prepare for (or remember) your walk by purchasing the *Bibbulmun Track on the South Coast* CD-ROM or the instructional *Getting on Track* video or DVD, intended to help walkers gear up for a Bibb Track epic. All of these items are available online at the **NatureBase Bookshop** (www.naturebase.net).

Look out for *In Praise of a National Park* by Lee and Geoff Fernie, a comprehensive rundown on the history of the national park.

Information Sources
Details of track conditions or section closures along the Bibbulmun Track are available on the **CALM website** (www.calm.wa.gov.au/tourism/bib_news) – be sure to check this page before you head out. The Bibbulmun Track Foundation (p276) is an excellent source of track information. Park information is available at CALM in Walpole (below).

Permits & Regulations
Camp fires are not permitted in Walpole–Nornalup National Park, so carry a fuel stove.

NEAREST TOWNS
Walpole
☎ 08 / pop 400
Surrounded entirely by Walpole–Nornalup National Park, Walpole is so inextricably linked to the large forests that it is almost

deserving of its own scientific name. The helpful **visitor information centre** (☎ 9840 1111; Pioneer Cottage, South Coast Hwy) sells Bibbulmun Track maps and guides, while **CALM** (☎ 9840 1027) has an office at the western end of town.

SLEEPING & EATING
Coalmine Beach Holiday Park (☎ 1800 670 026; www .coalminebeach.com.au; Coalmine Beach Rd; unpowered/powered sites for 2 $21/24, cabins $65-100; 🖳) has a great setting on the shore of Nornalup Inlet. There is a three-night minimum stay for cabins during school holidays and Easter. You walk through the park on Day 1, so you could consider starting here.

Tingle All Over (☎ 9840 1041; tingleallover2000 @yahoo.com.au; 61 Nockolds St; dm from $20, s/d $36/57; 🖳) is a basic hostel presented with a touch of care. Prepare yourself for the psychedelic carpets; they are bright enough to keep you awake at night.

The **Tree Top Walk Motel** (☎ 1800 420 777; www .treetopwalkmotel.com.au; Nockolds St; d $80-119; ❄ 🖳) has an opportunist name – the Tree Top Walk is about 20km away – but also large, neat rooms and Walpole's only genuine **restaurant** (mains $23-28; ☽ dinner).

In the Ampol service station, **Pioneer Store** (Nockolds St) is the best of Walpole's two supermarkets, with a decent range of supplies.

Eagle Rock Café (Nockolds St; mains $11-17) caters for walking appetites with its Kitchen Sink burger. You will just about need rope and karabiners to work your way around it.

GETTING THERE & AWAY
Walpole is on the South Coast Hwy, 120km south of Manjimup and 67km west of Denmark. The town is serviced by the daily **Transwa** (☎ 1300 662 205; www.transwa.wa.gov.au) bus between Perth ($54, 7½ hours) and Albany ($18, 1½ hours).

Peaceful Bay
☎ 08
In school holidays this shack town defies its name but at other times, with its beautiful bay almost enclosed by rocks, it suits it.

Burrowed into the peppermint trees, **Peaceful Bay Caravan Park** (☎ 9840 8060; www.valley ofthegiants.com.au/pbcaravanpark; unpowered/powered sites for 2 $10/12, on-site van per person $15) is basic but grassed and shady, with special prices (as above) for Bibb Track walkers. You can even roll out your sleeping mat inside a gypsy wagon ($15).

Peaceful Bay Chalets (☎ 9840 8169; www.valley ofthegiants.com.au/peacefulbaychalets; Peppermint Way; per person $20) is about 1km off the track and also has special walker rates (also as above). Whether you end up in the ultra-basic room or the party-sized house is at the discretion of the manager, though expect the former. There is free laundry to help you scrub up a bit.

The Peaceful Bay store is in the caravan park office. It has a small range of supplies and does basic takeaways; fish 'n' chips require 1½ hour's notice.

There is no public transport to Peaceful Bay but the Transwa Perth–Albany service stops at Bow Bridge, 8km away on the highway. If you are staying at the chalets, the manager may drive you out to Bow Bridge.

GETTING TO/FROM THE WALK

Walpole Taxi & Tours (☎ 08-9840 1041), run by the owners of Tingle All Over, operates a set-fare service between Walpole and Peaceful Bay ($45).

THE WALK
Day 1: Walpole to Frankland River Camp Site
4½–5 hours, 17.4km

From the highway at the western end of Walpole, walk south along Boronia St. After 300m turn right down a gravel track and then left onto the signposted Bibbulmun Track. Following the shore of **Walpole Inlet** you pass a jetty and, five minutes on, the track turns away from the inlet, coming to a Y-junction. Turn right, walking through bracken and kangaroo paw flowers for five minutes to reach a junction with a sandy track. Turn right and immediately right again, joining the Coalmine Beach Heritage Trail. Rounding Walpole Inlet, the track passes through heathland that's a rainbow of colour in spring. Cross Collier Creek on a boardwalk to enter Walpole–Nornalup National Park, and go through thick melaleuca, crossing sealed Knoll Dr to enter a car park. After checking out **Nornalup Inlet** straight ahead, turn left onto the sealed path, heading up into Coalmine Beach Holiday Park (p291), just over an hour from Walpole.

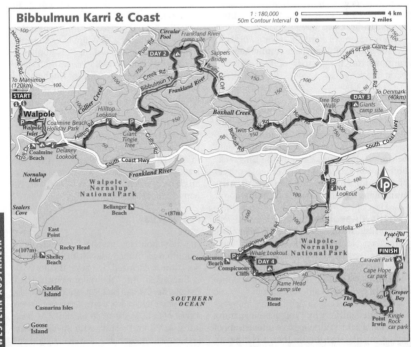

Bibbulmun Karri & Coast

BIBBULMUN TRACK

In all regards the Bibbulmun Track (commonly known as the Bibb Track) is one of the great long-distance walks in the country. The scenery is fantastic and varied, the walking can be as easy or as difficult as you like, and its walking infrastructure is the benchmark for all Australian trails.

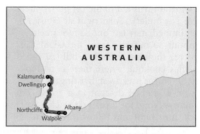

The 964km route begins in Kalamunda, on Perth's eastern fringe, and extends to Albany. Named after an Aboriginal people who walked long distances for ceremonial gatherings, it was conceived as an idea in the 1970s and completed in 1998. Using existing 4WD tracks and purpose-built walking trails, it has 48 camp sites, situated at roughly 20km intervals. Each site has a three-sided shelter with sleeping platforms, a picnic table, tent sites, toilets and a water tank. All facilities are free of charge.

Track signage is exceptional, with a yellow marker showing the Waugal, or rainbow serpent, every 200m (on average). Any temporary changes to the track are shown with white Waugal markers.

From Kalamunda, the route goes for around 200km through varied forests and over granite peaks to Dwellingup. There follows 50km through the forested Murray River valley, then karri and jarrah forests continue southwards for more than 350km to near Northcliffe. Islands of forest, rivers and plains (prone to flooding between July and November) lead down to the coast at Mandalay Beach and on to Walpole (another 130km). The track then heads up through tingle forest and back to the coast at Conspicuous Beach for the final 160km section to Albany.

The track passes through several small towns including Dwellingup, Pemberton, Northcliffe and Walpole, all useful for supplies and accommodation. One coastal inlet is crossed by boat, another by canoe and two must be waded.

Most people take around 55 to 60 days to walk the track in its entirety, though during the spring of 2005 a group walked it in less than 17 days (about 55km a day).

The track is managed by **CALM** (☎ 08-9334 0265; www.naturebase.net/tourism/bibbulmun_splash.html) with a lot of help from the **Bibbulmun Track Foundation** (☎ 08-9481 0551; www.bibbulmuntrack .org.au), a nonprofit community organisation. Both websites are a good starting point for any Bibb Tack wannabes.

CALM has published eight 1:50,000 topographical maps of the track and two superb pocket guides for the northern and southern sections, with succinct track notes and practical background information. These are available at CALM offices, visitor centres and CALM's online **NatureBase Bookshop** (www.naturebase.net).

About 200m beyond the caravan park (and ignoring a few vehicle turnouts) join a foot track heading away to the right, walking between the road and the inlet. Passing **Delaney Lookout**, with views along the inlet cliffs, you come to an unmarked junction. Turn right and say hello to the faster world as you cross the South Coast Hwy. Say hello also to the forest as you step from coastal heath into some of Australia's finest tall timber.

The track begins a gentle climb, swinging right and levelling out before turning left again and returning to the business of climbing. About 40 minutes from the road the track passes below **Hilltop Lookout**; wander up the few steps for a keyhole look at the coastal headlands and the eastern edge of Nornalup Inlet.

The track now takes in a fantastic bit of forest, passing by some impressive tingle trees, their branches like the waving arms of an octopus, and the taller, smoother karris. You will also see plenty of karri oaks. Thirty minutes from the lookout you come to a junction with a wide track. Take the right arm of the track, which leads straight on to a boardwalk around the **Giant Tingle Tree**, its hollowed trunk so wide that visitors used to park their cars inside it. Follow the hard-rolled track out, continuing straight on when it turns left to the car park (where there is a toilet). Turn right at Gully Rd, then immediately left onto a foot track.

About 30 minutes from the Giant Tingle Tree the track rounds a hill (so-called Douglas Lookout, where there is no lookout) and turns back west, twisting and turning on a gradual descent to a creek. Ten minutes beyond the creek you reach a 4WD track, turn right and follow it for 30 to 40 minutes. Keep a watch as you descend for glimpses of the Frankland River to your right. At the hairpin bend across a stream, take the foot track straight on and up to Creek Rd. Cross straight over and wander on to the Frankland River camp site, 20 minutes ahead. A possum with Rambo tendencies has staked a claim on the camp site and has been known to chew through backpacks to get at food. Use the supplied food box (and stick a rock on top of it).

Day 2: Frankland River Camp Site to Giants Camp Site
3½–4 hours, 13.9km

The track heads east from the hut, first along the river and then around a spur. Just beyond a steep flight of steps, turn right along a 4WD track, then quickly left. The track wanders up and down and arrives at Sappers Bridge across the **Frankland River** (45 minutes from camp). Cross it and turn right along Brainy Cut Off, climbing on this road for 10 minutes through karri and jarrah forest.

Turn right onto a walking track, heading through a magnificent stand of jarrah. Cross a creek, then a 4WD track and climb to unsealed Boxhall Rd (30 to 40 minutes from Sappers Bridge). Continue straight on, crossing the separate arms of Boxhall Creek. After the third bridge begin a steady climb, crossing Twin Creek Rd. There are a couple of potentially boggy creek crossings before you cross a 4WD track and descend to another slushy creek. A few minutes on, the wide track kinks right; take instead the unmarked path straight on. Tingle trees soon begin to reappear.

Turn right along unsealed Howe Rd and immediately left onto a narrow path. About 1km of overgrown track on, cross the sealed road and ascend to also cross a gravel road.

Veer left slightly to pick up the path into the **Tree Top Walk** (adult/child $6/2.50) car park, five minutes on. If you want to check out this world-class attraction (see opposite), leave your pack on the bench in view of the ticket office; staff will keep an eye on it for you.

From the Tree Top Walk entrance, continue east on the sealed path, turning left down steps to a boardwalk. Cut straight across a 4WD track, climbing steadily to a sharp left bend. Soon you begin the descent to Giants camp site (30 minutes from the Tree Top Walk), deep among tingle, karri and marri trees.

Day 3: Giants Camp Site to Rame Head Camp Site
4½–5 hours, 17.7km

As you begin for the highway this morning, you will pass some of the finest tingle trees of the walk.

Head east along a 4WD track, turning right after 200m. It's a gentle climb before you turn right then immediately left at the second 4WD track. Brush through the swordgrass, descending to cross the South Coast Hwy (45 minutes from camp).

Fifty metres beyond the highway, turn right along the formation of the former Denmark–Nornalup railway line. Almost immediately, you leave the forest, entering scrubby, sandy coastal country dominated by tea-trees and low gums. Cross a sandy vehicle track and then a swamp, coming to a wall of scrub about 20 minutes from the highway. Turn left here, crossing a creek and keeping to the right of a barbed-wire fence to re-enter the forest for a last look at a few tingle and karri trees. Climb on through tea-trees and grass trees, crossing one disused 4WD track, then veering right onto another. Swing right again after 50m to pass below **Nut Lookout**, with views east to West Cape Howe. The best views are just beyond the lookout, where the heath thins.

The track descends through mixed woodland and a skeletal, fire-burnt section of forest, crossing a sandy vehicle track and promptly joining another, turning right and following it as it reverts to a narrow track. Cross Nut Rd, continuing down through wildflower-peppered heath, then turning left and descending to unsealed Ficifolia Rd. This road is named after the red flowering gum (*Eucalyptus ficifolia*) you have been walking past. A rare find in the bush, they are a common and recognisable garden plant, especially when flowering between January and March.

Turn right and follow Ficifolia Rd for 400m, leaving it along a walking track to the left (one hour from Nut Lookout). This leads through heathland for about 600m before turning right. The sandy track wanders up and down through woodland. About 2km on, a steep descent leads to the edge of a small lake. From the swampy lake fringe, climb to a long sandy ridge. Turn left at the T-junction (Conspicuous Beach car park is to the right). At the next junction you can diverge left to a **whale-watching platform**, with a fine view of the beach – in spring you might see southern right and humpback whales. After this, follow the track to the right, go down some steps and along a boardwalk. Cross or bypass the small stream (depending on its depth) as you step onto **Conspicuous Beach** (one hour from Ficifolia Rd).

Turn left along the beach towards **Conspicuous Cliffs** and grind through soft sand for about 200m (until just past the whale-watching platform above). The track turns up into the dunes before dropping into a small swamp. Cut across the swamp below the sand blow and begin a circuitous ascent to the top of Conspicuous Cliffs. A fire in 2004 stripped most of the bush here but the wildflowers have returned with added intensity. About 30 minutes from the beach you reach a **high point** with magnificent views east and west. Good views of the rugged west side of limestone Rame Head also unfold as you continue – at about the same point the hut at Rame Head camp site comes into view. Five minutes on, turn left at a track junction to reach the hut, which has one of the best positions on the entire Bibbulmun Track, staring east along the coast.

Day 4: Rame Head Camp Site to Peaceful Bay
2¾–3¾ hours, 12.4km
From the hut toilet follow the wheel tracks northeast through heath and, seasonally, a burst of flowers. After 45 minutes cross a 4WD track and continue on the narrow walking trail, climbing along the ridge of a set of compacted dunes before dropping back down beside the 4WD track. The track soon begins veering back towards the coast, passing a phytophthora station and squelching through a swamp to reach a disused vehicle track. Turn right to meet a 4WD track, where you turn right and immediately left onto a walking trail, climbing through dunes to the beautiful beach at the **Gap** (1½ to two hours from Rame Head).

FOREST GIANTS
In WA's southwest, karri, tingle and jarrah trees are like a holy arboreal trinity. Found nowhere else in the world, they rule these forests with their height (karri) and their bulk (tingles). Karri can grow to 90m, making it one of the tallest trees in the world. It has a slender white trunk, turning pinkish in autumn, soaring 30m straight to the lowest branches.

There are three types of tingle tree – red, yellow and Rate's – and they occur only across a 6000-hectare area in Walpole–Nornalup National Park, between Deep River and Bow River. They are the only eucalyptus with buttressed trunks, and red tingles – the largest of the trees – can be as large as 16m around. Bushfires can burn through the heart of the trees, commonly leaving a huge hollow. The tree survives because its growth is concentrated in the outer layers of the trunk. Yellow and Rate's tingles can be difficult to distinguish from young red tingles.

Less spectacular, but more prevalent, is the jarrah, which has grooved, reddish-brown to grey bark. Among all these trees, you will also develop a fondness for the karri oak, with its cork-like wood and she-oak–like branchlets.

In the suitably named Valley of the Giants there is the opportunity to walk not only past some of these giants, but also atop them. The Tree Top Walk is one of WA's major tourist stops. Its centrepiece is an aerial walkway, 600m long and rising to 40m from the ground, offering a possum-like perspective on both tingles and karris. Also here is the Ancient Empire Walk, a 400m-long path through some of the most impressive tingles in the land. You will have seen lots of tingle trees before you get here, but none as furrowed and grumpy-looking as 'grandmother', a tree 12m around, 400 years old and bumpier than a desert track.

WESTERN AUSTRALIA

> **WARNING**
>
> Near Kingie Rock car park grows a bush with shiny green leaves called blister bush. For some people, contact with the bush can cause blisters, so steer clear.

At the beach's end follow the track through the scrub, meeting a 4WD track that turns down onto the rocks. Follow the smoothest line across the rocks to join a track that edges behind the rock platforms to a small **beach**. Cross this and turn inland, climbing several dunes en route to Castle Rock car park. Climb on to reach a trig point atop **Point Irwin** (30 to 40 minutes from the Gap) and an edge-of-the-world view of the Southern Ocean. West, you will see Rame Head and the distant Point Nuyts; east, the now-familiar West Cape Howe.

Rounding Point Irwin you turn north, passing through Kingie Rock car park – if you are lucky you might spot fur seals on the rocks below. The path continues around and onto the beach at **Groper Bay**. Cross the rocks at the beach's northern end to a small beach cut off from the sea by rocks. Turn left and then right on vehicle tracks at this beach's end to another small beach. Cross the rocks and one more longer beach before scampering over the dunes to the **Peaceful Bay** beach. About 200m along the sand a set of stairs leads up into the town (45 minutes to one hour from Point Irwin).

NANCY PEAK & DEVIL'S SLIDE

Duration	2½–3 hours
Distance	7km
Difficulty	easy–moderate
Start/Finish	Tree in the Rock picnic area
Nearest Town	Porongurup (right)
Transport	private

Summary Climb through unexpected slopes of karri forest to open granite domes and views of the Stirling Range and coast – the granite slabs are their own reward.

With the Stirling Range, the Porongurups are the only other true mountain range in southern WA. From a distance, they look like a standard run of hills but their beauty is in the detail. Just 12km long, and rising to 670m, they have a skin of granite and the most easterly karri trees in the country. Unusual rock formations are the range's party piece.

The range is protected by the 2500-hectare Porongurup National Park and has two main walking areas: Castle Rock and a selection of tracks around Nancy Peak and the Devil's Slide. The walk described here combines the trails in the latter area for an appealing half-day walk.

If none of that is enough to draw you here, there's the little matter of ending your walking day with a drop of red from the wineries at the foot of the range.

ENVIRONMENT

The Porongurups' bedrock is 1100-million-year-old granite, much of which is in full view across the granite domes that characterise the range. A second feature is the presence of a virtual island of karri trees, 100km east of the main areas of karri forest. The Porongurups receive less rainfall than other karri areas but the trees are fed by the extra runoff from the granite domes.

There are around 750 plant species along the range – most below the line where the karris take over the forest – including more than 70 orchids. Spring colour is dominated by wattles and hoveas.

PLANNING
Maps

CALM's 1:50,000 topographic map *Mt Barker & Porongurup* covers the walk.

Permits & Regulations

Camping is not permitted in the park.

NEAREST TOWN
Porongurup

☎ 08

Surrounded by both wilderness and wineries, there is a lot to like about tiny Porongurup, even if there isn't much here. The **Porongurup Range Tourist Park** (☎ 9853 1057; Porongurup Rd; unpowered/powered sites for 2 $18/20, cabins $55; 🖳) is large, attractive and grassy, with new owners planning to add a few motel-style units.

Porongurup Village Inn (☎ 9853 1110; www.porongurupinn.com.au; Porongurup Rd; s/d with shared bathroom $25/50, unit $80; 🖳) is attached to the general store and was refurbished in 2005. There is an in-house naturopath, and you are welcome to pick and cook your veggies from the garden. The store **tearooms** (mains $12-15) will prepare evening meals for guests if requested.

Next door, **Bolganup Homestead** (☎ 9853 1049/1102; www.bolganup.com.au; Porongurup Rd; d $95) has homestead and cottage accommodation on a 500-acre property abutting the national park. You can walk from the homestead across to the range, or stroll purpose-built kangaroo and wildflower walks.

If your timing is right, head 5km west out of town to perhaps Australia's most isolated Thai restaurant, **Maleeya's Thai Café** (☎ 9853 1123; 1376 Porongurup Rd; ☺ lunch & dinner Fri-Sun), which gets rave reviews. Otherwise, try the restaurant at **Karribank Country Retreat** (☎ 9853 1022, Porongurup Rd; mains $21 28; ☺ breakfast, lunch & dinner) for fine food with a view.

There is no public transport to Porongurup, but the Porongurup Village Inn can arrange guest pick-ups in Albany or Mt Barker with notice.

GETTING TO/FROM THE WALK

From Porongurup, take Bolganup Rd (opposite the caravan park) for 3km to its end at the Tree in the Rock picnic area.

THE WALK

Head northeast on the signposted Nancy Peak Circuit, crossing over a 4WD track to **Tree in the Rock**, where a karri tree grows out of a crevice in a large granite outcrop. Begin climbing through tall karri forest. As you

swing back west after 20 minutes, look up and you will see the sort of granite dome that characterises the range. A few minutes on, a short side track leads away left to the top of this **dome** for views across to the Devil's Slide, Hayward Peak and north to the jagged teeth of the Stirling Range.

Return to the main trail, which follows the ridge west. Climb onto the next granite slab, following the trodden line north through the lichen. Veer west again as you step onto a second slab to re-enter the bush. Clean your boots at the phytophthora station and climb another slab to the summit of **Hayward Peak**, with views north and south.

Continue along the ridge, rising to **Nancy Peak** (named after a cow), one hour from the car park. There are excellent views along the climb (especially of Twin Peaks, east along the ridge), though the summit is covered in thick, view-stealing scrub. Just beyond the summit you reach another slab of granite with an almost perfectly round boulder balanced atop it, and your best views yet of the ominous sheets of granite that form the Devil's Slide.

Descend west along the ridge to Morgan's View – you will have had better views along the ridge. A few minutes beyond Morgan's View, the track swings north, dropping off the ridge and descending more steeply into the simply named Pass. Cross straight over the Wansborough Walk Trail and begin up the opposite slope. Follow the ill-defined, trodden line through the lichen on the granite –

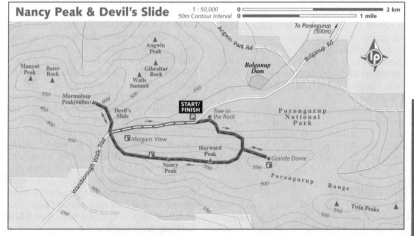

you are now on the **Devil's Slide** – heading up to a bridge that avoids a particularly slippery section of rock.

From the bridge the route becomes more of a track, climbing between the 'slides' of rock. In a few minutes you come to a steep bit of rock. The track appears to head onto the rock, but look to your left instead and you will see a white-topped stake. Follow this up through the scrub. Climb through two sets of steps to the granite boulders that form the summit of Marmabup Peak. Edge left around their base until the track climbs onto one of the flatter boulders, and follow the painted arrows up and around the rock to reach a break in the boulders. Climb through this and you pop out onto the summit of **Marmabup Peak** (660m), the highest point in the range (one hour from Nancy Peak). As well as the familiar wider view, you will also be looking down onto a host of granite domes.

Return to the Wansborough Walk Trail, turning left and descending through ever-more-impressive karri forest to reach the picnic area in 20 to 30 minutes.

STIRLING RANGE NATIONAL PARK

The Stirling Range is like a gift to mountain-starved WA. The only significant mountain chain in the state's south, you expect it to be worn down to a stub but it stands remarkably resilient. Stretching 65km east-to-west, the most striking feature of the range is the sharpness of its main ridge.

The national park was WA's third, established in 1913, though walking tracks weren't constructed until the 1960s. Today, it is inarguably the best mountain region for walkers in WA.

Phytophthora (see p47) is a problem in the park, and CALM has introduced strict control measures to try to limit its spread. Special protection areas, including the area around Yungermere Peak and a tract south of Stirling Range Dr, are out of bounds.

ENVIRONMENT

The range consists of tough sandstone, quartzite and slate, rising steeply from the surrounding plains up to 300m in the west

and 850m in the east. More than 1500 plant species have been recorded along the range, said to be more than the number of species in the UK. Of these, around 1100 are flowering plants, including about 80 endemic to the range. Woodlands of jarrah, marri and other eucalyptuses are widespread. The range is famed for its wildflowers, of which mountain bells, or Darwinias, are its trademark (see p275).

Most of the 35 species of mammal in the park are shyly nocturnal, though there is a chance you will see western grey kangaroos and western brush wallabies. Of the numerous species of bird, the smaller, colourful honeyeaters, wrens and robins are usually the most common.

PLANNING
When to Walk

Spring is prime time in the Stirling Range, with September and October the most profuse wildflower months. If you arrive late in the season and find few flowers near the trailheads, don't despair. From about November through January, the higher slopes are more likely to support wildflowers.

What to Bring

Even if the plains, foothills and lower peaks are bathed in sunshine, the summit of Bluff Knoll can be windy or shrouded in mist, and this mist and cloud can drop down with little warning. Bring your protective clothing.

Maps & Books

CALM's 1:50,000 map *Chester Pass & Ellen Peak* covers both walks in this section, though they look more like an architect's plans than a traditional topo. To venture further afield than the walks mentioned here, consider picking up the two-book series *Mountain Walks in the Stirling Range* by AT Morphet. They are usually available at Stirling Range Retreat (opposite).

CALM's *Mountains of Mystery* is the definitive natural history guide to the range, and includes chapters on plants, animals, walks and the human history of the area. Also published by CALM, *Wildflowers of the Stirling Range* will transform the pretty colours into names. Buy both ahead of your visit at CALM's **NatureBase Bookshop** (www.naturebase.net).

Information Sources

There is a ranger station at Moingup Spring (p300). There is also an information shelter as you turn onto Bluff Knoll Rd from Chester Pass Rd.

Park Fees & Regulations

Entry to the national park costs $9 per car (or $3 per motorcycle). Camping in the park is allowed only at Moingup Spring (p300).

ACCESS TOWN

See Albany (p289).

BLUFF KNOLL

Duration	2½–3 hours
Distance	6.2km
Difficulty	moderate
Start/Finish	Bluff Knoll car park
Nearest Town	Porongurup (p296)
Transport	shuttle

Summary Skirt high cliffs and thread through a myriad of wildflowers to scale the highest peak in southern Western Australia.

From its trailhead, Bluff Knoll's sheer sandstone escarpment looks unassailable but apart from a bit of sustained climbing, southern WA's highest mountain (1095m) offers a straightforward ascent. A clearly defined track leads up through a wide, well-hidden break in the cliffs to the summit plateau.

Though the walking is relatively straightforward, this climb should not be underestimated, for you must ascend around 640m into notoriously enigmatic weather. Regularly, there is a scarf of cloud draped over Bluff Knoll's shoulders, and this is the only place in WA that sees any real snow, even if only occasionally (up to 5cm has been recorded).

The mountain's Aboriginal name is Bular Miali, meaning 'many eyes', a reference to the many slits in the imposing escarpment. During spring and early summer, the track is a veritable avenue of wildflowers; it would be worth carrying a field guide so you can pick your sundews from your mountain bells.

NEAREST TOWN & FACILITIES

See Porongurup (p296).

Stirling Range Retreat

At the northern edge of the national park, with a great bush setting and eco-credentials, **Stirling Range Retreat** (☎ 08-9827 9229; www.stirling range.com.au; Chester Pass Rd; unpowered/powered sites for 2 $20/26, dm $20, cabins $59-120; 🖳 🖳) peers out onto Toll Peak and Mt Trio. It is not serviced by public transport but the hop-on hop-off Easyrider Backpacker Tours (p376) stops at the Retreat.

Bluff Knoll Cafe (mains $16-27; ☺ 8am-9pm), 200m south of the Stirling Range Retreat, cooks up mountain-sized serves of pub-style fare.

GETTING TO/FROM THE WALK

Around 200m south of the Stirling Range Retreat entrance (12km north of Moingup Spring), turn onto the signposted Bluff Knoll Rd. The car park is 8km along this sealed road. Stirling Range Retreat (above) runs a shuttle service to the trailhead ($15).

THE WALK

Start from the northern side of the car park, following the sealed path across to a rounded spur, where the climb really begins. Follow the crest of the spur east to reach a **creek** that plummets straight off the cliffs, bringing boulders like glacial erratics with it. Climb beside the creek for a couple of minutes before the track swings back southwest, cutting across the mountain to find a break in the cliffs in the gap between Bluff Knoll and Coyanarup Peak. Here, the

Bluff Knoll

1 : 50,000

50m Contour Interval

0 — 1 km
0 — 0.5 mile

To Stirling Range Retreat (8km)

Bluff Knoll Rd

START/FINISH

Stirling Range National Park

Bluff Knoll (1095m)

Coyanarup Peak (1042m)

woodland gives way to heathland, dotted with grass trees.

The track doubles back, ascending the summit ridge a few metres in from the line of the cliffs. As you skirt a rocky outcrop, a tiny side track to the left rewards you with **views** across a chain of lakes to the south – the Porongurup Range is just visible behind Coyanarup Peak. Bluff Knoll's **summit** is around 10 minutes further on, offering 360-degree views highlighted by lumpy Ellen Peak, and Toolbrunup Peak to the west. Retrace your steps to the car park.

TOOLBRUNUP PEAK

Duration	2½–3 hours
Distance	4km
Difficulty	moderate–demanding
Start/Finish	Toolbrunup car park
Nearest Town	Porongurup (p296)
Transport	shuttle

Summary A steep, rocky ascent with some scrambling to a superb view from the Stirling Range's second-highest summit.

Conceding a mere 43m in height to Bluff Knoll, Toolbrunup Peak offers a shorter but rather more gymnastic climb. If you are wanting something challenging while you are in the Stirlings, this sharp-tipped peak should be your first choice. You ascend about the same height as on Bluff Knoll – 600m – but in 2km instead of 3km, and you will need to be confident and agile to negotiate your way up (and especially down) the scree-choked gully at the heart of the climb. More so than on Bluff Knoll, you will feel that you are at the heart of the range as you stand atop Toolbrunup Peak. Watch as you climb for ripple marks on sandstone boulders – evidence that the rocks here once lay beneath an ancient sea.

NEAREST TOWN & FACILITIES

See Porongurup (p296).

Moingup Spring Camp Site

Immediately south of the Toolbrunup Rd turn-off, **Moingup Spring camp site** (per person $5) is on the grassy bank of Moingup Spring, with glimpses through the gum trees of Toolbrunup Peak. It has flush toilets and water tanks.

GETTING TO/FROM THE WALK

Access from Chester Pass Rd is along the signposted Toolbrunup Rd, 12km south of Stirling Range Retreat or 200m north of Moingup Spring camp site. The car park is at the end of the 4km-long gravel road. Stirling Range Retreat (p299) operates a shuttle service to the trailhead ($26).

THE WALK

The narrow track heads out through marri woodland and, seasonally, a colourful carpet of wildflowers. In 10 minutes it comes to a fairly deep gully and steepens to reach a scree drift. From here it gets serious about climbing. The forest becomes more open, giving way to thicket, until it reaches the foot of a long run of bouldery scree. The way up is clear enough, with yellow-topped stakes helping to show the route. The track makes a short, flattish chicane to the right, then follows the base of the cliffs steeply up to the main ridge (one to 1¼ hours from the start). Straight ahead are views of the western tail of the range, where the peaks look more like islands than a connected range. Turn right, scrambling through a narrow defile, along a wide ledge and then left for a final scramble up to the **summit**, with its comfortably flat rock slabs. The view stretches the length of the range, with the Porongurups away to the south.

Be prepared for a slow return to the car park, as you will need to step carefully on the descent through the scree.

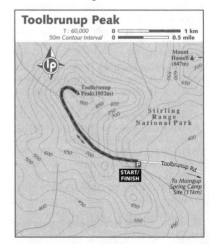

Toolbrunup Peak
1 : 60,000   0 ————— 1 km
50m Contour Interval   0 ————— 0.5 mile

STIRLING STROLLS

A good selection of the peaks in the Stirling Range can be reached on day walks. Bag the following, and you will feel like something of a Stirling specialist.

Mt Hassell (847m)

This thumb-like nib of rock looks like Toolbrunup Peak in miniature. This 2km walk begins on Stirling Range Dr, 4km west of Chester Pass Rd, and ends with a steep scramble up the summit dome.

Mt Trio (856m)

Offering the best views onto Toolbrunup Peak (climb in the morning for the best light), Mt Trio's name refers to its three separate summits, the westernmost being the highest. From the trailhead on Mt Trio Rd, it is a 500m climb to the summit. This 2km walk is good for viewing mountain bells.

Talyuberlup Peak (783m)

With a name that sounds like it has been gargled, Talyuberlup Peak is topped with rock spires, and the ascent requires some scrambling over rock ledges. The 2km walk begins on Stirling Range Dr, 21km from Chester Pass Rd.

Mt Magog (856m)

At 7km, this is a longer outing, close to Talyuberlup, climbing to Mt Magog's double summit. The overgrown trail begins at Mt Magog picnic area beside a short circuit road off Stirling Range Dr, about 27km west of Chester Pass Rd.

Ellen Peak (1012m)

The easternmost peak in the range, and offering the most difficult ascent, climbing 900m on a vague track to shapely Ellen Peak. Proficiency in navigation and route finding is crucial. The 22km walk begins from Gnowellen Rd, about 29km from Chester Pass Rd.

The major overnight outing in the park is along the Stirling Ridge. For details on this challenging walk, see below.

MORE WALKS

PERTH REGION
Coastal Plain Walking Trail

A good way to see some of the sand plains around Perth is to take this 55km trail between Yanchep National Park and Melaleuca Conservation Park.

Wandering through heath and wattle scrub, it makes for a relatively flat three-day walk. By camping at Ridges and Moitch camp sites, you have comfortable days of 16km, 20km and 10km.

CALM's 1:50,000 topographic maps *Yanchep* and *Muchea* cover the length of the track. Detailed track information is available from the rangers at **Yanchep National Park** (☎ 08-9561 1004).

Eagle's View Walk Trail

This 15km trail through John Forrest National Park (WA's first national park) was created by the Perth Bushwalkers Club in the mid-1990s. It loops around a northern section of the park, passing National Park and Hovea Falls and offering a mix of valley and ridge walking. It also has good views across Perth. The *Eagle's View Walk Trail* brochure, available at the registration point beside the trailhead, has a contour map sufficient for the walk.

STIRLING RANGE NATIONAL PARK
Stirling Ridge Walk

Often called the only alpine walk in WA, the Stirling Ridge connects Ellen Peak to Bluff Knoll and is one of the more demanding walks in the state. Though only 19km separates the two peaks you can expect it to take three days, with plenty of scrambling, steep climbs and descents, and potentially tricky route finding through thick bush – there is no marked track and the route is easy to lose. Nights are spent bivouacking in sheltered caves. This is a linear trail, and you will either need two vehicles or transport can be arranged through Stirling Range Retreat (p299).

Walkers must register with the **park ranger** (☎ 08-9827 9230). The 1:50,000 topographic map *Chester Pass & Ellen Peak* map covers the ridge.

TORNDIRRUP NATIONAL PARK
Bald Head

Information on the walk can be obtained from the CALM office (p290) in Albany. This small, popular park protects most of the rugged headland of Flinders Peninsula, 10km south of Albany. The park has some fantastic rock features and is worth general exploration, but for walkers the main attraction is Bald Head, the eastern point of the peninsula. This 10km return walk heads across Isthmus Hill and Limestone Head to Bald Head; you return along the same route. A fire burnt the peninsula in 2003 but it has recovered well.

A map is scarcely necessary but the NAT-MAP 1:100,000 topographic maps *Albany* and *Mt Barker* are useful for identifying the many features you will see as you walk. There is a caravan park on Frenchman Bay, near the trailhead.

CAPE LE GRAND NATIONAL PARK

Discover some of Australia's best beaches as you wander the 15km coastal trail through this park, 50km from Esperance. The trail connects Le Grand Beach to Rossiter Bay, passing through Hellfire Bay, Thistle Cove and Lucky Bay along the way. For an aerial perspective, climb to Frenchman Peak, with its granite summit undercut by a cave. For information on the park and walk, contact the Esperance office of **CALM** (☎ 08-9071 3733; 92 Dempster St). NATMAP's 1:100,000 topographic map *Merivale* covers most of the park. There are camping grounds at Lucky Bay and Le Grand Beach. Esperance can be reached from Perth by air or road, though you will need your own transport to reach the park.

NORTH OF PERTH
Kalbarri National Park

North of Geraldton, Kalbarri National Park protects a section of cliff-lined coast and a gorge carved by the Murchison River. Experienced and hardy walkers can follow the river for 38km – about four days – between Ross Graham Lookout and the Loop. There are no tracks and you will need to cross the river numerous times, but you will be rewarded with great viewpoints at Hawks Head and Z-Bend. The Murchison is brackish so search out seeps in the gorge walls for your drinking water. Walkers must register with the **park rangers** (☎ 08-9937 1140). NAT-MAP's 1:100,000 topographic map *Kalbarri* covers the area. The town of Kalbarri makes an excellent base, and can be reached from Perth by bus.

Mt Augustus

Despite popular perception, Uluru is not the world's largest rock, or even Australia's largest – Mt Augustus, or Burringurrah, in WA's Gascoyne region holds that honour. Twice the size of Uluru, it looks less dramatic because of partial vegetation cover but is still one for the walking scrapbook. The track to the summit begins at Beedoboondu (where you will find Aboriginal engravings) and climbs over 6km to the 1106m rock summit.

Camping is not permitted in Mt Augustus National Park, but there is camping and accommodation at **Mt Augustus Outback Tourist Resort** (☎ 08-9943 0527; unpowered/powered sites for 2 $18/22, d $80-140) at the foot of the rock. You will need your own vehicle to access this isolated mountain, about 500km inland from Carnarvon.

Mt Bruce

The gorges of spectacular Karijini National Park don't easily lend themselves to walks beyond a couple of hours but Mt Bruce, in the south of the park, does. The 9km return walk to the summit of WA's second-highest mountain (1235m) is accessed off Karijini Dr, and brings views over classic Pilbara country (think *Japanese Story*) dotted with spinifex, and down into Marandoo Mine. Expect to take four to five hours. NATMAP's 1:100,000 topographic map *Mt Bruce* will help identify the landscape. You will need your own vehicle to access this inland Pilbara region. Information is available from the **Karijini Visitor Centre** (☎ 08-9189 8121) inside the national park.

Piccaninnny Gorge

The World Heritage-listed Purnululu National Park, better known as the Bungle Bungles, protects a series of beehive-like sandstone domes. Between them are some spectacular gorges; the best of these for walkers is Piccaninny Gorge. This soaring gorge requires a 15km walk in, camping a night inside the gorge, then walking back out. Walkers must register at the visitor information centre at the park entrance. For an overall perspective carry NATMAP's 1:100,000 topographic maps *Linnekar* and *Osmond*. Halls Creek or Kununurra are your likely bases, though it is a long and brutal drive in wherever you begin. There are also two drive-up camp sites in the park. Information on the park and walk is available from the Kununurra office of **CALM** (☎ 08-9168 4200; Messmate Way).

Northern Territory

The Northern Territory delivers the Australia promised in postcards and calendars. Vast central deserts of red sand and timeless, weathered ranges merge with a tropical Top End where steaming (and crocodile-teeming) floodplains are backed by fissured escarpments that hold ancient art and primeval mystery. There are national parks that are World Heritage listed and others that are little known, even within Australia. Walking this challenging prehistoric terrain, you are aided by a sophisticated infrastructure of well-marked trails, solar-powered emergency phones and a walker registration system. What's more, national parks are co-managed with the land's traditional owners, helping walkers maximise their cultural experience.

The environments of the Top End and the Red Centre are starkly different, yet walking in either is a highly seasonal proposition. In the Top End you will be walking through diverse woodlands and rustling tall speargrass or up a craggy escarpment and across an exposed sandstone plateau. Water can be plentiful but the heat and humidity will challenge the fittest of walkers. The highlight of most Top End walks is the chance to plunge into a crystal clear pool or under a pummelling waterfall after a steamy workout. In the Centre, pleasant winter temperatures, which belie the unforgiving summers and the deserts' harsh reputation, encourage walkers to explore majestic ranges where pastel-hued panoramas, serene waterholes and perfect isolation are just part of the reward.

Wherever you go in 'the Territory' the horizons are vast and settlement is sparse. If you crave unpopulated vistas, unblemished starry nights and the exhilaration that only a remote and challenging location can awaken, then the Territory beckons.

HIGHLIGHTS

- Enjoying the high ridges and stunning chasms of the West MacDonnell Ranges along the demanding **Larapinta Trail** (p322)
- Reaching each day's camp site and its refreshing swimming hole on the exceptional **Jatbula Trail** (p315) in Nitmiluk National Park
- Exploring the amazing rock art at Nourlangie while tackling the **Barrk Sandstone Bushwalk** (p312) in Kakadu National Park
- Experiencing the peaceful grandeur of **Ormiston Gorge** and the textures and colours of **Ormiston Pound** (p321) in West MacDonnell National Park

---

■ TELEPHONE CODE: 08　　■ www.nt.gov.au/nreta/parks/　　■ www.travelnt.com

ENVIRONMENT

The majority of the Northern Territory is in the tropics, but only the northern quarter, the Top End, experiences the full impact of the monsoonal wet season, complete with spectacular electrical storms and flooding rains. This challenging climate has weathered the land for aeons, creating diverse habitats of woodland, rainforest, heath and expansive wetlands. While rainfall is highly seasonal, the great sandstone plateaus of Kakadu, Nitmiluk, Litchfield and Arnhem Land absorb sufficient water to release life-sustaining flows throughout the year.

Much of the rest of the Territory is classified as desert or semidesert: and it is mostly flat. Where there is topographical relief, the effect is dramatic. The archetypal outback of red sand, muted blue ranges and stark-white ghost gums belongs to the true Centre, around Alice Springs, with its temperate climate of low humidity and scant rainfall. The rivers are usually dry, their courses traced by majestic river red gums whose deep roots tap age-old soaks. Sheltering under rocky ramparts are isolated waterholes; these true oases secreted in the spare ranges are vital refuges for wildlife and hold significant cultural importance for traditional owners.

INFORMATION
When to Walk

Walks in the Top End are best undertaken from May through to September. There will be more water around in autumn, and temperatures and humidity will be most tolerable during winter. June and July are also the peak tourist times, though crowding on the trails is usually not a problem. The build-up to the Wet begins in October with increasing temperatures and humidity. During the wet season many walking trails and even access roads to parks may be cut by floodwaters and many trails are closed to walkers.

The best time to walk in the Centre is from April through to September when maximum temperatures range between a comfortable 20°C and 25°C. Overnight minimums are often below 0°C and significant rainfall is rare. Summer temperatures are extreme (40°C plus), which, combined with the scarcity of water, makes walking a potentially dangerous proposition.

Maps

MapsNT (www.ipe.nt.gov.au/whatwedo/landinformation/mapsnt/) produces a comprehensive 1:50,000 map series and a series of larger-scale topographic maps with a more limited coverage. MapsNT has offices in Darwin and Alice Springs, and the more popular sheets are often available in outdoor equipment shops in these cities. The 1:50,000 topographic sheets produced by **Geoscience Australia** (www.ga.gov.au) are also satisfactory. For maps covering individual walks, see Planning in the introduction to each walk.

TOP END'S SEASONAL CYCLE

The Aboriginal people of Kakadu recognise six seasons in the annual climatic cycle. These seasons are marked not only by observed changes in the weather but also its effect on plant growth and animal behaviour.

Gunmeleng This is the build-up to the Wet, and starts in mid-October. Humidity increases and temperatures rise to 35°C or more – and the number of mosquitoes, always high near water, rises to near plague proportions. By November, the thunderstorms have started, billabongs are replenished and waterbirds and fish disperse. Traditionally this is when the Aboriginal people made their seasonal move from the floodplains to the shelter of the escarpment.

Gudjuek The Wet proper continues through January, February and March, with violent thunderstorms and an abundance of plant and animal life thriving in the hot, moist conditions.

Banggereng In April, storms (known as 'knock 'em down' storms) flatten the speargrass, which during the course of the Wet has shot up to 2m in height.

Yekke The season of mists, when the air starts to dry out, extends from May to mid-June. The wetlands and waterfalls still have a lot of water. The first firing of the countryside begins.

Wurrgeng & Gurrung The most comfortable time to visit the Top End is during the late Dry, in July and August. This is when wildlife, especially birds, gathers in large numbers around shrinking billabongs.

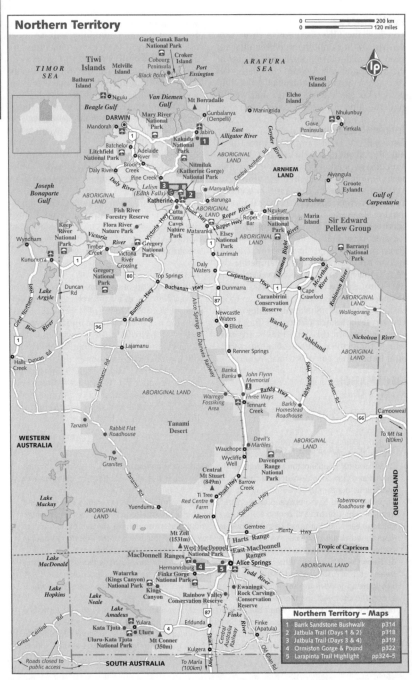

Northern Territory

Books

Lonely Planet's *Northern Territory & Central Australia* is highly recommended for more detailed information about the Northern Territory, while *A Field Guide to Central Australia* by Penny van Oosterzee is a comprehensive guide to the plants and wildlife of the Centre.

Information Sources

Tourism NT (☎ 13 67 68; www.travelnt com.au) operates several interstate and overseas information offices in addition to a comprehensive website. Regional tourism associations run very helpful visitor centres in Darwin (see p308) and Alice Springs (see p310).

The Northern Territory **Parks & Wildlife Service** (PWS; www.nt.gov.au/nreta/parks/) has its head office in Palmerston (see p308), near Darwin, and regional offices in Alice Springs (see p310) and Katherine (see p316). A lot of national park information is also available from Tourism NT offices and on the PWS website.

There are two main bushwalking clubs: the **Darwin Bushwalking Club** (☎ 8985 1484; www .bushwalking.org.au/dbc/; PO Box 41568, Casuarina 0811), which charges $30 for associate membership (6 months) before inviting you to join a walk; and the **Alice Springs Bushwalkers Association** (http://home.austarnet.com.au/longwalk/), an informal group that welcomes visitors to join walks.

Permits & Regulations

Permits must be organised in advance for the Jatbula Trail in Nitmiluk National Park (see p315) and for overnight walks in Kakadu National Park (see p312).

The voluntary **Overnight Walker Registration Scheme** (☎ 1300 650 730) is in operation across the state (except Kakadu, Nitmiluk and Uluru-Kata Tjuta National Parks) and is recommended for all overnight walks. You pay a $50 refundable deposit (or $200 a group) by credit card over the phone and tell them your walk details. Then, if you don't check out by noon of the day following your nominated completion date, they organise a search party.

During days of Total Fire Ban (see p54), all fires are forbidden, even fuel stoves.

Guided Walks

For guided walks on the Larapinta Trail see p323.

Willis's Walkabouts (☎ 8985 2134; www.bush walkingholidays.com.au) has a worldwide reputation and is probably one of the best organised and most original walking outfits in Australia. Walks from one to two weeks and longer in duration are tailored to the

---

ABORIGINAL ART & THE TOP END

Australian Aboriginal society has the longest continuous cultural history in the world, dating back at least 50,000 years, and walkers in the Top End are privileged to see first-hand a remarkable artistic heritage – the fascinating rock art of Kakadu and Arnhem Land.

Kakadu's Barrk Sandstone Bushwalk (p312 Kakadu National Park/Barrk Sandstone Bushwalk) boasts excellent art sites with examples of several artistic styles. Walkers can also see wonderful rock art at the Amphitheatre on day two of the Jatbula Trail (p315) in Nitmiluk National Park.

Kakadu alone contains over 5000 recorded art sites, some contemporary, some at least 20,000 years old. They record a changing world of animals long extinct, seasonal food sources, the arrival of Indonesian and European sailors, important ceremonies and the intriguing creation ancestors, such as the hauntingly beautiful *mimi*. The paintings have been classified into three roughly defined periods: Pre-estuarine, which is from the earliest paintings up to around 8000 years ago; Estuarine, which covers the period from 8000 to 2000 years ago, when rising sea levels flooded valleys, the climate warmed and the familiar X-ray art began; and Freshwater, from 2000 years ago, which includes the so-called contact art featuring Macassan and European subjects from about 500 up to 100 years ago.

For the local Aboriginal people the rock-art sites are a major source of traditional knowledge and a historical archive. The most recent paintings, some executed as recently as the 1980s, connect the present-day community with communities past. Older paintings are believed by many Aboriginal people to have been painted by spirit people, and depict creation legends and the development of Aboriginal law.

ability and the comfort expectation of the clients. Costs vary accordingly – from $1000 to over $3000 depending on logistics.

GATEWAYS
Darwin
☎ 08 / pop 71,350

Darwin's lively cosmopolitan character stems from its proximity to Asia and its standing as an essential watering hole on the traveller circuit. There are plenty of good restaurants and clubs where you'll enjoy the best food and nightlife in all of the Territory. Spend a few days here catching the markets and the other sights before heading to the bush.

INFORMATION
Tourism Top End (☎ 8936 2499; www.tourismtopend .com.au; cnr Knuckey & Mitchell Sts; ⏰ 8.30am-5.30pm Mon-Fri, 9am-3pm Sat, 10am-3pm Sun) Stocks numerous brochures and can book tours or accommodation. Free publications include *Destination Darwin & the Top End*, published twice yearly, and the annual *Top End Holiday Guide*. A full range of park notes on Top End national parks is available.

MapsNT (☎ 8999 7032; 1st fl, cnr Cavenagh & Bennett Sts; www.ipe.nt.gov.au/whatwedo/landinformation/ mapsnt/; ⏰ 8am-4pm Mon-Fri) Sells a full range of map products including large-scale topographic maps.

Parks & Wildlife Service (PWS; ☎ 8999 4555; www .nreta.nt.gov.au/parks//; 25 Chung Wha Tce, Palmerston) This head office and information centre is 18km south of Darwin. Tourism Top End in Darwin also has PWS information (though not the same expertise) and is more convenient.

SUPPLIES & EQUIPMENT
NT General Store (☎ 8981 8242; 42 Cavenagh St) stocks a good range of camping equipment, books and some maps and is centrally located. **Trek & Travel** (☎ 8985 4777; 1 Travers St, Coconut Grove) is about 7km north of the CBD and stocks the latest gear.

For self-catering there are three supermarkets in town. **Coles** (Mitchell Centre, 55-59 Mitchell St) is open 24 hours, while **Woolworths** (cnr Cavenagh & Whitfield Sts) is open to midnight most nights. There's another **Woolworths** (56 Smith St) near the corner of Smith and Knuckey Sts.

SLEEPING & EATING
There are plenty of caravan parks around Darwin but one of the best and closest is **Shady Glen Caravan Park** (☎ 8984 3330; www.shady

glen.com.au; cnr Farrell Cres & Stuart Hwy; unpowered/ powered sites for 2 $24/26, cabins from $75; ⬛ ⬛), which is indeed a shady park with immaculate facilities, camp kitchen, licensed shop and friendly staff.

As well as being host to numerous restaurants and bars, Mitchell St is the hostel and backpackers hot spot. **Darwin International YHA** (☎ 8981 3995; darwinyha@yhant.org.au; 69 Mitchell St; dm per YHA member/non-member $19-21/23-25, tw & d $53-70; ⬛ ⬛ ⬛) is a popular, convenient and friendly hostel adjacent to the Transit Centre. Across the street, **Melaleuca on Mitchell** (☎ 1300 723 437; www.melaleucaonmitchell .com.au; 52 Mitchell St; dm $30, s or d $95; ⬛ ⬛ ⬛) is a modern backpackers with characterless rooms but a great rooftop bar and pool area in which to unwind.

The quieter **Barramundi Lodge** (☎ 8941 6466; www.barramundilodge.com.au; 4 Gardens Rd, The Gardens; s/d $55/95; ⬛ ⬛) has spacious, old-fashioned rooms with TV and kitchenette; note that the bathrooms are communal.

Moving upmarket, the **Cherry Blossom Hotel** (☎ 8981 6734; fax 8941 3620; 108 The Esplanade; d $99; ⬛ ⬛) represents good value on the ritzy Esplanade. It is a friendly boutique hotel of 19 rooms, each with a double bed and a single. **Botanic Gardens Apartments** (☎ 8946 0300; www.botanicgardens.com.au; 17 Geranium St, Stuart Park;

d from $140, apt $190-300; ⊠ ⊡) has spacious motel rooms and apartments overlooking the botanic gardens. The three-bedroom apartments sleep up to six and boast a balcony, full cooking facilities and a laundry.

Darwin is easily the best place to eat in the Territory. Cullen Bay has a hip waterfront dining scene, while the food centre at Stokes Hill Wharf provides economical fish and chips and Asian stir-fries. However, no mention of Darwin dining could omit the tasty delights available at the **Mindil Beach Sunset Market** (☎ 8981 3454, off Gilruth Ave; ⊙ 5pm-10pm Thu & 4-9pm Sun May-Oct), a Darwin institution that draws huge crowds for its multicultural (especially Asian) street food.

Mitchell St has plenty of eateries for all budgets. For starched linen, enticing aromas and innovative Indian and Thai dishes follow your nose to **Hanuman** (☎ 8941 3500; 28 Mitchell St; mains $15-25; ⊙ lunch Mon-Fri & dinner daily). For alfresco waterfront dining try **Buzz Café** (☎ 8941 1141; The Slipway, Cullen Bay; mains $16-30; ⊙ lunch & dinner), a chic café/bar/restaurant furnished in polished teak and lava which makes a lovely spot for an afternoon drink and fusion fare.

GETTING THERE & AWAY
Air
Darwin International Airport receives international flights and is worth considering as a port of entry (see p372).

Domestic flights connect Darwin with all other Australian capital cities, as well as Alice Springs, Broome, Cairns, Kununurra and various regional destinations throughout the Top End.

Qantas (☎ 13 13 13; www.qantas.com.au) has direct daily services to Adelaide (one-way from $400), Alice Springs ($300), Brisbane ($350), Cairns ($340), Melbourne ($400), Perth ($500) and Sydney ($360).

Virgin Blue (☎ 13 67 89; www.virginblue.com.au) flies direct daily to/from Melbourne, Sydney and Brisbane for very similar prices.

The airport is 12km south of town. It's a $20 taxi ride or the **Darwin Airport Shuttle** (☎ 1800 358 945, 8981 5066) will pick up or drop off almost anywhere in the city centre for $8.50/17 one way/return.

Bus
Long-distance bus services are operated by **Greyhound Australia** (☎ 13 14 99; www.greyhound .com.au; Transit Centre, 69 Mitchell St; ⊙ 6am-3.45pm Mon-Fri, 6am-1.30pm Sat & Sun). Buses depart from the rear of the Transit Centre.

Darwin is serviced by daily services along three routes: the Western Australia route to/from Kununurra via Katherine; the Queensland route to/from Mount Isa via Three Ways (near Tennant Creek); or the central route to/from Alice Springs and Adelaide. Sample fares and times on the daily service to Adelaide ($496, 43 hours) are: Batchelor ($38, 1½ hours), Katherine ($70, 4½ hours), Tennant Creek ($185, 14 hours) and Alice Springs ($255, 22 hours).

For further information on interstate bus travel see p375.

Train
The *Ghan* operates twice weekly between Darwin and Adelaide via Alice Springs, with a third service in operation from May to July. The Darwin terminus is located on Berrimah Rd, about 18km from the city centre. A taxi fare into the centre is about $30, and there is a shuttle service to/from the Transit Centre for $10.

Adult fares for the service from Darwin to Alice Springs (12 hours) via Katherine are $240/880/1150 one way for day-nighter seats/sleeper cabins/1st-class (Gold Kangaroo) sleepers; Darwin–Adelaide (24 hours) fares are $440/1390/1830. Bookings can be made through **Trainways** (☎ 13 21 47; www.trainways.com .au). Discounted fares are sometimes offered.

Car
Most rental companies have agents in the city centre and are open daily. Avis, Budget, Hertz and Thrifty also have offices at the airport.

Avis (☎ 8981 9922; 89 Smith St)
Britz: Australia (☎ 8981 2081; 44 Stuart Hwy, Stuart Park) Campervan & 4WD specialists.
Budget (☎ 8981 9800; cnr Daly St & Doctors Gully Rd)
Europcar (☎ 8941 0300; 77 Cavenagh St)
Hertz (☎ 8941 0944; cnr Smith & Daly Sts)
Nifty Rent-A-Car (☎ 8941 7090; 86 Mitchell St) Usually has cheap deals.
Thrifty (☎ 8924 0000; 64 Stuart Hwy, Stuart Park)

Alice Springs
☎ 08 / pop 28,200
From a lonely telegraph station in the desert, Alice Springs, or 'Alice' as it's affectionately called, has grown into a thriving city (some

would say 'town') and the launching point of many an outback adventure. Uluru is five hours away, but it's the beautiful and adjacent MacDonnell Ranges that are the attraction for walkers.

INFORMATION

Central Australian Tourism Industry Association
(Catia; ☎ 8952 5800; www.centralaustraliantourism.com; 60 Gregory Tce; ☉ 8.30am-5.30pm Mon-Fri, 9am-4pm Sat & Sun) Stocks maps, brochures and PWS park notes.
MapsNT (☎ 8999 7032; www.ipe.nt.gov.au/whatwedo/landinformation/mapsnt//; 1st fl, Alice Springs Plaza, Todd Mall; ☉ 8am-4pm Mon-Fri) Stocks all kinds of maps including topographical sheets.
Parks & Wildlife Service (PWS; ☎ 8951 8250; www.nt.gov.au/nreta/parks//; Tom Hare Bldg, Arid Zone Research Institute, South Stuart Hwy; ☉ 8.30am-4.20pm Mon-Fri) Has expert staff, maps and park notes.

SUPPLIES & EQUIPMENT

Lone Dingo (☎ 8953 3866; 24 Parsons St) is the best and most central of Alice's outdoor stores.

There are several supermarkets around the centre including: **Coles** (cnr Gregory & Railway Tces; ☉ 24hr), **Woolworths** (Yeperenye Shopping Centre, cnr Hartley & Bath Sts; ☉ 7am-midnight Mon-Sat, 7am-10pm Sun) and **Bi-Lo** (Alice Plaza; ☉ 7am-9pm) at the north end of Todd Mall.

SLEEPING & EATING

The best-kept park in town is **MacDonnell Range Holiday Park** (☎ 8952 6111, 1800 808 373; www.macrange.com.au; Palm Pl; unpowered/powered sites for 2 $25/30, budget rooms $60, cabins $85-125, villas $135-150; ☒ ☐ ☒) with grassy sites, spotless amenities and good camp kitchens.

Right in the centre of town, **Pioneer YHA Hostel** (☎ 8952 8855; www.yha.com.au; cnr Leichhardt Tce & Parsons St; dm $23-27, tw & d $65, q $80; ☒ ☐ ☒) is clean, friendly and well run with a spacious kitchen, common room and outdoor area. Also convenient, inexpensive and just a short walk to the town mall, the **Desert Rose Inn** (☎ 8952 1411; www.desertroseinn.com.au; 15 Railway Tce; budget s/d $50/60, motel s/d $60/95; ☒ ☒) has budget rooms that share bathrooms, as well as standard motel rooms.

The **Gallery** (☎ 8953 3514; thegallery@outbacktravelshop.com.au; 16 Range Cres; s/d $120/150) is a beautiful stone B&B overlooking the golf course in a quiet part of town. There are three rooms with shared facilities and the owners speak five languages and are a mine of local knowledge. If a private tropical-style villa appeals,

then the **Desert Palms Resort** (☎ 8952 5977, 1800 678 037; www.desertpalms.com.au; 74 Barrett Dr; d/tr/q villas $120/135/145; ☒ ☐ ☒) with its rows of self-contained villas secluded behind palms and bougainvillea is an excellent choice. For a well-appointed private room in a central hotel, though, the **All Seasons Diplomat** (☎ 8952 8977; www.accorhotels.com.au; cnr Gregory Tce & Hartley St; budget/standard/deluxe d $70/135/155; ☒ ☐ ☒) is your best option.

There are plenty of cafés in and around Todd Mall, including the **Lane** (☎ 8952 5522; 58 Todd Mall; mains $12-28; ☉ lunch & dinner Tue-Sun), which serves for a casual lunch or intimate dinner. Try the tapas and wood-fired pizzas, or choose from the modern-Med menu. There's live entertainment on weekends.

For outback atmosphere head to **Bojangles** (☎ 8952 2873; 80 Todd St; mains $11-22, roast $13; ☉ lunch & dinner) with its 'gourmet Territorian' menu, including kebabs of croc, kangaroo, camel or emu served with quandong sauce. For more Australiana the **Overlanders Steakhouse** (☎ 8952 2159; www.overlanders.com.au; 72 Hartley St; mains $19-29; ☉ dinner) is an Alice institution. The ambience, like the king-size steaks and Darwin stubbies, is 'over the top'.

GETTING THERE & AWAY

Air

Qantas (☎ 13 13 13, 8950 5211; www.qantas.com.au; cnr Todd Mall & Parson St) and **Virgin Blue** (☎ 13 67 89; www.virginblue.com.au) operate daily flights to/from other capital cities. One-way fares from Alice include Adelaide (from $200), Brisbane ($270), Darwin ($300), Melbourne ($270), Sydney ($230), Perth ($300) and Hobart ($380). Check websites for latest timetables and fare offers.

The airport is 15km south of town, a $30 taxi ride or $12 with the **airport shuttle** (☎ 8953 0310).

Bus

Greyhound Australia (☎ 13 14 99; www.greyhound.com.au; Shop 3, 113 Todd St; office ☉ 6am-4pm Mon-Sat) has a daily service from Alice Springs to Yulara (for Uluru) and Adelaide, and a daily service to Darwin. Buses arrive at, and depart from, the office in Todd St, opposite Melankas.

Sample fares and times to various points include: Adelaide ($230, 21 hours), Tennant Creek ($130, 6½ hours), Katherine ($210, 15 hours), Darwin ($255, 22 hours) and Yulara ($85, 5 hours).

Train

The *Ghan* runs between Adelaide, Alice Springs and Darwin and is a classic way to enter or leave the Territory. There are two services weekly in each direction between Adelaide and Alice Springs throughout the year, and a third service from May to July. Heading north to Darwin, the train stops at Katherine for four hours, allowing a quick visit to the gorge.

It's a popular service, especially during winter, and bookings are essential – contact **Trainways** (☐ 13 21 47; www.trainways.com.au), or book through **Travel World** (☎ 8953 0488; Todd Mall). The **train station** (☉ noon-4.30pm Mon, 9am-1pm Thu, 10am-2pm Sat) is at the end of George Cres off Larapinta Dr.

Car

Alice Springs is a long way from anywhere and flying in and renting a car makes sense. All the major companies have offices in Alice Springs, and Avis, Budget, Hertz and Thrifty also have counters at the airport.

A conventional (2WD) vehicle will get you to trailheads in the MacDonnell Ranges (and out to Uluru and Kings Canyon).

Alice Camp 'n' Drive (☎ 8952 0099; www.alicecampndrive.com) Provides vehicles fully equipped for camping with swags (or tents), sleeping bags, cooking gear etc.

Avis (☎ 8953 5533; 52 Hartley St)

Budget (☎ 8952 8899; Shop 6, Capricornia Centre, Gregory Tce)

Europcar (☎ 13 13 90; 10 Gap Rd)

Hertz (☎ 8952 2644; 76 Hartley St)

Outback Auto Rentals (☎ 1800 652 133; www.outbackautorentals.com.au; 78 Todd St) Local company with cheap deals from $55 a day.

Thrifty (☎ 8952 9999; cnr Stott Tce & Hartley St)

KAKADU NATIONAL PARK

Kakadu National Park is one of Australia's greatest national assets. At almost 20,000 sq km it is the largest park in Australia, protecting a spectacular tropical ecosystem as well as an important concentration of Aboriginal rock art. Kakadu is more than a nature reserve; it is an acknowledgement of the traditional Aboriginal custodians and a leading example of the approach that combines the cultural interests of traditional owners with nature conservation. In 1992 the entire park attained World Heritage listing for cultural and ecological importance.

Throughout the park short, marked trails lead through different habitats to a variety of attractions – bird-filled billabongs, rock art and spectacular lookouts. There are also many possibilities for extended walks; however, there are no marked long-distance trails and a strict permit system regulates all overnight walks (see p312. What's more, publicity about possible routes is minimised, so the excellent 12km Barrk Sandstone Bushwalk described here is one of the longest marked trails in the park, and

---

BUSHWALKING & ABORIGINAL LAND

When the British arrived in Australia they colonised the continent on the basis of *terra nullius,* a British legal doctrine which claimed so-called 'unoccupied', or 'empty', land for the British Crown. It wasn't until 1976, and the Aboriginal Land Rights (NT) Act, that Aboriginal people could stake a claim on their traditional lands. At present almost half of the Territory has been claimed or is being claimed on behalf of the traditional owners.

It's important to realise that this is not about land ownership in a Western European sense. It's about having access to, and protection over, land which you have a spiritual and physical connection with. If a walker wanders into an art site meant only for clan Elders to see, or swims at a sacred site, there can be great and far-reaching repercussions. What's more, Aboriginal Elders feel personally responsible for the people on their land, including white folks wandering about in it. If a stranger out walking were to die, some Elders would take the view, 'I let the white fella onto our land, it's therefore my fault he died, I won't let it happen again'.

So it's important to obey the rules about walking on Aboriginal land. If you're asked not to visit or photograph a certain site, then don't. If you have to wait months for a permit to be approved, it's to stop you making a cultural gaffe that may not affect *you* very much, but could have deep repercussions for others.

a small taste of what's possible with a little more effort.

HISTORY

Kakadu is home to a number of different Aboriginal clans who have lived here for at least 23,000 years and possibly as long as 50,000 years. The name Kakadu comes from Gagadju, one of the languages spoken in the north of the region. Kakadu was proclaimed a national park in three stages. Stage One, the eastern and central part of the park including Ubirr, Nourlangie, Jim Jim and Twin Falls and Yellow Water Billabong, was declared in 1979. Stage Two, in the north, was declared in 1984 and gained World Heritage listing for its natural importance. Stage Three, in the south, was finally listed in 1991, bringing virtually the whole of the South Alligator River system within the park.

ENVIRONMENT

Forming a spectacular backdrop, the extensive Arnhem Land escarpment marks the boundary of the broad floodplains and the elevated Arnhem Land plateau. Depending on the season, water gently tumbles or explosively roars off the plateau to feed the rivers and floodplains below. These plains are covered in a patchwork of eucalyptus woodland, tall grasses and ephemeral billabongs and comprise 80% of the park. The seasonal wetlands are of international importance as feeding and breeding grounds for local and migratory birds. There are over 60 species of mammal in the park and, while many are small, nocturnal or shy, you are likely to see some of the six species of kangaroo and wallaby, including the beautiful black wallaroo, that inhabit the park. Among the numerous reptiles that live here, the potentially harmful crocodiles, both the freshwater and estuarine (or saltwater) species, are worthy of special mention and respect.

BARRK SANDSTONE BUSHWALK

Duration	5–7 hours
Distance	12km
Difficulty	moderate–demanding
Start/Finish	Nourlangie Rock car park
Nearest Town	Jabiru (p313)
Transport	private

Summary An excellent introduction to walking in Kakadu National Park, this walk links two important Aboriginal rock art sites via a rugged and challenging route up and over Nourlangie Rock.

This walk links Anbangbang and Nanguluwur, two of the most important Aboriginal rock art sites in Kakadu. These sites offer a visual record of traditional life and ceremony. Paintings show seasonal food sources, creation ancestors and the arrival of European sailors. Some paintings are contemporary, others possibly 30,000 years old.

The trail is well marked with orange triangle markers. This is just as well as the route across the top of the rock is full of small gullies and rocky hillocks, descents, climbs and geological mazes that are impossible to show on the map. Start walking

---

OVERNIGHT WALKS IN KAKADU

Permits are required for all overnight walks in Kakadu. Contact the **Permits Officer** (☎ 8938 1100, fax 8938 1115; PO Box 71, Jabiru, NT 0886) at Bowali visitor information centre for a permit application form, which should be returned with a copy of a topographical map (1:100,000 or 1:50,000) showing your proposed route and camp sites. No clues as to routes will be given by parks staff, but a number of recognised, unmarked routes lie along dry gorges and creeks in the sandstone plateau country southeast of Jabiru.

It takes at least seven days to process permits. June and July are the busiest times. Alternative routes are often worked out if there's a problem. Permits and bush camping are free.

Within 24 hours of finishing your walk, notify rangers on ☎ 8938 1179 (a dedicated line) and leave your name, date and permit number.

All walks are fuel stove only. Sleeping under a mosquito net is ideal in the Dry, when you'll also need a sleeping bag, while after September a tent and waterproof gear are necessary. Insect repellent is mandatory at all times.

early in the morning and carry at least 4L of water per person. Also note this is a one-way walk and the markers are not visible if you decide to turn around and backtrack.

When walking in the Nourlangie area, keep an eye out for black wallaroos (males are called barrks), which occur only in Kakadu and Arnhem Land. Also endemic to this region is the chestnut-quilled rock-pigeon. Listen for the whirr as they flee your arrival.

PLANNING
When to Walk
The dry season from April to September is the best time for visiting, and walking is best between May and July when temperatures are lower.

Maps & Books
The booklet *Kakadu National Park Visitor Guide and Maps* is available at Tourism Top End in Darwin and from the Bowali visitor information centre. Hema's 1:390,000 *Kakadu National Park* map and Auslig's 1:250,000 *Kakadu* map are good for planning and are widely available.

The whole park is covered by MapsNT's 1:50,000 series, available at the Bowali visitor information centre. The *Nourlangie Creek* map covers the Barrk Sandstone Bushwalk, but the relevant park notes are of more practical use.

Kakadu by Ian Morris gives an excellent background to the park, its wildlife, culture and people.

Information Sources
The **Bowali visitor information centre** (☎ 8938 1121; Kakadu Hwy; ⏰ 8am-5pm), 2.5km south of the Arnhem Hwy intersection, is open daily and has a café (with real coffee!), gift shop, library and film screenings. There are informative park notes for all the marked trails, topo maps, plus information on permits for overnight walks.

NEAREST TOWN & FACILITIES
Jabiru
☎ 08 / pop 1780
Jabiru, 260km from Darwin and 36km from Nourlangie Rock, on the Arnhem Hwy, is the service centre of Kakadu National Park. It has accommodation and a supermarket, post office and bank.

SLEEPING & EATING
Kakadu Lodge & Caravan Park (☎ 1800 811 154; www.aurora-resorts.com.au; Jabiru Dr; unpowered/powered sites for 2 $20/25, dm $31, lodge rooms $130, cabins $195-230; ❄ 🖥 🏊) is an impeccable resort with shade, gas barbecues, camp kitchens and a kiosk with Internet access, groceries and ice. The dorms and lodge rooms sleep four, while the comfortable cabins have en suite and kitchenette and sleep up to five. Overlooking the excellent pool is a good bistro.

Lakeview Park (☎ 8979 3144; www.lakeview kakadu.com.au; 27 Lakeside Dr; r for up to 4 people $85, d $110, cabins $180; ❄) Aboriginal-owned Lakeview Park is a good option for families and groups offering a range of tropical-designed bungalows. The fan-cooled budget rooms are also available to YHA members for $20 a bed. The doubles share a communal kitchen, bathroom and lounge, but have their own TV and fridge. The two-bedroom cabins sleep up to five people.

The odd-looking **Gagudju Crocodile Holiday Inn** (☎ 8979 9000; www.gagudju-dreaming.com; Flinders St; d $170-285; ❄ 🖥 🏊) is designed to resemble a crocodile when viewed from the air. The rooms are clean and comfortable if a little ordinary for the price. Try for one on the ground floor beside the central pool.

Self caterers will find the **Jabiru Foodland** (Jabiru Plaza; ⏰ 9am-5.30pm Mon-Fri, 9am-3pm Sat, 10am-2pm Sun & public holidays) supermarket is well stocked and even has a range of inexpensive camping equipment.

The **Kakadu Bakery** (☎ 8979 2320; Gregory Pl; ⏰ 7am-2pm Mon-Fri, 7am-1pm Sat) has fresh bread, cakes and pies; and you can get tasty fast food from the **Lightning Strike** (Civic Dr; ⏰ 10am-5pm Thu-Sun; meals $5-10), a tiny van parked down by the lake. The **Escarpment Restaurant** (Gagudju Crocodile Holiday Inn; ☎ 8979 9000; Flinders St; mains $25-30; ⏰ breakfast, lunch & dinner) serves inspired buffet and à la carte meals seasoned with bush ingredients, as well as delectable desserts.

GETTING THERE & AWAY
Greyhound Australia (☎ 13 14 99; www.greyhound .com.au) has a daily service between Darwin and Cooinda via Jabiru. The bus leaves Darwin at 6.30am, Jabiru at 10.15am, and arrives at Cooinda at 12.30pm. It departs Cooinda at 2.30pm, Jabiru at 4.10pm, and arrives in Darwin at 7pm. Fares from Darwin to Jabiru cost $43/82 one way/return.

URANIUM

Uranium was discovered in the Kakadu region as far back as 1953. Twelve small deposits in the southern reaches of the park were worked in the 1960s, then in 1970 three huge deposits, Ranger, Nabarlek (Arnhem Land) and Koongarra, were found, followed by Jabiluka in 1973. Scan any map of Kakadu and you will see the neat excisions of the Jabiluka, Ranger and Koongarra leases. The Ranger Uranium Mine started producing ore in 1981 and there followed an agreement to mine at Jabiluka negotiated with local Aboriginal people. Mine development at Jabiluka was delayed until 1996, however, due to oscillating Federal Government mining policy and growing concern that Aboriginal Elders had been coerced into signing the agreement.

The Jabiluka mine became the scene of sit-in demonstrations during 1998. A Unesco delegation inspected the mine site and reported that it would endanger Kakadu's World Heritage listing, a finding later contradicted by an Independent Science Panel. In 2003 stockpiled ore was returned into the mine and the decline tunnel leading into the deposit was backfilled as the mining company moved into dialogue with the traditional landowners, the Mirrar people.

In February 2005 the current owners of the Jabiluka mining lease, Energy Resources of Australia (ERA), signed an agreement that gave the Mirrar the deciding vote on any resumption of this controversial mining project. Under the deal ERA is allowed to continue to explore the lease, subject to Mirrar consent, and is allowed to ask for the re-opening of the mine every four years, beginning in 2006. Though it's unlikely the Mirrar will change their position, which is based on cultural and environmental concerns, the closure of the Ranger mine in 2010 will put the Mirrar under considerable pressure to find alternative sources of income.

Camping Grounds

Muirella Park (adult/child $5.40/free) is a national park camping ground 6km off the Kakadu Hwy and 7km south of the Nourlangie Rock turn-off. It's on an abandoned airstrip beside a paperbark-lined billabong. There are shaded barbecues and excellent amenities.

About 16km south of Jabiru on the Kakadu Hwy are the free **Malabanjbanjdju** camping grounds – one for caravans and one for tents. They are basic, with pit toilets the only amenities.

GETTING TO/FROM THE WALK

The turning for Nourlangie Rock is 21km south of Bowali Visitor Centre off Kakadu Hwy. The 12km sealed access road (open from 7am until sunset) leads to a car park (and toilet) close to the Anbangbang Galleries, at the start of the trail.

THE WALK

From the car park at the base of **Nourlangie Rock** (Burrunggui) follow the art sites trail past the **Anbangbang Shelter** to the **Anbangbang Gallery**. Don't miss any of the attractions while here; the art is superbly interpreted.

Just beyond the Anbangbang Gallery the trail forks. Go right following orange triangle markers steeply northeast up a rocky rise to **Gunwarddehwarde Lookout**. Bear right

off the little peak, before turning northwest down to a junction. Turn right and climb northeast up a gully before cutting right between two large rocks to a cliff – a waterfall in the Wet. Turn right (northeast) and begin the rocky climb to a stunning **lookout** with vistas of the floodplains and the escarpment (about 45 minutes from the start).

Head north across a low, wooded valley encircled by boulders. The path bends left, weaving across a boulder-strewn saddle

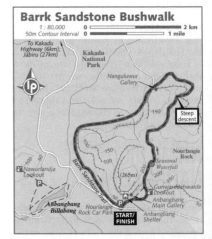

Barrk Sandstone Bushwalk

then heads west through sandstone pillars and conglomerate boulders south of the highest point of the rock (keep your eye on the orange markers). After passing a great **lookout**, the trail continues northeast, descending then climbing before threading between two huge boulders and dropping to a narrow gully. Turn left and head north to a wooded area hemmed in by stony hillocks. The trail continues north of the hillside, bearing right across the eastern flank before passing between a large outcrop and a precariously balanced boulder onto a saddle.

The trail then cuts back north before traversing northeast below the summit cliffs to a long, sloping slab of rock. Descend steeply east then turn left (northeast) and head through open woodland to a large cliff face, its base rutted with small caves. Turn right (east) along the cliff face and follow the dry creek east, then northeast, down to the valley floor.

The trail heads north across flat land into open eucalyptus woodland, then slowly swings west then southwest past the end of a dirt track to a T-junction. Take the left turn, leading to **Nanguluwur Gallery**, a long overhanging cliff which displays 30,000 years of Aboriginal rock art. Huge barramundi are displayed in X-ray style along with 'contact art' of sailing ships. Stencilled hand prints also feature here.

Continue southwest along the trail, which slowly curves west and after 30 minutes leads through a maze of boulders. Shortly afterwards the trail bears left (due south) then cuts up a rocky spur spread with sharp spinifex. After a short climb descend into a stone-scattered valley with great views of the Nourlangie's fiery red western cliffs.

Head southeast, crossing a stream 100m from the base of the cliffs, and after 10 minutes' walking through woodland the road becomes visible. Weave through several large rocks close to the road to return to Nourlangie Rock car park.

NITMILUK NATIONAL PARK

Originally called Katherine Gorge National Park, the area was renamed Nitmiluk (meaning 'Cicada Place') in 1989 when the Jawoyn Aboriginal people gained title to the land. They now jointly manage the park with the PWS.

Nitmiluk is a popular park, with the 13 sandstone sections of Katherine Gorge and the beautiful Leliyn (Edith Falls) its main attractions. A series of walks, some overnight, lead to various points along Katherine Gorge – which is perfect for exploring by canoe – and there is also a series of trails around Leliyn. However, there's much more to this 2920 sq km park, particularly some fine Jawoyn art sites and a variety of habitats, which can best be experienced on the Jatbula Trail linking Katherine Gorge to Leliyn.

JATBULA TRAIL

Duration	4 days
Distance	66km
Difficulty	moderate
Start	Nitmiluk Centre
Finish	Leliyn (Edith Falls)
Nearest Town	Katherine (p316)
Transport	shuttle

Summary A well-marked trail leading through varied woodland along the Arnhem Land escarpment in the heart of Jawoyn country. Attractions include rock art, tremendous waterfalls and perfectly positioned camp sites.

The Jatbula Trail links Katherine Gorge and Leliyn along the edge of the Arnhem Land escarpment, passing spectacular scenery, waterfalls, secluded swimming holes and Aboriginal art sites. Extra days are worth budgeting for as the camp sites en route have tremendous locations.

PLANNING
When to Walk

May (when there's plenty of water around) through to early September is the best time for walking. It's dry, with temperatures around 10°C overnight and 27°C during the day. From October to December it gets steadily hotter (up to 45°C) and more humid, with torrential storms a constant threat; the flies at this time can be maddening.

The Jatbula Trail may close for periods between October and April due to seasonal flooding.

What to Bring

Bring along a swimming costume for the crystal-clear and fish-teeming swimming holes. Sleeping under a mosquito net is ideal in the Dry, when you'll need a sleeping bag. Insect repellent is standard issue at all times, and after October a tent and waterproofs are required.

Maps & Books

MapsNT's 1:50,000 *Nitmiluk National Park* (widely available locally) displays the whole trail and is the only map you should need. However, you could also carry MapsNT's 1:50,000 *Katherine*, *Seventeen Mile*, and *Edith River* topo maps as a precaution.

The pocket-sized *Jawoyn Plant Identikit*, available in the Nitmiluk Centre, gives a fascinating insight into common plant use and is well worth carrying.

Information Sources

The **Nitmiluk Centre** (☎ 1800 089 103, 8972 1253; 🕑 7am-7pm Apr-Sep, 7am-5pm Oct-Mar), 30km northeast of Katherine at the entrance to Katherine Gorge, has excellent displays and information on the park's geology, wildlife, traditional owners and recent history. It is also the office of **Nitmiluk Tours**, which runs gorge tours and wet season access to the start of the Jatbula Trail. There's also a desk at the centre for the **Parks & Wildlife Service** (☎ 8972 1886), which has information sheets on a wide range of marked walking tracks.

Permits & Regulations

Permits aren't required for day walks, but are required for all overnight walks, along with a $50 deposit per party. (Note this is different to the *voluntary* Overnight Walker Registration Scheme.) Registration for overnight walks and camping permits ($3.30/night) are only available at the Nitmiluk Centre from 7am to 1pm. Camping permits are subject to availability and available only at the PWS desk at the Nitmiluk Centre, so apply well in advance. The Jatbula Trail can only be walked one way, from Katherine Gorge to Leliyn. The deposit is redeemable at Edith Falls Kiosk at the trail's end.

Checkpoints are dotted along the trail. Write your permit number, time of arrival and destination in each one. Use emergency call devices (ECDs) in an emergency only. Rangers actively discourage anyone starting the Jatbula Trail after about 1pm or walking alone.

NEAREST TOWN & FACILITIES
Katherine
☎ 08 / pop 6720

On the junction of the the Stuart Hwy and Victoria Hwy (which stretches all the way to the Kimberley), Katherine is the gateway to spectacular Nitmiluk National Park and a busy regional centre. It is the biggest town between Darwin and the Alice and a good place to buy supplies. The Katherine River, which cuts through the sandstone gorge at nearby Nitmiluk, flows through the town and represents the first permanent water north of Alice Springs.

The **Katherine Region Tourist Association** (☎ 8972 2650; www.krta.com.au; cnr Stuart Hwy & Lindsay St; 🕑 8.30am-5pm Mon-Fri, 9am-2pm (5pm dry season) Sat & Sun) stocks information on all areas of the Northern Territory, including PWS park notes. For further parks information visit the **Parks & Wildlife Service** (☎ 8973 8888; 32 Giles St).

Outback Disposals (☎ 8972 3456; 58 Katherine Tce) stocks a good range of camping gear.

SLEEPING & EATING

Kookaburra Lodge Backpackers (☎ 1800 808 211, 8971 0257; www.kookaburrabackpackers.com.au; cnr Lindsay & Third Sts; dm $19, s, d or tw $50; 🆒 🖳 🕮) is a well-run place a few minutes' walk from the transit centre. There's a kitchen in each dorm and the doubles have a TV and fridge. A free breakfast, bike and canoe hire, and YHA/VIP discounts are available.

On the road towards the gorge, **Knotts Crossing Resort** (☎ 8972 2511; www.knottscrossing .com.au; cnr Cameron & Giles Sts; unpowered/powered sites for 2 $18/22, d from $110, cabins from $58; 🆒 🕮) is set amid lush gardens. All powered sites have private bathrooms and there are spacious family rooms with kitchens, plus the excellent Katie's Bistro.

The friendly **Maud Creek Country Lodge** (☎ 8971 1814; www.maudcreeklodge.com.au; Gorge Rd; s/d $110/132, cottage d $165; 🆒 🕮) is just 6km from the gorge on a former cattle run where you can go walking, bird-watching and fishing, or just relax on the shady veranda. There are motel-style rooms and a self-contained cottage. A continental breakfast is supplied with all tariffs and the minibar is pegged at town prices.

If you're self-catering, **Woolworth's** (Oasis Shopping Centre; Katherine Tce; ⏰ 7am-10pm) is the cheapest place for hundreds of kilometres around to stock up on supplies.

Kumbidgee Lodge Tea Rooms (☎ 8971 0699; Gorge Rd; mains $7-18; ⏰ breakfast, lunch & dinner), 10km out of town towards the gorge, is a great spot to indulge in a hearty 'bush breakfast' ($12). The welcoming **Diggers Den Tavern & Restaurant** (☎ 8971 0422; 7 Victoria Hwy; mains $9-20; ⏰ lunch & dinner) has a small all-day menu till 6pm, then cranks up the kitchen with pizzas, pastas, steaks and, on Thursdays, a $10 buffet.

Katie's Bistro (☎ 8972 2511; Knotts Crossing Resort, cnr Giles & Cameron Sts; mains $19-28; ⏰ dinner) is regarded as Katherine's best restaurant. The dozen or so main courses may include Japanese hotpot or seared buffalo fillet as well as barra, steaks and one or two vegetarian options.

GETTING THERE & AWAY
Greyhound Australia (☎ 13 14 99; www.greyhound .com.au) buses between Darwin and Alice Springs, Queensland or Western Australia stop at Katherine's **Transit Centre** (☎ 8971 9999; 6 Katherine Tce). Typical fares and travel times for daily connections from Katherine are: Darwin ($70, 4½ hours), Alice Springs ($206, 15 hours), Tennant Creek ($135, eight hours) and Kununurra ($106, 4½ hours).

Nitmiluk National Park
At Katherine Gorge **Nitmiluk Caravan Park** (☎ 8972 1253; Nitmiluk Centre; unpowered/powered sites for 2 $19/23) has plenty of grass and shade and is well equipped with hot showers, toilets, barbecues and laundry. The licensed **Nitmiluk Bistro** (☎ 8972 1253; Nitmiluk Centre; mains $12-20; ⏰ breakfast, lunch & dinner) serves breakfasts, snacks and lunches, and occasionally puts on evening meals in the Dry.

At Leliyn (Edith Falls) the PWS **camping ground** (☎ 8975 4869; adult/child/family $8.80/4/19.50) has grassy sites, lots of shade, toilets, showers, a laundry and disabled facilities. Fees are paid at the **kiosk** (⏰ 8am-6pm), which sells good-value breakfasts, snacks and basic supplies. Nearby is a picnic area with gas barbecues and tables.

GETTING TO/FROM THE WALK
Travel North (☎ 8972 1044; Transit Centre, 6 Katherine Tce) runs a regular shuttle bus between

Katherine and the gorge to meet up with the gorge tours and on an 'as required' basis. Buses leave the Transit Centre at 8am, 12.15pm and 2.15pm and leave the gorge at 9am, 1pm and 5pm. The adult one-way/return fare is $15/22; children travel at half price. During the Wet walkers are ferried across the river by Nitmiluk Tours (see p315).

Things are more difficult from Leliyn, which is 20km from the Stuart Hwy and 60km north of Katherine. Contact **Dennis** (☎ 8971 0193, 0411 858 752), who does a shuttle ($40 one way for four people) from Leliyn to the gorge specifically for Jatbula Trail walkers. Otherwise contact the **Katherine Region Tourist Association** (☎ 8972 2650) for information on other local tour operators, or make inquiries at the kiosk.

THE WALK
Day 1: Nitmiluk Centre to Crystal Falls
5½–6½ hours, 23.5km
From the petrol station follow the sealed road east past the Youth Group Area then turn right onto the **Jatbula Trail**, following the blue triangle markers down to the Katherine River. Head upstream to a footbridge. Follow the 4WD track up the bank and then bear right onto a footpath leading northeast a short distance before turning north and arriving back on the 4WD track at the crossing of **Seventeen Mile Creek** in 30 minutes.

Cross to the east bank and follow the 4WD track through the open woodland of Seventeen Mile Valley to the right turn for **Northern Rockhole**, a spectacular seasonal waterfall 10 minutes away. Keep on the track as it climbs steadily up towards the escarpment, cutting east round a hill strewn with boulders and north over a pronounced gully. About 2¾ hours after setting out, and after passing the camp toilets, **Biddlecombe Cascades** is reached. Just 100m below the falls is the ECD and camp site (with barbecues), a good first-night stop if you've left in the late morning.

Crystal Falls, the next reliable water stop, is 12km away. From Biddlecombe Cascades move northwest along a trail leading upstream across some boggy ground to a boardwalk that leads across the creek – if there's been rain you may have to wade.

The trail now heads north, climbing gradually across open, flat ground strewn

NORTHERN TERRITORY

Jatbula Trail (Days 1 & 2)

1 : 160,000
50m Contour Interval

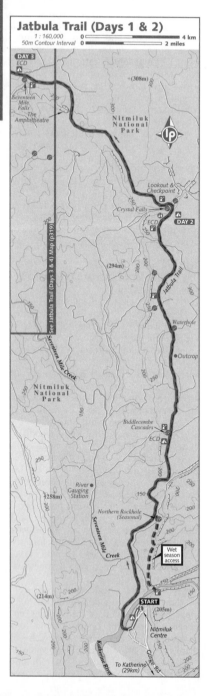

with boulders. After 45 minutes a corridor of rock is reached, and there are a few rocky sections to climb over as the trail follows a series of small creeks north, past a number of seasonal waterholes to an impressive rock outcrop.

Twisting and turning, the trail works its way over a series of gullies and hillocks and then drops down to cross a stream. Before the crossing, a sign points right to a beautiful waterhole 100m away. Ford the stream and continue heading northwest. In 30 minutes a faint path leads (left) to a **lookout**, after which the trail cuts northeast across a couple of (usually dry) creeks until it descends northwest to a permanent stream. Follow it downstream for a short while before crossing and heading northwest uphill to a lookout, ECD and toilet. Fifteen minutes on is **Crystal Falls** and a shady camp site (with barbecue) beside an excellent swimming hole.

Day 2: Crystal Falls to Seventeen Mile Falls
2½–3 hours, 11.5km

Cross the river downstream from the camp site and follow the trail up to a lookout and checkpoint above the 30m Crystal Falls. The trail climbs north then northwest to the summit plateau, before gradually bending west for the next hour through a series of shallow valleys, grassland and tall woodland. Eventually you will reach a sign directing you left down to the **Amphitheatre**. This wonderful curving rock art site is perched above a reliable stream and a remnant of monsoon rainforest sheltering huge numbers of birds and the occasional euro.

Seventeen Mile Falls is 3.5km away. From the Amphitheatre, the trail joins a rough 4WD track that heads west along, and then across, a creek. Five minutes later the trail bears left to a fantastic view point overlooking **Seventeen Mile Falls**. Continue north to Seventeen Mile Creek then go downstream to the falls. Cross to the true right bank and climb up to the camp site (with an ECD and barbecue but no other facilities).

Day 3: Seventeen Mile Falls to Sandy Camp Pool
5½–6 hours, 16.5km

The next 11km section to Edith River Crossing has no permanent water sources, so stock up at Seventeen Mile Falls.

Jatbula Trail (Days 3 & 4)

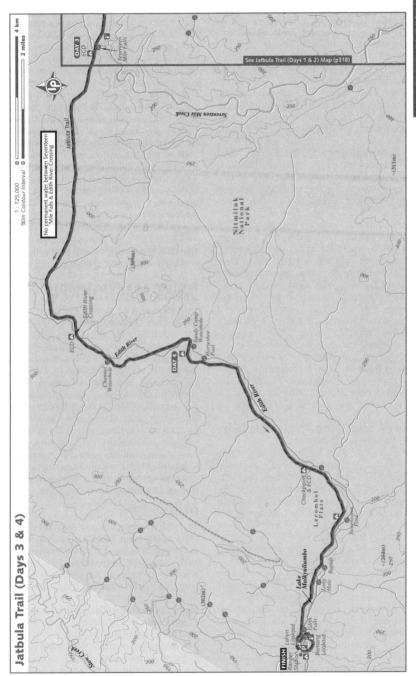

1 : 125,000
50m Contour Interval

0   0
2 miles 4 km

No permanent water between Seventeen
Mile Falls & Edith River Crossing

See Jatbula Trail (Days 1 & 2) Map (p318)

Seventeen Mile Falls

DAY 3
ECD

Jatbula Trail

Seventeen Mile Creek

Nitmiluk National Park

+(311m)

Edith River Crossing

ECD

Edith River

Channel Waterhole

(309m)

Sandy Camp Waterhole

Horseshoe Pool

DAY 4

Edith River

Checkpoint & ECD

Larombol Flats

Smetwah Pool

+(264m)

Lake Malkyullumbo

Long Hole Rapids

(302m)

Edith Falls

Ledym Lookout

FINISH
Ranger Station

Bemang Lookout

Sweet Creek

After initial bursts of heading west then north, the trail rolls west across gently sloping valleys and through patches of dense woodland. After about 90 minutes the top of the climb is reached and a descent into more rocky country begins, the trail making a sharp right turn (northwest) down among the tributaries of **Edith River**. With the presence of water the vegetation becomes lush, speargrass and spiral pandanus become common, and bird life is more evident. Upon reaching a sandy, seasonal creek, head south (downstream) to the rocky **Edith River Crossing**. Stepping stones lead across Edith River to a checkpoint and ECD. The camp site is nothing special, so it's better to continue to Sandy Camp, 5.5km to the south.

Follow the trusty blue triangles along the river bank for 200m and then up and over a series of rocky slopes to **Channel Waterhole**, a deep, narrow pool cut into the sandstone. Continue roughly south, close to the river, as the trail enters low dense woodland and then grassland. After about 45 minutes the river makes a sharp turn right (west) and the trail crosses it at the apex. Walk south between the river (on right) and a rocky outcrop (on left) through lush, dense woodland, soon to emerge into open grassland. **Sandy Camp Waterhole** is a short distance away – watch out for freshwater crocodiles in this superb, delightful spot. The best camp site is behind the western bank of the pool.

Day 4: Sandy Camp Waterhole to Leliyn
4–4½ hours, 14.5km

Head west, then south, following Edith River for 90 minutes as it bears southwest to Edith River South, where there's a checkpoint and ECD. The trail continues southwest, weaving past rocky outcrops and hills into **Lerombol Rainforest**, the largest pocket of rainforest along the Edith River. Forty-five minutes from Edith River South the trail swings west across a muddy stream and cuts south through boggy ground to the bank of Edith River. Turn right and walk across the slabs of rock to **Sweetwater Pool**. If you're lucky you may see the resident freshies in the beautiful, wide pool. The water channels through the top end are quite spectacular and at the southern end is a great camp site. There are barbecues and a toilet. Although Leliyn is only 4.3km away, it's well worth spending an extra night here.

The well-defined trail edges along the river to reach **Long Hole**, another good swimming spot, in 30 minutes. The trail then continues downstream for another 15 minutes (avoid the service trail on the right) before turning right to begin a short, sharp climb away from the river. Turn sharply left (west) at the top and ride out the now zigzagging trail to a rocky saddle and T-junction with a wide, easy tourist trail. Turn right for an unexceptional 630m descent to the car park or left onto the Leliyn Trail leading to Leliyn Lookout (a little 20m side track), down through **Upper Pool** (you can swim here) and up to **Bemang Lookout**, which gives great views of the whole, dramatic Leliyn area. The camp site is 1km from here.

The large pool at the base of **Leliyn** (Edith Falls) is great for swimming and fish-watching, but closed between 7pm and 7am, so no late-night skinny dipping.

WEST MACDONNELL NATIONAL PARK

Encompassing an unbroken section of the MacDonnell Ranges from the Stuart Hwy just north of Alice Springs to Mt Zeil, 170km to the west, this outstanding park protects 1333 sq km of varied arid habitats. Jagged, sparsely vegetated ridges, deep gorges, spinifex plains, dry creeks and permanent, tree-lined waterholes afford a ruggedly beautiful setting. Tourism is concentrated at 10 small 'sights', where it is easy to lose the crowds on short trails or launch onto the superb Larapinta Trail (see p322) to experience the heart of the ranges.

ENVIRONMENT

The vivid landscape of the West MacDonnell Ranges was formed 350 million years ago when massive earth movements created a mountain range of quartzite several kilometres high. Although significantly weathered and eroded, Mt Zeil (1531m), in the far northwest of the park, remains the highest point in the Territory.

The usually dry creeks, their banks shaded by stately river red gums, weave between stony ridges and through wide valleys carpeted in yellowing spinifex, soft to the eye but sharp to touch. Spinifex provides food and shelter for numerous mammals, including common wallaroos, tiny dunnarts and spinifex hopping-mice, as well as birds such as zebra finches, spinifex pigeons and rufous-crowned emu-wrens. Deep in the ranges, secluded gorges shelter moisture-loving plants such as ferns and the MacDonnell Ranges cycad, relicts of a wetter climate 22 million years ago.

With permanent water and diverse flora and fauna, the area has supported the Western Arrernte Aboriginal people for thousands of years. The Western Arrernte maintain a strong link with the park, and the waterhole at Ormiston Gorge (Kwartetwenne) is just one of many sacred sites.

PLANNING
When to Walk
The ideal time to walk is between April and September when maximum daily temperatures hover around 20°C; you should walk before 11am and after 3.30pm at either end of this period. It gets incredibly hot (40°C-plus) between October and March. June and July are the coldest months (-10°C has been recorded), although nights are cold even in summer. Statistics will tell you that most rainfall occurs in the summer, but rainfall is low and unreliable.

What to Bring
The terrain is rocky, so sturdy boots will save your feet. In winter bring warm clothes and a sleeping bag comfortable below 0°C – you'll need a fleece jacket year-round. Sun protection is essential and a swimming costume is recommended.

Maps
The ranges from Alice Springs to Standley Chasm are covered by MapsNT's 1:50,000 *Alice Springs*, *Simpsons Gap* and *Brinkley* topographic maps (laid over aerial photographs). The 1:50,000 coverage does not stretch to Ormiston Gorge, although Ormiston Pound and Mt Giles are covered by an accurate sketch map available with park notes from PWS offices (see above) and the PWS website (see p323).

MapsNT's 1:250,000 *West MacDonnell National Park* map covers the park and includes blow-ups of the main tourist areas. For map recommendations for the Larapinta Trail see p323.

Information Sources
There are PWS visitor centres at **Ormiston Gorge** (☎ 8956 7799; ☉ 5am-8pm) and **Simpsons Gap** (☎ 8955 0310; ☉ 5am-8pm) where you can register, find the latest information and catch evening talks and slide shows between May and October. A number of water tanks have been installed in the park, but check with the rangers on their levels, as well as the levels of the numerous waterholes and springs.

Permits & Regulations
If you plan to walk for more than a day in the West MacDonnell Ranges, you should use the voluntary Overnight Walker Registration Scheme (see p307).

Fuel stoves are encouraged and fires may be banned between October and April. There are free camp sites throughout the park, but camping is banned – or discouraged – at sites of significance to Aboriginal people and at major wildlife watering holes (eg Fish Hole, Spring Gap and Bond Gap).

ORMISTON GORGE & POUND

Duration	3½–4 hours
Distance	7.5km
Difficulty	easy–moderate
Start/Finish	Ormiston Gorge visitor centre
Nearest Town	Alice Springs (p309)
Transport	shuttle

Summary A beautiful short walk that offers great vistas of the stunning natural basin of Ormiston Pound before returning via permanent waterholes under the red ramparts of spectacular Ormiston Gorge.

Ormiston Gorge is one of the main attractions in West MacDonnell National Park. There's a large waterhole suitable for swimming, it's a dramatic (short) walk into the gorge and facilities are good. Day visitors, however, rarely wander into the arid Ormiston Pound east of the gorge, where a fascinating landscape awaits.

The walk described is easily completed in half a day, but you can overnight at Bowmans Gap, a short detour off the marked Pound Walk. Set off early for a great view of the sunlit gorge. Alternatively, the afternoon's soft light on the Pound is also worth the walk. Remember to carry a full day's supply of water. Through this habitat flows Ormiston Creek, a tributary of the 100 million-year-old Finke River, which flows south into the Simpson Desert and is one of the oldest rivers in the world.

NEAREST TOWN & FACILITIES
See Alice Springs (p309).

Ormiston Gorge
The gorge is 140km west of Alice Springs via the Larapinta and Namatjira Drives. Close to Ormiston Gorge, **Glen Helen Resort** (☎ 8956 7489; www.glenhelen.com.au; Namatjira Dr; unpowered/powered sites for 2 $20/22, dm without/with linen $20/30, d $160) has a range of accommodation, an idyllic back veranda, occasional live music and the excellent **Namatjira Restaurant** (mains $21-29).

Ormiston Gorge camping ground (adult/child/family $6.60/3.30/16), adjacent to the gorge car park, has hot showers, toilets (with disabled facilities), picnic tables and free gas barbecues. Get here early for the best sites.

Alice Wanderer (☎ 8952 2111; www.alicewanderer .com.au; seat on existing tour $55, private shuttle for 1 or 2 $200) and **Emu Run** (☎ 8953 7057; www.emurun.com .au; seat on existing tour $99) offer transfers from Alice Springs. **Glen Helen Resort** (☎ 8956 7489; www.glenhelen.com.au) also runs transfers from Alice Springs to Glen Helen and other trailheads in the park.

THE WALK
From the visitor centre walk southeast beside the access road, crossing Ormiston Creek after five minutes to follow yellow trail markers for the Pound Walk. Head 20m downstream before turning left, off the Larapinta Trail (marked with blue triangles), and heading uphill thorough a network of dry gullies and over small rocky hillocks to a saddle, the gateway to **Ormiston Pound**, reached in 45 minutes. From the saddle, there's a 100m scramble up to a fantastic view point (signposted) on the exposed ridge to the north.

From the saddle, descend east, bearing right (south) behind and around the pronounced hillock and then turn north dropping down into the Pound. After 20 minutes weaving through spinifex and low scrub **Ormiston Creek**, with a 'guard of honour' of river red gums, is reached. It's

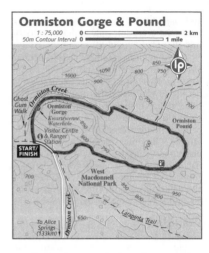

Ormiston Gorge & Pound

usually dry, but waterholes will persist after heavy rains. At this point you could turn off the Pound Walk and head upstream (northeast) towards Bowmans Gap. Otherwise, head towards the looming red gorge – you may find the yellow-on-white trail markers hard to spot in this section – crossing over a large meander in Ormiston Creek and then along the creek's rocky left bank into the brick-red **Ormiston Gorge**. After about 40 minutes the creek swings left to the large waterhole, Kwartetwenne. The visitor centre is five minutes south. Alternatively, go via the Ghost Gum Walk (on the right, west) which leads up to a view point.

LARAPINTA TRAIL HIGHLIGHT

Duration	2 days
Distance	38.6km
Difficulty	moderate
Start	Standley Chasm (p324)
Finish	Simpsons Gap
Nearest Town	Alice Springs (p309)
Transport	shuttle
Summary	Sample one of Australia's finest long-distance trails, crossing between two of the West MacDonnells' most popular natural attractions.

Simpsons Gap and Standley Chasm are among the most famous of the multitude of West MacDonnell gorges but they are also bookends to a chain of peaks, gorges and waterholes – classic central Australian imagery – accessible only to those prepared to walk.

The route described here covers sections two and three of the Larapinta Trail, in reverse. This direction has been selected because it places the afternoon sun at your back, rather than in your face. As a snapshot of the greater Larapinta, there are few better or more accessible sections of trail to sample. The route scrambles along a creek bed, up to a ridge with views that seem eternal, and through castaway gorges that you could have to yourself for days. In between you'll pass through the sort of spinifex, mallee and mulga country that furnishes the entire trail.

Begin early from Standley Chasm on day one and there's a chance to see black-footed rock wallabies along Angkale Creek.

PLANNING
Maps
The most useful maps can be downloaded free from the **Parks & Wildlife Service** website (www.nt.gov.au/nreta/parks/walks/larapinta.html). Hit the 'Walking the Trail' link to access maps and information sheets on each section. The maps look like black blurs on screen but they print well and are better than MapsNT's topographic maps, which don't show the trail.

Guided Walks
Trek Larapinta (☎ 8953 2933; www.treklarapinta.com .au; 3 days $550, 5 days $990, 8 days $1584) Offers an end-to-end walk (20 days, $2970) once a year.
Willis's Walkabouts (☎ 8985 2134; www.bushwalking holidays.com.au) An eight-day Larapinta East walk ($1050) and a seven-day Larapinta West Walk ($1125), or the two combined ($1850).

LARAPINTA TRAIL

Completed in 2002, the Larapinta Trail is the newest, and certainly among the finest, of Australia's long-distance walking tracks. Meandering between and along the parallel ridges that form the West MacDonnell Ranges, it extends 223km from the Alice Springs Telegraph Station to Mt Sonder (1380m), the ranges' most prominent peak. Switching between the desert plains, dolomite foothills and sharp quartzite ridges of the ranges, the trail is the most intimate way to experience the Red Centre.

Divided into 12 sections of between 13km and 31km in length, with water sources no more than 33km apart, the trail doesn't require Herculean strength or marathon endurance to complete. Many sections end beside one of the ranges' popular gorges, creating a selection of possible trailheads and making it possible to sample the trail on day walks or overnight wanders, or to stretch it out to around 16 fairly comfortable days. Food drops can be made at the Standley Chasm and Ormiston Gorge kiosks, Glen Helen Resort and a shed at the Serpentine Gorge camp site, while it's also a simple task to bury a box of food in the sandy creek bed below Ellery Creek Big Hole. The trail is marked throughout with blue triangles and kilometre posts.

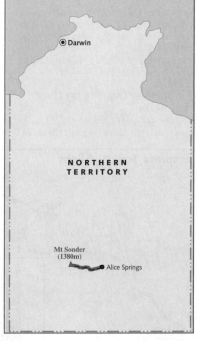

Alice Wanderer and Emu Run (see p322) offer transfers to points along the trail, as does **Glen Helen Resort** (☎ 8956 7489; www.glenhelen.com.au).

World Expeditions (☎ 1300 720 000; www.worldexped itions.com.au; 8 days $1750, 14 days end-to-end $2990)

NEAREST TOWN & FACILITIES

See Alice Springs (p309).

Standley Chasm

Standley Chasm (☎ 8956 7440; entry $7, camping per person $3) has walker-only camping on a small, uneven grassed area at the edge of the visitor car park. Tents are not allowed up between 8am and 5pm. The kiosk sells drinks, hamburgers and other fat and sugar fixes.

Alice Wanderer (☎ 8952 2111; www.alicewanderer .com.au; seat on existing tour $30, private shuttle $95) and **Emu Run** (☎ 8953 7057; www.emurun.com.au; seat on existing tour $30) offer transfers from Alice Springs.

GETTING TO/FROM THE WALK

For details on getting to Standley Chasm, see p324. From Simpsons Gap, Alice Wanderer can also deliver you to Alice Springs (seat on existing tour $25, private shuttle $75). You can walk to Alice from Simpsons Gap by continuing along section one of the Larapinta Trail, which offers great views from Euro Ridge. It's 23.8km to the telegraph station and another 4km into Alice.

THE WALK
Day 1: Standley Chasm to Jay Creek
4–5 hours, 14.1km

From the car park, follow the Standley Chasm trail north along Angkale Creek. In a few minutes, the signposted Larapinta Trail turns sharply uphill, leaving you a choice of routes. The trail proper ascends sharply to **Larapinta Hill** for views of the creek and the ranges to the south, before returning to the creek bed after about 30 minutes.

If you're feeling dexterous, the more interesting route is through **Standley Chasm**, turning left up the creek bed at its end. Scramble over boulders and wobble up a dead tree-cum-ladder to enter a second, narrower **chasm**. At its end, climb the polished chute of rock, drop your pack and squirm through the narrow hole in the rockfall, pulling your pack up behind you. About 100m upstream, and 30 minutes from the car park, you rejoin the Larapinta Trail and almost immediately come to Angkale Junction.

Turn northeast (right), ascending to a saddle then dropping back down into a wide valley. A stony creek bed becomes your path, threading through a set of rock outcrops. At the first outcrop, the trail skirts a 10m-high waterfall (almost certainly dry) by edging left along the top of the shelf before descending in steps on the rougher rock at the edge. At a smaller waterfall in the second outcrop, the easiest route down is to the right of the main drop.

Continue along and beside the creek bed (which is overgrown with scrub and MacDonnell Range cycads, a fern-like relict that once rubbed fronds with the dinosaurs) to reach **Millers Flat** (1¼ hours from Angkale

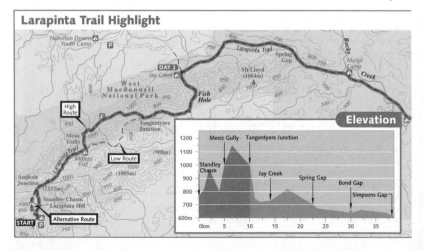

Larapinta Trail Highlight

Junction). Set between rocky peaks, Millers Flat is a great camp site if you fancy a short day, though you'll need to carry in water from Standley Chasm.

At the signposted junction at Millers Flat, you again have a selection of routes: low or high. The low route (4km, one to 1¼ hours) continues along the creek bed to a saddle, but unless you have a real aversion to great views and a bit of climbing, the ridge-top trail is recommended. This route heads north (left), climbing 200m through the prominent **Mesic Gully**. Pinched between red walls and thick with cycads, it's more like a steep gorge than a humble gully. Turn east (right) at the small saddle at its head, and continue climbing through the bluffs.

As you walk along the ridge, look behind to watch the rugged Chewings Range emerge into view. The rounded summit of Brinkley Bluff – the key feature of section four of the Larapinta Trail – is the most prominent peak. To the north, on the plain, the buildings of Hamilton Downs Youth Camp also come into view.

Thirty minutes from the top of Mesic Gully you reach the ridge's **high point** (1148m) and a spectacular view. To the southeast, below the sharpened point of an escarpment ridge, Alice Springs is just visible. The tilted escarpment of Arenge Bluff is to its left.

Continue along the ridge until the trail drapes away southeast, descending 350m on a spur to rejoin the low route at Tangentyere Junction, about one hour from the lookout.

Turn east (left) and walk through mulga woodland interspersed with ghost gums and bloodwoods, rounding the range and climbing first above and then into a gorge at the northern end of **Fish Hole** (45 minutes from Tangentyere Junction). This waterhole is significant to the local Aboriginal people, who request that you leave no trace of your visit. Camping isn't allowed. Follow the creek bed north as it bends through the range, emerging on to the plain and the **Jay Creek camp site**, with water tanks, after about 30 minutes.

Day 2: Jay Creek to Simpsons Gap
6½–7½ hours, 24.5km

From Jay Creek the track heads east, along the foot of the Chewings Range, climbing gently through mulga and the red, tubular flowers of the desert fuchsia. After about 40 minutes it turns on to a more substantial line of hills, briefly doubling back then continuing east along the low ridge, with good views across to the Chewings Range.

Amble along the ridge for about an hour until the track drops away southeast and into the small gorge at **Spring Gap** (1¾ hours from Jay Creek). There's a wonderful spring-fed pool inside the gap but with water tanks just 3.5km ahead at Mulga Camp, it's unlikely you'll need it as a drinking source. It's also an important wildlife refuge, so camping is prohibited.

Beyond the pool, the path follows the west (right) side of the gorge, returning you to the southern side of the Chewings Range and following the creek and its river red gums for about 30 minutes. It then crosses through mulga-covered hills for another 30 minutes to the water tanks, picnic tables and toilet at **Mulga Camp**, set unsurprisingly in a tall stand of mulga trees on an alluvial flat. As you approach the camp you'll see the impressive Arenge Bluff beginning to appear over the ridge lines.

The trail follows Rocky Creek southeast out of the camp before crossing through woodland again. Atop low cliffs above Rocky Creek, it rounds the southern flank of **Arenge Bluff**, with its imposing escarpment, to reach a burr-filled camp site about one hour from Mulga Camp.

Climb back above the creek and beside Arenge Bluff as it slopes away towards **Bond Gap**, reached 30 minutes from the camp site.

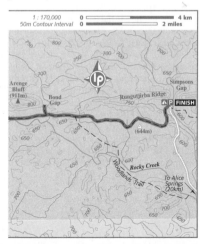

The trail cuts south of the gap but a side track leads to the reedy pool at its entrance. Camping is discouraged here in order to protect wildlife.

Return to the main trail, which rolls east through a rocky landscape, slowly edging away from the sharpened tip of Rungutjirba Ridge, which is a continuation of the escarpment that began at Arenge Bluff. As the trail draws level with the obvious gap in the range it swings north, skirting a small hill and passing the walkers' camp site to arrive at **Simpsons Gap** (two to 2½ hours from Bond Gap).

MORE WALKS

LITCHFIELD NATIONAL PARK
Table Top Track

This 39km, three- to five-day circuit takes in Litchfield's major sights and is rated moderate–difficult. However, shorter walks are possible, with alternative access points and designated campsites located at Florence Falls, Greenant Creek, Wangi Falls and Walker Creek. Overnight walkers are encouraged to register (see p307). Up-to-date information is available from the Batchelor office of the **PWS** (☎ 8976 0282) and the Darwin visitor information centre. The track is closed in the Wet – usually starting at the end of September – and the re-opening date depends on rainfall and is highly variable. MapsNT's 1:30,000 *Litchfield National Park* and 1:50,000 *Mt Tolmer* and *Rum Jungle* maps cover the area.

WEST MACDONNELL NATIONAL PARK
Mt Giles

This two- to three-day walk from Ormiston Gorge visitor centre is roughly 18km each way, with the last 3km a difficult climb to the peak of Mt Giles (1389m). It's graded as demanding and is suited to experienced walkers only: once you're off the marked Pound Walk track that leads into Ormiston Pound, it's up to you. There's an unreliable water source at the base of the mountain close to the best camp site – certainly don't

depend on it. It is possible – and rewarding – to camp on the summit of Mt Giles, but you'll need to hump all your water up there. A detailed map showing the suggested route west through the Pound, camp sites, and recommended routes up the southern spur is available from PWS offices (p308) and the PWS website (www.nt.gov.au/nreta /parks).

Redbank Gorge to Mt Sonder

This route, 8km in each direction, takes you from beautiful Redbank Gorge to the summit of the West MacDonnells' most striking peak (and its fourth highest at 1380m). It's the final (or first) stage of the Larapinta Trail but is worth the walk in its own right. The climb follows a wide ridge, shaped like the figure of a sleeping woman when seen from many points, most of the way to a view that incorporates many of central Australia's finest features: Mt Zeil, Haast Bluff, Gosses Bluff, Mt Giles, the Napperby Salt Lakes and Glen Helen Gorge. There's a camp site (with water tank) beside the trailhead, on the bank of Redbank Creek. From here the Larapinta Trail heads east to Glen Helen Gorge and Ormiston Pound (two to three days). The best map is the one for section 12 downloadable from the PWS website (www.nt.gov.au/nreta/parks).

WATARRKA NATIONAL PARK
Giles Track

Although this park, about 300km southwest of Alice Springs, is something of a tourist magnet, it contains an excellent one-way overnight walk. From Kathleen Spring the Giles Track traverses 22km northwest below the George Gill Range before descending into the 'Garden of Eden' in Kings Canyon. Camping is above Lilla (Reedy Creek) and there are a number of semipermanent springs en route. Contact the **PWS ranger** (☎ 8951 8250) for detailed track notes and sketch map (not available on the PWS website). As well as camping, **Kings Canyon Resort** (☎ 1300 134 044) provides budget and luxurious accommodation. You will need your own transport to reach the park.

Queensland

It's sunny, warm and the only state where more people want to come than want to leave! It's the 'Sunshine State' – Australia's great escape and a powerful magnet for southerners creeping northward for less complicated lifestyles and sun-drenched holidays.

Five regions in Queensland are World Heritage–listed and three of them can be explored through walks that are featured in this chapter. Australia's Great Dividing Range begins amid the Wet Tropics region in the far north and here lies Queensland's highest peak – Mt Bartle Frere – where walkers can still experience Jurassic plants from Gondwana days. Also in the Wet Tropics, there's a sense of romance as you roam Hinchinbrook Island's beaches and camp under starry skies. Freshwater lakes and pristine beaches lure walkers to the world's largest sandbar, Fraser Island, with its unique ecosystem and genetically pure dingo population. Queensland's southern doorway leads to the Central Eastern Rainforests Reserves region and Lamington National Park's subtropical rainforests, with Australia's most extensive walking track network (160km).

In the past, Queensland may not have ranked as highly as some southern states as a bushwalking destination, but the secret's out. Come and share the outdoors with the locals.

HIGHLIGHTS

- Cracking a coconut under starry skies at **Hinchinbrook Island** (p349)
- Splashing cool mountain water on your face in **Lamington National Park** (p335)
- Ripping off your boots, running through the sand and plunging into Lake McKenzie on **Fraser Island** (p342)
- Congratulating yourself after hauling up to Queensland's rooftop, **Mt Bartle Frere** (p353)

■ TELEPHONE CODE: 07   ■ www.epa.qld.gov.au   ■ www.queenslandholidays.com.au

QUEENSLAND

ENVIRONMENT

Queensland's a land of contrasts, five times bigger than Japan and twice as big as Texas. Hot, wet summers characterise the tropical north, but along the southern highlands snow has been known to fall. Some places get only 150mm of rain a year, while others experience up to 4000mm.

The Great Dividing Range is Queensland's backbone and separates the well-watered coast from the inland's rolling plains. Sun-baked islands and beaches give way to mountainous rainforests and eucalypt glades. Descending westward, taller trees are replaced by stunted mulga and acacia scrub, eventually petering out to the Outback's spinifex grasses.

Queensland's home to Australia's most endangered mammal, the northern hairy-nosed wombat. Once found as far south as Victoria, it now lives only in a small national park in the tropics. Lungfish are unique to Queensland – they can live in water or on land. Queensland has more bird species than any other state or territory. One of the most striking is the large, flightless cassowary, a primitive bird restricted to dense northern rainforests and now endangered even there.

Queensland has been subjected to sustained and government-supported environmental vandalism – 4.5 million hectares of brigalow (eucalypt) scrub was cleared from north Queensland to the New South Wales (NSW) border in one nine-year period. Seventy-five percent of its rainforests were felled and some mangrove nurseries remain threatened by urban development.

Fortunately, there are now 223 national parks protecting its natural areas – havens for adventure seekers.

INFORMATION
When to Walk

Queensland has an undeserved reputation as being 'too hot for walking', but try visiting its rainforests during summer: temperatures are guaranteed to be degrees cooler than lower coastal areas. Rain is common (most falls between January and March, which is also the cyclone season for the northern two-thirds of the state), but the heady perfume of a wet forest enhances your experience. Winter's the time to walk its coastal islands.

Maps

Hema's 1:2,500,000 *Queensland State Map* and its associated regional maps are great for travel planning. Sunmap has a 1:2,500,000 state map, regional maps and a series of 1:25,000 and 1:50,000 topographic maps. Individual maps are listed in the Planning sections for each walk.

Books

Lonely Planet's *Queensland* gives a great overview of the state's jewels, charms, people and peculiarities. Queensland Museum publishes an excellent series of environmental and natural history books including *Wild Places, Wild Plants* and *Wildlife,* all with stunning colour photos. *Take A Walk in Queensland's National Parks – Southern Zone,* by John and Lyn Daly, is a comprehensive guide for that region. Townsville to Cooktown is admirably covered by *Tropical Walking Tracks,* a series of five booklets by Kym Dungey and Jane Whytlaw. Paul Curtis' *The Travellers' Guide to North Queensland* has over 50 walks and scenic drives.

Information Sources

Most cities and towns have visitor information centres, often staffed by knowledgeable and helpful volunteers, though don't expect too much info about specific walks.

National Parks Association of Queensland (NPAQ; (☎ 3367 0878; www.npaq.org.au) Leading community voice for conservation since 1930, it organises comprehensive bushwalking and camping programs.

Queensland Federation of Bushwalking Clubs (www.geocities.com/qfbwc) Maintains a list of state-wide affiliated bushwalking clubs.

Queensland Parks & Wildlife Service (QPWS; ☎ 3227 8185; www.epa.qld.gov.au) Manages national parks.

Queensland Travel Centre (☎ 13 88 33; www.queenslandwalks.com.au) A Tourism Queensland innovation that walks you through the state from the coast to the Outback. Whether you're after a short walk or a multiday hike, the new website has it covered and also provides useful links to other sites.

Permits & Regulations

Permits are necessary for camping in national parks. Contact **QPWS** (☎ 13 13 04; www.qld.gov.au/camping; sites for 2 $8). Some parks require contact with local rangers; these are mentioned in the specific walks. Permits for Green Mountains (p335), Great Walk Fraser Island (p342) and the Thorsborne Trail

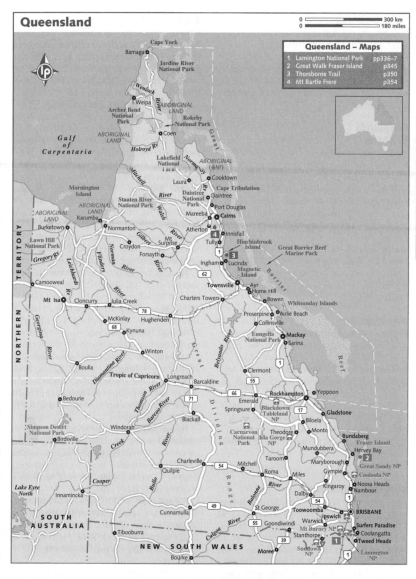

(p349) may need to be secured months in advance. QPWS encourages walkers visiting remote areas to complete bushwalking registration forms, which are available online or from QPWS offices.

Most areas are 'fuel stove' only. During Total Fire Ban days (p46/47), all fires are forbidden, even fuel stoves.

Guided Walks

K2 Extreme (☎ 3257 3310; www.k2extreme.com.au; 140 Wickham St, Fortitude Valley; yearly membership $70) Caters for beginner and experienced adventurers, who can walk, climb, kayak or cycle in Queensland's southeast.

Torre Mountaincraft (☎ 3870 2699; www.torre mountaincraft.com.au; 205 Moggill Rd, Taringa) Offers abseiling and climbing on world-acclaimed Kangaroo Point cliffs, plus canoeing and mountain biking.

Wooroonooran Safaris (☎ 1300 661 113; wooroonooran-safaris.com.au) Conducts guided day tours to less-crowded, less-commercialised beauty spots, especially Wooroonooran National Park. Their most popular naturalist-guided walk is the 19km Goldfield Trail, offered as a one-day tour.

GATEWAYS
Brisbane
☎ 07 / pop 1.5 million

Australia's most laid-back capital city, Brisbane is home to South Bank Parklands with its own lifeguard-patrolled free beach (that's no fee, not no clothes) opposite the city centre; Brisbanites gather here to celebrate special occasions. There are several heritage walks around town and if you miss seeing a koala in the bush, there's always **Lone Pine Koala Sanctuary** (☎ 3378 1366; www .koala.net; Jesmond Rd, Fig Tree Pocket; adult/child/family $19/14/49; ☯ 8.30am-5pm), Australia's largest koala sanctuary.

INFORMATION
Brisbane visitor information centre (☎ 3229 5918; www.ourbrisbane.com; Queen Street Mall; ☯ 9am-5.30pm Mon-Thu, 9am-7pm Fri, 9am-5pm Sat, 9.30am-4.30pm Sun) Download maps for Brisbane River Heritage Trail and RiverWalk, a trail connecting over 20km of paths, roads, bridges and parks along Brisbane River.

QPWS (☎ 3227 8185; www.epa.qld.gov.au; 160 Ann St; ☯ 8.30am-5pm Mon-Fri) Customer service centre sells maps and books, and can organise permits.

World Wide Maps and Guides (☎ 3221 4330; www .worldwidemaps.com.au; Shop 30, Anzac Sq Arcade) The best place to buy maps.

SUPPLIES & EQUIPMENT
You can buy quality adventure/outdoor gear from specialty shops, including **K2** (☎ 3854 1340), **Mountain Designs** (☎ 3216 1866) and **Paddy Pallin** (☎ 3252 4408), which are all on Wickham St in Fortitude Valley, while **Kathmandu** (☎ 3252 8054; 728 Ann St) is just up the road. Torre Mountaincraft (p329) sells and hires out equipment, and several suburban camping stores stock cheaper gear or sell brand names at competitive prices.

Supermarkets in Brisbane's CBD include **Coles Express** (Myer Centre, 91 Queen St) and **Woolworths** (MacArthur Bldg, cnr Queen & Edward Sts). There's a **Foodworks Supermarket** (Brunswick St, Fortitude Valley) in Valley Metro Plaza.

SLEEPING & EATING
Check the net (www.ourbrisbane.com) for a list of Brisbane's accommodation houses or **Brisbane Visitors Accommodation Service** (☎ 3236 2020; bristrav@tpg.com.au; 3rd fl, Roma St Transit Centre; ☯ 8am-5.30pm Mon-Fri, 8.30am-4pm Sat & Sun) will find a bed to suit your budget.

Newmarket Gardens Caravan Park (☎ 3356 1458; www.newmarketgardens.com.au; 199 Ashgrove Ave, Ashgrove; unpowered/powered sites for 2 $22/23, lodge rooms for 2 $45, cabins for 2 $75-95; ☐) is the closest to the city and buses stop out the front. Linen hire is available and there are free barbecues and a fridge.

Bunk Brisbane (☎ 1800 682 865; www.bunk brisbane.com.au; cnr Ann & Gipps Sts, Fortitude Valley; dm $16-25, s/d $45/70; ☒ ☐ ☒), winner of Queensland Tourism's Backpacker Accommodation award, has taken hostels to another level. Birdee Num Num Bar has $5 meals from 6pm and daily upbeat entertainment.

Painted bright orange, **Brisbane City Backpackers**, (☎ 1800 062 572; www.citybackpackers .com; 380 Upper Roma St; dm $17-26, s/d $55-75/60-80; ☒ ☐ ☒) is 400m from the transit centre. Fiddlers Elbow Pub has nightly entertainment and The Cafe serves good food, focusing on backpacker budgets.

Explorers Inn (☎ 1800 6288; www.explorers.com .au; cnr George & Turbot Sts; r $85; ☒ ☐) is Brisbane's cheapest three-star accommodation and is just 150m from the transit centre. Its licensed barbecue opens daily and $10 will get you a main meal.

Snooze Inn Hotel (☎ 1800 655 805; www.snoozeinn .com.au; 383 St Pauls Tce; s/d/tw $90/100/110; ☒ ☐) in cosmopolitan Fortitude Valley, is new and fifteen minutes' walk from Brisbane's centre. There are over 200 eateries within walking distance.

Il Mondo (☎ 3392 0111; www.ilmondo.com.au; 25-35 Rotherham St, Kangaroo Point; r $100-135, f $165-350; ☒ ☒) is close to the city and convenient to the start of Brisbane River Heritage Trail and RiverWalk. Savini Restaurant, downstairs, serves dinner.

City food courts serve the usual ready-to-go food, but Brisbane's great climate makes eating outdoors especially enjoyable. Stacks of cafés cater for all cuisines.

On South Bank's boardwalk, **Chez Laila** (☎ 3846 3402; mains $9-24; ☯ breakfast, lunch & dinner) overlooks Brisbane River to the city. Its signature dish is an authentic Lebanese platter, big enough for two.

Among West End's eclectic café set, **Ouzeri** (☎ 3846 5800; cnr Boundary & Russell Sts; lunch $13-16; ❤ lunch & dinner daily) comes recommended by local bushwalkers. Greek and Italian fare is served with lashings of live Greek music on Friday and Saturday. Lunches are huge and scrumptious.

The best place to sample native cuisine is **Tukka Restaurant** (☎ 3846 6333; 145 Boundary St, West End; mains $21-31; ❤ dinner daily, lunch Sun) Its platter of game meats, native berries, bush dukkah and Australian cheeses is a hit and comes in at $19 per person.

GETTING THERE & AWAY

The national highway bypasses the city centre via Gateway Motorway (M1), connecting the Gold and Sunshine Coasts via the Pacific and Bruce Hwys. The Pacific Motorway (M3) leaves the city, joining M1 at Eight Mile Plains. Take Ipswich (M2) or Logan (M6) Motorways to head west.

Air

Qantas (☎ 13 13 13; www.qantas.com.au; 247 Adelaide St; ❤ 8.30am-5pm Mon-Fri, 9am-1pm Sat) has international and domestic flights servicing Brisbane. QantasLink and their affiliate airlines service metropolitan and regional Australia, while **Virgin Blue** (☎ 13 67 89; www.virginblue.com.au) and **Jetstar** (☎ 13 15 38; www.jetstar.com.au) generally tout cheaper fares for on-line bookings.

Buses and the Airtrain (right) run to and from the airport.

Bus

TransInfo (☎ 13 12 30; www.transinfo.qld.gov.au) is the bus and train hotline for Brisbane and Queensland's southeast.

Brisbane Transit Centre (☎ 3236 2528; www.brisbanetransitcentre.com.au; Roma St; ❤ 4.30am-midnight Sun-Thu, 24 hr Fri & Sat) is the nucleus for interstate and regional coach arrivals and departures. Booking desks are on level three.

Greyhound Australia (☎ 13 14 99; www.greyhound.com.au) Operates services from Brisbane to Cairns ($200, 29 hours, four daily) and Brisbane to Sydney ($100, 17 hours, five daily).

Premier Motor Service (☎ 13 34 10; www.premierms.com.au) links Australia's east coast from Melbourne to Cairns. Services include Brisbane to Cairns ($175, 29 hours, daily) and Brisbane to Sydney ($70, 14 hours, two daily).

Coachtrans (☎ 1300 664 700; www.coachtrans.com.au) operates Skytrans transfers from the airport to Brisbane Transit Centre and accommodation in the CBD (adult/child $9/11, half hourly, 5.30am to 11pm) as well as the Gold Coast ($35, hourly, 6.15am to 11pm).

Train

State and interstate trains arrive and depart from Roma St Railway Station, below the transit centre.

Queensland Rail (☎ 13 22 32; www.traveltrain.com.au) runs the high-speed *Tilt Train* from Brisbane to Cairns ($300, 24 hours, Monday and Friday). The slower *Sunlander* also travels this route ($200, 32 hours, Sunday, Tuesday and Thursday).

Citytrain (☎ 13 16 17; www.qr.com.au) runs from **Central Station** (cnr Ann & Edward Sts) to the Gold and Sunshine Coasts.

Airtrain (☎ 3215 5000; www.airtrain.com.au; ❤ 6am-7pm daily) links Brisbane's airport with the city centre ($12) and the Gold Coast ($24) every 30 minutes.

Car Rental

ABC Integra Network (☎ 1800 067 414; www.abcintegra.com.au; 398 St Pauls Tce, Fortitude Valley) says it will beat the majors by up to 40%, while **Abel** (☎ 1800 131 429; www.abel.com.au; level 1, Brisbane Transit Centre) rents over the net from $45 per day, all-inclusive.

Cairns

☎ 07 / pop 98,981

Unashamedly the tourist capital of Queensland's tropical north, Cairns is hugged by World Heritage-listed Wet Tropics rainforests. An adventurers' playground, outdoorsy folk get adrenalin rushes from bushwalking, bungee jumping, kayaking, snorkelling, diving and everything in between.

INFORMATION

The Esplanade's eateries, accommodation and booking centres all peddle the 'ultimate' tourist experiences.

Absells Chart & Map Centre (☎ 4041 2699; Andrejic Arcade, 55 Lake St) Stocks an extensive range of guidebooks and maps.

Gateway Discovery Centre (☎ 4051 3588; www.tropicalaustralia.com.au; 51 Esplanade; ❤ 8.30am-6.30pm) Helpful for general info and walking track brochures.

QPWS (☎ 4046 6600; www.epa.qld.gov.au; 5b Sheridan St; ❤ 8.30am-5pm Mon-Fri) Gives park information, issues permits and has a good collection of books. Get topographic and tourist maps from the third floor.

SUPPLIES & EQUIPMENT

City Place Disposals (☎ 4051 6040; 46-48 Shields St) has lower-end camping and walking equipment, including gas canister refills, and hires out three-person tents. **Adventure Equipment** (☎ 4031 2669; 133 Grafton St) is into better-quality gear and hires kayaks and canoes. It's not a booking agent so provides sound advice on local adventure spots.

For self-caterers there's a **Woolworths** (Sheridan St) and two supermarkets in Cairns Central Shopping Centre. For the ultimate in fresh fruit and vegies, visit **Rusty's Bazaar** (Grafton St; ☯ 6am-6pm Fri, 6am-3pm Sat & Sun).

SLEEPING & EATING

Gateway Discovery Centre (☎ 4051 3588; 51 Esplanade; ☯ 8.30am-6.30pm) arranges accommodation throughout Cairns and the region.

Cairns Coconut Caravan Resort (☎ 4054 6644; www.coconut.com.au; cnr Bruce Hwy & Anderson Rd; unpowered sites for 2 $32-38, powered sites for 2 $34-40, cabin d $55-75; 🔀 🖳 🖳) has a courtesy bus to the city and there's a campers' kitchen, mini-mart and lots of free fitness activities. It's meticulously maintained by a swarm of worker bees.

Opposite the train station, **Gecko's Backpackers** (☎ 1800 011 344; www.geckosbackpackers.com .au; 187 Bunda St; dm $21, s $31-35, d $46-48; 🔀 🖳 🖳) has renovated Queenslander homes that are bright and clean. Linen is supplied and they'll store extra luggage if you're off walking.

At **Caravella Backpackers** (☎ 4051 2159, 4031 5680; www.caravella.com.au; 77 & 149 Esplanade; dm/s $20/40, tw & d $45-65; 🔀 🖳 🖳) the bright, spacious rooms have fridges, and the big community kitchens are ideal for preparing trail food.

The 'backpacker' in the name of **Gilligan's Backpackers Resort** (☎ 4041 6566; www.gilligans backpackers.com.au; 57-89 Grafton St; dm $26-28, r $90; 🔀 🖳 🖳) decries its class. It has combined resort-style surroundings with upmarket budget accommodation. Social activities revolve around the pool, deck bar and a mezzanine bar that looks like a sheik's communal bedroom.

The Balinese Motel (☎ 4051 9922; www.balinese .com.au; 215 Lake St; s $90, tw & d $100; 🔀 🖳 🖳) is centrally located and decorated with unique Balinese-style furnishings. Included

are free airport transfers and a continental breakfast. There's a communal kitchen for self-caterers.

Fig Tree Lodge (☎ 1800 068 090; www.figtreelodge .com.au; 253 Sheridan St; r $110-130; 🔀 🖳 🖳) Get a home-away-from-home feel in this open-plan resort, set among cool, tropical gardens. Studio rooms have kitchenettes. In the heart of the lodge is a restaurant and Irish-style bar, famous for serious steaks and Guinness.

Cairns is a city of international cuisine. Locally recommended **Swiss Cake & Coffee Shop** (☎ 4051 6393; 93 Grafton St; dishes $6-11; ☯ breakfast & lunch Mon-Sat) serves the ultimate European, home-made cakes and slices with excellent coffee. Its salads are the best.

A local bushwalkers' hangout, **City Walk Cafe** (☎ 4051 5075; cnr Shields & Lake Sts; dishes $8-12; ☯ breakfast, lunch & dinner Mon-Sat) has hearty brunches, snacks, sangas and vegie meals.

A top travellers' haunt, **The Woolshed** (☎ 4031 6304; 24 Shields St; meals $12-16; ☯ dinner) serves up huge steaks. Several hostels promote free dinners here. These entree-sized meals can be upgraded to heartier meals for five to six dollars. You might need to queue outside waiting for a seat.

GETTING THERE & AWAY

Air

The international terminal allows visitors to hop on or hop off in Cairns.

Qantas (☎ 13 13 13; www.qantas.com.au; cnr Shields & Lake Sts), its affiliate **Jetstar** (☎ 13 15 38; www .jetstar.com.au) and **Virgin Blue** (☎ 13 67 89; www .virginblue.com.au) fly between Brisbane and Cairns (from $140, two hours).

Australia Coach (☎ 4048 8355; per person $8) runs the Airporter bus to the city. A taxi is around $15.

Bus

Buses operate from the **Cairns Transit Centre** (☎ 4051 5899; Trinity Wharf, Lake St; ☯ 8.30am-5.30pm daily). See Bus p331 for details of fares and schedules.

Train

Cairns Railway Station (☎ 4036 9249; Bunda St) is the arrival and departure point for inter-state trains.

Queensland Rail (☎ 13 22 32; www.traveltrain .com.au) operates the *Tilt Train* from Cairns to Brisbane ($300, 24 hours, Sunday and

Wednesday). The slower *Sunlander* also travels this route ($200, 32 hours) on Tuesday, Thursday and Saturday.

Car Rental

Majors are represented at the airport and in town. Town's the place for cheaper deals. Most start from $29 per day, plus charges. Some offer one-way rentals and 4WDs.

All Day Car Rentals (☎ 4031 3348; www.cairns-car -rentals.com; 1/62 Abbott St)

Billabong Car Rentals (☎ 1800 354 299; www.billa bongrentals.com.au; 134 Sheridan St)

LAMINGTON NATIONAL PARK

Lamington's rainforest-clad slopes form part of the Scenic Rim, a chain of mountains encircling Queensland's most populated and accessible areas – Brisbane and the Gold Coast. Lamington, like most of the rim, is World Heritage–listed and protects one of the world's largest stands of subtropical rainforest. With most of these forests falling to the logger's axe, it's quite the privilege to be able to explore this ancient landscape.

Lamington is all about walking, smelling, seeing, hearing and feeling the rainforest.

HISTORY

Dairy farmers, and loggers attracted by 'red gold' (the prized cedar trees), arrived in the mid 1800s. Surprisingly, a grazier and the son of a prominent timber miller were two of the first to lobby for creation of the park. Named for an early Queensland governor (not the Australian chocolate-coated cake), Lord Lamington only visited the park once, supposedly shooting a koala to mark the occasion!

Men using picks and shovels were employed during the Depression to construct the graded tracks. Today, Lamington boasts over 160km of walking tracks winding through lush rainforests to panoramic lookouts and over 500 waterfalls. An easy walk along the 22km Border Track links Green Mountains (commonly known as O'Reilly's) and Binna Burra. Most walking tracks start at these trailheads and radiate from this route.

ENVIRONMENT

Wollumbin (Mt Warning), Australia's largest shield volcano, erupted 22 million years ago. Continual weathering of its lava flows produced Lamington's creeks, rivers, valleys and escarpments. Wollumbin's original height is estimated at 2000m. Today the plug stands 1157m and is visible from many of Lamington's lookouts.

Lamington's rainforests nurture over 200 rare or threatened plants and animals. Trees with massive buttressed trunks, liana vines and orchids and the aptly named strangler figs, flame trees, stinging trees, wait-a-while vines, elkhorns, staghorns and crows-nest ferns all flourish. Fairylands of Antarctic beech forests are at their northernmost extent; the root stock of some are estimated to be more than 5000 years old.

Listen for the melodious song of the elusive Albert's lyrebird mimicking bush sounds to attract a female companion. Few walkers are lucky enough to see his display ritual. Distinctive calls of catbirds, whipbirds and riflebirds resonate throughout the forest. Brilliant black-and-yellow regent bowerbirds are regularly seen at O'Reilly's, and king parrots and crimson rosellas are easily spotted.

Pademelons graze near camp sites at dawn and dusk, while spotlighting reveals possums, gliders and bandicoots. Along the tracks you may meet shiny black land mullets (skinks about 30cm long with a 20cm girth), goannas and non-venomous carpet pythons. An encounter with the bright-blue, pugnacious Lamington spiny cray will have it hissing and snapping its pincers as it retreats.

PLANNING
When to Walk

Lamington's temperate climate brings in walkers year-round. You can enjoy an invigorating swim under a waterfall in summer (rain and thunderstorms are common at this time, but after all it is a 'rainforest'). Don't fancy rain? Then walk in winter. Days are crisp but nights can be freezing. Spring attracts birders and flower enthusiasts to the heathlands.

No bush camping is allowed during December and January. Rangers close some tracks in adverse conditions but there's always something open.

QUEENSLAND

QUEENSLAND

What to Bring

Insect repellent or other deterrents are essential to discourage leeches (see the boxed text opposite) and ticks. Apply liberally to your socks, boots, gaiters and exposed skin.

Maps & Books

Day walkers can use the free maps from the visitor information centres (below). Hema's 1:35,000 *Lamington National Park* displays walking tracks in different colours. Sunmap's 1:25,000 *Beechmont* and *Tyalgum* topographic maps should be carried by overnight walkers. Maps are available from stockists (p330) or at O'Reilly's and Binna Burra gift shops.

Bernard O'Reilly's *Green Mountains* gives a graphic account of his 1937 search and rescue efforts following one of Queensland's best-known aircraft crashes. Reading it before walking through Lamington's seemingly impenetrable forests engenders admiration for his superior bushcraft. O'Reilly's gift shop sells the book.

Information Sources

Walkers and naturalists with a passion for the park staff visitor information centres at **Green Mountains** (☎ 5544 0634) and **Binna Burra** (☎ 5533 3584) on weekends and school holidays. They give sound advice about current conditions. Contact rangers on the same numbers.

Permits & Regulations

Bush camping (☎ 5544 0634; sites for 2 $8, limit 6 people, maximum stay per site 1 night) is restricted and phone bookings are essential. Binna Burra's remote sites are closed indefinitely because of the risk of tree falls. Fuel stoves are mandatory.

> **WARNING**
>
> Giant stinging trees (gympie gympies) invade storm-damaged areas or tree-fall breaks. Identified by distinctive dinner-plate shaped leaves, pock-marked with holes from insect attack, their severe 'sting' can last for days. When touched, fine silica hairs (even from dead leaves) penetrate your skin and release a painful irritant. Antidotes include bikini wax strips to remove the painful hairs (a tad embarrassing for guys at the pharmacy) or local anaesthetic lotions. These trees are the topic of many camp site myths – caution is required when bush toileting!

Guided Walks

O'Reilly's Rainforest Guesthouse (p337) has a comprehensive program of guided activities. Binna Burra Mountain Lodge (p339) offers abseiling (10m to 90m), half- and one-day guided track walks and one-day, off-track walks. Activities are offered to campers and day-trippers. Both provide transfers for those walking the 22km Border Track.

ACCESS TOWN

Gold Coast

☎ 07 / pop 376,500

This holiday hot-spot is just an hour south of Brisbane. It's glitzy, it's plastic, it's expensive, it's fast and just very Gold Coast. If you want to escape the hype, drift in and out on your way to some great hinterland walking.

There are almost as many tour desks as hotels, but for central information visit **Surfers Paradise visitor information centre** (☎ 5538 4419; www.goldcoasttourism.com.au; Cavill Ave Mall; 8.30am-5.30pm Mon-Fri, 8.30am-5pm Sat, 9am-4pm Sun). For a comprehensive range of camping gear see **Nerang Disposals & Camping** (☎ 5596 4434; 10 Spencer Rd, Nerang). There are supermarkets in all big shopping centres and throughout the suburbs.

SLEEPING & EATING

Stay Oz (☎ 1800 359 830; www.stayoz.com.au; Transit Centre, Surfers Paradise) Helpful for accommodation and travel services.

Surrounded by eateries and continually being refurbished, **British Arms YHA Hostel** (☎ 1800 680 269; www.britisharms.com.au; Mariners Cove, Main Beach; dm $22-26, r $60;) is near the beach, just five minutes' walk from Seaworld. There's a free bus to/from Surfers' transit centre.

For self-caterers, **Club Surfers Apartments** (☎ 5531 5244; www.clubsurfers.com.au; 2877 Gold Coast Hwy, Surfers Paradise; r $90-150;) is near the beach and a short stroll to the café scene.

Chateau Beachside (☎ 5538 1022; www.chateaubeachside.com.au; cnr Esplanade & Elkhorn Ave, Surfers Paradise; s/d $110-145, f $120-150;) is a high-rise complex in the heart of Surfers,

---

BEAT THE LEECH

Rainforests are notorious for leeches and some novices panic just thinking about them! It's probably because these black, worm-like passengers suck your blood, then swell until they drop off. You then start bleeding. But don't worry – they're not a death threat and after a while you'll find yourself picking off these little critters as a matter of course.

Leeches are most active during rain, when they escape from their burrows in the leaf-litter or drop from trees. They usually home in on your feet and ankles, making their way through shoelace eyelets and your socks, or they may even travel quietly up your leg to other intimate parts. You can't feel them attaching because their saliva contains a local anaesthetic; you bleed because it also contains an anticoagulant.

While some reach for the saltshaker to dislodge them, others flick them off or let them feed and then drop off. Deterrents come in several forms, most of which cause the leeches to vomit and fall off. Insect repellent (not environmentally friendly), eucalyptus oil, tea-tree oil, vinegar, lemon juice or salt sprinkled between two layers of finely woven socks have all been tried. No matter what, leeches seem to be winning the rainforest war!

---

opposite the beach. Rooms are spacious and have spectacular ocean views. Ask about special off-peak rates.

You'll never go hungry on the Gold Coast. There's everything from quick eats to fine dining in this multicultural melting pot.

For great Aussie seafood – from bugs to barra – head for **Sonatas** (☎ 5526 9904; cnr Surf Pde & Queensland Ave, Broadbeach; mains $15-25; ☽ breakfast, lunch & dinner). It's popular with locals and also serves vegie meals.

Watch the world go by in the outdoor dining area at **Costa D'ora Italian Restaurant** (☎ 5538 5203; 27 Orchid Ave, Surfers Paradise; dishes $10-35; ☽ lunch & dinner). The pasta-and-cappuccino lunch deal is a bargain.

GETTING THERE & AWAY

Coolangatta's Gold Coast Airport is 25km south of Surfers Paradise. **Qantas** (☎ 13 13 13; www.qantas.com.au; 3047 Gold Coast Hwy, Surfers Paradise) and **Jetstar** (☎ 13 15 38; www.jetstar.com.au) fly from Sydney (from $110, 1½ hours) and Melbourne (from $155, two hours) daily.

Greyhound Australia (☎ 13 14 99; www.greyhound .com.au) runs from Brisbane to Surfers Paradise ($22, 1½ hours, seven per day), while **Premier Motor Service** (☎ 13 34 10; www.premierms .com.au) travels the same route ($15, 1½ hours, two per day).

Citytrain and Airtrain (p331) have multiple services from Brisbane's city ($8.70, one hour) and airport ($23, 1½ hours) to **Nerang Railway Station** (☎ 5527 4921) where a bus connects to Binna Burra (p339).

All buses stop at the Southport, Surfers Paradise and Coolangatta Transit Centres.

Connections to Green Mountains leave from **Surfers Paradise Transit Centre** (☎ 5584 3700; 10 Beach Rd, Surfers Paradise).

GREEN MOUNTAINS

Duration	2 days
Distance	28.9km
Difficulty	moderate
Start/Finish	Border Track trailhead
Nearest Town	Gold Coast (opposite)
Transport	bus

Summary This walk showcases Green Mountains' finest – pristine subtropical rainforests, mossy gorges, cascading waterfalls and sweeping panoramas. Fourteen creek crossings add adventure to some of Lamington's best-loved tracks.

As you stroll along the track, pause to enjoy the unique sounds of this ancient forest: the screech of a catbird, the crash of a falling log, a whisper of breeze in the canopy or the soothing sound of a gurgling cascade. All add to the enjoyment of walking to a remote camp in one of Queensland's favourite parks. Feeling fit? Extend Day 1 with a challenging, more rugged deviation that crisscrosses West Canungra Creek (see Side Trip p338).

Before leaving Green Mountains, experience life in the canopy on Australia's first tree-top walk. A 180m suspended walkway leads you through tree-tops, 15m above the ground. There is no need to book and, best of all, it's free.

QUEENSLAND

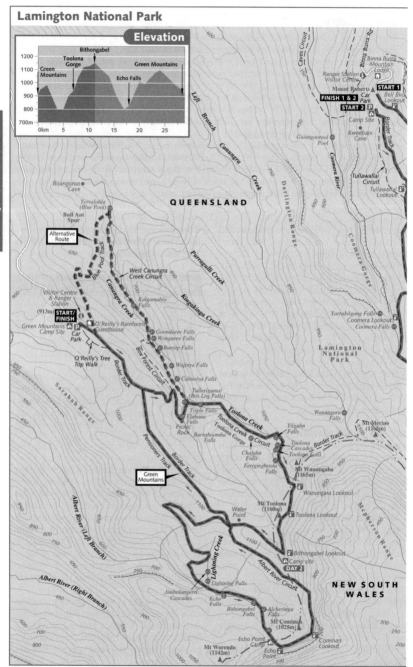

Lamington National Park

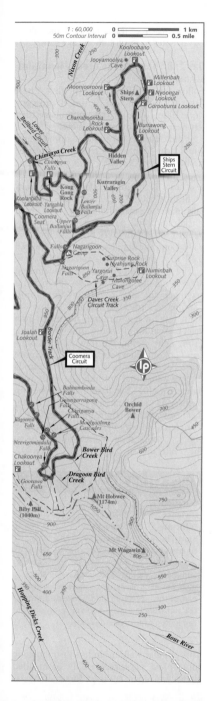

NEAREST TOWN & FACILITIES
See the Gold Coast (p334).

Green Mountains
O'Reilly's kiosk sells basic walkers' needs including noodles, gas cylinders, metho and spare tent pegs. There are no ATMs, so cash up in Brisbane or the Gold Coast.

Book your Green Mountains camp sites at **QPWS** (☎ 3227 8185; www.epa.qld.gov.au; per person/family $4/16) and enjoy rainforest settings and hot showers. **O'Reilly's Rainforest Guesthouse** (☎ 1800 688 722; www.oreillys.com.au; s/d from $145/290; 🖳) has a range of accommodation, most with magnificent mountain views. Lodgers and campers can sample their country-style cooking. View the mountains from the café verandah (best value – burger and drink $15), experience sunset from the Rainforest Bar (meals $15 to $20) or enjoy à la carte meals in the guesthouse dining room.

GETTING TO/FROM THE WALK
Allow two hours from Brisbane or 1½ hours from the Gold Coast via Nerang and Canungra. It's a winding, sealed road from here. **Australian Day Tours** (☎ 3236 4155; www.day tours.com.au) run from Brisbane Transit Centre ($70 return, daily). **Mountain Coach Company** (☎ 5524 4249; fax 5524 8013) operates from Gold Coast Airport or Surfers Paradise Transit Centre ($70 return, daily).

THE WALK
Day 1: Green Mountains to Bithongabel
4–4½ hours, 11.2km

Follow the Border Track for 1.7km and turn left on to the Toolona Creek Circuit track. Zigzag downhill past huge brush boxes with distinctive salmon-pink trunks and fibrous bark socks. Veer right at the next junction towards **Picnic Rock** – your first creek crossing and possibly your first encounter with a Lamington spiny cray.

Walk to the next junction and detour 70m left to **Elabana Falls**, the park's most photographed. Back at the junction, continue to the creek crossing at Triple Falls, but be careful: the mossy rocks can be treacherous. The track winds gradually uphill, passing several waterfalls, and challenges you with four creek crossings before reaching the steep, moss-covered walls of **Toolona Gorge**.

After winding past Chalahn Falls, Toolona Cascades and dramatic Toolona

Falls, the canopy opens slightly near Ee-rigingboola Falls. The track winds uphill, crosses Toolona Creek twice (collect overnight water) and passes a stand of Antarctic beech before rejoining the Border Track. It's worth another detour, 75m left, to visit **Wanungara Lookout**. On a fine day, you can see northeast to Stradbroke Island, east to Wollumbin and southeast to Byron Bay.

From the previous junction, the Border Track enters NSW en route to Toolona Lookout. Ten minutes on is the 'wedding tree', a huge, moss-covered Antarctic beech – the site of many nuptials. The track meanders 400m through lush rainforest to **Bithongabel Lookout** and the cleared camp site (no facilities), back in Queensland. If you need extra water, follow the Border Track northwest (towards Green Mountains) for 1km and look for a water sign, 200m before the Albert River Circuit junction.

ALTERNATIVE ROUTE: VIA WEST CANUNGRA CREEK
3½–4 hours, 10.6km

If you feel 18.2km for Day 1 is within your capabilities, this variation is worthwhile. Don't attempt it if water levels are high.

Leave the Border Track 250m from O'Reilly's and head downhill, crossing several creeks on the way to **Yerralahla** (Blue Pool). This deep pool is always cold, even in midsummer.

Turn sharp right near the pool and head south, upstream beside West Canungra Creek. The track crosses the creek and its tributaries several times and some crossings get tricky after rain. Track quality deteriorates as you wind from side to side, passing fern-clad cliffs and a few short zigzags on the way to Kalgamahla Falls. Continue upstream past the falls to another crossing below Wongaree Falls. Masses of Christmas orchids flower here in December and January, and you may spot the blue Lamington spiny cray, especially following rain.

Soon you will reach Box Forest Circuit track junction on the right. Continue ahead past several cascades to Caboolya Falls. The track climbs again, passing a rill before crossing Toolona Creek. When you reach a junction, a short detour right leads to **Box Log Falls** in a small gorge. The main track winds gently uphill to another junction. Turn right to visit beautiful **Elabana Falls** before returning

to Toolona Creek track. Turn left and follow Day 1 notes to reach Bithongabel camp.

Day 2: Bithongabel to Green Mountains
6–7 hours, 17.7km

Follow the Border Track to the first Albert River Circuit junction. Ignore it and continue 100m to the second junction and turn left near more Antarctic beeches.

Wind downhill for about 40 minutes and you'll hear Lightning Creek gurgling over Jimbolongerri Cascades. Swing right, zigzag downhill past several smaller waterfalls and cross Lightning Creek, upstream from Lightning Falls. (The 30m side track to **Echo Falls** makes a great photo stop.) The main track leads uphill, past three more waterfalls before crossing the creek below Bithongabel Falls. Continue uphill beside a moss-covered bank to Alcheringa, the final waterfall.

The track climbs past a storm-damaged area to a bush camp site on the right, a staging point for adventurous forays into Lamington's trackless regions. Follow the main track a few hundred metres to **Echo Point Lookout** for views towards Wollumbin. From Echo Point, the trail passes Cominan Lookout, then goes downhill past more moss-covered banks (home to thousands of **glow-worms** that sprinkle the walls with light at night). You'll soon reach the top of the ridge near a stately Antarctic beech; head downhill to rejoin the Border Track. Turn left, go downhill for 3.2km to Toolona Creek turnoff, then retrace your steps to the trailhead.

SHIPS STERN CIRCUIT

Duration	6 hours
Distance	19km
Difficulty	moderate
Start/Finish	Binna Burra car park
Nearest Towns	Gold Coast (p334))
Transport	bus

Summary Aboriginal legends, a ship-shaped bluff and steps hewn from a sheer rock face are part of this adventure. Add a towering waterfall and stunning views and you're on one of Lamington's most varied walks.

This popular walk meanders through cool, subtropical rainforest, shady palm-filled glades and open eucalypt forest. Banksias attract hordes of honeyeaters around July, and orchids and other wildflowers peak in September. Allow time to linger at the lookouts and don't miss the climb to Charraboomba Rock. You won't be disappointed!

NEAREST TOWN & FACILITIES

See the Gold Coast (p334).

Binna Burra

Binna Burra's gift shops have limited groceries, maps and books. There are no ATMs, so cash up in Brisbane or the Gold Coast.

SLEEPING & EATING

Enjoy peace and quiet at **Binna Burra Mountain Lodge** (☎ 1800 074 260; www.binnaburralodge.com.au; unpowered/powered sites for 2 $22/29, 2-/4-bed on-site safari tents $50/70, lodge packages per person from $100; 🖥) where the attached camping ground has hot showers, laundry, communal cooking shelters with coin-operated barbecues. Linen hire is available for safari tents. The Tea House has café-style meals, plus barbecue packs from $9.50, while packed lunches ($16) are available from the Lodge if ordered the night before. Campers can dine at the Cliff Top Dining Room, but book first.

GETTING THERE & AWAY

Allow 1½ hours from Brisbane or one hour from the Gold Coast along a winding, sealed road, via Nerang and Beechmont.

Binna Burra buses collect visitors daily from **Gold Coast Airport** (🕙 1.30pm, return per person $50) and the Airtrain (p331) at **Nerang Railway Station** (🕙 2pm, return per person $50). Book with the Binna Burra Mountain Lodge.

THE WALK

From the car park, walk 300m back down the road to the grassy saddle and head southeast along the signposted track. Head past a huge tallowwood known affectionately as 'Big Foot'. Ignore Bellbird Lookout track, cross Chiminya Creek and pass another track to Yangahla Lookout. Zigzag downhill to **Koolanbilba Lookout**, an exposed rocky bluff where there are superb views. Wind further downhill between the two halves of Kong Gong Rock and cross the creek again before reaching a junction.

Ignore Lower Bellbird Circuit turn-off and descend between towering brush boxes,

estimated to be 1200 years old. Don't miss the ancient red cedar crowding the left of the track. If this 50m giant weren't so isolated, it would have been felled by loggers. The track leads beside a wide, rocky gully to another junction. Before turning left, it's worth taking a 600m detour to the base of **Lower Ballunjui Falls** where Nixon Creek tumbles over a two-tiered, 150m cliff. You could cool off in the pool, but it'll be a teeth-chattering experience!

Back at the junction, descend through a grove of piccabeens flanking boulder-choked Nixon Creek, then climb high above its left bank. Cross Chiminya Creek, swing right across Nixon Creek, then head uphill, passing a slot guarding Hidden Valley, a small palm-filled oasis. Continue beside cliffs, fenced with an avenue of palms. Aboriginal people knew this area as 'skeleton caves', and believe loose rocks below the cliff were thrown by spirits defending the caves.

At the next junction, take a 330m detour up to **Charraboomba Rock**. Climb 85 steps etched into the rock and follow a scrubby track to the edge of an exposed cliff. Panoramic views centre on Egg Rock and Kurraragin Valley. Back at the junction, the track leads 100m to Moonjooroora Lookout. It levels, closely following the Ships Stern escarpment to another junction. Turn left and walk 100m to the end of **Kooloobano Point** on the sharp end of Ships Stern. Great views at this halfway point make an obvious lunch spot.

Return to the track, veer left uphill past Milleribah, Nyoongai, Gorooburra Lookouts and Burrawong Lookouts. Woollumbin towers over the Tweed Valley. Beyond Gorooburra, the track divides briefly – the right branch has the best western views. Vegetation alternates between rainforest and eucalypt forest. The track rejoins near Burrawong Lookout. At the next junction, if you're still feeling fit, it's only 1.4km to a vantage point near the head of **Upper Ballunjui Falls**. The views are great, but you need to allow one hour for the return trip and it's still 5km back to Binna Burra.

The main track climbs past Ballunjui Cascades and continues beside lush tree ferns in Nixon Creek, to Nagarigoon Falls. Just beyond, you reach Nagarigoon Clearing, once the site of a beautiful remote

QUEENSLAND

camp. A few minutes later you come to Daves Creek track. Turn right and walk 15 to 20 minutes to the Border Track. From here it's only 2.3km on relatively level track to Binna Burra.

COOMERA CIRCUIT

Duration	8 hours
Distance	17.5km
Difficulty	moderate
Start/Finish	Binna Burra car park
Nearest Towns	Gold Coast (p334)
Transport	bus

Summary Views into the 160m Coomera Gorge are awesome. Coomera Crevice splits the head of the gorge and cradles the plummeting Coomera Falls. Definitely one of the best waterfall hikes in Lamington.

There are more than 500 waterfalls in Lamington, and this walk (considered one of the prettiest) visits one of the most famous. Giant brush box trees give way to glossy green lilies and ferns as you descend to the gorge. And there are plenty more waterfalls as you crisscross the river six times on the way back uphill.

Go to the lookout and back (11km return) for a shorter walk, but be warned, you'll be missing some serious scenery upstream of the falls.

NEAREST TOWNS & FACILITIES

See the Gold Coast (p334) and Binna Burra (p339).

THE WALK

Set out along the Border Track and walk gradually uphill for 1.9km to the Coomera Seat where the track splits. Take the middle branch and head downhill. You'll often see blue, golf ball-sized fruit from quandong trees, a favourite food of pigeons, fruit-doves and parrots, so keep your eyes open.

Dappled light filters through the canopy as the track descends, crossing three rills. It passes through a patch of open eucalypt forest then sidles along the edge of a ferny gully. As you re-enter eucalypt forest, note the massive old tree on the right with burls on its trunk. These are usually caused by insect attack and are prized by wood-turners.

Continue downhill past an exposed rocky outcrop on the cliff edge. There are great views across Coomera Valley to the Darlington Range. The track then descends through a blanket of sedge, and hugs the cliff until it reaches **Coomera Lookout**, which hangs precariously over the edge. Take time to soak up the superb views of Coomera Falls (64m) and neighbouring Yarrabilgong Falls (150m).

Beyond the lookout, the track continues along a very narrow ledge beside the beautiful Coomera Crevice. Runnels of water constantly tumble into this crevice, nourishing lilies that cling to the sheer, mossy cliffs. Follow the ledge to the first crossing where large lichen-flecked boulders fill the riverbed. After two more crossings, zig-zag uphill on the right bank for about 15 minutes to reach the base of **Bahnamboola Falls**. As you wind uphill, two side tracks will lead you to vantage points overlooking the falls. Beyond the falls, cross Barrajum Creek below another small cascade and continue uphill to a side track, which leads to **Kagoonya Falls**. These falls stay in view as you ascend.

Cross Gwongarragong Creek and head past Gwongarragong Falls towards the fourth river crossing. A few minutes later, cross a flat rocky slab below Moolgoolong Cascades. Wind past Chigigunya Falls, then cross Bower Bird Creek before skirting around a lily-filled gully at **Dragoon Bird Creek**. Look around the edge of the clear shallow pools – you may see blue spiny crays.

After the fifth crossing, meander uphill past Goorawa Falls (the last for the day), and then cross the river for the final time. A few minutes later, rejoin the Border Track, 7.6km from Binna Burra. Turn left, cross two more fern-filled creeks and continue on, ignoring the Mt Hobwee track on the right. Follow the gently graded track uphill to **Joalah Lookout** for good views across Woggunba Valley to Springbrook Plateau and the Pacific Ocean. This sunny clearing has long been home to yellow-faced whip snakes, but recently a fat blue-tongued lizard has taken up residence, possibly displacing the snakes. The track leads north past Daves Creek track, to the Coomera Seat. From here, retrace your steps to the beginning of the walk.

FRASER ISLAND

Fraser's up there among Australia's out-standing natural places – international and Australian visitors flock here to swim in un-polluted lakes, relax along sandy beaches, walk through lofty rainforests, slide down mobile sandblows and marvel at cliffs of coloured sands.

Walkers jealously guarded Fraser's se-crets for years, content that most visitors only frequented popular beauty spots. But the secret is out, partly because the Queens-land Government allocated heaps of money to create six world-class walking tracks throughout the state, showcasing three World Heritage–listed areas. They're called 'Great Walks' and Fraser Island's Great Walk was the first, meaning that increasing numbers of visitors are now appreciating the island's inner beauty on foot.

HISTORY

The traditional owners called Fraser Island *K'gari*, meaning 'paradise'. Theirs was a self-sufficient lifestyle to be envied – unlimited seafood and forests providing material for shelters, canoes, fishing tackle and a cool escape on summer days.

That great seafarer, James Cook, penned the first record of the island. Matthew Flinders was the first Englishman to stand on its shores, noting, 'Nothing can be im-agined more barren than this peninsula'. Didn't he get it wrong!

Captain James Fraser and his young wife Eliza were among survivors shipwrecked in 1836. They drifted for weeks before landing on Fraser. Seized by Aboriginal people and subjected to harsh treatment, some eventu-ally escaped to the mainland – including Eliza. Her dramatic 'account' won world-wide notoriety and she is immortalised in the island's name.

Fraser's mineral sands were mined until late last century and logging its tall forests was condoned until just before World Her-itage listing in 1992.

ENVIRONMENT

Fraser is another world. It's a gigantic (120km by 15km) vegetated sandbar. Over a few million years, shifting ocean currents

---

PRISTINE LAKES AND CRYSTAL CREEKS

Sand is the key to Fraser's formation, but it's water that's made it so special. Many regard Fraser's lakes and creeks as its most distinctive assets. Each has its own character: some mysterious and some moody, while others are just beautiful. With an average annual rainfall of 1600mm and a huge natural aquifer channelling rainwater that fell 60 to 100 years ago, it's no wonder Fraser is adorned with fast-flowing creeks and 40-plus lakes.

Over half the world's perched (dune) lakes, including the world's largest (Lake Boomanjin) nestle on Fraser. Perched lakes occur above the water table. Almost impermeable organic matter and sand hold water in depressions between the dunes. Some, like Lake McKenzie, are crystal-clear, their waters percolating through sand, while others, including Lake Boomanjin, are tannin-stained from decaying vegetation. Lake Bowaraddy (120m above sea level), in the island's north, is one of the world's highest perched lakes. Water is so pure that these lakes support few plants and animals, and most have only two or three fish species.

Window lakes are less common. They form when ground level falls below the water table. Lake Wabby, the island's deepest, is an example of this type. It's also known as a barrage lake, caused by mobile Hammerstone Sandblow damming the waters of a natural spring and encroaching on its shores. Unlike the others, it supports several fish species.

Three species of turtle live in the lakes. Please don't feed them, or the fish, as it upsets the natural balance of aquatic life.

Many creeks drain the island. Some, like Wanggoolba at Central Station, flow silently past ancient *Angiopteris* ferns, the largest fern fronds in the world. Others like Eli, north of Happy Valley, spill millions of litres of water per hour into the ocean.

Help preserve Fraser's fragile creeks and lakes by not polluting their waters. Most don't have streams filling or draining them, so foreign matter can be trapped for many years. Try a T-shirt instead of sunscreen when swimming!

QUEENSLAND

have stolen and deposited sands from northern NSW. The dune systems still evolve – changing before your eyes.

But how do Fraser's forests survive on a bed of sand? They draw mineral nourishment from sand and absorb trace minerals washed into the sand by rain. Vegetation decays and recycles these minerals. As successive dunes form, deeper nutrient layers develop, supporting diverse forest types and the state's most extensive heathlands.

Fraser is a buffer zone for seagrasses, critical for dugong and green turtle populations. Watch for migrating whales as they swim north in cooler months, then return to Antarctica with their young during warmer climes.

You'll identify hosts of seabirds. Look for pied oystercatchers, running along on skinny, red legs. The female may be trying to spirit her chicks away from harm, while the male of the family feigns a broken wing to distract would-be predators or inquisitive humans.

PLANNING
When to Walk

Fraser offers something year-round. Despite heat, possible tropical storms or persistent rain, summer and autumn (22°C to 28°C) are most popular with campers. Annoying insects decline in cooler months from March, although mosquitoes and sandflies will always inhabit swampy areas. Winter and spring are definitely the best for walking. Chances of rain are reduced, especially after June, when temperatures settle between 14°C and 21°C and wildflowers are at their best.

Designated walkers' camps mean you needn't share your site with hordes of people, even during school holidays and long weekends.

What to Bring

Take fuel stoves, warm clothes for chilly nights and insect repellents to banish March flies and other peskies. A $1 coin will get you a hot shower at Central Station.

Maps

The QPWS 1:50,000 topographic map *Great Walk Fraser Island* is all you'll need. They also issue information brochures about the Great Walk.

Information Sources

It's best to gather information from www .epa.qld.gov.au before heading for Fraser. There's an historical display of the island at Central Station.

Permits & Regulations

For camping and vehicle permits visit www .qld.gov.au/camping or call ☎ 13 13 04.

Fraser is a 4WD-only area and permits must be displayed on your windscreen. Collect them from **QPWS Brisbane** (☎ 3227 8185; www.epa.qld.gov.au, 160 Ann St; ⓧ 8.30am-5pm Mon-Fri), **QPWS Maryborough** (☎ 4121 1800; cnr Alice & Lennox Sts; ⓧ 9am-5pm daily), **QPWS Rainbow Beach** (☎ 5486 3160; Rainbow Beach Rd; ⓧ 7am-4pm daily) or ask about other collection points.

Guided Walks

Kingfisher Bay Resort (☎ 1800 072 555; www.king fisherbay.com) offers ranger-guided eco walks for guests and day visitors. Swim and walk on a two- or three-day, all-inclusive Cool Dingo tour, staying at its **Wilderness Lodge** (2-4 bed r from $240-280; 🐾). 4WD coaches transport you to beauty spots.

GREAT WALK FRASER ISLAND

Duration	5 days
Distance	83.8km
Difficulty	moderate
Start/Finish	Dilli Village/Happy Valley
Nearest Town	Hervey Bay (opposite)
Transport	ferry, 4WD taxi

Summary Nowhere else in the world can you walk beside towering rainforests, vast wildflower heathlands, ancient permanent streams and expansive sandblows to a lake that's so clear you can see turtles on the bottom.

Fraser needs to be the world's largest sand island to contain all its jewels. Meandering through Fraser's magical paradise you'll be following ancient trading pathways of Butchulla people, and logging roads and tramways that served a bygone forest industry. Naturally, a cool dip in one of its iconic lakes becomes part of your day.

Several access points provide links to the Great Walk or enable smaller sections to be walked. The side trip from Central Station to Pile Valley is an absolute must, so it's been included in the total distance for Day 2.

WARNINGS

■ Keep out of the surf. Strong rips are common and sharks, stingers and box jellyfish are likely to be lurking.

■ Take care walking along Seventy-Five Mile Beach. It's a designated highway and it's really hard to hear vehicles above the crash of the surf. Sleeping unprotected in the sand dunes is not cool. 4WDs use these areas and have run over hung-over tourists.

■ Be dingo-safe (see the boxed text p340).

NEAREST TOWN & FACILITIES
Hervey Bay

☎ 07 / pop 36,100

This peaceful, seaside town has just been voted 'Australia's happiest place to live'. It's Australia's whale-watching capital and the most convenient launching place for Fraser Island trips. **Hervey Bay visitor information centre** (☎ 1800 811 728; www.herveybay.qld.gov.au; cnr Maryborough-Hervey Bay & Urraween Rds; 8.30am-5pm Mon-Fri, 10am-4pm Sat & Sun) is best for advice on accommodation and tours. **Great Outdoors** (☎ 4194 0622; 2 Boat Harbour Dr) and **The Camping Company** (☎ 4124 7233; 108 Boat Harbour Dr) have a huge range of tents and camping gear. The smaller **Torquay Disposals & Camping** (☎ 4125 6511; 424 Esplanade) is central and has everything you need for a hiking trip to Fraser.

SLEEPING & EATING

Beachfront Tourist Park (☎ 4125 1578; www.beachfronttouristparks.com.au; Esplanade, Torquay; unpowered/powered sites for 2, $19/24) is on the beach and has a family atmosphere.

Set in bushland, **Colonial Cabins Resort** (☎ 1800 818 280; www.coloniallogcabins.com.au; Boat Harbour Dr, Urangan; dm/r from $20/50;) is a spotlessly clean YHA backpackers that has a bar and eatery. It also offers fully self-contained accommodation.

Koala's Beach Resort (☎ 1800 354 535; www.koalaadventures.com; 408 Esplanade; dm/r $25/70;), a VIP backpacker resort opposite the beach, has a party atmosphere.

Rates at **Lakeside B&B** (☎ 4128 9448; www.herveybaybedandbreakfast.com; 29 Lido Pde, Hervey Bay; d $120-150;) include breakfast, and the lakeside spa makes this a perfect place to unwind after your Fraser hike.

Locally recommended **Bayaroma Cafe** (☎ 4125 1515; 428 Esplanade; dishes $5.50-17; breakfast & lunch) is a popular haunt. It has the best coffee in town, and home-made biscuits and cakes are a speciality.

Still one of the most popular eateries in town, **Black Dog Cafe** (☎ 4124 3177; 381 Esplanade, Torquay; mains $10-20; lunch & dinner) has a great atmosphere and excellent staff. Meals range from sushi to club sambos, ribs to seafood salads. Check out the blackboard specials.

Licensed, waterfront **Cafe Balaena** (☎ 4125 4799; Shop 7, Hervey Bay Tourist Terminal, Buccaneer Ave, Urangan; mains $10 27; breakfast, lunch & dinner) has been serving the world since the early 90s. Dine with locals and enjoy huge meals and salads, and mouthwatering seafood.

GETTING THERE & AWAY

Hervey Bay is 300km north of Brisbane, and 25km east of the Bruce Hwy.

Sunshine Express (☎ 13 13 13; www.sunshineexpress.com.au) flies between Brisbane and Hervey Bay ($120, one hour, daily).

Greyhound Australia (☎ 13 14 99; www.greyhound.com.au) and **Premier Motor Service** (☎ 13 34 10; www.premierms.com.au) have daily services ($32 to $50) from Brisbane to Hervey Bay's **Bay Central Coach Terminal** (☎ 4124 4000; Bay Central Shopping Centre, Boat Harbour Dr). Catch Bus No 5 ($2.80) for the 7km ride to Urangan Marina to transfer to Fraser Island.

Suntours (☎ 1300 735 301; 449 Esplanade, Torquay) run from Brisbane to Hervey Bay, stopping at the coach terminal and Urangan Marina ($45, four hours, two per day).

Queensland Rail (☎ 13 22 32; www.traveltrain.com.au) connects Brisbane with Maryborough via the *Tilt Train* ($65, five hours, Sunday and Friday), where a Trainlink bus ($5.90) transfers to Hervey Bay.

Fraser Island

Near the trailhead at **Dilli Village Environmental Education Camp** (☎ 4127 9130; sites for 2 $20, bunkhouse per person $20, cabins $60, maximum 3 people), you can leave vehicles for $5 per day. 'Village' in the name doesn't mean shops – there's nothing here except the camp.

You can self-cater or eat and drink in the bar and bistro at **Fraser Island Wilderness Retreat** (☎ 1800 063 933; www.fraserislandco.com.au; r $140-180 1-3 people, f $180-220 up to 5 people;) at Happy Valley (the end of the trail). There's a general store and fuel next door.

Kingfisher Bay Resort (☎ 1800 072 555; www .kingfisherbay.com; r $270-300, max 3 adults; ❎ ❑) is the ultimate treat before and after your walk. Visit the Sandbar (open to day-trippers) or the Maheno or Seabelle Restaurants for that pre- and post-walk indulgence. There's also a bakery, general store and fuel.

GETTING TO/FROM THE WALK

Vehicle and passenger ferries operate from Hervey Bay. **Kingfisher Fast Cat** (☎ 1800 072 555) leaves Urangan Marina for Kingfisher Bay ($50 return, 30 minutes, six per day).

Fraser Venture (☎ 1800 072 555; vehicle/walker $120/20 return) runs a ferry from River Heads to Wanggoolba Creek (30 minutes, three per day), while the *Fraser Dawn* connects Urangan Marina with Moon Point.

Aussie Trax (☎ 1800 249 330; www.fraserisland4wd .com.au) at Kingfisher Bay Resort provides pick-ups and drop-offs, hires hiking and camping gear and can arrange food packages. Three-day deals ($300 per person, extra days $60) include equipment, food, permits and maps.

Fraser Island Taxi Service (☎ 4127 9188, 0429 379 188; www.fraserservice.com.au) transports walkers and arranges food drops to/from anywhere on the island. It's the only cab, so bookings are essential. Kingfisher Bay–Dilli Village is $105, while Happy Valley–Kingfisher Bay will set you back $120 (up to five passengers for each service).

THE WALK
Day 1: Dilli Village to Lake Benaroon
5 hours, 13.5km

Follow a sandy road west from Dilli Village to a boardwalk spanning a wetland. Head uphill through coastal woodland before curving right, beside a swampy area. Crest a sandy ridge dotted with bloodwoods and scribbly gums and follow it northeast, then west to a cluster of twisted angophoras with distinctive pink trunks.

About an hour from the start, the track leads through a long sandy swale to a junction. Turn right and clamber uphill to the top of **Wongi Sandblow** for stunning coastal views. Back at the junction, follow a level track through macrozamias (Aboriginal people leached poison from their red fruits, then pounded them to make flour). Wind downhill, cross a firebreak and continue below banksias and bloodwoods to the

dingo-proof enclosure surrounding a walkers' camp. Head past the car-based camping ground to **Lake Boomanjin**. Casuarina needles and gum leaves blanket the track as you head north along the soft, sandy shore. Cross a few tannin-stained rills, then curve east around the lake to a junction.

Turn left towards Lake Benaroon and climb north. The track winds up and down along a ridge covered with leaf-litter and peppered with sedge and macrozamias. After crossing several fallen logs, Lake Benaroon comes into view through regenerating brush box and blackbutt. Descend again and veer left beside the lake towards a junction at the camp site.

Day 2: Lake Benaroon to Central Station
5 hours, 12.1km

From the junction, the track passes melaleucas fringing the lake, then veers away into banksia woodland. It curves around a swampy depression before reaching **Lake Birrabeen** – a good swimming spot.

Veering east from the lake, the trees become taller as you enter a stand of majestic blackbutts. Meander through undulating terrain, passing the stumps of long-felled trees, before cresting a ridge lined with brush box and satinay – the Fraser Island turpentine. (Satinays were once prized for their ability to withstand marine borer attack. Many were felled during the late 1800s and early 1900s for wharf planking and piles; some were used during construction of the Suez Canal and others to rebuild London Docks after WWII.)

Continue downhill, curve past a water tank and descend a set of steps to cross a sandy road. Turn right at the next road and head past Pile Valley track to Central Station camping ground. This huge enclosure has elevated storage lockers to keep food away from marauding goannas.

Select a camp site and return to Central Station. A narrow bitumen road leads steeply downhill from the day use area to a boardwalk beside crystal-clear **Wanggoolba Creek**. Walk past Basin Lake turnoff and continue towards Pile Valley. There's a viewing platform beside a huge angiopteris fern, a species dating from Gondwanan times.

At the next junction, veer left and continue beside the creek. Head through tall piccabeen palms to the appropriately named

Great Walk Fraser Island

1 : 185,000
50m Contour Interval

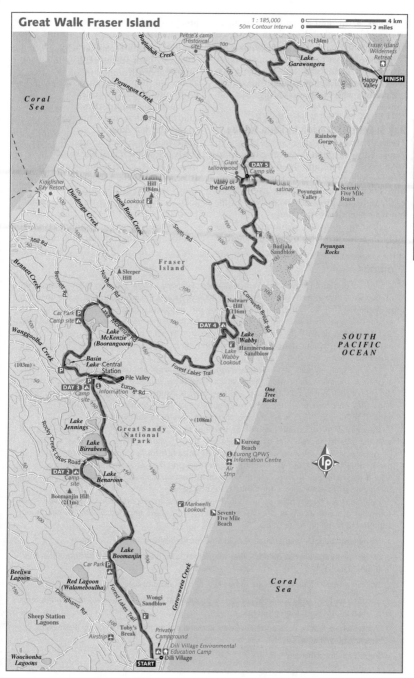

QUEENSLAND

Pile Valley. Turn right at the next two junctions and head uphill through an avenue of towering kauri pine. The other pines with tessellated bark are slash pines, part of an early 1900s plantation. There's one more road to cross before returning to the camping ground where you can indulge in a hot shower.

Day 3: Central Station to Lake Wabby
7 hours, 18.5km

Walk back through Central Station to Wanggoolba Creek and Basin Lake turnoff. Head uphill, along a sandy ridge to a junction. Small but beautiful **Basin Lake** is 150m to the right. It's probably too early to swim, but it's certainly worth a look.

Back at the junction, climb gradually to an old road. Turn left downhill to another junction and continue towards Lake McKenzie. Skirt a swampy depression before reaching a walkers' camp, then follow the fence to the shores of stunningly beautiful **Lake McKenzie**. You'll rarely find yourself alone, but despite the crowds, a swim here is an unforgettable experience.

The track climbs northwards along a soft, sandy road. At the top of the ridge, a walking track veers left downhill and becomes firm underfoot. It curves around the lake and levels below a stand of blackbutts, towering over a dense understorey of macrozamias. It's cool below the canopy as you head towards the next sandy road, where the track follows an old logging tramline to another junction. Turn left towards Lake Wabby.

Climb north over several low rises, cross another road and crest one final ridge before

---

DINGOS

Dingos are one of Australia's most efficient killers. Evolving in Asia, probably from a subspecies of grey wolf, they arrived with sailors around 4000 years ago. Their hunting skills were honed to perfection as they slunk through our grasslands and woodlands, colonising all areas of Australia except Tasmania. They were probably responsible for the demise of Tasmanian tigers (thylacines) and Tasmanian devils from the mainland. Because of Fraser's isolation, its dingos have rarely interbred with domestic dogs and they are among the most genetically pure. They have roamed Fraser for several thousand years.

They are small animals, less than knee-high, watchfully aloof and never friendly, but irresistibly appealing. Their ears are pointed; their coats usually yellow, striped with white on their chests and the tips of their bushy tails and feet, and they have a distinctive trotting gait. Unlike domestic dogs, they only have one litter of up to six pups a year and rear them in a den until they're old enough to hunt for themselves. Instead of barking, they have a mournful howl.

They gather in packs, and establish and defend territorial rights. They'll hunt alone for small animals, rodents, reptiles and birds, but engage in pack warfare when larger prey is targeted. Dingos are natural scavengers, always looking for an easy feed. By nature's standards they're not overly cruel or savage, but we need to respect them and their environment. Let them grow up wild; if they scrounge from people they lose their hunting skills and become aggressive. Sadly, these dingos may be culled – for habits taught by people.

Fatalities from dingos have occurred in recent years, so it's important to be dingo-safe. Make sure your group is aware of the basics (on-the-spot fines are imposed on foolish people not adhering to common sense rules):

- Never feed dingos – wild animals should fend for themselves.
- Never encourage or coax dingos – they might look loveable, but they can be aggressive and unpredictable.
- Walk in groups – lone walkers are more likely to be stalked or bailed up.
- Secure your food and rubbish in containers provided at camps – dingos will rip through tents to steal unprotected food or scraps.
- If threatened, remain calm and back away, keeping eye contact with the dog. If attacked, defend yourself aggressively.
- Report all dingo incidents.

winding downhill to a junction at the walkers' camp. Leave your packs and contour around the edge of a ridge, past the car park to **Lake Wabby Lookout** for great views across Hammerstone Sandblow.

Feel like a romp on the sandblow? Head downhill through tall scribbly gums to Valley of the Giants track junction. Ignore it and continue 500m ahead. Climb a wide finger of soft sand to crest the sandblow, then descend to **Lake Wabby**. It's a great spot to cool off. Before returning to camp, collect water at the car park.

Day 4: Lake Wabby to Valley of the Giants
6 hours, 20km

Retrace yesterday's steps to Valley of the Giants turnoff. Go left and climb through casuarinas to the ridge top. When you reach a road, continue ahead on a service trail covered with leaf-litter. Open forest surrounding the high dunes gives way to rainforest as you continue climbing. A walking track veers right, away from the road, and leads through piccabeen palms to another road.

Continue through closed forest on a gentle gradient, high above the valley floor. Cross a few steep ridges, then climb to a signed junction. Drop your packs and walk 600m east, along a eucalypt-lined ridge to the base of a huge dune. A short climb leads to **Badjala Sandblow** and great coastal views.

Back at the junction, head north downhill into tall forest. Occasional tree stumps remind us of Fraser's logging days. The terrain levels below a cool stand of rainforest where purple lilly-pilly berries litter the ground. Turn right at the next two junctions and continue to a third where a 3km side track leads to the island's tallest satinay.

Follow the main track left, downhill through beautiful forest to another junction. It's worth dropping your packs to visit **Fraser's tallest tallowwood**, 1300m to the left. Its diameter is 3.6m and it's believed to be around 1000 years old. After hugging the tree, return to the junction and follow the main track 400m to the camp site.

Day 5: Valley of the Giants to Happy Valley
7 hours, 19.7km

Follow the old tramway route through lush rainforest and climb gradually past a storm-damaged area. This section of forest was heavily logged and is now revegetated with spindly eucalypts, all vying for the sunlight.

Crest a ridge, descend to cross another road and veer right along a walking track. Huge sawtooth banksia leaves blanket the track as you approach another road. Turn right, continue to a T-junction and go right again. (The left-hand track leads 500m to Petries Logging Camp but all traces have now been removed.)

Head northeast uphill to a stand of satinays, towering above piccabeens. This marks the start of a long, steep climb high above the valley floor. The track contours around a ridge and descends southeast to a disused 4WD track. Continue past melaleuca wetlands, cross another ridge and swing right, away from the road. Head past a walkers' camp to **Lake Garawongera**, one of Fraser's most attractive perched lakes. It's a great place for a swim, but because of its fragile environment, you're asked to eat in the picnic area.

From here, follow a hard-packed road around the western edge of the lake. The walking track swings right, away from the road and leads east around the lake. You may hear wompoo fruit-doves as you climb to the top of a long, sandy ridge. Head downhill and look for a tree blazed by early surveyors. At the next road, veer right through a gate, climb another ridge and contour along the left of a gully between tall dunes. Crest a low hill, descend to a road and turn left down steps to a picnic area at the end of the walk – but not the end of the day. **Happy Valley Pub** is just 200m along the road.

HINCHINBROOK ISLAND

Hinchinbrook is a huge 35km-long island wilderness in the state's tropical north. It's Australia's largest (and by far Queensland's most rugged) island national park.

Crossing Hinchinbrook Channel's seagrass beds you're confronted by huge granite mountains. These hulking sentinels of the wilderness watch over the island – from fragile mangrove forests on its western shores, to sandy palm-lined beaches, sweeping bays and rugged headlands on its east coast. After completing the Thorsborne Trail, those same mountains seem to

QUEENSLAND

WARNINGS

- Don't swim in the sea during box jellyfish season (October to April). These jellyfish are the world's most venomous. Transparent tentacles up to 3m long contain millions of stinging cells. Contact can cause severe shock, respiratory failure and cardiac arrest.

- Estuarine crocodiles (salties), the world's largest reptiles, inhabit creeks, rivers, lagoons and coastlines. Sightings around North and South Zoe Creeks are common. Heed the signs and be extremely cautious during breeding season (September to April).

- Native rats will chew through packs and tents (and pretty much anything else) looking for food. Use the metal, rat-proof boxes at camp sites or suspend food above the ground (although the rats are famous for their ingenuity – even leaping from the top of your tent to try to reach hanging food!).

- Heavy rain and high tides make creek crossings dangerous. If in doubt, wait till low tide or turn back.

---

congratulate us, knowing we will share their wish to protect all that is wild and beautiful on Hinchinbrook.

ENVIRONMENT

Hinchinbrook is surrounded by the Great Barrier Reef Marine Park. These fascinating waters cover fringing reefs and are home to marine grazers including dugongs and green turtles. Its mangrove forests are important breeding grounds for a host of marine life, and are some of Australia's richest and most diverse.

Several mountains, often shrouded in clouds, exceed 1000m. They're covered with tropical rainforests, open woodlands and fragile heathlands and cradle spectacular waterfalls and deep plunge pools.

PLANNING
When to Walk

The cooler, drier months between April and September are best for walking. Heavy rain is common in the hot, humid months between December and March, but prepare for rain at any time. Extremely dry or wet conditions, cyclone threats and controlled burning can force trail closures.

What to Bring

Long-sleeved shirts, trousers and a tent will stop mozzies, sandflies and March flies carrying you away during the night, and insect repellent will help to keep them under control during the day. Raincoats are invaluable and light sandals are great for crossing creeks. For beach camping, carry a length of cord or fishing line to hang food above the

ground – away from the island's infamous marauding native rats.

Maps & Books

The QPWS *Thorsborne Trail* map and guide can be downloaded when booking your permit (below). Collect tide timetables from the Rainforest & Reef visitor information centre (below).

Hinchinbrook Island – The Land Time Forgot, by Arthur and Margaret Thorsborne, has a wealth of natural history information. For an inspiring read, Warren MacDonald's *One Step Beyond* details his ordeal when trapped beneath a one-tonne rock while climbing Mt Bowen. He was rescued two days later and had both legs amputated. He's since climbed Africa's Kilimanjaro, America's El Capitan and Tasmania's Federation Peak. Don't ever complain about blisters!

Information Sources

Cardwell's **Rainforest & Reef visitor information centre** (☎ 4066 8601; 79 Victoria St; ☿ 8am-4.30pm) provides up-to-date info. View the excellent 15-minute video *Without a Trace* before walking the trail. The centre also houses the QPWS office.

Permits & Regulations

Permits are essential and are issued by the **QPWS** (☎ 13 13 04; www.qld.gov.au). There's a limit of 40 people on the trail at any one time, and groups are limited to six. Book at least 12 months in advance for holiday times. Note that special permits are required to climb any mountain other than Nina Peak, and fuel stoves are mandatory (no fires).

THORSBORNE TRAIL

Duration	4 days
Distance	32km
Difficulty	moderate
Start/Finish	Ramsay Bay/George Point
Nearest Town	Cardwell (below), Lucinda (right)
Transport	ferry/bus

Summary Curved sandy bays, cool tropical rainforests, idyllic rock pools, cascading waterfalls and stunning vistas conspire to create an unforgettable island experience.

This trail is included on most short lists of the world's 'best treks'. It's named for local conservationist, the late Arthur Thorsborne, who with wife Margaret spent years monitoring pied (Torresian) imperial-pigeons. This migratory white bird with black outer wing feathers and tail tip nests here in summer. The trail follows the east coast and can be walked in either direction. Orange markers point north to south, and yellow south to north. Walking north to south allows a side trip to Nina Peak for spectacular views on Day 1, while you're still fresh, and finishes with an easy walk along the beach on Day 4. Add a swim in plunge pools at Zoe and Mulligan Falls on Days 2 and 3 and you have a recipe for a memorable walk.

NEAREST TOWNS
Cardwell
☎ 07 / pop 1420

Separated from the ocean by the Bruce Hwy, this sprawling town is your departure point for the trail. The Rainforest & Reef visitor information centre (opposite) books accommodation and tours. **Cardwell Hardware** (☎ 4066 8521; 71 Victoria St) sells basic camping supplies. There are several ATMs on the main drag.

SLEEPING & EATING
Hinchinbrook Hostel (YHA) (☎ 4066 8648; www .kookaburraholidaypark.com.au; 175 Bruce Hwy; unpowered/ powered sites for 2 $18/22, dm/s/d $18/35/40; ✕ 🖳 🖲) has excellent facilities and also offers villas, motel units and cabins. It hires out camping gear from trowels to backpacks.

Spotlessly clean **Cardwell Central Backpackers** (☎ 4066 8404; www.cardwellbackpackers.com .au; 6 Brasenose St; dm $18, d $35; 🖳 🖲) is a tastefully renovated squash court with a great feel, just 200m from the bus stop.

Mudbrick Manor (☎ 4066 2299; www.mudbrick manor.com.au; 13 Stoney Creek Rd; s/d $75/100; ✕ 🖲) offers more upmarket B&B style stays. Staff will collect you from the bus and drop you at the ferry.

The only supermarket is at the town's northern end. For quality home-made meals, try **Annie's Kitchen** (☎ 4066 8818; 107 Victoria St; dishes $7-14; ☾ breakfast, lunch & dinner).

Enjoy ocean breezes, a view through coconut palms to Hinchinbrook Island and tasty meals at **Marine Hotel** (☎ 4066 8662; Victoria St; dishes $8-16; ☾ lunch & dinner). Aussie-style fish or steak sandwiches and hearty steak salads are good value.

GETTING THERE & AWAY
Cardwell is 165km north of Townsville, or 184km south of Cairns, opposite the northern tip of Hinchinbrook.

Greyhound Australia (☎ 13 14 99; www.grey hound.com.au) has services to Cardwell from Cairns ($31, three hours, six per day) and Brisbane ($185, 26 hours, four per day). **Premier Motor Service** (☎ 13 34 10; www.premierms.com .au) also connects to Cairns ($24, four hours) and Brisbane ($165, 26 hours).

Cardwell is on the route of the high-speed *Tilt Train*, which runs from Brisbane ($290, 21 hours, Monday and Friday) and Cairns ($55, 3½ hours, Sunday and Wednesday). The *Sunlander* also stops here, departing Brisbane ($200, 26 hours, Sunday, Tuesday and Thursday) and Cairns ($40, four hours, Tuesday, Thursday and Saturday). Book with **Queensland Rail** (☎ 13 22 32; www.traveltrain.com.au).

Lucinda
☎ 07 / pop 783

This tiny fishing port is the southern approach to Hinchinbrook Island. Fuel and limited supplies are available. There's an ATM at the shop, near the beach.

Wanderers Holiday Village (☎ 4777 8213; www .wanderers-lucinda.com.au; Bruce Pde; unpowered/pow ered sites for 2 $20/24, cabins from $70; ✕ 🖲) Will transport guests to/from the boat ramp (per person $5).

GETTING TO/FROM THE WALK
Ferry operators will store luggage and arrange to transfer it to the other end. Free EPIRBs are available on request.

Hinchinbrook Island Ferries (☎ 4066 8270; www .hinchinbrookferries.com.au) leave Port Hinchinbrook

Marina at 9am and drop off or collect walkers at Ramsay Bay at 11.30am ($60). The service is daily from May to October, and runs Sunday, Wednesday and Friday from November to January and during April. There are no services in February and March.

Hinchinbrook Wilderness Safaris (☎ 4777 8307; www.hinchinbrookwildernesssafaris.com.au) runs a ferry between George Point and Lucinda ($50) daily between April and October (other times on demand). Departures are tide-dependent and bookings are essential.

Ingham Travel (☎ 4776 5666) provides a service between Lucinda and Cardwell ($25 per person for a minimum two people) by appointment. It will also transfer walkers to/from Townsville Airport to Lucinda or Cardwell ($70, two hours, three per day Monday-Thursday, two per day Friday, on demand Saturday & Sunday).

THE WALK
Day 1: Ramsay Bay to Little Ramsay Bay
4 hours, 6.5km

From the jetty follow a boardwalk to a sandy swale behind the dunes and make your way to **Ramsay Bay**. Follow its beautiful shoreline to a marked track near granite boulders at the end of the beach.

Head inland, climbing to a low ridge, then cross shallow gullies flanked with stringybarks before descending to Black-sand Beach. Water in a lagoon behind the beach is often brackish and shouldn't be relied upon. Follow the beach south to three huge paperbarks flanking a track leading uphill. Cross several shallow gullies before reaching a saddle. (The unmarked track to Nina Peak leads southwest; see the Side Trip opposite.)

Descend, cross more shallow gullies and follow a watercourse down to the mangrove-lined tidal reaches of Nina Creek. You may get wet feet skirting this swampy area. Cross two boulder-filled creek beds on the way to a low ridge, before descending to a camping ground at Nina Bay's northern end.

Follow the coastline and scramble across pink rocks to a track leading steeply up a short cliff. It levels out through casuarinas and grass trees before emerging at the northern end of **Boulder Bay**. Cross sloping granite slabs to the beach and hop over boulders to a small sandy patch. Climb another rocky outcrop and continue uphill

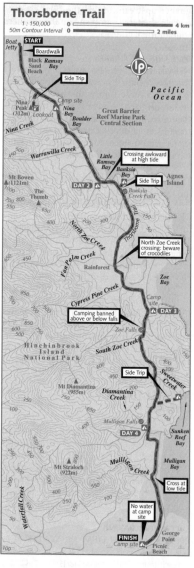

through thin, woody acacias and casuarinas to the ridge top. The track descends, following a rocky watercourse to Little Ramsay Bay. Head down the beach to a large tidal creek. (A footpad on the northern side leads 50m through the scrub, past a lagoon, to the creek bed. This is usually a reliable water point, but you may need to rock hop further upstream.) Ford the tidal creek to reach a sheltered camp site on the southern edge of the lagoon.

SIDE TRIP: NINA PEAK
1½ hours return, 1km, 220m ascent

A distinct path leads steeply uphill to an exposed granite slab with sweeping views across Ramsay Bay. Continue uphill through grass trees, casuarinas and tea-trees to the summit. There are great views across Mt Bowen's craggy cliffs and beyond to mangrove-lined Missionary Bay. Move around the summit for views in all directions before returning to the main track.

Day 2: Little Ramsay Bay to Zoe Bay
6 hours, 10.5km

Mt Bowen dominates the skyline as you walk along the beach. Cross a small tidal creek (may be difficult at high tide) and scramble around a rocky headland to the next stony beach – a secluded, alternative camp site. Rock hop around the next headland to another small beach. At the southern end a track leads uphill, on the left of a shallow watercourse. The gradient increases as you approach the ridge top. Ignore a false trail on the left and continue for five minutes to a signed track leading to Banksia Bay.

The Thorsborne Trail descends past a small, mossy cliff before reaching a pool at the head of a permanent cascade in **Banksia Creek**. Cross black, lichen-stained rocks and continue uphill beside the creek to a saddle dividing the watersheds of Banksia and Zoe Bays. Banksias line the track as you descend, following a bouldery creek bed. After a few minutes of rock hopping, the track leads sharply left uphill, then right, paralleling the creek. Look for old-growth stringybarks as you head into a cool section of forest.

Continue southwest around a swampy plain dotted with paperbarks. Cross several rocky creek beds, avoiding the tendrils of aptly named lawyer vines, sometimes called wait-a-while.

Cross a few gullies, then descend steeply to an expanse of lichen-stained rocks in North Zoe Creek. (Crocodiles have been sighted here.) Cross diagonally and head upstream beside **Fan Palm Creek**. This permanent creek is a good spot to cool off.

Ford again near a huge fan palm on the eastern bank, cross another tributary and continue past a bog below tall palms where the trail becomes indistinct. Cross more gullies flanked with nasty bits of lawyer vine and red beech trees with distinct red, flaky bark, before reaching **Cypress Pine Creek**. You'll almost certainly hear the distinctive 'wollack-a-woo' of wompoo fruit-doves. They love feeding on blue quandong berries.

The track passes a massive paperbark, the start of a paperbark swamp. Skirt the swamp, passing unusual granite monoliths that appear totally misplaced on the edge of a rainforest. Continue across another boggy, mangrove-lined creek and look for an enormous brush-turkey mound on the left. A few minutes later you pass more quandongs, beeches and paperbarks before emerging at **Zoe Bay**. Walk right 400m, to the camp site at South Zoe Creek. Heed the crocodile signs – they're not for decoration! To collect water, follow the Zoe Falls track for about 15 minutes to a creek crossing. After walking this far, you'll probably want to continue 100m for a swim below beautiful **Zoe Falls**.

SIDE TRIP: BANKSIA BAY
1 hour, 600m

A well-defined track leads around the side of a ridge, then descends steeply to an alternative camp site beside the bay. There's plenty of mangroves, but not a banksia in sight! It's worth exploring this rocky beach.

Day 3: Zoe Bay to Mulligan Falls
4½ hours, 7.5km

Return to Zoe Falls and climb a stony track to a slot in a rock slab, where a knotted rope aids your ascent. Continue climbing to the head of the falls. Sweeping views across Zoe Bay from smooth granite slabs are a real highlight. It's hard to leave this spot, but shoulder your pack and head upstream to a crossing. The track parallels the creek, crossing it several times.

Continue through open forest, above the right bank of South Zoe Creek. The gradient increases as you traverse more rocky gullies, before the final creek crossing. Look for turtles and crays in the small, rocky pools.

Ascend across a carpet of casuarina needles to a broad, rocky slab at a saddle. This is the highest point (220m) on the track. Contour around the ridge and descend

QUEENSLAND

to cross **Sweetwater Creek**. Vegetation alternates between rainforest and dry open forest as you cross more gullies. There are glimpses of Sunken Reef Bay and Lucinda Jetty through the trees. Raw sugar is conveyed 5.6km along this jetty to ship-loaders. One of the longest of its type in the world, it dips 1.2m over its length, following the curvature of the earth. Continue downhill to a junction where a track leads to Sunken Reef Bay.

Take care on slippery casuarina needles as the Thorsborne Trail heads downhill to the broad, boulder-choked **Diamantina Creek**. These boulders are treacherous when wet! Veer right, diagonally upstream to locate the track on the opposite bank.

Leave the creek and climb southwest through open forest, high above the creek. There are good views across Mulligan Bay to the Palm Islands as you contour around a steep-sided ridge. Descend past a balancing granite tor to a series of rocky steps. Wind past more boulders to a junction. Turn left and walk 40m to the camp site. **Mulligan Falls** and a magic swimming hole is 100m beyond here.

SIDE TRIP: SUNKEN REEF BAY
1 hour, 1.4km, 100m descent

To visit this secluded bay littered with oddly-shaped driftwood pieces, turn left and head east along an almost level track for a few minutes, then descend steeply to the beach. If the lagoon is full, follow its southern edge to the beach. The bay makes an ideal alternative camp site. Collect water from Sweetwater Creek at the northern end of the beach.

Day 4: Mulligan Falls to George Point
2½ hours, 7.5km

There's no reliable water today, so collect enough from Mulligan Falls. A clear track leads through rainforest, crossing a rocky creek bed. The forest opens as you approach the next creek and veer right around a paperbark swamp. Cross another muddy creek bed with a tangle of exposed tree roots snaking across the surface. Then cross several more creeks, separated by swamps before winding left and right, avoiding thick tangles of lawyer vine until you emerge at the beach. Turn right and walk to **Mulligan Creek**. This easy low-tide crossing can rise to

waist-height or worse at high tide, so carry a tide table and time your crossing. There are great views of Mt Diamantina before you round the point. Walk 200m to a lone coconut palm marking the ferry pick-up point and entrance to the camp site.

WOOROONOORAN NATIONAL PARK

Part of the World Heritage–listed Wet Tropics region, Wooroonooran is a remote haven that's off the beaten tourist tracks – a huge plus for walkers. This is a land of wild rivers and ancient, mystical mountain massifs blanketed by 140-million-year-old rainforests.

Fit, experienced bushwalkers are lured to Mt Bartle Frere to bag the state's highest peak. As a bonus, they can appreciate the Wet Tropics' fragile ecosystems and the complex web of life they support.

ENVIRONMENT

Across the Bellenden Ker Range, tropical rainforests grow from foothills to mountain summits. Growing continuously since our island continent was connected to Gondwana, they contain an almost complete record of the evolution of plant life on earth. Large-leafed, large-trunked plants from the lowlands give way to stunted, closed-canopy plants in the uplands.

Many plant and wildlife species are unique to the region. Golden bowerbirds occur only in rainforests at altitudes above 900m. They build a bower of sticks, one pile higher than the other and joined by a branch forming a display perch. The bower may be up to 3m high, and contrary to their southern cousins who decorate in blue, these male birds prefer yellows and creams. Rare orchids are a favourite – a sure way to attract a bird!

It's not only plants that grow huge up here: giant moths (some with 25cm wingspans), 20cm caterpillars and frogs, and scrub pythons up to 8m long (the world's fourth-largest snake) thrive in the lush, fertile conditions.

On a prettier note, bright butterflies, including the brilliant blue Ulysses, may flit past you on the track.

PLANNING
When to Walk

This is Australia's wettest place, where annual rainfalls around 10m have been recorded – check the conditions before hiking. Majuba Creek rises and falls very quickly, often forcing track closures. May to September is drier and the best time to walk, while the Wet (October to March) is extremely hot and humid.

What to Bring

A sunny day at the bottom of the range can often deteriorate to wet, windy and freezing conditions at the top. Wet-weather gear, warm clothing and a good tent are essential. Carry enough food for an extra night, as it's easy to run out of daylight on the long second day of the walk. Leeches are always lurking (see the boxed text p335).

Maps

The well-defined track is marked by orange triangles. The QPWS *Bartle Frere Trail Guide* (available from park offices) shows the route. Sunmap's 1:50,000 topographic map *Bartle Frere* supplements the guide.

Information Sources

QPWS Cairns (☎ 4046 6600; www.epa.qld.gov.au) should be the first contact for current park conditions. Rangers are also based at **Josephine Falls** (☎ 4067 6304), but spend most of their time in the field.

Permits & Regulations

Book camping permits ($8 per night for two people) online with the **QPWS** (www.epa .qld.gov.au). There's no camping at Josephine Falls car park. Fuel stoves are mandatory.

MT BARTLE FRERE	
Duration	2 days
Distance	19km
Difficulty	demanding
Start/Finish	Josephine Falls car park
Nearest Towns	Cairns (p331) and
	Innisfail (right)
Transport	private or bus
	(with 8km road walk)

Summary It's steep and it's tough, but anyone who has experienced a fine day atop Queensland's tallest peak will say that exhilaration overcomes fatigue.

If you're lucky to hit the summit in sunshine, the panorama is awesome. Explorer and adventurer, Christie Palmerston, was the first European to scale this lofty peak, back in 1886. Today, you'll follow a route pushed by gold miners and adventurers through rainforest, mountain heath and an extensive boulder field to the summit.

But climbing a 1622m mountain from near sea level is never easy, and attempting the return trip in one day is not recommended. There's no reliable water near Eastern Camp, so if a high camp is planned, water must be lugged up from Big Rock Camp.

The best approach is to walk 3km to Big Rock Camp on Day 1, then test your fitness with a climb to Broken Nose. (This isn't possible if you've walked from the bus stop on the Bruce Hwy.) There are often great views from this 962m peak, even when the summit's cloudy. If you can't complete the side trip to Broken Nose in four hours, then you'll struggle to reach the summit of Bartle Frere the next day and return to the car park before the rainforest canopy forces an early sundown.

NEAREST TOWNS

See Cairns (p331).

Innisfail

☎ 07 / pop 8530
On the Bruce Hwy, 83km south of Cairns, Innisfail is predominantly a sugar town. It's one of the last largish towns in tropical Queensland untouched by the tourist boom and has an easy laid-back country charm.

Innisfail visitor information centre (☎ 4063 2655; www.innisfailtourism.com.au; Bruce Hwy, Mourilyan; ⏰ 9am-4pm Mon-Fri, 9am-3pm Sat & Sun) can supply walk brochures listing the town's famous Art Deco buildings. **Northern Stock Supplies** (☎ 4061 1674; 131 Edith St) is the town's camping specialist. There are supermarkets in town.

SLEEPING & EATING

Just south of town, **Mango Tree Tourist Park** (☎ 1800 008 789; www.mangotreepark.com.au; Couche St; unpowered/powered sites for 2 $22/25, cabins for 2 from $80; ⚇ ⚑) has a camp kitchen and free barbecues.

Codge Lodge (☎ 0428 820 105; www.codgelodge .com; 63 Rankin St; dm/r $20/25; ⚇ ⚏ ⚑), in a large Queenslander home, is run by a banana farmer. It also does meals.

On Innisfail's southern side, **Barrier Reef Motel** (☎ 4061 4988; www.barrierreefmotel.com.au; Bruce Hwy; s/r $85/95; 🅿 🖳) is clean and tidy. It also has a restaurant and bar so you don't have to go far!

Family-owned **Oliveri's Continental Deli** (☎ 4061 3354; 41 Edith St; sandwiches $6.50; ⏱ breakfast & lunch, Mon-Sat) has been serving European fare since 1930s. It carries extensive ranges of delicacies from Australia and abroad to top *pannini* and lunch rolls.

For authentic Italian meals in a town with many Italians try **Roscoe's Piazza** (☎ 4061 6888; 3b Ernest St; mains $12-16; ⏱ lunch & dinner). It's licensed and specialises in pastas, pizzas and seafood.

GETTING THERE & AWAY
Premier Motor Service (☎ 13 34 10; www.premierms .com.au) travels daily from Cairns ($16, 1¼ hours). **Greyhound Australia** (☎ 13 14 99; www .greyhound.com.au) does the same route for $23 (seven daily).

Queensland Rail (☎ 13 22 32; www.traveltrain.com .au) services stop on the way to and from Cairns: *Tilt Train* ($35, 1¾ hours, Sunday and Wednesday) and *Sunlander* ($23, 1¾ hours, Tuesday, Thursday and Saturday).

GETTING TO/FROM THE WALK
Josephine Falls car park is 75km south of Cairns or 30km north of Innisfail. Leave the Bruce Hwy just south of Miriwinni, and drive 8km to the trailhead.

Mission Beach Dunk Island Connections (☎ 4059 2709; www.missionbeachdunkconnections .au) drops walkers at Josephine Falls turn-off from Cairns or Innisfail ($14, three daily). From here it's an 8km road slog to the trailhead.

THE WALK
Day 1: Josephine Falls Car Park to Big Rock Camp & Broken Nose
6 hours, 7km, 860m ascent, 460m descent

A well-defined track enters lowland rain-forest and leads uphill. Cross a tributary of Majuba Creek and climb below liana vines swinging from the canopy. Cross several shallow gullies and head through a storm-damaged area before climbing between two huge boulders, 2km from the start.

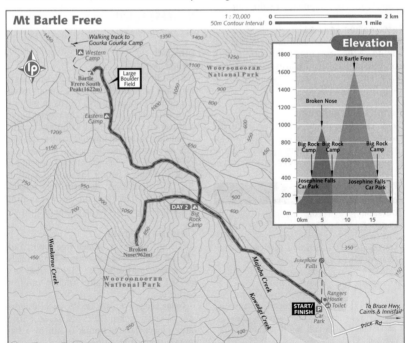

Follow the undulating spine of a narrow ridge and cross the boulder-choked bed of **Majuba Creek**. Climb to the crest of the ridge separating Kowadgi and Majuba Creeks. The blue egg-shaped fruit on the track is from grey milkwood trees. Be warned – most rainforest fruits are toxic in their natural state!

A myriad of bird calls complement the sounds of the forest as you follow the ridge to another storm-damaged area, 3km from the start. The ridge narrows and the track hugs its spine, high above the creek. Cross a jumble of mossy boulders to a clearing in a rainforest glade at **Big Rock Camp**.

A bright, sunny day often ends with a sudden squall, so make camp beside the permanent creek before setting out for Broken Nose. A signposted track leads steeply uphill past the trunk of a stately red cedar that lost its crown during a 2005 storm. Continue uphill below a dense rainforest canopy to crest the summit ridge. The track makes a distinct turn south, following the eastern edge of the ridge to a small col below **Broken Nose**. From here, it's 10 minutes to an exposed, flat rocky overhang with views across Russell River Valley. Care is definitely required. After enjoying the views, retrace your steps to the camp site.

Day 2: Big Rock Camp to Bartle Frere Summit & Josephine Falls Car Park
10 hours, 12km, 1100m ascent, 1500m descent

Collect water for the return trip, cross the creek and head steeply uphill. The track climbs between boulders and a muddy bank, then winds uphill to crest a spur. It passes close to the edge where there are views into the creek bed, then swings sharply right and almost levels out, making the walking pleasant.

After passing rounded granite boulders, look for a massive Johnson River satin ash on the right with roots from a strangler fig snaking their way down the trunk. In 50 years or so, they will almost engulf this tree. The gradient lessens near the 4km point and the narrow ridge drops off steeply on both sides. Exposed tree roots aid the climb when you reach a steep 3m mud bank. Continue up the ridge, taking care on tree roots crisscrossing the track. At a massive granite boulder, the track swings left and continues uphill.

The climb is unrelenting until you reach a U-shaped gully on the right, filled with helmholtzia lilies. You may cop a blast of cool sea air whipping up the gully. After another slog uphill, the track levels slightly near large orania palms. Tree roots crisscross the track as you approach drier forest, before reaching a helipad on the ridge top. (This has been used for several rescues of injured or lost bushwalkers.) A rough track leads left downhill to the exposed **Eastern Camp**.

Follow an eroded path uphill through low heath to the start of a massive lichen-stained boulder field. Orange arrows define the route but extreme care is required – especially if the rocks are damp. Occasional stainless steel brackets have been bolted to the boulders where stumpy legs once struggled. From October to December, you may see striking red flowers of Australia's only native rhododendron. Continue uphill through the boulders to a level spot on the ridge top. Views stretch across Russell River Valley. Climb steeply for a few minutes to a clearing on the summit. The views are from an exposed boulder to the left. Have a well-earned rest, and then descend Queensland's tallest mountain to Big Rock Camp, via the same route. Remember, you should allow 1½ hours to walk from camp to the car park.

MORE WALKS

SOUTHEAST QUEENSLAND
Daves Creek Circuit
From Binna Burra (p339) section of Lamington National Park, this 12km day walk is the park's most botanically diverse. Winding through rainforest, eucalypt forest and open heathlands, you're bound to see something flowering year-round. There are several lookouts with uninterrupted vistas of the Gold Coast's hinterland and even a cave resembling an ancient dining room. Add a rock that's a 'surprise' and a couple of creek crossings and you'll have a great day. Collect track maps from the visitor information centre.

Mt Barney
You'll need private transport but Mt Barney, southwest of Brisbane, is a bushwalker's mecca with some of Queensland's toughest routes. The classic circuit up Southeast Ridge and down Peasant's, is one of the 'easiest',

but there's no 'easy' way to scale this mountain. The 17km day or overnight challenge starts and finishes at Yellow Pinch car park and passes through woodlands and rainforests. There's a camp near the summit with good water. Camping permits are required (p328). Navigation skills are essential; use Sunmap's 1:25,000 *Mt Lindesay* topographic map. The route is described in Queensland's *Take A Walk* book (p328).

Brisbane Forest Park

Brisbane Forest Park (☎ 3300 4855; www.brisbane forestpark.qld.gov.au) is a huge expanse of rainforest and eucalypt woodland 12km northwest of Brisbane. Graded tracks lead through Walk-About Creek and Mts Nebo, Glorious and Samson sections. England Creek and Northbrook Gorge have day and overnight routes for experienced hikers. An extensive ranger-guided *Go Bush* program includes full-day bushwalks, off-track adventure walks and evening activities. Bookings are essential. Get maps from QPWS information centre in Brisbane (p330) or the park information centre. Frequent buses (Route 385) run from the city to park headquarters.

SUNSHINE COAST
Glass House Mountains

Near the Sunshine Coast, the distinctive volcanic plugs of Glass House Mountains rise above coastal plains. Bushwalkers have been bagging Glass House summits for years but more recently rock climbing is drawing crowds. Several peaks including Mts Ngungun and Elimbah are easily walked. Mts Beerwah and Tibrogargan offer more challenging routes for walkers who don't mind a bit of air and a tricky track. Queensland's *Take A Walk* book (p328) details most routes. Contact rangers at **Maleny** (☎ 5494 3983) for added info.

Cooloola Wilderness Trail

This easy three-day, 46km trail roughly follows Eliza Fraser's mainland route after she escaped from her Aboriginal captors on Fraser Island (p341). It starts at East Mullen car park on Rainbow Beach Rd, and leads through wallum heathland, passing a

pair of camp sites at lagoons, before reaching Harrys camping area, beside the Noosa River. The tea-tree stained river, renowned for its spectacular reflections, is a canoers' paradise. The trail continues through littoral rainforest to Elanda Point, on Lake Cootharaba. You can hire canoes here. Organise permits in advance (p328); limits apply. For track notes and maps contact **QPWS** (☎ 5449 7364) at Elanda Point.

CENTRAL HIGHLANDS
Carnarvon Gorge

An oasis in the semiarid heart of Queensland, this walk features towering sandstone cliffs, decked with palms and rainforests, that form spectacular steep-sided gorges. Carnarvon Creek winds through the main gorge where sandstone overhangs are galleries for some of Australia's best Aboriginal art. There's 21km of tracks from short strolls to overnighters. Battleship Spur is a must. It's best done as a two- or three-day walk, following the main gorge (19 creek crossings) and camping at Big Bend; permits are required (p328). Next day, climb to the spur. **QPWS** (☎ 4984 4505) at Carnarvon Gorge has walk details. Commercial camping grounds are located within a few kilometres of the park – details are available on the QPWS website (www.epa.qld.gov.au).

THE WET TROPICS
Goldfield Trail

Prospectors and loggers followed Aboriginal trading routes through Bellenden Ker Range in northern Queensland. The Goldfield Trail follows one of these routes between Queensland's two highest peaks. It's a spectacular walk, starting at The Boulders Scenic Reserve and camping area near Babinda, 60km south of Cairns. Winding through lush, tropical rainforest to a saddle between the two peaks, it descends to cross East Mulgrave River at a popular swimming hole. It continues beside the river, to a picnic and camping area at Goldsborough section of Wooroonooran National Park. Contact **QPWS** (☎ 4046 6600; www.epa.qld.gov.au; 5b Sheridan St; ☯ 8.30am-5pm Mon-Fri) in Cairns or Wooroonooran Safaris (p330) for more information.

QUEENSLAND

Walkers Directory

PRACTICALITIES

- To get a few more walking ideas, or just to feel part of the scene, pick up a copy of *Wild* or *Outdoor Australia* magazines.

- Videos you might buy or watch will be based on the PAL system, also used in New Zealand and most of Europe.

- Use a three-pin adaptor (different from British three-pin adaptors) to plug into the electricity supply (240V AC, 50Hz).

- Australia uses the metric system: you will buy your milk and petrol in litres, and you will walk kilometres.

ACCOMMODATION

It's easy to get a good night's sleep in Australia, which offers everything from the tent-pegged confines of camping grounds and the communal space of hostels to gourmet breakfasts in guesthouses, chaperoned farmstays and all-inclusive resorts, plus the full gamut of hotel and motel lodgings.

In most areas you will find seasonal price variations. During the high season over summer (December to February) and

---

BOOK ACCOMMODATION ONLINE

For more accommodation reviews and recommendations by Lonely Planet authors, check out the online booking service at www.lonelyplanet.com. You'll find the true, insider low-down on the best places to stay. Reviews are thorough and independent. Best of all, you can book online.

---

at other peak times, particularly school and public holidays, prices are usually at their highest, whereas outside these times you will find useful discounts and lower walk-in rates. One exception is the Top End, where the Wet season (roughly October to March) is the low season, and prices can drop substantially.

The weekend escape is a notion that figures prominently in the Australian psyche, meaning accommodation from Friday night through to Sunday can be in greater demand (and pricier) in major holiday areas.

Camping & Caravan Parks

Caravan parks are thick on the ground in Australia – you will find one in just about every town (or roadhouse) that imagines itself to have a tourist attraction or three. Camping is the cheapest option you will find in the country, with the nightly cost for two people usually between $15 and $25, or slightly more for a powered site. Almost all caravan parks are equipped with hot showers, flush toilets and laundry facilities, and frequently a pool and barbecues. Many have old on-site caravans for rent, though it is more likely they will have on-site cabins. Cabin sizes and facilities vary, but expect to pay $60 to $120 for two people in a cabin with a kitchenette. If you intend doing a lot of caravanning or camping, consider joining one of the major chains such as **Big 4** (www.big4.com.au), which offers 10% discounts at member parks.

Walkers will usually find themselves with the option of staying at designated camp sites in national parks. These normally cost between $4 and $10 per person. It is rare for them to have showers, and most toilets are the great Aussie long-drop – part of the bush experience, if nothing else. Running water is a rarity but there is almost always a water tank. National park camping grounds invariably also have better locations than caravan parks.

CAMPING ON THE WALK

Now *this* is camping. You have walked all day and there is a flat piece of earth, grass or sand contoured to fit your back. On most walks in this book you will need to camp, and camp sites are as variable as the walking terrain you will encounter. They might be relatively plush, park-cleared areas, furnished with water tanks, pit toilets and picnic tables, or they might be as simple as a patch of dirt polished clear by previous tents. Whatever the facilities, camp sites are almost universally positioned near a water source – it is wise practice to check ahead with park authorities about water levels, especially in summer or autumn. For some suggestions about minimising your impact while camping, see the boxed text p24.

Guesthouses & B&Bs

B&Bs in Australia might be restored miners' cottages, converted barns, rambling old houses, upmarket country manors, beach-side bungalows or a simple bedroom in a family home (though invariably they will be more floral than the Chelsea Flower Show). Prices are typically around $80 to $150 (per double), though in cutesy weekender destinations such as the Blue Mountains and Mornington Peninsula this might just be your deposit.

B&Bs are mostly going to be places you snuggle into before or after you have walked, but if you are on a trail such as the Surf Coast Walk (p140) there is the option to get comfy by staying in B&Bs during your walk.

Local tourist offices can usually provide a list of places. For places listed online, try www.babs.com.au.

Hostels

Hostels are a highly social but low-cost fixture of the Australian accommodation scene. Not all dorms are same-sex rooms –

WALKING CLUBS

To add a social flavour to your walking, you might consider joining a walking club. Typically, a walking club will organise regular day walks and an occasional multiday walk, with club meetings around once a month. Many clubs also organise other activities, such as cycling and kayaking. There are numerous walking clubs around Australia, most of which are covered by statewide umbrella organisations: clubs in the Australian Capital Territory are covered by the Confederation of Bushwalking Clubs NSW, and in the Northern Territory by the Walking Federation of South Australia, while a peak national body, **Bushwalking Australia** (www.bushwalkingaustralia.org .au) was created in 2003.

The websites of the state federations can be an excellent resource for finding the right club for you, though if it's pure trail information you are after it is usually best to begin with national park authorities or tourist centres.

- **Confederation of Bushwalking Clubs NSW** (☎ 02-9290 2060; www.bushwalking.org.au) Represents around 60 clubs; website addresses for many can be found on the confederation's site.
- **Federation of Tasmania Bushwalking Clubs** (www.bushwalkingaustralia.org/html/taspage.html) Represents nine clubs.
- **Federation of Victorian Walking Clubs** (☎ 03-9455 1876; http://home.vicnet.net.au/~vicwalk) Represents more than 70 clubs.
- **Federation of Western Australian Bushwalkers** (☎ 08-9362 1614; www.bushwalkingaustralia.org/ html/wapage.html) Six member clubs.
- **Queensland Federation of Bushwalking Clubs** (www.geocities.com/qfbwc) Twenty-five affiliated clubs.
- **Walking Federation of South Australia** (☎ 08-8361 2491; www.walkingsa.org.au) Around 40 member clubs.

double-check if you are after a single-sex dorm. Dorm rates are usually around $20 to $30, with doubles typically around $50 to $65 (without bathroom). The website www.hostelaustralia.com lists hostels throughout the country.

Most hostels are aligned to different organisations, and membership of each entitles you to discounts on your stay and usually also for transport, tours and activities. There are around 140 hostel franchisees of **VIP Backpackers** (☎ 1800 724 833, 07-3395 6111; www.vipbackpackers.com; annual membership $39) in Australia, while **Nomads Backpackers** (☎ 02-9232 7788; www.nomadsworld.com; annual membership $34) has several dozen franchisees across Australia.

However, the most prominent hostel organisation is the **Youth Hostels Association** (YHA; ☎ 02-9261 1111; www.yha.com.au; annual membership $52), which has around 130 hostels across the country. Nightly charges are between $10 and $30 for members, while most hostels also take non-YHA members for an additional $3.50. YHA hostels provide varying levels of accommodation, from the austere simplicity of wilderness hostels to city-centre buildings with a café-bar and some en suite rooms. Most of the accommodation is in small dormitories (bunk rooms), although many hostels also provide twin rooms and even doubles. They have 24-hour access, cooking facilities, a communal area with a TV, laundry facilities and, in larger hostels, travel booking offices. There is often a maximum-stay period (usually five to seven days). Bed linen is provided (sleeping bags are not welcomed due to hygiene concerns) in all hostels except those in wilderness areas, where you will need your own sleeping sheet.

Australia also has numerous independent hostels, with fierce competition for the backpacker dollar prompting high standards and plenty of enticements, such as free breakfasts, courtesy buses and discount meal vouchers. They range from run-down hotels trying to fill empty rooms, to converted motels, to purpose-built hostels, often with the best facilities but sometimes too big and impersonal – avoid 'we love to party' places if you are in an introspective mood. The best places tend to be the smaller, more intimate hostels where the owner is also the manager.

Some hostels will only admit overseas backpackers; this mainly applies to city hostels that have had problems with locals sleeping over and bothering the backpackers. Hostels that discourage or ban Aussies say it is only a rowdy minority that makes trouble, and will often just ask for identification in order to deter potential troublemakers, but it can be annoying and discriminatory for people trying to genuinely travel in their own country.

Hotels & Motels

Except for pubs, the hotels that exist in cities or well-touristed places are generally of the business or luxury variety (insert the name of your favourite chain here), where you get a comfortable, anonymous and mod con–filled room. Typically, they have a pool, restaurant/café, room service and various other facilities. For these hotels this book generally quotes 'rack rates' (official advertised rates), though significant discounts can be offered when business is quiet, or by booking online.

Motels offer comfortable midrange accommodation and can be found all over Australia. Most motels are modern and generic – you will find tea- and coffee-making facilities, fridge, TV, air-con and bathroom. Some might contain a microwave, while a small number have a full kitchen. You will generally pay between $80 and $140 for a room.

To book ahead, you could try a service such as **Australian Accommodation Agency** (☎ 1800 626 822; www.hotel-reservation-australia.com), which offers rooms at around 250 capital-city hotels.

Huts

Australia is not the European Alps, where you can wander between mountain refuges with just a sleeping bag in your pack and the knowledge that somebody else is waiting to cook your meal at night. Australian tracks with huts are the exception not the norm: the Bibbulmun Track (p293) has an exceptional set-up, with three-sided shelters spaced a day's walk apart; there are simple timber huts in the High Country; and the Overland Track (p214) can – in principle – be walked staying each night in a hut, though places are not guaranteed so you should never set out under this assumption.

Pubs

For the budget traveller, hotels in Australia are the ones that serve beer, and are commonly known as pubs (from the term 'public house'). In country towns, pubs are invariably found in the town centre. Many pubs were built during boom times, so they are often among the largest, most extravagant buildings in town. In tourist areas some of these pubs have been restored as heritage buildings, but generally the rooms remain small, old fashioned and weathered, with a long amble down the hall to the bathroom.

You can sometimes rent a single room at a country pub for not too much more than a hostel dorm, and you will also be in the social heart of the town. But if you are a light sleeper, avoid booking a room right above the bar and check whether a band is playing downstairs that night (especially on Friday and Saturday nights).

Standard pubs have singles/doubles with shared facilities starting at around $35/55, or more if you want a private bathroom. Few have a separate reception area – make inquiries in the bar.

BUSINESS HOURS

Hours vary a little from state to state, but most shops and businesses open about 9am and close at 5pm Monday to Friday, with Saturday hours usually from 9am to either noon or 5pm. Sunday trading is becoming increasingly common, but is currently limited to major cities and, to a lesser extent, regional Victoria. In most towns there are usually one or two late shopping nights a week, normally Thursday and/or Friday, when doors stay open until about 9pm. Most supermarkets are open till at least 8pm and are sometimes open 24 hours in larger centres. Milk bars (general stores) and convenience stores often open until late.

Banks are normally open from 9.30am to 4pm Monday to Thursday and until 5pm on Friday. Some large city branches are open from 8am to 6pm weekdays, and a few are also open until 9pm on Friday. Post offices are open from 9am to 5pm Monday to Friday, but you can also buy stamps on Saturday morning at post office agencies (operated from newsagencies) and from Australia Post shops in all the major cities.

Restaurants typically open at noon for lunch, and 6pm to 7pm for dinner. They normally dish out food until at least 9pm (later on Friday and Saturday), while the main restaurant strips in large cities usually open longer hours throughout the week. Cafés tend to be all-day affairs that either close around 5pm or continue into the night. Pubs usually serve food from noon to 2pm and 6pm to 8pm. Pubs and bars often open for drinking at lunchtime and continue well into the evening, particularly from Thursday to Saturday.

CHILDREN

Walking with your kids is very different from walking as you knew it BC (Before Children). Fortunately if you can adjust happily to living with children, you will probably also enjoy walking with them.

You will be well aware of the assertion that kids slow you down, and that is never truer than when you set out on a walk. There is an age when children go at exactly your pace because you have carried them all the way (a good backpack built for the purpose is worth its weight in chocolate), but their increasing weight, and a growing determination to get down and do everything for themselves, means that phase soon passes. Once your first child is too big or too independent for the backpack, you simply have to scale down your expectations of distance and speed.

This is when the fun really starts. No longer another item to be carried – at least, not all the time – a walking child must be factored into your planning. Rather than get part-way into a walk and ask yourself in desperation, 'Why are we doing this?', make this the first question you ask. While walking driven by stats (kilometres covered, peaks bagged) is not likely to work with kids, other important goals can surface: fun and a sense of something accomplished together; and joy in the wonders of the natural world.

Easy and small is a good way to start. Too hard, and what should be fun can become an ordeal for all, especially the child. Don't overlook time for play. A game of hide and seek during lunch might be the highlight of your child's day on the track. A few simple toys or a favourite book brought along can make a huge difference. Play can also transform the walking itself: a simple stroll in the bush becomes a bear hunt in an enchanted forest.

Walks in this book that are particularly suitable for children include Bouddi Coast (p55), Wentworth Falls & Valley of Waters (p66), Werribee Gorge (p130), Surf Coast Walk (p140) and Nancy Peak & Devil's Slide (p296). For a longer outing with older children you might consider the Bibbulmun Karri & Coast (p290) walk, the Thorsborne Trail (p349) or the Coast Track (p58).

CLIMATE

Australia's climate typically errs on the hot side, but as should be expected from the sixth-largest country on the planet, there is tremendous variation. The southern third of the country has cold (though generally not freezing) winters (June to August). Tasmania and the High Country in Victoria and New South Wales (NSW) get particularly chilly (at Crackenback, above Thredbo, the average July maximum temperature is 0.1°C). Summers (December to February) in the south are pleasant and warm, though sequences of days above 36°C are quite common. Spring (September to November) and autumn (March to May) are transition months, offering comfortable conditions throughout the south.

As you head north the climate changes dramatically – 40% of the continent lies north of the Tropic of Capricorn. Seasonal variations become fewer until, in the far north around Darwin and Cairns, you are in the monsoon belt where there are basically just two seasons: hot and wet, and hot and dry. The Dry roughly lasts from April to September, and the Wet from October to March; the build-up to the Wet (from early October) is often when the humidity is at its highest. The centre of the continent is arid – hot and dry during the day, but often bitterly cold at night.

Outside of Antarctica, Australia is the driest continent; more than half the country receives less than 300mm of rain annually. The wettest place in the country is Mt Bellenden Ker, near Mt Bartle Frere (p353), with an average of around 8m a year. Rainfall decreases steadily away from the coast; a large part of the interior receives less than 100mm annually.

See When to Walk (p20) for details on how the seasons might influence your walking plans. Also see Climate charts (pp362–3) for destination-specific information.

Weather Information

The best source of weather information is the website of the **Bureau of Meteorology** (BoM; www.bom.gov.au), which includes detailed regional forecasts and all kinds of warnings. Some national park offices also post daily local forecasts to help you keep a watch on the heat or approaching rain.

A weather factor of principal importance to walkers is that of Total Fire Ban days (see p25). These are publicised widely in the media, with fire weather warnings also listed on the BoM website.

For a good overview of climate averages for destinations throughout Australia, take a look at www.weatherbase.com.

CUSTOMS

When entering Australia you can bring most articles in free of duty provided that customs is satisfied they are for personal use and that you will be taking them with you when you leave. There is a duty-free quota per person of 2.25L of alcohol, 250 cigarettes and dutiable goods up to the value of $900.

There are duty-free shops at international airports and in their associated cities, though many goods are not really much (if at all) cheaper duty-free. Alcohol and cigarettes are certainly cheaper duty-free, though, as they are heavily taxed in Australia.

For further information on customs regulations, contact the **Australian Customs Service** (☎ 1300 363 263; www.customs.gov.au).

EMBASSIES & CONSULATES
Australian Embassies & Consulates

The website of the **Department of Foreign Affairs & Trade** (www.dfat.gov.au) provides a full listing of all Australian diplomatic missions overseas.

Canada Ottawa (☎ 613-236 0841; www.ahc-ottawa.org; suite 710, 50 O'Connor St, Ottawa, Ontario K1P 6L2) Also in Vancouver and Toronto.

France Paris (☎ 01 40 59 33 00; www.france.embassy .gov.au; 4 Rue Jean Rey, Paris 75724 Cedex 15)

Germany Berlin (☎ 030-880 08 80; www.australian -embassy.de; Wallstrasse 76-79, Berlin 10179) Also in Frankfurt.

Indonesia Jakarta (☎ 0212-550 5555; www.austembjak .or.id; Jalan HR Rasuna Said Kav C15-16, Jakarta Selatan 12940) Also in Medan (Sumatra) and Denpasar (Bali).

Ireland Dublin (☎ 01-664 5300; www.australianembassy .ie; 7th fl, Fitzwilton House, Wilton Tce, Dublin 2)

Climate

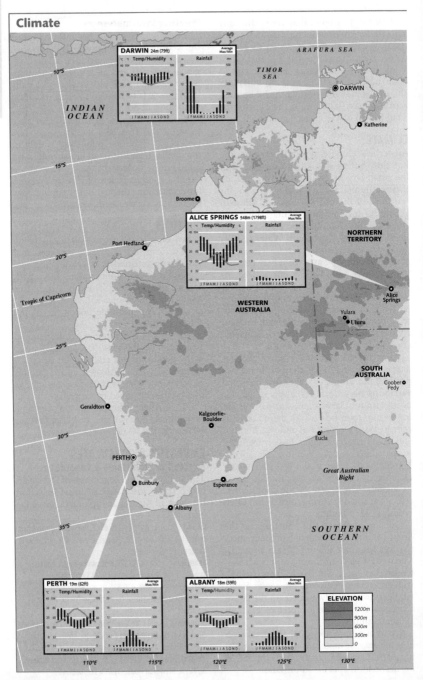

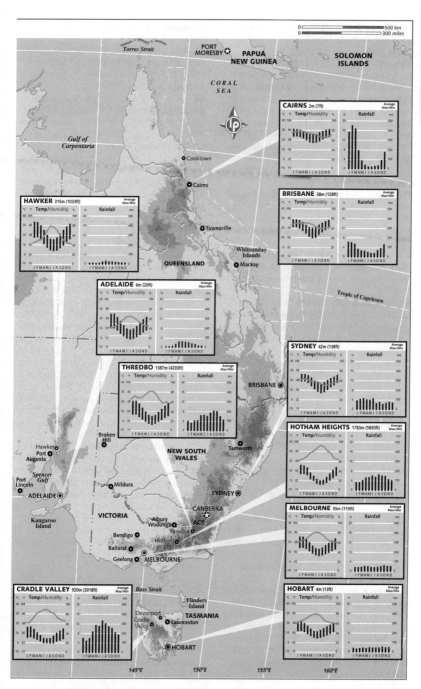

Japan Tokyo (☎ 0352-324 111; www.australia.or.jp; 2-1-14 Mita, Minato-Ku, Tokyo 108-8361) Also in Osaka, Nagoya, Sendai, Sapporo and Fukuoka City.

Malaysia Kuala Lumpur (☎ 032-146 5555; www.australia .org.my; 6 Jalan Yap Kwan Seng, Kuala Lumpur 50450) Also in Penang, Kuching (Sarawak) and Kota Kinabalu (Sabah).

Netherlands The Hague (☎ 0703-10 82 00; www .australian-embassy.nl; Carnegielaan 4, The Hague 2517 KH)

New Zealand Wellington (☎ 04-473 6411; www.australia .org.nz; 72-76 Hobson St, Thorndon, Wellington); Auckland (☎ 09-921 8800; level 7, Price Waterhouse Coopers Tower, 186-194 Quay St, Auckland)

Singapore (☎ 6836 4100; www.singapore.embassy.gov .au; 25 Napier Rd, Singapore 258507)

Thailand Bangkok (☎ 0 2344 6300; www.austembassy .or.th; 37 South Sathorn Rd, Bangkok 10120)

UK London (☎ 020-7379 4334; www.australia.org.uk; Australia House, the Strand, London WC2B 4LA) Also in Edinburgh.

USA Washington DC (☎ 202-797 3000; www.austemb.org; 1601 Massachusetts Ave, Washington DC NW 20036-2273) Also in Los Angeles, New York and other major cities.

Embassies & Consulates in Australia

Canada Canberra (☎ 02-6270 4000; www.dfait-maeci.gc .ca/australia; Commonwealth Ave, Canberra, ACT 2600); Sydney (☎ 02-9364 3000; level 5, 111 Harrington St, Sydney, NSW 2000)

France Canberra (☎ 02-6216 0100; www.ambafrance -au.org; 6 Perth Ave, Yarralumla, ACT 2600); Sydney (☎ 02-9261 5779; level 26, St Martins Tower, 31 Market St, Sydney, NSW 2000)

Germany Canberra (☎ 02-6270 1911; www.german embassy.org.au; 119 Empire Circuit, Yarralumla, ACT 2600); Sydney (☎ 02-9328 7733; 13 Trelawney St, Woollahra, NSW 2025); Melbourne (☎ 03-9864 6888; 480 Punt Rd, South Yarra, Vic 3141)

Ireland Canberra (☎ 02-6273 3022; irishemb@cyberone .com.au; 20 Arkana St, Yarralumla, ACT 2600); Sydney (☎ 02-9231 6999; level 30, 400 George St, Sydney, NSW 2000)

Japan Canberra (☎ 02-6273 3244; www.japan.org.au; 112 Empire Circuit, Yarralumla, ACT 2600); Sydney (☎ 02-9231 3455; level 34, Colonial Centre, 52 Martin Pl, Sydney, NSW 2000)

Malaysia Sydney (☎ 02-9327 7596; 67 Victoria Rd, Bellevue Hill, NSW 2023)

Netherlands Canberra (☎ 02-6220 9400; www.netherlands .org.au; 120 Empire Circuit, Yarralumla, ACT 2600); Sydney (☎ 02-9387 6644; level 23, tower 2, Westfield Bondi Junction, 101 Grafton St, Bondi Junction, NSW 2022)

New Zealand Canberra (☎ 02-6270 4211; www.nzembassy .com/australia; Commonwealth Ave, Canberra, ACT 2600); Sydney (☎ 02-8256 2000; level 10, 55 Hunter St, Sydney, NSW 2001)

Singapore Canberra (☎ 02-6273 3944; 17 Forster Cres, Yarralumla, ACT 2600)

Thailand Canberra (☎ 02-6273 1149; rtecanberra@mfa .go.th; 111 Empire Circuit, Yarralumla, ACT 2600); Sydney (☎ 02-9241 2542; http://thaisydney.idx.com.au; level 8, 131 Macquarie St, Sydney, NSW 2000)

UK Canberra (☎ 02-6270 6666; http://bhc.britaus.net/ default.asp; Commonwealth Ave, Yarralumla, ACT 2600); Sydney (☎ 02-9247 7521; 16th fl, 1 Macquarie Pl, Sydney, NSW 2000); Melbourne (☎ 03-9652 1600; 17th fl, 90 Collins St, Melbourne, Vic 3000)

USA Canberra (☎ 02-6214 5600; http://usembassy-australia .state.gov/index.html; 21 Moonah Pl, Yarralumla, ACT 2600); Sydney (☎ 02-9373 9200; level 10, 19-29 Martin Pl, Sydney, NSW 2000); Melbourne (☎ 03-9526 5900; 553 St Kilda Rd, Melbourne, Vic 3004)

FOOD & DRINK
Local Food & Drink

Australia is not known for having a unique cuisine, but many people are surprised by the range and quality of food available in restaurants, markets, delicatessens and cafés, especially in the major cities but often in less populated places as well. Australians have coined their own phrase, Modern Australian (Mod Oz), to describe their cuisine. If it's a melange of East and West, it's Mod Oz. If it's not authentically French or Italian, it's Mod Oz – the term is an attempt to classify the unclassifiable. It doesn't really alter from one region to another, but some influences are obvious, such as the Italian migration to Melbourne and the Southeast Asian migration to Darwin.

Vegetarian eateries and vegetarian selections in nonvegie places (including menu choices for vegans and coeliac sufferers) are becoming more common in large cities and are forging a stronger presence in the smaller towns visited by tourists, though rural Australia – as exemplified by pub grub – mostly continues its stolid dedication to meat. Those who enjoy a pre- or postdigestive cigarette will need to go outside, as smoking has been made illegal in most enclosed public places in all Australian states and territories, including indoor cafés, restaurants, clubs and (sometimes only at meal times) pub dining areas.

Not many actual dishes can lay claim to being uniquely Australian. Even the humble 'pav' (pavlova), the meringue dessert with cream and passionfruit, may be from New Zealand. Ditto for lamingtons, large cubes

---

RECIPE ON THE RUN *Andrew Bain*

Gourmets, look away now. One of my favourite meals on the track is the sort of thing your mum might have called 'surprise soup': a bit of this, a bit of that. But it is light, filling and actually tastes pretty good (for camp food anyway). The following recipe is for two people:

- 250g couscous
- a handful of pistachio nuts or cashews
- two sachets of tomato paste
- a half packet of dried peas and carrots
- mixed herbs
- stock cube

Stir the tomato paste and stock cube into water, add the dried vegetables and bring to the boil. After a few minutes, add mixed herbs and couscous. Boil for about one minute, then remove from heat and let the couscous sit in the hot water. Add the nuts, stir and eat.

Chocolate-chip-cookie chaser optional but welcome.

---

of cake dipped in chocolate and rolled in desiccated coconut. The nearest thing you will find to a truly local experience is to eat some of the wildlife – kangaroo, emu or crocodile – that you have been admiring as you walk.

On the Walk

You will almost certainly be self-catering as you walk, meaning you will need to carry your food and, in most places, a stove (p393). For a walk of two or three days you will be able to carry some fresh food, but beyond this you will need to fall back on dried walking staples such as pasta, rice, legumes, flat breads and muesli. If you carry commercially produced, freeze-dried meals you will be relieved of much of the menu planning but often also much of the taste. Scroggin – a trail mix of nuts, dried fruit and often chocolate – is almost de rigueur for snacking as you walk, though chocolate always seems a great idea in the supermarket but less so by the time the Aussie heat has melted it to a paste.

It makes good sense to compartmentalise your food packing, keeping it all together or at least in some easily found order. The temptation when packing is to fill those small and awkward gaps in your pack with muesli bars and that squeeze pack of Vegemite, but you might rue your decision when you are pulling everything from your pack just to find a snack or spread.

For a bit of inspiration beyond pasta a la bland, pick up a copy of *The Outdoor Gourmet* by Michael Hampton.

BUYING FOOD

You'll find some sort of grocery store in most Australian towns, though not all are sufficiently stocked to satisfy walkers' specific needs. In this book, supermarkets and other self-catering options are listed in the town descriptions. Where possible, we have noted where you will need to shop elsewhere in order to find a decent range of goods.

WILD FOOD

Nibbling on bush tucker is a great idea in principle, but distinguishing edible fruits

---

WATER

Australia has some of the finest drinking water in the world (you might disagree if you have only tasted it from Adelaide's taps), though drinking from streams on your walks without treating the water is not advised. Rarely can you be certain that another person or animal hasn't contaminated it upstream. Some treatments, especially iodine, can leave an unpalatable flavour in the water – if this is a concern, think about carrying powdered flavour sachets such as Tang. For information on treating water, see the boxed text p385.

from inedible is difficult to the untrained eye. Some foods also require multiple forms of preparation just to make them edible, so pick cautiously as you wander. For more on bush tucker and a selection of guidebooks about identifying it, see the boxed text (p31).

HOLIDAYS
Public Holidays
The following is a list of the main national public holidays. Each state and territory also has its own public holidays, such as bank holidays and Labour Day, and (this being Australia) major horse races. For precise dates check locally.

New Year's Day 1 January
Australia Day 26 January
Easter (Good Friday to Easter Monday inclusive) March/April
Anzac Day 25 April
Queen's Birthday (except WA) Second Monday in June
Queen's Birthday (WA) Last Monday in September
Christmas Day 25 December
Boxing Day 26 December

School Holidays
The Christmas holiday season, from about mid-December to late January, is the main school break – it is the time you are most likely to find transport and accommodation booked out, and crowds on the popular walking tracks. There are three shorter school holiday periods during the year. Dates vary by a week or two from state to state, but they fall roughly from early to mid-April, late June to mid-July and late September to early October.

INSURANCE
Don't underestimate the importance of a good travel insurance policy that covers theft, loss and medical problems – nothing is guaranteed to ruin your walking plans quicker than an accident on the trail or having that brand-new digital camera stolen. Most policies offer lower and higher medical-expense options; the higher ones are chiefly for countries that have extremely high medical costs, such as the USA. Australia is usually at the lower end of the price chain. There is a wide variety of policies available, so compare the small print.

Some policies specifically exclude designated 'dangerous activities'. For some insurance companies this can mean bushwalking, so check the small type to make sure the policy you choose fully covers you for your walking plans.

You may prefer a policy that pays doctors or hospitals directly rather than requiring you to pay on the spot and claim later. If you have to claim later make sure you keep all documentation. Check that the policy covers ambulances and emergency medical evacuations by air – an airlift from a remote walking track can also disable your savings.

Worldwide cover to travellers from over 44 countries is available online at www .lonelyplanet.com/travel_services. For information on health insurance, see p381. For information on vehicle insurance, see p378.

INTERNET ACCESS
Internet cafés have become so ubiquitous throughout Australia it is easy to imagine that bytes and not bites are now a menu item. Connection speeds and prices vary significantly, but they all offer straightforward Internet access. Most public libraries also have Internet access, though this is provided primarily for research needs, not for travellers to check their email, so head for an Internet café. You will find them in cities, sizable towns and pretty much anywhere else that travellers congregate. The cost ranges from $3 per hour in cut-throat places such as Sydney's King's Cross to $10 per hour in more remote locations. The average is about $6 per hour, usually with a minimum of 10 minutes' access. Most youth hostels and backpacker places can hook you up, as can many hotels and caravan parks. Telecentres (community centres providing web access and other hi-tech facilities to locals and visitors) provide Internet access in remote areas of Western Australia (WA), South Australia (SA) and NSW, while Tasmania has set up access centres in numerous local libraries and schools.

Free web-based email services include **Yahoo** (www.yahoo.com), **MSN Hotmail** (www.hotmail .com) and **Excite** (www.excite.com). See p23 for some useful sites when planning your trip.

MAPS
When packing for a walk, a good map is as essential as your sleeping bag and boots – we do not recommend setting out on any bushwalk without a map. Learn to read its features and how it translates the land. That

way, you will not only be more likely to navigate yourself out of any difficulty, but your enjoyment will also be enhanced by the ability to use the map to identify everything you are seeing and passing.

In the Planning section of each walk in this book you will find details of the best maps to carry.

MAPS IN THIS BOOK

Our maps are based on the best available references, sometimes combined with GPS data collected in the field. They are intended to show the general route of the walk and should always be used in conjunction with the maps suggested in the walk description. For information on symbols used on our maps, see the legend on the back page.

Buying Maps

It is a good idea to stock up on all the walking maps you will need in capital cities. Each capital has at least one decent map shop – you will find them listed under Information in each chapter's Gateway section – but there are few outside these cities. Small-scale maps showing the entire country or state or a region are plentiful and can also be purchased at map shops, visitor information centres, some newsagents and even petrol stations. If you want to get a head start, the **Melbourne Map Centre** (☎ 03-9569 5472; www.melbmap.com.au) has online purchasing, and stocks topographic maps and road maps from around the country.

Large-Scale Maps

The most common map scale used for walking is 1:50,000 (2cm on the map equalling 1km), providing enough detail to make navigation generally straightforward. For some popular and short walks you will even find dedicated 1:25,000 topographic maps. Maps at 1:50,000 are available for most walks.

Geoscience Australia (www.ga.gov.au), Australia's national mapping division, produces a 1:100,000 NATMAP colour topographical series that covers the entire coast and hinterland, but not a lot of the outback. It lacks the detail for reliable route finding so is generally useful only for orientation and identification of landscape features.

Most states have an official mapping agency that produces large-scale colour topographical maps suitable for walking. There are also dedicated national park maps to some of the most popular parks.

Small-Scale Maps

Good-quality road maps are plentiful. The various state motoring organisations are a dependable source of road maps, while local tourist offices usually supply free maps, though the quality varies.

Lonely Planet publishes handy fold-out city maps of Sydney and Melbourne. City street guides, such as those produced by Ausway (publishers of *Melway* and *Sydway*), Gregorys and UBD, are useful for in-depth urban navigation but they are expensive, bulky and only worth getting if you intend to do a lot of city driving.

If you are planning on plenty of touring between walks, a car touring atlas such as *Explore Australia* will be useful, with maps that cover the entire country and blurbs on most towns along the way.

MONEY

Australia's currency is the Australian dollar, comprising 100 cents. Although the smallest coin in circulation is 5c, prices are marked in single cents, and the total price rounded to the nearest 5c when you pay. The Australian dollar has stabilised in recent times, after slipping to around US$0.50 in 2003 – see the inside front cover for exchange rates at the time of writing. For an idea of local costs, see p20.

Unless otherwise stated, all prices in this book are given in Australian dollars.

ATMs

ATMs are plentiful throughout Australia, though don't expect to find them too far off the beaten track or in very small towns. Most ATMs accept cards issued by other banks and are linked to international networks.

Credit & Debit Cards

Arguably the best way to carry most of your money around is in the form of a plastic card. Australia is well and truly a card-carrying society, and credit cards such as Visa and MasterCard are widely accepted for everything from a hostel bed to a restaurant meal, and are pretty much essential (in lieu of a large deposit) for hiring a car. They can also be used to get cash advances over the counter at banks and from many ATMs, depending on the card, though these transactions incur immediate interest. Charge cards such as Diners Club and American Express (Amex) are not as widely accepted.

The obvious danger with credit cards is maxing out your limit and racking up a steaming pile of debt and interest charges. A safer option is a debit card from which you can draw money directly from your bank account using ATMs, banks or Eftpos devices. Any card connected to the international banking network (Cirrus, Maestro, Plus and Eurocard) should work, provided you know your PIN. The most flexible option is to carry both a credit and a debit card.

Exchanging Money
Changing foreign currency or travellers cheques is usually no problem at banks throughout Australia, or at licensed moneychangers such as Travelex or Amex in cities and major towns. Black-market exchange is almost unheard of.

On the Walk
If you are going to be incurring costs as you walk, such as camping fees or snacks, cash is going to be your only real option – rangers who come around to collect your $5 don't carry credit-card swipers. As you leave the last town before your walk, replenish your cash supply.

Taxes & Refunds
The Goods and Services Tax (GST) is a flat 10% tax on all goods and services – accommodation, eating out, transport, electrical goods, books, clothing etc. There are exceptions, however, such as basic foods (milk, bread, fruits and vegetables). By law the tax is included in the quoted or shelf prices, so all prices in this book are GST-inclusive. International air and sea travel to/from Australia is GST-free, as is domestic air travel when purchased outside Australia by non-residents.

If you are an overseas resident and purchase new or second-hand goods with a total minimum value of $300 from any one supplier no more than 30 days before you leave Australia, you are entitled under the Tourist Refund Scheme (TRS) to a refund of any GST paid. The scheme doesn't apply to all goods but mainly to those taken with you as hand luggage or worn onto the plane or ship. Also note that the refund is valid for goods bought from more than one supplier, but only if at least $300 is spent in each. For more details, contact the **Australian Customs Service** (☎ 1300 363 263; www.customs.gov.au).

Tipping
Tipping is the exception rather than the norm in Australia, though by some law of the jungle it is expected in more expensive restaurants – 10% of the bill is the usual amount if you think the food and service has warranted it. Nobody is going to be offended if you tip, but some people will happily think they have taken you for a ride (in more than their taxi) if you are extravagant about it.

Travellers Cheques
The ubiquity and convenience of internationally linked credit- and debit-card facilities in Australia means that travellers cheques are not heavily relied upon. Nevertheless, Amex, Thomas Cook and other well-known international brands of travellers cheques are easily exchanged. Transactions at their bureaux are commission-free if you use their cheques, while local banks charge hefty fees (often in excess of $7 per transaction) for the same service. You need to present your passport for identification when cashing travellers cheques. There are no notable restrictions on importing or exporting travellers cheques.

PERMITS & FEES
National Park Fees
It is becoming more commonplace to be charged an entry fee on arrival at a national park – this can range from a bit of chump change to $16 a day at Kosciuszko National Park. Only Queensland allows free access to all of its national parks.

Increasingly you can also buy park passes that allow you entry into all, or a selection of, national parks in each state. Each state has its own system and pricing – for details see the Information sections at the start of each regional chapter. Individual park entry fees are detailed in the relevant sections inside the regional chapters.

PUBLIC & PRIVATE PROPERTY

If you have travelled to Australia from the UK, toss away the notion of 'right to roam' – there is no legal public right of way across private land in Australia. Private property here is a possession as cherished as the three family cars, so treat with respect those signs that declare 'Trespassers Prosecuted' (and especially the few that suggest 'Trespassers will be Shot').

Most walks in this book are on public land; ie land owned by the government. A couple of the Northern Territory walks are also in national parks to which Aboriginal people hold title and for which it is essential to obtain an entry permit. Some short sections of walks in this book do cross private land, the access to which has been granted by the owner. When walking these sections, respect any conditions, close gates (if they are closed when you get to them) and avoid spooking any livestock.

Walking Permits

As some tracks in Australia grappled with their increasing popularity, it became inevitable that permit systems would be implemented. What used to be a free-and-easy walk on the Overland Track (p214) is now regulated by a permit system (at least between November and April), as is the Thorsborne Trail (p349), Prom Southern Circuit (p176), Croajingolong Coast Walk (p182) and Jatbula Trail (p315). For permit details see the Planning sections for each of these walks.

If walking any of these tracks be sure to plan well ahead – permits on the Thorsborne Trail in holiday periods will need to be booked up to a year in advance.

TELEPHONE

Local calls from private phones cost 18c to 30c, while local calls from public phones cost 50c; both allow unlimited talk time. Calls to mobile phones attract higher rates and are timed. Long-distance calls are cheaper during off-peak hours – generally between 7pm and 7am.

International calls from Australia are cheap and subject to specials that reduce the rates even more, so it is worth shopping around. When calling overseas you will need to dial the international access code from Australia (☎ 0011 or ☎ 0018), the country code and then the area code (without the initial 0). In addition, certain operators will have you dial a special code to access their service.

If dialling Australia from overseas, the country code is ☎ 61 and you need to drop the 0 in state/territory area codes.

Numbers starting with ☎ 190 are usually recorded information services, charged at anything from 35c to $5 or more per minute (more from mobiles and payphones). To make a reverse-charge (collect) call from any public or private phone, dial ☎ 1800-REVERSE (738 3773) or ☎ 12 550. Toll-free numbers (prefix ☎ 1800) can be called free of charge from almost anywhere in Australia, although they may not be accessible from certain areas or from mobile phones. Calls to numbers starting with ☎ 13 or ☎ 1300 are charged at the rate of a local call – the numbers can usually be dialled Australia-wide, but may be applicable only to a specific state or district. Telephone numbers beginning with ☎ 1800, ☎ 13 or ☎ 1300 cannot be dialled from outside Australia.

Mobile Phones

Local numbers with the prefixes ☎ 04xx or ☎ 04xxx belong to mobile phones. Australia's two mobile networks, digital GSM and digital CDMA, service more than 90% of the population but leave vast tracts of the country uncovered. The east coast, southeast and southwest have good reception, but elsewhere (apart from major towns) it is haphazard or nonexistent.

Australia's digital network is compatible with GSM 900 and 1800 (used in Europe), but generally not with the systems used in the USA or Japan. It is easy and cheap enough to get connected short term as the main service providers have prepaid mobile systems. Buy a starter kit, which may include a phone or, if you have your own phone, a SIM card (around $15) and a prepaid charge card. The calls tend to be dearer than with standard contracts, but there are no connection fees or line-rental charges and you can buy the recharge cards at convenience stores and newsagents.

TAKING PHOTOS OUTDOORS *Gareth McCormack & Grant Dixon*

For walkers, photography can be a vexed issue – all that magnificent scenery, but such weight and space restrictions on what photographic equipment you can carry. With a little care and planning it is possible to maximise your chance of taking great photos on the trail.

Light & Filters In fine weather, the best light is early and late in the day. In strong sunlight and in mountain, desert and coastal areas where the light is often intense, a polarising filter can improve colour saturation and reduce haze. On overcast days the soft light can be great for shooting wildflowers, forest interiors and running water, and an 81A warming filter can be useful. If you use slide film, a graduated filter will help to balance unevenly lit landscapes.

Equipment There is a plethora of film and digital-camera models now available, but the best results are still obtained using single-lens reflex (SLR) models. If you need to travel light carry a zoom lens in the 28mm to 70mm range (or the digital equivalent), and if your sole purpose is landscapes consider carrying just a single wide-angle lens (24mm). A tripod is essential for really good images and there are some excellent lightweight models available. Otherwise you can improvise with a trekking pole, pack or even a pile of rocks.

Camera Care Keep your gear dry and protect it from humidity – a few zip-lock freezer bags can be used to double wrap camera gear. Sturdy cameras will normally work fine in freezing conditions. Take care when bringing a camera from one temperature extreme to another; if moisture condenses on the camera parts make sure it dries thoroughly before going back into the cold. Standard camera batteries have a much shorter life in the cold. In hot areas, keep film as cool as possible, especially after it has been exposed.

For a thorough grounding on outdoor and on-the-road photography, read Lonely Planet's *Landscape Photography* by Peter Eastway or *Travel Photography* by Richard I'Anson. Also highly recommended is the outdoor photography classic *Mountain Light* by Galen Rowell.

Phone Codes

For long-distance calls, Australia uses four STD (Subscriber Trunk Dialling) area codes. Area-code boundaries don't necessarily coincide with state borders – NSW, for example, uses each of the four neighbouring codes – but the main area codes are as follows:

State/Territory	Area code
ACT	☎ 02
NSW	☎ 02
NT	☎ 08
QLD	☎ 07
SA	☎ 08
TAS	☎ 03
VIC	☎ 03
WA	☎ 08

Phonecards

A variety of phonecards can be bought at newsagents, hostels and post offices for a fixed dollar value (usually $10, $20 etc) and can be used with any public or private phone by dialling a toll-free access number and then the PIN number on the card. Some public phones also accept credit cards.

TIME

Australia is divided into three time zones: the Western Standard Time zone (GMT/UTC plus eight hours) covers WA; Central Standard Time (plus 9½ hours) covers the Northern Territory (NT) and SA; and Eastern Standard Time (plus 10 hours) covers Tasmania, Victoria, NSW, the Australian Capital Territory and Queensland. So when it is noon in WA, it's 1.30pm in the NT and SA, and 2pm in the rest of the country.

'Daylight saving' here is as complex as calculus. Clocks are put forward an hour in most states during the warmer months (October to March), but WA, the NT and Qld stay on standard time, while in Tasmania daylight saving starts a month earlier than in SA, Victoria, the ACT and NSW. Also see the World Time Zones map (p411).

TOURIST INFORMATION

Tourism Australia (☎ 02-9360 1111; www.australia.com) is the peak national tourist organisation. The website (which comes in 10 languages) is a good planning resource, though not heavy on walking information. That said, run a search for 'bushwalk' and you will uncover a good thumbnail selection of options.

Within Australia, tourist information is disseminated by various regional and local offices. In this book, the main state and territory tourism authorities are listed in the introductory Information Sources section of each chapter. Almost every major town in Australia seems to maintain a tourist office of some type, providing local info not readily available from the state offices. Invariably, local offices have better knowledge of walking tracks than state offices or Tourism Australia, and even at this micro-level you will usually find it better to chat with park authorities than the all-encompassing visitor information centres. Details of local tourism offices are given in the relevant city and town sections throughout this book.

Tourist Offices Abroad

Tourism Australia agents can supply various publications on Australia, including a number of handy fact sheets on topics such as camping, fishing, skiing and national parks, plus a handy map for a small fee. This literature is only distributed overseas, but local travellers can download and print the information from the Tourism Australia website.

Some countries with Tourism Australia offices:

Germany (☎ 069-2740 0622; Neue Mainzer Strasse 22, Frankfurt D 60311)

Japan (☎ 0352-140 720; New Otani Garden Court Bldg 28F, 4-1 Kioi-cho Chiyoda-ku, Tokyo 102-0094)

New Zealand (☎ 09-915 2826; level 3, 125 the Strand, Parnell, Auckland)

Singapore (☎ 6255 4555; 101 Thomson Rd, United Sq 08-03, Singapore 307591)

Thailand (☎ 0 2670 0640; unit 1614, 16th fl, River Wing East, Empire Tower, 195 South Sathorn Rd, Yannawa, Sathorn, Bangkok 10120)

UK (☎ 020-7438 4601; 6th fl, Australia House, Melbourne Place/Strand, London WC2B 4LG)

USA (☎ 310-695 3200; 6100 Center Dr, Los Angeles CA 90045)

VISAS

All visitors to Australia need a visa – only New Zealand nationals are exempt, and even they receive a 'special category' visa on arrival. Application forms for the several types of visa are available from Australian diplomatic missions overseas (p361), travel agents or the website of the **Department of Immigration & Multicultural & Indigenous Affairs** (Dimia; ☎ 13 18 81; www.immi.gov.au).

However, most visitors get their visa in the form of an Electronic Travel Authority (ETA) through any travel agent or overseas airline registered with the International Air Transport Association (IATA). They make the application directly when you buy a ticket and issue the ETA, which replaces the usual visa stamped in your passport. It is common practice for travel agents to charge a fee of around US$15 for issuing an ETA. This system is available to passport holders of 32 countries, including the UK, the USA and Canada, most European and Scandinavian countries, Malaysia, Singapore, Japan and South Korea.

You can also apply for the ETA online (www.eta.immi.gov.au), which attracts a nonrefundable service charge of $20.

If you are a passport holder from outside the 32 ETA nations, or you want to stay longer than three months, you will need to apply for a visa through an embassy or consulate. Standard visas (which cost $65) allow one (in some cases multiple) entry for a stay of up to three months, and are valid for use within 12 months of issue. A long-stay tourist visa (also $65) can allow a visit of up to a year.

Transport

GETTING THERE & AWAY

ENTERING THE COUNTRY

Arrival in Australia is a straightforward affair, with only the usual customs declarations (p361) to endure. However, as an island nation, Australia has strict quarantine requirements. If you are bringing in equipment such as boots and a tent, they will need to be clean or you might find them getting a spit and polish from quarantine officers.

There are no restrictions on citizens of foreign countries entering Australia – if you have a visa (p371), you should be fine.

AIR

There are myriad airlines and air fares to choose from if you are flying from Asia, Europe or North America. If you plan to fly at a particularly popular time (Christmas is notoriously difficult for Sydney and Melbourne) or on a particularly popular route (such as Hong Kong, Bangkok or Singapore to Sydney or Melbourne), make your arrangements well in advance of your trip.

The high season for flights into Australia is roughly over summer (December to February), with the shoulder months being around October/November and March/April. The low season is basically winter (June to August), a bonus if you are thinking of walking in the Northern Territory or Queensland.

Airports & Airlines

Australia has several international gateways, with Sydney and Melbourne being the busiest. International airports of use to walkers:

Adelaide (code ADL; ☎ 08-8308 9211; www.aal.com.au)
Brisbane (code BNE; ☎ 07-3406 3088; www.brisbaneairport.com.au)
Cairns (code CNS; ☎ 07-4052 9703; www.cairnsport.com.au/airport)
Darwin (code DRW; ☎ 08-8920 1811; www.ntapl.com.au)
Melbourne (Tullamarine; code MEL; ☎ 03-9297 1600; www.melbourne-airport.com.au)
Perth (code PER; ☎ 08-9478 8888; www.perthairport.net.au)
Sydney (Kingsford Smith; code SYD; ☎ 02-9667 9111; www.sydneyairport.com.au)

Australia's overseas carrier is **Qantas** (airline code QF; ☎ 13 13 13; www.qantas.com.au; hub Kingsford Smith Airport, Sydney), which – as anybody who has seen the movie *Rainman* can testify – is regarded as one of the world's safest airlines. It flies chiefly to destinations across Europe, North America, Asia and the Pacific.

A subsidiary of Qantas, **Australian Airlines** (airline code AO; ☎ 1300 799 798; www.australianairlines.com.au; hub Kingsford Smith Airport, Sydney) flies between Cairns (with connections to the Gold Coast) and Japan, Hong Kong and Singapore. It also flies between Bali and Perth, Sydney and Melbourne.

Airlines that service Australia include the following (all phone numbers listed are for dialling from within Australia):
Air Canada (airline code AC; ☎ 1300 655 767; www.aircanada.ca; hub Pearson International Airport, Toronto)

Air New Zealand (airline code NZ; ☎ 13 24 76; www
.airnz.com.au; hub Auckland International Airport)

British Airways (airline code BA; ☎ 1300 767 177;
www.britishairways.com; hub Heathrow Airport, London)

Cathay Pacific (airline code CX; ☎ 13 17 47; www
.cathaypacific.com; hub Hong Kong International Airport)

China Airlines (airline code CI; ☎ 02-9231 3336; www
.china-airlines.com; hub Chiang Kai Shek Airport, Taipei)

Emirates (airline code EK; ☎ 1300 303 777; www.emirates
.com; hub Dubai International Airport)

Freedom Air (airline code SJ; ☎ 1800 122 000; www
.freedomair.com; hub Auckland International Airport)

Garuda Indonesia (airline code GA; ☎ 1300 365
330; www.garuda-indonesia.com; hub Soekarno-Hatta
International Airport, Jakarta)

Gulf Air (airline code GF; ☎ 1300 366 337; www.gulfairco
.com; hub Abu Dhabi International Airport)

Hawaiian Airlines (airline code HA; ☎ 02 9244 2377;
www.hawaiianairlines.com.au; hub Honolulu International
Airport, Hawaii)

Japan Airlines (airline code JL; ☎ 02-9272 1111; www
.jal.com; hub Narita Airport, Tokyo)

KLM (airline code KL; ☎ 1300 303 747; www.klm.com;
hub Schiphol Airport, Amsterdam)

Lufthansa (airline code LH; ☎ 1300 655 727; www
.lufthansa.com; hub Frankfurt Airport)

Malaysia Airlines (airline code MH; ☎ 13 26 27; www
.malaysiaairlines.com; hub Kuala Lumpur International
Airport)

Pacific Blue (airline code DJ; ☎ 13 16 45; www.flypacific
blue.com; hub Brisbane Airport)

Royal Brunei Airlines (airline code BI; ☎ 1300 721 271;
www.bruneiair.com; hub Bandar Seri Begawan Airport)

Singapore Airlines (airline code SQ; ☎ 13 10 11; www
.singaporeair.com.au; hub Changi International Airport,
Singapore)

South African Airways (airline code SA; ☎ 1800 221
699; ww4.flysaa.com; hub Johannesburg International
Airport)

Thai Airways International (airline code TG; ☎ 1300
651 960; www.thaiairways.com; hub Bangkok International
Airport)

United Airlines (airline code UA; ☎ 13 17 77; www.united
.com; hub Los Angeles International Airport)

DEPARTURE TAX

Travellers leaving Australia are slugged a
departure tax of $38, but this is incorpo-
rated into the price of your air ticket.

Tickets

Automated online ticket sales work well if
you are doing a simple one-way or return

BAGGAGE RESTRICTIONS

Airlines impose tight restrictions on carry-
on baggage. No sharp implements of any
kind are allowed onto the plane, so pack
items such as pocket knives, camping cut-
lery and first-aid kits into your checked luggage or they'll be confiscated.

If you are carrying a camping stove you
should remember that airlines ban liquid
fuels and gas cartridges from all baggage,
both check-through and carry-on. Empty
all fuel bottles, wash them to be rid of the
scent of fuel and buy what you need at your
destination.

TRANSPORT

trip on specified dates, but are no substitute
for a travel agent with the low-down on
special deals, strategies for avoiding stopovers and other useful advice.

If you are flying to Australia from the
other side of the globe, round-the-world
(RTW) tickets can be a real bargain. They
are generally put together by the three biggest airline alliances – **Star Alliance** (www.star
alliance.com), **Oneworld** (www.oneworldalliance.com)
and **Skyteam** (www.skyteam.com). An alternative
type of RTW ticket can be put together by a
travel agent. These are usually more expensive than airline RTW fares but allow you
to create your own itinerary.

For online ticket bookings, start with the
following websites:

Air Brokers (www.airbrokers.com) US site specialising in
cheap tickets.

Cheap Flights (www.cheapflights.com) Informative site
with specials, airline information and flight searches.

Cheapest Flights (www.cheapestflights.co.uk) Worldwide
flights from the UK.

Expedia (www.expedia.msn.com) Microsoft's travel site;
mainly USA related.

Flight Centre (www.flightcentre.com) Respected operator.
Site links to Australia, New Zealand, UK, USA, Canada and
South Africa sites.

Flights.com (www.flights.com) International site; offers
cheap fares and an easy-to-search database.

Roundtheworldflights.com (www.roundtheworld
flights.com) Allows you to build your own trips from the
UK with up to six stops.

STA Travel (www.statravel.com) Prominent in international
student travel but you don't have to be a student; site linked
to worldwide STA sites.

Travel Online (www.travelonline.co.nz) Good place to
check worldwide flights from New Zealand.

Travelocity (www.travelocity.com) US site that allows you to search fares (in US dollars) to/from practically anywhere.

Asia

Most Asian countries offer competitive airfare deals, with Bangkok, Singapore and Hong Kong the best cities in which to find discount tickets.

Flights between Hong Kong and Australia are notoriously heavily booked. Flights to/from Bangkok and Singapore are often part of the longer Europe-to-Australia route so are also in demand. Plan your preferred itinerary well in advance.

You can get cheap short-hop flights between Darwin and Indonesia. Royal Brunei Airlines flies between Darwin and Bandar Seri Begawan, while Malaysia Airlines flies from Kuala Lumpur.

A couple of Asian agents:

Phoenix Services (☎ 2722 7378) Based in Hong Kong.
STA Travel Bangkok (☎ 02-236 0262; www.statravel.co .th); Singapore (☎ 6737 7188; www.statravel.com.sg); Tokyo (☎ 03-5391-2922; www.statravel.co.jp)

Canada

Most flights from Toronto and Vancouver stop at one US city such as Los Angeles or Honolulu before heading on to Australia. Air fares from Canadian discount ticket sellers (consolidators) tend to be about 10% higher than those sold in the USA.
Travel CUTS (☎ 866-246-9762; www.travelcuts.com) is Canada's national student travel agency and has offices in all major cities.

Qantas, Air Canada, Air New Zealand, Japan Airlines and United all fly from Canada to Australia.

Continental Europe

From major European destinations, most flights travel to Australia via one of the Asian cities. Some flights are also routed through London before arriving in Australia via Singapore, Bangkok, Hong Kong or Kuala Lumpur.

In Germany good travel agencies include **STA Travel** (☎ 069-7430 3292; www.statravel.de). A good place to check out in the Netherlands is **Holland International** (☎ 0900-8858; www.holland international.nl).

In France try **OTU Voyages** (☎ 01 40 29 12 22; www.otu.fr), a student/youth specialist with offices in many French cities. Other recommendations include **Voyageurs du Monde** (www .vdm.com/vdm) and **Nouvelles Frontières** (☎ 08 25 00 07 47; www.nouvelles-frontieres.fr/nf) – again, both companies have branches around France.

New Zealand

Air New Zealand and Qantas operate a network of flights linking key New Zealand cities with most major Australian cities, while quite a few other international airlines include New Zealand and Australia on their Asia–Pacific routes. Emirates flies to Sydney, Melbourne and Brisbane from Auckland, and to Sydney only from Christchurch.

Another trans-Tasman option is the no-frills budget airline Freedom Air, an Air New Zealand subsidiary that offers direct flights between destinations on Australia's east coast and six New Zealand cities.

Pacific Blue, a subsidiary of budget airline Virgin Blue, flies from Christchurch, Wellington and Auckland to a number of Australian cities.

There is usually not a significant difference in price between seasons, as this is a popular route year-round. Agents with numerous branches and reasonably priced fares:

House of Travel (www.houseoftravel.co.nz)
STA Travel (☎ 0508 782 872; www.statravel.co.nz)

UK & Ireland

There are two routes from the UK: the western route via the USA and the Pacific; and the eastern route via the Middle East and Asia. Flights are usually cheaper and more frequent on the latter. Some of the best deals are with Emirates, Gulf Air, Malaysia Airlines, Japan Airlines and Thai Airways International. British Airways, Singapore Airlines and Qantas generally have higher fares but may offer a more direct route.

Discount air travel is big business in London. Advertisements for travel agencies appear in the travel pages of the weekend broadsheet newspapers, as well as in *Time Out*, in the *Evening Standard* and in the free magazine *TNT*.

Popular agencies in the UK:

Flight Centre (☎ 0870-499 0040; www.flightcentre.co.uk)
STA Travel (☎ 0870-160 0599; www.statravel.co.uk)
Trailfinders (☎ 0845-058 5858; www.trailfinders.co.uk)

USA

Most flights between the USA and Australia travel to/from the west coast, with the bulk routed through Los Angeles but some coming through San Francisco. Numerous airlines offer flights via Asia or various Pacific islands.

San Francisco is the USA's ticket consolidator capital, although good deals can be found in Los Angeles, New York and other big cities. **STA Travel** (☎ 800-781 4040; www.statravel .com) has offices all over the USA.

GETTING AROUND

AIR
Airlines in Australia
Qantas (p372) is the country's chief domestic airline, and is represented at the so-called 'budget' end of the national air-travel market by its subsidiary **Jetstar** (☎ 13 15 38; www .jetstar.com.au), which flies to 15 east-coast destinations from Cairns to Hobart, and also to Adelaide. Another highly competitive carrier that flies all over Australia is **Virgin Blue** (☎ 13 67 89; www.virginblue.com.au).

Australia has many smaller operators flying regional routes, including the following:

Australian Airlines (☎ 13 13 13; www.australianairlines .com.au) Qantas subsidiary flying between Cairns and both the Gold Coast and Sydney.

Regional Express (Rex; ☎ 13 17 13; www.regional express.com.au) Flies to Sydney, Melbourne, Adelaide and regional centres in NSW, Victoria, SA and Tasmania, including Cooma, Devonport and Kangaroo Island.

Skywest (☎ 1300 660 088; www.skywest.com.au) Flies from Perth to many West Australian towns, including Albany, plus Darwin.

Air Passes
With discounting now the norm, air passes are no longer great value. Qantas' Boomerang Pass can only be purchased overseas and involves buying coupons for either short-haul flights (up to 1200km), or multizone sectors (including New Zealand and the Pacific). You must purchase a minimum of two coupons before you arrive in Australia, and once here you can buy more.

Regional Express has the Rex Backpacker scheme, where international travellers with a VIP, YHA, ISIC or IYTC card can buy one/two months of unlimited travel on the airline; it applies to standby fares only.

BOAT
Australia might be an island nation but there are few opportunities to practically

use the ocean as a means of transport. Ferries likely to be of use to walkers:

SeaLink (☎ 13 13 01; www.sealink.com.au) Vehicle ferries between Cape Jervis (out of Adelaide) and Kangaroo Island.

Spirit of Tasmania (☎ 1800 634 906; www.spiritof tasmania.com.au) High-speed vehicle ferries between Devonport (Tasmania) and both Sydney and Melbourne.

Ferries or shuttles also serve Hinchinbrook Island (p349) and Fraser Island (p344).

BUS
Australia's extensive bus network makes a relatively cheap and reliable way to get around, though it can be a tedious means of travel. Most buses are equipped with air-con, toilets and videos, and all are smoke-free. Small towns eschew formal bus terminals for a single drop-off/pick-up point, usually outside a post office, newsagent or shop.

A national bus network is provided by **Greyhound Australia** (☎ 13 14 99; www.greyhound .com.au). Fares purchased online are roughly 5% cheaper than over-the-counter tickets; fares purchased by phone incur a $4 booking fee.

Due to convoluted licensing arrangements involving some regional bus operators, there are some states and areas in Australia – namely SA, Victoria and parts of NSW and northern Queensland – where you cannot buy a Greyhound ticket to travel between destinations within that state/area. Instead, your ticket needs to take you out of the region or across a state/territory border. For example, you cannot get on a Greyhound bus in Melbourne and get off in Ballarat, but you can travel from Melbourne to Bordertown just across the border in SA. This situation does not apply to bus passes, which can be used freely.

Other operators running key routes:

Firefly Express (☎ 1300 730 740; www.fireflyexpress.com .au) Runs between Sydney and Adelaide through Melbourne.

Premier Motor Service (☎ 13 34 10; www.premierms .com.au) Covers the east coast between Cairns and Melbourne.

Premier Stateliner (☎ 08-8415 5555; www.premier stateliner.com.au) Services towns around SA, including Port Augusta and Port Germein.

Redline Coaches (☎ 1300 360 000; www.tasredline.com .au) Services Hobart, Launceston and Tasmania's north and east coasts.

TassieLink (☎ 1300 300 520; www.tassielink.com.au) Covers Tasmania extensively, with dedicated walker services in summer.

Transwa (☎ 1300 662 205; www.transwa.wa.gov.au) Destinations include Albany, Walpole, Dunsborough and Augusta out of Perth.

V/Line (☎ 13 61 96; www.vline.com.au) Services to most major Victorian towns and cities.

Bus Passes

The following Greyhound passes are subject to a 10% discount for members of YHA, VIP, Nomads and other approved organisations, as well as seniors/pensioners.

The popular range of Aussie Explorer Passes gives you from one month to a year to cover a set route – there are 24 routes in all and the time of validity depends on the distance of the route. You can't backtrack, but if you find a route that suits you it generally works out cheaper than other passes. The Aussie Highlights pass ($1430), for instance, allows you one year to loop around Australia's eastern half from Sydney, through Melbourne, Adelaide, Alice Springs, Darwin, Cairns, Townsville and Brisbane, taking in many of the walks in this book. Or there are one-way passes such as the Outback and Reef Explorer Pass ($800), giving you six months to travel from Sydney through Brisbane, Townsville, Cairns, Katherine and Darwin.

The Aussie Kilometre Pass is the simplest pass and gives you a specified amount of travel, starting at 2000km and going up in increments of 1000km to a maximum of 20,000km. The pass is valid for 12 months and you can travel where and in what direction you like, and stop as many times as you like. For example, a 2000km pass ($300) will get you from Cairns to Brisbane, 4000km ($540) from Cairns to Melbourne, and 12,000km ($1370) will cover a loop from Sydney through Melbourne, Adelaide, central Australia, Darwin, Cairns and back to Sydney. Side trips or destinations off the main route (such as Kakadu) may be calculated at double the actual kilometres travelled. Phone at least a day ahead to reserve a seat if you are using this pass.

Hop-on Hop-off Buses

Many of the backpacker-style buses that are so ubiquitous around Australia operate only set tours, making them impractical for walkers, but some do offer hop-on hop-off services that can be a cost-effective alternative to the big bus companies. The buses are usually smaller, you will meet lots of other travellers and the drivers sometimes double as tour guides. Conversely, some travellers find the tour-group mentality and inherent limitations don't suit them. Discounts for students and members of hostel organisations are usually available.

Easyrider Backpacker Tours (☎ 1300 308 477; www.easyridertours.com.au) Runs tours with hop-on hop-off options through WA. Of most use to walkers is the Southern Curl tour, passing through Dunsborough, Augusta, Walpole and Albany.

Oz Experience (☎ 1300 300 287; www.ozexperience.com) Highly social buses – for better or worse – that cover central, northern and eastern Australia. Travel is one-directional and passes are valid for up to 12 months with unlimited stops.

Wayward Bus (☎ 1300 653 510; www.waywardbus.com.au) Most trips with this reputable company allow you to get on or off where you like. The Classic Coast route runs between Adelaide and Melbourne along the Great Ocean Road. Trips also run to Alice Springs, Kangaroo Island and Flinders Ranges, Kosciuszko, Nitmiluk and Kakadu National Parks.

Reservations

Over summer, school holidays and public holidays, book well ahead on the more popular routes such as intercity and east-coast services.

CAR & MOTORCYCLE

Many of Australia's best walking tracks are a long way from the reach of public transport, so having your own vehicle is not only an asset but also often a necessity.

Automobile Associations

Each state (and the NT) has its own automobile association, providing emergency breakdown services, excellent touring maps and detailed guides to accommodation and camping grounds. They all have reciprocal arrangements with each other (and overseas), so if you're a member of the NRMA in NSW, for example, you can use RACV facilities in Victoria. Similarly, if you are a member of the AAA in the USA, you can use any of the Australian organisations' facilities. Bring proof of your membership.

Association details for each state:

Automobile Association of the Northern Territory (AANT; ☎ 08-8981 3837; www.aant.com.au)

National Roads & Motorists Association (NRMA; ☎ 13 11 22; www.mynrma.com.au) In NSW and the ACT.

Royal Automobile Association of South Australia (RAA; ☎ 08-8202 4600; www.raa.net)

Royal Automobile Club of Queensland (RACQ; ☎ 13 19 05; www.racq.com.au)
Royal Automobile Club of Tasmania (RACT; ☎ 13 27 22; www.ract.com.au)
Royal Automobile Club of Victoria (RACV; ☎ 13 19 55; www.racv.com.au)
Royal Automobile Club of Western Australia (RACWA; ☎ 13 17 03; www.rac.com.au)

Driving Licence

You can generally use your home country's driving licence in Australia, as long as it is in English (otherwise you will need a certified translation) and carries your photograph for identification. You can also use an International Driving Permit (IDP), which must be supported by your home licence. It is easy enough to get an IDP – just go to your home country's automobile association and it should issue it on the spot. The permits are valid for 12 months.

Fuel & Spare Parts

Fuel (predominantly unleaded and diesel) is available from service stations sporting well-known international brand names. LPG (liquefied petroleum gas) is not always stocked at more remote roadhouses; if you are on gas it is safer to have dual-fuel capacity.

Prices vary from place to place but basically fuel is heavily taxed and continues to rise in price, much to the disgust of local motorists, though it is still relatively cheap compared with Europe. Once in the bush, prices soar – in outback NT and Queensland, or along the Nullarbor, prices can be up to 50% higher than in the cities.

Distances between roadhouses can be long in the outback, but not so long that you need worry about running out of fuel. The greatest distance between fuel stops along Highway One is around 300km along the west coast, which is outside the area of any walks in this book. While many roadhouses on are open 24 hours, this does not apply to every fuel stop and you can't always rely on them to be open in the dead of night.

The further you get from the cities, the better it is to be in a Holden or Ford. Spare parts are easy to find for these vehicles, but less so for some other makes.

Hire

For cheaper alternatives to the big-name international car-hire firms, try one of the many local outfits. Remember, though, that if you want to travel a significant distance you will want unlimited kilometres, and that cheap car hire often comes with serious restrictions.

You must be at least 21 years old to hire from most firms – if you are under 25 you may have to pay a surcharge. It is cheaper if you rent for a week or more and there are often low-season and weekend discounts. Credit cards are the usual payment method.

Large firms sometimes offer one-way rentals (eg pick up a car in Adelaide and leave it in Sydney) but there are many limitations, including a substantial drop-off fee.

Major companies offer a choice: either unlimited kilometres, or 100km or so a day free plus so many cents per kilometre over this.

Daily rates in cities or on the east coast are typically about $55 to $60 daily for a small car (Holden Barina, Ford Festiva, Hyundai Excel), about $65 to $80 daily for a medium car (Mitsubishi Magna, Toyota Camry) and $85 to $100 daily for a big car (Holden Commodore, Ford Falcon), all including insurance. A small 4WD (Suzuki Vitara, Toyota Rav4) is about $85 to $100 a day, while a large 4WD such as a Toyota Landcruiser is at least $150, which should include insurance and some free kilometres (100km to 200km a day, or sometimes unlimited). You can compare prices between companies at www.carhire.com.au.

Rental companies with offices in the capital cities include the following:
Airport Rent-A-Car (☎ 1800 331 033; www.airportrentacar.com.au)
Apex (☎ 1800 777 779; www.apexrentacar.com.au)
Avis (☎ 13 63 33; www.avis.com.au)
Budget (☎ 1300 794 344; www.budget.com.au)
Europcar (☎ 1300 131 390; www.deltaeuropcar.com.au)
Hertz (☎ 13 30 39; www.hertz.com.au)
Rent-a-Bomb (☎ 13 15 53; www.rentabomb.com.au) Offices in NSW, Victoria and Queensland.
Thrifty (☎ 1300 367 227; www.thrifty.com.au)

If you prefer a campervan with a bad paint job, join the backpacker scene with **Wicked Campers** (☎ 1800 246 869; www.wickedcampers.com.au).

For a less orthodox form of car rental check out **Ezi-Ride** (☎ 07-5559 5938; www.ezi-ride.com), an organised car-pooling scheme that brings together travellers who are prepared to pay for lifts and drivers looking for cash-paying passengers. Also check out the possibilities for long-distance lifts on the virtual notice board www.needaride.com.au.

Insurance

In Australia, third-party personal injury insurance is included in the vehicle registration fee, ensuring that every registered vehicle carries at least minimum insurance. We recommend extending that minimum to at least third-party property insurance, which covers damage to other vehicles (and property) in an accident – minor collisions can be amazingly expensive.

When it comes to hire cars, understand your liability in the event of an accident. Rather than risk paying out thousands of dollars, you can pay an additional daily amount to the rental company to reduce the excess you pay in the event of an accident. If travelling on dirt roads in a rental vehicle you will not be covered by insurance unless you have a 4WD. Also, most companies' insurance won't cover the cost of damage to glass (including the windscreen) or tyres.

Note that some companies won't cover you for accidents that occur between dusk and dawn while driving in the outback, so be prepared to confine your driving to daylight hours.

Road Conditions

Multilane highways are relatively uncommon in Australia, but all major routes are sealed and have two lanes. The starting points of several walks are on unsealed roads – some gravel-road driving is inevitable if you want to access areas such as the Victorian Alps. Always carry spare parts, such as fan belts and radiator hoses, if you are heading into the bush on dirt roads.

Road Hazards

Kangaroos are common hazards on country roads and can cause a lot of damage if you hit one. They are most active at dawn and dusk, and often travel in groups. If one hops across the road in front of you, slow right down – its mates may be close behind. Many Australians avoid travelling after dark because of the risk posed by animals. Cattle join kangaroos as hazards in the outback.

If you are travelling at night and a large animal does appear in front of you, hit the

---

INTERSTATE QUARANTINE

Restrictions on the movement of fruit, vegetables, plants and flowers between states apply in Australia in an attempt to prevent the spread of pests and diseases such as fruit fly and grape phylloxera. There are quarantine inspection posts at some state borders and dump bins at airports. Some inspection posts are manned, with quarantine officers entitled to search your vehicle for undeclared items, so save your fruit and veg shopping until you are across the border. For a list of restrictions between each state, see the **Travellers' Guide to Interstate Quarantine** (www.agric.nsw.gov .au/reader/4699).

---

brakes, dip your lights (so you don't continue to dazzle and confuse it) and avoid swerving if you can – people have been killed in accidents caused by swerving to miss animals.

Away from the cities you may also meet road trains. These are huge trucks (a prime mover plus two or three trailers) that can be more than 50m long in the Top End and west, so you need about 1km to overtake one. When a road train approaches on a narrow sealed road, slow down and pull over – if it has to put its wheels off the road to pass, the shower of stones it tosses up could shatter your windscreen.

Another hazard is driver fatigue. Driving long distances (particularly in hot weather) can be so tiring you might fall asleep at the wheel. It is not uncommon and the consequences can be unthinkable. On a long haul, stop and rest about every two hours – do some exercise, change drivers or have a coffee.

Road Rules

Australians drive on the left-hand side of the road and all cars are right-hand drive. An important road rule is 'give way to the right' – if an intersection is unmarked, you must give way to vehicles coming from your right.

The general speed limit in built-up areas is 60km/h, but this has been reduced to 50km/h (and in some cases 40km/h) on residential streets in most states – keep an eye out for signs. Near schools, the limit is

40km/h in the morning and afternoon, and is often stringently policed. On the open highway it is usually 100km/h or 110km/h. In the NT there is no speed limit outside built-up areas (except along the Lasseter Hwy to Uluru, where the limit is 110km/h). Police have speed radar guns and cameras, and are fond of using them.

Oncoming drivers who flash their lights at you may be giving you a friendly warning of a speed camera ahead, or they may be telling you that your headlights are not on. Try not to get caught doing it yourself, since it is illegal.

All new cars in Australia have seat belts back and front, and it is the law to wear them; you are likely to get a fine if you don't. Small children must be belted into an approved safety seat. Talking on a mobile phone when driving is also illegal.

Drink-driving remains a real problem. Serious attempts to reduce the resulting road toll áre ongoing and random breathtests are not uncommon in built-up areas. If you are caught with a blood-alcohol level of more than 0.05%, expect a hefty fine and the loss of your licence.

HITCHING

Hitching is never entirely safe and we don't recommend it. Travellers who decide to hitch should understand that they are taking a small but potentially serious risk. People who do choose to hitch will be safer if they travel in pairs and let someone know where they are planning to go. In Australia, the hitching signal can be a thumbs up or a downward-pointed finger.

TRAIN

Long-distance rail travel in Australia is something you do because you really want to – because it is neither cheaper nor more convenient, and it certainly isn't fast. Trains are likely to be of little practical use to walkers, as stations are rarely near trailheads. Exceptions include the Coast Track (p58), Red Hands Cave (p64) and the Yurrebilla Trail (p253).

Rail services within each state are run by that state's rail body. The three major interstate services in Australia are operated by **Great Southern Railway** (☎ 13 21 47; www.gsr .com.au), namely the *Indian Pacific* between Sydney and Perth, the *Overland* between Melbourne and Adelaide, and the *Ghan* between Adelaide and Darwin via Alice Springs and Katherine.

CountryLink (☎ 13 22 32; www.countrylink.info) is a rail and coach operation that visits destinations in NSW, the ACT, Queensland and Victoria.

Reservations

As the railway-booking system is computerised, any station (other than those on suburban lines) can make a booking for any journey throughout the country. For telephone reservations call ☎ 13 22 32; this will connect you to the nearest main-line station.

Discounted tickets work on a first-come, first-served quota basis, so it helps to book in advance.

Train Passes

The Great Southern Railway Pass ($590), available only to non-Australian residents, allows unlimited travel on the rail network for a period of six months. With the pass you will be travelling in a 'Daynighter' reclining seat and not a cabin. You need to book all seats at least 24 hours in advance.

CountryLink offers two passes. The East Coast Discovery Pass ($400) allows one-way economy travel between Melbourne

---

LOCAL TRANSPORT TO/FROM WALKS

In a country with as much land and as few major roads as Australia, it's inevitable that public transport is going to be of limited use to most walkers. In response to this, an industry of shuttle services has developed around the most popular trails, so that there are private operators – often accommodation owners – throughout the country that whisk walkers to and from trailheads. In one case (Walpole in Western Australia) the town's taxi service even grew from its origin as a walkers' shuttle.

Around 14 of the walking regions in this book have dedicated shuttle services. For service details, see the relevant sections in the regional chapters.

TRANSPORT

and Cairns (in either direction) with unlimited stopovers, and is valid for six months. It is available to Australian residents and overseas visitors. Shorter sections, such as Sydney to Cairns, are also available. The Backtracker Rail Pass is available only to non-Australian residents, and allows for travel on the entire CountryLink network.

There are four versions: 14 days ($220), one month ($260), three months ($280) and six months ($390).

The Austrail Flexi-Pass allows you to travel on any Great Southern Railway, CountryLink and Queensland Rail routes for either 15 days ($870) or 22 days ($1210) over a six-month period.

Health & Safety

Australia's greatest hazards are more topographical than infectious – you are more likely to twist an ankle on the trail than you are to be felled by disease. Some tropical maladies such as malaria and yellow fever are unheard of, as are diseases of insanitation such as cholera and typhoid. By taking care to treat the water you drink along the tracks, covering yourself against the sun and walking with basic caution, you are likely only to carry this chapter as ballast.

BEFORE YOU GO

Since most vaccines don't produce immunity until at least two weeks after they are given, visit a physician four to eight weeks before departure. Ask your doctor for an International Certificate of Vaccination (known as 'the yellow booklet'), which will list all the vaccinations you have received. This is mandatory for countries that require proof of yellow fever vaccination upon entry (sometimes required in Australia; see right).

Bring medications in their original labelled containers. A signed and dated letter from your doctor describing your medical conditions and medications, including generic names, is a good idea. If carrying syringes or needles be sure to have a doctor's letter stating their medical necessity.

Some walks in this book are physically demanding and most require a reasonable level of fitness. Even if you are tackling the easiest walks, it pays to be relatively fit, rather than launch straight into them after months of sedentary living. If you are aiming for the demanding walks, good fitness is essential.

Unless you are a regular walker, start your get-fit campaign at least a month before your visit. Take a vigorous walk of about an hour, two or three times per week and gradually extend the duration of your outings as the departure date nears. If you plan to carry a full backpack on walks, take a loaded pack on some of your training jaunts.

INSURANCE

If your health insurance doesn't cover you for medical expenses abroad, consider getting extra insurance. Make sure this covers you for walking and remote-area rescue.

Medicare doesn't cover ambulance costs, though ambulance service is free for Queensland and Tasmanian residents. Residents of other states (and Queenslanders and Tasmanians walking outside of their home states) should check their health insurance covers them for remote-area ambulance rescue services. Some health insurers offer ambulance-only cover for around $30 a year, and in Victoria, SA and country WA you can take out ambulance cover direct with the ambulance service.

REQUIRED & RECOMMENDED VACCINATIONS

If you are entering Australia within six days of having stayed overnight or longer in a yellow fever-infected country, you will need proof of yellow fever vaccination. For a full list of these countries visit the **World Health Organization** (WHO; www.who.int/wer/) website or the **Centers for Disease Control & Prevention** (www.cdc.gov/travel/yb/outline.htm£2) website.

If you are really worried about health when travelling, there are a few vaccinations you could consider for Australia. The WHO recommends that all travellers should be covered for diphtheria, tetanus, measles, mumps, rubella, chickenpox and polio, as well as hepatitis B, regardless of their destination. While Australia has high levels of childhood vaccination coverage, outbreaks of these diseases do occur.

MEDICAL CHECK LIST

- ☐ Acetaminophen (paracetamol) or aspirin
- ☐ Adhesive or paper tape
- ☐ Antibacterial ointment for cuts and abrasions
- ☐ Antibiotics
- ☐ Antidiarrhoeal drugs (eg loperamide)
- ☐ Antihistamines (for hay fever and allergic reactions)
- ☐ Anti-inflammatory drugs (eg ibuprofen)
- ☐ Bandages, gauze swabs, gauze rolls
- ☐ Elasticised support bandage
- ☐ Iodine tablets or water filter (for water purification)
- ☐ Nonadhesive dressing
- ☐ Oral rehydration salts
- ☐ Paper stitches
- ☐ Permethrin-containing insect spray for clothing, tents and bed nets
- ☐ Scissors, safety pins, tweezers
- ☐ Sterile alcohol wipes
- ☐ Steroid cream or cortisone (for allergic rashes)
- ☐ Sticking plasters (Band-Aids, blister plasters)
- ☐ Sutures
- ☐ Syringes and needles – ask your doctor for a note explaining why you have them
- ☐ Thermometer

Also see the equipment check list, p392.

INTERNET RESOURCES

There is a wealth of travel health advice to be found on the Internet. The **WHO** (www.who.int/ith) publishes a superb book called *International Travel and Health,* which is revised annually and is available online at no cost. Another website of general interest is **MD Travel Health** (www.mdtravelhealth.com), which provides complete travel health recommendations for every country and is updated daily.

It is usually a good idea to consult your government's travel health website before departure, if one is available:

Canada (www.travelhealth.gc.ca)
UK (www.doh.gov.uk)
USA (www.cdc.gov/travel)

FURTHER READING

Lonely Planet's *Healthy Travel Australia, NZ & the Pacific* is a handy, pocket-sized guide packed with useful information, including pre-trip planning, emergency first aid, immunisation and disease information and what to do if you get sick on the road.

Australian First Aid, published by St John Ambulance, is a good general reference, while *Remote Area First Aid,* also from St John Ambulance, is one for the backpack, offering quick reference on the injuries you might encounter on the trail. Both books can be purchased from **St John Ambulance** (www.ambulance.net.au).

IN AUSTRALIA

AVAILABILITY & COST OF HEALTH CARE

Australia has an excellent health-care system. It is a mixture of privately run medical clinics and hospitals alongside a system of public hospitals funded by the Australian government. The Medicare system covers Australian residents for some health-care costs. Visitors from countries with which Australia has a reciprocal health-care agreement are eligible for benefits specified under the Medicare program. Agreements are currently in place with New Zealand, the UK, the Netherlands, Sweden, Finland, Italy, Malta and Ireland – check the details before departing these countries. In general the agreements provide for any episode of ill-health that requires prompt medical attention. For further details, visit www.health.gov.au/pubs/mbs/mbs3/medicare.htm.

Preparing for a Walk

On many of Australia's walking tracks, there is likely to be a significant delay in emergency services reaching you in the event of serious accident or illness, which makes an increased level of self-reliance and preparation essential. Consider taking a wilderness first-aid course, such as those offered at the **Wilderness Medicine Institute** (www.wmi.net.au). Take a comprehensive first-aid kit that's appropriate for your activities, and ensure that you have adequate means of communication. Australia has extensive mobile phone coverage but additional radio communication is important in remote areas.

INFECTIOUS DISEASES
Dengue Fever

Dengue fever occurs in northern Queensland – particularly from October to March – during the wet season. Also known as 'breakbone fever', because of the severe muscular pains that accompany it, this viral disease is spread by a species of mosquito that feeds primarily during the day. Most people will recover in just a few days; however, more severe forms of this disease can occur, particularly in residents or visitors who are exposed to another strain of the virus (there are four types) in a subsequent season.

Giardiasis

Giardiasis is widespread in waterways around Australia. Drinking untreated water from streams and lakes is not recommended. Use water filters and boil or treat water with iodine to help prevent the disease. Symptoms consist of intermittent foul-smelling diarrhoea, abdominal bloating and wind. Effective treatment is available (tinidazole or metronidazole).

Meningococcal Disease

This disease occurs worldwide and is a risk if you have prolonged stays in dormitory-style accommodation. A vaccine exists for some types of this disease, namely meningococcal A, C, Y and W. No vaccine is presently available for the viral type of meningitis.

Ross River Fever

The Ross River virus occurs throughout Australia and is spread by mosquitoes living in marshy areas. As well as fever, it causes headache, joint and muscular pains and a rash, and resolves after five to seven days.

Tick Typhus

Cases of tick typhus have been reported throughout Australia, but are predominantly found in Queensland and New South Wales. A week or so after being bitten, a dark area forms around the bite, followed by a rash and possible fever, headache and inflamed lymph nodes. The disease is treatable with antibiotics (doxycycline), so see a doctor if you suspect you have been bitten. Seek local advice on areas where ticks pose

---

COMMON AILMENTS

Blisters

To avoid blisters make sure your boots are well worn in before you hit the trail. Your boots should fit comfortably with enough room to move your toes; boots that are too big or too small will cause blisters. Make sure socks fit properly and are specifically made for walkers; even then, check to make sure there are no seams across the widest part of your foot. Wet and muddy socks can also cause blisters, so even on a day walk pack a spare pair of socks. Keep your toenails clipped but not too short. If you do feel a blister coming on, treat it sooner rather then later. Apply a simple sticking plaster, or preferably a special blister plaster that acts as a second skin.

Fatigue

More injuries happen towards the end of the day rather than earlier, when you are fresher. Although tiredness can simply be a nuisance on an easy walk, it can be life-threatening on narrow, exposed ridges or in bad weather. You should never set out on a walk that is beyond your capabilities on the day. If you feel below par, have a day off. To reduce the risk, don't push yourself too hard – take a rest every hour or two and build in a good-length lunch break. Towards the end of the day, reduce the pace and increase your concentration. You should also eat properly throughout the day; nuts, dried fruit and chocolate are all good energy-giving snack foods.

Knee Strain

Many walkers feel the judder on long, steep descents. Although you can't eliminate strain on the knee joints when dropping steeply, you can reduce it by taking shorter steps that leave your legs slightly bent and ensure that your heel hits the ground before the rest of your foot. Some walkers find that tubular bandages help, while others use hi-tech, strap-on supports. Walking poles are very effective in taking some of the weight off the knees.

HEALTH & SAFETY

a danger and always check your skin carefully for ticks after walking in a danger area such as a tropical forest. An insect repellent can help, and walkers in tick-infested areas should consider having their boots and trousers impregnated with benzyl benzoate and dibutylphthalate (see Ticks, right, for advice on removal).

ENVIRONMENTAL HAZARDS
Bites & Stings
LEECHES
Often present in damp rainforest conditions, leeches attach themselves to your skin to suck your blood. Trekkers often get them on their legs or in their boots. Salt or a lighted cigarette end will make them fall off. Do not pull them off, as the bite is then more likely to become infected. Clean and apply pressure if the point of attachment is bleeding. An insect repellent may keep them away.

SNAKES
Australian snakes have a fearful reputation that is justified in terms of the potency of their venom, but unjustified in terms of the actual risk to walkers. Snakes are usually quite timid and, in most instances, will move away if disturbed. They have only small fangs, making it easy to prevent bites to the lower limbs (where 80% of bites occur) by wearing protective clothing (such as gaiters) when walking.

In all cases of confirmed or suspected bites, preventing the spread of toxic venom can be achieved by applying pressure to the wound and immobilising the area with a splint or sling before seeking medical attention. Firmly wrap an elastic bandage (you can improvise with a T-shirt) around the entire limb, but not so tight as to cut off the circulation. Along with immobilisation, this is a life-saving first-aid measure.

SPIDERS
Australia has a number of poisonous spiders. The Sydney funnel-web spider causes severe local pain, as well as generalised symptoms (vomiting, abdominal pain and sweating). An antivenin exists, so apply pressure to the wound and immobilise the area before transferring to a hospital.

Redback spiders are found throughout the country. Bites cause increasing pain at the site, followed by profuse sweating and generalised symptoms (including muscular weakness, sweating at the site of the bite and nausea). First aid includes application of ice or cold packs to the bite, then transfer to hospital.

White-tailed spider bites may cause an ulcer that is very slow and difficult to heal. Clean the wound thoroughly and seek medical assistance.

TICKS
Always check all over your body if you have been walking through a potentially tick-infested area as ticks can cause skin infections and other more serious diseases. Ticks are most active from spring to autumn, especially where there are plenty of sheep or deer. They usually lurk in overhanging vegetation, so avoid bush-bashing if possible.

If a tick is found attached to the skin, press down around the tick's head with tweezers, grab the head and gently pull upwards. Avoid pulling the rear of the body as this may squeeze the tick's gut contents through its mouth into your skin, increasing the risk of infection and disease. Smearing chemicals on the tick will not make it let go and is not recommended.

Heat Exhaustion & Heatstroke
Very hot weather occurs year-round in northern Australia and during summer for most of the country. When arriving from a temperate or cold climate, remember that it takes two weeks for acclimatisation to occur. Before the body is acclimatised, an excessive amount of salt is lost in perspiration, so increasing the salt in your diet is vital.

Heat exhaustion occurs when fluid intake does not keep up with fluid loss. Symptoms include dizziness, fainting, fatigue, not sweating very much (or at all) nausea or vomiting. The skin is usually pale, cool and clammy. Treatment consists of rest in a cool, shady place and fluid replacement with water or diluted sports drinks.

Heatstroke is a severe form of heat illness that occurs after fluid depletion or extreme heat challenge from heavy exercise. This is a true medical emergency, with heating of the brain leading to disorientation, hallucinations and seizures. Prevent heatstroke by maintaining an adequate fluid intake to ensure the continued passage of clear and copious urine, especially during physical exertion.

Dehydration is also a risk. The first symptoms are weakness, thirst and passing small amounts of very concentrated urine. This may progress to drowsiness, dizziness or fainting on standing up, and finally, coma. It is easy to forget how much fluid you are losing via perspiration while you are walking, particularly if a strong breeze is drying your skin quickly. You should always maintain a good fluid intake – a minimum of 3L a day is recommended.

Hypothermia
Hypothermia is a significant risk, especially during winter in southern parts of Australia. Strong winds produce a high chill factor that can result in hypothermia even in moderately cool temperatures. Early signs include the inability to perform fine movements (such as doing up buttons), shivering and a bad case of the 'umbles' (fumbles, mumbles, grumbles, stumbles). The key elements of treatment include moving out of the cold, changing out of any wet clothing into dry clothes with windproof and waterproof layers, adding insulation and providing fuel (water and carbohydrate) to allow shivering, which builds the internal temperature. In severe hypothermia, shivering actually stops – this is a medical emergency requiring rapid medical attention in addition to the above measures.

Insect-Borne Illnesses
Various insects can be a source of irritation and, in Australia, may be the source of specific diseases (such as dengue fever and Ross River fever). Protection from mosquitoes, sandflies, ticks and leeches can be achieved by a combination of the following strategies:

- Cover up by wearing loose-fitting, long-sleeved clothing.
- Applying 30% DEET to all exposed skin and repeating every three to four hours.
- Impregnating clothing with permethrin (an insecticide that kills insects but is believed to be safe for humans).

Ultraviolet (UV) Light Exposure
Australia has one of the highest rates of skin cancer in the world. Monitor your exposure

---

> **WATER**
>
> Tap water is universally safe in Australia, but all other water should be treated. This can be done by boiling it for around five minutes, filtering it or chemically disinfecting it (with iodine tablets, available from outdoor-equipment suppliers and pharmacies) to prevent travellers diarrhoea and giardia. Too much iodine (prolonged use for several weeks) can be harmful – for longer walking trips buy a filter instead.

to direct sunlight closely. Slap on the sunscreen and a barrier cream for your nose and lips, wear a broad-brimmed hat and protect your eyes with good quality sunglasses with UV lenses, particularly when walking near water, sand or snow. Ultraviolet exposure is greatest between 10am and 4pm, so be particularly vigilant about skin exposure during these times. Always use 30+ sunscreen, apply it 30 minutes before going into the sun and repeat regularly to minimise damage.

TRAUMATIC INJURIES
Detailed first-aid instruction is outside the scope of this book, but here are some basic points. You should consider taking a first-aid course (see p382) before hitting the trail to ensure you know what to do in the event of an injury.

Major Accidents
Falling or having something fall on you, resulting in head injuries or fractures, is always possible when walking, especially if you are crossing steep slopes or unstable terrain. Following is some basic advice on what to do in the event of a major accident. If a person suffers a major fall:

- Make sure you and other people with you are not in danger.
- Assess the injured person's condition.
- Stabilise any injuries, such as bleeding wounds or broken bones.
- Seek medical attention (see p388).

If the person is unconscious, immediately check whether they are breathing (clear their airway if it is blocked) and check whether they have a pulse – feel the side of the neck rather than the wrist. If they are

HEALTH & SAFETY

not breathing but have a pulse, you should start mouth-to-mouth resuscitation immediately. In these circumstances it is best to move the person as little as possible in case their neck or back is broken.

Check for wounds and broken bones – ask the person where they have pain if they are conscious, otherwise gently inspect them all over (including their back and the back of the head), moving them as little as possible. Control any bleeding by applying firm pressure to the wound. Bleeding from the nose or ear may indicate a fractured skull. Do not give the person anything by mouth, especially if they are unconscious.

You will have to manage the person for shock. Raise their legs above heart level (unless their legs are fractured); dress any wounds and immobilise any fractures; loosen tight clothing; keep the person warm by covering them with a blanket or other dry clothing; and insulate them from the ground if possible, but do not heat them.

Some general points to bear in mind:

■ Simple fractures take several weeks to heal, so they do not need fixing straight away, but they should be immobilised to protect them from further injury. Compound fractures (those associated with open wounds) need urgent treatment.

■ If you do have to splint a broken bone, remember to check regularly that the splint is not cutting off the circulation to the hand or foot.

■ Most cases of brief unconsciousness are not associated with any serious internal injury to the brain but, as a general rule of thumb, any person who has been knocked unconscious should be watched for deterioration. If they do deteriorate, seek medical attention straight away.

Sprains

Ankle and knee sprains are common injuries among walkers. To help prevent ankle sprains, be sure to wear boots that provide adequate ankle support. If you do suffer a sprain, immobilise the joint with a firm bandage, and, if feasible, immerse the foot in cold water. Once you reach shelter, relieve pain and swelling by keeping the joint elevated for the first 24 hours and, where possible, by putting ice on the swollen joint. For more severe sprains, seek medical attention.

SAFETY ON THE WALK

You can significantly reduce the chance of getting into difficulties by taking a few simple precautions. These are listed in the boxed text on opposite. A list of the clothes and equipment you should carry is on p392.

CROSSING RIVERS

Sudden downpours can speedily turn a gentle stream into a raging torrent. If you are in any doubt about the safety of a crossing, look for a safer passage upstream or wait. If the rain is short-lived, it should subside quickly.

If you decide it is essential to cross (late in the day, for example), look for a wide, relatively shallow stretch of the stream rather than a bend. Take off your trousers and socks, but keep your boots on to prevent injury. Put dry, warm clothes and a towel in a plastic bag near the top of your pack. Before stepping out from the bank, unclip your chest strap and belt buckle. This makes it easier to slip out of your backpack and swim to safety if you lose your balance and are swept downstream. Use a walking pole or stick, grasped in both hands, on the upstream side as a third leg, or go arm in arm with a companion, clasping at the wrist, and cross side-on to the flow, taking short steps.

BUSHFIRE

Bushfires occur every summer in Australian national parks, bushland areas and even cities. The chances of getting caught in one while walking are slight but it is wise to be familiar with the precautions.

Before leaving on a walk in summer, check the weather report. Fire danger warnings are usually publicised by national park agencies and visitor centres. Remember that on days of Total Fire Ban even the use of a fuel stove is banned.

If you are caught in a fire, don't start running unless there is a clear escape route, and remember that fire travels faster uphill than downhill. Seek shelter in a creek, wet gully, drain, under a concrete bridge, in a rocky outcrop, an open area with little or no vegetation or a recently burnt area. Don't enter still water as there's a chance of being boiled alive. Clear the area around your shelter of

---

WALK SAFETY – BASIC RULES

▪ Allow plenty of time to accomplish a walk before dark, particularly when daylight hours are shorter.

▪ Study the route carefully before setting out, noting the possible escape routes and the point of no return (where it is quicker to continue than to turn back). Monitor your progress during the day against the time estimated for the walk, and keep an eye on the weather.

▪ It is wise not to walk alone. Always leave details of your intended route, number of people in your group, and expected return time with someone responsible before you set off; let that person know when you return.

▪ Before setting off, make sure you have a relevant map, compass and whistle, and that you know the weather forecast for the area for the next 24 hours.

---

leaves, twigs or flammable material. Cover exposed skin with clothing (preferably woollen), soft earth or anything that will give protection from the heat. Keep low and breathe air close to the ground where it's cooler and there's less smoke. Don't leave your shelter until the fire has passed.

If you're in a vehicle, don't drive along a road obscured by fire and smoke, and don't leave your vehicle. Park as far as possible from any flammable material. Close all windows and vents and turn on the headlights. Lie on the floor and cover yourself with a blanket or any cloth that will shield you from the heat. If you must continue driving, do so slowly with headlights on and watch out for fallen trees, firefighting vehicles and firefighters.

LIGHTNING

If a storm brews, avoid exposed areas. Lightning has a penchant for crests, lone trees, small depressions, gullies and caves, as well as wet ground. If you are caught out in the open, try to curl up as tightly as possible with your feet together and keep a layer of insulation between you and the ground. Place metal objects such as metal-frame backpacks and walking poles away from you.

RESCUE & EVACUATION

If someone in your group is injured or falls ill and can't move, leave somebody with them while another person goes for help. They should take clear written details of the location and condition of the victim, and of helicopter landing conditions. If there are only two of you, leave the injured person with as much warm clothing, food and water as it is sensible to spare, plus the

whistle and torch. Mark the position with something conspicuous – an orange bivvy bag, or perhaps a large stone cross on the ground. Remember, the rescue effort might be slow, perhaps taking days to remove the injured person.

Emergency Communications & Equipment

Communications equipment has brought the entire world into speaking range. Adventurers are calling home from the Poles and the summit of Mt Everest, so it is not surprising that the scope for emergency communications on a bushwalk has also grown tremendously in recent years. Mobile phones and Emergency Position Indicating Radio Beacons (EPIRB) could be of use if you are in need of emergency treatment or help. A Global Positioning System (GPS) receiver (p390) may help you avoid some emergency situations, though there is no substitute for good old bush sense and map and compass skills.

When you ring an emergency service, be ready to give information on where an accident occurred, how many people are injured and the injuries sustained. If a helicopter needs to come in, explain also the terrain and the weather conditions at the place of the accident.

TELEPHONE

Australia's GSM and CDMA mobile-phone networks currently cover around 98% of the country's population but this translates to less than 14% of the land area. That said, most of the walks in this book are in the areas of general coverage. You should not expect uninterrupted reception as you are walking – and you may not get reception anywhere on some walks – but you will often find points along a walk (usually mountain peaks or hilltops) where your phone will work. This makes your mobile phone a useful emergency tool, though be sure to carry it in something waterproof.

From a mobile phone you should ring the standard emergency number (☎ 000). If you don't have mobile-phone reception, and you have a GSM phone, you can dial ☎ 112; this will connect you to an emergency call service if another carrier has network coverage in the area. Check with your mobile service provider if you are not certain which network you are on.

EPIRB

EPIRBs transmit a signal when activated that is picked up by a satellite, which then transmits the beacon's position to an emergency service. EPIRBs are becoming more commonplace among walkers, and Service Tasmania (p193) and the Snowy Region Visitor Centre (p86) now hire out beacons to walkers.

Traditionally, walkers have used analogue 121.5MHz beacons, but from February 2009 these will no longer be detected by satellites, leaving the digital 406MHz system as the only option. These beacons are available and usable now, though they are bigger, more expensive and require registration (in order that authorities know whose beacon has been set off). For further information on the frequency change, check out the **Australian Maritime Safety Authority** (http://beacons .amsa.gov.au/) website.

DISTRESS SIGNALS

If you need to call for help, use these internationally recognised emergency signals. Give six short signals, such as a whistle, a yell or the flash of a light, at 10-second intervals, followed by a minute of rest. Repeat the sequence until you get a response. If the responder knows the signals, this will be three signals at 20-second intervals, followed by a minute's pause and a repetition of the sequence.

Search & Rescue Organisations

Search and rescue operations in Australia are the responsibility of the police force in each state, with the assistance of various professional and voluntary organisations. The latter usually include experienced and trained bushwalkers. In an emergency, call ☎ 000 (on a GSM mobile phone you can also call ☎ 112 – see p387).

In NSW only, you can contact the **Bushwalkers Wilderness Rescue Squad** (☎ 13 22 22 pager 6277321), a volunteer service provided by the Confederation of Bushwalking Clubs. It is a pager service so somebody will ring you back.

Helicopter Rescue & Evacuation

If a helicopter arrives on the scene, there are a couple of conventions you should be familiar with. Standing face on to the chopper:

- Arms up in the shape of a letter 'V' means 'I/We need help'.
- Arms in a straight diagonal line (like one line of a letter X) means 'All OK'.

For the helicopter to land, there must be a cleared space of 25m x 25m, with a flat landing pad area of 6m x 6m. The helicopter will fly into the wind when landing. In cases of extreme emergency, where no landing area is available, a person or harness might be lowered. Take extreme care to avoid the rotors when approaching a landed helicopter.

Clothing & Equipment

You don't need to spend a fortune on gear to enjoy walking, but you do need to think carefully about what you pack to ensure you are comfortable and prepared for an emergency. Taking the right clothing and equipment can make the difference between an enjoyable day out or a cold and miserable one; in extreme situations, it can even mean the difference between life and death.

The gear you need will depend on the type of walking you plan to do. For day walks, clothing, footwear and a backpack are the major items; in some parts of the country you might get away with very little of the first mentioned. For longer walks or those in the mountains, especially if you are camping, the list becomes longer.

We recommend spending as much as you can afford on good walking boots, a rain jacket and a sweater or fleece jacket. These are likely to be among your most expensive items but are a sound investment, as they should last for years.

As for non-essentials – such as that Tolstoy tome you might be considering for the long evenings – think about applying the bushwalkers' two-use principle: each item should have at least two uses before you pack it. Your shoulders will thank you.

The following section is not exhaustive; for more advice visit outdoor stores, talk to fellow walkers and read product reviews in outdoor magazines.

CLOTHING

For clothing considerations specific to the mountains, see the boxed text p39.

Layering

A secret of comfortable walking is to wear several layers of light clothing, which you can easily take off or put on as you warm up or cool down. Most walkers use three main layers: a base layer next to the skin; an insulating layer; and an outer, shell layer for protection from wind, rain and snow.

For the upper body, the base layer is typically a shirt of synthetic material such as polypropylene, with its ability to wick moisture away from the body and reduce chilling. The insulating layer retains heat

---

PIONEER PADDY

Australia's thriving walking gear industry was born in 1930 in a Sydney suburban bedroom belonging to Frank 'Paddy' Pallin, who had migrated to Australia from Yorkshire four years earlier. A keen walker, he soon began exploring the bushland on the fringes of Sydney and in the still largely unexplored Blue Mountains.

Losing his hated office job at the start of the Great Depression, he seized the chance to turn his recreation into income, setting about designing and making lightweight walking gear in his home. He moved the business to a small city premises in 1934.

After a disastrous fire in his shop and factory in the early 1950s the business went from strength to strength, with its own city shop in the 1970s and expansion state-wide and interstate during the 1980s. 'Paddymade' gear in those days covered the full range: backpacks, sleeping bags, tents, clothing and camping equipment. Many innovative items were developed – double sleeping bags, H-frame packs, self-standing lightweight water buckets and even highly prized pink wool socks, known as 'Paddy's Pinkies'.

Paddy remained active throughout his life, learning to cross-country ski in his 50s and trekking in Nepal in his 70th year; he died aged 91 in 1991. Paddy Pallin is still a family business, although the range of Paddymade gear has narrowed and other reputable brands are sold in its many shops located throughout the country.

next to your body, and is often a windproof synthetic fleece or down jacket. The outer shell consists of a waterproof jacket that also protects against cold wind.

For the lower body, the layers generally consist of either shorts or loose-fitting trousers, polypropylene 'long-john' underwear and waterproof overtrousers.

Waterproof Shells

Australia may be mostly arid but many of its walks are in the wettest parts of the country – Mt Bartle Frere is about *the* wettest place – so you are going to need good rain protection. Traditionally, this has been a rain jacket and overtrousers, though a relatively new arrival on the market is the 'soft

shell' jacket, offering protection from cold, wind and light rain. It can be used in place of the insulating layer and waterproof layer, ie one jacket instead of two, but should only be considered for areas unlikely to receive heavy rains.

The ideal specifications for a rain jacket are a breathable, waterproof fabric, a hood that is roomy enough to cover headwear but still allows peripheral vision, capacious map pocket and a heavy-gauge zip protected by a storm flap.

Overtrousers can be restrictive – and the only thing you might hear while walking is your legs rubbing together – but can be a godsend in really wet conditions. As the name suggests, they are worn over your

---

NAVIGATION EQUIPMENT

Maps & Compass

You should always carry a good map of the area in which you are walking (see p366), and know how to read it. Before setting off on your walk, ensure that you understand the contours and the map symbols, plus the main ridge and river systems in the area. Also familiarise yourself with the true north–south directions and the general direction in which you are heading. On the trail, try to identify major landforms such as mountain ranges and gorges, and locate them on your map. This will give you a better understanding of the region's geography.

Buy a compass and learn how to use it. The attraction of magnetic north varies in different parts of the world, so compasses need to be balanced accordingly. Compass manufacturers have divided the world into five zones. Make sure your compass is balanced for your destination zone. There are also 'universal' compasses on the market that can be used anywhere in the world.

1	Base plate
2	Direction of travel arrow
3	Dash
4	Bezel
5	Meridian lines
6	Needle
7	Red end
8	N (north point)

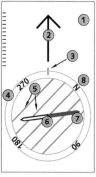

How to Use a Compass

This is a very basic introduction to using a compass and will only be of assistance if you are proficient in map reading. For simplicity, it doesn't take magnetic variation into account. Before using a compass we recommend you obtain further instruction.

Reading a Compass

Hold the compass flat in the palm of your hand. Rotate the bezel (4) so the red end (7) of the needle (6) points to the N (north point; 8) on the bezel. The bearing is read from the dash (3) under the bezel.

Orienting the Map

To orient the map so that it aligns with the ground, place the compass flat on the map. Rotate the map until the needle is parallel with the map's north/south grid lines and the red end is pointing to north on the map. You can now identify features around you by aligning them with labelled features on the map.

trousers, offering waterproofing for your legs. Choose a model with slits for pocket access and long leg zips so that you can pull them on and off over your boots.

Footwear

Your footwear will be your friend or your enemy, so choose carefully. The first decision you will make is between boots and shoes. Runners or walking shoes are fine over easy terrain, but for more difficult trails – and across rocks and scree – the ankle support offered by boots is invaluable. Nonslip soles (such as Vibram) provide the best grip. Buy boots in warm conditions or go for a walk before trying them on, so that your feet can expand slightly, as they would on a walk.

Most walkers carry either a pair of thongs (flip-flops) or sandals. These will relieve your feet from the heavy boots at night or during rest stops, and sandals are also useful for fording waterways that are above the height of your boots.

GAITERS

If you are going to be walking through snow, deep mud or scratchy vegetation, or you are worried about snakes, consider using gaiters to protect your legs and keep your socks dry. If you are heading across buttongrass plains in Tasmania, you will think gaiters the best thing since internal-frame backpacks, and they will also help prevent spinifex stabs if you are walking

Taking a Bearing from the Map

Draw a line on the map between your starting point and your destination. Place the edge of the compass on this line with the direction of travel arrow (2) pointing towards your destination. Rotate the bezel until the meridian lines (5) are parallel with the north/south grid lines on the map and the N points to north on the map. Read the bearing from the dash.

Following a Bearing

Rotate the bezel so that the intended bearing is in line with the dash. Place the compass flat in the palm of your hand and rotate the base plate (1) until the red end points to N on the bezel. The direction of travel arrow will now point in the direction you need to walk.

Determining Your Bearing

Rotate the bezel so the red end points to the N. Place the compass flat in the palm of your hand and rotate the base plate until the direction of travel arrow points in the direction in which you have been walking/hiking/trekking. Read your bearing from the dash.

GPS

Originally developed by the US Department of Defense, the Global Positioning System (GPS) is a network of more than 20 earth-orbiting satellites that continually beam encoded signals back to earth. Small, computer-driven devices (GPS receivers) can decode these signals to give users an extremely accurate reading of their location – to within a few metres, anywhere on the planet, at any time of day, in almost any weather. The cheapest hand-held GPS receivers now cost around $250 (although these may not have a built-in averaging system that minimises signal errors). Other important factors to consider when buying a GPS receiver are its weight and battery life.

Remember that a GPS receiver is of little use to walkers unless used with an accurate topographical map. The receiver simply gives your position, which you must then locate on the local map. GPS receivers will only work properly in the open. The signals from a crucial satellite may be blocked (or bounce off rock or water) directly below high cliffs, near large bodies of water or in dense tree cover and give inaccurate readings. GPS receivers are more vulnerable to breakdowns (including dead batteries) than the humble magnetic compass – a low-tech device that has served navigators faithfully for centuries – so don't rely on them entirely.

For a complete rundown on GPS use, consider picking up a copy of a book such as *GPS Made Easy* by Lawrence Letham.

EQUIPMENT CHECK LIST

This list is a general guide to the things you might take on a walk. Your list will vary depending on the kind of walking you are doing, whether you are camping or planning to stay in huts or B&Bs, and on the terrain, weather conditions and time of year.

Clothing

- ☐ boots and spare laces
- ☐ down jacket
- ☐ gaiters
- ☐ hat (warm), scarf and gloves
- ☐ overtrousers (waterproof)
- ☐ rain jacket
- ☐ runners (training shoes), sandals or thongs (flip flops)
- ☐ shorts and trousers or skirt
- ☐ socks and underwear
- ☐ sunhat
- ☐ sweater or fleece jacket
- ☐ thermal underwear
- ☐ T-shirt and long-sleeved shirt with collar

Equipment

- ☐ backpack with waterproof liner
- ☐ first-aid kit*
- ☐ food and snacks (high energy) and one day's emergency supplies
- ☐ insect repellent
- ☐ map, compass and guidebook
- ☐ map case or clip-seal plastic bags
- ☐ plastic bags (for carrying rubbish)
- ☐ pocket knife
- ☐ sunglasses
- ☐ sunscreen and lip balm
- ☐ survival bag or blanket
- ☐ toilet paper and trowel
- ☐ torch (flashlight) or headlamp, spare batteries and globe (bulb)
- ☐ water container
- ☐ whistle

Overnight Walks

- ☐ cooking, eating and drinking utensils
- ☐ dishwashing items
- ☐ matches and lighter
- ☐ sewing/repair kit
- ☐ sleeping bag and bag liner/inner sheet
- ☐ sleeping mat
- ☐ spare cord
- ☐ stove and fuel
- ☐ tent, pegs, poles and guy ropes
- ☐ toiletries
- ☐ towel
- ☐ water purification tablets, iodine or filter

Optional Items

- ☐ altimeter
- ☐ backpack cover (waterproof, slip-on)
- ☐ binoculars
- ☐ camera, film and batteries
- ☐ candle
- ☐ emergency distress beacon
- ☐ GPS receiver
- ☐ groundsheet
- ☐ mobile phone**
- ☐ mosquito net
- ☐ notebook and pen
- ☐ swimming costume
- ☐ walking poles
- ☐ watch

* see the First-Aid Check List (p382)
** see Mobile Phones (p369)

something like the Larapinta Trail. Elsewhere, builder-style gaiters that cover just the tops of your boots to keep out stones and dirt can be useful.

SOCKS

Socks with a high proportion of wool are more comfortable when worn for successive days without washing. They should be free of ridged seams in the toes and heels. Spare socks are equally valuable, especially in wet conditions.

EQUIPMENT
Backpack
For day walks, a day-pack (30L to 40L) will usually suffice, but for multiday walks you will need a backpack of between 45L and 90L capacity. A good backpack should be made of strong fabric such as canvas or Cordura, contain a lightweight internal or external frame and an adjustable, well-padded harness that evenly distributes weight. Even if the manufacturer claims your pack is waterproof, use heavy-duty liners.

Sleeping Bag & Mat
Down fillings are warmer than synthetic for the same weight and bulk, but unlike synthetic fillings do not retain warmth when wet. Mummy bags are the best shape for weight and warmth. The rating (eg –5°C) is the coldest temperature at which you should feel comfortable in the bag (though the ratings are notoriously unreliable).

An inner sheet helps keep your sleeping bag clean, as well as adding an insulating layer. Silk inners are lightest, but they also come in cotton or polypropylene.

Self-inflating sleeping mats work like a thin air cushion between you and the ground; they also insulate from the cold. Foam mats are a low-cost, but less comfortable, alternative.

Stoves
Fuel stoves fall roughly into three categories: multifuel, methylated spirits (ethyl alcohol) and butane gas. Multifuel stoves are small, efficient and ideal for places where a reliable fuel supply is difficult to find. However, they tend to be sooty (prime them with methylated spirits to avoid this) and can require frequent maintenance. Stoves running on methylated spirits are slower

---

STOVE FUEL

Super-refined petrol for stoves, known in Australia as Shellite, is available from outdoor stores and hardware stores, usually in 1L bottles. Most such stoves will also take unleaded petrol, which can be easily obtained at any service station.

Methylated spirits in Australia is not colour-dyed as in some countries, and is widely available in supermarkets, and hardware and outdoor shops. Gas canisters also can be purchased at outdoor shops.

---

and less efficient, but are safe, clean and easy to use. Butane gas stoves are clean and reliable but can be slow, and the gas canisters can be awkward to carry and a potential litter problem.

Tent
A three-season tent will fulfil the requirements of most walkers. The floor and the outer shell, or fly, should have taped or sealed seams and covered zips to stop leaks. Most walkers find tents of around 2kg to 3kg a comfortable carrying weight. Dome- and tunnel-shaped tents handle windy conditions better than flat-sided tents.

BUYING & HIRING LOCALLY
Australia is no bargain basement for outdoor clothing and equipment, but prices are reasonable. In each state capital you will find the following major outdoor chains:
Kathmandu (www.kathmandu.com.au)
Mountain Designs (www.mountaindesigns.com.au)
Paddy Pallin (www.paddypallin.com.au)
Snowgum (www.snowgum.com.au) Not in Brisbane or Adelaide.

For addresses in each city, see the appropriate regional chapters.

Hiring of equipment and clothing is not common.

CLOTHING & EQUIPMENT

Glossary

Visitors from abroad who think Australian is simply a weird variation of English/American may quickly find themselves lost in a strange collection of Australian words. The meaning of some words in Australia completely differs from those in other English-speaking countries, while others are derived from Aboriginal languages, or from the slang used by early convict settlers. This includes many words pertaining to the landscape, flora and fauna that are relevant to the walker. The list that follows focuses primarily on words that walkers may come across. Lonely Planet also publishes an *Australian Phrasebook*, which is an introduction to both Australian English and some Aboriginal languages.

arête – narrow ridge, particularly between glacial valleys
anticline – arch-shaped fold in rock in which rock layers are upwardly convex
arid – having little or no rain; arid regions are usually defined as those receiving less than 250mm of rain

bezel – the rotating dial on a compass
billabong – ox-bow bend in a river cut off by receding waters
billy – small cooking pot
bivouac or **bivvy** – makeshift shelter used in the open; large waterproof sleeping sack used for this purpose
boardwalk – walkway made of timber planks
bore – artesian well
brumby – wild horse
bush, the – undeveloped areas away from the city
bush-bash – to force your way through pathless bush
bushfire – fire in bushland
bush tucker – indigenous foods, found naturally in the *bush*
bushwalking – hiking, tramping, trekking or walking; walking for pleasure in the *bush*
buttress – pillar-like rock formation protruding from a hillside

cairn – pile of stones marking a walking route, a summit or a prominent geographical feature
CALM – Department of Conservation & Land Management in Western Australia
camp site – area suitable for camping, often without facilities
camping ground – designated camping area with facilities
canyon – *gorge* or ravine, usually formed by a river
cascade – small waterfall
Centre, the – the arid region in Australia's centre
circuit – walk that starts and ends at the same point

contour – line on a *topographic* map connecting points of the same altitude; to move across a slope along the same level
cooee – call used to locate people over long distances; within shouting distance, close ('to be within cooee of...')
creek – small watercourse or stream
cuesta – long low ridge with a steep *escarpment* and a gentle back slope
cyclone – violent tropical storm, confined to northern Australia

damper – bread traditionally made of flour and water and cooked in the ashes of a campfire
DEH – Department for Environment & Heritage in South Australia
dieback – microscopic fungus called *Phytophthora cinnamomi*, which attacks, and usually kills, some species of native plants
dolerite – coarse-grained volcanic rock
Dreaming – the ancient period for Aboriginal people when totemic ancestors formed the landscape, made the laws and created the people who would inherit the landscape
Dry, the – dry season in northern Australia (April to September)
duckboards – see *boardwalk*

ECD – Emergency Call Device; solar powered phones installed along walking trails
EPIRB – Emergency Position Indicating Radio Beacon
erratic – boulder carried by a glacier and deposited some distance from its origin
escarpment – line of cliffs along the edge of a ridge

fire trail – 4WD track, usually in national parks, built for fire-fighting vehicles
ford – to cross a river by wading
fork – point where a path splits into two
freshie – freshwater crocodile (usually harmless)
fuel stove – cooker, usually portable, using liquid fuel or gas canisters
fuel-stove-only area – area where campfires are banned

gap – *saddle* or pass; low point on a ridge or between peaks
Gondwana – ancient supercontinent that included modern Australia, Africa, Antarctica, South America and the Indian subcontinent
gorge – large, steep-sided valley, usually surrounded by cliffs
GPS – Global Positioning System; an electronic means of accurately fixing location using microwave satellite signals
granite – light-coloured, coarse-grained volcanic rock

grid reference – method of fixing location by using the numbered horizontal and vertical lines (grid) on *topographical* maps
GST – Goods and Services Tax
gully – small valley
gum tree – eucalyptus tree

hut – simple building used for accommodation, mainly in national parks, generally unsupervised and without facilities

inlet – indentation in the coast, usually with a narrow opening to the sea
isthmus – narrow stretch of land connecting two larger landmasses

jumper – sweater or pullover

limestone – sedimentary rock composed mainly of calcium carbonate
logbook – book or register at the start and finish of a walk to record walkers' movements; also in huts as a visitors' book
loop – see *circuit*

mallee – a group of eucalyptuses with multiple stems; the northwest of Victoria
management track – 4WD track in national park used by park rangers
mangrove – coastal tree that grows in salt water
midden – mound of discarded shells and bone fragments

outback – remote, sparsely inhabited interior areas of Australia
outlet – of a lake, an opening that permits water to flow away

pad – indistinct informal track, usually made by animals, also by walkers
Parks Victoria – Victoria's state-based national park agency
plateau – elevated area of land that is almost level
pound – broad-basin valley created by the uplifting and sinking of land

QPWS – Queensland Parks & Wildlife Service

ranger – on-site park management official
ridgeline – crest of a ridge, often used for travel through alpine areas
runoff – rainfall running into creeks and rivers as surface water

saddle – pass or gap; low point on a ridge or between summits
saltie – saltwater crocodile (dangerous); properly known as an estuarine crocodile

sandbar – ridge of sand in the sea or a river, often uncovered at low tide
sandblow – large, unstable dune of sand that is slowly driven forward by a prevailing wind
sandstone – sedimentary rock comprised of sand grains
scree – weathered rock fragments at the foot of a cliff or on a hillside
scrub – low dense vegetation
semiarid – characterised by low rainfall and scrubby vegetation
Shellite – liquid fuel derived from petroleum and used in camp stoves
sidle – to *contour*
sinkhole – depression in limestone through which surface streams sometimes disappear
snow line – level below which snow seldom falls or lies on the ground
snow plain – open grassed area in alpine country, usually surrounded by snow gums
snow poles – route markers used in alpine areas
spot height – altitude of minor features, marked on *topographical* maps
spur – small ridge that leads up from a valley to a main ridge
station – large sheep or cattle farm
swale – sandy depression between sand dunes
swimming hole – large pool on a creek or river, safe for swimming
switchback – route that follows a zigzag course up or down a steep incline
syncline – basin-shaped fold in rock in which rock layers are downwardly convex

tarn – small alpine lake
Top End – northern part of the Northern Territory
topographic – showing the surface configuration of a region; with contours
torch – flashlight
Total Fire Ban – prohibition of all open flames on days of extreme fire danger
tor – high, bare, rocky hill
track – formed route for use by walkers (walking track) or vehicles (4WD track)
tree line – highest natural level of tree growth
trig point – triangulation point; point used in triangulation as a basis for mapping
tucker – food
true left/true right bank – side of a riverbank as you face downstream

waterhole – small pool or lake
Wet, the – rainy season in the north (October to March)
wildfire – bushfire out of control
World Heritage Area (WHA) – area included on a list of places deemed by Unesco to be of world significance

Behind the Scenes

THIS BOOK

This guidebook was commissioned in Lonely Planet's Melbourne office, and produced by the following:

Commissioning Editor Marg Toohey, Ben Handicott
Coordinating Editor Pete Cruttenden
Coordinating Cartographer David Connolly
Coordinating Layout Designer Jim Hsu
Managing Editor Jennifer Garrett
Managing Cartographer Corie Waddell
Assisting Editors Nigel Chin, David Andrew, Jeanette Wall, Lutie Clark, Nick Tapp
Assisting Cartographers Amanda Sierp, Piotr Czajkowski, Simon Tillema
Assisting Layout Designer Carlos Solarte
Cover Designer Wendy Wright
Project Manager Glenn van der Knijff, Eoin Dunlevy
Thanks to Glenn Beanland, Sally Darmody, Brendan Dempsey, Ryan Evans, James Hardy, Laura Jane, Katie Lynch, Wayne Murphy, Trent Paton, Stephanie Pearson, Paul Piaia, Wibowo Rusli, Jacqui Saunders, Cara Smith, Gerard Walker, Celia Wood

THANKS
ANDREW BAIN

Thanks foremost to Mark Grundy for surviving 16 days (and some lentil drag) with me on the Larapinta Trail, then backing up again for a second walk. To Lindsay Brown also for company on the Great Ocean Walk. For the beds, thanks to Matt Brown and Carina Tan-Van Baren, Stephanie Potts and my mum and dad. The knowledge of a legion of park rangers has been invaluable – thanks to all who were of assistance. To Marg and Ben for mak-

ing the cut and thrust of writing the book entirely painless, Corie for help with maps, Lindsay, Ian, Grant, Glenn, John and Lyn for making my job easier, and Janette, Kiri and Cooper for enduring my absences, both when I was away and at home.

LINDSAY BROWN

Thanks to Dion Brugman and colleagues in the Northern Territory Tourist Commission, and to all the rangers that assisted with updating the national park and trail information, particularly Norm Greenfield at Nitmiluk. Thanks to Marg, Ben and Corie at LP, and fellow walker and coordinating author Andrew Bain.

IAN CONNELLAN

The expert attention of several past and present land and environment managers greatly sharpened NSW walks information. Ian Brown helped with useful leads. Thanks to NPWS staff Aine Gliddon, Aileen Bell, Pat Hall, Dan Smillie, Barbara Webster and Anton Ingarfield. Six Foot Track Heritage Trust administrator Jon Guyver was especially diligent. Walking partners included my daughter Tess, nephews Andrew and Matthew and 75-year-old father Norman – watching Dad march steadily up an 800m vertical ascent was a research highlight. Veechi Stuart came for lunch atop Ruined Castle. There's no better long-walk partner than my calm and companionable brother David (have you packed the first-aid kit, hmmm?). Thanks to Jane, Adam, Therese and Mum for staying home while others went out to play.

THE LONELY PLANET STORY

The story begins with a classic travel adventure: Tony and Maureen Wheeler's 1972 journey across Europe and Asia to Australia. There was no useful information about the overland trail then, so Tony and Maureen published the first Lonely Planet guidebook to meet a growing need.

From a kitchen table, Lonely Planet has grown to become the largest independent travel publisher in the world, with offices in Melbourne (Australia), Oakland (USA) and London (UK). Today Lonely Planet guidebooks cover the globe. There is an ever-growing list of books and information in a variety of media. Some things haven't changed. The main aim is still to make it possible for adventurous travellers to get out there – to explore and better understand the world.

At Lonely Planet we believe travellers can make a positive contribution to the countries they visit – if they respect their host communities and spend their money wisely. Every year 5% of company profit is donated to charities around the world.

JOHN & LYN DALY
Thanks to Oliver from Wooroonooran Safaris for inviting us to tag along with his guides on a training trip across Mt Bartle Frere. Trees and plants in this unique region now have special meaning, thanks to Caitlin's extensive knowledge and enthusiasm. Thanks Linus, from Binna Burra Lodge, for continually promoting Queensland bushwalking, and Luke (one of his guides) for teaching us heaps more about our own backyard. Kaye and the other folk at Kingfisher Bay were an enormous help when we researched their part of paradise and planned Fraser Island's Great Walk. Bushwalking is always more enjoyable in the company of friends and we continue to discover and rediscover special places with our friends from NPAQ and Brisbane Bushwalkers Club – thanks. As usual QPWS park staff rallied behind our requests for assistance. And special thanks to Marg Toohey from Lonely Planet for her encouragement, patience and help and to Corie Wadell for her assistance with the maps.

GLENN VAN DER KNIJFF
I'd particularly like to thank Commissioning Editor at Lonely Planet Marg Toohey for giving me the opportunity to update and improve the High Country sections of the New South Wales and Victoria chapters, as well as to coordinating author Andrew Bain for support and advice on my submission.

GRANT DIXON
Thanks to various Tasmanian Parks & Wildlife Service staff, in particular Stuart Graham, Rebecca Johnson, Terry Reid, David Clarke, Dick Dwyer, Greg Peters and Stuart Dudgeon, for useful information and feedback. Wellington Park's Michael Easton and Margie Jenkin were similarly helpful. Ian Housholdt provided suggestions and comment on The Land text. Thanks to Andrew Bain, and Marg Toohey at Lonely Planet, for keeping the whole show on the road, and to my partner Rhonda for assistance throughout.

OUR READERS
Many thanks to the travellers who used the last edition and wrote to us with helpful hints, useful advice and interesting anecdotes:

Liz Abbott, Steven & Cath Abbott, Thelma Anderson, Raymond Ang, Erin Arsenault, Paul Dixon, Paul Evenblij, Neil Glick, Aine Gliddon, Jonathan Ide, James Lamb, Tony Lang, Chai Lee, Gabrielle Methou, Keith Moon, Russell O'Brien, Thomas Palfy, Noelene Proud, Melinda Richards, Tobias Roller, David Rutter, Andrew Sharpe, Helen Spurling, Matt Wielgosz, John Willems

ACKNOWLEDGMENTS
Many thanks to the following for the use of their content:

Globe on back cover ©Mountain High Maps 1993 Digital Wisdom, Inc.

Walking in Australia incorporates data that is copyright Commonwealth of Australia 2006. The data has been used in *Walking in Australia* with the permission of the Commonwealth. The Commonwealth has not evaluated the data as altered and incorporated within *Walking in Australia*, and therefore gives no warranty regarding its accuracy, completeness, currency or suitability for any particular purpose.

Index

INDEX

INDEX

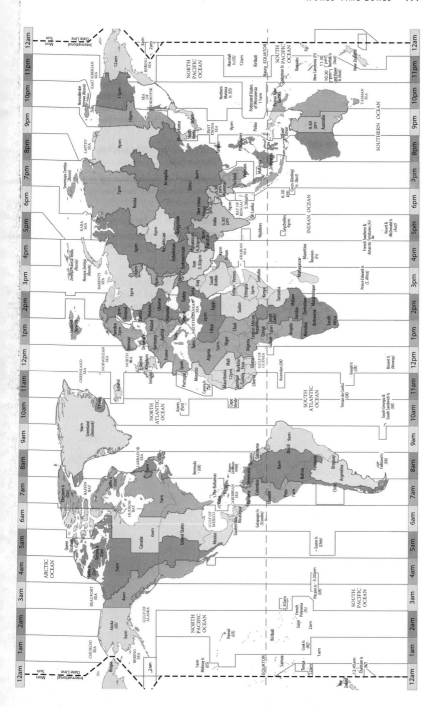

LONELY PLANET OFFICES

Australia
Head Office
Locked Bag 1, Footscray, Victoria 3011
☎ 03 8379 8000, fax 03 8379 8111
talk2us@lonelyplanet.com.au

USA
150 Linden St, Oakland, CA 94607
☎ 510 893 8555, toll free 800 275 8555
fax 510 893 8572
info@lonelyplanet.com

UK
72-82 Rosebery Ave,
Clerkenwell, London EC1R 4RW
☎ 020 7841 9000, fax 020 7841 9001
go@lonelyplanet.co.uk

Published by Lonely Planet Publications Pty Ltd
ABN 36 005 607 983

Cover photographs: Picnic Rocks, Mt William National Park – Tasmania, Australian Scenics (front); view from Mt Geryon above the Overland Track – Tasmania, Hugh Watts/Lonely Planet Images (back). Many of the images in this guide are available for licensing from Lonely Planet Images: www.lonelyplanetimages.com.

Printed through Colorcraft Ltd, Hong Kong.
Printed in China